The Enemy of the New Man

George L. Mosse Series
in Modern European Cultural and
Intellectual History

Advisory Board

The Enemy
of the New Man

Homosexuality in Fascist Italy

Lorenzo Benadusi

Translated by
Suzanne Dingee
and
Jennifer Pudney

The University of Wisconsin Press

Publication of this volume has been made possible, in part, through support from the **George L. Mosse Program** at the University of Wisconsin–Madison. The translation of this book has been funded by **SEPS**—Segretariato Europeo per le Pubblicazioni Scientifiche.

S·E·P·S
SEGRETARIATO EUROPEO PER LE PUBBLICAZIONI SCIENTIFICHE

Via Val d'Aposa 7—40123 Bologna—Italy
seps@seps.it—www.seps.it

The University of Wisconsin Press
1930 Monroe Street, 3rd Floor
Madison, Wisconsin 53711-2059
uwpress.wisc.edu

3 Henrietta Street
London WCE 8LU, England
eurospanbookstore.com

Originally published as *Il nemico dell'uomo nuovo: L'omosessualità nell'esperimento totalitario fascista*
© 2005 Giangiacomo Feltrinelli Editore Milano

Library of Congress Cataloging-in-Publication Data
Benadusi, Lorenzo, 1973–
[Nemico dell'uomo nuovo. English]
The enemy of the new man : homosexuality in fascist Italy / Lorenzo Benadusi ;
translated by Suzanne Dingee and Jennifer Pudney.
p.   cm. — (George L. Mosse series in modern European cultural and intellectual history)
Originally published as Il nemico dell'uomo nuovo:
L'omosessualità nell'esperimento totalitario fascista. Milano : Feltrinelli, 2005.
ISBN 978-0-299-28390-2 (cloth: alk. paper)
ISBN 978-0-299-28393-3 (e-book)
1. Fascism—Italy—History.   2. Masculinity—Italy—History—20th century.
3. Gay men—Italy—History—20th century.   4. Fascism and sex—Italy.
5. Italy—History—1922–1945.   I. Dingee, Suzanne.   II. Pudney, Jennifer.   III. Title.
IV. Series: George L. Mosse series in modern European cultural and intellectual history.
DG571.B437813   2012
306.76′62094509041—dc23
2011019926

To Elena

who made my return home so welcome

Contents

Foreword

EMILIO GENTILE

Let us imagine an Italian in Fascist Italy at the beginning of the 1940s who wanted to know something more about how Fascism viewed homosexuality and what the eventual punishment for being homosexual might have been. Of course, our Italian already knew that public opinion in Fascist Italy, like in Liberal Italy, severely condemned homosexuality as did Catholic morality, for being an acquired immoral vice or a congenital passion that led to depravity and degenerate behavior because it went against nature and was harmful for the health and integrity of the race. He also knew that Fascism considered homosexuals the "enemies of the new man." As Lorenzo Benadusi explains in this book, homosexuals "upset national order, raised doubts about the basic values of Fascist morality, and damaged national prestige with acts that were universally considered perverse. They risked corrupting anyone who came in contact with them and put the country's future at risk by shirking their duty to procreate, the foundation of the nation's might. Moreover, they undermined the country's internal unity by confusing the roles of the sexes" (see chap. 4). However, our Italian would probably be surprised to find that while the other "enemies of the new man," the bourgeois and the Jew, were sonorously berated by the regime's obsessive newspaper propaganda and daily hate campaign, little was written about homosexuality and homosexuals. And even when the regime's newspapers mentioned homosexuality it was never straightforward but allusive and general in manner. For example, they compared homosexuality to sexual

habits that clashed with the regime's demographic policy that was based on
the supremacy of men over women and acclaimed the large family as a moral
and political duty. Homosexuality was also likened to the modern tendency to
"masculinize women" and "femininize men": in a widely read book published
in 1929 titled *Fecondità e potenza* (Fertility and Power) the phrase "social homosexuality" was used to "indicate that there were equal rights and customs for men
and women, in life and on the job." Those accused of being homosexuals were
anti-Fascists, the self-centered hedonist bourgeois who were reluctant to change
their lifestyles to conform to the Fascist new man's style, the Jews and democratic
populations who were considered degenerate and decadent because they were
not sufficiently reproductive. One of the regime's journalists maintained that
"the most despicable and most disgraceful vice, unknown even to beasts, is widespread in America more than any other country and is a sign of an unthinkably
low and filthy moral level."

Now let us imagine that our Italian in Fascist Italy was not satisfied with
what he read in the newspapers and wanted to have more precise information
about how homosexuals were dealt with by the regime. He first consulted
the *Enciclopedia Italiana.* The entry "homosexuality" referred him to "sexology,"
where under the subheading "Sexual Psychopathology" there was a paragraph
titled "Perversions relative to the object," which "include all cases in which the
object of sexual intercourse is different from that of all normal cases of eroticism."
In the paragraph, homosexuality is defined as "consisting of the search for an
individual of the same sex as the 'object'; it is the most notorious and frequently
studied of the sexual perversions. . . . [I]n some states homosexuality is punishable
as such pursuant to the law, but in others it is only penalized along with other
perversions when it becomes a public scandal or in some way damages others."
Now our Italian had obtained some information, but he still did not know what
punishment was provided for in the Italian legal system. Therefore, he consulted
a well-known book on the matter, *La sessuologia nel codice penale italiano* (Sexology
in the Italian Criminal Code) by Giuseppe Falco, professor in the Forensic
Medicine Department as well as head of the School for Forensic Police. Our
Italian learned from the introduction to the book that in Italy the problem of
sex "does not attract the widespread attention and interest that it does in other
countries." This depends on the fact that there are "some forms of moral and
religious discretion that prevent any in-depth discussion of such delicate arguments because dealing with them could clash with prevalent traditional ideas
and feelings" and also on the fact that "certain sex-related abnormal and pathological conditions are less frequent in our country than elsewhere." In the fourth
chapter, titled "Psicopatie sessuali e criminalità sessuali" (Sexual Psychopathy
and Sexual Crimes), after reading about sadism, masochism, necrophilism,

fetishism, zoophilia, pedophilia, and exhibitionism, our Italian finally got to homosexuality defined as a "sexual abnormality that concerns Forensic Medicine because it is often the cause of crimes or events that, even if not criminal offences, upset public order and offend public decency and morality." To better understand the meaning of this unfathomable phrase, our Italian consulted the new Criminal Code effective since 1931 but did not find any article that provides for the crime of "homosexuality." However, when he pursued the matter he discovered in the volumes containing the drafts of the new code that there had actually been a proposal to consider homosexuality a criminal offense, but that it had been eliminated from the final text. Apparently, the commission did not think it necessary to provide for such a crime "because fortunately Italy can proudly say that homosexuality, that abominable vice, is not so common among us as to warrant the lawmakers' attention." Nevertheless, "in similar cases the most severe punishment for sexual assault, corruption of minors, and offence to public decency should be applied." By excluding homosexuality from the Criminal Code the commission had wanted to avoid spreading the idea that "the vice is much more serious and common than it really is."

At this point our imaginary Italian could consider his research complete, because he could not have learned anything more about the Fascist regime's treatment of homosexuals except from first-hand information or rumors. From the very beginning the Fascist regime had decided to adopt a "strategy of concealment" regarding homosexuality. Consequently, any attempt on the part of Italians to learn more would probably have raised suspicion within the regime's watchful police force. However, to be precise, for almost fifty years it was impossible for Italians in the Italian Republic to know what the condition of homosexuals had been under Fascist rule since, after the collapse of Fascism the "strategy of concealment" was followed by a "concealment of silence," or the indifference of historiography toward the issue of homosexuality and homosexuals during that period. Until the mid-1980s an Italian could not have learned anything more about the matter than his predecessor: neither from supplements to the *Enciclopedia Italiana* nor from studies of the Fascist era. As a matter of fact, incongruously in the seventies an Italian who saw the films *Salò o le centoventi giornate di Sodoma* (*Salò, or the 120 Days of Sodom*) by Pier Paolo Pasolini or *Novecento* (*1900*) by Bernardo Bertolucci was easily led to believe that the Fascists themselves were homosexuals devoted to all sorts of depravity. As Benadusi recalls, the cinema world and fiction used "homosexuality as a metaphor for cruelty, perversion, and . . . corruption," and therefore painted the Fascists "as grotesque executioners, addicted to all kinds of vices and depravity" thus re-proposing "the same negative stereotype of homosexuality spread by the Fascists, . . . transferring the image from the persecuted to the persecutors."

The indifference of historiography to the problem of homosexuality during the Fascist period lasted until the late 1980s, when the first studies appeared. They were limited to giving a general overview or to the investigation of some particular aspect. Certainly the publication in Italian of three books by George L. Mosse, *Il razzismo in Europa* (1980; *Toward the Final Solution: A History of European Racism*), *Sessualità e nazionalismo* (1984; *Nationalism and Sexuality*), and *L'immagine dell'uomo* (1997; *The Image Man*) contributed to ending this indifference. Benadusi clearly states that Mosse's work inspired him to carry out the research that subsequently led to the publication of this book. Furthermore, Benadusi also deserves credit for being the first to undertake a detailed and structured investigation of homosexuality during Fascism, conducted according to historiographical criteria based on numerous published and unpublished sources and on an extensive knowledge of Italian and foreign historiography. However, I must add that while the main theme of the book regards the Fascist policy on homosexuality, it also provides an insight into the problem of homosexuality in Italian history during the liberal and Fascist periods. As a result, we are well informed of the premises and origins of the Fascist attitude toward homosexuality and better equipped to examine what Fascism carried over from the previous homophobic traditions of the Catholic Church, from positivism and nationalism, and also to better understand how much of the attitude and state action toward homosexuals was new or *specifically Fascist*. Based on a wealth of documents and evidence, Benadusi is able to show for the first time how important the sexual issue was for the anthropological revolution in the totalitarian venture where the problem of homosexuality was only one particular aspect of Fascism's eugenic, birthrate, and racist policies.

Benadusi has studied the Fascist policy toward homosexuality from its cultural, social, medical, juridical, political, and police point of view and given ample account of human vicissitudes taking into consideration ordinary people as well as some very important public figures. Because they were or were alleged to be homosexuals they were the victims of police repression or ended up ensnared in the web of defamation, persecution, blackmail, and ostracism that meant they were banned from public life. Nevertheless, the repressive measures of Fascism against homosexuals were less radical and cruel than those adopted by the Nazi regime. Homosexuality in Germany became a crime in 1871 pursuant to article 175 of the Imperial Criminal Code, but during the Second Empire a movement was organized to protect the rights of homosexuals, and while the Weimar Republic was in force homosexuals enjoyed greater tolerance. However, as soon as he came into power Hitler undertook a fiercely repressive campaign against homosexuality and used it as a political weapon within his own Nazi movement. As a result, in June 1934 the head of the SA, Ernst Röhm, a homosexual, and his collaborators were assassinated. The slaughter was publicly justified by accusing the victims of conspiracy and saying that the Führer wished to free the Germans from sexual perverts. The following year harsher punishment was provided for in article 175, and in 1936 the Reich set up a central office under the supervision of SS head Heinrich Himmler to combat homosexuality and abortion. The aim was not only repression but total elimination to protect the race's integrity and health. About 50,000 people were condemned for being homosexuals by the Nazi regime. Of these 10,000 or perhaps 15,000 died in concentration camps. In Italy as well the persecution of homosexuals was justified by the need to defend the race's health and integrity, but the methods were not as cruel and inhumane as those used by the Nazi regime. We do not know exactly how many people were condemned for being homosexuals by Italy's Fascist regime. From the documents in the state's central archives, consulted by Lorenzo Benadusi, it seems that about 300 people accused of pederasty were sentenced and exiled to forced residence, whereas 88 political detainees were considered homosexuals.

The comparison with Nazi Germany does not mitigate the gravity of the persecution of homosexuals in Fascist Italy but, as Benadusi explains thanks to his well-documented study, it helps us to better understand the peculiarity of the Fascist sexual policy and its repression of homosexuality. It did not come as a consequence of the introduction of the racial laws, nor was it an attempt to imitate Germany as many people have written. Its origin was to be found in Fascism's anthropological and political concepts and above all in its desire to carry out an anthropological revolution to change the Italian character and customs so as to create a new race made up of men and women entirely devoted to the state.

As an important element in the campaign to regenerate the Italians, the persecution of homosexuals acquired particular political significance not only in the fight against "an enemy of the new man" but became an internal political weapon to be used by the Fascist Party leaders, as happened in Germany. Thanks to the many unpublished documents Benadusi was able to access, his book discloses more precisely the importance and function of homosexuality, or rather the accusation of being homosexual, in the regime's internal power struggle, where often brutal or slanderous methods were common. The book treats these matters without yielding to scandalous narrative or sensationalism even when the situation was very tempting, as in the case of Prince Umberto of Savoy or the three Fascist Party national secretaries accused of being homosexuals. Benadusi examines these cases, like many others that concern figures of the regime, simply to understand their *political significance* because they can help us gain a better grasp of more complex political situations such as the relationship between the monarchy and Fascism or the internal struggle among the regime's leaders, or more generally to better understand the reasons for, the ideas behind, and the modes of behavior during the anthropological revolution within the sphere of the totalitarian venture.

In order to examine the precisely political aspect of the issue of "homosexuality" within the Fascist regime, Benadusi makes use of the interpretation of Fascism as the Italian "pathway to totalitarianism." It seems to me that the book's theme consists of a clash between continuity and novelty within the Fascist totalitarian venture, and that the author continually tries to reconstruct and interpret historical events as realistically as possible without allowing himself to be influenced by theoretical suppositions, which in studies of historical periods, and especially of the Fascist era, often end up imposing themselves consciously or unconsciously on the historian, making it impossible for him or her to have an unbiased and realistic view of the events examined as they actually emerge from the study. Benadusi deserves credit for having dealt with the issue from an unprejudiced point of view. With this book we have left behind the fabrications, dissertations, digressions, and theoretical disquisitions on the rhetoric of virility and Fascism's phallic essence with the inevitable reference to the phallic symbol of the club and the Duce's shaved head that up to now have made up the content of most studies of the relationship between Fascism and sexuality.

Benadusi develops his investigation, his reasoning, and his considerations and evaluations within a concrete historical context. He analyzes from a historical viewpoint the matrixes, origins, and development of the Fascist concept of man and sexuality and the regime's policy of persecution and repression of homosexuals. In this way he contributes considerably to what is known about the particular features of the Fascist totalitarian venture and how it actually operated in everyday life; thus, from this point of view, the book goes beyond its specific subject. Benadusi's considerations regarding the Fascist concept of the new man, virility, the relationship between the sexes, racism, tradition, the "double morality," and the ambiguity and contradiction between practicing and preaching, as well as his final considerations on the relationship between the political concept of sexuality and the regime's actual policy implementing the anthropological revolution, are also particularly important for an assessment of the overall results of the study in view of the general and more controversial debate over Fascist totalitarianism. I agree with most of Benadusi's conclusive considerations but would like to add some comments that emerge from the research itself.

A first series of considerations relate to the comparison between "civilian respectability" and "respectability in uniform" that Benadusi calls attention to in the conclusion and that, to a certain extent, is the essence of his interpretation of the political significance given to sexuality and homosexuality in the Fascist totalitarian venture. Benadusi maintains that "respectability in uniform" was never actually completed as demonstrated by the repeated call to demolish resistance and make a clean sweep of all "dead ground." I think it appropriate here to clarify that on the basis of the formulation developed, "respectability in uniform" was not so much an ideal to be achieved compared to the "civilian respectability," as it was in itself a reality in terms of mentality, custom, and behavior. This emerges not from theoretical propositions but from the actual experience of Fascism and is represented by Italian men and women who were integrated into the regime's organization and, for this reason, claimed to be the true incarnation of the Fascist man and woman embodying all that was then valid for "civilian respectability."

I would also like to make a few comments about the figure of the Fascist new man, who was identified above all with a virile, warrior-type male, and about the corresponding figure of the Fascist new woman, depicted as wife and mother and subjugated to male supremacy and vigorously devoted to the "political" function of producing children for the Fascist state. In both cases they definitely represent the type of male and female that Fascism tried to create within its totalitarian regime. However, I think the historiographical representation of Fascism's new man and woman, described only by their virile, warrior-like sexual characteristics, would limit the understanding of the other aspects of the Fascist anthropological concept. These aspects originated not from abstract theoretical statements but from the actual development of the totalitarian venture, from the way men and women were involved in the venture that conditioned every aspect of their existence, including sexual intercourse, their families, and their private lives. The experimental construction of a "new civilization" seen as a civilization of the masses, as the totalitarian and all-pervasive organization of a collective existence, as the organization of the working population into corporatives, introduced into the lives of real men and women living in Fascist Italy anthropological elements that conferred new common characteristics on the Fascist male and female types while also confirming the difference and hierarchy between the sexes. To a certain extent the fact of *being an organized collective* transcended the sexual status and the virile, warrior-like image and became identified, in a wider sense, mainly with the function of "citizens entirely devoted to the state." An important aspect of this new anthropological dimension that emerged from the totalitarian venture concerns women and "female citizen activists," as evidenced in an innovative study conducted by Maria Fraddosio about twenty years ago on female activism. Where male anthropology is concerned, an assessment of the new aspects introduced in the concept of the "new man" by the totalitarian venture is in the early stages; the study of Fascist university groups by Luca La Rovere highlights the usefulness of this new perspective also for male organizations.

I think Benadusi sensed the importance of the new organizational and functional dimension of Fascist anthropology but chose not to investigate it further, perhaps because he is still somehow influenced by the tendency, widespread among those researching Fascism, to take for granted that there was a permanent separation within Italian Fascism "between theoretical statements and practical applications, . . . between ideology and political action"; that the above-mentioned separation must be taken as a theoretical precondition for analysis; and that consequently the historian's task is to proceed with a sort of examination, based on the principle of coherence or noncontradiction, so as to highlight, whenever it occurs, the discord between aspiration and realization or between intuition and behavior.

In studies of a historical nature the method of separating theoretical statements from practical actions or intentions from realization tends to disconcert historians. I believe this is partly due to the assumption that a Fascist totalitarian ideology existed prior to Fascism's concrete policy. As a result, in order to evaluate the concrete policy it must be compared to the presumed preceding theories and ideologies so as to verify if it was realized or not, which inevitably brings us to the obvious conclusion that it was not realized. In my opinion, therefore, this method is not the most appropriate historic procedure for understanding the Fascist totalitarian venture and the effects it had on the lives of millions of men and women, because its application establishes inevitably, as if it were a natural law, the fact that confirms the assumption: that a contradiction or incoherence always existed between theoretical statements and actions or between intentions and realization. The equally inevitable conclusion this method leads to is that Fascism's totalitarian aspirations were not realized because the totalitarian venture was a failure. Establishing that the Fascist venture ended up as a failure cannot be transformed, in my opinion, into a failure of the Fascist theory, which is projected retroactively over the whole Fascist period, thus reducing the totalitarian venture to a mere ideological statement that was continually contradicted by the practical realizations. A similar theory seems historically sterile because it will keep confirming itself whether it is confirmed by history's inflexible irony or by the research of a historian who limits the method of evaluation to a comparison between aspiration and actions or between intentions and realization. Perhaps a more fruitful method would be to understand that from the historical point of view aspirations and intentions are an integral part of human experience, and for this reason they, too, are a historic reality and as such should be examined.

It is evident from reading this book and the brief comments I have made that there is a need for a new approach in the study of the Fascist totalitarian venture, one that would know how to evaluate the concrete historical experience within the inseparable reality of intentions and actions or aspirations and realization, ascertained and defined by their effective historical expression. This approach would reject abstract logical models projected onto a historic reality where incoherence and contradiction are nothing more than the constant manifestation of history's supreme irony. Steps forward in this direction will be made when those studying the Fascist period understand that totalitarianism was a method not a goal. Apart from my comments and evaluation of the author's final considerations it seems to me that the actual results of his study point to this new approach as the best way to gain greater historical knowledge and understanding of the Fascist totalitarian venture.

Acknowledgments

The idea for this book came to me after reading the work of George L. Mosse, whose studies, like Ariadne's thread, were able to guide me during some difficult moments. A heartfelt thanks to Emilio Gentile; his comments, which always led to queries and new considerations, encouraged me to look at issues from multiple points of view and to critically evaluate interpretations that are often taken for granted. I express my deepest gratitude to Simona Colarizi for her unflagging attention to every detail, her ability to mete out criticism and encouragement with perspicacity and gentleness, her interest, not only in the methodological and interpretational problems of the research, but the practical and human problems common among young researchers, which have made this book possible. Many people and institutions also helped me complete this book. I was facilitated in this endeavor thanks to the advice of friends and scholars, the cooperation of numerous librarians, and the courteous helpfulness of the officials at the Italian Central State Archive. Of the many people to whom I am indebted, particular thanks goes to the people in the Italian Studies Department at Brown University who gave me the opportunity to continue my studies and introduced me to many of the positive aspects of the American university system. Collaborating with Suzanne Stewart-Steinberg and the activities I participated in at the Cogut Center were crucial for broadening my interests and rethinking many aspects of my research. My deepest thanks to John Tortorice who, during my stay at the University of Wisconsin in Madison, first proposed publishing the book in English. It is to him that I owe its publication in the United States. Our close friendship and his continued support and advice have been enormously helpful throughout this endeavor. In closing, I would like to thank Suzanne Dingee and Jennifer Pudney for their fine work in translating an often complex Italian manuscript into English. I would also like to thank Stephen Marth who edited the translation of the book with great competence and precision, not limiting himself to a simple rereading of the manuscript in its pre-publication phase, but working closely together with me to resolve any interpretive problems.

Glossary

arruso—Sicilian term for a homosexual

autorizzazione maritale—Civil Code requirement for husbands to authorize wives' property transactions and legal actions

carabinieri—special unit of the Italian army that carries out police duties

confino—a police measure that placed individuals considered dangerous under house arrest somewhere distant from their normal place of residence

domiclio coatto—confinement measure used in Liberal Italy

fascio—local organization of the Fascist Party

federale—secretary of Fascist Party provincial federations

gerarca—authority of the Fascist regime

OVRA—internal organization of the political police whose task was the "vigilance and repression of anti-fascism"

P.NF—National Fascist Party

podestà—Fascist head of municipal government

Polizia Politica—secret police assigned to political investigation

prefect—state official in charge of province

ras—local Fascist leader

squadrista / squadrismo—armed Fascist squads and their violent actions

Testo Unico—in Italian law, the phrase refers to a group of laws that deal with the same topic; in this specific case, the issue was public security

Ventennio—the Fascist twenty years (1922–43)

The Enemy of the New Man

Introduction

Against Nature:
Masculinity and Homosexuality

Those who obey God, instinct and custom are disgusted by homosexuals and call them monsters against nature. However, these unfortunate persons are not always different from other men as regards the rest.

GIOVANNI PAPINI,
Rapporto sugli uomini

—Did you have sexual intercourse with the accused?
—Yes.
—What did he seem like to you?
—A pederast.
—Do you believe he availed himself of fiendish arts etc.?
—Against nature.

ALDO PALAZZESCHI,
Il codice di Perelà

In 2000, when I began doing research on homosexuality and Fascism, the argument was all but ignored in Italy. Fascism's repression of homosexuality did not even receive attention at the gay pride festival in Rome that summer, despite the enormous media attention surrounding the event. It was as though the homosexual community had taken center stage out of nowhere without a history. For an American reader who is used to finding entire sections in

bookstores dedicated to gay studies, it would be hard to imagine that in Italy
the subject is in many ways still considered taboo: an insult used to smear the
name of one's rival in political campaigns, to delegitimize an opponent, to
marginalize a classmate or a neighbor. Scientific publications on the argument
are rare; a university course on the subject would be unthinkable. On the other
hand, homosexuality has gained a lot of public visibility. It is debated in newspapers, utilized by the fashion industry, and appears often in advertisements.
Television shows and movies include it as a theme, and there are a number of
openly gay celebrities. It is a relationship of ambivalence, an attitude that
fluctuates between moral disapproval and curiosity. Homosexuality is still
considered something strange and abnormal in Italy, something to be ignored
or exploited for its eccentricity.

Studying homosexuality is considered unusual and likewise, by default,
those who study it are thought to be unusual. Believe it or not, "Are you homosexual?" was the question I received most often when presenting the book.
After awhile, I began asking in response, "Why doesn't anyone ever ask me if I
am Fascist?" Paradoxically, studying Fascism is considered completely natural,
while studying homosexuality means you must be a homosexual.

I actually became interested in the subject while researching the historical
evolution of the male image and the concept of masculinity, something George
Mosse's book *The Culture of Western Europe* (Chicago: Rand McNally, 1961) had
inspired me to reflect upon when I first read it as an undergraduate. When
reading Mosse's book, history confronted me for the first time with new questions
and concerns about behavior, mentality, and lifestyle, all of them within a
specific political and cultural context. Only later did I realize that Mosse had
written about and developed these themes in other books. In that first reading,
however, I discovered an approach to historiography that was and continues to
be incredibly suggestive and fruitful. From research on the male image in Italian
nationalism and futurism, I moved on to Fascism and decided to dedicate
specific attention to this overlooked subject, which is of course closely intertwined with the history of masculinity.

As with any new investigation, my fascination with these unfamiliar discoveries went side by side with the difficulty of addressing a series of disparate
subjects: jurisprudence and law, science and medicine, religion and politics.
Readers cited the breadth of the study as one of the book's main characteristics
when it came out in 2005, and critics positively emphasized the freshness of the
research, the abundance of documentation, and the endeavor to discuss homosexuality within a more general interpretation of the research on Fascism. The
body of research on the subject has grown since the book's publication, shedding
light on some of the specific conditions of the lives of homosexuals and lesbians

during the interwar period. At the same time, the first documentaries on the subject have been produced, and Italy's national newspapers are beginning to talk about a topic that has been obscured for way too long.

Translating the book into English provides the opportunity to give greater attention to certain aspects of the research and to explicate some assessments about the relationship between Fascism and sexuality. In particular, it is important to investigate the modalities, diffusion, motivations, and strategies with which Fascism repressed homosexuality, all of which might provide some indication of the ways in which Fascism's repression of homosexuality differs from that of other countries and other historical periods. The repression of homosexuality does not begin with Fascism, nor is it a unique prerogative since it happens in other democratic countries in the interwar years, such as France, England, and the Weimar Republic.[1] During the Fascist Ventennio, there is a typically Italian attitude toward homosexuality, closely connected to the influence of Catholic morality, which is worth analyzing and defining in relation to other contexts. For example, the observations made by George Chauncey on the male homosexual community in New York may be applicable to the Italian context, where until the end of the Second World War the cultural and linguistic distinction between homosexuality and heterosexuality was made on the basis of gender roles rather than sexual behavior.[2] Chauncey explains how there were effeminate homosexuals ("fairy," "sissy," "pansy"), more conventional homosexuals ("queers"), and masculine heterosexuals who participated in occasional relationships ("trade"), but that only the "fairies" and "queers" were actually considered abnormal. Those who accepted the proposals of these so-called fairies and queers did not forfeit their masculinity, since their role in the relationship was an active, masculine one. In many ways, this is the same model we find in Milan, Naples, and Catania under Fascism, although the reasons for which homosexual behavior did not automatically result in the formation of a homosexual identity are different.

Most relevant in the case of Italian Fascism, and in German Nazism as well, is the complex nature of the relationship between rules and transgressions, hegemonic and subaltern identities, individuals who hold power and those who are subjected to it, and dominant and marginal bodies. The very existence of rules presupposes the possibility of violating them, creating the coexistence of prescribed and transgressive behaviors. Within a dictatorial regime, subjectivities are negotiated through precarious forms of compromise, comparable to the "regulatory fictions" that Judith Butler talks about in *Gender Trouble*, discursive constructions that break down more easily the more rigid they are.[3] The concept of hegemonic masculinity itself, used in a Gramscian sense by the Australian sociologist Connell—the overly virile, traditional, misogynous, homophobic, and aggressive connotation of man that marks his every expression—is so evident in Fascism and Nazism that it almost obscures all those forms that do not conform to this model.[4] For example, in Italy Fascism's initiative to reinforce the masculinity of its citizens inevitably clashed with the values of individualism, bourgeois respectability, and Catholic morality, which were incompatible with the idea of the Fascist New Man who represented a form of virility based on masculine exuberance and aggression rather than moderation and self-control. Also in regard to Germany, Dagmar Herzog has demonstrated that it is inaccurate to think of the Third Reich solely in terms of sexual repression and that "all the ugly aspects of Nazi sexual politics and other politics were not embedded in a broader antisexual attitude, as so many scholars have surmised, but, rather, coexisted with (however conventional and conformity-inducing) injunctions and encouragements to the majority of Germans to seek and experience sexual pleasure."[5] Annette Timm maintains that "while extolling the virtues of the chaste Aryan family, Nazi leaders simultaneously provided support for various kinds of extramarital sex: first of all prostitution. . . . So the regime's sponsorship of prostitution greatly complicates the idealized imagery of Nazism's support for a nation of chaste families."[6] In addition, the development of the German nudist movement shows that there was not solely a climate of sexual conservatism and puritanism under Nazi rule.[7] The idea, then, of totalitarian regimes as reigns of repression should be reconsidered, in particular in relation to the impulses toward greater openness that were inevitable in a period of such rapid social and economic change. Also, in regard to sexuality, Fascism and Nazism try to balance the destructive and the conservative impulses, activism and the protection of traditional morality, and order and change.

I am not in the least attempting to deny the repressive nature of these regimes, which were always more and more attentive to law and order, but rather to underline how sexuality was simultaneously repressed and promoted, both regulated and incentivized. The effects of this ambivalent attitude are apparent in relation to homosexuality: both in Nazism's invocation of the tie between Bund and Eros, with the tension between the latent homosexuality of respectable society and the homoerotism of the Mannerbund, and in Fascism, in terms of the very conditions of life for homosexuals. During the Ventennio, Italy continued to be a kingdom of masculine Fascist virility but also a paradise for "eccentric love," a destination for the homosexual tourism of foreigners attracted by the country's "libertine" primitivism. Shifting from an abstract history of homosexuality based on ideas to one centered around an analysis of practices and behavior would give us a better understanding of the ways in which homosexuals adapted to the norms of society. Indeed, it is most likely the absence of just such a history that has led to the idea that the Ventennio was solely repressive and dismal. From the few existing interviews, a much more nuanced vision of the period emerges, one characterized by marginalization but also by the possibility of living one's own homosexuality with a certain liberty. At times, even the victims of Fascist repression express nostalgia for a period in which, despite the restrictions and condemnation, it was easy to have love affairs with heterosexuals who were willing to have relationships with another man. Grahm Robb's questioning of the idea that Victorian England, and the entire nineteenth century in general, was the century of sexphobia, of repression toward "vices and perversions" is applicable to Fascist Italy as well.[8] Starting from this very question, this study on homosexuality under Fascism covers the period from the end of the nineteenth century up until the Fascist Ventennio, when the stereotype of the virile male was at its height. In this period, a new idea of masculinity takes shape as a point of comparison to its effeminate counterpart, helping to define, through a negative opposition, the attributes of an ideal type model.

Abundant literature on the problem of how male identity is formed and transformed is now available and has become part of the larger discipline of men's history. The ample debate on gender, in which supporters of essentialist theories argue that it is a natural and biological fact, while constructivists posit that it is a largely social and cultural construction, surely contributed to opening the way for this research. The first essay to really draw attention to women but also men was written by Natalie Zemon Davis, who in 1976 claimed that researchers should be interested in the "history of both women and men, that we should not be working only on the subjected sex any more than an historian of class can focus exclusively on peasants."[9] Her studies were taken up again and fully developed in the 1980s, following the linguistic turn in the social sciences and the reception of poststructuralist theories. Above all Joan Scott, in her famous article "Gender: A Useful Category of Historical Analysis," used gender as a key to understanding the discursive underpinnings of historical evolution.[10] From these initial investigations a series of studies have been done, beginning in Anglo-Saxon countries, Germany, and France, and finally making their way to Italy, where the first study on the history of men was published in an issue dedicated to *Uomini* (Men) in the women's history review *Memoria*,[11] and by Maurizio Vaudagna in *Rivista di storia contemporanea*,[12] without however giving rise to a new sector of studies dedicated to the subject.

In Italy, the field of men's studies is still emerging: there is no history of masculinity that analyzes the Italian case in detail, and studies by foreign historians of Italy (usually considered only as a term of comparison for studies centered on other nations) have often given misleading interpretations based on clichés rather than on a documented reconstruction.[13] The reluctance of

Italian historians to deal with the subject derives in part from a certain wariness toward cultural studies in general but is also due to Italian historiography's focus on questions of politics and its extremely rigorous methodological approach. This approach becomes difficult when dealing with the details of inquiries on the borderline between various disciplines, such as the history of the body, science, and ideas; or cultural anthropology and historical sociology. Certainly, the subject of masculinity appears in Italian historiography, but as a particular aspect within broader, more comprehensive political, cultural, and social histories, and not as an autonomous object of study.

Italy's delay in investigating the history of masculinity has also had repercussions for the study of homosexuality, an area of study that has yet to acquire the dignity of a true research field in Italian academia. In addition, the reluctance of scholars to make use of contributions from other disciplines has impeded the investigation of an interdisciplinary subject like homosexuality. After twenty years, John D'Emilio's observations on gay history still have a certain resonance for Italy:

> In comparison to what we knew a scant fifteen years ago about the history
> of male homosexuality, the wealth of writing already produced has advanced
> our knowledge considerably. In comparison to what one would like to know,
> gay history is still in its infancy. Laboring in this field promises to open new
> vistas of understanding about the past—and about the present.[14]

Compared with what is happening in other countries, Italian historiography continues to dedicate little attention to homosexuality. The majority of studies carried out on the subject have come from sociologists, literary historians, or activists from GLBT movements (gay, lesbian, bisexual, transsexual, and transgender). The publishing houses have mostly ignored books on the history of homosexuality written in other languages. In fact, most of the fundamental texts on the subject have yet to be translated into Italian. Apart from an occasional mention in works dealing with broader subjects, there have been few specific contributions. Only in the last few years has the subject been more systematically approached. The results of these forays have greatly added to our understanding of the Fascist period as well. In fact, the word "homosexuality" has finally appeared in a recently published dictionary on Fascism.[15]

In any case, the important part played by Fascism in redefining masculinity should certainly not be underestimated. The regime embodied the most evident attempt to transform the Italian people, physically and sexually. The history of homosexuality in this phase of Italian history, then, is constantly correlated with virility, making it possible to better reconstruct the image of man promoted by Fascism. In my opinion, the evolution of the concept of virility that had begun at the end of the nineteenth century reached its climax in the Ventennio. It is not that the image of the new Fascist man was already in place before Mussolini came to power; rather, when defining the new man the regime took a series of elements that were already part of Italian culture and modified them. The new Fascist man was an exaggerated version of the sum of the various features of the pre-Fascist man: the idealized virile man was a mythical image that captivated society because it was founded on real elements; it was a feasible aspiration, a future model already based in the present.

Thus, the history of homosexuality is useful to clarify some historiographical problems linked to the interpretation of Fascism and especially to its totalitarian nature and its relation to modernity. It sheds light on many questions surrounding Fascism: how the model of virility imposed by the regime pervaded society; the scope of Fascism's totalitarian design; the successes and failures of the plan to anthropologically revolutionize Italians; the mechanisms used to create a masculine identity that conformed to ideological requirements; how intolerant Fascist racism was; the means and strategies used to repress transgressive behavior; how much politics interfered in the private sphere, and the relation between traditional morality and the new Fascist morality. The extent to which the regime's attitude toward homosexuality was the legacy of a long tradition and how much Fascism fostered the survival of a stereotype capable of conforming, with few alterations, to the republican culture that followed are some of the most important questions that this study attempts to answer.

In conclusion, it is necessary to explain the use of some words whose significance does not always coincide with their current use. As used in the book, the term "homosexuality" refers exclusively to male homosexuality and the term "pederasty," the prevalent expression used during the Fascist regime, has the same meaning and goes beyond its literal one.[16] I shall also use some other synonymous terms for "homosexual,"[17] a neologism invented by the Hungarian writer Kàroly Mària Benkert in 1869. These other terms, coined at the end of the 1800s, include "urningo" (or "urnigo") and "uranist" and derive from Plato's *Symposium*, where love between men was considered to be related to Aphrodite Urania. To avoid excessive repetition, at times the word "homosexuality" has been substituted with "sodomy," "sexual inversion," and "intersexuality," terms that were widely used during the Ventennio. Although "androgyny" and "hermaphroditism" are also used as synonyms for homosexuality, they refer to a genital conformation rather than a sexual tendency. I have used the word "homosexuality" in the singular, but it will always have a plural meaning. As André Gide pointed out back in 1911, there are many kinds of homosexuality.[18] I hope that the truth of this statement will be even more evident by the end of this work, in which many possible variations of homosexuality will be dealt with: equal sentimental unions and male prostitution, transsexuality and bisexuality, Platonic love and carnal love, occasional sexual intercourse and monogamous relationships, effeminate behavior and over-virile behavior, the transvestite and the family man.[19] On the other hand, I use the term "homo-eroticism" to mean a general attraction between men, without necessary sexual implications, while the term "homophobia" is associated with both the fear of homosexuality and that of having one's own masculinity questioned, which arises from the contempt for effeminate men.[20]

I

The Making
of the Virile Italian

He appeared as a completely new model Italian virility, whose equal could only
be found somewhere many years back in history.

MARIO CARLI,
L'Italiano di Mussolini

Spreading the Masculine Model

After the unification of Italy, the difficult task of "making Italians," of national-
izing the masses, meant not only spreading the ideal of a common nation but
creating conformity in behavior, habits, and lifestyle, something the kaleido-
scope of Italian regions lacked, so much so that it seriously jeopardized the
creation of a unified state. The socioeconomic and cultural differences between
the poorer and wealthier regions were reflected in the physical appearance of
the new citizens as well. In poorer areas, malnutrition and poverty led to high
infant mortality rates and condemned survivors to live with signs of poverty
impressed on their bodies in the form of short, thin, and delicate statures and
shallow chests. Surveys of southern Italy and the first statistical findings regarding
the population's health and anthropometric data clearly showed the need for
widespread regeneration.[1] The body and character of the Italian people had to
be molded according to the necessities of the new national state. It was imperative
to create a minimum of anthropological homogeneity through moral, behavioral,
and health standards. The link between "body and nation" was indivisible;

health, physical fitness, and masculinity were considered indispensable moral values for everyone and above all necessary for the country.[2] The body, which represented the nation just like the flag, the anthem, or national holidays, was to represent ideal beauty and be a living monument capable of conveying to the masses the values and virtues needed to increase their domestic cohesion.[3] "Physiological patriotism,"[4] achieved by forming strong, healthy individuals, would make a physically homogeneous population possible and foster the creation of a national identity.

The major supporters of the nation's greatness, those who promoted the supremacy of Italy and the establishment of an internationally prominent third Rome, also emphasized the pressing need for a deep-rooted anthropological revolution capable of eliminating the weaknesses and flaws of Italians and creating a radically new man.[5] Already during the Giolitti era,[6] palingenetic objectives—once the domain of religion—characterized the nation's radical political and cultural movements, which believed that a complete transformation of human nature was necessary for building a new society. Such a profound "revolution of the spirit" was passed off as an overall change in Italy's political and economic sphere, but it also encompassed culture, customs, and mentality, as well as the psyche, character, and physical and moral make up of Italians.[7] The "new, young" intellectual avant-garde aristocracy, endowed with the ability to view politics as a comprehensive activity capable of molding the modern conscience of the new Italian, of implementing a spiritual and physical regeneration, and of renewing a decadent, materialistic society, was supposed to lead the renewal process. Therefore, a new lay religion was needed to rediscover the ethical meaning of existence, to renew faith in national myths and ideals. This is how Emilio Gentile describes the cultural modernization project of the avant-garde movements active in pre-Fascist Italy, which "sought to be 'religious' movements and to give a new meaning to life and to the world, spreading that meaning through modern myths for the education of the masses and their integration to the national State offering them the collective awareness of the nation as a community of values and destiny."[8] It was exactly their desire to be the "preachers" of the nation's rebirth and the leaders in regenerating Italians that made the Futurists, the revolutionary syndicalists, the nationalists, the members of La Voce and the proselytes of D'Annunzio into relentless adversaries of the liberal ruling class. They were the declared enemies of Italietta, a nation without backbone or dreams, resigned to accepting their meritocracy. And even if Alberto Asor Rosa tells us that "at its origins, this total denial of the present is no more than a conscious expression of the intellectual class's *deprecatio temporum*,[9] it is sufficient to read Papini to understand why minds and spirits were so attracted by the call for a revolution:

The most revolutionary idea consists in changing people's sentiments, in clearing their minds and making them younger, in teaching them boldness and folly. Upon changing man's spirit all desired external changes shall follow spontaneously easily and naturally. The real revolution is in the mind and not at the barricades.[10]

Moreover, Asor Rosa himself admits that in the rejection of Giolitti's Italy there was already "a positive outlook, the search for a new culture, a new morality and, in the end, a combination of all these efforts, the search for a *new man*,"[11] as the foundation for the realization of a new state.[12] The spread of a new mentality focused on regeneration and revolution and aimed at substituting outdated values, ideals, and myths, cast doubt on the previously held belief in unyielding and inevitable progress toward a better society. This widened the gap between those who believed that by changing society, one could change men, and those who thought that in order to transform society, it was indispensable to alter men, to carry out an outright anthropological revolution. Confidence in the belief that freely and rationally deliberated choices fostered the amelioration of man was slowly being replaced with the conviction that only through external action would it be possible to change man's nature.

In this concept of politics as a regenerative activity that could legitimately invade all spheres of an individual's life so as to mold and remake him lay the premises for the total submission of personal liberties to the mission of the party or state. Politics deprived people of the possibility for self-determination and reduced them to mere objects in the hands of a superior power that claimed the right to shape them mentally and physically according to a predetermined ideological formula. The extent to which these developments contained the germ of totalitarianism is easily understandable. In point of fact, the legacy of early twentieth-century avant-garde movements and radical anti-Giolitti nationalism will prove to have a direct effect on the creation of the new Fascist pedagogical program.

Benito Mussolini's dream, bolstered by the cultural movements, was to have "wholly virgin generations" born and brought up within Fascism, capable of expressing and implementing all the potential inherent in its ideology. For the Duce, Fascism was the "greatest experiment of remaking the Italians in our history. It is as though Fascism takes the Italians one by one to form them according to the national rules." Mussolini also said, "Sometimes I like the idea of laboratory generations, the idea of creating the warrior class that is always ready to die, or the class of inventors who pursue the secrets of mysteries, or judges, or the class of great industrialists, famous explorers or great governors."[13] The desire to regenerate Italians in their habits and character was combined with the totalitarian intention to create "a species of man, a new man, a whole man, one who is the same man in his family, in society, and in the state."[14]

As George Mosse has highlighted in his works on the bond between sexuality and nationalism, the palingenetic approach of politics in regards to men had a particular impact in the sexual sphere, the guarantor of a perpetuating lineage of strong, virile warriors.[15] The uncertainty and insecurity that accompanied modernization in all of the more advanced Western countries increased the need for firm beliefs capable of providing a foundation for one's convictions. The risk of intolerance was inherent in the search for a rigid paradigm of human behavior. The influence of Nietzsche's Overman theory and his conviction that the evolution of history was cyclical undermined people's confidence in reason, progress, and the strength of society[16] precisely because such beliefs were persuasive enough to compel people to sacrifice their own freedom[17] in the name of a higher authority capable of guaranteeing the primary links and bonds that mass society tended to tear asunder. The result was an almost obsessive conformism considered indispensable for establishing a globally shared set of norms and values necessary to ensure the disciplining of the collective to state power.

The search for a new identity and collective order also influenced the male image and the model of masculinity that, with the spread of nationalism, had increasingly become associated with "warrior-like" characteristics. Since a strong, powerful nation had to be made up of virile men, masculinity was associated with the ability to fight for the homeland; it became symbolic of virtue, health, vigor, and national regeneration. Confusion about gender, then, was considered a serious threat to the goal of orienting people, while virility became an indispensable requisite, necessary for consolidating a sense of belonging in society, of being accepted by society, as well as becoming by right a member of the national community. Such is the context in which the attempt to redefine masculinity and virilize Italian men should be situated. The exaltation of virility originated from within those movements that referred most to the strength of the nation, Italianism, activism, and youthfulness and aimed to increase demographic growth, physical vigor, and social renewal through instruction on hygiene and public health. These aspirations were not always well received by the state, and they did not always manage to have a great effect on collective behavior; yet they were destined to have a certain importance in the creation of a "male stereotype,"[18] a stereotype so widespread throughout the culture of the early twentieth century as to be commonly considered the model of reference.

Sport, Heroism, and Youth

From the nationalist point of view, young men had to be ready to go to war, an eventuality for which Italy, lest it remain marginal in the international field, needed to be prepared. Therefore, in order to develop the strength and courage necessary to triumph and dominate, Italians needed to be trained and restored mentally as well as physically—according to the old saying *mens sana in corpore sano* (a sound mind in a sound body).[19] As Enrico Corradini wrote, "The virtues of the body stimulate many virtues of the soul."[20] Indeed, virility, considered the most important male virtue, was thought to be the perfect balance of a strong, vigorous body and an energetic, strong-willed soul. The truly virile man was able to harmonize mind and body; he had exceptional self-control and was able to control his passions and his body. Every effort had to be put forth to create the most energetic, strongest, healthiest, and best-looking men possible; men endowed with "all the masculine virtues, such as courage, boldness, and the generosity of risking one's life for a noble cause, determination, sincerity of character, and the ability to look friend or foe straight in the eye."[21] Pedagogic efforts needed to be directed at bringing up "more valid, more agile and more physically beautiful young Italians so that they would also be more valid, agile, and beautiful mentally."[22] Greater importance and more time were to be given to physical education, because a well-trained, vigorous, stronger body reflected a noble soul, good moral fiber, and a well-balanced mind. Furthermore, as highlighted by Gaetano Bonetta,[23] liberal Italy had always considered gymnastics indispensable to the preparation of citizens for military service and for realizing the myth of the militarily mobilized nation.[24] Sports events also had an important role because they brought international prestige to Italy. In addition, they taught young people how to compete, created in them a sense of team spirit, and brought them closer to nationalism, which, according to Andrea Busetto "schooled them in discipline, virtue, sacrifice, and heroism."[25] An extremely "virile education" was seen as indispensable so that students would be prepared to "make their life cause one with that of the nation."[26] The nationalist review *Il Regno* suggested organizing "impressive ancient Roman games," in which young Italians "would be able to demonstrate their prowess and strength," proof that the nation had "a lot of blood running through its new veins."[27] A vigorous life fueled by competitiveness in sports was deemed necessary because "a nation's material strength is contingent on the physical development of its children."[28] According to the Futurists, sport was an indisputable sign of superiority, emblematic of modernity's energetic and vital spirit; their movement was the "intellectual program of young Italian males taught to love violent sports, eager for temerarious novelty and hungry for a life filled with adventure, energy and daily heroism."[29] Physical education became a proper school of courage because it taught students to "consider life a battle that could only be won by the most virtuous and strong willed."[30] Warfare required an athletic, aggressive temperament, and athletics showed "the civilian version of the soldier, the athlete as a combatant in a civilian clash."[31]

This is the context for the Associazione nationalista italiana's (Italian Nationalist Association) request for "an immediate increase in school and after-school activities aimed directly at encouraging militaristic behavior in young men and an effective increase in physical education, considered fundamental to the physical and moral training of the army."[32] The institutions responded to this appeal by fostering sports related to and most suited to promoting the nation's historic accomplishments; these ranged from gymnastics to fencing, from target shooting to alpinism. "In this way the state established strategies of discipline and control connected to military instruction, with the scope of defending the country and improving the population both physically and mentally. In other words, they sought to create citizen–soldiers."[33] However, this did not mean that sports were widely practiced in Italy; it was more of a cultural myth than a real activity engaged in by millions of citizens. This exaltation of physical fitness and the importance given to masculinity and athleticism served as the premise for the creation of the myth of the political leader–athlete.[34] The extraordinary quality of the figure of the athlete, scornful of danger, inherently courageous and heroic conveyed the idea of a natural winner in sports and politics. The political leader, narcissistically presumed to possess physical superiority, also had to provide evidence of his aptitude for sport and his unequalled athletic ability. The appeal of an athletic politician that would find its maximum expression and the culmination of its suggestive powers in the figure of Mussolini could only be generated in a country permeated by the importance of sport but little inclined to practice it.

Therefore, the image of masculinity was most perfectly represented by the athlete whose specific physical characteristics had to be strength, youth, agility, and beauty. The model of the virile male had many aspects in common with the classic athlete, rendered eternal in sculpture. Western European culture, moreover, was greatly influenced by Hellenic aesthetic ideals.[35] According to Scipio Sighele, for example, "the ideal type of man was represented by the young Greeks and Romans leaving the gymnasium." Ancient art, which portrayed "chests that breathe easily, trunks that are planted sturdily on the hips, and sinewy legs that nimbly support the whole body, did not concern itself as ours does about the height of a forehead, the curl of a scornful lip or the frown of an angry brow." Sighele longed for a return to the ancient Greek ideals of physical beauty whose "harmonious ideal" of sculpture should continue to be adopted by modern society.[36] Enrico Corradini as well believed the ideal of eternal beauty resided in Greek sculpture:

> I searched the Uffizi Gallery in Florence for the famous *Lottatori* [*Wrestlers*] and saw once again in the movement of muscles and nerves sculpted in

marble, the image of beauty preserved for centuries and millennia. And I understood the art of Greece and Athens. An art that established the beauty of strength and agility, the beauty of life for centuries and millennia.[37]

The strong influence of classicism was particularly evident during Fascism, which made it its emblem.[38] The statues that decorate the Fascist-built Stadio dei Marmi in Rome exemplified Fascism's new man even if the balance between strength and harmony so magnificently achieved in ancient Greece was, in this case, disproportionately in favor of power and masculinity. The tendency of Fascism's "heroic nude" was to combine beauty with an impressively muscular body, a grim face, and a plastic martial, gladiatorial pose.[39]

> A virile man's appearance—Guido Mazza maintained—may express distinction but not aestheticism. His beauty is made up of contrasts not consonance; not of nuances but of harshness; a male face must be the expression of the race and not of harmony.[40]

This enhancement of the aesthetic aspects linked with an aggressive and hypermasculine image began thanks to nationalism and its proposal of classicism as a conduit for the emergence of a new morality based on the exaltation of aggressive and heroic energies that would counter the Christian philosophy of renunciation.[41] Ancient Rome's "heroic morality" would prepare Italians for life's difficulties, strengthening their willpower and reviving their spirit and body. A concrete example of how much the country's greatness depended on the masculinity of its men was provided by the Roman legionnaires who, according to Francesco Coppola, embodied all the masculine virtues that the war would instill in the "new Italian people": "The perfect harmony of discipline and liberty, justice and power, will and intelligence, . . . awareness, meditated resolve, steadfastness even when faced with adversity and danger, composure even if expressing the joy of a victory, a heart free of anger, hard and fast subordination to Divine and human laws, perfect dignity, absolute self-control of one's passions, a morality on par with the valor of the race and its virtues."[42] The nationalist movement's references to Rome did not only mean tying it to the past; indeed, the real novelty lay in combining tradition with modernity. A new type of man would be formed through the "marvelous and harmonious combination of two civilizations, the ancient and the modern." In other words, he would be the perfect synthesis of ancient Roman and modern American virtues:

> *The new man*, the man of the twentieth century and the future, the typical American so incredibly strong and perfect for work and play, for his ideas and muscular strength, for peace and war *mens sana in corpore sano*; the man

who derives from the ancient and the modern man, the Greco-Roman
Anglo-Saxon.[43]

Accelerated industrialization brought with it the need to rebuild masculinity to enable individuals to cope with the new challenges of the modern
world. Men, fascinated by speed and capable of dominating machines, were the
real heroes of the future. Motorists, race car drivers, aviators, and submarine
helmsmen made up the image of the new man because, with machines as their
armor like medieval knights, they fearlessly faced modern tournaments: auto
races, endless skies, and bottomless oceans. Chivalry was still the ideal model of
masculinity, characterized by poise, composure, sense of honor, pride, and
courage. Only by participating in modern competitions that truly tested one's
strength would it be possible to manifest these ideals again. Heroic deeds, death,
and sacrifice accepted with intuitive detachment were in fact the virile characteristics of the medieval knight as well as the modern sportsman and record
holder. Not by chance then does the protofuturist Mario Morasso use the image
of the race car driver, the new hero of the machine, to reincarnate the myth of
the fearless, virtuous knight. The birth of a "new chivalry of the twentieth-
century" would fulfill the full expression of masculinity.[44] These new warriors
would acquire the physical qualities and temperament of past heroes and put
them to good use for the country. The modern young man "was receiving more
effective schooling in the potential of energy than any other." Through machines,
energy was a force on which to exercise conquest, domination, and heroism,
and in doing so, demonstrate their manly courage.[45] The automobile would
reawaken the dormant warrior qualities in men because it "repositions modern
males in situations tantamount to those experienced by men employing weapons
in moments of grave peril, and teaches them to challenge death serenely." "On
the one hand, driving an automobile reinvigorates and eliminates effeminate or
dainty manners and dress; it makes one tougher, more accustomed to exertion;
to making quick decisions; on the other hand, driving makes one ill tempered,
increases hostility toward other men, reduces volition and produces a kind of
analgesia and moral indifference toward oneself and others. As everyone can
see, these make excellent qualities for combat."[46] Competitiveness served to
educate new generations in the ways of a virile existence, to prepare them for the
battle of life and to form individuals capable of employing their aggressiveness
for the benefit of the nation.[47]

The Futurists and nationalists—and to a certain extent the members of La
Voce and revolutionary syndicalists—helped define and spread an image of men
based on the exaltation of masculinity. Young men were to be molded according
to authoritarian pedagogical methods consisting of orders, discipline and

hierarchy, exercises in domination and fighting, sport and physical education, and games and contests.[48] Only a "vigorous education of adolescents" and the cult of heroism would be able to temper the weak, effeminate character of a people known abroad for their sunshine and mandolins. The dream of creating a proper militia of young men who would be able to consolidate national identity by manifesting their virile Italian characteristics led Pasquale Turiello to contemplate the introduction of paramilitary training for boys and girls. Claiming it "urgent that the weak ministers, deputies, and magistrates be followed by a more virile generation,"[49] he suggested organizing school battalions, militarized high schools, groups of young explorers, as well as marches and choral singing. In this backdrop the warrior, the fighter and the citizen-soldier became emblematic of masculinity. Enrico Corradini also thought the new male should symbolize life and victory: "His gaze should be fixed straight ahead and direct; his forehead should be low and firm; his mouth should be tight-lipped and unyielding, and his strength should be equal to his ardor and volition."[50] His appearance should reflect the extent of his courage and character with an "extraordinarily prominent profile from forehead to chin, the mark of true fighters and conquerors; he should have sharp, square features, in other words, a face similar to a sword's blade, the mark of resoluteness, aggressiveness, and strong willpower."[51]

In these ways, nationalism added a new fundamental aspect to the predominant nineteenth-century male stereotype: aggressiveness. The male body needed to be similar to a warrior's lest he be caught unprepared for combat, a duel, or a war. Daring, courage, and physical strength were extremely important. As a result, virility, brute force, and courage were exalted over capability, dexterity, and cleverness bringing about the "militarization of masculinity."[52] The new man's body was to express his virile strength. Like sport, warfare was also instrumental in consolidating the male identity, a sort of initiation to virility. The outbreak of World War I further supported this point of view, which endured in sporting events after the war was over. As George Mosse noted, "sports were considered a peacetime continuation of the war, the best surviving test of masculinity."[53]

Furthermore, the indivisible link established between virility and activeness accentuated the aggressive aspects of masculinity because "real men" were defined as those possessing great vitality. The conflict between the "active man of practical reason and the contemplative man of pure reason" would be resolved with the victory of the former, the only men capable of facing the challenges of modernity.[54] People incapable of action were considered weak and passive, similar to women. Consequently, it was necessary to attack those "tired, effeminate spirits who prefer feminine words to male actions."[55] The criticism leveled

at peace and quiet, inactivity, and lack of strength in favor of virility led the
radical nationalist movements and later Fascism to reject the bourgeois mentality.
In light of the mandate that the *new man* had to be energetic, courageous, and
fervently agonistic, the attack on the passivity and lack of heroism typical of
the bourgeoisie was inevitable. The potbellied type in his dressing gown and
slippers was far removed from this model of virility and risked being taken for
an effeminate milksop.

During the Giolitti era the Socialists were not the only ones to be anti-
bourgeoisie; the same sentiment was expressed by the radical nationalist movements, whose criticism, however, was limited to mores and mentality and not
concerned with political or economic aspects.[56] This sentiment was fruit of a
classist opposition insofar as the term "*bourgeois* did not so much imply a *social*
category, characterized by private property, as it did a *moral* one characterized
by a sense of privacy."[57] The bourgeois or middle-class person, concerned only
with his personal interests, was depicted as an individual whose only ideals
were humanitarianism and pacifism; a refined, idle egoist incapable of real political commitment. The first decade of the twentieth century, wrote Salvatore
Francesco Romano, saw the "formation of the typical middle-class figure who,
according to his contemporaries, was reluctant and even opposed to heroic
enthusiasm and adventure, convinced of the advantages of peaceful economic
development, and expressive of his humanitarian ideas. He enjoyed the comforts
of life, looked after his own interests carefully, and was essentially conservative
and philistine despite his liberal ideas. This caricature of the average Giolitti-era
bourgeois was to become so widespread that the words *borghese* [bourgeois] and
borghesia [bourgeoisie] in Italian are almost exclusively associated with this
specific controversial moral significance."[58] This stereotypical image of the
bourgeois man also included his appearance. For Papini, for example, "your
classic 'fat bourgeois' was a man who thought first and foremost about filling
his stomach and his wallet."[59]

Bourgeoisie also expressed a generational revolt. Following the changes
brought about in the new century by the advent of modernity, the younger
generation was contesting the mentality, habits, and values of their fathers and
expressing their desire for transformation.[60] During such a period of rapid
change, the behavioral models that had guided the choices of their fathers
now seemed useless to the younger generation.[61] Since virility meant vigor and
youthfulness, it was necessary to make room for the new generations in the
same way that, on an international level, the young, energetic nations would
oust old nations from their undeserved positions of prominence. Such hostility
on the part of the younger middle-class toward the bourgeois order established
by their elders was pleasantly described by George Mosse as the "anti-bourgeois

bourgeois revolution."[62] Most of the young people openly rebelling "against positivism, materialism, and the lifestyle of their fathers belonged to a select group of bourgeois high school and university students. Bored and dissatisfied, they were looking for excitement, novelty, and adventure; something that would give their lives some significance. Giuseppe Prezzolini himself acknowledged that they could afford to scorn the past and the middle class because they were sustained by the very same milieu.[63] People from all the anti-Giolitti movements that developed in Italy at the beginning of the twentieth century became spokespeople of the young and their dissatisfaction contributing to the creation and diffusion of the myth of youth and the cult of youthfulness.[64]

In an anthropological contraposition between youth and old age, the traditional distinguishing traits of the young—immaturity, inexperience, impulsiveness, and ingenuity—were translated into their opposites—resoluteness, enthusiasm, courage, and physical and moral vigor. Being young meant keeping pace with the times, being able to decipher and interpret the future so as to build a different and better world. "War against old age," against "the predominance of white hair," against "the tyranny of old age." became the slogans of the early twentieth century generational revolt.[65] Electing themselves representatives of the young—of their needs and dissatisfaction with the liberal State—the nationalists, like the members of La Voce and the Futurists, considered themselves the only ones capable of uniting the young generation that was eager for change.[66]

With the outbreak of World War I the generational awareness of those who took part in it was further consolidated, but, as Robert Wohl said, "What bound the generation of 1914 together was not just their experiences during the war, as many of them later came to believe, but the fact that they grew up and formulated their first ideas in the world from which the war issued, a world framed by two dates, 1900 and 1914."[67] After the war, the Futurists, the *arditi*, and the *squadristi* reconnected with the generational revolt of the beginning of the century, proposing a new regime more suited to the younger generation. The myth of youthfulness and its connection to virility merged with Fascist ideology to recreate an antiliberal climate and reignite the desire for a complete change.

The Sexual Sphere

However, within the radical nationalist movements there were some differences about the idea of virility that involved, above all, aspects linked to the sexual sphere. For example, the Futurists viewed virility as sexual drive, an instinctive libidinous impulse toward erotic satisfaction and the freedom to express one's sexuality.[68] Masculinity was expressed as "contempt for women," who became instruments for pleasure used to increase the number of new conquests and to give vent to the senses and sensual pleasure.[69] However, as historian Renzo De Felice notes, "What might have seemed like antifeminism was actually the denial of sentimental and nostalgic love, traditional love, or lascivious and obsessively erotic love. It was a rejection of 'horrible and heavy' love, the sort that 'hinders the progress of men' and perpetuates the inferiority of women, preventing them from being modern."[70] Indeed, despite declarations that "the weaknesses of the race" had to be overcome so that Italians could "finally appear very virile, very new and very Italian,"[71] the Futurists' political program would have granted women active and passive suffrage, eliminated the marital authorization law (*autorizzazione maritale*), and abolished the institutions of marriage and the family. It also called for the legalization of divorce, scoffed at the excess importance given to virginity, renounced jealousy, and foresaw the "gradual advent of free love and state-owned children." The proposed program would have meant throwing out the time-held conventions of bourgeois society and respectability by a libertarian, anticonformist force unknown to the nationalists and the Fascists. The futurist conception of life as a permanent party to be lived beyond the limits of ordinary morality made them little inclined to channel their vitality into rigid conventions.[72] Futurist Italo Tavolato's *Contro la morale sessuale* (Against Sexual Morality) and *Elogio alla prostituzione* (Praise of Prostitution) are examples of this total openness toward the basic instincts of men.[73] The most sacred and fundamental right was the "right to sexual intercourse" promoted by Mario Morasso, who praised masculinity to such an extent that he separated sex from the sphere of love, affection, and the communion of the senses.[74] Paradoxically, in this vision the female had to disappear because her "tyrannical love" threatened male virility and heroism.[75] In *Mafarka il futurista* (Mafarka the Futurist) F. T. Marinetti created a character endowed with inhuman virile powers: an African king who steals the gift of procreation from woman by single-handedly generating a new life through willpower alone.[76] The constant references to virility in Marinetti's works, which often associated aggressiveness with masculinity and military success with sexual prowess, were based on an image of men as brutish, always in the grip of passion.[77] Futurist aesthetics substituted the languor of the decadents with an eruption of irrepressible vitality and replaced sentiment with coitus.[78] Nevertheless, if "hyper-sensuality,"[79] "marriage,"[80] and "female extravagance"[81] encouraged "male effeminacy" and the "development of pederasty," because they hindered the expression of warrior-like virtues, the banning of women and the birth of exclusively male social relations also generated a sort of "homosexual panic."[82] In fact, the obscene, a characteristic element of Futurist style, art and poetry,[83] was continuously expressed in sexually oriented metaphors in which homosexuality was used as an instrument to mock adversaries and show irreverent contempt for their passé mentality. But homosexuality was considered detestable only when it appeared in the form of effeminate behavior, revealing the absence of courage and exuberance. Marinetti, in his *Taccuini* (Notebooks) clearly illustrated this point of view:

> October 8, 1918: The Lt. sculptor Antonio Maraini arrived late. He was distinguished, effeminate, and serious when he spoke. He had the typical delicateness of homosexuals. Intelligent. With him was a nice Englishman, 28, a refined and distinguished air force major. Jim S. Barnes was an elegant, well-educated pederast who never simpered shamelessly. But you can feel that he does not have the predatory hold or the attack strength of a real man. He was as hesitant about sex (at 28) as one might be at 15. He heard me speak in London in a dark room, funereally buried under the black silk of Monroe's Poetry Bookshop. This had all the symptoms of homosexuality as well. There were no clear signs of aggressive virility, only a vague poetic desire for a faraway woman idealized to the point of being abstract.[84]

In his opinion virility was not so much the opposite of homosexuality but rather of effeminacy (languor, passivity, sentimentality, and mawkishness). Paradoxically, therefore, Marinetti thought pederasts were useful because they could satisfy such typical aspects of the female mentality as "sentimental complications, exquisitely abstruse notions and unproductive tenderness" that a real man—the copulating instrument, cold, violent, and lacking in tenderness—was not capable of satisfying. It was a good idea, therefore, to have "a homosexual friend as a usual guest around the house, as a sentimental, refined, delicate, and somewhat sickly relief for one's girlfriend or lover."[85] Certainly, Marinetti never theorized any other use for a homosexual friend. Actually, to halt the spread of the Nuova Internazionale degli invertiti (New International of Homosexuals) he proposed to "immediately provide the widespread distribution of free prostitutes."[86] However, he was not shocked by homosexuality. Indeed, his continuous criticism of social taboos, his constant search for extreme paradoxes, for liberation from bourgeois hypocrisies, and for complete satisfaction of the senses, as well as his disdain for conventions and prejudices and his desire to experience all forms of pleasure, led him away from ever considering sexual perversions too negatively. In his speech "Discorso futurista agli inglesi" (Futurist Speech to the English), given before the Lyceum Club in London, Marinetti scolded the English for their puritanism and bigotry and criticized the condemnation of Oscar Wilde as being "lugubrious and ridiculous":

> The intellectuals of Europe will never forgive you. Did you not cry out in all your newspapers that it was time to open the windows because the

plague was over? It is natural that almost all of your twenty-year-old boys
are homosexuals for a while in such a formal, hypocritical environment, so
set in its ways. This perfectly respectable taste of theirs develops because of
a kind of intensified *camaraderie* and friendship that occurs in sports activities
before they turn thirty and have to start working and putting their lives in
order. That is when they suddenly return from Sodom, become engaged
to a girl who brazenly wears low-cut dresses, and are quick to severely
condemn those who are inverts from birth, the false men, the half women,
who don't mend their ways.[87]

Homosexuality was to be disdained only when associated with the decadence
and extreme romanticism of a repressive society that suffocated the primary
instincts of men. Every individual was allowed "every freedom save the right to
be cowardly" or to preserve the past, now dead and buried.[88] Also, from this
point of view pederasty was not part of Marinetti's world because any attempt
to recreate a society like the Greek one, based on the educational value of the
adult–adolescent relationship, was a step backward for him; cultural traditionalism was to be avoided but without condemning homosexuality as an individual
choice. In fact, the Futurist poet treated the matter much more liberally than
most of his contemporaries. So much so that Aldo Palazzeschi, despite his
maniacal reservation regarding his private life, openly confessed his love for a
"lovely" young man "of about twenty," to Marinetti with the knowledge that
he would find an understanding listener.[89]

The nationalists' attitude toward sexuality was very different indeed. They
linked virility with self-control and set domination over instinct and passion.
Sex was to be channeled within the limits of the national ethic in order to fulfill
its natural purpose of procreation within matrimony. Assigning a specific
political value to sexuality led to the explicit disciplining of sex, viewed as a
"fundamental element of national identity." Morality served to establish rigid
behavioral norms to avoid anarchy and the corruption of customs. As a result,
the nation would become the realm of moral laws, and every action was to
be carried out in its interest. The state would guarantee respect of its ethical
dictates through widespread education and by submitting citizens to a process
of normative internalization. Iron discipline as well as self-constraint and
control over one's passions served to orient individual choices toward a public
end. According to Sighele, "relative chastity denotes a condition of superiority
in a people and an individual. For the individual it is a sign of self-control and
self-confidence that will enable him to put the energy he would have wasted on
pleasure to good use in other fields. For a people it is its strength to conquer and
civilize the world. Superiority in the growth of a race is largely due to its physical

health: a population that is weak because of sensual excess will have a short-lived civilization."[90] Likewise, "young people need to be reminded that even if chastity cannot be an absolute rule it should be an exercise, an exercise in will-power that keeps the body healthy and elevates the spirit."[91] Self-control created a balance between two apparent dichotomies: action and discipline. A rigid division and classification of roles and behavior, a uniformity of customs, and the moralization of the sexual sphere could be achieved through adherence to bourgeois rules of respectability. Nationalism channeled sexuality into bourgeois conformism, smoothing over the most unsettling aspects of virility, and consequently managed to define "ideal types" while "closing off all routes of escape from the respectable world."[92] The rejection of all that differed from the proposed male model further aggravated an already dichotomized view of reality and increased the head-on opposition between *amico* (friend) and *nemico* (enemy), between *tipi* (types) and *controtipi* (counter types). An identity formed through rigid contrasts and determined by debasing and rejecting the opposing identity made *il diverso* (the other) a focal point of nationalist ideology. Whoever lacked the characteristics of the ideal type was easily identifiable and was considered an enemy of society, an "outsider" out of step with the standards and values of the nation.

In its explicit separation of the sexes and extreme exaltation of masculinity, nationalism was deeply misogynous and hostile toward the mixing of gender roles. Both homosexuality and feminism, a "movement made up of old maids or unsexed people,"[93] "truly ugly women, viragoes, bony, dried-up damsels and witches,"[94] were intolerable for those who viewed virility as an indisputable requisite. Calling someone a cowardly eunuch was considered an offense reserved for one's worst enemies. Homosexuality was considered an unnatural defect common in morally, mentally, and physically inferior individuals; males had to carry themselves with military bearing and demonstrate their masculinity by maintaining an athletic body. According to Mario Morasso, "homosexuals had a different nervous system"; they were "eunuchs, both physically and morally; they were hypocritical and incapable of important or powerful actions or of any good activities whatsoever."[95] For Sighele, they represented "the strangest, the filthiest and, fortunately, the rarest of unions that two people can form—a monstrous parody of love."[96] Consequently, society should severely punish any "abnormal" behavior and stress the differences between genders. Masculinity was based on virility and founded exclusively on heterosexuality, to be interpreted, however, as male domination over women to the point of radical misogyny. G. Papini, expressing his masculinity, stated that his book *Maschilità* was about male matters and was written for men "who were supposed to be bold, fearless, a bit crazy and, above all, to have the courage to be beastly, brutal, savage, strong, energetic, tough and proud. Those who deviated from this rule were "effeminate men," "women behind a virile mask and name," "weak men with female traits," or "weak women with male traits." In the end this led to the same conclusions reached by the Futurists: men should free themselves from love for women because loving them meant becoming their slaves.[97]

For the nationalists the standard by which they defined and judged people and their behavior was masculinity; "the line between modern masculinity and its enemies had to be sharply drawn," wrote George Mosse.[98] Thus, virility became a political instrument used to criticize one's adversaries by portraying them as effeminate: the Socialists, for example, were described as power hungry, "frenetic little devils, half men with an evil and cowardly spirit whose long-standing ambition makes them dangerously ferocious like the eunuchs of Byzantium with their shrill voices."[99] The class war and those in favor of the proletariat represented the "dream of the *eunuchs* who deceive themselves that they are men: little men pretending to be warriors."[100] The Socialists had beastly instincts that made them subhuman at the opposite extreme of the male stereotype. The Liberals, instead, were described as "decadent men, very decadent,"[101] passive, old and weak, with an "average temperament, not strong, not rich, not agile, neither energetic nor resolute."[102]

The nationalists' attitude, aimed at dehumanizing political rivals and depriving them of their respect and dignity, added to the already substational foundation for Fascism's subsequent fanatical opposition of *amico* (friend) and *nemico* (enemy). Although this verbal aggression had not yet escalated to concrete violence, as would come about with the Fascist squadrons, the radical nationalist movements had already demoted their adversaries to negative stereotypes, most often by underlining their lack of virility. Often comparing their rivals to women or to old people for their lack of strength and resoluteness, they sought to combine the contestation of the programs and ideas of their rivals with an attack on their disposition.[103] The enemy par excellence was Giolitti, a man who lacked courage and morality, and who "thought Italians were innately inept at war, a miserable population of females";[104] he was "an old shoe" with "the mentality of his wife, Rossa, a little Piedmontese woman with a small brain. Giolitti has the mentality of a housewife, and on top of that, he is a bureaucrat and a criminal."[105] Francesco Nitti, depicted as a person who lacked virility and ideals, a loudmouth, was no better. Like all impotent people, he showed little dedication to his political agenda and likewise had the personality of a defeated man.[106]

The contrasting images of the young, virile, and athletic new man and the lazy, potbellied, and shortsighted elderly democrat were used by the antiliberal, anti-Giolitti movements to create a grotesque caricature of their political rival.

Among the opposing political parties, there was an anthropological difference that gave great aesthetic and political importance to one's physical appearance. Each party's ideology proposed a standard of beauty to which the body was supposed to conform, becoming the outward manifestation of inward diversity. By leveling the distinction between physical, sensory, and moral qualities it was possible to "mythologize the world of politics by physiognomizing it" and to believe that somatic deformation could be employed to prove an adversary's inferiority.[107] In this way, the human body became a *politicum*; a battlefield on which a series of contradictions could express themselves publicly: young/old; black/white; healthy/sick; strong/weak; normal/abnormal; male/female.

Fascist Revision

The use of stereotypes against one's political foe would also characterize Fascism, which accentuated the same opposition of human types that began with nationalism. Thus, wrote Emilio Gentile, "liberalism and socialism portrayed not only two political concepts but also two types of people: the bourgeois man and the obsequious man of the crowd against which the 'militia party' began forming a new type, the Fascist man. . . . The Fascist revolution, therefore, was also to be a battle of youth against old age, of vitality against rationality. The struggle was not between ideologies but types of individuals. At stake was the model of a new type of man."[108] Political foes were insulted and ridiculed (not only verbally), and very often their virility was the object of these disparagements. The repeated recourse to laxatives and castor oil served to openly illustrate the cowardice of anti-Fascists, individuals who were scared "shitless"—not only metaphorically. Shaving the enemy's beard and shearing his head was another method used to divest them of their masculinity. In some cases these forms of humiliation were so barbaric that they reached the point where the most obstinate opponents of the regime were sodomized.[109] The *squadristi* used violence to establish their own masculinity at the expense of their enemy's. Shedding an enemy's blood was a form of initiation into virility. The Fascists tried to legitimize this use of violence by situating it within the noble framework of an honor code, by defining it as "surgical, intelligent and chivalrous" without in practice ever eliminating bullying, brutality, and gratuitous cruelty.[110] Resolutely accepting the use of force reasserted one's Fascist pride and served to consolidate the militia party's camaraderie. Fascist ritual adopted symbolism connected with the bold exhibition of one's masculinity; in fact, invocations of the "holy club" preceded punitive expeditions by the Blackshirts "carried out as playful exercises in virility,"[111] which often ended with an affirmation of one's potency in the form of a collective visit to a brothel. The repeated use of sex-related adjectives such as "male," "virile," and "potent" as opposed to "female," "impotent," and "cowardly" was aimed at establishing camaraderie in a community of males that was cohesive yet constantly impelled to demonstrate and boast their personal courage and strength in respect to the next. Even the Fascist lifestyle was supposed to stress the martial nature of a militia whose "military appearance was intended to give Italy a new male virility."[112] The regime, through the image of the new man and the male stereotype connected with it, tried to enhance its self-representation and highlight the difference of those who did not conform to that model.

The ideal of virility propagated by the national radical movements provided the base on which to build the new mentality of the Blackshirts. The new Fascist male was in many ways, "the continuation of a stereotype that had its roots in nineteenth-century nationalism. No matter how free he felt to explore new regions, his ancestors were the youths who had waged the generational war at the end of the century."[113] The Fascists, however, personalized the male stereotype that was commonly accepted at the beginning of the twentieth century, adding new features more closely connected to the war experience. The effect that the war had on the image of manhood was not lost on Mussolini, who understood that the men who had fought in the trenches provided a new human potential that could be used for his political plan. The legacy of the fighters, the *arditi* and *squadristi,* was added to the magma of cultural movements: socialism and nationalism, the La Voce milieu, Futurism, D'Annunzism, and idealism. From this complex mixture the Duce molded a new political elite determined to bring down the liberal state in view of the achievement of his own ideal of the male through the complete transformation and regeneration of Italians. Fascism integrated the different nuances given to masculinity at the turn of the century into a new synthesis and exploited them for all their meanings and implications, depending on the moment or situation. The regime reformulated the male image and adopted such means as symbols, rites, and ceremonies to guarantee its diffusion. As a totalitarian dictatorship, Fascism's aim was to reach and mold every Italian. This applied to both men and women and involved the creation of strict models of femininity and masculinity, of motherhood and fatherhood on the basis of the values expressed in the ideology.[114]

As we have seen, virility and the war-mongering values connected with it (the essence of political participation during Fascism) resulted in the development of "new mythologies and manifestations of aggressiveness and manly vigor," by the mass media in order to publicly assert a "typical Fascist model of male identity."[115] Propaganda helped spread the image of masculinity as being aggressive, authoritarian, and soldierly through iconographic representation, the exaltation of physical education and youthfulness, and the public exposure of the Duce's body as a model of virility and political culture.[116] Also pedagogy, the virile education of young men, aimed at the "heroic resurrection of the new Italian," was meant to create a insurmountable barrier against the spread of foreign trends that tended to confuse genders, gradually making males more effeminate and females more masculine.[117] As the well-known jurist Giuseppe Maggiore stated peremptorily:

> Fascism is male. It loves danger, dislikes chitchat, and scorns courting; because of its natural roughness, it uses its fists when necessary; Fascism is as hard as stone; a far cry from the sweet texture of candied fruit that— like the soul of a woman—hides a hard, teeth-cracking pit inside. That suffices to determine its sex. . . . In short, Fascism arouses virility against any sort of effeminateness or weakness of the spirit. It is also against the Petrarchism of poetry, the mysticism of religion, the democratization and liberalization of politics, against dandyism and leniency at school. Is there anything more masculine than that?[118]

Virility—the pride and prerogative of the Italian race: "a virile population of dominators and lovers who are always armed, natural born leaders, made for sexual supremacy"[119]—was firmly linked to the warrior image. Fascist men lived in a permanent state of war; their virility was based on courage and heroic actions. The task of the "bestial morality that embodied the new ethical type, be it individual, class, people, or race," was to bring back the vitality and warrior spirit of ancient Rome after centuries of servitude and resignation.[120]

The continuous display of male chauvinism by the Fascists has been interpreted in different ways: in Wilhelm Reich's psychoanalytic vision it is considered the expression of the average, sexually repressed man's structurally irrational character; in Carlo Emilio Gadda's grotesque literary caricature of the matter it is seen as the emblem of a "favist era"; Bruno Wanrooij links the regime's "phallocracy" to a crisis of identity and men's social role following the First World War; while for Alfredo Capone the need to reassert masculinity was because there was also the need to repropose a collective demonstration of sexuality.[121] In my opinion, Fascism's exaltation of virility was the outcome of its project to create a "new man," which meant transforming every aspect of citizen's lives, from behavior in public to behavior in private. The aim was explained clearly by Mussolini in 1932: "How we eat, dress, work, sleep and all of our everyday habits need to be reformed."[122] Only by constantly reproposing this ideal of virility could it become a standardized mental and normative framework, capable of clearly outlining gender identity and normal sexual behavior. Consequently, tolerance diminished toward anyone who did not conform to the accepted model proposed by the antibourgeois campaign, which, in its attempt to create a completely Fascist morality and lifestyle with virility as its main prerequisite, opened battle against celibate, sedentary, and weak men, targeting through clear allusions, impotency, and pederasty.

Fascism, therefore, marked the apex of the stereotype of masculinity, virility, courage, and aggressiveness. Physical fitness was considered so important that anyone who was "different" was to be held in contempt. Meanwhile the conflict between type and countertype, between male and anti-male, reached such exasperated levels that it opened the door to racism. Real males were muscular and virile, vigorous and in good shape. They wore the fierce look of warriors, strong and bold, and were always ready and eager to go to war or conquer a woman. On the other hand, non-males had frail effeminate bodies and delicate features. They were shy and gentle, they moved gracefully, easily became emotional, and were timidly affectionate with the gentle sex. By stressing the importance of virility and sacrificing freedom and tolerance for order, conformism, and internal cohesion, Fascism "carried intolerance against those who were different and useless to an extreme, thus turning the question into something that no longer concerned society and its customs but the nation and its survival."[123] The prescribed ideal served as a guide for every aspect of citizens' lives, from morality to custom, from their way of thinking to their actions. Rigid criteria had to be established in order to facilitate this clear-cut separation between normal and abnormal, between those who were "in" and those who were "out." These criteria were necessary to identify and classify actions, behavior, and people with absolute certainty. Because of their scientific nature, medicine and law facilitated the prevention of various forms of deviation. Medical and juridical prestige combined with religious precepts served to establish and spread the stereotype of the outcast that inevitably concerned those men who did not measure up to the image of virility wanted by the regime.

2

The Discovery
of Homosexuality

Although he could not fully understand why, he had always been aware of his
solitude; he had the sensation he was the Only One thrown in the middle of
men and women who loved each other, who embraced one another and had
children together. But now he knew there were *others like him*, and this fact, instead
of giving him comfort, frightened him to death.

PIERO SANTI,
Ombre Rosse

Science and Medicine:
Rejecting and Defining Homosexuality

In the nineteenth century the continuous avoidance of any reference to
homosexuality—a taboo subject of such unspeakable indecency and immorality
that even classical Greek and Latin texts were censored to avoid corrupting the
honest reader—was destined to clash with the new scientific interest in sexuality.[1]
Yet the "conspiracy of silence" regarding "abnormal" sexual behavior was broken
in the late nineteenth century.[2] While being one of history's most sex-phobic
periods, it also strove, with its mythologizing of science as a "new creed," to
unmask the mysteries of human existence.[3] In this context, sex became a central
object of interest and a key to interpreting illnesses, anxieties, and neuroses.
National states could not ignore an element of such relevancy for their citizens'
health and hygiene and the possible cause of social and moral ills; as a result,
besides establishing evermore clearly what was permitted and what was not,
what was normal and what was pathological, they were driven to discipline all

31

expressions of sex according to the nation's demographic, economic, and eugenic requirements. A veritable apparatus of normalization was created, structured around the judicial and medical control of perversions so as to identify and analyze "perverse" sexual habits and discipline them back to normal in order to protect society and the race.[4] Since stigmatizing deviant behavior was seen as the best way to internalize correct sexual habits, normality was almost exclusively described in relation to the pathological.[5] At the height of the positivist era, with the birth of sexology and the transformation of sexuality from a private to a public fact, homosexuality became a field for enthusiastic investigation for doctors, psychiatrists, criminologists, biologists, and anthropologists. Between the nineteenth and twentieth centuries with a "multiple implantation of 'perversions,'"[6] the focus shifted to marginal forms of sexuality: pederasty, onanism, fetishism, masochism, and numerous other sexual anomalies. The courtroom, doctor's office, insane asylum, hospital ward, penitentiary cell, and reformatory were full of these abnormal individuals, considered somewhere between crazy and criminal, sick and depraved. As Michel Foucault described it, homosexuality ceased being sinful behavior and became a species, an individual whose own body bore the signs of his perversion:

> As defined by the ancient civil or canonical codes, sodomy was a category of forbidden acts; their perpetrator was nothing more than the juridical subject of them. The nineteenth-century homosexual became a personage, a past, a case history, and a childhood, in addition to being a type of life, a life form, and a morphology, with an indiscreet anatomy and possibly a mysterious physiology. Nothing that went into this total composition was unaffected by his sexuality. It was everywhere present to him: at the root of all his actions. . . . The sodomite had been a temporary aberration; the homosexual was now a species.[7]

Despite criticism of Foucault's theory and the disagreement among experts as to what period marked the beginning of the creation of "modern homosexuals," certainly the medicalization of perversions contributed to this type of behavior being considered the expression of an orientation or a particular identity, and not occasional or momentary acts performed by normal individuals.[8] Instead of merely judging what was considered immoral behavior, once psychiatrists, doctors, and psychologists were faced with the figure of the sodomite, they were inclined to study and analyze him as a person with a deviant tendency. After having investigated the immoral behavior, the next step was to investigate the immoral individual himself—his nature, his body, and his soul— in order to individuate the characteristics of his abnormality.[9] "A whole web of discourses, special knowledges, analyses, and injunctions"[10] was applied to homosexuals: their lives and actions began to be studied; their bodies were measured, and their genitals examined; their anatomy, features, gestures, and poses were inspected. They were questioned; their habits, desires, and sensations were investigated; attempts were made to reconstruct their childhood as well as that of family members in an attempt to pinpoint their degeneration as an inherited trait. They were kept under observation and made to submit to experimentation and treatment; from being considered freaks or despicable libertines they became human guinea pigs, medical records, or faces placed in some kind of criminal anthropology museum.[11]

While until the middle of the nineteenth century homosexuality had principally been the concern of magistrates and theologians, doctors now replaced them, substituting for virtue and sin their allegedly scientific classification of behavior into categories of natural and unnatural, normal and abnormal, healthy and pathological. Science came to the rescue of morality by providing the categories necessary to offset ethical–religious abhorrence with a medical explanation. Alongside the prohibitions there were suggestions and recommendations relative to diseases caused by indecent and disorderly sexual habits. Acts described as being unnatural and monstrous not only offended God's law, but such conduct was dangerous for the health of society and those who practiced acts of this kind. The syncretism of religious precepts and medical prescriptions created a sort of alliance between science and faith, transforming moral theology into a medical–pastoral science and medicine into a set of ethical–behavioral precepts. Little by little, interest in homosexual relationships shifted from the fields of religion, philosophy, and morality into those of biology, criminal anthropology, psychiatry, and science in general: as perversions became a matter for investigation, a growing number of scholars formulated theories as to their origin and the best way to cure them. Thus the idea of homosexuality, supported by Karl Heinrich Ulrichs, began to spread. It postulated a third sex, a separate, intermediate sex characterized by a female soul in a male body.[12]

However, doctors and researchers—sometimes using pseudonyms so as to protect their good names and scientific reputations—unmasked homosexuality unwillingly, compelled by the need to understand, repress, or treat such immoral behavior. Those who dealt with such a risqué subject for the first time felt the burden of the endeavor, but above all they wondered whether they should continue to hide this abominable behavior from the public. Assuming that all deviations from heterosexual and procreative relationships were unnatural, immoral, and pathological aberrations, they were inclined to condemn pederasty and considered it a dangerous disease for society. Therefore, there was a continuous tension between the epistemological vocation of doctors and scientists and their ethical principles, between the "desire to know" and the fear that exposing such immorality might cause it to spread. Medical studies that informed the population of the negative effects caused by similar behavior might have contaminated readers or revealed latent perversions in the case of potential homosexuals. Fear and false ideas created the real need for counseling homosexuals in order to help them fully understand the mysteries surrounding their nature. Science could answer their questions regarding the reasons, causes, and remedies for their "secret illness," while giving them the confirmation necessary to assess their nature. This would enable them to understand the difference between weakness and illness and to realize to what extent they should feel they were the victims of a hostile society or guilty of immoral behavior. Furthermore, instead of increasing a guilty feeling in homosexuals, science could help them realize that they were not the only individuals in the world attracted to people of their own sex; that they were not "alone in this miserable veil of tears to carry the burden of their disease."[13] As Auguste Forel, a Swiss psychiatrist and homosexual, noted: for those who lived out their "diversity" in solitude, science could even be a sort of liberation:

> Believe me, professor, fighting an instinct, with the obligation not to succumb is terrible. As Heine said, "I withstood it but do not ask me how." As soon as I read your book I realized that I am not as despicable a creature as I had thought just because I wish to satisfy my sexual desires in the arms of a willing friend.[14]

Anyone who tried to deal with homosexuality was therefore faced with the dilemma of whether or not to deny its existence; whether or not to eliminate any trace of this sordid behavior in order to safeguard citizens or to create an apparatus of norms and knowledge from studies and institutions within the medical, juridical, and administrative fields that would work to repress, treat, or, quite simply, understand it. Many were hesitant about extending scientific enquiry to such unnatural, monstrous behavior. It was commonly thought that "it was disgusting to speak of such things." It was feared that it might "turn peoples' attention to even more squalid cases."[15] In other words, the doubt that remained was whether speaking of homosexuality somehow legitimized it.[16]

In my opinion this fear, or rather this obsession with taboo and "indecent topics" whose very mention might be contaminating, is extremely important for historically contextualizing the way in which homosexuality was approached. Foucault underestimated the importance of this kind of self-censorship, although he was absolutely right in maintaining that the polymorphic interweaving of power, knowledge, and sexuality produces not only repression, prohibition, denial, and false ideas, but also truth and scientific knowledge. The question remains, however, as to how to weigh these negative and positive aspects that, at least in the Italian context, seem to be unbalanced in favor of negation as opposed to a more liberating approach of discovery and understanding. Of course, from a broader perspective, the interaction that scientific development activated at the end of the nineteenth century between sexuality as a private matter and sexuality as a public problem opened the way for public discussion of the topic, which would eventually emerge from the shadows with all of the liberating conse-quences attached. Nevertheless, from the first postwar period up to long after World War II the desire to learn about the "revolting practice of homosexuality" was greatly overshadowed by the desire to ignore it.[17] Even so, there were many in favor of a more open attitude or, at least, more willing to try to understand the problem, in the name of science and education, so as to better cope with its effects without creating scandal. Although the study of homosexuality did not necessarily imply a complete lack of negative judgment, it was the best way to "avoid applying a general rule of disapproval to the phenomenon and to consider it without moral, religious, or even social prejudices and limitations."[18]

Degeneration and the Crisis of Masculinity

Heightened interest in homosexuality was brought on not only by the birth of sexology as field of scientific study but also by women's emancipation, which seemed to generate a rapid masculinization of women, a crisis of male virility, and even a feminization of men.[19] Because it was inseparably linked to that "dark side of progress" known as degeneration, homosexuality could not continue to be ignored, above all at a time when the phenomenon appeared to be progressively more widespread.[20] As a result, the subject of perversion acquired such interest that by the end of the century there were hundreds of publications, articles, and essays on this new branch of knowledge.[21] Although Italy was a few years behind others, by the second half of the nineteenth century there was a flourishing of studies on sexual practices that had been considered morally unnatural until then. Following the example set by the fathers of sexology (Ambroise Tardieu, Havelock Ellis, Richard von Krafft-Ebing, Auguste Forel, Ivan Bloch, Edward Carpenter, Albert Moll, Magnus Hirschfeld) Italian scientists were inspired to deal with topics tied to eroticism and found themselves face to face with a little-studied phenomenon, the inversion of sexual instinct.[22] This opened the door onto a hitherto unexplored world in which homosexuality was connected with complicated cases of people whose sex was undetermined.[23] In this way both effeminate men and "bearded women"[24] raised the problem of sexual identity: these were the beginnings of very complex considerations as to the connection between genetic inheritance and environmental conditioning, between physiology and psychology, between genitalia and the determination of gender; as to the difference between male and female; as to the possible contrast between nature and culture, between anatomy and behavioral character-istics, which once again raised, in an alarming way, questions regarding the relationship between biological identity and sexual orientation. The new theory on bisexuality risked replacing the idea of sexual dimorphism based on genital differences that had recently begun to replace the old monosexual model.[25]

However, the influence of criminal anthropology tended to preclude the possibility of fully developing these considerations, as it strongly conditioned modes of analyzing and treating homosexuality that continued to be viewed as an anomaly, a field suitable for investigation only by those who studied deviancy. In other words, the "cult of normality" and the "culture of degeneration"—so dear to anthropologists and intellectuals in general—led people to face the problem of homosexuality with a whole series of prejudices that were scarcely of a scientific nature. Cesare Lombroso's studies gave ever more credit to the idea that homosexuality was due to a form of arrested development, to some form of atavism caused by organic factors or to "sickly genes."[26] "Invert love," wrote Lombroso, "reminds us of the horrors of the Lesbians or Socratics." He explains: "perhaps it goes back to the hermaphroditism that Darwin divined in our earliest ancestors and that can be distinguished in the first months of a fetus's life and, as Hoffman also noted, in the analogy of the two sexes that I discovered in delinquents."[27] Between the nineteenth and twentieth centuries, the theory of degeneration, which showed how steps toward progress could be impeded by obstacles and relapses, had become the paradigm for confronting homosexuality; everyone had to frame their discussion of homosexuality in these terms because it lent "greater authority in indicating the outward signs of the abnormality by making a private vice a public one."[28] Therefore, homosexuals were viewed as diseased or abnormal, guilty of threatening the procreation of the species and disturbing the natural order of life.[29]

This homophobic climate was further encouraged by studies of adolescent homosexuality, such as those published in Le "amicizie" di collegio (Boarding School "Friendships").[30] More and more often researchers were ready to confirm that boarding school life was conducive to "a boy developing sexually related mental disorders" because masturbation led to mutual onanism and to group pederasty masked as platonic friendships. "The flame," namely, love between two young boys, the "deception of sexual instinct" could die out as one grew older but could also turn into a permanent perversion.[31] The idea that homosexuality was widespread in boarding schools made parents so worried about the virility of their sons that they insisted on the problem of la coppia cineda (adolescent effeminate couples) being treated in medical and pedagogical literature.

However, it was the sociological investigation of the journalist and writer Paolo Valera that really uncovered this "hidden" world, made up of meeting places for pederasts, the streets, hotels, and haunts where male prostitution was practiced. Suddenly homosexuality was far more widespread than anyone could or would have wanted to imagine. In Valera's gritty *Milano sconosciuta*, he described a modern Sodom and Gomorrah.[32] A few years later, in *Amori bestiali* (Beastly love), the author devoted himself to exploring the corrupt bourgeoisie, known for its unspeakable vices and abominable depravity.[33] One of the causes of their decadent behavior was precisely homosexuality. "Oscar Wildism" had not disappeared with the death of the "high priest of perversions," who embodied the "most disgusting lust in the world"; as a matter of fact, it increased day by day, penetrating Milan as well as the other major European cities. Oscar Wilde was proof that "the bestial instincts of pederasts, men who love other men, are stronger than all the social clamor against them," because "those who have abandoned themselves in animal-like amusement so as to please the new women, are so depraved that they will continue on their filthy course even if all of society should rise up to find them and beat them."[34]

Furthermore, the Oscar Wilde affair had demonstrated that the spread of homosexuality was determined by cultural factors and was thus induced when aestheticism exalts elegance and demeanor to a point of bordering on androgyny. This was particularly true in Decadentism where criticism of bourgeois order was symbolized by the figure the hermaphrodite, by those who were characterized by both male and female aspects, while the image of the effeminate dandy on the one hand, and the virago and femme fatale on the other, were metaphors for transgression.[35] Therefore, according to the well-known Anglicist Mario Praz, the search for enjoyment and lust typical of decadent culture inevitably led to a cult of androgyny and the practice of homosexuality.[36] At a time when the model of virility was in crisis because of rapidly spreading "effeminacy," the aesthetic ideal of the "new males," based on the permeation of masculinity and femininity, had become so fashionable that "in public places anyone horrified by sexual inversion is considered old-fashioned."[37] Valera wrote:

> Look at them—they themselves have changed. The bosom that was once a woman's beauty has now become the male's. The new men wear close-fitting jackets with padded chests and shoulders. Their hairstyle resembles that of Pre-Raphaelite virgins. Their hair is long, parted in the middle and wavy; they have no mustaches; they wear leather bracelets with dials and gold chains around their wrists.[38]

Interest in homosexuality was augmented by the growing concern about a gradual extinction of the virile male, with the advent of modernity and the rapid decline of masculinity. Industrialization and the birth of feminism seemed to constitute a serious threat to male domination,[39] because the cultural, social, and technological changes that took place between the nineteenth and twentieth centuries risked jeopardizing the hegemony of males, destroying all of the certainties on which patriarchal society was based. Homophobia and misogyny served, therefore, to protect male identity and confront anxieties and fears related to impotency and the loss of virility.[40] Male security had to be defended by reconfirming male virility, strength, and aggressiveness and by identifying all possible causes of effeminacy. It is not surprising then that in the early years of the twentieth century, concern about the spread of homosexuality was so great that it generated huge scandals such as those of Oscar Wilde in England or the entourage of the emperor in Germany.

The Italian press also attacked the indecent behavior of the Germans, guilty of having exposed the unfortunate social evil of homosexuality on an international level. The court of Wilhelm II was the scene of a sensational court case against homosexuality involving a group of people close to one of the emperor's most intimate friends and advisors, Count Philipp Eulenburg.[41] Books and satirical drawings also ridiculed the homosexual practices of the Prussian Army and General Moltke.[42] Germans were again accused of homosexuality during World War I in an attempt to demonize and discredit the enemy by depicting him as monstrous and perverse. The insults directed at the "pederastic" and "degenerate" Teutonic population became crueler and more insistent. German soldiers were described as effeminate, and Wilhelm's cabinet was seen as a den of depraved ministers. Newspapers for Italian soldiers tried to ridicule the Germans by alluding to their homosexuality in comic strips, songs, parodies, and caricatures.[43] According to the journalist Silvano Fasulo, the world was at the mercy of a "gang of forty or fifty degenerate, blood-thirsty megalomaniacs, sexual perverts whose graves we must work to dig independently of the events of the war."[44] Guido Podrecca, former editor of the socialist paper *L'Asino* agreed with Fasulo. According to him, pederasty in Germany had reached enormous proportions and was developing into a dangerous entwinement of homosexuality with politics, sadism, cruelty, and domination. "At all social levels in Germany pederasty prevailed alongside *Kultur*," and life at the courts of Louis II of Bavaria and Wilhelm II was proof of this.[45] In other words, "love, which in Paris, like in Venice and Rome, is flirting, passion, joyful serenading, and poetry, in Berlin becomes—among mugs of beer, sparring, farts and burps—a brutal embrace, the outburst of the Jew who, groping among the tables, confuses the sexes and ends up homosexual."[46]

Germany had started the war to draw attention away from the problem of pederasty and to provide its irremediably corrupt population with an image of virility. According to Giuseppe Senizza, homosexuality was an inherent German trait; their cult of strength, their "harsh and rough manners, bluntly and brutally virile," their cult of domination, militarism, cruelty, and war inevitably led them to disdain "meekness and gentleness, in other words, the weakness typical of femininity."[47] In the opinion of the Honorable Luigi Maria Bossi, founder of the anti-German league in Italy, it was best "to distance oneself from Berlin and its mission to resurrect Sodom and Gomorrah," by railing against the "man wives" or men who are "similar to representatives of the *third sex* [and] who admire and defend German culture."[48] Italian Socialists were also to be despised because by declaring their neutrality it was as if they had been "sodomized."[49]

On the other hand the war had strong repercussions on male identity.[50] The consequences were not, however, unequivocal; the exaltation of virility, intended as aggressiveness and courage, went hand in hand with a silent erosion of these values.[51] Not all of the soldiers were able to overcome the test of virility that combat provided. Shell shock, fear, insubordination, apathy, and hysteria were all syndromes that did not conform well to the image of the temerarious warrior, disdainful of danger.[52] Given the objective difficulty of realizing and universalizing such an emphatic type of masculinity, homosexuals could be a bad example for the soldiers; so much so that in order to avoid contagion it was thought appropriate to keep them away from the front and to reform them.[53] Even the homoerotic implications of wartime camaraderie had to be canceled out by emphasizing the values of strength, battle, and the conquest.[54] But, above all, it was the myth of the First World War, created during its immediate aftermath, that spread the stereotype of the aggressive soldier and exalted masculinity to the point of brutality.[55]

Veterans also perceived the new social standing that women had gained during the war as a threat. The greater level of public visibility gained by women scared men, who were determined to defend their dominance at all cost.[56] Moreover, the war had demonstrated the importance of technology in a brutally dramatic manner. Men by now crushed by the power of "machines" had to reassert their virility; they did so by taming a new unruly "woman," the automobile.[57] The impersonal and materialistic society of the masses, along with the mechanization of everyday life tended, in fact, to make men evermore similar to women. Above all, this was true in the cities, where laziness and constant exposure to stimuli and temptation fostered the spread of vice, perversion, and even "abnormal love affairs." Urbanization and industrialization brought greater comfort and wealth and tended to level gender differences. The mechanization of work and the growth of the service industry reduced the need for strength and physical resistance and lessened the difference between male and female occupations. A regeneration of masculinity was needed through the rediscovery of the [male] body, as well as by fighting homosexuality and the confusion of the sexes. The population's decadence had to be dealt with by strengthening and expanding hygienic and physical education. Before the war, Senator Paolo Mantegazza had stated that "our rachitic civilization manufactures semi-eunuchs by the hundreds,"[58] while the physiologist Angelo Mosso had reported on the dangers caused by inactivity: reduction of sturdiness and endurance, weakening of the nerves, and the gradual loss of virility. However, there was no need for false alarms, the "effeminacy of the Latin race" was not an "organic or constitutional defect but an educational one" that could be remedied through physical exercise, sport, and outdoor games.[59]

These suggestions were taken up again by the Fascists, who championed the revival of Italians and hurled curses "against the easy life," against impotence and homosexuality. Young, prolific, and energetic nations like Italy were supposed to oust those plutocratic nations characterized by their decadence and sterility. The English and French were seen as living examples of the negative effects of the wrong type of modernity because they had been transformed by luxury and affluence into sterile, effeminate individuals, devoid of heroism.[60] After the test of virility provided by World War I, the democratic spirit had to be abandoned in order to prevent the spread of lax mores and to emphasize gender differences. Angelo Ventrone noted:

> Democracy, in its attempt to reconcile opponents, a characteristic thought to be essentially feminine, appeared to many as a consequence and, at the same time, a cause of the emasculation of the spirit, whereas a violent and radical confrontation able to separate and establish hierarchy, to reestablish the qualitative differences between men and nations, seemed like the pharmaceutical needed to counter this dangerous process.[61]

In the Fascist viewpoint, increasing the virility of the spirit as well as the body was the antidote needed to offset the decadence and diminishing birth rate. The regime's demographic concept, following in the wake of a positivist tradition, reiterated that the only way to stop degeneration was through a true "reclamation of human beings."[62] Thus, despite widespread criticism, Lombrosian ideas became popular again in the 1920s and 1930s, when several disciples of the Turin criminologist—in particular, Salvatore Ottolenghi, Mario Carrara, Antonio Marro, Benigno Di Tullio and Nicola Pende—returned to exploring the physical makeup of criminals, shedding new light on the morpho-physiological characteristics of deviants. This also had an influence on the way pederasty was treated. Sexual identity was still an exclusively biological matter, a plain and simple anatomical fact, while the homosexual continued to have a precise physiognomy and to be seen as an abnormal being to be watched, studied, and treated.

The Body and Behavior, the Basis of Racism

Thanks to Lombroso and his definition of what was considered the norm, based on the study of its negative opposite,[63] the pederast became a particular type of human being, an individual with unmistakable physiological traits that were proof of his perversion. The search for objectively quantifiable factors, for a set of signs or characteristics that would enable one to identify degenerates, drove Lombroso and his disciples to search out homosexuals in the unlikeliest of places,[64] in order to study them, measure them, and observe their posture, behavior, aptitudes, tattoos, and tell-tale identifying marks.[65] To understand their habits so as to better understand their nature, it was necessary to be able to decipher their particular jargon, their system of identification, and their secret codes. The conventional language used by pederasts to recognize each other— offering a light, asking for a cigarette, touching one ear, or winking—had to be deciphered. All of these tactics were adopted in order to veil the secret nature of those defending their privacy through a specialized jargon; a jargon capable of "hiding not only the love affairs but also the shame that went with sexually inverted relationships" through the employment of a special phraseology to disguise thoughts and sentiments that were "horrible for a *normal* human being."[66] Even the pioneering studies of the ethnologist Raffaele Corso on Italian erotic folklore confirmed a wide range of words in dialect used to describe both passive and active pederasts, while the works of Abele De Blasio and Emanuele Mirabella served to discover such a language used by the criminal world.[67]

The identification of homosexuals was not therefore dependent on a determined behavior, but on the degree to which it corresponded to stereotypes established according to characteristic signs to be deciphered and catalogued by an anthropologist. Every unusual trait had to have a naturalistic biological explanation that was scientifically understandable and demonstrable. In this way, however, clichés, the collective imagination, and prejudice disguised as scientific reason became indisputable knowledge. The fact that some particular traits were taken to be the symptoms of an arrest in the normal growth process created a close link between aesthetic and moral judgments and physical, biological and natural principles. The bodies and "faces of degeneration" mirrored the soul, character, and disposition of a subject being studied.[68] External physical differences reflected internal, organic anomalies; appearance, physiognomy, and demeanor were indicators for identifying deviants and perverts. Thus, criminal anthropology was destined to become an "unfortunate science" that tried to distinguish healthy from unhealthy, normal from abnormal; that opposed beauty to ugliness, and usual to unusual in an attempt to determine whether or not an individual was dangerous.[69] Lombroso's studies contributed significantly to the formulation of a model of the lunatic or perverted criminal type, and were instrumental in the categorization of deviant behaviors as pathologies and their nosographic classification. Nevertheless, not all of the results of Lombroso's studies were so negative. Considering science an instrument of regeneration, a means by which deviants might be rendered inoffensive and treatable, favored the shift from repressing abnormal individuals to isolating them. All children considered errors of evolution—the born criminal, the lunatic, the epileptic, the genius, the prostitute, or the homosexual—were people who, for some sort of biological reason or ill-fated hereditary predestination, were far removed from the normal individual without, however, being responsible for their actions, which were due to hereditary defects. Due to the muddling of these various anomalies—lunatics with criminals, pathologies with teratogenetic degenerations, illegal actions with immoral conduct, and mental illness with constitutional defects—the immediate consequences did not much improve the lives of deviants who were put in insane asylums instead of prisons.

Lombroso's theories on homosexuality were destined to leave their mark on Italian medical and scientific culture, and in particular on the *Archivio di psichiatria e scienze penali ed antropolgia criminale* (Archives of Penal Psychiatry and Science and Criminal Anthropology).[70] A clear-cut distinction remained between natural and unnatural acts, and pederasty continued to be viewed as the result of degeneration, a genetic flaw whose external signs were evident in pederasts' behavior and morphology.[71] In its research, however, medicine was conditioned by a stereotypical image of homosexuals; the attention of psychiatrists, magistrates, criminal lawyers, policemen, doctors, and anthropologists was focused above all on sexual inverts; on men who lacked the characteristics of the virile male and assumed the behavior and mannerisms of women. Homosexuals were almost exclusively identified with the figure of the effeminate male. It was for this very reason that they became the object of contempt. In a society where women were relegated to a secondary and inferior role compared with men, sexual passivity was suspect and considered negative behavior. Consequently, only the one who assumed the passive role in the sexual relationship was seen as different, to be studied, recorded, and classified. As the words of Vito Massarotti clearly illustrate, condemnation of sexually passive partners, relative to that of those who assumed the typically male role, was common and widespread:

Some homosexuals love to be possessed, to play the woman's role; they are the so-called passive partners. Others instead maintain their male role during coitus—they are the active partners. Often the two forms exist in the same individual, one prevalent and the other provisional or to please one's lover. . . . Men who love other men passively, and this is the most serious form of sexual degeneration and the lowest on the scale, feel and think like women.[72]

The Aristotelian image of woman as a passive subject was so deeply rooted that the identification of homosexuality with passivity was inevitable. As Luigi Pasolli said, "The fact that men are aggressive and active in manifesting their sexuality and women are passive, is something that goes without saying."[73] Men were biologically catabolic, that is, mobile and active, whereas women were metabolic, in other words, stationary and passive.[74] Therefore, if a male took on the passive role common to the female he was considered "abnormal" while, according to this logic, a male who expressed his sexuality actively, even if with another male, was, all things considered, acting in a "normal" manner, because he retained his virility.[75] The difference between active and passive—very often a formal division and not a substantial one—was considered particularly important in Italy and in other Mediterranean cultures, because it allowed a large number of heterosexuals to consider sexual intercourse with passive pederasts perfectly normal.[76] For those studying the subject, homosexuality was perhaps more widespread among Anglo-Saxon and Germanic populations than in those of the Roman Mediterranean. In Latin and southern European countries, however, there were certainly "many bisexual individuals who regularly prefer heterosexual intercourse but are not averse to sexual relations with members of their own sex."[77] Not surprisingly then, it was a known fact that among Sicilians and Neapolitans "there was a deeply rooted idea that whoever took a passive role during anal and oral intercourse was obscene, while whoever took an active role was not."[78] What we would define today as bisexuality was perceived as heterosexual and not deviant behavior, whereas passive, effeminate behavior among homosexuals was strongly condemned. Even the most understanding, tolerant experts studying homosexuality, together with the militant supporters of rights for homosexuals, despised homosexuals who assumed the appearances and behaviors typical of women, and expressed anxiety over the gradual disintegration of male/female dualism.

For example, according to Marc André Raffalovich, "one could admit that (as a general rule) the greater the morality of a unisex, the less effeminate he is." The only uranians worthy of respect were those who "being more masculine than the normal man" felt passion for their own sex and so despised women that they found too disgusting to look or act like.[79] On the other hand, a similar consideration was expressed by André Gide in *Corydon*[80] and Marcel Proust in *In Search of Lost Time*,[81] in which hatred for the "damned race"—homosexuals, degenerates with a feminine appearance—was combined with an attempt to defend their virility from anyone questioning it.[82]

Because pederasts were defined as the passive partners, their physical and psychological characteristics, their behavior, and their habits were entirely similar to those of women: their love of jewelry, makeup, and perfume; the way they swayed their hips when walking, the blushing and the flirtatious lowering of their eyes, their languid movements, and their delicate appearance; their love of gossip and lies, their emotionality, their weak character, their unreliability, their vanity and excitability. Their bodies clearly showed female traits: the absence of hair on their face or bodies, their wide hips, their wavy hair, their hypertrophic breasts capable of secreting milk,[83] their soft, smooth skin, the disproportionate length of their torsos with respect to the lower part of their bodies, the rounded profile of their faces, their short teeth, and the particular shape of their ears and skull. In those who regularly practiced sodomy, physical signs included "a funnel-shaped anus, dilation of the anus, disappearance of the usual skin wrinkles, the appearance of fissures."[84]

This approach, based on the descriptive image of a typical pederast, began to be questioned by those who did not consider these physical characteristics and features as being caused by sodomy, but as the mark of homosexuality, which they maintained was congenital. A funnel-shaped anus or "penis typical of canines" could not be considered indications of a pederastic relationship because these anomalies predated the "perverted" sexual practice. The diagnosis of passive pederasty by analyzing the anus created scientific debate among experts who tended not to give much importance to such simple indications anymore.[85] The Italian school of medical examiners maintained that these signs of passive pederasty were purely illusory, devoid of scientific or diagnostic value, and were only useful when linked with other, more reliable data. Despite the efforts of medical experts to demolish "old theories according to which the signs that more or less characterized a passive homosexual confirmed an individual's tendency to submit passively to unnatural sexual intercourse," and notwithstanding the fact that "the so-called funnel-shaped anus was by now deprived of any significance, as was the relaxation of the anus's external sphincter because they were not connected with a person's perverse habits but were constitutional,"[86] the police continued to carefully inspect the rectums of people suspected of sodomy.

In an attempt to confute these outdated convictions, medical examiner Giuseppe Falco tried to demonstrate that homosexuality was congenital by analyzing several volumes of photographs of naked young men in effeminate poses. The photos had been seized from a German photo studio and later donated by the police academy's forensic sciences department to the criminal museum of Rome. According to Falco, the analyzed photos proved without any doubt that degenerative mental and sexual anomalies were clearly related to degenerative physical abnormalities in the external genitals and in secondary sexual attributes. In fact, most of the young men exhibited a "feminine physiognomy and manner," as well as "wide hips and feminine buttocks and thighs," but above all, there were recurrent anomalies in the conformation of their genitals." Therefore, there was a hormonal and nervous-system correlation between mental abnormalities and genital anomalies, with the latter representing "degenerative anthropological stigmas that accompanied the psychosexual tendency."[87] This did not actually change the organicist approach, because the only novelty was that these marks were considered peculiar, making homosexuals a sort of separate species, as though their anomalies had been established at birth and not through the practice of pederasty. Once a pederast was identified, every effort was made to locate a confirmation of this in his body. Likewise, once particular features and genital characteristics were discovered, it was easy to link them with an analogous mental abnormality.

Looking for the diverse physical stigmas in homosexuals induced the general population to consider homosexuals' behavior irrevocably linked to their biological system. The determination of moral qualities and character was based on the extent to which they deviated from the norm, from the benchmark of the white, adult male defined by his mental health, virility, and heterosexuality. The other, the one who differed from this model, was condemned to represent that which was negative, abnormal, monstrous, and unnatural. Biology, thus, justified an a priori discrimination whereby diversity was the symptom of abnormality and inferiority. Science became a weapon for racism, capable of legitimizing prejudice and a dichotomous view of reality. The tendency toward axiological polarizations based on binary categories—man/woman, active/passive, virile/effeminate, natural/unnatural, moral/immoral—created the premise for the isolation and dehumanization of homosexuals.

The studies carried out by George Mosse were fundamental for understanding the link between sexuality and racism that, on the one hand, led to classifying those who were sexually different from the norm as a separate race and, on the other hand, the ascription of sexual diversity to the so-called inferior races. According to Mosse, hatred of homosexuals had been created by the bourgeois society of the nineteenth century, through their intolerance of any conflation of the sexes or the questioning of the superiority of the heterosexual male. A reversal of gender roles could have endangered the coherence of norms, leading to decadence. The image of the virile man, taken as a model of equilibrium and beauty, had to be safeguarded from all those who deviated from this stereotype. For this reason, racism employed the concepts of degeneration and virility: masculinity served, in fact, to clearly define the boundary between vice and virtue, between normal and abnormal, between natural and unnatural. Meanwhile, thanks to the specter of degeneration, the dangers involved in violating these divisions could easily be perceived. The infamous counter-image of the pederast was necessary to give scientific support to the century-old public hatred of homosexuals and clearly define the boundaries of respectability; making the other easily identifiable was the best way to legitimize their marginalization and clearly outline standards of behavior and the ideal type. Thus, racism did not invent stereotypes, but racial theorists used them to establish hierarchies and to discriminate against those who did not conform to appropriate customs and traditions.[88] The need for conformity, necessary for guaranteeing greater national cohesion, justified the intolerance and exclusion of those who were different, whose integration meant complete assimilation to the rules of respectability. Mosse wrote: "Solitude was the price exacted for abnormal behavior, and the outsider . . . was supposed to live a lonely life and die a lonely death. If he tried to enter society he had to pay the price of admission."[89] In other words, homosexuals were obliged to find their "happiness in the ghetto,"[90] in an underground world that they could leave only by renouncing their identity, rejecting every feminine aspect, and declaring their virility publicly. Well aware of the social condemnation with which pederasty was judged, they were obliged to keep their real identities a secret out of fear that their neighbors, friends, colleagues, and even their closest relatives might learn of their orientation, a discovery that would have caused an abrupt change of behavior in their regard, making them suffer the weight of disapproval.[91]

Competing Schools of Thought

Matters of sexuality could not be ignored by Fascism, which, with its totalitarian aim of transforming every aspect of citizens' lives in conformity with its ideological precepts, was impelled to make sex a primary interest of the State, whose task it was to manage collective behavior in order to achieve greatness and power for the nation. Consequently, never had sex been of such political importance as during Fascism: preventive medicine, the safeguarding of traditional morality, health, and population growth fell under government jurisdiction.

Although Fascism's position regarding sex was extensive and ranged from demography to eugenics, from hygiene to education, when it came to "illicit" sexuality its attitude was quite different. It was considered best not to speak of such subjects and was forbidden to refer to or allude to subjects that were not considered edifying for a regime that made virility one of its cornerstones. The positivist era's *desire for knowledge* was, therefore, checked by Fascism, which permitted only discussion about "normal" sexuality, and through censorship, denial and repression inevitably inhibited the study of homosexuality. Fascism's influence on science, then, was not irrelevant. Mussolini himself, particularly in the field of medicine, was aware of the importance of overseeing and controlling the methods and uses of research, in particular regarding doctors; guarantors of the health and morality of Italians, they were also viewed as instrumental figures for "the defense of the Regime and the evolution of the Fascist Revolution," and of course politically influential in relation to their patients.[92] The link between science and Fascism has been closely analyzed by Roberto Maiocchi, who revealed the readiness of doctors to comply with the regime's demands.[93] This relationship was not merely instrumental or imposed from above, but resulted from a true commonality of objectives and a certain concurrence of ideas. The medical studies carried out adapted perfectly to the new atmosphere that had been created with the regime's legislative involvement in the health sector. Fascism did not, therefore, silence science or obscure knowledge; it did, however, facilitate the diffusion of research to which it was congenial and, in doing so, conditioned the competition between different schools of thought.

The homosexuality question is a clear example of this. Also, in this case the influence exercised over people and scientific and cultural institutions allowed for the prevalence of one school of thought over another. The pressure, exerted more or less explicitly by Fascism on the way so-called sexual anomalies should be treated, fostered their categorization as perversions and consolidated a viewpoint of intolerance and incomprehension that existed in the French scientific community. Robert A. Nye's considerations on the process of medicalization and pathologization of sexual identity in France between the nineteenth and twentieth centuries are valid to a certain extent for Italy, where Fascism exalted virility, valorized the concept of honor, and left very little room for love outside of matrimony and reproduction.[94] Elsewhere Bloch, Forel, Ellis, and Hirschfeld maintained that "the function of sex has gained a significance and purpose above and beyond the mere propagation and preservation of the species."[95] Consequently the psychological and erotic aspects of sexuality did not necessarily have to be tied to procreation. This point of view was unacceptable in a country like Italy where doctors, psychologists, and psychiatrists considered all sexual behavior beyond the scope of reproduction to be deviant; Homosexuality, judged with extreme severity, was at the top of this list. Based on a series of stereotypes widespread in civil society and shared by the regime, most depictions of homosexuals were small-minded and intolerant. Medicine, then, contributed to establishing a link between sexual perversion, disease, weakness, and femininity, turning a medical diagnosis of one's homosexuality into a judgment of his respectability.

Competition among schools of thought vying for the last word on the nature of perversions encouraged the proliferation of the most unfathomable theories. Doctors, psychiatrists, and anthropologists wrote volumes trying to understand, above all, whether pederasty was a congenital disease or an acquired vice. However, the interest in the causes of homosexuality revealed that the matter was of scientific importance for the fact that homosexual behavior was considered unnatural and abnormal. As John Boswell rightly noted, no one questioned, for example, the cause of heterosexuality or right-handedness, because that which is accepted as normal does not require an explanation.[96] The numerous studies of homosexuality led to a series of theories that can be divided loosely into two categories, organic and psychological. The former can be further subdivided into biological and endocrinal and the latter into psychiatric and psychoanalytical.

In Italy, due to Fascism and the strong influence of Lombroso, organicist paradigms predominated, while positions more attentive to the more psychological aspects of sexual inversion were less common. Theorists who thought homosexuality was due to biological factors located its origin in either genetic (hereditary) or physical (constitutional) anomalies. For some, however, homosexuality was the consequence of another perversion, onanism; whoever practiced the solitary habit too frequently was irredeemably destined to sink to the lowest levels of perversion, to the point of practicing reciprocal masturbation and even sodomy.[97] There were also those who traced the causes of homosexuality to such things as the fear of being infected with syphilis, the desire not to have children, the curiosity of libertines (who were always looking for new forms of titillation), excessive sexual urge, perception of a bad odor emanated by women, unrequited love, or sexual abuse suffered at an early age.

For promoters of the school of thought linking pederasty and physical anomalies, attraction toward members of one's own sex stemmed from a malformation of the genitals. Particularly fanciful in his explanation was Paolo Mantegazza, who located the cause of homosexuality in an anatomical abnormality that directed the spinal nerves that govern sensual pleasure toward the rectum instead of the genitals.

Active pederasts also had an abnormality that made them want to feel *penis circumclusum* (the desire for tightness). Therefore the origin of sodomy was to be found in nerve centers, even though Mantegazza did not entirely exclude psychological factors such as passion: "sinful, revolting, disgusting if you want, but passion."[98] Doctor Annunziato La Cara also believed sexual inversion was a congenital physiological disease, in this case caused by atavism and epilepsy. He did, however, introduce the thesis that homosexuality was linked with old age: in his opinion an elderly man had "an inclination for pederasty and all other sorts of unnatural obscene libidinous behavior," as demonstrated by the exceptional spread of perversions in older nations as compared with younger ones.[99] The second edition (1924) of La Cara's book *La base organica dei pervertimenti sessuali* (The Organic Basis of Sexual Perversions) is particularly interesting because it clearly shows just how central the body had become again after a period of decline for organicism. Unlike many foreign studies, La Cara's simply rejected homosexuality as a mental disorder or spiritual malady and identified in perverts "anomalies in the external genital organs as well as in the nerve impulses from the genital organs to the cerebral cortex." Even mental disorders were caused by biological defects; the body conditioned the mind and not the reverse. Theories linking sexual inversion to psychological causes were clamorously debunked by notoriously homosexual, yet extremely illustrious figures, such as Michelangelo and Julius Caesar, who certainly could not be classified as morally insane. More than twenty years after the first edition, the organicist theory of the origin of sexual inversion appeared to be confirmed by important scientific information coming from endocrinology and the new theory of psychological bisexuality announced by Otto Weininger in his book *Sesso e carattere* (Sex and Character).[100] La Cara ended his study with "the though not rosy, at least ample hope" that sexual perversions could finally be fought and cured through endocrinology. This branch of medical science, despite being at its beginnings, had resurrected the biological explanation for homosexuality, providing organicist nosography with another weapon with which to fight psychoanalysis for the final word on the causes and effects of pederasty.

During the twenty years of Fascist rule, endocrinology was considered the leading discipline for the study of homosexuality. The regime gave these studies substantial support and boasted about the results obtained by this new branch of medicine. Endocrinology became the *trait d'union* between Fascism and Lombrosian thought thanks to the theory of constitutional homosexuality it provided the instruments needed to rehabilitate traditional physiognomy and recover the biological determinism of sexual deviance maintained by the anthropological and organicist vision. Studies carried out by Giacinto Viola on the physical constitution of individuals,[101] in other words on the idea that people could be identified and classified on the basis of morphological and functional characteristics, resurrected from the ashes of Lombrosoism the conviction that homosexuality was due to a congenital abnormality recognizable in certain hormonal disorders. Nicola Pende, in particular, investigated the link between endocrinology and "constitutional science" in his search to find a connection between "hormonal and organic anomalies" and an individual's personality. In spite of the still predominant concern about social defense and the claim that it was possible to identify a criminal or a pervert before that person committed an illegal or immoral act, supporters of the constitutional theory of homosexuality did not want to be too closely connected with the organicist approach, maintaining that constitutional factors could only decide predetermined behaviors.[102] According to Pende it was possible, thanks to the new science of *human biotypology* and the study of an individual's particular endocrinal structure, to decode the link between body and mind.[103] Biotypology, applied to all fields of modern knowledge, became a necessary instrument for the nation's well-being—the aim of "orthogenesis is to form the healthy, well-proportioned men our regime wants."[104] The eugenic implications of this approach were evident: by means of "constitutional hormonology" it would be possible to achieve the Fascist dream of anthropologically transforming Italians. Pende, who had become a staunch supporter of the regime, was considered essential for establishing a harmonious relationship with the scientific community and for lending credibility to the *Manifesto della razza* (Manifesto of the Race).[105] Fascism was the political instrument for the actual implementation of medical biology; in 1936 Pende wrote, "Modern medical biological thought not only identifies itself with Mussolini's coherent and correlative political doctrine, but it must identify itself with the philosophy of the Fascist nation."[106] Thus *orthogenetic science* became the emblem of Fascist progress and a means of "continually improving the nation's biological balance, ridding it as much as possible of the mediocre and the unproductive, of precocious invalids, of the weak and the morally and the intellectually mediocre."[107]

Pende's investigation of endocrinology led to an interest in problems relative to sexuality and, in particular, homosexuality. During his long academic career he would eventually gain international renown and come to be considered a true visionary for his work on the subject. An individual's sex was not only determined by the genital glands but also by the "overall hormonal system," which, in the case of hormonal disorders, caused sexual instinct to deviate.[108] Pende referred to the most recent discoveries in embryology and linked the theory of bisexuality to that of endocrinology. In his opinion the existence of a physiological hermaphroditism in the sex glands—with elements of the opposite sex present in a latent state—created potential for bisexuality, which however tended to resolve itself with a prevalence of male hormones in males and female hormones in females. As could be verified anatomically in the genital glands of sexual inverts, homosexuality occurred when there were too many female hormones in a male body.[109]

As we have said, Pende was well aware of the connection between these matters and Fascism's totalitarian plan, intent on increasing the population and disciplining the sexual sphere of its citizens:

> Today the problem of intersexuality, in its theoretical and practical aspects, cannot be ignored given the Fascist movement's goal of maximizing fertility and sexually normalizing Italians.[110]

Pende's intention was to develop a trend in eugenics based on the enhancement of positive, constructive eugenics, with the ultimate goal of increasing the population and improving Italians. The regime considered him an important asset in its demographic battle, although with his own particular approach. His efforts in the sphere of demographics and health were not concentrated as much on those who did not want to procreate as on those who were not able to procreate because of disease, physical defects, or mental illness. The physiological causes for the decreased birth rate were to be combated with the scientific weapons of endocrinology, and the best way to increase the study of these problems and cure such patients was to create a group of specialized clinics where the pathologies that caused impotence could be treated. In the eyes of Fascism the project was praiseworthy, but it was never fully implemented due to impediments brought on by the war.[111] Apart from treatment centers there were also other ways to increase virility in men and cure the scourge of pederasty. One such method was massive and prolonged treatment with hormones.

Foreign scientists, however, willing to bend science and medicine for uses that were inhuman and horrifying, developed far more invasive methods. For example, Eugen Steinach became well known for his studies on the testicles of homosexuals carried out with the aim of finding final proof of the origin of bisexuality. By transplanting ovaries into castrated male animals, this Austrian psychiatrist was able to cause the development of typical female characteristics, and similarly, by transplanting testicles into sterilized female animals, he was able stimulate the appearance of male characteristics.[112] The possibility of changing the sex of animals seemed like a scientific miracle. A number of studies and experiments followed in many places confirming the results obtained by Steinach. In Italy, there was a blossoming of studies on gender acquisition and transformation that resulted in fanciful conjectures regarding the possibility of determining the sex of babies not yet born or on what elements favored the birth of males instead of females. According to Gina Lombroso-Ferrero, who like her father supported endocrinological treatments, the outcome of Steinach's experiments made it feasible to foresee mitigating and curing the deviant physical and mental characteristics of sexual psychopaths.[113]

These experiments were not limited, however, to animals. The same procedures were performed on men. Steinach himself, together with his colleague Lichtenstern, applied his findings to six homosexuals who first underwent castration and then the implantation of testicles taken from heterosexuals. The results obtained were highly praised by Ferdinando De Napoli, who commented on these transplants:

> The results obtained by Lichtenstern are worthy of note particularly those on homosexuals. He has made them like the other men of their sex; he has made them act, think, and love like normal men (and we shall see how differently they act not only in the sphere of sex but in many spiritual demonstrations, these poor inverts!). He has made them different by transplanting good material after removing the bad, abnormal, defective material, which made these unhappy creatures appear to be insane, or worse, depraved for so long. Isn't it, therefore, the material that predominates, influences, guides, and alters even the spirit?[114]

Even better known were the gland transplants carried out by the Russian surgeon Serge Voronoff. These experiments, unfortunately notorious because they were used in Nazi concentration camps, envisaged replacing the testicles of homosexuals with those of monkeys.[115] The transplants were supposed to "cure" endocrinal dysfunctions in subjects in which testicular extracts had not given satisfactory results and transform effeminate homosexuals into energetic, virile men. In theory, Voronoff's aim was to restore virility in elderly men, but the applications were much less humanitarian and focused on sexual anomalies, above all inversion and impotence. This new treatment was well received in Italy as well, where they even coined the neologism *to voronoffize*,[116] and where Enrico Morselli, among its various supporters, strongly praised its advantages:

> Individuals affected with sexual inversion in whom the secondary sexual characteristics are not very accentuated and whose instinct directs them toward the sterility of homosexual satisfaction, could have their perversion corrected thanks to the implantation of testicles that would awaken or strengthen their deviant or abnormal virility. This is a problem that sexologists should tackle: in fact, as Giuseppe Vidoni has demonstrated, a good number of these homosexuals, including the passive ones, present eunuch-like characteristics caused by the defective activity of their genital hormones; together with their eunuch-like appearance they also have a weak, apathetic,

indolent frame of mind that is often combined with mental deficiency.
Transplanting an active male gland could help them emerge from their
state of physical, mental, and social inferiority and consequently attenuate,
in the realm of civil society, the revolting plague of male prostitution.[117]

In France, as in Spain and Germany, doctors and psychiatrists "implanted
testicles" in men who had suffered wounds to their genitals in war, in individuals
with eunuch-like forms, as well as in "neuropathic homosexuals."[118] Therefore,
Voronoff was not the only one to devise such disputable remedies to solve the
problem of sexual inversion, although most experts proposed less invasive
treatments, including dietary measures and education through gymnastics; a
virile approach to the education of boys in order to prepare them for the battles
of life and to extract them from the excessive tenderness of their mothers;
instruction about sex to prevent precocious sexual experiences and to stimulate
the right amount of restraint, and so forth.

Thanks to the possible applications of endocrinology in the sexual field,
Pende's theory that homosexuality was caused by an anomaly in the endocrine
system gained ever greater credit and was taken up and further developed by
one of the most important sexologists of the twentieth century, the Spaniard
Gregorio Marañón.[119] Studies on the relationship between the endocrine
glands and homosexuality became, therefore, the point of departure for a
constantly developing trend in research.[120] The considerable attention given to
the endocrine and chromosomic aspects of sexual inversion, together with the
substantial influence of Otto Weininger's book *Sesso e carattere*,[121] were the main
reasons for the success of the theory of bisexuality, or intersexuality. According
to this theory, a person's sex was determined by the chromosome complement
but, since an embryo was sexually undifferentiated in the first weeks after
conception, it was the hormones that favored one sex over the other. Since this
preliminary bisexuality was never completely overcome in each individual, there
was a certain degree of intersexuality that varied from person to person, resulting
in some hypermasculine and some hyperfeminine individuals, but also a wide
range of in-betweens, among which were homosexuals. In the end these studies
often adopted the concept of intersexuality in order to reconfirm the dichotomies
of male/female; active/passive; virile/effeminate.

Fascist ideologues themselves, admirers of the Manichean dualism of this
view of reality based on the juxtaposition of opposites, used theories about
intersexual states and, in particular, Weininger's work to confirm the fundamental
value of "masculinity." For example, Mussolini read *Sesso e carattere* and kept
other books by Italian researchers on matters regarding intersexuality in his
library.[122] As a result, these theories could be bent for instrumental use and

manipulated to perpetuate the fear and contempt of homosexuals, who were seen as proof of the continuous battle between the male and female elements of the human personality. Not surprisingly, then, Marañon's endocrinological considerations were also highly regarded for the negative opinion they expressed about the feminization of men and the masculinization of women. Marañon wrote:

> The femininization of men is a regressive phenomenon, one might say almost negative; while the masculinization of women is a phenomenon that, apart from its pathological nature, we might consider progressive, in a certain sense positive. . . . For a man to appear feminine it only takes a passive influence. But for a woman to look like a man an active impulse that overcomes her femininity is necessary.[123]

The male sex returned, then, to being the perfect state of sexuality, and with clear reference to Weininger and his misogyny, the greater the distance from the virile model the greater the regression to a lower level on the human scale. Contempt for women and the exaltation of men also characterized the works of Ferdinando De Napoli. He was an avid supporter of the theory of bisexuality and one of the major promulgators of Weininger in Italy. The layout of his two weighty volumes on matters regarding sexuality traced almost to the letter that of *Sesso e carattere*.[124] Also, De Napoli thought homosexuality was an "endocrine-based psychological anomaly," and that the only explanation for this was to be found in the embryo's original bisexuality, which left traces in the body and soul, two separate spheres that were linked but distinct, both having male and female characteristics. There could be physical or mental bisexuality, capable of generating cases of hermaphroditism or sexual inversion.[125] However, the psychological factors were always relatable to the physical ones, because the organic state of the nervous system and the brain conditioned the psyche, and not vice versa. Homosexuality was to be treated with hormones that would strengthen the masculine element in men and the feminine element in women. De Napoli himself carried out trials on some homosexuals and obtained satisfactory results by treating them with "Viroglandolo" tablets.[126]

The concept of bisexuality formulated by Weininger, the "poor man's Freud,"[127] was linked to the approach of Marañon, Freud's substitute,"[128] and became the point of reference for Italian researchers interested in matters involving sexuality and homosexuality.[129] This hindered the influence of psychoanalysis and consolidated the Lombrosian organicist approach.[130] The theory of intersexuality was in perfect harmony with the campaign undertaken by Fascism to *masculinize men and feminize women*.[131] This task—"the great task of the future generations"—was even more necessary in order to complete the work of nature that, in "this mixture of somatic and functional characteristics of the sexes," was rarely able to form a man who was 100 percent male or a woman who was 100 percent female. Therefore, if gender remained somehow precarious due to the conflict between these two antagonistic hormones, and the opposite sex remained stuck in a person's body and soul like a thorn, it was necessary to expel it by masculinizing young boys as much as possible and feminizing young girls so as to eradicate any residual sexual ambiguity.

According to Angelo Signorelli, Fascism should be given credit for having begun this "splendid" undertaking. In his book *Sesso intersesso supersesso*, Signorelli tried to link his theory of "male femininity," namely the relationship between the male and female elements present in an individual or a nation, with the political actions undertaken by Mussolini. His theory postulated a division between the pure sex and intersex of people with both male and female characteristics. The pure male was active and mobile, courageous and combative, energetic and willful, conquering and itinerant, capable of dominating himself and others; the pure female was immobile and passive, irrational and maternal, housewifely and busy. Taking the Gospel as his example, Signorelli identified the pure male with the figure of Paul (the pure female with Martha); the normal male or first degree intersexual with Peter (the female with Mary); and the effeminate or second degree intersexual with John (the female with Mary Magdalene). Concerning this last group, there was an accentuated intersexuality in the female direction. Sexual inversion, however, was yet another state that could be represented by the figure of Judas. Thus:

> The disproportionate exaltation of Paul's masculinity and of John's femininity leads to hybridism, inversion, and degeneration. Sexual inverts who have had their moment of glory and about whom a certain type of foreign literature is so concerned, are to be found at the two extremes, that is beyond the masculinity of Paul and beyond the femininity of John, and their division in actives and passives is explained by their predominant male or female characteristics. Probably Judas belonged to the group of feminized males . . . who betray just like jealous females.[132]

In Italy there were still many males with a prominent female intersexuality. They were the homebodies, the lovers of the quiet life, who were jealous, vain, loquacious, addicted to food and sensuality, easily seduced, and submissive. Nevertheless, the First World War and, above all, the advent of Fascism had awakened the pure male; the regime was "turning many Johns (who had slipped into the feminine male-group) into Peters and Pauls." Even if the period of decadence that had been brought about by excessive feminization was over, it was necessary to continue "intensifying masculinization in order to compete with the male countries and inseminate the boundless and abundant number of Italian women."[133] In other words, Fascism had brought back the virile male capable of procreating, dominating, and conquering. Unfortunately, however, in the case of women there had not been an analogous development because there were too many Mary Magdalenes who wanted sexual equality; they were active and performed male jobs; too many were out to conquer men and too few were interested in having children. In Signorelli's opinion, the study of different forms of sexuality was necessary in order to create what he called the "supersex," in other words, the maximum strengthening of individuals according to their particular constitution and based on their degree of masculinity and femininity. The reinforcement of male qualities like strength, creativity, and intelligence was intended to coincide with the strengthening of female qualities such as beauty, maternity, and morality. The new heroes could only be individuals capable of combining these two principles, heroes of action and thought, dominators from a political as well as a cultural point of view. The "supersex" had, however, already been born in the "Latin land" and was actively operative in the guise of Mussolini. His square-cut masculine face sculpted with the sensibility of an artist made him the emblem of the "supersex." The rudimentary female and male elements, maternal and paternal, were fused in the figure of the Duce: intelligence, sentiment, and willpower worked together to create a unique masterpiece. He was, therefore, an example of this perfect balance, a synthesis of the best masculine and feminine qualities, a virile man but not brutish, creative but not irrational. Signorelli ended his work with the following invocation: "*May Italy's males be more masculine and its females more feminine. From their union the new Italian will be born: instinct-form, sentiment-will, faith-reason.*"[134]

The fear that a sexual hybridization could develop was, after all, implicit in the theory of bisexuality, which itself should be credited with having laid the groundwork for considering homosexuality a latent potentiality; a predisposition present to a greater or lesser degree in all people. Therefore, homosexuality, unlike immoral behavior, was independent of individual will. The endocrinal origin of sexual inversion made those affected by it people to be pitied, not condemned: pederasty was an organic dysfunction and not a sin or a crime. Quite incredibly, no doctor, endocrinologist, or psychologist ever asked himself whether a man might love another man simply out of natural inclination; if passion was involved, it was always considered an abnormal sentiment, a disease, or in any case an imperfection that called for treatment, if not punishment. This was a step toward establishing the level of responsibility of pederasts in criminal proceedings. The division between the supporters of the constitutional or endogenous theory of homosexuality and those of the acquired or exogenous theory of homosexuality meant that the courts made a distinction between homosexuals who were suffering from an illness and those who were perverse. Inverts and congenital homosexuals were not responsible for their behavior, while perverts and transgressive homosexuals behaved this way on purpose. Thus, "while inverts are dangerous, perverts are all the more so. They can approach young boys more easily because they do not appear so repulsive but they are able to take hold of them very quickly, albeit not as profoundly as inverts."[135]

This distinction between organic and acquired homosexuality was the foundation for psychiatrist Giulio Moglie's classification according to which sexual inversion was a congenital disease, "a truly degenerative symptom," while sexual perversion was due to an ethical defect.[136] According to Moglie there could be homosexual perverts who lacked morality and were ready to indulge in their "abnormal" tendency as if it were "natural," and homosexuals with strong ethical principles who were deeply anguished, depressed, and saddened over a necessity "they felt was brutally abnormal and profoundly immoral." In other words, he who accepted his "abnormality" and considered the physiological act perfectly moral or those who tried to find a justification by resorting to examples from antiquity or "pseudoscientific" theories were considered perverse, whereas only those who were disgusted and ashamed of their nature deserved comprehension." These homosexuals were "true wretches who appealed, for the most part in vain, to medicine, religion, or the distraction of work to help them to free themselves from their vices and escape insult. And so Émile Zola maintained: 'You would not condemn a hunchback for being born hunchback. Why should we condemn a man who acts like a woman if he was born half woman?' These cases clearly show that inversion is not perversion, or at least not only perversion or solely the expression of a mental abnormality."[137]

It was the psychiatrist's job, then, to determine whether the abnormal behavior of homosexuals was of a congenital or an acquired nature in order to determine their level of responsibility. Subsequently, on the basis of these homosexuals' ability to reason, psychiatrists assessed whether to send them to an insane asylum or declare them incapacitated. In terms of psychiatric expertise, the studies of Augusto Murri and Lorenzo Ellero were considered the reference point. The latter was convinced that homosexuality was a sign of serious mental degeneracy, the effects of which were only manifested in the erotic and senti- mental lives of those affected. If homosexuality was not accompanied by an evident form of mental alienation, it did not determine civil incapacity, even though those induced to spend excessively large amounts in order to satisfy their sexual yearnings were to be deprived of the ability to manage their own finances.[138] Furthermore, psychiatrists were called on to assess whether or not to annul marriages involving homosexuals and to establish their irresponsibility or partial responsibility in the event that they committed crimes.[139]

Psychiatrists questioned whether mental derangement was the result of homosexuality or vice versa. The question was dealt with in psychiatry manuals where psychologists also confronted the matter and tried to establish whether sexual inversion was a mental illness or a psychopathic sexual perversion.[140] Sante De Sanctis, one of the founders of Italian psychology, was convinced that homosexuality almost always depended on external factors and was, unfortunately, much more frequent than people thought. He maintained that "whereas congenital sexual inversion of a biological nature is rare, the acquired form is incredibly common (imitative, due to immorality, professional) and is practiced in the most depraved manner."[141] Another famous psychiatrist, Enrico Morselli, also president of the Società freniatrica italiana (Italian Phreniatric Society) was of the same opinion: homosexuality was mainly due to "unwholesome and abnormal associations, or the continuation of or reliving of sexual experiences suffered in the past" and only to a lesser extent to a congenital perversion stemming from a constitutional anomaly.[142]

The discipline of psychoanalysis, which as mentioned above had great difficulty affirming itself against the Catholic Church's condemnation and the scientific community's hostility, had a very different approach.[143] The few studies undertaken at the beginning of the century were further reduced in number with the consolidation of Fascism and, in particular, with the enforcement of the racial laws and the consequent exiting of many prominent psychoanalysts from the country. One should not underestimate the extent to which Freud's own vision of sexuality created resistance to psychoanalytic theories in Italy, a country in which bourgeois conformism, Catholic morality, and nationalism's emphasis on self-control had laid the ground for a series of firmly rooted sexual taboos. There was also a more banal reason why people were distrustful of this new direction of research. Michel David wrote:

> At the bottom of every rejection of psychoanalysis there is a more or less conscious fear that the "pathological" might substitute the "normal" in the image that man has of himself or that a community creates so as to explain itself to itself. A kind of self-defense mechanism induces us to make a clear division between "normal" or "healthy" and "abnormal" or "unhealthy." Everything that is thought to be abnormal is put in the "other" category by means of a hasty but consoling mechanism supported by largely mythical arguments. Thus, in Italy in particular, there was an exaggerated emphasis on what was considered normal and healthy so as to nip psychoanalysis in the bud throughout the various cultural streams.[144]

This sort of repression of psychoanalysis was due, finally, to the influence exercised on sexology by Lombroso and his medical-anthropological school of thought. The pretext of assigning organic factors to every abnormality, thereby limiting the study of human beings almost exclusively to the anatomical and physical–chemical sphere made it impossible for Freud's ideas regarding sexuality to develop and thwarted the formation of a more tolerant and understanding attitude toward homosexuality. In fact, psychoanalysis substituted the concept of illness with perversion despite the fact that it continued to consider "sexual deviations" pathologies. The difference between the so-called normal individual and the abnormal one was not qualitative but quantitative: the same sexual components were active in both types, including the inclination toward perversion, which often created neuroses and suffering brought on by the inability to express themselves freely. Therefore, it was absurd to maintain that homosexuals were an isolated group with specific characteristics that differentiated them from other individuals, because there were no constitutional peculiarities to distinguish sexual inverts from normal people. Freud's position with regard to sexual inversion was quite conciliatory and indulgent.[145]

In Italy the first person to take up and discuss the theories of sexuality developed by Freud was Gustavo Modena, the deputy director of an insane asylum in Ancona, who wrote an essay on the subject in which he openly dealt with the problem of homosexuality, among other things.[146] His intention was to make psychoanalysis known to the public because "many aspects of Freud's theories of sexuality deserve to be more widely studied, analyzed, and criticized: the same can be said about his ideas regarding sexuality in children and his concept of sexual perversion."[147] Modena's research did not go unnoticed; the psychologist Roberto Greco Assaglioli delivered a paper called "Trasformazione e sublimazione delle energie sessuali" (Transformation and Sublimation of Sexual Energies) at a conference organized in 1910 by La Voce.[148] For these first researchers of Freud, the virtue of his psychoanalytic theory lay in his having intuited the importance of sexuality vis-à-vis the insurgence of psychoneuroses, having discovered the existence of infantile libido, and having widened scientific investigation to new areas of research. Soon after, La Voce began regularly addressing the problem of sex and, at times, though marginally, also the topic of sexual inversion. Giuseppe Prezzolini, for example, included a specific paragraph on homosexuality listing the most recent foreign works and the latest Italian publications on the matter, in a bibliography of sexology that he edited.[149]

This initial interest in psychoanalysis was considerably dampened with the consolidation of the Fascist dictatorship. Unfortunately, this coincided with the most positive period for Freudism—1930 to 1934[150]—when thanks to the activity

of Edoardo Weiss a serious scientific debate about the theories of psychoanalysis
was beginning to develop; a debate that with the publication of his *Elementi di
psicoanalisi* (the Basics of Psychoanalysis) extended beyond a limited circle of
specialists.[151] However, when the *Rivista Italiana di Psicoanalisi* (the Italian Review
of Psychoanalysis) was closed, vetoed by both the Vatican and Fascism, Freudian-
ism began its decline and later reached a point of total silence during the period
of the racial laws. The most innovative contributions to the study of homosexuality, coming from studies carried out by foreign psychoanalysts, went unnoticed by Italian culture, which set up a sort of impenetrable barrier against
northern theories of sexual inversion. Psychoanalytic ideas on sexuality were
an easy target for the Fascist press, which criticized the Oedipus complex and
its theory that perversions were inherently part of every individual. In an attempt
to ridicule psychoanalysis, Anton Giulio Bragaglia summarized the issue coarsely,
saying, "We are all pederasts," affirming triumphantly that he did not at all
consider himself such.[152]

　　Despite the growing hostility toward psychoanalysis, this new branch was
given ample attention in the *Enciclopedia Italiana* (Italian Encyclopedia), over-
seen by Giovanni Gentile. Two of the entry's collaborators, Emilio Servadio
and Weiss, were disliked by psychiatrists and opposed by Fascist culture precisely
because of the way they dealt with subjects linked with psychology.[153] All this
illustrates that the *Enciclopedia* had obtained a certain amount of autonomy from
the regime and that Fascism had resigned itself to the impossibility of obtaining
total obedience from the cultural world, which was ready to violate the conspiracy
of silence imposed by Mussolini on such awkward issues as sexuality and
homosexuality. One of these entries was *omosessualità* (homosexuality), which
appeared as a cross-reference to *sessologia* (sexology), which in turn was located
under the lemma *scienze mediche* (medical science), edited by Nicola Pende and
Giacinto Viola. Despite Pende's hostility toward psychoanalysis, he assigned
Servadio the entry *sessologia*, which held the entry *psicopatologia sessuale* (sexual
psychopathology), which in turn also discussed *omosessualità*.[154] The approach of
psychoanalysis to the problem and its focus on the complexity of the phenomenon
encouraged people to question widespread prejudices regarding the matter,
such as the old-fashioned organicist approach that ascribed particular characteristics to pederasts and depicted them as effeminate and lacking virility; the
disputable division between active and passive homosexuals; and the absurd
conviction that homosexuality originated from disease, genetic flaws, or self-
evident psychic abnormalities.

　　In general, the diffusion of psychoanalytical theories within the field of
sexology was very limited, in part because of sexology's juridical and criminal

slant and its almost exclusive link with legal medicine.[155] It is not surprising that the psychoanalyst Cesare Musatti authored the entry *omosessualità* in the *Dizionario di criminologia* (Dictionary of Criminology) edited by Pende, Niceforo, and Eugenio Florian and published in 1943 by Vallardi.[156] In the entry, Musatti openly criticized theories that postulated endocrinological or somatic causes for homosexuality while upholding the validity of psychoanalytic studies as a more plausible explanation. In his opinion, homosexuality was a form of neurosis; however, social causes favored the insurgence of the mental disorders so often found in sexual inverts. In fact, because they had to hide their condition and were subject to social disapproval, they developed psychoneuroses as well as a tendency toward criminal activity. Feeling isolated and not defended by the law, living a clandestine existence in an effort not to reveal their true sexual orientation, homosexuals were obliged to protect their own interests and defend themselves without recourse to any competent authority, and often ended up violating the law. Musatti's social perspective did not imply a distancing from the psycho-analytic approach, which he thought also served to destroy the stereotypical image of homosexuality. A whole series of false ideas had developed around a simple difference of sexual behavior, making it impossible to correct the errors of interpretation that over time had become clichés. For example, this is how Musatti highlighted the social importance ascribed to the difference between active and passive homosexuals:

> The concept according to which active homosexuality is distinguished from passive homosexuality is erroneous: even if in some instances there are homosexuals whose behavior is mainly active, such prevalence is never absolute; and it is for the most part due to principles of evaluation whereby, for example, a man feels that his behavior is not so different from that of a normal male if he practices, or says he practices, an active form of homosexuality. It is also a mistake to believe another concept (connected to this first one) according to which male homosexual activity consists exclusively or prevalently in the practice of *coitus per anum*.[157]

Furthermore, it was absurd to establish a natural connection between homosexuality and asocial behavior that, at the most, might be the result of external factors and, in particular, society's ostracism of homosexuals. The most modern aspect of Musatti's work, thanks also to his psychoanalytical approach, was to consider homosexuals on equal grounds with heterosexuals, distinguishable only by their sexual orientation. For Musatti, homosexuals were just as virtuous and intelligent as heterosexuals, and both could have perverse and criminal tendencies.

La Rassegna di studi sessuali

Basing his thesis on different assumptions, Aldo Mieli, a "pioneer" supporter of the movement for homosexual rights, came to similar conclusions.[158] Mieli was also the founder of the Società italiana per lo studio delle questioni sessuali (Italian Society for the Study of Sexual Questions). The aim of the society, set up in 1921, was to "spread serious and carefully pondered knowledge relative to sexual matters, to provide greater portions of the population with opinions and standards regarding hygiene as well as considerations on pedagogy and morality, in the best interest of society and good health."[159] Mieli proposed dealing with all aspects of sexuality through an approach open to the most modern scientific discoveries, which would stimulate medical, sociological, juridical, anthropological, and philosophical investigations and inaugurate an extensive debate on sexual issues capable of getting the general public involved and influencing the government's policies with the drafting of laws and measures on the subject. The society's official journal, the bimonthly *La Rassegna di studi sessuali* (The Sexual Studies Review), was edited by Mieli himself and was characterized by the diversity of its contributors and its openness to various points of view on sexuality: all opinions were in fact accepted and counterbalanced through a lively written exchange between supporters of opposing theses. Perhaps the journal's refusal to take a definite "reactionary and subversive progressive" side,[160] its antidogmatic attitude that was critical of any preconceived moralism disconnected from logical scientific arguments, was both the journal's strength and weakness, because it suffered from not being attached to any specific school of thought.

As Bruno Wanrooij justly noted, the society helped to secularize the debate over sexuality, but by shifting the discussion onto a purely scientific level, it was not able to involve the masses. This does not mean, however, that this choice pacified initial battles in favor of implementing sexual reform; on the contrary, it sustained these battles with a wealth of knowledge capable in time of taking root and bearing fruit.[161] Proof of this comes directly from how Mieli systematically confronted the question of homosexuality in his journal through a juxtaposition of different theories that brought the lively debates of the most famous international sexologists to Italy. *La Rassegna di studi sessuali* became a sort of free port where homosexuality could be discussed without necessarily considering it a negative thing to be corrected, cured, or fought. For this reason the journal slowly ended up being isolated and incapable of defending itself against the Fascist tide, which, as it advanced inexorably, tried to repress any mention of pederasty.

Aldo Mieli came from a background that Fascism surely disliked. He was born in Livorno on December 4, 1879, into a wealthy Jewish family. At a very young age he combined his love for scientific subjects—in particular, chemistry and math—with a precocious political commitment, in particular in support of socialism. He was expelled from the socialist association (il Circolo socialista) and the sharecroppers' union (la Lega di resistenza), founded by Mieli himself. Accused of passive pederasty, he was also obliged, in 1903, to resign from his office as a town councilor in Chianciano, a position he had undertaken two years earlier when he was still a student at the University of Pisa. Disheartened by the way he was treated, Mieli abandoned active politics to devote his time to study and travel abroad. He received a degree in chemistry, and thanks to Stanislao Cannizzaro and Emanuele Paternò he was soon appointed assistant in the chemistry laboratory at Rome University. Some time after that he qualified as a university teacher.[162] Mieli became involved in politics once again during the interventionist agitation in 1914–15. In an article published in *Lavoratore* (the Worker), the Socialist paper of Sartiano (Siena), Mieli reasserted that he was an internationalist and pacifist and criticized both interventionism and Giolittian and pro-German neutrality.[163] The war, a sort of metaphor of hatred, inspired the preface to his *Libro dell'amore* (Book of Love, 1916), in which he tried to "bare his soul" but also to reform a field that was soon to be defined with "a new word not commonly used," sexology:

> In the name of love, sincerity, and knowledge, and with a clear conscience,
> I have dealt with the most profound and delicate problems. I challenge
> and have little regard for laws, customs, and conventions. Because I reject
> that which is false, that which is not the fruit of love. And if laws, customs,
> uses, and conventions serve hatred and falseness, I shall want nothing to do
> with them.[164]

Mieli's approach to sexual matters was based on steadfast scientific rigor. His position was embedded in a positivist view of knowledge, critical toward idealism's "meaningless" but open to the most vanguard branches of knowledge.[165] No dogmatism or a priori dismissal was to preclude the acquisition of new scientific truths. False modesty and old prejudices were to be overcome by adopting an objective point of view: only by dealing with sexuality scientifically could so many harmful clichés be contradicted.

La Rassegna di studi sessuali was born in 1921 with this goal in mind. It encouraged discussion of matters that in the rest of Europe, and particularly in Germany, were stirring the interest of an ever-wider public: in Italy they were approached with hypocrisy. The journal was, therefore, instrumental in spreading information and "educating the educators,"[166] in keeping with Mieli's intention to make it a publication "open to all approaches, and one that would deal with all problems relative to sexual matters with impartiality and seriousness.[167] Contributions from a large number of collaborators were intended to foster fruitful debate and enrich the wealth of information on the subject. From the start, *La Rassegna di studi sessuali* published contrary or contradictory theories postulated by a group of very mixed collaborators: Catholic moralists, progressive laymen, disciples of the Lombroso school, psychologists, endocrinologists, sexologists, anthropologists, philosophers, scientists, doctors, jurists, and also writers and artists.[168] Despite the considerable diversity of the group, during the years the journal was edited by Mieli it was characterized by its particularly bold and innovative positions out of sync with the cultural and political climate of the period, especially with regard to sexual morality and considerations of homosexuality. According to Carola Susani, within the labyrinth of ideas, the only connecting thread was the continuous reference to homosexuality and the articles of Mieli and Proteus.[169] The latter was a well-known biologist and assiduous collaborator of the journal. Unfortunately, his true identity remains uncertain.

It has been hypothesized that Mieli himself was Proteus, but this seems implausible: Mieli had no reason to hide his identity, seeing as he had already signed even more explicit articles in favor of an open, nonmoralistic approach to homosexuality. Secondly, Proteus's positions did not always coincide with those of *Rassengna*'s editor. It seems much more probable that Proteus was a pseudonym for Pende, in light of the fact that they both adopted an endocrinological and constitutionalist approach to the problems connected with sexuality and showed an interest in the hormonal and biological aspects of homosexuality.[170] Further evidence in favor of this hypothesis is the strange absence of articles in the journal that are published by Pende, who was a member of the board of directors and was also vice president of the Società italiana per lo studio delle questioni sessuali.

It is hard to understand why he did not write for his own newspaper in spite of the fact that his name was among the journal's collaborators and his interest in such matters was well known. However, there are also some good reasons to doubt this pairing: for example, Proteus reviewed Pende's books, openly appreciating and praising them but at the same time criticizing some aspects and making some suggestions.[171] Furthermore while his reflections on homosexuality are very similar to Pende's, they seem to be a little to too progressive. It is also possible, however, that Pende used that very pseudonym in order to avoid discrediting his image by linking his name with overly progressive proposals, which might have left him vulnerable to criticism, especially considering the climate of narrow-mindedness and hostility surrounding homosexuality at the time.[172]

It is necessary, then, to carefully analyze the positions of Mieli and Proteus relative to homosexuality in order to demonstrate their different points of view and the novelty of their approach to the argument. Mieli, in particular, tried to prove that homosexuals could be perfectly normal men. In his opinion, studies had always approached sexual inversion as an abnormal behavior or illness and had only considered those who least conformed to the model of virility. Science had made the mistake of placing too much emphasis on hermaphrodites, transvestites, and effeminate men, and had neglected studies on homosexuals without any abnormal physical characteristics. Sexual inversion should not be the concern of doctors or psychiatrists but naturalists "who would approach the problem without the conventional concerns and, above all, without wanting to *cure* it. It should be studied in the same way as, for example, the habits of animals or the metamorphoses of the earth."[173] The absolute novelty of Mieli's message was precisely his desire to consider homosexuality a completely natural fact, not something to cure but to be analyzed with a high degree of objectivity. He believed that science was the means for overcoming false information because it went beyond simple moral judgment and brought hope for a more objective approach that would trigger a new phase in the study of homosexuality: it was time to radically change the way this unresolved matter was investigated by starting with the study of homosexuality in "normal" people. For Mieli, the idea that male homosexuality was always accompanied by female somatic characteristics was unacceptable: there was a certain amount of inherent bi-sexuality to everyone, independent, however, of somatic traits. For Mieli, the majority of homosexuals did actually show female characteristics, but this did not constitute an absolute rule; for example, some homosexuals were completely masculine, both physically and mentally. Pederasty, too, considered the act of *immissio membri in anum*, was simply a way to perform the sexual act and not an indicator capable of revealing the normal or abnormal nature of an individual.

Mieli, seconding with some reservation Hans Blüher's idea that male homosexuality was at the basis of human society, held that homoeroticism was a necessary means for the development of civilization.[174] Greece was a perfect example because there, "homosexual love had contributed more than hetero-sexual love to the development of art and had been of great social influence in education, games, and in all of public life."[175] His vehement defense of homo-sexuality led him to oppose all attempts to condemn private and consensual intercourse between adult individuals and to criticize those who, like the well-known dermatologist Giovanni Franceschini, were ignorant about the issues and sought to resolve them by punishing homosexuals and putting them in jail.[176] Equally fierce was his censure of the way in which newspapers reported events involving homosexuality. In January 1922, *Popolo Romano* reported on the

suicide of two lovers; the fact was harshly judged an "unmentionable relationship between two wicked individuals who as a result of their *horrible nefariousness*
had decided to commit such an extreme gesture. According to Mieli, if it was
totally out of place to speak of *nefarious actions* from the scientific point of view,
it was downright "criminal" to do so from a practical and social one: "because
homoerotic love affairs, like heterosexual ones, may range from the most
sublimely pure to the filthiest prostitution." The inane insults of people like the
reporter in question were much more serious than the "noble" sentiment that
united the two young men. The climate of social condemnation that surrounded
homosexuality was to blame for the suicide: the hostility of people toward those
who committed no other crime than that of being different from the majority
was to blame for his great distress.[177]

Criticism of the concept of normalcy was also central to Proteus's analysis
of homosexuality. In two articles published in *La Rassegna di studi sessuali,* and
then together in 1928 under the title *Moralità e sessualità* (Morality and Sexuality),[178]
he tried to demonstrate that sexual inversion was only one of the many ways in
which Nature expressed itself. In his opinion, the very existence of "sexual
deviation" was proof that sexual instinct did not perform the function of species
preservation but originated from a "need to eliminate the germinal substance."[179]
Once sex was no longer tied exclusively to the purpose of procreation, homosexuality became a perfectly natural phenomenon. According to Proteus, in
fact, individual hormone variations determined constitutional and personality
difference, frequently causing sexual deviations. The so-called sexual abnormalities were simple variations determined by inherited, individual, organic,
and constitutional factors, making homosexuality, then, contingent on the
individual endocrine formula. Endocrinology was responsible for demonstrating the
organic and constitutional origin of sexual inversion.[180] Furthermore, this new
scientific approach was decisive in resolving a whole series of problems relative
to sexuality that up to then had been the exclusive province of religion and
morality, "which, unable to resolve them rationally, surrounded them with
dogmatic precepts and arbitrary prejudices."[181]

Proteus was severely critical of those who still mixed up scientific investigation
with moral judgment on the question of sexual inversion, those who arrived at
the point of condemnation and contempt of homosexuals. It made no sense to
go on comparing normality with abnormality when in reality "only by dint of
habit and psychological associations" were they distinct from one another. As
Ludovico Limentani had rightly observed, it was wrong to expect that the "the
moral conscience of he who acts and he who passes judgment should be identical:
the latter approves or disapproves of the behavior of the former based on whether
it appears to conform to the same obligations that he feels or professes."[182]

Proteus was attempting to explain homosexuality on the basis of the law of errors, according to which there is always a large number of variations in all natural phenomena.[183] In his opinion, any social or moral judgment of what was supposed to be considered abnormal was entirely subjective, because normality was simply determined by the frequency with which a given behavior manifested itself, and it had not been "at all demonstrated that the values so far considered normal actually correspond to the most frequent behavior; probably they do not."[184] In order to establish normal sexual behavior, the frequency of variation had to be studied. In doing so however, it would be apparent that male and female characteristics were almost always mixed. Therefore the definition of "normal" sexuality was based on the ridiculous conviction that there was a clear distinction between the sexes, while in reality this was rare. The individual endocrine formula was too varied from person to person to make it possible to establish a universal model of masculinity and femininity. As such, the condemnation of homosexuality was predicated on unfounded assumptions:

> "Masculine" females and "effeminate" males are generally viewed with a greater or lesser degree of repugnance; as a result, they are exposed, in some countries, to judicial proceedings and everywhere to relatively appalling social persecution. This is because their behavior does not match up with the expectation that their personality arouses in others. In the mind of the observer, the labels male and female correspond to a determined "normal type" of person, and consequently also to a determined conduct and personality. This "type" is inexorably set out, as though preordained, so much so that any deviation away from conformism seems offensive, contradictory, and incomprehensible. . . . In the case of the virago and the effeminate male the expectation was not fulfilled because it was based on an unrealistic and arbitrary mental model.[185]

Only by analyzing deviations from the average could the difference between normal and abnormal behavior be determined rationally. Thus, sexual anomalies had "nothing to do with morality" but belonged to the sphere of biological research. Furthermore, the equation of the abnormal with the unusual had very significant practical and social repercussions on how homosexuality was considered. In fact, homoeroticism—although not always predominant, since only rarely did bisexuality assume particularly marked forms—was, however, "a simple *variation* of certain somatic and psychological characteristics, and as such neither moral nor immoral.[186] It was incorrect, then, to judge a homosexual—or for that matter a person with red hair—just because they represented an exception.

Starting from his biological approach, Proteus came to understand the subjective and relative nature of ethics. Morality changed from one period to the next, from one society to another and from person to person. For example, homosexuality was highly regarded and valued in ancient times and during the Renaissance. Given the fact that morality is a "historically evolving and changing product," "when our conscience considers certain actions good or bad per se, this will always be a judgment based on habit.[187] It was precisely Proteus's analysis of the relationship between morality and sexuality that enabled him to openly criticize contemporary behavior and morality. Maintaining that "morality can be substantially equated with liberty," Proteus's articles almost come across as an apology for diversity.[188] Since universal and objective morality did not exist, true freedom consisted in fully developing one's personality following one's natural inclination without forcing oneself to conform to the models imposed by society. Rules and moral imperatives were not meant to be imposed through "social force"; it was possible for each individual to distinguish himself from others without jeopardizing the freedom of other individuals but, at the same time, without being subject to externally established moral principles.

> Humanity—in all its elements, in the diversity of beings that represent it—has the right to be respected, insofar as nothing is without importance: each life, each type of activity, each action adds to the concept of human, that is, of everything he might be or do. . . . We must act so that all men may develop the faculties that nature has granted them, in other words develop their personalities fully. Unfortunately, society tends to enslave not only their bodies but their intelligence and will as well; it imposes a sort of rough psychological camouflage on its members, the denial of social progress.[189]

According to Proteus, individualism should overcome "conformism the father of tyranny, philistinism, and falsehood." Unfortunately there were still too many "positivists," "for whom society is everything and the individual nothing." The slow march toward acknowledging diversity had just begun, "until quite recently all individuals manifesting *behavioral* aberrations were ostracized by society and had to pay dearly for being different." Regretfully, Proteus ascertained that where sexuality was concerned, the old false, hypocritical mentality had not changed: "Here more than ever we can see the ever powerful effects of prejudice and conformism; here more than ever we can see how they are the main cause of unhappiness in our society."[190] Fear of being judged, of appearing different from others, or "arousing prejudice and social quarantine," were all forms of enslavement that limited the freedom of expression of human personalities. Social pressure exerted on the sexual sphere and the repression of instinct were so strong that they caused unhappiness and neuroses.

I know many admirable people whose full development has been inhibited by the repression of sexual tendencies that do not conform with those of the group; or who, having renounced the current morality, find themselves judged and condemned by a naïve, ferocious, impersonal and anonymous force.[191]

Conformism and not homosexuality was the true disease that needed to be cured by overcoming the need to act according to traditional morality. Therefore, Proteus called for a review of traditional ethics, and with the following words proclaimed the need to "protest and rise up with all our strength" against intolerance:

We ask that all good men stand up and fight the conformism and imitation that continue to dominate social life; to combat the atmosphere of intolerance and the persecution that inevitably accompanies passive and ignorant imitation. Just think that even what concerns one's own conscience is not allowed or tolerated when it clashes with the ideas or even the prejudice of public opinion! Those who desire happiness for men must hope for their liberation from the tyranny of the spirit of the horde and social prejudice. Until this condition is achieved no progress will be made toward happiness.[192]

This defense of individualism and diversity was in complete contrast with efforts being made by Fascism to create a "harmonious collective" capable of subordinating the individual's interests to those of the nation and of creating a uniformity of behavior and lifestyle among Italians. The dream of a regimented nation in uniform marching forward to make the country great was incompatible with the desire to let each individual freely express his own personality. For this very reason it seems unlikely that Pende—already prepared to subject science to Fascist orthodoxy—was behind the penname Proteus.[193]

Mieli's and Proteus's innovative positions were well received by *La Rassegna di studi sessuali*, though there was no dearth of contrasting opinions or condemnation and contempt for homosexuals.[194] One of the journal's main characteristics was "its spirit of great open-mindedness, a stranger to prejudice, something inconceivable in men of science." Its aim was always to combine the fight against "falsehood and false modesty" with the scientific investigation of sexual phenomena. All aspects of homosexuality were examined. Attention was even given to the ways in which it was dealt with in literature. In 1923 Filippo De Pisis published an article in *La Rassegna* titled "Psicologia e l'arte narrativa in Italia" in which he analyzed homoeroticism in literature. In 1925 André Gide's *Corydon* received an excellent review, heavily criticizing "French philistinism," which in the name of bourgeois morality had attacked this extremely important book that "shed new and unprecedented light" on the matter of homosexuality.[195]

The *Rassengna*'s attitude toward psychoanalysis was much more critical. According to Proteus, the importance of psychological factors in determining homosexuality needed to be reconsidered. He attributed the origin of so-called sexual anomalies to organic factors alone, claiming, consequently, that theories postulating "pseudo-psychological and pseudo-moral" causes for homosexuality were incorrect. Regarding these matters it was necessary to *think biologically*, to focus on "inherited traits, constitutional factors, and the complicated mechanism of internal secretion." Pende maintained that the organic base determined and conditioned the mind and not vice versa: "The hormonal composition together with the whole of inherited and constitutional factors determine the psychological state from which sexual anomalies originate."[196] Hormones influenced both the sexual and the psychological spheres by conditioning emotions, sentiments, and desires; the "emotional index of each individual was directly connected to the functional index of his endocrine system."[197] Emotions could be aroused by administering hormones (for example, injections of adrenaline) that functioned as regulators for the whole human organism.

Not all of *La Rassegna*'s collaborators were so critical toward psychological theories of sexual inversion; within the journal, psychology and endocrinology were in constant dialogue, and although interest in the latter predominated this did not altogether suffocate interest in the former. Mieli himself was an attentive observer of this new way of investigating the sexual sphere. Though he had some reservations about Freudism as a therapeutic practice, he appreciated its theoretical value and acknowledged that Freud had "easily resolved many fundamental questions,"[198] and had understood how the impossibility of indulging one's sexual inclinations created internal conflicts that could lead to serious psychological disorders. A truly scientific approach to sexual inversion had to be based on the comparison and analysis of all the most important intellectual contributions, including psychoanalysis.

La Rassegna's new viewpoint on homosexuality, an unjustly condemned and vilified behavior, was continuously corroborated by the most innovative foreign studies. The work of Edward Carpenter was particularly well received. The English literature teacher Guido Ferrando examined Carpenter's concept of an "intermediate sex" in detail.[199] Carpenter's "brilliant" ideas were thought to be fundamental in shedding new light on sexual inversion. His new approach linked homosexuality to emotions for the first time. Homoeroticism was not a form of immoral degeneration, but one of many different forms for expressing love; and "no matter how varied, anomalous and unusual the circumstances and combinations in which love is manifested, it must be treated by society with the greatest respect as a law unto itself, the most sacred and profound law of human nature."[200] Carpenter managed to show how, in most cases, the affectional relationship between persons of the same sex, based on sentiments rather than physical needs, found its highest expression in friendship. Here, love took on one of its "most perfect forms" because sexual needs were present but subordinate to spiritual needs. Since the best qualities of both sexes were combined in homosexuals, it was possible that "homosexual people might one day form the avantgarde of a great movement that will transform everyday life putting the bonds of personal affection and compassion in the place of other types of legal or interested exterior bonds that now typify our society."[201]

However, the greatest external contribution to *La Rassegna di studi sessuali* came from German sexologists. The very birth of the journal was largely due to its connection to the organization for the study of sexual matters and the defense of homosexuals' rights founded some years before in Germany. Magnus Hirschfeld, a doctor internationally known for his battle for the decriminalization of homosexuality, founded the Comitato scientifico umanitario, or CSU (Humanitarian Scientific Committee), in 1897. The association was actively committed to promoting research on "intermediate sex types" and to pressuring the government to abrogate paragraph 175 of the German criminal code, which outlawed homosexual relationships.[202] Hirschfeld is credited with having considered sexual inversion a physiological factor, not to be judged unnatural. His activity moreover stimulated the birth of other movements for the defense of homosexuals' rights that often voiced even more libertarian demands, as in the case of the journal *Der Eigene*, edited by Adolfo Brand, or that of Benedict Friedländer, who thought homosexuality was neither unnatural nor abnormal. To a certain extent *La Rassegna di studi sessuali* imitated the CSU yearbook (*Jahrbuch für sexualle Zurischenstufen*)—a yearbook on intermediate sexual stages and an endless source of medical information for sexologists around the world. Mieli probably learned of Hirschfeld's activity during a stay in Germany. The two formed a fast friendship, and in fact when *La Rassegna di studi sessuali* was set up, Mieli was listed among the members of the CSU and collaborated actively with his famous German colleague, who was sent to Italy in 1922 for a series of conferences on homosexuality. From the very first issue of *La Rassegna*, Mieli informed readers of Hirschfeld's work. He particularly praised the Institut für Sexualwissenschaft (Institute for Sexual Science) set up in Berlin in 1919 with the aim of studying sexual inversion and collecting available material for a specialized library as well as a space in which to welcome, defend, advise, and help homosexuals.[203] As a result of Hirschfeld's efforts, the first congress of the World League for Sexual Reform was held in Berlin in September 1921. Mieli participated as the Italian representative. He was invited to give the second talk on attempts at sexual reform in Italy, right after Hirschfeld's inaugural address.[204] After having denounced Italy's delayed progression in the sphere of sexology, and expressing a favorable opinion on divorce and the introduction of sex education, Mieli also stated his regret that there was still prejudice against homosexuality:

> Even if Italy doesn't have an article 175 like Germany's, which continuously keeps the public's attention focused on the matter, that doesn't mean that we shouldn't work at destroying the prejudices that, while demonstrating true scientific incomprehension, are left over from medieval barbarianism.[205]

Mieli's visit to the German capital must have left a strong impression on him, because of the seriousness with which studies on intermediate sexual types were carried out; and also for the pride and willingness with which homosexuals displayed their sexual identity without living in duplicity. There were cafés, dance halls, and other spots exclusively for homosexuals. Life in Berlin during the Weimar Republic offered an image of a new world where sexual inversion, in spite of the strict laws, was so widespread that a movement was founded to protect the rights of homosexuals.[206] Mieli was strongly impressed by all this, although after several other trips to the German capital he discovered he did not agree with some aspects of underground Berlin that were excessively provocative and that ended up hindering its efforts to give homosexuality a respectable image:

> In Berlin, I was interested in the study of intermediate sexual types. And Berlin was a suitable place for such studies. While such forms, homosexuality in particular, can exist anywhere, in no other place was such an odd form of organization established as in the German city. In this way, what was hidden so carefully elsewhere was manifested in broad daylight in Germany through organizations mostly promoted for noble purposes but among which there were also some overly audacious manifestations.[207]

In many German cities, homosexual associations were set up that, besides organizing meetings to discuss sexual inversion, followed the example of the journal *Die Freundschaft* and published insertions by people looking for jobs, partners, or meeting places for homosexuals. In Berlin there was even a theater (Theater des Eros) that specialized in homosexually themed performances. At the same time, Professor Karsch Haak had begun publishing the journal *Uranos* and Max Marcuse the *Zeitschrift für Sexualwissenschaft*, which he transformed into the *Handwörterbuch der Sexualwissenschaften* in 1924. While leafing through the pages, Mieli thought with regret about a country where "scientifically valid books can be printed and sold, while in Italy buyers are few and far between, university libraries lack funds, professors are paid very little, and finance sharks and millionaires are worried about everything but culture."[208]

In any case, Germany's example encouraged Mieli to undertake the responsibility of organizing the second World Congress of the League for Sexual Reform, to be held in Rome in June 1922.[209] He then proceeded to examine the theories of Hirschfeld, whose temperance he so admired along with his scientific rigor. Mieli considered his studies on sexual inversion free of arbitrary moral judgment and protective of people's most elementary rights.[210] The ideas of Krafft-Ebing appeared obsolete compared to those of this modern sexologist who was responsible for substituting the concept of sexual psychopathy with sexual pathology.[211] In spite of the fact that he considered Hirschfeld's work of fundamental importance, particularly *Die Homosexualität des Mannes und des Weibes* (1914), Mieli did not agree with the German doctor's explanation of "intermediate degrees of sexual manifestations," which he considered too focused on endocrinological aspects that undoubtedly had considerable physiological repercussions, but much less influence on the psychological sphere. The psychological inclination in favor of one or the other sex was still not fully explained: "With regard to homosexuality, or better, the attraction of an individual for persons of their own sex," wrote Mieli, "Hirschfeld's concept of the psychological factors is too crudely materialistic and separates homosexuality and heterosexuality too cleanly in spite of the fact that they are connected by the intermediate state represented by bisexuals."[212]

As time went by *La Rassegna di studi sessuali* became more and more vehement in its denouncement of the prejudices and false information surrounding sexual inversion. Mieli's and Proteus's disassociation from those who despised homosexuals and considered them criminals was greatly influential with collaborators of the journal, whose ties with the CSU became even stronger and more fruitful. Their aim was to keep Italy informed about the progress being made in Germany with regard to homosexuals.[213] Despite its harsh criminal code, for over fifty years German researchers had considered homosexuality a phenomenon to be studied through science rather than a vice or perversion. In fact, the motivation of the German movement for the rights of homosexuals was thought to have come as a direct reaction to the harshness with which unnatural relationships were punished: article 175 seemed to have prompted to some degree the realization that it was necessary to come out and fight against unjust persecution. With a pinch of bitterness, the Germans noted:

In France and Italy where homosexual acts between adults occurring inside closed places are not punished by law, the need to protest is not felt to the same degree as among German homosexuals. And this despite the fact that in these countries there is social contempt of homosexuals and conditions that would fully justify a general movement on their part. If nothing else, to enlighten the cultured and help them understand homosexuality, in light of modern scientific data that acknowledges that it is almost always the result of a particular constitution and a congenital state.[214]

In a short time, *La Rassegna di studi sessuali* had acquired ever-greater credit, and the Società italiana per lo studio delle questioni sessuali had become a model for other countries. In fact, Mieli considered it the "best organized and the most successful compared with similar organizations abroad."[215] Presided over by Professor Silvestro Baglioni (Mieli was secretary) it was divided into various groups, one of which was dedicated to the study of intermediate sexual types.[216] The society had sent four representatives to the first International Congress on Sexology held in Berlin on October 10–16, 1926, and had been chosen to organize the second congress to be held in Rome in 1929,[217] thus gaining entrance as a founding member of the newly formed International Sexology Society. However, despite these important acknowledgments, Baglioni himself noted that most intellectuals—educators, artists, and writers—were not yet members of the society.[218]

In his talk at the Berlin congress, on the development in Italy of related studies, Mieli referred explicitly to the work begun by the Fascist government to solve problems connected with sexuality. In particular, he emphasized the regime's energetic fight against prostitution, venereal disease, abortion, and neo-Malthusianism. Mieli thought highly of the new impetus with which the regime had begun to deal with sexual problems.[219] With the Fascists in power, *La Rassegna* would inevitably have to measure itself with a new political force so alert to problems concerning population growth and sexual issues. Therefore, although Mieli had criticized the regime during the Matteotti crisis,[220] beginning in 1924 the journal added the word "eugenics" to its title, thus becoming the official publication of the Società italiana di genetica e di eugenica (Italian Society for Genetics and Eugenics) and the Lega italiana contro il pericolo venereo (Italian League for the Prevention of Venereal Disease). In 1927 further specifications were added to the title: *Rassegna di studi sessuali, demografia ed eugenica* (Journal of Sexual, Demographic and Eugenic Studies). The change was not only superficial but involved the journal's entire layout, which now allowed even more space for topics regarding demographics and foreign publications on eugenics. It published several passages from Mussolini's Ascension Day Speech and even praised the regime's health and welfare policy. Some of the journal's positions taken before the advent of Fascism were toned down, for example concerning the taxation of unmarried men. Mieli himself, who in January 1922 had openly criticized the introduction of a law of this sort, deeming it as "unjust, immoral and barbaric as could possibly be imaginable,"[221] assumed a more conciliatory attitude and only stressed that the introduction of the new tax should not cancel out the state's position in favor of abstinence from marriage for those who were not fit for it, due to illness or problems of a psychological nature. More worrisome than the economic burden on unmarried men was the social pressure exerted on those who did not marry. According to Mieli, "above all from a moral point of view the state should facilitate the lives of those that the state wants to keep from proliferating so that they will not enter into marriage out of desperation, which would reap even more painful fruits."[222]

In 1928, when Mieli moved to France, the journal took on a totally different face. Among the editorial staff, Corrado Gini became increasingly important and turned *La Rassegna* into a pulpit from which to express his ideas regarding demographics and race. By 1931, following the official transfer of the journal's editorship to Silvestro Baglioni, Cesare Artom, and Corrado Gini, there was little left of Mieli's innovative, audacious spirit: the matter of homosexuality had become increasingly marginal and the issues ever more sporadic. It is not clear why Mieli moved to France, but it seems that it was not for political reasons. He did not carry out anti-Fascist activities and was by then an esteemed scholar, recognized worldwide for his research on the history of science and sexology; so much so that Giovanni Gentile included him in the first list of contributors to the *Enciclopedia Italiana* (Italian Encyclopedia; Milan: Bestetti and Rome: Tuminelli, presumed date 1925), responsible for the section on the history of chemistry and the editing of some entries in the section on chemistry and the history of science.[223] Certainly, as Claudio Pogliano observed, "In Italy under the fully established Fascist regime Mieli would have had to continue to—in his own words—'go up and down someone else's stairway,' tolerated just enough not to have to fully 'conform.'"[224] Most likely, apart from the atmosphere of the period, the decision to emigrate was made for financial reasons. He took with him his extensive library, which he donated in exchange for an annuity at the Centre de Synthèse, where he became a contributor. In fact, Mieli had used his wealthy estate to subsidize his research and, at his own expense, had created the publishing company Leonardo da Vinci to publish journals and books on science and sexology. The publishing house's failure was the mainspring that prompted him to leave Italy and seek refuge in France.[225]

However, in 1929 the police again took interest in Mieli after finding his name in the diary of the anarchist Camillo Berneri.[226] Furthermore, the frequent visits he received in Paris from Gino Chiappini and Angelo Pisani, the managers of his estate, aroused suspicion about his "sexual abnormality."[227] Despite all this, only in the summer of 1939 did Mieli's presence in France become dangerous enough to prompt him to leave the country. For him, a Jew and a homosexual, the only solution in the face of an advancing Nazi front was to leave Europe.

He went to Buenos Aires, taking his library with him and obtained a teaching post at the Universidad del Litoral (Santa Fe), where he was charged with founding and directing South America's first institute of science and history. His interest in sexology had diminished by then but, in the eulogy written on the occasion of Hirschfeld's death one could sense that he had not completely given up hope that true sexual reform was possible. In 1948, at the end of a tormented existence, Mieli took stock of his life and summarized his efforts to enable science to enlighten a world that was still full of dark areas, prejudices, and misinformation:

> In Italy, Fascism has destroyed all movements for redemption by introducing a true reign of hate. However, there is no doubt that I have been able to awaken a sense of human solidarity in some souls. For years I have fought, written, and taken action in support of a better comprehension of sexual life in an effort to overcome strongly rooted false ideas and proclaim a kingdom of physical and spiritual love. I am sure I have obtained some results and convinced some dubious souls. However, it appeared as though all my efforts had ended in failure when another morality based on power, imposition, and superstition began to dominate and reduce populations to slavery.[228]

Actually, after Mieli's flight from Italy his work to spread scientific knowledge about sexuality by means of *La Rassegna* continued thanks to the commitment of Edoardo Tinto, a publisher in Rome, who also carried on the proposal to set up a new university chair in sexology in order to spread sex education, at least in universities. Toward the end of the 1920s Tinto began a series called *La Biblioteca dei curiosi* (A Library for Curious People), in which he published essays on sexual topics meant to collect "interesting, entertaining, and culturally stimulating monographs" based on an "unbiased scientific concept of morality" that would be fit for the general public. The price of one lira for each book was supposed to make it accessible to all and favor the spread of "popular culture." As evidenced by the list of publications, the matter of homosexuality figured frequently among the series' proposals.[229] Between 1932 and 1934 in the *Biblioteca dei curiosi*, Tinto published the *Dizionario di sessuologia a dispense* (Dictionary of Sexology in installments), many of whose contributors were Italy's most important sexologists. Often they supported very advanced theories of sexuality and homosexuality and were convinced that sex had to be separated from religious morality because, as Hirschfeld had declared, "Believing that sexuality is in itself sinful is a charming fairytale that, owing to its long-lasting influence on the minds of children and adults has almost assumed the characteristics of a *spiritual epidemic*."[230] The intention was to devote ample space to sexual anomalies — "the most important area within the sphere of sexology" — the investigation of which had made great strides thanks to endocrinology. Right under the entry "Anomalies," Tinto reiterated the necessity of distinguishing between science and morality, and after stating that he agreed with Proteus's biological-constitutional theory, he wrote:

> Are the factors that we call "abnormal" scientifically so? Who and what has correctly established where normalcy ends and abnormality begins? . . . Ignorance has made it seem easy to separate sexual phenomena into the categories of normal and abnormal; but if we stop for a moment to consider all the physiological variations and we base our determination of an event on frequency, we shall be surprised to discover how extremely difficult it is to establish which phenomenon should qualify as normal and which as abnormal.[231]

The ambitious plan to publish a popular work about sexuality was short lived. Soon after the first few issues of the *Dizionario di sessuologia* were published, it was removed from the national libraries, as were other books on sexual matters edited by Tinto.[232]

The "desire for knowledge" clashed with the Fascists' desire to control. Sexuality, and in particular pederasty, could not escape the regime's ever watchful eye, ready to censor and silence free discussion of such delicate issues. The end of *La Rassegna di studi sessuali* and the *Biblioteca dei curiosi* is a perfect example of the pressure exerted by Fascism to steer science toward ideological objectives. Most likely Mieli's works had been possible because of his considerable economic resources. Self-financing, however, was not always easy for researchers, who had to bend to the will of others in order to exercise their professions in a dignified manner. In the 1930s, with the acceleration of Fascism's totalitarian project, science lost more and more of its autonomy, and widespread censorship pervaded every aspect of sexuality that did not conform to Fascist ethics. According to Giuseppe Falco, head of the police academy's forensics department, Mieli's works "did not attract great public interest except for a few biologists, medical examiners, and specialists on venereal disease"; the Fascist state, instead, had for the first time paid "great attention" to sexology, as was substantiated by the new social and criminal laws.[233] The success of some of these books published on sexuality effectively showed an increased interest in such topics but, at the same time, induced the regime to make greater efforts to maintain conformity. Under Fascism, sexuality and its "abnormal" forms became problems of national interest to be dealt with, above all, by the law and the police. The interest in sexology about which Falco spoke was not aimed at bettering the understanding of the matter but at disciplining its every manifestation in view of demographic growth and the protection of morality and public order. It is not surprising then that the Lega universale per la riforma sessuale (Universal League for Sexual Reform), the organization headed by Ellis, Forel, and Hirschfeld whose purpose was dealing with sexual problems, also came under the scrutiny of the police. The activities undertaken by Hirschfeld in favor of homosexuals and his "dangerous propaganda regarding sexual issues" were bitterly criticized. The league's congressional activities were carefully watched over so that they might be structured around the "most transparent materialism." According to the police, the scientific veneer of discussions about sexual matters was in fact "only a pretext to hide a lot of moral depravity."[234]

3

Sodomy

Sin or Crime

Nevertheless, I much prefer sin (if that is what it is) to a denial of self which leads to self-destruction.

MARGUERITE YOURCENAR,
Alexis

The Church and Sodomy

The rise of Fascism seemed to ease the Church's growing concern with the rapidly changing nature of sexual morality brought on by modernity and accelerated by the First World War. For the Church, the secularization taking place collided with morality, creating a divergence between sacred Christian principles and the lifestyle of citizens, official religious precepts, and everyday life. Once sexual behavior was no longer bound to the intentions assigned it by religion, the sacred began to be progressively eclipsed, threatening the Church's influence over a society in which new fashions, hedonism, and unrestrained vice were rampant. Corruption augmented forms of perversion, including sexual perversion; only the defense of traditional morality would make it possible to safeguard social order. From this point of view, with the advent of Fascism there could be perfect collaboration with the state, which in turn would rigorously watch over the habits of citizens and undertake a demographic project aimed at increasing the nation's population. In fact, the regime shared many

79

values with the Catholic church: respect for discipline, promotion and defense
of the family, distinct male and female roles, and the importance of matrimony
and procreation. Although this moral convergence did not always correspond
to an agreement about the ultimate purpose of sexual behavior, Fascism considered the Church's commitment to monitor and correct deviant behavior
positively. This shared viewpoint, above all in the 1920s when the Fascist totalitarian venture was in its early stages, favored the signing of the Concordat, which
officially acknowledged the Church's supremacy in directing the morality of its
followers. Consequently, in 1930, the traditional image of the family and sexuality
were reasserted in the encyclical *Casti Connubi*, in which Pope Pius XI openly
condemned the lax morals brought about by the country's sudden modernization.
Sexuality was supposed to fulfill "its natural reproductive virtue"; great was the
offense of those who violated "the law of God and Nature."[1] A crusade was
launched against indecent behavior that stressed the importance of self-control
over one's sexual impulses. It called for chastity and moderation, fundamental
virtues of a good Catholic and the only antidote against these new licentious
habits.

The Church's efforts to safeguard traditional morality were to be implemented by spreading Christian values throughout society. However, as the
regime was consolidated and its totalitarian plan accelerated, reasons for friction
inevitably arose between the Catholic Church and the new political religion of
Fascism that was so eager to permeate the whole of society with its values.[2]
Fearing the Church might hinder the complete fascistization of Italians, yet
not undervaluing the impact of Catholicism, Mussolini used the convergence
between throne and altar and the trinomial "God—Country—Family" instrumentally to increase his power in view of attaining a position of supremacy.
Similarities and differences of interest created a dialectical relationship between
Fascism and the Holy See. This "marriage of convenience" became increasingly
turbulent in the 1930s as the regime became more and more totalitarian. The
Catholic male did not differ greatly from Fascism's new man with regard to
masculinity and reproductive capacity. The two also shared a patriarchal vision of
the relationship between the sexes, were both hostile toward the emancipation of women, and believed in maintaining gender roles distinct from one
another. Males should be active, strong willed, and of the utmost integrity;
females should be mothers, wives, and protectors of the hearth. Virility was a
fundamental value for Fascism and the Church as clearly exemplified by Luigi
Gedda's slogan "strong and pure": a true man was first of all a prolific father, a
man of character, a master of sensuality.[3] The specific features of the Catholic
model were listed, one by one, in a book by the Dominican Ferdinando A.
Vuillermet, bearing the meaningful title *Siate uomini, alla conquista della virilità*

(Be Men, Conquer Virility).[4] In fact, the author was trying to diffuse the cardinal principles of educating young men in matters of masculinity, the first of which was to reject a lifestyle based exclusively on "luxury, affluence, comfort, entertainment and pleasure." Only by harmonizing the virtue of chastity with that of virility would it be possible to resist the temptations of lust and to avoid weakening one's willpower in the ephemeral search for pleasure. Control over one's passions continued to be a sign of virility; reason enlightened by religious precepts, rather than instinct, should guide sexual behavior. The new generations that grew up under Fascism perfectly embodied the aesthetic ideal of beauty and the value of purity. Vuillermet congratulated them on their virile appearance with the following words:

> How beautiful this generation is of pure young men, their foreheads marked with virility! Seeing them is a joy. Their noble faces, their refined behavior, the dignity of their lives make them seductive and attractive. Nobody can resist such beauty.[5]

Nevertheless, there were differences between the regime and the church's visions of the male, not only regarding their view on aggressiveness but also on the role of the husband and father within the family. In the Catholic vision, within the family the man should not only exercise control and domineeringly make the most important decisions; it was also his duty to guarantee the holiness of matrimony and the correct education of his children. Education, in fact, was the reason for most of the friction between Fascism and the Church; the clash with Azione Cattolica (Catholic Action), which culminated in a real crisis in 1931 and again in 1938, originated in a dispute over the control of society and the new generations. As Renzo De Felice rightly notes, although they shared some common points, Mussolini saw Christianity as a "pernicious doctrine of renunciation and humiliation that corrupted and emasculated men and the population."[6] Catholicism's humanitarian pacifism was the complete opposite of the bellicose martial spirit with which young men were educated in Fascist organizations. Furthermore, compared to Fascism, the Church extolled self-control and the domination of one's passions with the goal of leading a chaste and pure life. Instead, the regime emphasized a more unrestrained and transgressive masculinity, allowing for the satisfaction of sexual needs implicit in a healthy and explosive virility, to the extent that it tolerated giving in to carnal temptations so as to gratify one's own sexual exuberance.

Despite all this, Fascism preferred leaving the job of controlling the sexual behavior of its citizens to Catholicism, which guaranteed the respect of proper habits understood as heterosexuality, purity, faithfulness, and the conservation of gender divisions. Therefore, all forms of pleasure that departed from this mold continued to be criminalized, including extramarital relationships or those whose purpose was not reproductive. Reproduction was one of the main reasons for the Church's almost obsessive interest in matters regarding sexuality. Priests were charged with watching over the behavior of the faithful, of warning them of the dangers of lust. Its control over sexuality steadily became more meticulous, above all thanks to confession, a valuable instrument for investigating the most intimate aspects and secrets of a repentant sinner's private life. Studies by Foucault provide evidence of the important social effects of confession, among which, in particular, is the amplification of the discourse on sex.[7] In spite of itself, the Church actually favored an increase in discourse about sexual perversions because of its need to correct and set sinners on the right path. As a result, there was more talk about sex, but in the form of secrecy, something to confess in a whisper, kneeling, and with a bowed head.[8]

The sacrament of repentance, instrumental for the interiorizing of norms, the safeguarding of morality, and the repression of instinct, perversion, and temptations of the flesh, made it possible to classify sexual behavior and provided the parameters for distinguishing what was natural from what was unnatural, what was admissible from what was inadmissible, venial from mortal sins. Individual actions were placed on a scale of values that made sexuality appear monstrous, though forgivable, when expressed in ways different from those prescribed by the Church. Confession was supposed to allow homosexuals to investigate their nature, understand their sexual orientation, and express their agony; but this sort of self-analysis, because it remained closed within the walls of the confessional, only augmented homosexuals' sense of isolation and abnormality. Just as refusal of absolution magnified the sense of isolation and the anxiety over damnation, forgiveness did little to overcome the idea that sodomy was sinful, immoral, and unnatural. The need for contrition in order to obtain the remittance of one's sins led to a deeper awareness about one's most intimate inclinations as well as the translation of the most irrational desires into logical discourse. Like being on the couch of a psychoanalyst, in the confessional a repentant sinner also learned the words for describing his pleasures, but unlike the psychoanalyst, the priest was there to increase his sense of guilt, not to help free him from it. Homosexuals experienced a clash between impulsive desire and the rational evaluation of behavior that was judged unnatural: they felt understood and forgiven, but precisely for this reason, all the more guilty. In fact, as Pino Lucà Trombetta states:

> The strict disciplining of sexual drive required by the system of contrition
> presupposes a high degree of interiorization of moral norms that would
> make one's behavior seem legitimate not only because of external pressure

but above all because it seemed "natural" and was triggered somewhat spontaneously from within the individual himself. Only under these conditions would violation of the norms prompt, in the individual, an acute sense of wrongdoing and such a painful internal schism as to induce immediate obedience.[9]

The confessor who entered the private lives of the faithful had to be cautious and careful not to overstep the boundary beyond which it might upset the sensitivity of repentant sinners by asking them for too many details, and thus become counterproductive. By asking them about the most intimate details of their private lives, even their thoughts and sexual fantasies, confessors risked producing the negative effect of making indecent practices known to people who were pure and decent and whose ignorance was thought to be much more useful than their knowledge. Instilling doubt and perplexity in the souls of the innocent about their own sexual conduct might have driven them to commit sins that were previously unknown to them. Apart from its investigative aspect, this interference in the private lives of believers, meant to bring their sexuality back inside the institution of marriage and for the sole purpose of reproduction, led in the end to stricter controls and the condemnation of "impure acts" carried out in a sinful way and for a sinful purpose.

Many pages were devoted to sexual perversions and homosexuality in publications on theology, surveys of morality, and handbooks for confessors.[10] In fact, carnal sins were divided into two categories: those that were consistent with nature and those that were against nature; in other words, all types of behavior not geared toward reproduction, such as masturbation, sexual intercourse during pregnancy, and anal coitus. It was the confessor's task to warn repentant sinners of the seriousness of sodomy, which was condemned by the Bible. One particular handbook for confessors published in 1885 and widely used in Italy is a good example of the manner with which the matter was dealt. It provided a series of detailed pieces of advice on how to deal with such sins as lust and the violation of marital duties.[11] The author, Monsignor Bouvet, Bishop of Le Mans, clearly expressed his concern about referring explicitly to such dangerous subject matters. He was so concerned that he felt he should justify himself—*escusatio non petita*—for having raised "this lewd, indelicate and reprehensible subject," clarifying that he had done so reluctantly, out of necessity, "invoking the supreme help of God." Once again, sex was being discussed but only after apologizing and recommending that the book be kept well hidden from seminarians lest they fall prey to "sins of indecency."[12] Only priests and deacons were allowed to deal with similar matters so that they would be well prepared for the ministry of confession. Due to the lack of specific publications on how to face sexuality, there was the risk that anxiety and uncertainty might befall those charged with this delicate office. According to Monsignor Bouvet, sodomy was in all respects a lustful act, a "monstrous wickedness" caused by the unnatural desire to "use sex wrongfully." It was considered a grave sin "for the horror it arouses universally; for its true and manifest moral deformity; for the unprecedented punishment inflicted by God on the five cities soiled by this contamination; for the epistle of Saint Paul to the Romans . . . ; for the grave penalties decreed in Canon Law and particularly in the papal bull against homosexual priests, *Horrendum illud scelus*, issued by Pius V; for the vehemence with which all the holy fathers of the Church have inveighed against this crime." The bishop thought it superfluous to discuss the appropriateness of asking repentant people to specify whether during homosexual acts they had played an active or a passive role. He thought it was better not to enter into too much detail, although many theologians believed the sin to be more serious when a passive man violated nature by voluntarily allowing himself to be sodomized.[13] In any case, all lustful behavior had serious psychological, moral, and physical consequences that required remedies of a religious (prayer and contrition), ethical (useful suggestions for and recommended readings), and medical nature. Only "venereal contact" between persons of the same sex, kissing or sitting on another's lap, did not constitute mortal sins. They were, however, considered obscene acts that should be avoided and severely condemned.[14]

Don Renato Louvel, the Father Superior of the seminary at Séez, was equally severe in his condemnation of homosexuality. He wrote a handbook for confessors, containing a series of suggestions on how to handle sexual sins, that was widely distributed in Italy starting in the mid-1800s. With regard to sodomy, Louvel invited future confessors to "find out who supplied the act and who received and in what proportion each took part in this crime." In fact, "there is a natural difference between the sin of submitting voluntarily to corruption and that of only cooperating with the pulsations of someone else, because not refusing to enjoy is completely different than procuring pleasure from another."[15] Homosexuality was such a filthy act, according to Father Louvel, that the only words that could condemn it were those of the Bible describing the overthrow of Sodom and Gomorrah:

> And for that, God abandoned them to shameful passions since their women changed the use of nature into another against nature. Equally, the men rejected the natural use of the women and burned with desire for each other, the males practicing a despicable action on the males, and received for this the penalty of becoming blind. Because they did not want to acknowledge the Lord, He abandoned them to their depraved senses so that they could do disgraceful things to one another.[16]

Eroticism was to be directed toward reproduction alone. All acts that deviated from this goal were considered impure. "Educating the young in chastity" would preserve them from vice because uncontrolled lust distracted individuals from holiness and replaced faith with the quest for material pleasure.[17] "Dispersal of the seed" was a serious sin, and sodomy was even more serious, because it violated the law of nature *criminen de spendere seminem extra vas naturale*. However, the Church's battle against homosexuality and sexual deviance also required efforts to understand and investigate such matters. Acts that deviated from legitimate sexuality were to be criminalized but at the same time understood and corrected. In order to defend Catholic ethics, it was not enough to merely censure every reference to sex; it was necessary to discuss all unorthodox behavior as well by analyzing and studying the works of scientists and doctors. The increasing importance of science breached even the Church's traditional sexphobia. The Church combined science's explanation of the dangers involved in some "unnatural acts" such as sodomy—that caused physical and psychological decay—with its moral anathema against anyone who did not obey the precepts imposed by religion. Although religion and medicine continued to fight for the monopoly over sex-related issues and morality, little by little the Church tended to reinforce its doctrine with certified scientific contributions without, however, renouncing its supremacy. Even though the Catholic pastoral established a series of prohibitions relative to sexual practices that had little to do with science, its remedies for curbing the spread of sinful behavior were no longer limited to acts of contrition but included medical and social measures.

Scientific theories that concerned the various carnal sins could not be ignored by priests whose task it was to teach their followers correct sexual behavior and show them the spiritual and physical risks of immoral conduct. The *Rivista medica per il clero* (Medical Journal for the Clergy), first published in 1930, was a review specifically for confessors that aimed at helping them understand the link between physical and moral illnesses. Father Agostino Gemelli, whose opinions on sexual problems were rooted in an attentive study of pertinent scientific literature, also thought it necessary to have a variety of knowledge so as to properly evaluate the biological, moral, spiritual, and religious aspects of such a socially important matter.[18] Even if the interest in sexuality manifested in the early 1900s was on the wane and the books and reviews on the subject had by then been moved to the depositories of libraries, it was necessary to reawaken people's interest. This had to be done, however, without making overly audacious statements—like Mieli had—that might contaminate the purity of the young.[19] Likewise, it was important not to fall into the distorted pansexuality of psychoanalysis, whose only merit was having developed the fundamental concept of sublimation in relation to sexual instincts. Instead, the task of morality and religion was to infuse the souls of adolescents with chastity and purity: "Be chaste, be pure and you will be strong in the productive life that awaits you, you will be an example to follow."[20] Father Gemelli also researched the problem of homosexuality, and in 1943 he dedicated a study in Latin to hermaphroditism and intersexuality. His approach was strictly organicistic, eliminating all reference to Freud and openly criticizing "pseudoscientific" books that divulged sex to youngsters. The major sexologists of the time, Hirschfeld and Marañon and others, were banned, so to speak: Hirschfeld was described as "iudaeus germanus" ("expressio illarum falsae scientiae generic litterarum in quibus Hirschfeld iudaeus excellit, qui turba scriptorium vulgo propinavit"); Marañon "clarus biologus hispanicus" was mentioned because he "fuit inter seditiosos rubros in seditione hispanica."[21]

Less famous than Father Gemelli but with close ties to the Vatican, Angelico Arrighini also made recourse to medicine in his defense of Catholic ethics on sexuality. Against vice and uncontrolled passion—the ills of modern society— the aim of his books was to provide confessors and educators with the necessary instruments for establishing "the moral and somatic therapy" that would cure these diseases. Passions were natural instincts that, if expressed in excess or defect, led to libertinism and sexual perversion. Arrighini also agreed with the endocrinological doctrines according to which hormone dysfunction could cause a male to end up somewhere in between reason and insanity, leaving him in the grip of his own instincts and turning him into an immoral and irreligious person. The ideal man was dispassionate, "a normal man, the classic type" with a free personality, self-confident and without any abnormal desires, without any predominant ideas, and capable of keeping his instincts under control.[22] Confession was useful to help him regain control over his passions, but even more useful were the new endocrinologic drugs that recreated the body's correct hormonal balance. Pende and Marañon wrote fundamental works on the subject, but the most complete treatise remained Magnus Hirschfeld's. Steinach's experiments were the best proof for demonstrating that hormone treatment was a reliable cure for pederasty, because only organotherapy was able to bring about a change in the *individual's endocrine formula*. Arrighini admitted he had used such treatment on two homosexuals: one, an *occasional* homosexual who had become a *habitual* one during his stay at the front; the other, a *congenital* homosexual with *passive* characteristics. He had given the two unfortunate men tablets of *viroglandolo*. In the first case, he obtained excellent results, but in the second, the results were negligible. Although unaware, the Catholic moralist turned "apprentice witchdoctor" had formed a different position from the Church regarding "inverted sexual tendencies." Homosexuality was no longer a sin, a perversion, or an immoral act chosen voluntarily; it was a "deformity and an illness" to be cured with medicine or corrected with hormonal mixtures, not simply repressed.[23] All passionate people considered dangerous for society were to be treated "the same as psychopaths: instead of sentencing them to imprisonment where they would suffer unjust punishment that would only worsen their condition, they should be hospitalized in a clinic, which they could eventually leave when cured or at least when they were much better."[24]

On the other hand, the Church considered homosexuality an immoral behavior that was to be corrected in a sacramental environment and repressed by law. Canon law provided expressly for the crime of sodomy and divided this libidinous act against nature into three separate types: *sodomy* in the given sense of the word, which was in turn subdivided into perfect sodomy if occurring between people of the same sex (*concubitus masculi cum masculo aut foeminae cum femina*) and imperfect sodomy if between persons of a different sex (*non servato debito vase*); *bestialitas*, the union with animals; and *mollities*, masturbation.[25] Punishment was particularly severe for these acts that violated the Divine Law of reproduction and upset natural order, and in the instance that the offender was a member of the clergy, it even reached the point of dismissal from the order. For laypeople the sanctions were far less severe and limited almost exclusively to habitual homosexuals or, in other words, those who practiced sodomy *iterates vices frequentium et quasi de consuetudine*. Everyone else eluded public punishment, something the Church avoided out of fear of *vitatio schandali* and as not to disturb the souls of its followers. Those who were notorious sodomites had to be punished, because failure to do so would have caused scandal.[26] Canon law also dealt with homosexuality in relation to the rules and regulations of marriage, which could be dissolved if not consummated or annulled because of impotence. "That abominable vice caused disgust and dishonor for the wife"; therefore, it was sufficient to be certain of a husband's homosexuality to presume that the marriage had not been consummated whether the husband was actually capable of performing the sexual act or not. The tendency of the Sacred Rota was to pronounce the marital bond legally broken in the case of impotence caused by sodomy.[27]

Criminal Law and Homosexuality

The state, like the canon, also had to deal with the problem of homosexuality, arming itself with all the necessary instruments for repressing deviant sexual behavior. With the advent of secularization, sodomy, long considered an act committed against the laws of God and nature, crossed into the secular realm and became the object of widespread legal debates on whether or not to make it a crime punishable by law. As we have seen, medical studies on the causes of "monstrous love" led to the question of whether homosexuals were criminals to be condemned or sick individuals in need of treatment. Jurists were therefore obliged to refer to doctors in order to assess the responsibilities of those who were dragged or let themselves be dragged into the world of perversion. Experts were faced with a series of problems to be solved: if the law was independent of Catholic ethics, sodomy would be judged only on the basis of its danger to society; whether a homosexual was able to avoid such reprehensible behavior; if his immoral conduct depended on a rational choice or biological factors independent of his will; whether specific laws against pederasty would be able to eliminate this plague or if more effective measures should be employed.

These difficult problems were finally being faced after a long and tortuous path. On the other hand, homosexuals had been criminalized, condemned, punished, and tortured for centuries. Such criminalization varied from period to period and country to country, but in actual fact it had been around for long enough to provide the legal instruments necessary to severely punish unnatural libidinous acts. Pederasty continued to be harshly repressed in Germany and England in particular. In fact, during the first decades of the nineteenth century in Great Britain about fifty executions for "buggery" were recorded, and there was no reduction in the number of people sentenced to prison or forced labor for this crime during the remainder of the century.[28]

In countries where the influence of the Enlightenment had led people to criticize the brutality with which "monstrous love" was fought, the penalties against those who committed such crimes were slowly reduced, leading eventually to the elimination of the harshest sanctions. With the increasing competence of nation-states, actively concerned with the health, education, and welfare of their citizens, there also came the idea that the harsh repression of sodomy should be replaced with widespread prevention.[29] The diffusion of the Napoleonic Code, which called for an absolute distinction between religion and law, and morality from law, further influenced the approach to sexuality, an individual freedom belonging to the private sphere outside of the state's jurisdiction, barring cases in which the freedom of others was violated. This principle was adopted by the preunification codes in Italy, which, taking the French code as a model, had eliminated sodomy from the list of punishable acts.[30] Thus, on the basis of this new legal model, only homosexual affairs that came about without the consent of one of the partners were punishable by law. The words of an Italian jurist writing at the beginning of the nineteenth century clearly express the need to not confuse religious precepts with the impositions of the law, to leave unnatural sexual acts out of the criminal code:

> The religious zeal of many legislators invests itself with the right to avenge
> offenses to nature (against Greek love, lesbianism, and homosexuality) and

goes further, to the point of wanting to punish those who are guilty with axe and fire. But the sacred indignation that is inevitably aroused in moral breasts at the sight of such abominations should not ever move us to praise the ferocious ideas of those lawmakers. The public authorities should have no other purpose than the protection of the rights of the social body and the individuals who compose it; certainly not out of spite for the wrongs that individuals do to their own detriment and shame. . . . Apart from that, what could soil the codes, the tribunals and public hearings? Criminal laws on such filth would not instill moral doctrines in the population; they would only create scandal. . . . If Governments are wise, they will educate their citizens about these vices with stable and healthy institutions instead of criminal precepts; with the constant exception of cases in which public decency, the sacred property of the population, comes to be insulted.[31]

Homosexuality remained such an abominable vice that it was better not to list it among criminal offenses. It was such a delicate subject that it was preferable not to allow it to enter the courtroom lest it set a bad example; only overt insults to public morality called for the state's involvement in trials against those guilty of "such filth." These are the reasons for the exclusion of homosexuality as an indictable offense from almost all preunification civil codes, with the exception of the Austro-Hungarian Code in force in the Lombardo–Veneto region and that of the Kingdom of Sardinia.[32] As correctly noted by Giovanni Dall'Orto, the importance of this innovation was revolutionary, to say the least, and contrasted with prevailing attitudes in the rest of the Western world, where sodomy was still a crime punishable by death.[33]

This way of dealing with homosexuality changed after the birth of the unified state, when the need to create a coherent civil code led to a sweeping transformation of the legal system. While awaiting the formulation of a new national criminal code, the Savoys decided to extend their code to the rest of the country. However, in the Kingdom of Sardinia, which had reintroduced prerevolutionary legislation after the fall of Napoleon, article 425 on homosexual relationships had also reappeared.[34] As a result, the newborn Kingdom of Italy adopted this same article that "inflicted severe punishment on any kind of unnatural libidinous act committed with violence or that caused a scandal or, even with no sign of the aforementioned, gave rise to legal action.[35] Nevertheless, in 1861 the Commission of Deputies charged with extending the 1859 Sardinian penal code to the rest of southern Italy decided to abolish article 425 throughout the Kingdom of the Two Sicilies, where the Neapolitan criminal code, which did not provide for the crime of homosexuality, had been in force for years.[36] The decision was motivated as follows:

Events of incontinence are not punishable unless the law has been violated, public decency has been offended, or violence has been committed against one's personal decency, such as in the case of rape, abduction, or an attack on decency. Yet, the commission, pointing to the traditions of our previous legislation for this last type of crime, warns that it will have to divest of juridical effectiveness the penalty established by the code for unnatural libidinous acts when they are not accompanied by violence and refer to the punishment for rape with violence when there has been violence.[37]

In practice, for several years the situation was ambiguous: in the North, homosexual relationships between consenting adults were punished, while in the South this type of act was completely decriminalized, even if the courts could, however, take action in the case of unnatural libidinous acts if they caused a public scandal or could be considered an insult to decency and morality. By acting in this way, the commission acknowledged the particularity of Mediterranean culture, which considered it normal, above all in the period of adolescence, to have limited homosexual experiences. This same culture, which scorned pederasty and resisted its official legitimization, tended to tolerate those who played an active role in the relationship, judging it on the basis of the mental categories used for heterosexuality.[38] Therefore, the "particular disposition" of the southern population, those citizens who in the eyes of the Piedmontese political leaders were so different from the rest of the inhabitants of Italy, influenced the decision to not consider homosexuality a crime, thus avoiding the negative effects of a repressive law. The lower-class ceremony known as the *figliata*, a fake marriage between men, was evidence of the particular relationship that Neapolitan culture had with homosexuality. In the southern regions, this "ancient ceremony sacred to the homosexual cult" that imitated the nuptial rites between husband and wife, was in fact quite common.[39] The ceremony took place at an inn where there happened to be "the lover, an accordion and a guitar player, and a group of 'fairies' surrounding the timid . . . young maiden."[40] It ended with the wedding night and the subsequent ascertainment of the marriage's consummation.

The conviction that there was a racial difference between northerners and southerners in the sexual sphere as well acquired ever-greater credibility and, in 1901, after the publication of a book by Alfredo Niceforo, *Italiani del Nord, e italiani del Sud* (Italians of the North and Italians of the South), took on the characteristics of an actual scientific certainty.[41] Anthropological studies confirmed the existence of "two Italies, dissimilar in their customs, civilization and race," each having "the traces of a lively physical and moral dissimilarity indelibly impressed on their physiognomy."[42] The particular customs and habits

of the South required a considerable adaptation of the norms, because it was
not always possible to apply decisions coming from the center to an area where
the population was so anthropologically different from that of the North.
Where homosexuality was concerned, then, the proposal to implement what
Raffaele Romanelli defined as "the impossible command" or, in other words,
the belief in the ability to "educate Italians by force" through the state's
maieutic mission" had to be scrapped.[43] The commission itself did not regard
the code's extension to the southern regions as an attempt to "Piedmontize,"
but rather as an instrument that would "free Neapolitans" by enabling them to
enjoy the innovations intended to ensure citizens greater protection and more
rights. "The legislative innovations" were to be extended to the whole nation,
respecting, however, the "Neapolitan juridical traditions, which satisfy the
needs of justice, science, and civilization,"[44] Evidently, not entering homosexuality as a crime was one of these traditions.

The problem of this legislative inconsistency between North and South
came up again in 1865, with the proposal to extend the 1859 Sardinian code to
Tuscany, with the modifications adopted for the Neapolitan regions.[45] The
matter was definitively resolved in 1889, when the Zanardelli code came into
effect and decriminalized homosexuality throughout the nation.[46] The decision
was reached after a lengthy debate that carefully assessed whether or not
homosexual relationships should be considered criminal offenses. The clash
between the abolitionists and those who were in favor of considering homosexuality a crime was resolved in typical fashion by not mentioning unnatural
libidinous acts directly but having them figure, when occurring together with
violence or public attention, under the categories of rape or insult to public
decency.[47] The parliamentary member Villa, in his report before the Chamber
of Deputies, motivated the decision as follows:

> Criminal law is the protector and avenger of rights; it cannot legitimately
> explicate its action in cases where violations to these rights are not met.
> Incontinence is without any doubt a sin and a sin that sometimes manifests
> itself repulsively, but this by itself cannot be punished by legislators
> without entering into the realm of repressive guidance. Incontinence may
> become a crime and is punishable only when it violates an individual or
> social right. It is by logical and rigorous deduction from these fundamental
> principles of the right to punish to which the laws being examined pay
> their respect; let us not see reproduced among them any crimes that, only
> because of their moral ugliness, are still in the code in force. Thus, unnatural
> libidinous acts when not accompanied by violence or scandal are now
> excised from the category of actions prosecutable by law.[48]

The law was meant to protect personal and social rights while taking care not to transform sins into crimes. Despite the hostility and severe judgment of such sexual behavior expressed in the language used, the liberal approach was aimed at defending the private lives of individuals from interference on the part of the state and public morality as well as guaranteeing the separation between private and public spheres.[49] Minister of Justice Giuseppe Zanardelli, loyal to these principles, explained why homosexuality should not be dealt with in the penal code:

> The current draft law, in conformity with previous ones, draws inspiration from this fundamental concept: whereas it is necessary to harshly repress events that may cause evident and considerable damage to families or that are contrary to public decency, *the legislator must not invade the field of morality.* The law's criminal sanctions should not indiscriminately affect all events that offend moral conduct and the order of families but only those that manifest the characteristics of violence, insult, fraud or scandal, the repression of which is in the best interest of society.[50]

Homosexuality was considered a "disgusting" behavior, but if practiced in private between consenting adults, it was outside of the dominion of the law. The liberal ruling class thought it was up to religion to deal with sexual matters. The Catholic Church alone had the task of watching over morality and of controlling and repressing homosexuality. This concept was clearly expressed in Giampaolo Tolomei's comment on the Zanardelli penal code:

> In the celebrated controversy over the punishment of unnatural libidinous acts and incest, the new code has been informed by both science and public conscience. It represses these acts as crimes in the name of rape when committed with true or alleged violence, because they damage the rights of personal dignity and freedom, which must be scrupulously protected by the state. It represses them as crimes even when committed without violence, in the case of incest or insult to decency when they offend the sacred rights of public morality; otherwise it leaves them to be sanctioned by religion and personal conscience.[51]

Church and state had different roles, and despite continuous attempts at interference, it was useful for both to keep their dominions of action separate. The role the Catholic Church had had in establishing morality and controlling sexual mores is considered by many researchers to be the main reason for the different ways in which homosexuality has been treated in Catholic countries compared to Protestant ones.[52] According to those who sustained this point of view, Catholic countries were more indulgent toward homosexual behavior because it was the Church's task to repress such behavior, while in Protestant countries this task belonged to the state. Giovanni Dall'Orto defended this thesis by comparing penal codes:

> If we take note of the nations that abandoned lawful persecution of homosexuality starting in the nineteenth century (France, Italy, Spain, Portugal, the Republics of Latin America, even Pilsudski's Fascist Poland) we recognize that they are all Catholic countries. Even in Germany, before unification, Catholic Bavaria decriminalized homosexuality while Protestant Prussia never did. The most exemplary case is perhaps Holland, which followed the Napoleonic code as long as the population was Catholic, but introduced antihomosexual laws after the independence of Belgium (when the Catholics became a minority).[53]

Their relationship with the Church was not the only reason the liberal ruling class did not punish homosexuality. As Zanardelli explained in his report, behind this decision there was also a social motivation :

> The draft law says nothing about unnatural libidinous acts, because with respect to them, as Giovanni Carmignani states, "it is more beneficial, in regards to public example, *to ignore the vice* rather than to make the penalties that repress it known." These libidinous acts are also included among those that are indictable in the case of violence, when minors are involved or when they create public scandal, however without them being in any way indicated as the object of special measures.[54]

The legislator's choice was perfectly in line with tradition: many years later the advantages of not criminalizing homosexuality, as clearly evidenced by Giovanni Carmignani at the beginning of the nineteenth century, were once again relevant.[55] The best way to deal with this "vice" was to not talk about it, to deny it even existed, and to avoid risky disquisitions on its nature and dangers. That the code did not mention unnatural libidinous acts was seen as a positive thing: "Cautious politics teaches us that it is not in the interest of public justice or morals to reveal, in the form of clamorous court sentences, certain obscene acts that have remained hidden in the shadows of secrecy."[56]

Dr. G. Bruni was of the same opinion. He challenged the commonly held stance that homosexuality was punishable in the case of sexual perverts guilty of unnatural libidinous acts performed out of vice, curiosity, or imitation, yet not punishable when the sexual inversion was a result of illness or congenital flaws.[57] According to Dr. Bruni, it was the police's job to keep social order by protecting the honesty and morality of citizens through moral laws. These, however, should not have anything in common with criminal law and, furthermore, the preventive measures were to remain distinct from measures of punishment. Besides being useless, it was also harmful to reestablish "the persecution of an immoral act that did not have the characteristics of *physical or moral violence, or scandal*. The regulations against homosexuality had been abolished to prevent "the legal system from penetrating the secrets of private lives in search of events wrapped in mystery only to regale the public with the often uncertain and always scandalous result of its difficult investigations.[58] Unnatural libidinous acts were simply immoral actions that, if committed clandestinely and with the consent of the partners, did not violate any law. Without a crime, there could be no penalty. Consequently, only the morality and the ethical censure of those involved could reduce and eradicate these forms of perversion." Dr. Bruni, therefore, praised the Italian penal code for the fact that it did not contain an article against homosexuality. He summarized the advantages of this choice in his concluding comments:

> The repression of these *unmentionable vices* is a matter of ethics and conscience: resorting to criminal sanctions in cases in which owing to secrecy there is no resultant upsetting of the legal social order would do more harm than good.[59]

This concept was expressed with similar clarity in the *Enciclopedia di diritto penale italiano* (Encyclopedia of Italian Criminal Law):

> However repulsive such events are, they should not be recorded and punished. For it is preferable for public morality that they remain buried in darkness and ignored. . . . "The Zanardelli Code," for this reason, has consecrated a scientific principle that is in unison with public conscience, in other words, that the censure of vices and *corruttela* [moral corruption] belong to the law of ethics and that criminal law should not punish them unless they appear as an evident violation of rights; sodomy and bestiality do not present such violations except when they represent an attack on the freedom of a person or on public decency.[60]

In reality, not everybody felt so lenient about homosexual relationships, a repulsive crime that "not only damages the body but also corrupts morality."[61] Alfredo Niceforo, for example, was a strong opponent of the decriminalization of pederasty. He hoped for a return to "energetic and firm" measures that would prevent and repress sexual crimes, and believed that ignoring the vice in the hope that it might not spread was infantile and lax reasoning; what better deterrent could there be than fear of harsh punishment. Medicine, and particularly psychiatry, thought it important to determine to what degree the immoral behavior was a voluntary act or not through a careful analysis of the passive pederast's psyche. Thus, in cases of an acquired habit "in which the individual submits to pederasty unwillingly," owing to illness or contingent factors, the homosexual should be treated like a minor, considered mentally incompetent and as such not criminally indictable. "The incubus who demands pederasty" needed to be punished, as was the case, on the other hand, for anyone corrupting a minor. The integration of these two approaches, medical and juridical, was only feasible through the reintroduction of article 425 of the Sardinian penal code; "and when the measure is once again adopted it will be clear how illogical today's legislator has been in denying his protection to men who, due to a wretched sexual environment almost always caused by our miserable social conditions, have been thrown into a state of psychic distress, which has deprived them almost entirely of their wills, making them not only equivalent to minors but often inferior to them.[62]

Similar criticism of Zanardelli's approach toward "deviant" sexual behavior was expressed in the *Digesto italiano* (Italian Digest). Sexual inverts, or rather "true homosexuals, psychopaths from birth or those who became so as a result of an internal rift and the agony undergone from social shame" were not fully responsible; they necessitated treatment, not punishment. All other pederasts, however, were to suffer the full severity of criminal law "the particular horror of this act of incontinence that violates the rights and the laws of nature should have alerted our legislators to the need to be stricter, to act to protect public morality from the influence of depravity."[63] Even Enrico Morselli pointed out the "numerous shortcomings of the permissive code, which was not sufficiently disapproving of certain sexual acts such as pederasty.[64] For others, ignoring the vice was only a form of "ignorant bliss"; taking criminal action against homosexuals was indispensable, because "those who commit sex-related crimes are the champions of human degeneration—homosexuals, lesbians, those lacking self-control, and necrophiliacs—the outcome of which is not only the monstrous sexual act itself but the noncontinuation of the species."[65]

Despite these negative observations, the debate over the criminalization of pederasty eventually quieted down.[66] The silence that results from its decriminalization, however, also blocked the possibility of creating a movement for homosexuals' rights. According to Dall'Orto, this stratagem was born of an "unwritten agreement between the state and homosexuals that, all told, awarded some advantages to each side: the state guaranteed relative impunity for their private relationships, and in exchange it was assured that the heterosexual and patriarchal model of life would not be contested publicly.[67]

The Rocco Code

This kind of compromise risked appearing inadequate for Fascism, which was attempting to consolidate its power by boasting about its moral rigor and its commitment to reforming the customs and all other aspects of citizens' lives, the sexual sphere included. The slogan "virilize the nation" was not quite compatible with the decriminalization of pederasty. Therefore, when the time came to replace the Zanardelli Code with a Fascist one, the problem of introducing a specific article against homosexual relationships came up again.

On December 24, 1925, the government in power began discussing the reform of the Penal Code. According to the Minister of Justice, Alfredo Rocco, this was a fundamental step in order to affirm the principles of Fascism as well as Italy's juridical supremacy. Furthermore it was an opportune moment to overcome, once and for all, the heated debate between the traditional school of thought and the positivist school by linking the principles of criminal responsibility and the importance of punishment to the use of new preventive measures (for example, administrative and judicial security measures) aimed at defending the state from potential delinquents.[68] The best way to integrate the legal, anthropological, and sociological sciences was to give as much weight to the crime as the criminal, to stress prevention as much as repression. Alongside the traditional school's fixed-term sanctions, understood as retribution for the crime committed and meant to discourage criminal activity were the positivist school's indefinite sanctions that were dependent on the length of time for which a criminal was considered dangerous and intended to be an instrument of prevention and social defense. Actually the new code made instrumental use of these two schools of legal thought because within this adoption of a binary system of punishment there lay a new technical-legal school approach that utilized some traditional and some positivist principles toward authoritarian, repressive and threatening ends.[69]

The Minister of Justice, together with a small group of jurists, headed by Arturo Rocco, father of the technical-legal school of thought, drafted a preliminary penal code to be submitted to a panel of legal experts, chosen by Mussolini. As consultants, they were to examine, criticized and propose corrections to the code. The panel's suggestions were to take into account observations from scientific and political publications as well as the opinion of the Appeals courts, the forensic department and some university law departments. Although not binding, these opinions were considered useful for the development of a final text that could become a model for other states to follow. In 1927, after less than two years, the preliminary version was presented. It was drafted in accordance with the fundamental criteria that had motivated the reform: to overcome the rift between the two schools of thought; to harden the system of punishment; better defend the state and the economy; guarantee the respect of religious expression, particularly manifestations of the Catholic religion; "*to strengthen the protection of the family and public morality*"; "*to protect the integrity and the future of the race*."[70] Increasing the protection of interests was in harmony with the Fascist concept of the state's moral superiority with respect to the individual. The penal code served, above all, to defend the ethical foundation of the authoritarian state based on respect for moral decency, the family, religion and the integrity and health of the race. Because of the importance attributed to the safeguarding of public morality, a specific article, number 528, against homosexual relationships was introduced in the draft, among other offenses consider insults to public decency and sexual honor. The text was as follows:

> Article 528—Homosexual Relationships: Anyone who . . . performs libidinous acts on persons of the same sex, or consents to such acts, is punishable by imprisonment from six months to three years if the events cause public scandal.
>
> The penalty is imprisonment from one to five years: if the person guilty is over twenty-one years old and commits the act on a person under eighteen years of age; or if the act is performed habitually or for profit.[71]

Homosexuality, then, was punishable only in cases where the relationship created public scandal. In addition, in the instance that such actions had been carried out habitually or for profit the law called for imprisonment.

According to legislature the new "crime" of pederasty needed to be disciplined in so much as it violated the "aim of the sexual act, conservation of the species" and the way in which sex should be practiced. Unnatural libidinous acts constituted a blatant insult to decency and morality. Fascism's sanctioning of them was in line with its new policy, "oriented toward a more effective protection of the physical and moral health of the race." Young people had to be protected from the various manifestations of immorality and obscenity that were spreading so alarmingly as a result of a loosening of social mores caused by the war. New instruments of repression were needed to put a stop to this worrying trend; but above all it was necessary to cast aside "the demo-liberal legislative tendency by which public authorities pretended to ignore the immoral practices being perpetrated behind domestic walls." In other words, in the Fascist state, the need to protect public morality, a collective asset, justified limiting the freedom of individuals, obliging them to uniform their private habits to the ethics of the regime.

The innovations introduced in the morality and decency draft law on the matter were not limited to condemning homosexual relationships but also covered: seduction through insincere promise of matrimony, birth control practices and the exploitation of prostitution. Furthermore, punishments for sexual crimes and the publication of obscene material were made more severe. More protective measures for minors were also included. One of Fascism's main objectives was to reinvigorate public morality. By way of the new penal code, then, it tried to give itself the power needed to "educate the people by restoring morality."[72] The most significant innovation, however, regarded the introduction of a new asset to be protected: the physical and moral health of the race. The fight against the spread of neo-Malthusian theories and against homosexuality was the result of this profound change, of the desire to anthropologically transform Italians; one means of doing this was through special legislation. Anyone who hindered or limited procreation was a dangerous enemy of the Fascist state, which had turned the campaign to increase the nation's population into a dogma for its citizens' sexual behavior.

Of course, during the commission's meetings the debate explored whether the crime of homosexuality originated from genetic, constitutional factors or if it was the result of an individual's free choice. The first interpretation, stubbornly supported by the Humanitarian Scientific Committee, in favor of decriminalizing homosexuality, was rejected. The prevailing viewpoint judged libidinous acts between persons of the same sex as an indication of perversion; whether active or passive, homosexuality was a bilateral crime involving both partners. This applied to men and women although in cases of lesbianism (tribadism etc.), which was "considered the most despicable of all, it was almost impossible to prove the homosexual relationship." Habitual offense was considered an aggravating condition and resulted in more severe punishment, as was the case if an active homosexual were to commit the act with a consenting minor (this did not apply in cases where the minor was the active partner).[73]

The preliminary draft of the penal code was submitted to the approval of a Ministerial commission chaired by the Attorney General of the Supreme Court of Appeals, Giovanni Appiani, and made up of magistrates, law professors and lawyers. It gathered observations and proposals from people knowledgeable about the matter and from organizations, entities and institutes concerned with criminal law. This extensive work is collected in twenty-three volumes and is a valuable source for reconstructing the various opinions on the draft law and the procedure that led to the final version of the code in 1930. This material, in particular, enables us to understand the reasons for deleting article 528 from the final version, despite the chorus of voices that agreed with the part about crimes against public morality and decency. There was unanimous approval in favor of the institution of harsher measures against such crimes and the need for better tutelage of morality and the family. The legislation was viewed as the realization of Catholic ethics and the fight undertaken by the state to defend "sound traditions and the destiny of future generations." Professor Battaglini of the University of Pavia commented on the criteria that had inspired the legislature in this matter: "strengthening and protecting morality and decency are worthy of the warmest welcome and are in conformity with the regime's own aims to reestablish moral values."[74]

There was also general agreement over the intention to fill in gaps in previous legislation by introducing new measures; particularly popular for these slots were those measures against homosexual relations. For example, the Court of Appeals in Aquila considered it important to punish this new type of "crime" because, together with incest, it represented one of the most disgusting crimes and was an insult to the "the general publics most elementary sense of morality." Homosexuality was always referred to in extremely negative terms: it was a "moral plague"; "a sexual deviance, detrimental to the race's moral health"; a "crime that most seriously offended moral sensibility"; "a sickening unnatural degeneration." Professor Del Giudice of the University of Naples criticized the German abolitionist movement, which, maintaining that homosexuality was not punishable as a "crime" because it was caused by irreducible constitutional factors, had allowed "effeminate homosexuals to be seen walking around town wearing women's dresses as long as they had a medical certificate confirming their illness." More convincing in his opinion were the theories of experts who found homosexuality to be "a perversion or an immoral habit due to exogenous and misogynous factors (environment, examples, imitation, particular circumstances and living conditions)." Therefore, an excessive application of the law was not necessary, since by referring to the opinion of medical experts, judges would be able to decide as best as possible what measures to take. A lawyer, Mr. Piero Marsich, who commented on article 528, drew the same conclusions.

> With regard to homosexuality I think the legislature has taken the appropriate measures. It is impossible to think of seconding the abolitionist vote, which is inspired by legal methods of reconciliation, or with nations who have such sound morals that they do not need restraints, or with countries of such relaxed morals that they refuse them: the draft code, which is not excessively repressive and punishes the event only when public scandal originates, is fully acceptable.

Some people even suggested abolishing the "public scandal" requisite, claiming that it was implicit in all homosexual relationships because all unnatural libidinous acts were, per se, scandalous; social needs required maximum severity in punishing these acts as soon as they were known.[75] Many liked the draft because of its directness, for having set aside false legislative modesty and made a return, somehow, to the Sardinian code that severely punished homosexual relationships.[76] The introduction of article 528 filled "a gap that had been the cause of concern for some time" and realized "a productive return to traditional morality."[77] Some jurists, when praising the code's educational aspects, remarked that repressing homosexuality had not only an ethical aim but also "an important political one" because "a strong state is one in which the people have more vigorous morals."[78]

Of the various opinions expressed, the comments coming from the Law School at the Università Cattolica del Sacro Cuore provided an interesting version of how sexual crimes and homosexuality were judged in the ecclesiastical world. The university's president, Agostino Gemelli, openly praised the draft code because it was "created on the basis of healthy and sound moral criteria," and because it respected Italians' Christian sentiments. He particularly praised the commonalities with the Catholic School of Law, which rejected both the positivist and the traditional approach: the first, which had employed new discoveries made in anthropology and psychology, was criticized for its materialistic view of life that abolished free will; the second, had not taken into consideration the subjective factors of the crime and had underestimated the effectiveness of preventive measures. Catholic researchers were therefore in favor of the new penal code because it managed to combine the best aspects of the two schools of thought and arrive at an effectively moralizing outcome.[79] Similar approval was also expressed by Father Francesco Gavotti, the head secretary of morality for *Azione Cattolica*, who complemented the draft code suggesting, however, stricter punishment for crimes against public decency and morality. The physical and moral defense of the race, the tutelage of mores and the integrity of the family needed to be guaranteed through the direct action of public justice. "Criminal actions . . . against all that which, together with procreation and moral sanity, ensures the vitality, strength and greatness of the State" had to be prosecuted. They could not be considered detrimental to one's private rights alone.[80] Furthermore, the link between religion and morality was favorably accepted, as was the attempt to harmonize criminal law with the eternal laws of Catholic morality: according to the Supreme Court of Appeals sentence, with the new code, "the moral sensibility of the masses, which acts as a strong restraint against misconduct, will take strength from the restored influence of religious sentiment in public and private life."[81] Equally well received was the government's acknowledgement that "true morality is that established in the Gospel of Christ, its interpretation, its tradition, its Catholic teachings and in God's Ten Commandments."[82] Regarding practices against procreation, article 528 on homosexual relationships was generally regarded positively.

> The new measure that attacks these extremely despicable acts is certainly excellent. However, the wording of article 528 could be improved by substituting the words "between persons" with "on persons" and eliminating the parenthesis "if the event creates public scandal" as it is superfluous and

dangerous; either the event is known only to those who are guilty and then that would surely not be prosecutable, or it is known to others and, in that case, the scandal has already taken place.[83]

The national Committee for Public Morality was of the same opinion. It suggested considering public scandal an aggravating circumstance rather than a necessary condition for the "crime to exist. Despite the reassertion that it was fundamental to make crimes against morality directly prosecutable and that prostitution had to be stopped, the Committee was pleased that many of the requests put forward on these delicate matters several years before were finally being taken into consideration. Since 1902, during their various national meetings, the League for Public Morality had been petitioning greater legislative rigor and now the Fascist State was achieving this by making the punishment for sexual crimes more severe. The committee's chairperson, Adolfo Bettazzi, particularly liked the articles of the new code regarding the protection of minors, the family, and the morality and integrity of the race. He advised endowing the vice squad in each and every police station with specialized agents and assigning the best men to this fundamental service. Many such suggestions were made, among them was the proposal to introduce a new "extremely strict and somewhat punitive" moral code. Giovanni Agnese suggested assembling a special police corps and Fascist militia to save the nation from the decadence caused by the rapid spread of vice and sensuality; however, in order to win the fight against immorality it was necessary to intensify the laws, create specific tribunals dedicated solely to crimes against morality, and to reintroduce flogging "for crimes such as rape, adultery, the corruption of women, procuring or *unnatural sexual acts.*[84]

The Italian Association of Forensic Medicine, influenced by the positivist school and particularly concerned with sexual crimes, suggested clearly differentiating between *heterosexual and homosexual physical acts and rape*, claiming that libidinous acts between persons of the same sex, both ethically and legally, were much more serious than the rape of a woman by a man.[85] On the other hand, there was no mention of homosexuality in the comments sent to the ministerial commission by the *Italian Society for Sexology, Demography and Eugenics*, which simply expressed its positive opinion of the new measure incriminating the act of contagion, for its indispensable preventive function. The same cannot be said for *La Rassegna di studi sessuali, demografici ed eugenica* whose position was the complete opposite of that which had led to the introduction of article 528. In the review, which had always maintained that homosexuality was congenital, Proteus published an article on the reasons why pederasty should not be considered a

crime. After some customary praise of the code for having given so much attention to sexual matters, the author clearly expressed his disappointment over the
new law that went against the most accredited theories of sexologists. Criminalizing homosexuality in imitation of foreign penal codes meant ignoring the fact
that this type of behavior was due, in most cases, to "hereditary or very often
somatic factors, rather than being an acquired vice."[86] Other shortcomings of
the code were the uncertain definition given for the words "habitual" and
"public scandal" and the fact that no account was taken of the different sort of
impact that such a crime would have in big cities versus small towns where
homosexual relationships would be easily discovered. Furthermore, punishing
homosexuals would fuel an endless series of extortions by unscrupulous delinquents ready to speculate against citizens who were guilty of nothing more
than having different sexual tendencies. The measures would increase scandal
rather than diminishing it and would provoke the suicide of even more desperate
people being coerced by squalid blackmailers. Lastly, the effects of imitation had
not been taken into account: a healthy population like the Italians should not
publicize this kind of private behavior so as not to awaken the spirit of imitation
in individuals with latent homosexual inclinations. The article ended with an
appeal to Rocco, asking him not to introduce the measure, which was incompatible with the modernity and originality of the new code. However,
the final words were addressed to Mussolini who was the only one capable of
eliminating article 528:

> We are confident that in his wisdom and unfailing intuition, Benito
> Mussolini will renew the gesture of Napoleon who eliminated some
> measures against homosexuals that the commission of jurists in charge of
> reforming the French criminal code had decided to propose.[87]

Proteus's suggestions, put forward so cleverly by referring to Napoleon and
the French criminal code, were partially accepted. The comments on the draft
code were analyzed carefully and despite the fact that most opinions praised
the new article against homosexual relationships, the commission decided to
eliminate it during its session on July 7, 1925. As clear from the meeting's minutes,
this decision had nothing to do with a benevolent attitude toward homosexuality
or with a position of tolerance but was the result of a deep-seated aversion
for "this type of perversion." Punishing homosexual relationships would have
given foreign countries the impression that in Italy this practice was widespread
enough to require legislative measures while a population as virile as the Italians
should not even be remotely worried about this "dangerous vice." Why should
the code deal with a "crime" that was, first and foremost, a sin and as such
treatable at the "tribunal of repentance; given also the extensive damage to the

family inherent in such procedures"? The Church, which had always been charged with protecting sexual morality, should exercise control over and prevention of homosexuality. Instead, the State should consider these lurid relationships between persons of the same sex an insult to decency, and as such punishable on the grounds of this article without having to create *ex novo* a specific law "whose inclusion in the code arouses true aesthetic and moral repugnance." This abdication of supremacy as the authority on the moral conduct is a step back for Fascism in its relationship with the Church. This choice was born from the conviction that the best way to repress homosexuality was to deny its existence, to eliminate all traces of it and hide all possible reference to it. This conviction was clearly expressed in the words of one of the commission's members:

> The less certain things are mentioned the better it is. Was it necessary to mention this vice and give it a form ? I don't think so. . . . The country is healthy enough to renounce the creation of a new article that would only imply that the vice is much more serious and widespread than it really is. Homosexuality is a type and an appellation that you read about in books on sexual pathologies and forensic medicine, particularly in foreign ones. It should not leave their pages to become infamous as a criminal action.

The by then widely consolidated convention of concealment continued to prevail, as it fit in perfectly with the Fascist vision aimed at spreading an image of the regime as the domain of morality, of supreme ethical purpose, capable of building a flawless, virile society.

As a result there were as many arguments in favor of including measures against the "crime" of homosexuality in the new code as there were reasons for eliminating it altogether. First of all, there had to be proof that sodomy had taken place by means of an inquiry that would inevitably arouse clamor and scandal; in other words, the sort of negative publicity that should be avoided at all cost. Secondly, as Vincenzo Manzini stressed, in order to introduce new sanctions the vices to be repressed had to be alarmingly widespread and this was not true for homosexuality, a practice that was practically nonexistent among Italian Fascist males. Thirdly, the police watched homosexuals carefully; the strict application of police measures was sufficient to "uproot this noxious weed." Essentially, those who exercised male prostitution and incorrigible pederasts had to be driven out of society through security measures while the healthy portion of the population needed to be kept in the dark about this "abominable perversion." Furthermore, it was always possible to take criminal action against an "insult to decency" under article 527, the "corruption of a minor" if the relationship involved a minor, or the crime of rape, if it was not consensual. The fight against homosexuality was also supplemented by a few amendments that the commission accepted. These amendments worsened the punishment for an "insult to decency" in the event that homosexual-type behavior was involved and listed homosexual intercourse under "obscene behavior" even when it occurred on private premises, as long as it produced scandal. When the time came for the final vote, the commission decided unanimously to eliminate article 528 from the code.[88] The chair of the commission summarized briefly the main reasons for such a drastic decision:

> a) It is not necessary to provide a measure for this crime because fortunately Italy can proudly say that this abominable vice is not so widespread among us as to justify legislative intervention;
> b) In similar cases it is possible to resort to and apply the most severe punishment for such crimes as rape, corruption of minors and insult to decency

And then Appiani concluded by mentioning the hasty, pragmatic measures Fascism took to repress homosexuality:

> It is a well known fact that for habitual professionals of this vice, in truth quite rare and either imported or exploited by foreigners, the police enforce their security measures, detention included, immediately and very effectively.[89]

After this lengthy procedure, the final draft was sent to the Senate and the Chamber of Deputies to be reviewed by a special inter-parliamentary commission that met on November 14, 1929, and whose opinions were not binding but were to be considered in the drafting of the final text of the code. This new commission was subdivided into three sub-committees. Senator Garofalo chaired the third of these, in charge of examining the eighth clause on crimes against public morality and decency, among which article 528 had been entered initially. The article, praised when the code was first drafted, was by now definitively eliminated and the second commission, as well, confirmed the motives that had led to its being discarded.

On March 22, 1930, the inter-parliamentary commission, having concluded its work, expressed approval of the code's protection of the moral and physical health of the race as well as its introduction of more severe measures against sexual crimes, even if "in the case of the more repugnant and horrifying crimes" punishment would have to be further intensified.[90] In his speech Rocco himself spoke approvingly of the harshness of punishment for crimes against decency and sexual honor that was in harmony with the attempt to curb the "spread of vice, against which the Fascist government has been fighting for years through various measures including police methods." The Minister of Justice also mentioned article 528 and briefly outlined the steps that had led to its elimination. He also recalled the almost total hostility toward the new measure, which "fortunately" was unnecessary since "this terrible vice" was not widespread enough in Italy to require a new law.[91] Thus the new criminal code, voted in on October 19, 1930, became effective on July 1, 1931, without any mention of homosexuality as a "crime," although the debate on the subject was far from being over.

The Legal Debate

The issue was brought up again by Vincenzo Manzini, an attorney who had been on the ministerial commission assessing the preliminary draft of the criminal code and who, at the time, had voted in favor of eliminating article 528. In spite of this, the illustrious jurist described the disinterest in the law on pederasty as "a false distinction between morality and law, and an excessive and damagingly tolerant attitude toward the most degenerate sexual vice."[92] In his opinion, the law's intrusion in the field of ethics represented no threat, nor was there a problem with restricting individual freedom because not only was it legitimate to incriminate acts condemned by the common morality but it was indispensable. Only a "pro-pederast" could defend such depravity and not consider homosexuality immoral and shameful. Manzini found it unexplainable that the "Fascist code could omit the incrimination of sodomy, especially since the Fascists were quite comfortable expressing their ideas on the matter" through the use of their action squads that forcibly repressed pederasty. Homosexuality—continued Manzini— "is also harmful for the race, not only because it is mentally degrading for those affected but also because it corrupts sexual instinct and tampers with procreation." Unnatural lust was such a dangerous vice that in all the civilizations where the State had not intervened forcefully against it, a slow but inexorable decline began to take place. The example of Greece and ancient Rome should be an admonishment against the spread of this sexual practice, which was the cause of much moral and physical degeneration. Although Italians were repulsed by homosexuality this dangerous behavior could be exported, particularly from England and Germany, even to a healthy nation like Italy. Only a severe criminal system could prevent the spread of this "most horrible vice." Modernity, affluence, the search for pleasure and the good life, a taste for luxury and a refined lifestyle, better means of travel and communication as well as the tendency of wealthy people to spend their vacations traveling around Europe, all favored the imported diffusion of homosexuality into Mediterranean countries. Those who thought sodomy was an "uncontrollable pathological degeneration" were wrong; even if Manzini did not exclude the existence of psychopathic pederasts, he was convinced that most of them practiced sodomy out of habit. Furthermore, it was not sufficient to treat homosexuality as a crime only in cases of violence or when it created a scandal because "there is always a scandal when, in one way or another, news circulates about an unnatural libidinous event."[93]

The critique of the jurist Mario Manfredini was even more severe. He claimed that in not punishing pederasty, the Rocco code was actually "defending immorality" and permitting the practice of an "antisocial activity that caused decadence, violated the protected interests of the population and was completely self-serving."[94] With this permissive line of conduct the State renounced safeguarding the social good that derived from the protection of heterosexuality, which was the only guarantee of the race's progress. At the same time it showed unjustifiable indifference toward "normal" sex behavior, which was not "protected per se, but only in relation to other concerns." In fact, pederasty was repressed only when it infringed on public decency or sexual freedom whereas, because of its detrimental effects on population growth, it should have always been punished.[95] The separation between morality and law obscured the fact that homosexuality was not only an immoral act but also a criminal one, in so much as it completely violated the laws of nature. Proper sexual behavior was an objective reality and anyone who violated it endangered society and its fundamental principles. It was the State's duty to repress "unnatural physical acts" in order to avoid widespread degeneration. Threatening the preservation of the race and endangering the "social right to normality" were not only highly questionable individual choices but also actual "crimes" that required the most severe punishment. Manfredini's words left no doubt about that:

> Silence represents one of the most serious deficiencies in our legal system because it protects true delinquency: such is this activity that destroys the natural laws of relationships.[96]

Nor was the decriminalization of homosexuality in an attempt to avoid scandals and blackmail justifiable; any crime could have given rise to such unpleasant problems. Greater leniency in the penal code, resulting from concern about "intruding upon morality's perfective sphere," gave the impression that pederasty was just a bad habit, instead of a dangerous form of deviation.[97] Any violation of natural laws—originating in antisocial individuals, psychopaths or physically degenerate individuals—contributed to social decline. From Manfredini's point of view, informed by a positivist idea of nature as a given fact, regulated by rationally deductible laws that were unbreachable, deviance coincided with criminality. The State should require citizens to practice sexual behavior that was "neither harmful nor dangerous" and which was not detrimental to the institution of the family. Consequently although the code did not provide for rape of one's own spouse because a woman was bound by marriage to satisfy her husband's sexual desires, unnatural sexual intercourse committed by a husband on a wife was criminally prosecutable.[98]

Fascism's attention to the family, with the aim of making it a political subject fully aligned with the regime's directives, was yet another stimulating factor for the condemnation of homosexuality. In relation to the family, the link between citizen and state, the guarantor of social order, pederasty was seen as a disintegrating factor. For those who concerned themselves with such matters, as for example, the editor of *Il secolo fascista* Giuseppe Attilio Fanelli—who was busy drafting a new domestic code meant to form "new moral beings"—it was necessary to "give new impetus to the laws against the sexual deviations that lead to homosexuality." It was Fascism's duty to preserve the relationship between the sexes by introducing a "rigorous law against deviation" that would better protect birthrights.[99] In addition, to ensure prosperity and cohesion within the family, which "one achieves on the basis of masculinity," it was necessary to establish the "husband's absolute supremacy" and fully respect the principle of authority.[100]

The debate between those favoring criminalizing homosexuality and those that continued to ignore the vice, also regarded opinions on the countries that had adopted specific laws against pederasty. It is no surprise, then, that early-twentieth-century Germany was criticized for its homophobic legislation that had encouraged the creation of a dangerous homosexual rights movement. The State's repression had actually transformed hideouts of perversion into centers for open discussion about these "awkward" matters. For example, in 1909 the *Rivista penale* (Criminal Review) commented on the German campaign against the antihomosexual provisions:

> German homosexuals have come out of the shadows where they usually hide to show themselves in broad daylight, to meet in Berlin and to be interviewed by newspapers and magazines. Article 175 of the criminal code that incriminates homosexual acts even if they occur within the four walls of a lonely room with mutual consent, has produced this effect and has resulted in a campaign that wants to abolish the provision and has opened a heated debate on homosexuality.[101]

An attack on article 175 of the German code was also launched by Giacomo Perrando:

> As regards the repression of homosexuality, let us not follow the example of the regrettable provisions of the German code's well known art. 175. These and other immoralities and perversions should not be fought with

inquisitions of one's private and intimate life. The law should only interfere
in the instance of a public offense. Prevention should only resort to the
already mentioned educational reform of customs.[102]

Criminal action against pederasty did not cause the phenomenon to disappear but rather had the great disadvantage of creating committed homosexual militants. Thus "even in countries where homosexuality is considered a
"crime," not only does it remain but it becomes enveloped in a dangerous aura
of public attention that contributes to its diffusion among those predisposed
and often provokes the worst forms of blackmail."[103] On the other hand, however, Germany, Switzerland, Austria, Hungary and England were to be praised
for providing expressly for the "crime" of homosexuality and, in doing so,
responding to "society's moral needs."[104] Almost everyone agreed, however,
that the *Comitato scientifico umanitario* (Humanitarian Scientific Committee),
involved for several years in defending the rights of pederasts, should be
condemned. Of course the harshest criticism of those supporting the abolition of
article 175 came from Manzini who expressed his joy over their failure stating:

> The German homosexual *pro sodomy* campaign was unprecedented and
> repulsive. The Reichstag had the good sense to reject a petition signed by
> 5000 well-known philosodomites, backed by a certain scientific-literary
> committee to abolish the incrimination of sodomy, at the time considered
> a "crime" by the German criminal code. Actually, instead of suppressing
> art. 175 of the code, the Parliamentary Committee for Reform intensified
> the punishment extending the measure to include women.[105]

With the advent of Nazism and the intensification of antihomosexual legislation the comparison with Germany prompted a reconsideration of the effectiveness of legal measures for repressing homosexuality. In 1936, for example, the
Anthropological, Psychiatric and Forensic Medicine Archives published an article
on the matter in which it compared the Italian criminal code to the German
one.[106] Legislation in these countries testified to the State's effort to effectively
protect the family and the race through the harsh repression of sexual crimes
and, in particular, perversions that were spreading and causing the "degeneration
of the race." The author of the article, Guglielmo Guareschi, openly defended
the positivist school, the first to draw attention to the delinquent, without
neglecting the crime. This approach was indispensable for sexual crimes in
which the criminal's personality strongly influenced the form of the crime. The
numerous amendments to the German criminal code,[107] introduced in 1935,
which went as far as to punished even the manifestation of homosexual thoughts,
were considered important innovations but also an example of how morality

could vary from country to country depending on the race, the lifestyle, the level of civilization, the environment and the traditions, as demonstrated by the different laws against unnatural libidinous acts.

The German theory that the lack of a punishment for pederasty would allow "unlimited homosexual activity," did not convince Guareschi who believed this approach would only repress homosexuality as an immoral behavior and not as a crime: "if pederasty is punished merely for the fact that it is an immoral act and, therefore, dangerous for society, it could be objected that the law cannot punish immorality per se, otherwise masturbation should, at least in theory, be punished as well." Furthermore, often homosexuals were not responsible for their depravity because their "abnormality" was determined by an "aberration in their physical-psychic-sexual structure." Only prostitutes, those who are habitual pederasts for financial gain, should be punished because their activities, apart from the fact that they caused public scandal, and "endangered society's interest in preservation and reproduction," were always "antisocial and the cause of degenerative decadence."[108]

Despite criticism over the failure to criminalize homosexuality, the regime's reproductive plan, aimed at increasing the nation's demographic power and defending the health of the race, was almost unanimously supported by the jurists, as was the Fascist attempt to introduce legislative measures in the Rocco code that would have safeguarded the integrity of the race.[109] The most important of these condemned birthrate restrictions and the spread of neo-Malthusianism and criminalized the endorsement of birth control practices (article 553), all clearly expressing the Fascist policy in favor of the "demographic expansion of the race."[110] However the totalitarian intent hidden behind the introduction of this opinion-related crime was not apparent to most. Likewise, no one was aware of the possible racist implications of the concepts of racial integrity and health. As a matter of fact, one of the most liked aspects of the criminal reform was its exceptional new title to be listed among the various headings indicating different types of crime: "crimes against the integrity and health of the race."[111] Specific articles against abortion, the spreading of syphilis and blennorrhagia (art. 554), and procured impotence fell under this new heading.[112] This last article also affected transvestites and transsexuals who were denied the possibility of undergoing sex changes; procured impotence together with the crime of self-mutilation were sufficient deterrents against surgeries that adapt genital organs to sexual leanings.[113] Even the sale of contraceptives was severely forbidden. Permission to use contraceptives and authorization for therapeutic abortions were granted only for health reasons and to avoid the contagion of dangerous diseases. From the Fascist point of view the nation was an organism whose vitality depended directly on the vigor of its citizens; consequently anyone who jeopardized the country's population growth was an enemy of the state; their behavior, an offense to its livelihood.

The regime's almost spasmodic concern with population growth and protecting the race's integrity and health was not in contradiction with the decision to decriminalize homosexuality, nor did it mean that the State was unconcerned about this type of behavior. The truth of the matter was that the State had concluded that a strategy of silence, like that adopted in the liberal system, was the most effective way to repress pederasty. The strategy of not talking about homosexuality, denying that it existed or pretending that it did not occur amongst Italians, is illustrated by a 1926 passage in *Il Popolo d'Italia* under the heading *Perversioni* (perversions), which criticized, in no uncertain terms, the position of those who had condemned England for persecuting an artist of Oscar Wilde's stature:

> We must take care to keep our people pure, vigilant and in good health, and even if we enjoyed the play *Lady Windermere's Fan* or praised *The House of Pomegranates* or *The (Prisoner's) Ballad of Reading Gaol* where this mediocre poet and writer does strike some deeply human notes, the Italian newspapers—*that are read by all*—should keep silent about the epistolary documentation of shameful diseases, left to the public under vaguely literary pretexts. *Silence is the only respectful form of pity for the dead and prevention from contagion for the living.*[114]

Direct legal action against homosexuality was effectively substituted by its demonization, while virility was exalted and protected through repressive measures of control.

4

The Repression
of Homosexuality

Some thought that freedom was lost forever and that one's privacy, anomalies
and even the state of one's health lay within the competence of the authorities.

PIERO CHIARA,
Il Balordo

Total Institutions

Although there was no specific law regarding the "crime" of homosexuality,
the repression of the "vice," as well as the persecution of any behavior that did
not conform to state-imposed rules, were the basic instruments that Fascism
implemented in its attempt to completely regenerate Italian society and the
Italian people. Mussolini expressed this prerogative very clearly as early as
1923: "Where consensus lacks, we will use force. Regarding all the measures the
government will take, even the toughest, citizens will have to face the dilemma
of either accepting them out of a noble spirit of patriotism or being subjected
to them."[1] Alongside "the factory of consent,"[2] the repressive measures were in
full swing, with the double aim of forcing non-Fascists into silence and obedience
while subjecting them, through violence or the threat thereof, to an educative
process of fascistization.

In his Ascension Day speech at the chamber on May 26, 1927, Mussolini
praised the role of the police force: "Before feeling the need for culture, Man
felt the need for order. Historically speaking, the policeman preceded the
professor in a certain sense, because if there isn't an efficient, armed police

force, laws remain nothing more than words."[3] The aim was to achieve a full-fledged totalitarian police state that would control society and its individuals, despite the Duce's refusal of this definition:

> The Fascist state cannot be considered a police state because it has not limited and does not limit itself simply to a negative defense of an existent and consolidated political reality. On the contrary, day after day and with great effort it has created and is creating a new political reality, a new order, destined to express and bring into effect the most profound ethical and civil needs of our nation's civilization, as well as its desire to live and be powerful in the world.[4]

Conceiving of the "State as the universal, ethical will," the creator of laws and the sole entity justified in suppressing freedom gave the police the duty of enforcing the law and protecting its institutions. The notion that national interests came before those of the individual meant that protecting the citizen was secondary to defending the state from those whose behavior or ideas were not in line with Fascist doctrine. The individual himself was subordinate to the needs and morality of the state, understood as an ethical institution that made a clear and rigid distinction between good and evil and produced moral energy, giving religious value to life.[5] Rocco clearly expressed this new concept in his speech to the chamber on May 16, 1925:

> The state is not only a legal organism, it is and must be an ethical one as well. (*Expressions of approval.*) The state must be the guardian of public morality and claim this morality; it must take care of the citizens' souls as well as their bodies. And in the name of this most noble duty, the state must intervene and repress falsehood, corruption, and every kind of deviation from and degeneracy of public and private morality.[6]

Fascism's action may be described as a global politicization of existence. The state intervened directly in the private lives of citizens, with the scope of transforming their mental processes, moods, actions, thoughts, lifestyles, and, regarding virility, their sentiments and sexual behavior as well in order to make them conform to the regime's policies. The new, strong and virile Fascist male was to be achieved by using both coercion and persuasion. In order to safeguard the physical and moral health of citizens, which Mussolini had called the "absolute condition for a people to live and progress," the authorities had "to persevere without pause or hesitation as a moralizing force," keeping a careful watch "so that the germs of corruption do not ruin and wipe out the people's vital energies."[7] In short, where education and convincing fell short of its task of making Italian men more virile, coercion was used.

Fundamental to the totalitarian dimension of Fascism was its aspiration to completely transform individuals. This inevitably required establishing "*the paramount importance of political action*," in other words, totalitarianism understood as the complete submission of what is *private* into the *public*,[8] as well as the ability of the state to intervene in the minds and bodies of its citizens.[9] The birth of an ethical state, where morality and politics were inextricably intertwined, meant an even greater social control of sexuality and severer punishment for any behavior that deviated from sexual practices considered to be "normal." Disrespect for the criteria of preestablished forms of virility resulted in expulsion from society in order to protect the community from a negative example. Homosexuals upset national order, raised doubts about the basic values of Fascist morality, and damaged national prestige with acts that were universally considered perverse. They risked corrupting anyone who came in contact with them and put the country's future at risk by shirking their duty to procreate, the foundation of the nation's might. Moreover, they undermined the country's internal unity by confusing the roles of the sexes.

As stated before, the repression of homosexuality had a long history (death sentences, burnings at the stake, torture, imprisonment, and punishments) that had only begun to die out toward the end of the eighteenth century. This repression had not ended; the forms and ways of practicing it had only changed. On the contrary, according to Romano Canosa, in the nineteenth century, there was a new push to punish any sexual deviation "with a semblance of legal condemnation and censure." It had certainly become evident that "it was culturally impossible to continue handling sexual deviation with the same marked methods of the past." However, society in the nineteenth century "was still not sexually free." Even if its criminal law was less repressive than before, it was not ready to make further concessions because "what it grants, it grants reluctantly, more as an inevitable consequence of the failure of the traditional repressive state model than a voluntary choice in favor of more sexual freedom."[10] From this point of view, the Fascists rejected such failure and took new repressive actions against various kinds of sexual deviation, even giving a political identity to the fight against pederasty, to the point of considering homosexuality not only a danger to society but the living antithesis of the new Fascist male. Although under Fascism there was less legal severity in comparison with the past, internment was increasingly used as an instrument of repression. Indeed, most homosexuals who fell into the hands of the police during Fascism ended up in confinement (*confino*), prison, or insane asylums.

Along with concentration camps, such "total institutions," in the words of sociologist Erving Goffman, are places where "a large number of like-situated individuals, cut off from the wider society for an appreciable period of time, together lead an enclosed, formally administered round of life." That they had an "encompassing or total character"—"symbolized by the barrier to social intercourse with the outside"[11]—made them an extreme solution for those who had not submitted to the model imposed by the state, who broke the rules, or whose very existence undermined the foundations of Fascist society. Foucault maintained that power manifests itself in its most despotic incarnation in these institutions by claiming authority over a moral value that in turn becomes an instrument for the domination of good over evil, order over disorder, the licit over the illicit, and normality over abnormality.[12]

Fixing rigid behavioral rules and models tended inevitably to expand the category of what was considered deviant and to strengthen repression against those who did not accept the values expressed by the ideology—seen not in relative terms but as absolute and unchangeable imperatives. Deviants who refused to follow the rules were considered obstacles to keeping social and political order and became rebels from which the regime had to liberate itself. They were excluded from the world of "normal citizens" and committed to one of the various total institutions that took on a double task: educative, radically changing the inmates' personalities; and repressive, isolating anyone who expressed his own sexual, religious, political, or racial diversity. As De Felice pointed out, for Mussolini, repressive measures for those who deviated from the average collective behavior was just as necessary as education for making Fascists out of the Italians. Those who did not become Fascists spontaneously were made to do so through coercion. Mussolini was so convinced of this that he confided to Yvon De Begnac that "he thought it was possible to turn Jews into Aryans, something that Hitler considered a violation of the laws of nature and perhaps the worst heresy ever uttered."[13] In this, the Duce considered himself a doctor and surgeon, a "doctor who does not neglect symptoms,"[14] who has "the pulse of the nation in his hand,"[15] who can make a diagnosis and proceed to cut out the sick part. In his view, he should have been recognized as the savior of the country, "the press all over the world will have to admit that Fascist surgery is really courageous and timely."[16]

In these expressions, the comparison with surgery, already used in relation to violence, became a metaphor for the efforts made by Fascism to cure the nation's sick body by removing, where necessary, the parts that were incurably sick. Political adversaries and nonconformists were considered harmful viruses or infectiously sick people, against whom it was necessary to act with drastic cures. Total institutions, particularly *confino*, were a big part of this work of social purification and cure. The Duce himself said that *confino* was "social hygiene, a national preventive treatment. These individuals are removed from circulation just like a doctor isolates an infectious person."[17] Many of the Duce's metaphors regarded land reclamation. For example, as stagnant water was drained off malaria infested land, so social reclamation—or "human reclamation," to use Dino Grandi's definition—was carried out on society's body.[18] Then there was the reference to purging, a topos of Fascist rhetoric, which Mussolini used in an interview with a *New York Herald* correspondent. In fact, he compared *confino* to a "social laxative that tends to rid the country of numerous and harmful influences."[19] For Leonardo Musci, within this ideological framework, *confino* gave the system that controlled social and political deviations an extremely totalitarian character; in particular because it became "the repressive political instrument par excellence, even more so than the special court that had a more limited range of intervention, both quantitatively and politically."[20] It was the most efficient method of repressing homosexuality, because it was extremely easy to strike all "those who in their disorderly or immoral lifestyle do not observe the ethical rules laid down by the law, without harming or tarnishing it."[21]

Confino

The use of *confino* as a preventive measure dated back to the years just after unification and evolved out of forced residence (*domicilio coatto*), which had the double function of defending society from common-law offenses while also serving as a useful political instrument against "dangerous classes" representing a threat.[22] The lack of objective requirements for indicating with certainty who was liable under this administrative measure had made "preventive measures inevitably ambiguous," "entrusted to bodies that were traditionally accustomed to considering political opponents, as well as delinquents, enemies of public order."[23] *Confino* was, thus, a legal anomaly, a punishment applied to something that was not defined a crime. It often received criticism because, when put into practice, it usually failed to reform those involved and, on the contrary, more often became a sort of "advanced school for perfecting the crime."[24] On November 6, 1926, *domicilio coatto* was changed to *confino*,[25] when the police regulation Testo Unico P.S. was approved, resulting in important changes to the organization of the police force, most importantly providing it with the instruments necessary to carry out widespread repression of every possible form of dissent. The innovations, writes Paolo Carucci, consisted in "a different relationship between state and society, in new meanings being attributed to expressions like 'public order,' 'state security,' 'public morality,' and 'moral behavior,' in broadening the concept of 'subversive' and 'political suspect,' and in giving political significance to social and private problems (like abortion and homosexuality, for example)."[26] The totalitarian project to make public and private behavior conform to the regime's policies broadened the police's ability to intervene in the private sphere of citizens in a manner that did not aim exclusively at limiting subjective rights. The Fascist state's duty was not only to protect public morality but to encourage it as well. The Liberals had been mistaken by not pursuing "important aims of public interest," by not transforming the state into the "moralizer of the masses."[27]

In this case as well, the Fascists changed liberal institutions or laws to suit their own needs by modifying rules and procedures with the intent of reaching their political goal. Although *confino* was similar to *domicilio coatto*, it was enforced according to different criteria. In particular, it emphasized the more authoritarian aspects of the preceding legislation. As Musci points out, "to suit its totalitarian aims, the regime modified preexisting structures, often bending them to extreme measures, in the same way it did in other institutional sectors and areas of social life when these structures lent themselves to such modifications. In this particular case, the fundamental interpretative change was to have applied a measure to political opponents en masse that had mainly been (even if not exclusively) destined for social outcasts, such as common delinquents or rebels."[28] It was just this continuity with the authoritarian elements of the post-Risorgimento state's organization that made it difficult to perceive the break with the past that was gradually taking place, offering in some way an appearance of legitimacy to these liberticidal measures.[29] However, upon closer examination, the break was there: compared to *domicilio coatto*, *confino* took on a permanent political value; it was used as a basic instrument for repressing anti-Fascism and was a preventive measure used "to protect national and state order," which operated outside the limits of jurisdictional control. The new provincial commission regulation provided that the provincial commission for cautioning and *confino* was made up of the prefect (who was in charge), the chief police officer, the commander of the *carabinieri* (Italy's military police force), a ranking officer of the voluntary militia for national security, and the king's district attorney.[30] Those subject to *confino* included victims of slander and all those who "are a threat to public safety and carry out or have expressed the intention to carry out activities aimed at subverting the political, economic or social directives and regulations of the state, as well as those who oppose or hinder the actions of the state, or indulge in any activity that would damage national interests."[31]

Consequently, the measure became increasingly arbitrary, punishing not only illegal actions but people's intentions as well. Furthermore, the vagueness of expressions like "national interests" led to a significant increase in the kinds of behavior considered incriminating. In fact, a person received *confino* if only presumed to be socially or politically dangerous, or simply if rumored to oppose the regime. Moreover, the commission that judged him was mainly formed of the same persons who had accused him. Its presiding judge was always a minority with respect to the four other members. Evidence supporting the accusation was not necessary. The police chief's word was per se considered evidence enough to arrive at a verdict. Thus, anyone even suspected of carrying out activities against the Fascist regime could be deprived of their liberty. Within ten days of the court order, the accused had the right to turn to the Appeals Commission within the Ministry of the Interior.[32] However, in practice there was no chance at defending oneself. The sentence was not made public, the defense was suppressed, witnesses were not admitted, often there was no interrogation, and, in some cases, the reason why the accused was subjected to the provincial commission was not even made known.

Confino could last from one to five years; however, this could be lengthened, in cases in which the detainee violated regulations of his *confino* before his sentence had been served; in some cases, when the period had been served, a new sentence could automatically begin. The Ministry of the Interior established the *confino* location: theoretically, it was possible to send the person to any town in the kingdom, as long as it was not their hometown. However, in most cases, islands or small villages in southern Italy were used as *confino* locations. These preventative measures, outside of the realm of legal influence, allowed the Fascist regime to avoid getting involved in political ordeals with the court, which was not always in line with it, and save itself a great deal of time, even though the accused were deprived of the civil right to a regular trial. Cesare Rossi made an interesting comment about this:

> Often the sentences of judges who, despite everything, still respected the constitutional state, were not willingly accepted by the aspiring dictator. He wanted to reduce his opponents; to have them chained, isolated and bewildered, in front of his judges, and he wanted to commit them to trial so quickly that the examining magistrate would not have time to split hairs over procedures and laws.[33]

The absence of even the slightest form of protection of civil rights, increased the investigators' efficiency and made the repressive action faster while avoiding unpleasant public scandal. The threat of *confino* hung like a sword of Damocles over the heads of Italians; in its arbitrariness, it indiscriminately threatened to strike anyone. As Lussu wrote:

> *Confino* is the regime's masterpiece: the fear of being sent there looms over everyone. It is much more efficacious for Fascism than the actual infliction of the punishment. A punishment involves few people, a threat is for everyone. The law indicates various types of adversaries that can be condemned to *confino*. It is a sort of didactic game for the Regime. The fact

is that everybody can be sent there because not only the law is revolutionary
but its interpretation is as well. . . . What counts is not the text of the law
but the possibility of applying it at will.[34]

Confino, then, carried out a double function: preventive and repressive;
preventive, because it extricated those who had not yet committed any crime,
but who were considered potentially capable of doing so; repressive, because it
struck those who had committed crimes, even if they had already served a
sentence for the crime. At any rate, the measure was essentially unjust in both
cases. On one hand, *confino* preempted the suspected dangerous behavior of an
individual even though it was, as Davide Petrini pointed out, a *praeter delictum*
measure rather than *ante delictum* protection. The police were considered infallibly
capable of establishing the potential danger of a person, basing their decision
on facts without any legal precedent, as, for example, in the case of behaviors
considered dangerous for public morality.[35] On the other hand, the repressive
function was completely illegitimate, because it was carried out without any
regard for the basic right to trial. In fact, *confino* was also applied as an alternative
to judicial action when the alleged offender was acquitted in a trial in an ordinary
court or in the special court for the defense of the state (Tribunale Speciale per
la difesa dello Stato).[36] As Laura Grimaldi points out, in a certain way, "assigning
confino became a way of correcting judges, a type of *errata* of their sentences, of
the courts and the special court itself." *Confino* and jail ended up being "com-
municating vessels, often the former either continuing the imprisonment or
substituting the latter in the case of an acquittal."[37] Furthermore, the extremely
ambiguous regulations of *confino* and its streamlined procedure made it an efficient
blackmailing weapon to extort confessions in the absence of proof.

Such widespread use of police measures even worried the Minister of the
Interior, who tried to check its discretionary power by establishing criteria for
applying the preventive measures. He invited the prefects not to carry out
repressive actions "en masse, because while it seems extremely easy, it would
not meet the aims of the law but, on the contrary, would end up compromising
them."[38] Repressive action was to be carried out "discreetly" and "intelligently"
to avoid creating martyrs, alarming the population, and making opposition to
the regime too evident. Focused action, aimed and directed at a chosen few
would be doubly functional: it would serve as a warning for all those who had
not, for the moment, been sent to *confino*, while maintaining Fascism's image as
a fair, not overly repressive regime.

This strategy of varying, on a case-by-case basis, the measures taken against
opponents of the regime, the idea of setting an example for many by punishing
one, was destined to be a constant factor during the Ventennio. Mussolini

himself wished not to alarm the population by sending too many people to *confino*. He was anxious to diminish the number of anti-Fascists while strengthening the image of Fascism abroad where, thanks to information supplied by exiles, the use of police measures had been heavily criticized.[39] In his Ascension Day speech, May 26, 1927, Mussolini's reference to those condemned to *confino* is extremely interesting:

> How many people have been sent to *confino*? It's about time we made it known, as abroad there is talk of 200,000 and in Milan alone reportedly 26,000 have been rounded up. Above all, this is stupid as well as base. In the meantime, let's make a distinction between the two kinds of condemned: criminals and those sent for political reasons. I hope nobody wants to feel sorry for the delinquents sent to *confino*. Usually they are real scoundrels, thieves, pimps and drug dealers who must be removed rapidly from society, usurers, etc. The number of these *confinati comuni* [common criminal detainees] may increase. In all there are 1,527 of them. [Voices shouting: "Too few! Too few!"] Now let's look at the *confinati politici* [political detainees]: 1,541 individuals have been warned, 959 have been cautioned, and 698 are on the islands. I defy anyone to say that these modest figures are incorrect. But none of these *confinati* wants to be anti-Fascist, and some of them look as if they are Fascists.[40]

The distinction between confinement for common criminals (*confino comune*) and confinement for political detainees (*confino politico*) that Mussolini referred to was particularly problematic, so much so that, in February 1927, the provincial commissions were asked to specify on the basis of which subsection the injunction had been issued.[41] *Confino comune* was meant to remove those considered undoubtedly guilty from society, even if there was insufficient proof to charge them. In some circumstances it could fill a legislative gap, as in the case of homosexuality, in others it was used to overcome procedural difficulties, as in the case of rape. The code provided that it was only possible to proceed against this crime if someone lodged a complaint, with the result that often the guilty parties were not accused for fear of making the dishonor of the victim public. However, *confino* was most frequently employed for habitual criminals with long criminal records, considered to be inveterate.[42] Lastly, it was an instrument for controlling social outcasts: drunkards, the unemployed, the mentally ill, prostitutes, vagabonds, and beggars, all of whom were sent to distant islands, both because they were thought to be potential subversives and because the sight of them damaged the regime's public image. The Fascists did not actually make much distinction between *confinati politici* and *confinati comuni*, as they believed that the privation of the latter group could easily turn them into political opponents of the government. On November 8, 1926, Undersecretary of the Interior Giacomo Suardo had sent a telegraphic notice to the prefects stating that the "battle against those who disturb and plot against the regime must not neglect petty delinquents, as it is not a question of two distinct battles but of two faces of a single initiative with a common aim: to ensure the peace and tranquility of the workers and producers."[43] The same endemic lack of space in the colonies was due mainly to the ever-increasing number of detainees,[44] who were forced to live segregated.[45] It was even harder to make a distinction if we consider that interns described as "politici" were often just "deviators" — individuals that unwittingly expressed anti-Fascist sentiments through actions that did not conform to Fascist ideology, through something said when drunk, a funny story told simply to entertain, general complaints against the government, unorthodox religious practices, or lifestyles considered antisocial and antinational. Furthermore, it was the prevailing custom to give *confino politico*, almost as reduced sentence, to the public officials and functionaries of the Fascist Party guilty of common-law offenses. In comparison to the *confinati politici*, the treatment of *confinati comuni* was much more severe. In addition to being subjected to greater temporal and geographical restrictions, they were forced to share large dark rooms without floors, windows, or facilities. Moreover, because *confinati comuni* had to survive on only four liras a day instead of ten, they often ended up prey to moneylenders or became outright slaves to their employers, who could hold them as prisoners and lock them up every evening.

In practice, the real distinction between political and nonpolitical detainees was made by the *confinati* of the colonies themselves, where there were three separate groups: the *confinati comuni* who were still called "*coatti*" ("forced residents"), those who were really *confinati politici*, and other criminals, contemptuously called "Manchurians," who were treated in the same way as the *confinati politici*.[46] This conflation offended the anti-Fascists who had been condemned for their ideals and now found themselves regarded on the same level as delinquents and Manchurians. From their memoirs, it is clear that the anti-Fascists ended up disliking the others intensely.[47] The political interns accused the Manchurians of helping the colony directors; in fact, the authorities used the *confinati comuni* to do the hardest work for very low pay and used them as spies among the *confinati politici*. According to Mario Magri, the regime intended to further humiliate the anti-Fascists by obliging them to live together with "corrupt men who had never thought of carrying out any political activity." It was not, then, by chance that the requests to be separated from the "criminals" were constantly rejected; "the police have always maintained that we were all birds of a feather."[48] On the other hand, the *confinati comuni* were quite happy to enjoy social structures like the cafeterias, stores, schools and libraries organized by the *confinati politici*, a practice that sometimes sparked fights, brawls, and acts of vengeance or violence.

Even though in some cases the division between *confinati politici* and *confinati comuni* was expressly provided for by regulation,[49] the different ways of living this experience ended up strongly emphasizing this distinction. It was natural for former party comrades or people who had the same ideas and ideals to mix together, leading to numerous small, separate communities, strongly united among themselves but rigidly closed to outsiders. Umberto Terracini wrote that "there were two parallel, enemy organizations living together on these islands, silently, angrily, and eternally challenging each other: the official one of the *confino* colony . . . and the other of the mainly left-wing groups, distinguished by their political tendencies (communists, Gaullists, and anarchists) and, from a certain point on, by their nationality (Albanians, Ethiopians and Greeks)."[50] As well as for ideological and national reasons, detainees of similar origins or socio-economic level often aggregated.

Although the detainees did not have differently colored triangles sewn on their clothes, as was customary in the Nazi concentration camps, in their "spontaneous" gatherings—*confinati politici*, mafia members, homosexuals, prostitutes, Jehovah's Witnesses, gypsies, and Yugoslavs—each group became a living symbol of a particular human type to be eliminated from civil society. From this point of view, the penal colonies had a racist quality as well, insofar as they led to the exclusion and persecution of all those who were considered to be different. The detainees themselves had so completely interiorized this division among themselves that they had difficulty recognizing their shared lot. Nevertheless, there were numerous exceptions to this extremely negative picture.[51] In the colonies where there was no rigid separation into groups, *confino* became a useful occasion to cultivate dialogue among different expressions of anti-Fascism. This intermingling fostered education and gave the interns the chance to express their ideological beliefs, spread political culture, reflect on the reasons for their political ideas, and become more directly aware of the reality and living conditions of the poorer classes. Thus, an exchange was set up whereby the anti-Fascists passed on values and knowledge to criminals, leading them to develop an interest in politics and take anti-Fascist positions.

Hence, there was a motley assortment of people in the colonies. It is enough to think that among the *confinati politici* there were homosexuals, doctors and midwives accused of inducing abortion and attacks on the race, bankrupted people, embezzlers, rustlers, usurers, suspected spies, drug-pushers, beggars, mentally ill people, and vagabonds. As Rosa Spadafora pointed out, most of them were sent to *confino* "for petty crimes (swindling, arbitrarily raising prices and rents, money trafficking, lending money on usury, indecent behavior, etc.)

or, at the most, for behavior that could be called 'generally dangerous' (anonymous statements, stirring up rebellion against local authorities, spreading alarming news, breaking the law on the defense of the race, etc.)."[52] The presence of such a heterogeneous group of detainees clearly shows that this repressive measure was employed against every kind of deviation and was used not only to fight political opposition, but as a means of limiting various forms of social dissent. The special court was considered the most suitable tool for repressing organized anti-Fascism, while *confino* was aimed at the indistinct mass made up of discontented people, gossipmongers, people considered bad examples for society, and individuals whose suspicious backgrounds might be fertile ground for the seeds of anti-Fascism. In short, "by widening the public sphere to include sectors that up until then had been private, the regime itself ended up encouraging an existential anti-Fascism, whose dimensions have yet to be explored on a historiographical level."[53] Further research on this argument could widen our interpretive perspective on Fascism by placing political opponents, in the true sense of the term, side by side with the various apolitical manifestations of dissent, which expressed themselves in lifestyle choices considered transgressive of the Fascist order.[54] In my opinion, this should not, however, be considered "mass dissent" or true anti-Fascism,[55] because this "generic and primitive tendency toward insurrection" expressed "by irregulars, by those abandoned by society, by those who do not accept the political system and by every kind of outsider" is not the fruit of well-defined political beliefs,[56] but comes above all from poverty and wretchedness. It was the great disparity between the legal and the real country, between state and civil society that fomented the protest of people who belonged to social strata that were completely extraneous to politics. Furthermore, by broadening the category of those considered subversive, Fascism gave political value to these kinds of antisocial behavior.

Confino was often resorted to for its efficiency and ease; in fact, the chief police officer needed only to propose somebody's name for it to be submitted to the provincial commission. In some cases an accurate investigation had been carried out beforehand, but quite often simply an anonymous declaration, a tip-off, or a confidential report was enough. The person involved was arrested immediately and did not always appear before the commission, but waited in prison for an order that would establish his *confino* location. Life in the penal colonies was certainly not a "holiday."[57] It began with an extremely uncomfortable trip from the person's hometown to a distant destination. The detainees were handcuffed and, with chains linking their wrists together, were crammed into boiling hot or freezing carriage cells, depending on the season, where they passed many hours without drinking or eating, their movements limited by the chains, and their arms swollen from the tight handcuffs. Sometimes it took days and days to reach the penal colony, and once there, the interns had to carry out a gesture of submission by signing the "permanence agreement" with all the rules that had to be respected.[58] There were restrictions on their movements and designated curfews, and they were forbidden to speak of politics, gather in groups, or go to shows, public places, bars, coffee shops, or restaurants. During the daytime the detainees were constantly checked on, and the most dangerous ones were followed. At night, there were surprise inspections for those living in private homes. Those housed in dormitories were locked in until the following morning. The excessively generic obligation to behave well and not give rise to suspicion gave the colony directors total power over the detainees, including the possibility of inflicting harsh punishment at their discretion. In some cases the regulation was applied in a very severe fashion, in others cases, not. This arbitrariness left the detainees with the impression that they might be punished for any reason at all.[59]

Seen in this light, *confino* was a type of total institution. Life in these penal colonies was irreconcilable with past experiences: one's daily rhythm was altered, there was limited space, detainees were isolated from the outside world, their individuality was erased, and they were forced to submit to authority. As Antonio Gramsci wrote to his sister-in-law, "It's impossible to imagine the atmosphere on the island of Ustica, how we live there, because it is an absolutely exceptional, it is different from any normal experience of cohabitation."[60] This completely abnormal situation, the violent uprooting from one's life and family, and the sudden deprivation of one's civil rights and freedom, was meant to make detainees lose their past identities, to erase their personalities. *Confino* was made even harsher by the continuous provocations and bullying of the MVSN militiamen (the *militia volontaria per la sicurezza nazionale*, the volunteer militia for national security, commonly called the *camicie nere*, the Blackshirts), who even beat, tortured, and threatened the detainees in some cases.[61] According to Leonardo Musci, the militiamen became even more violent, especially after Carlo Rosselli, Emilio Lussu, and Francesco Saverio Nitti escaped from Lipari in July 1929, and began carrying out a "depressive repression" by openly ignoring the regulations and making the political detainees feel even more at the mercy of their persecutors.[62] This arbitrary abuse of power was intended to weaken the detainees' resistance, making them ready to accept every kind of ill treatment in order to obtain more human living conditions. Officially, the disciplinary board (made up of the colony director, the local doctor, and the priest) was responsible for punishing those who did not observe the obligations imposed by the permanence agreement; however, punishment was often summarily applied by the militiamen themselves, who openly ignored the regulation.[63]

Life in *confino* would become even harsher after the 1929 crisis, when the government allowance (*mazzetta*) was reduced from ten to five liras. Consequently, it was difficult for the detainees to adequately provide for themselves,

especially on the islands, where provisions were lacking, the prices imposed by
the shopkeepers were inflated, and there was a constant scarcity of work. Cold
weather and malnutrition caused illnesses, but also the death of some who did
not receive sufficient medical assistance. Despite the restrictions on drinking,
instances of alcoholism increased, while during the war tuberculosis spread
alarmingly. In some cases the psychological disturbance of the injustice suffered,
the incomprehensibility and unacceptability of this new existence, created such
serious mental disorders that hospitalization in insane asylums was necessary.
Insane asylums became supplementary forms of *confino* and vice versa, even
though persecution complexes, signs of mental derangement, nervous break-
downs, and schizophrenic behavior were written off by colony directors as
attempts on the part of detainees to be freed. On the other hand, when doctors
themselves were not sure if mentally ill patients or people with mental disorders
should be confined to insane asylums, they were removed from society and sent
to the colonies.

The hardships of the *confinati* also affected their families: parents, wives, and
children were left without financial support and forced to suffer poverty and
humiliation in order to survive. This is proved by the great number of requests
for help—pardon for a relative or a subsidy for his family—sent to Mussolini,
the Ministry of Interior, the chief of police, and the prefect. The Duce was not
indifferent to these appeals and granted pardons quite generously. Because
confino was meant to be educative as well, at times, those who had behaved well
and had openly submitted to Fascism were freed. In addition, this served to
strengthen Mussolini's image as a good and just man capable of pardoning those
who had erred; at the same time it served to present an image of anti-Fascists
ready to submit to Fascism. Particular anniversaries, like the decennial celebration
of the March on Rome or the proclamation of the empire, were favorite occasions
for acts of clemency, all-embracing amnesties, and pardons. However, once the
detainees were freed, their lives were not easy: it was difficult to find work, the
oppressive police surveillance persisted, and in cases in which they had been
freed before the established period of *confino* was up, they had to undergo a two-
year period of cautioning, not to mention the difficulties that they faced in re-
establishing relationships.

Life in the Colonies

The history of repression of homosexuals is closely tied to the use of *confino*. In
fact, *confino* was one of the main instruments used against those whom the police
considered "pederasts." Already during the liberal period, "devotees of Sodom"
were among those sentenced to *domicilio coatto*—those "who had lost their moral

sensibility." Not surprisingly, as Avellino police chief, Giuseppe Damiani, testified in 1905, a small dwelling on the island of Ustica had been purposefully set aside for "passive sodomites, degenerated human forms recognized and branded with disgrace." In his book on *confino*, Damiani expressed his deep repulsion for them:

> They are the worst detainees of all, not because of their past or for the same common crimes they have committed, but for the enormous, disgraceful crime they commit on themselves. They are passive pederasts. Who knows the instincts and the mysterious forces they obey in abasing themselves so ignominiously. I have met a lot of these despicable and repulsive persons. . . . These individuals have not sufficiently developed physically and intellectually, so that they must be considered inferior to other men, although such depraved youths do not always bear these stigmata of degeneracy. That there was such a small number of them does not mean that there are only a few in the colony; it only reflects the known sodomites, the ones that do not hide their obscenity. They offer their favors to the first to come by for the paltry sum of two or three coins; their favorite places are grottoes or among the rows of prickly-pear cacti in the country.[64]

This kind of individual was to be isolated in order to prevent "perverse" practices from spreading among the detainees, some of whom were already accustomed to going to male brothels. According to Dr. Emanuele Mirabella, in most of the cases in the Favignana colony, "the majority of passive sodomites are hysterical interns; nicknamed *femminelle* (sissies), their sense of morality is very weak, and their consciences are perverted."[65]

Only through a specific study could one reconstruct the extent to which *domicilio coatto* was employed against homosexuals in the liberal period. In any case we can affirm that, thanks to new police instruments, repressive acts against homosexuals became harsher and more intrusive with Fascism; compared to the preceding period, more people were persecuted, especially since pederasty was by then officially considered a form of deviant behavior. Detailed instructions on the monitoring of homosexuals stated that every police station was to identify and register the pederasts in their province so that they might feel the threat of *confino* looming over them. Meanwhile, the prefect's office was ordered to immediately open a special file entitled "Repression of Pederasty" (*Repressione pederastia*), with a report of the investigation carried out and a list of the people in *confino* for this reason. Unfortunately there are no records of this in the police division's sector of the Central Archives of the State. The only file there is from Florence, while in the other cases, there is only a reference to *confino comune* in the files on general affairs for provinces. Despite this lack of records, one can imagine that

Table 1. Political detainees in *confino* for pederasty

YEAR	TOWN	INTERNS
1931	Ascoli Piceno	1
1934	Rome	1
1935	Milan	2
	Novara	1
1936	Florence	2
	Milan	1
	Rome	1
	Udine	1
1937	Florence	1
	Genoa	1
	Venice	2
Total 1931–1937		**14**
1938	Florence	5
	L'Aquila	1
	Piacenza	1
	Trieste	1
1939	Catania	46
	Florence	3
	Palermo	5
	Rome	1
	Salerno	3
	Sondrio	1
	Vercelli	1
1940	Pavia	1
	Turin	2
1941	Rome	2
	Udine	1
Total 1938–1941		**74**
Total		**88**

once homosexuality had become a proper category, repressive action against it was diffused among almost all the ninety Italian provinces. Nevertheless, it is difficult to know exactly how many people were sent to *confino* because they were thought to be homosexuals. We can only be certain that there were 88 *confinati politici* registered in the police records (see table 1),[66] and that altogether they were given over 400 years of *confino*, keeping in mind that homosexuals were almost always given the maximum penalty. However, as with the other kinds of interns, the number of years actually spent in the colonies were almost always reduced by an act of clemency on the part of the Duce.

The number of *confinati comuni* should be added to that of *confinati politici* (see table 2). The former number regarding criminals is not easy to detect, as the reports of the provincial commissions only cover the three-year period 1937–39, and do not always indicate the reasons for the conviction.[67]

Documents discovered in the central state record office show that there were about 300 *confinati comuni* charged with pederasty; unfortunately there are only 38 personal files (see table 3).[68] The approximately 300 delinquents in *confino* however, made up only a small part of the whole, which can be inferred from the fact that of these 300, a good 196 were pederasts who had been on the islands of Ustica and Favignana in the summer of 1942. In July 1942, it had been decided, at the behest of the Department of the Navy, to evacuate these two islands as it was expected that the punishment of *confino* would be reduced to a warning for those who had already served two thirds of their sentence. Consequently the police Department had drawn up a list of all the pederasts in the two colonies, indicating those who were to be released.[69]

Most of the homosexuals in *confino* openly displayed their sexual orientation, either because they were prostitutes or because "having caught the disease common to passive pederasts and lost all restraints of decency," they tended "to make their depravity known publicly."[70] They were poor, generally of lower social classes, with a life of hardship and difficulty behind them. Most of them were illiterate and employed in lowly jobs that were more often than not irregular (many of them were tailors and waiters, some were barbers, cobblers and day-laborers, but there were also five priests). The majority of them were unmarried and had very little interest in politics. They were all registered as apolitical. Anyone registered as a member of the PNF (Partito nazionale fascista, the National Fascist Party) was automatically expelled because of the evident contradiction between belonging to the Fascist party and behaving in a way that was anthropologically opposed to Mussolini's Italian male.[71] Apart from a few exceptions,[72] the repression of presumed pederasts was rather sporadic and incidental; *confino* represented, in fact, an extreme solution, while cautioning and warning[73] were preferred for the fact that they instilled fear, forcing suspects

Table 2. Number of common criminal detainees in *confino* for pederasty, divided into towns

TOWNS	INTERNS
Agrigento	1
Ancona	8
Arezzo	1
Avellino	1
Bari	3
Bologna	8
Bolzano	1
Brescia	2
Cagliari	10
Catania	21
Catanzaro	1
Como	1
Cremona	1
Cuneo	2
Enna	1
Florence	5
Fiume	9
Forlì	2
Genoa	14
L'Aquila	2
Littoria	1
Leghorn	8
Lucca	3
Mantova	14
Milan	2
Naples	5
Novara	3
Nuoro	1
Padua	6
Palermo	13
Parma	1
Pavia	1
Perugia	3
Pola	2
Potenza	4
Ravenna	1
Reggio Calabria	6
Rome	35
Rovigo	1
Salerno	6
Siracusa	1
Turin	6
Trapani	3
Trieste	1
Udine	1
Venice	38
Vercelli	23
Verona	9
Vicenza	6
Total	**298**

Table 3. Files in the Archivio Centrale dello Stato on common criminal detainees in *confino* for pederasty

YEAR	TOWN	INTERNS
1927	Venice	4
1929	Rovigo	1
	Venice	2
1934	Avellino	1
	Catania	4
	Rome	1
	Venice	5
1935	Brescia	1
	Palermo	1
	Parma	1
	Venice	3
1936	Venice	1
1937	Ancona	1
	Bari	1
	Cagliari	1
	Milan	2
	Naples	1
	Palermo	1
	Turin	1
	Venice	2
1938	Ancona	1
	Genoa	1
	Naples	2
1939	Palermo	2
1940	Catania	1
	Palermo	1
	Pola	1
Total		**44**

to be more prudent and discreet.[74] Homosexuals were continually stopped and taken to the police station to be interrogated; they spent days and days in prison before being registered in the police records and released with the fear of new roundups and harsher measures. Sending homosexuals to *confino* created too many problems for the authorities and so, when possible, they tried to limit employing it. For example, the prefect for Potenza, Ottavio Dinale, thought that the 16 pederasts in *confino* in the various towns in his province represented "an extremely dangerous center for infection due to their physiological density" and, since *"pederasts are constantly on the look-out*, get sensuously excited and reach out yearningly toward new prey on whom they can vent their irrepressible and bestial instincts," they should be locked up in prisons or penal colonies, because keeping them in towns on the mainland was "a contradiction in terms for a regime that has established a miracle of institutions and initiatives for the physical and spiritual health of the race."[75]

Furthermore, many were convinced that pederasts could mend their ways and give up their "sordid vice"; in short, a bit of strength of will was enough to get on the path to a "normal" life. Only those who persisted in their perversion and "on the path they had fatally undertaken" ended up in *confino*, a place reserved for "incorrigible" pederasts who continued to cause scandal. Extreme severity was reserved for those who openly professed their homosexuality; while the regime was more tolerant toward those who were careful to preserve an immaculate public image and not reveal their sexual tendencies.[76] Only those who openly showed their "depravity" were considered a threat to the nation's future. Consequently *confino* served as a threat for "all those who, though more discreet about it, are nevertheless addicted to pederasty, as well as for those young people who are already on their way to depravity."[77]

In an attempt to prevent the negative effects of public actions against sexual "deviations," the Fascists themselves made an effort not to overly publicize their repression of pederasty. In this case as well, the intention was not to alarm the population but to make homosexuality—a slight to national honor and prestige and a "vice" that did not belong to a virile people like the Italians—as inconspicuous as possible. This "repressive tolerance,"[78] Marcuse's categorized it, concealed a wide range of coercive measures, including preventive police actions, expulsion from society, public derision, losing one's job, insults, beatings and castor-oil, all of which were used to isolate and condemn homosexuals to civil death. Even before the intervention of the police, the family, neighbors, and priest or doctor of the pederast tried to inhibit and reeducate him by showing him the mistake he was making. In rural tradition there was even a ritual called the *chiarivari*, whose aim was to redefine the boundaries of gender that had been violated, by punishing the transgressor through derision and public humiliation. The members of the community claimed the right to express their disapproval of relationships they considered irregular and of sexually perverted behavior, not only by keeping a simple check on suspected pederasts and morally condemning them, but also by "using more aggressive and potentially dangerous rituals, whose names differed from region to region in Italy: *scampanata, cembolata, trimpellata, mattinata, cecconata, ciabre* etc. These rituals targeted different kinds of transgression: adultery, homosexuality and conflicts between husbands and wives where the former were beaten by the latter."[79] With the wane of these public rituals against these "traitors of the race," weapons such as satire, slander, insults and derision, which in the climate introduced by Fascism, extended their range of action to such an extent that they often turned out to be more efficacious than cautioning and *confino*. As a result, the repression suffered by homosexuals during the Fascist Ventennio was much more widespread than what emerges from the relatively small number of detainees.

In any case, due to the incomplete nature of the archives, the little work done on this subject has been at times inaccurate. Giovanni Dall'Orto and Gianfranco Goretti, among the first to tackle the issue, situated the persecution of homosexuals within Fascist racial policy, putting it in direct relation with the 1938 racial laws. This idea was taken up again more recently by Patrizia Dogliani, according to whom "the persecution of homosexuals by the Fascist regime" should be situated within the "general chapter of their racial and sexphobic policies." Nevertheless, the same author herself inevitably had to acknowledge that "the nature of the offense, and therefore whether it could be punished or not, was left uncertain" and that "in Italy, the magazine *La Difesa della Razza* (In Defense of the Race) never treated the issue openly in the most fervent years of racist propaganda.[80] Consequently, this interpretation, which, moreover, limits the period of persecution to the three-year span from 1936–1939—those in which an attempt was apparently made to imitate Nazi Germany in this field as well—is not entirely convincing.[81] As mentioned before, the repression of homosexuals, on the contrary, has a long tradition—even before the rise of Fascism—including the use of *confino* as a tool for driving pederasts out of society. Undoubtedly we can agree that the use of repressive action increased concomitantly with the racial laws. However, it seems that this increased severity should be understood, not in terms of a sudden increase in racism, but rather in relation to the attempt to give imperial Italy a more virile and martial aspect and to the accelerated move toward totalitarianism that shaped all the regime's policies in that period.[82] It is true that the creation of the racial laws represent a fundamental moment for the development of anti-Semitism. The aversion toward homosexuals, however, certainly did not arise then but has its origins in the implicit racism of the model of a new man, something that is present in Fascism from the beginning. The first homosexuals put into *confino* in the 1920s were also considered a threat to the race: in their police files they were always described as "dangerous for the integrity and health of the race," which later became simply "dangerous for the integrity of the race."

In light of this, I find it unconvincing to maintain that homosexuality took on political significance precisely in 1938. Dall'Orto and Goretti explain that those sent to *confino* for pederasty were classified as political on the basis of the link between racial laws and the persecution of homosexuals, which also explains why their numbers increased beginning in 1938.[83] If this were so, the reason why homosexuals, considered political interns from 1936 to 1939, suddenly went back to being listed as criminals in 1940, would be incomprehensible since racism had certainly not disappeared in that year. Even harder to understand would be why, in 1939, there were also cases of pederasts recorded in the lists of *confinati comuni*. In my opinion, on the contrary, it clearly emerges from the documents that those in *confino* for pederasty were still considered *confinati comuni* and that the extraordinary increase in their numbers in 1939 should not be linked to the racial laws but to the mass roundups that took place that year in Catania, with at least 46 people sent to *confino* on the Tremiti islands. Secondly, people often without criminal records, with a high social position or with an important public function, were recorded as political detainees and were given better treatment. These included priests, those with influential backers or individuals who, besides being considered pederasts, were accused of politically incorrect behavior, like criticizing the regime or ridiculing the prestige of the nation and the race. Nevertheless the main reason was another, and more simple, if we consider that, from 1937 on the Tremiti islands became a colony used exclusively for *confinati politici*: apart from the reason for the conviction, anyone who ended up on the Tremiti islands was therefore listed as a political detainee.[84]

In 1937, after an on-the-spot inspection of the Tremiti islands to suggest the steps necessary for transforming them into colonies for *confinati politici*, the police inspector Raffaele Capobianco advised the Department of the Interior to keep about fifty criminal interns in the two dormitories on San Domino (one of the three islands of the archipelago) because they would be useful for farm work and did not need close surveillance. The recommendation not to use this island for *confinati politici* was due to its topography that, "as it slopes down to the sea, [offers] numerous possibilities for escape, consequently making a considerable number of police officers necessary to guard the detainees."[85] Capobianco's suggestion was accepted by the Ministry of the Interior that decided to keep only about 60 pederasts on San Domino, concentrating all the other *confinati politici* on the main island of San Nicola, with the intention of creating a special place for homosexuals, keeping them isolated and separated from all the other detainees. As the file of the *confinati comuni* reveals, the island of San Domino had been used as a *confino* location for homosexuals following the 1935 ministry provision specifying that the pederasts sent to the Tremiti islands had to stay on San Domino in a house set aside exclusively for them.[86] The presence of homosexual detainees on the Tremiti islands had created a proper scandal, so much so that in 1936 an enquiry was carried out regarding the discipline and administration of the colony as well as the conduct of its director, Cavaliere Fusco, who was accused, among other things, of having homosexual intercourse with a detainee sent there for passive pederasty. The engagement of the pederast in *domicilio coatto* as a housekeeper in his own home had given rise to comments and gossip, even if later inspections showed that these suspicions were unfounded.[87]

If the Tremiti islands were considered the harshest *confino* site, life on San Domino was even more difficult: at that time the island was almost completely uninhabited, lacking a sewage system and water, without any work opportunities and in constant lack of food supplies due to difficult connections with the mainland. Mario Magri thus described the homosexuals' life on San Domino:

> On San Domino there was a colony of *"signorine"* (young ladies) as they were commonly called by the administration as well: there were about a hundred perverts, almost all of them from Catania and other Sicilian towns. These poor devils, who also included some good artisans and even professors, lived in terrible conditions. They were given four liras a day and were crammed into two filthy wooden huts, surrounded by a barbed wire fence that left them only a few square meters in which to move about. They had to go to San Nicola to reach the administration office and the infirmary, taken there by boat and guarded by a police officer. About fifteen of them arrived every day. They were very elegant, smartly dressed, with eye makeup and flowing hair. They walked arm-in-arm, calling each other by women's names and glancing around languidly and provocatively. They were not allowed to speak to us and limited themselves to sighing, smiling and singing love songs. Every now and then there were fights in the dormitory caused by jealousy, they scratched each other's faces and pulled each other's hair until the guards arrested the rivals.[88]

There were various reasons why the police considered homosexuals a threat to society. Above all, they created scandal, upsetting the moral sensibility of the public; they corrupted inexperienced young men and they damaged the prestige and integrity of the race because they jeopardized the institution of the family and contributed to spreading a perversion that was harmful for the nation. As repression was almost exclusively directed toward the passive pederast, police roundups mostly targeted male prostitutes, particularly those who solicited men publicly or flaunted feminine behavior. Public morality was brought into question by such an open violation of the canons of Fascist virility, which considered passivity to be a typically feminine characteristic. Active homosexuals, who behaved like "normal" men in public, were treated more indulgently, even though their "perverse" habits encouraged "the deplorable scourge of passive pederasty." In his study of the Catanian interns, Goretti revealed how this rigid division between exclusively (active) male behavior and exclusively (passive) female behavior was so rooted in society that it was interiorized by homosexuals themselves. For the majority of them, sexuality had to express itself in the form of one of the two predetermined roles, the dominating and active role of males and the subordinate passive one of females. Therefore, they had not yet acquired the characteristics of "modern homosexuals":[89] their choice of partner was exogamous, their relationships as couples were asymmetric and their meeting places were almost always impromptu, varied and secret. Their relationships were structured around the polarization of identity and roles, based on an asymmetry that was not only sexual but also social: active and passive, effeminate and masculine, rich and poor. According to Goretti the very lack of a paradigm different from that for heterosexuals kept the various groups of homosexuals in Fascist Italy from forming a proper subculture. In short, the life of their universe was so conditioned by the surrounding culture that they were prevented from developing alternative values capable of questioning the dominating model, of claiming their own identity and asserting their diversity.

The police regarded pederasts as effeminate individuals who were sexually passive and who submitted to anal intercourse, often for money. According to Catania's police chief, Alfonso Molina, a certain Antonio P. was a good example of this image, "a typical pederast because of his deep-rooted depravity, his physical features and his behavior," who "does not hide his depraved feminine tendencies and even goes by the pet name 'Ninetta.' Furthermore he boasts that he has a lot of lovers that he usually copulates with in secluded places where he has sometimes been caught in lustful and disgusting positions."[90] However, even without explicitly feminine traits, at times the tone of voice was enough to report a "passive." For example, Giuseppe L.P. with his "lean face, deep-set eyes, flaring nostrils and thick lips, seems like a perfectly sensual type. He could be considered a fortunate male if his voice did not give him away and the life he led was not evidence of his sexual perversion."[91] The police chief subjected all those accused of pederasty to a medical examination, in order to "objectively" confirm they were homosexuals.[92] After the unfortunate person was arrested, often only on the grounds of malicious gossip, and after a rigorous interrogation, he was taken to a government clinic for venereal diseases where he underwent a rectal analysis that was, once and for all, supposed to confirm his pederasty.

The medical certificates bore various and horribly detailed reports, for example: "occasional pederast, not accustomed to regular intercourse," or "accustomed to habitual preternatural intercourse," or "not habitual;" also "funnel-shaped anus," "cornet-shaped anus," "typical wear of overused anus . . . centripetal-type rhagades," "relaxed sphincters," "anal rhagades and rectal caruncle," "shallow rhagades or relative wearing of the sphincter," "damaged perianal plexus," "venereal-type ulcerations," "anal ulcerations and condilomas,"

"suffering from chronic syphiloma of the anus," "afflicted with syphilis transmitted via the anus." These signs were considered unmistakable proof of the vice,
as were anal scars and fistulas; it is, however, easy to imagine how superficial
the medical examination was, a simple formality that served to exculpate the
alleged homosexual on only two occasions. In the case of Barbaro M., whose
brother was a doctor, there was a real battle between the testimonies of the
prosecution and defense, without a final diagnosis ever being reached. Then,
after the umpteenth inconclusive examination ordered by the provincial commission, the police chief called for a further examination by the provincial doctor
of Foggia who was responsible for the Tremiti penal colonies, to which the
unlucky suspect had already been sent in the meantime. Using a pin, the doctor
tried to confirm that the former was a pederast, concluding his legal examination
with a report that left little doubt as to its scientific value: "torn asshole."
Consequently the appeal was rejected once and for all."[93]

It was not easy for the police to explain the causes of this "sexual perversion."
Following prevailing medical opinion, homosexuality was considered a mental
propensity, while pederasty was thought to be either a congenital disease or an
acquired vice. Theoretically this distinction could be very important, in that if
it were a disease, some kind of treatment would be prescribed with hospitalization
in a clinic or confinement to an insane asylum. On the contrary, if it were a vice
acquired because of the depravity of the accused, repression and punishment
with prison or *confino* were justified. Thus the police and *carabinieri* investigated
the detainee's childhood and family background, "his medical records" and the
hereditary factors, environmental and immediate factors that may have led the
individual "to practice this abominable vice." Sexual abuse when young, living
in contact with other homosexuals or with degenerate parents and relatives
were all considered possible causes of passive pederasty. For example, a Catanian
youth was considered a congenital invert because "since his childhood he had
been very fond of everything that was feminine, revealing a tendency toward
perversion. When he was adolescent, this tendency degenerated into pederasty.
Led astray by this disease that was almost congenital, he lost all sense of modesty,
freely showing and even flaunting his perverted sensuality."[94] In cases in which
one's homosexuality was judged to be an "abominable vice" and not congenital,
the contempt, disgust and moral and material condemnation of the "depraved
person" was even greater, as proved by the police description of another eighteen
year old Catanian detainee: "this wreck of a youth, who has rejected his sex out
of vice rather than congenital intention, is a real attack on our customs and on
the health of our young men."

However, a sure diagnosis was not always arrived at; in such cases, it was
openly declared: "we do not know if he is given over to pederasty because of
congenital sexual perversion or because the perversion is acquired." This

continuous wavering between vice or disease did not replace the standard conviction that homosexuality depended largely on the will of the individual, too weak or too attracted to the vice not to resist being dragged into such "abnormal practices." Even if considered an illness, at the core of the homosexuality lay a moral perversion. Police reports clearly indicated the pederast's responsibility. Depending on the case, one might read:

> "He succumbed to the goddess of pleasure against nature and was overcome by the vice of pederasty." "Keeping the bad company of degenerates instilled the vice of pederasty in him." "Since he was a boy he has dedicated himself to the immoral practice of passive pederasty, until with the worsening of the vice, it has become a physiological necessity." "He has practiced pederasty since he was a boy, a congenital vice that he has been unable to repress." "An obscene and obstinate passive pederast who caught the disease of passive pederasty." "As time passed his vice became almost pathological, so much so that recently he has been incapable of calming his evil desires, on the contrary he has almost unwittingly flaunted them." "Born homosexual, he practices pederasty without restraint; it is a vice from which he can no longer break free." "Rather than concentrate on his studies he preferred moral perversion, contracting the disease of passive pederasty, which he has stubbornly practiced ever since."

The endless ambiguity between vice and disease was used by homosexuals themselves following the same mental framework as those who judged them. In their written defenses, they were very often ready to recognize that it was a "vice" and not their natural tendency or instinct, which were still "those of their masculine virility." They tried to conform to the widespread stereotype of the virile man; they pointed out that they were engaged or about to be married or as a screen they noted that they had fought in the war or intended to go as volunteers. In short, it was only a banal error of youth, due to their inexperience or to having been sexually abused. Very few openly acknowledged they were homosexuals, but considered it a real disease that should be treated and not repressed through violence or the revoking of their liberty. For example, one *confinato* wrote: "I have never offended public morality because I know the law very well. I am an orphan; fate and destiny have given me this disease—why am I to blame? Why punish me? Perhaps serving the sentence will cure me?"[95]

An elderly teacher from Ancona more stubbornly maintained his unpunishability and claimed he had fallen victim to a disease. He had had various convictions for indecent behavior, corruption of minors and soliciting licentious practices and had been forced to leave teaching. However, his troubles were not over: in 1932 he was cautioned about his homosexual tendencies and, after failing to comply with the obligations of the caution, was convicted several times and put on probation. Exasperated by this persecution he began a stubborn battle against the restrictive measures taken against him. In a series of letters sent to high-ranking state personalities he gave detailed reasons, upholding that the repression was illegitimate and asking for justice. He even wrote directly to the Duce pleading his cause:

> No educated person could honestly doubt that the moral defect afflicting me and for which the law makes no provisions (the law does not deal with sexual intercourse, which is ignored unless it takes place in particular circumstances) is an illness of the spirit (psycopathia sexualis), an unwelcome gift cruelly given to me by nature. . . . If this were not so, otherwise why not, by analogy, call the blind, the hunchbacked, the crippled etc. to answer for their physical defects that are less serious than mine, which is incurable?

To convict him was unjust "almost as if the psychopathy that torments me revealed an act of will, a pose, a deliberately eccentric behavior!" Not only the authorities continually harassed him but also some citizens that led him to report a person to the police, something he could have done "every day, indeed several times a day." In the letters he sent to the king and the undersecretary of the Interior, he underscored that the judges in one of his many trials had reduced his sentence for partial insanity, acknowledging his psychopathy. His only blame was having been an "unfortunate victim of his own nature." Not even this appeal served to stop the police from tormenting the teacher. Once again they took action against him, seizing his railway pass because he could have used it to evade police surveillance and go to the seaside resorts on the Adriatic in summer, where he might "easily satisfy his perverted instincts." In addition, in the same year, 1936, he was caught with a minor in his home during a police inspection and ended up once again under trial. Also this time he managed to avoid being convicted. The acquittal "so emboldened him that he pinned a notice on his front door announcing the news to his fellow-tenants," the very ones who had reported him. However, due to his offenses against public morality and indecent behavior, but also because of the continuous complaints of his neighbors, the elderly teacher was considered a threat to social order and the peace and morals of the family, and as such, one who should be sent away from Ancona once and for all. As a result, he was sent to *confino comune* in 1937, something he had vainly tried to avoid with a line of reasoning, totally incompatible with the repressive philosophy of the Fascist regime. The defendant opposed the measure, believing it absurd to consider "an occasional pathological episode" dangerous for public security and even more unreasonable to think that *confino* was the most suitable remedy, because "the internment of a person, just or not, for petty common offenses should be inferred exclusively from his police record and not from the moralistic opinions of individuals or the collective, however respectable they may be." In the opinion of the police, these were merely the usual attempts to "defend his vile inclination toward homosexual activities by advancing the idea that the natural perversion of his senses gave him the right to satisfy his insane desires, which he considered unpunishable by law." While still in *confino*, and after having served half of his sentence, he submitted a new request to be sent to a clinic at his own expense for rehabilitation. The prefect agreed to the request with the stipulation however that "this passive pederast be prohibited from returning to the province of Ancona"; however, the Minister of the Interior decided to reject the request.[96]

In another case, it was a sergeant major of the *carabinieri* who proposed leniency for detainee from Salerno who was "given to passive pederasty," recommending isolation in a rehabilitation clinic instead in hopes of curing this serious disease through moral restoration.[97] Sometimes it was the detainee's family members themselves who entreated the authorities to prescribe such solutions. Such was the case of a mother who, after questioning the legitimacy of *confino* for persons like her son, who had never been involved in activities that "harmed national interests,"[98] suggested medical treatment instead of punishment for those afflicted with this "disease":

> There are many unfortunate people afflicted by this disease and it is unfair to flog, and severely punish, those who, on the contrary, need treatment. Now, if it is true that pederasty is a disease, there is no one who cannot see that the measures of the new police regulation, which was created to curb and correct delinquency, are not the best remedy for this case.[99]

These words were destined to go unheeded, if we consider how deep-rooted and widespread the moral and cultural repugnance was for homosexuals. The cultural tools the Fascist police and most of the population were equipped with, did not leave room for understanding sexual "difference." The assumption that sexual intercourse, as a law of nature, was an exclusively male-female exchange, inevitably led to the opinion that homosexual relationships were illicit. Setting aside the causes of homosexuality, passive pederasts were always considered abnormal individuals without good qualities, who even if they possessed any, were incapable of using them for any aim other than satisfying their own perversion.

The fact that in some cases the police had taken repressive action to satisfy popular request, shows how widespread this mentality was. There were other cases similar to that of the Ancona teacher. For example, in 1938 *confino* was proposed for a tailor from Piacenza after he had been beaten up in a street in the center of Borgonovo because he was held to be responsible for trying to corrupt a youth. The entire town was greatly satisfied with the news. In place of an official complaint, which had not been lodged in an attempt at avoiding further scandal, "the townspeople expected exemplary punishment for this sinister individual who had revealed the mental derangement of a homosexual." Consequently the provincial commission of Piacenza decided to send him to *confino* for five years.[100] The same thing happened in Salerno where, after repeated complaints from the townspeople about a youth who wandered around the town streets "day and night, walking and moving in a feminine way, wearing lipstick and clothes that attracted the attention of passers-by, most of whom became nauseated,"[101] the boy was sentenced to *confino*. A deep revulsion for homosexuals, "despised and shunned by all decent people," emerged from the many complaints and anonymous letters that arrived at the police station, so much so that many detainees in *confino* for pederasty who filed an appeal were rejected in order to avoid disappointing the public, who were certainly against these detainees being freed.

It was often the case that homosexuality created difficulties in family relation-ships: parents and relatives did not always manage to understand those who, in their opinion, behaved so unconventionally that they were despised by the whole community. This contempt also affected the families, who were obliged to bear the shame of having a "degenerate" son. In small villages where respect-ability and honor were extremely important values, and where it was more difficult to remain anonymous, even a single piece of gossip or the suspicion that a person was a homosexual could ruin their life and that of their whole family forever. Homosexuals were not only obliged to live in loneliness but sometimes they were expelled from their families, where living together had become impossible after long and useless attempts to lead them back to the straight and narrow way, at times "without sparing thrashings and food depriva-tion."[102] Nevertheless it should be pointed out that, once the suspects had fallen into the hands of the police and were faced with measures like *confino*, even the severest parents ended up defending their own sons, begging for mercy and repeatedly asking for leniency on their behalf. Although they usually shared the widespread negative opinion of homosexuality, the bonds of affection prevailed and spurred them to try to help their dear ones in any way possible.[103] Moreover, having a young son sent to *confino* brought a family into even more disrepute and created serious financial difficulty, especially if his parents were elderly or unemployed. The many letters sent to Mussolini, Rachele (Mussolini's wife), the police chief and the Minister of the Interior repeatedly mention the disgrace it caused. For example, a young student of Paternò defended himself against the accusation of passive pederasty in his letter to the appeals commission saying:

Now I wholeheartedly rebel against this defamatory classification and beseech that this mark that stains my dignity as a man and citizen be wiped clean. It inevitably reflects on my entire family and on my poor sister who lives in a small town, rife with gossip, is still unmarried, and is without means. Her future will be irremediably compromised by this accusation that I contest. I protest strongly against this undeserved disgrace in the name of my family, which has never wavered in the face of sacrifice.[104]

Where the family life of homosexuals was certainly not easy, the situation was even more difficult at work and in public. Those found guilty of offenses against morality had their party cards immediately confiscated, and quite often lost their jobs. For example, because of his homosexuality, Maurizio B., who was sent to *confino* in 1935 by the Novara provincial commission, was degraded from army captain to soldier and later discharged permanently; he then lost his job with a company that ran large hotels. The effect on his political curriculum was just as devastating: although he had taken part in the March on Rome, to avoid making his expulsion from the party public, he was first obliged to leave it and was later was struck off the Fascist membership list and even off the servicemen's association list. At the same time he suffered a kind of continuous persecution from the Stresa political secretary and from the local party officials (*gerarchi*). Unemployed, reduced to hunger and to living in a barn for some time, he sent a series of appeals, accusations and anonymous letters to take revenge on those who had ruined him; in response he was accused of instigating discord within the PNF and discrediting its institutions. Thus, as he had "also shown he was dangerous because of his incurable sexual perversion," he was sentenced to five years of *confino*.[105]

Popular hostility led to the creation of homosexual groups that met in autonomous and hidden places or in those reserved exclusively for men, where they could freely express their identity. Nevertheless, this secrecy prevented any widespread solidarity or the birth of a movement to defend and protect homosexuals' rights—which, in any case, would have been unthinkable under a Fascist regime.[106] One's only defense was to keep his sexual tendency even more private, or to deny or lie about one's identity, by conforming to the standard model imposed. Homosexuals made themselves inconspicuous and pretended to be like everybody else, without making their claims known publicly. Doing so would have been difficult, since persecution—striking above all those who publicly revealed their homosexuality—was aimed at uneducated people belonging to the lower classes. Furthermore, without some newsworthy event capable of shaking public opinion, like Oscar Wilde's trial in England or the scandal surrounding the emperor of Germany, Wilhelm II's, entourage, public opinion in Italy was never involved in a debate on homosexuality. Consequently, criticism of the repression of pederasty never took root, even among intellectuals.

This kind of ghetto where homosexuals were forced to hide in order to prevent public morality from invading their private lives, continued in *confino* as well. Theirs remained a world apart, within a world apart. They were outcasts, mocked by the other detainees and by the locals. Nevertheless, a memoir describing life on the Tremiti islands reveals that those who managed to escape police supervision and work as prostitutes had a wide range of clients, including even Fascists and *carabinieri*.[107] It was just this isolation, meant to prevent these episodes, that made the homosexuals an extremely united group. This community of "sisters"—as the colony directors called them—did not lack true love stories, episodes of jealousy and violent fights triggered by passion, which called for the intervention of the disciplinary commission. Although the pederasts were separated from the rest of the detainees it was not easy for the latter, who were forced to observe sexual abstinence to escape temptation and "infection." When writing about his experiences of *confino* on the island of Ponza, Giorgio Amendola included some interesting comments on this subject:

> Obligatory sexual abstinence was agonizing. Masturbation gave the only relief, but we made a reciprocal effort to keep each other in check, to prevent excessive use being made of it. We all suffered from strong collective sexual repression. For example it was forbidden to display photographs from some illustrated weeklies that were considered pornographic. Even the photograph of a pair of legs became provocative. Self-control, discipline and strict puritan morality were required in order to avoid the danger of degeneracy. Despite the early permissive upbringing my mother gave me, something of that harsh self-discipline is still part of my character, and it comes out in the negative opinion of the overvalued importance given to sex in present-day life. Italian historicism's criticism of psychoanalysis as a general philosophy and not a medical science, expressed in other terms by the Stalinist interpretation of Marxism, has become customary for me, a rejection of the so-called uncontrolled release of sexual impulses. It is no coincidence that out of thousands and thousands of *confinati politici*, severely punished by being sent away from their political groups, the number of cases of homosexuality could be counted on the fingers of one hand. I was brought up in a highly permissive atmosphere and spent long periods of time on Capri, where homosexuals were more or less accepted, and yet I too realized that this self-discipline was necessary. Whatever one's opinion

of homosexuality, nobody can deny what a disaster it would have caused
in a segregated and starved community, forced to live in such a state. The
only way for us not to give in was to uphold our pride as communists.[108]

Amendola's words demonstrate how political identity was important enough
to influence sexual behavior: harsh self-discipline resulting from an ideologically
imposed morality and "the pride of being communist," were considered the
only ways for conserving one's "purity" from the "danger of degeneracy."
Besides, for those in *confino* who could not afford to send for their families, sexual
continence might last many years, giving rise to strong temptations and leading
to homosexual relationships. For example, Giovanni Ansaldo describes how
relationships between detainees on the island of Lipari and the young islanders
often became homoerotic:

> Most of the detainees were forced to lead a life of sexual abstinence.
> There were two prostitutes in the village, but I had not even seen them.
> However, it seems they were so foul that many (even those who were not
> very finicky) scorned them. Quite naturally, then, there was a lot of talk on
> the subject, and unconsciously sexual impulses looked for other forms of
> gratification, at least in one's imagination. I should add at once that I did
> not hear of any specific acts of pederasty. The detainees were generally
> people who, although they were quite crazy when it came to politics, knew
> how to keep strong moral self-control and whose "unconscious," to use a
> Freudian term, was constantly checked by social inhibitions. Nevertheless,
> certain *nuances* in the behavior of many of the detainees did not go un-
> noticed. Let me explain. Down at the sea cliffs there was often a swarm of
> young village boys who were there for the same reason as we were, to go
> swimming; it was inevitable that they ended up taking part in the diving
> and games of the more boisterous detainees. This diving and playing
> games became an easy pretext for the more impatient adults to fondle the
> boys' bare buttocks and thighs and linger over touches and caresses whose
> meaning could not be mistaken and that nobody in fact misunderstood,
> adults and children alike.[109]

Once again, memoirs on *confino* testify to the ubiquity of the stereotype
of homosexuals as womanly, ready to carry out a woman's work and to turn
aggressive when quarrelling with a rival over a strong and sturdy male. Alfredo
Misuri described them as: "smooth-skinned, effeminate young men who became
'the detainees' women' and who used nom de guerre like: Carmen, Tosca,
Cabiria etc. When a name became popular and was copied by others in the
colony, the result was: Carmen the second, Tosca the second, and so on. They

were 'the laundresses' or 'the ironers' for their companions. They preferred the
more robust ones and fought over them tooth and nail."[110] Especially on the island
of Ustica, among the *confinati comuni*, "there were many who went around wearing
their hair in ringlets, with lipstick and eye-shadow." Like with the town prostitutes,
the colony doctor examined them once a week.[111] Cesira Fiori as well did not
hide her distaste for these people that she believed belonged in hospitals instead
of *confino* on the Sicilian island:

> .   Sometimes, sarcastic laughter, little cries, simpering and stupid giggling
> could be heard in the long, sloping square that the church of San Barto-
> licchio overlooks, with its two flights of steps. The noises came from passing
> perverts who imitated women, their faces roughly made up. Nausea?
> Pity? Either way, revolt against the blindness of those who had sent them
> down there to attract attention, instead of to the hospital. They were put
> in small, separate dormitories, but there were some that let themselves be
> passed from one lodging to another, corrupting the normal detainees and
> getting beaten up by them as well. Women were forbidden goods, and so! . . .
> There was one who called himself Nanninella, a Roman from San Lorenzo,
> with bleached hair, bright red lipstick on a pretty, chubby, delicate face
> with just a light blond fuzz; the look in his eyes was sick, ashen. He stuffed
> his shirt with two balls to look like breasts, his voice was high-pitched,
> honeyed, and refined, and he was always accompanied by his two little
> girlfriends. . . . The young boys enjoyed the scene. . . . So did the islanders.
> So did the police officers.[112]

The two categories used to define these people who imitated women were
always 'normal' and 'abnormal.' Like circus performers, they attracted attention
and amused people. This evidence of how widespread the antihomosexual
mentality was helps us to understand the introjection of moral condemnation
on the part of the passive pederasts themselves. The incapacity to accept their
own identity—claiming it proudly, was naturally unthinkable in those times—
and the a priori forgoing of their rights, prevented the formation of a collective
awareness and the possibility of getting organized, of influencing the dominant
cultural model. The problems for those given *confino* for pederasty did not end
after they had served their sentence. Once they were freed they were subjected
to two years of cautioning, and they rarely managed to find a job. It was even
difficult to seek refuge in a religious community, as a detainee from Catania
tried vainly to do, after being freed in 1940 from the Tremiti islands and being
refused permission to enter an Augustinian convent by the police. After years
spent in *confino*, life was no longer the same for homosexuals, both because of
the fear of further punishment and the continuous scrutiny of the police, their

families and their neighbors. The memoirs of a former detainee at Goretti explains this new situation clearly:

> We could not go back to a normal life, we were under surveillance. We were given two years of cautioning and every now and then we had to go to the police station and sign. I didn't even see the others any more, because of this thing, the war, as well. Then, with the observation of mothers and fathers, we couldn't do what we had before, do you understand? We had to be more careful, also because we were told that if we were caught again we would never be freed. We were terrified.[113]

Considering the authorities' discretionary power in inflicting *confino*,[114] we should analyze, in particular, the repression carried out in those towns where, because homosexuality was so widespread, or the police chief was over-zealous, or simply because the files were not lost, there was a conspicuous number of people persecuted for their believed homosexuality.

Catania

Interestingly enough, the battle against homosexuals seems to have been particularly tough in Catania, a town where, as Vitalian Brancati described it, male sexual conceit prevailed, where virilism was carried to the extreme, and where hot-blooded men and Don Juans with a passion for women abounded.[115] Police action intensified in 1927 when some individuals, recognized passive pederasts, descended on the streets in women's clothing during the carnival festivities. The men were arrested, photographed, registered and given a warning. In August of the same year, the same course of action was taken against another twenty homosexuals accused of criminal association, rape, indecent behavior and the corruption of minors. The police had discovered a group of former detainees and offenders who had carried out "lustful acts and unnatural sexual intercourse in boats at the port or marina, using violence and threats and harming numerous boys" forced to suffer this "disgraceful slavery."[116] Some of these boys, most of whom were abandoned or had run away from home, little by little had become "accustomed to this sordid depravity," working as prostitutes for a few coins, cigarettes or some food. The nicknames of some of the members of the gang, like *Strazza causi* (trouser tearer) o *Turi u Purpu* (Salvatore the octopus), left no doubt about their bent for pedophilia and pederasty. The trial ended in February 1929, with eighteen of the defendants being sentenced to terms of imprisonment ranging from one to nine years.[117] The sentence was not particularly harsh because "the waif and stray victims, in their depravity," had fostered the crime, in fact the boys had ended up "agreeing willingly to have sexual intercourse."[118]

Some years later, in 1930, following the murder of a pederast the police intensified their investigation of homosexual circles by watching places where homosexuals commonly met, such as dance halls and public urinals. The police also made night raids on private homes used for male prostitution, which resulted in scenes of panic among the clients who were forced to jump out of the windows to escape. In 1934, the provincial commission of Catania delivered the first sentences for passive pederasty. Following a proposal of the police, five men who had already been warned were given *confino comune*. Already in 1927 two of them had been accused of indecent behavior and soliciting and were consequently convicted, while all of them had been repeatedly taken into custody by the vice squads as a public security measure. Since the offenders were passive pederasts, they were sentenced to five years of *confino* for offenses against public morality and decency. In his report to the prefect, the police chief informed him of the particular situation in Catania where:

> Despite the large-scale measures and constant police surveillance, it has been impossible to put a stop to the scourge of pederasty; the unsatisfactory results of the measures adopted so far are due solely to the stubbornness and indifference of the most rebellious degenerates of this kind, who run any risk in order to satisfy their perversion and continue to infest their surroundings.[119]

A detailed description of their activity expresses all the resentment and disgust for those who suffered from "one of the most disgusting kinds of degeneracy that afflict society: pederasty." For example, when speaking of a coal merchant of Catania, the chief police officer wrote:

> A pimp addicted to the *most shameful sexual perversion*, pederasty, who has dragged unknowing and needy boys into this *vile trade*, profoundly offending all moral and ethical laws. . . . He has managed to found a real school that enables him to launch other pederasts in society, choosing them among needy and defenseless boys who turned to him for a few cigarettes or liras. (my italics)

The police thought that the pederasts were driven to solicit people around town to satisfy their "insane desires," giving serious scandal and threatening public health and morality. Particularly alarming was the spread of pederasty among youths, endangering their health and irreparably infecting them with this tremendous vice whose bad effects "not even science was capable of correcting." As the prefect wrote to the Minister of the Interior, these "despicable and immoral beings" were socially dangerous and therefore, "out of regard for the work of moral improvement that the Regime is carrying out," they should be sent to *confino* in order to wipe out this "breeding-ground of infection and corruption."[120]

The police stepped up their investigations in October 1937, after the murder of another wealthy homosexual, a case that was still unsolved after two years of investigations. Consequently, in 1939 Alfonso Molina, the new police chief of Catania, decided to intensify the repressive battle against pederasts, proposing fifty-three offenders for *confino*, forty-six of whom were accepted. Mussolini in person had agreed to send the first twenty "passive pederasts" of Catania to *confino*, intending to authorize the police to carry out further measures to clean up the town. As aforementioned, they were considered *confinati comuni*. However, since they were all sent to San Domino on the Tremiti islands, the Office for political detainees handled them.[121]

The fact that most of the Catanians given *confino* for homosexuality (in addition to Catania, the repression had involved Paterno, Adrano and Riposto as well) were "arrusi,"[122] who managed to find clients quite easily, testifies to the diffusion of male prostitution. Women's limited freedom, respect for honor, and the value of virginity, typical of Sicilian culture, made prematrimonial relationships between men and women difficult. Public life was reserved exclusively for men. In the absence of women, who were relegated to domestic life under the strict supervision of relatives, men sometimes ended up considering it perfectly natural to satisfy their sexual needs with youths ready to prostitute themselves for money or pleasure.[123] Thus, thanks also to the spread of what doctors called "pederasty as compensation" and what Gianni De Martino called "ethnic homosexuality,"[124] a hidden city had developed with special places for men only, as well as brothels for male prostitution. However, homosexuals only openly displayed their sexual tendency on particular occasions, for example, during carnival or dancing seasons, when some of them dressed as women, breaking the Fascist law that forbade the wearing of costumes in public.

In this particular situation, the police chief, Molina, had undertaken a real crusade against the homosexuals of his province. By promising immediate release, he was able to coerce those taken into custody into giving him the names of other pederast and lengthen the list to be submitted to the provincial commission for *confino*. From what one victim said, we can gather that quite often it was enough just to have met someone under investigation to risk being sent to a penal colony. "Can a person approach a pederast or is that an offense against decent behavior? Does that mean he is a pederast or that he will become one? Well then, half of Italy should be sent to *confino*, because I think that any honest citizen can meet a serious and correct pederast without being sullied by the same defect." The police chief certainly did not fall for such reasoning; there was proof that this teacher, who had fallen into the hands of the police, was guilty, because he had gone to a dance party in the home of someone considered a pederast.[125]

Besides, Molina had a lot of experience repressing homosexuality since his appointment as police chief of Salerno, he had gained the praise of the prefect for the efficiency with which he had dealt with prostitution and pederasty. The latter's report says that the manner in which he had increased preventive and repressive police measures against indecent behavior and in order to protect the family had been "intelligent and firm." Because of his vigilance against prostitution, against "idle people and vagabonds in order to defend population growth," he was appointed as head police chief of Salerno.[126] Molina then moved to Avellino, where he stayed until 1938 and where he continued his campaign against homosexuals as harshly and uncompromisingly as before, as demonstrated by the case of Salvatore M., a passive pederast called "Nanninella," with a criminal record for theft, soliciting, indecent behavior and corruption of minors, who had already been locked up in the Aversa insane asylum in 1932 for his "very serious sexual perversion." However, as soon as "Nanninella" was discharged from the mental home, he "took up his immoral life again, wandering through the streets, wearing his hair and behaving like a woman and urging youths to be licentious. Some of these latter caught venereal diseases from sexual intercourse with him." As a result, in May 1934, the police chief recommended he be given five years of *confino comune*, as "he had shown he had no intention of leading an honest life, and was, because of his immoral behavior, a danger to society and public security.[127]

These precedents partially explain the harshness of the repression carried out in Catania, where Molina had arrived in February 1938, to discover a vast and deep-rooted homosexual world, imbricated in the city's social structure. The police chief's ideas on the problem were very precise: pederasty was a kind of perversion that gave rise to male prostitution; in fact, pederasts were entirely similar to female prostitutes, even if they did not always live off this activity. Police reports on homosexuals depicted them as individuals who "practice a shameful vice and know all the tricks and arts of seduction, and who, like whores, are shameless and deceitful liars." They had the same "tendencies and lifestyles as prostitutes," ready "to do it like females," in order to satisfy "male desires." On the sidewalks of Via Etnea, in Piazza Roma, in the Quartiere Duomo, at Castello Ursino, in the Villa Bellini gardens, on the beach, or in the special dance hall in Piazza Sant'Antonio, the Catanian pederasts looked for clients they could take into dark streets, out-of-the-way places, or the countryside, for fear of the police. However well hidden this activity was, the police were convinced that pederasty was widespread enough to be a public threat, especially to those youths attracted by this sexual degeneracy. To the homophobic police chief, the cinemas and coffee shops already seemed 'infected' by pederasts and their admirers and clients who had invaded the city and who organized parties in private homes and places of entertainment, turning dance halls into "stock exchanges for the pricing of pederasts." Molina sent reports to the provincial commission for *confino*, where he explained in detail how homosexuality in Catania had passed from being a hidden practice to a public scandal:

> The scourge of pederasty in this province's capital is worsening and spreading because youths who were unsuspected up to now have turned out to be so taken by this form of sexual degeneracy, both passive and active, that they very often end up with venereal diseases. In the past, one rarely saw a pederast going to a coffee shop or dance hall or wandering around in crowded streets; even more rarely was he publicly accompanied by young lovers or clients. Before, pederasts and their admirers preferred lonely streets where they could avoid jibes and lewd comments; which were generally despised, not only by more timid homosexuals but also by those considered to be bold and unscrupulous but who were, after all, morally sound. Nowadays we can see that a lot of spontaneous and natural disgust has been overcome, and we must sadly admit that some coffee shops, dance halls, seaside and mountain resorts, according to the seasons, welcome these sick people, and that youths of all social classes publicly seek this company, preferring their love and thus becoming enfeebled and brutish.

Traditional repressive measures were no longer enough. Homosexuals had invented every possible ways of avoiding police checks:[128]

> Those who are able to set up small quarters that are furnished charmingly and invitingly, with resort to the most diverse expedients, not excluding theft, to find the means so that they, too, can have a hospitable place. Out of vanity or petty jealousy, they all brag about the conquests that they try to hang on to, at any cost. On the other hand, when the youths are not expressly invited, they are drawn to those houses, some out of curiosity, others by the temptation to smoke a free cigarette. After having seen it, all of them wanted to try it and afterwards, they always return. . . . Therefore I think it is essential to intervene with more drastic measures in the interest of public decency and the well-being of our race, so that the breeding-ground of this disease can be attacked and cauterized. In the absence of a particular law, we must resort, in the case of the more obstinate offenders, to the use of *confino*.

Faced with the imminent "spread of sexual degeneracy," the only remedy was to send all of the city's pederasts to *confino* for as long as possible, and since Molina had the last word on the provincial commission, they were inevitably convicted. Even though some declared themselves to be active pederasts, the obtuse mentality and rigid bureaucratic models led police officials to consider them all passive; not by chance, it was extremely difficult to classify homosexuals who were married with children. A shepherd from Cibali was considered "one of the most complicated cases of pederasty, just for this reason. As he is both active and passive, his pederasty may be considered acquired rather than rather than congenital, and is consequently more despicable for the fact that he is married. It is difficult to keep a check on him because he carries out his abominable activity in the Cibali suburb and in the country among his goats, following their example."[129] On the contrary, the clients of the male prostitutes, who were usually well-off and seemingly virile, ran no risk from the police measures because, being considered active, their only wrong-doing was in choosing degenerate individuals as the objects on which to vent to their masculine sexuality. Yet their impunity, besides discontenting the detainees,[130] encouraged the spread of male prostitution, which usually involved street-boys bought with cigarettes, sweets or a few liras. The result was that, despite the many repressive measures against passive pederasts, homosexuality had not yet been completely eradicated from Catania. Consequently, in 1940 Molina thought about eliminating all privileges. In his opinion, once "professional homosexuals" had been sent away, there was the danger that the remaining active ones would turned "their lust exclusively against youths who were inexperienced and not sufficiently protected and watched over, thus undoing the benefits" of the actions taken against passive pederasts. Molina's detailed report explained the strategy carried out by the police to charge active pederasts as well, suppressing pederasty once and for all:

> The serious problem of pederasty in this city was faced and resolved, in part, by sending a large number of passive pederasts to *confino*. However, to be able to declare that the city has been effectively cured, as provided for by the ministerial law of 14-1-1939, N. 10.11500, it was necessary to proceed against active pederasts as well, the so-called sexual exploiters of those degenerates—the perverted and depraved—who, as sexual anomalies, must be followed more closely by the police, both because their exploitation of youths for mere sadistic enjoyment is harmful and because it involves profit, blackmail and crime, and harms elderly people as well. In any case, it is certain that these degenerates break certain regulations of penal law, upset family peace and worry the police. . . . Now, all these perverts walking free can no longer be tolerated . . . with the intention of resolving this second aspect of the problem of "sexual anomalies," that afflicts this provincial capital, this office, while continuing investigations to round up other passive

pederasts, has decided to identify active pederasts and gather evidence confirming their specific and dangerous tendency.[131]

Nevertheless, very few active pederasts were actually sent to *confino*, as many of them were well-to-do people with the means necessary to bury the scandal, making it difficult for the police to gather proof and identify them "both because these active pederasts lack specific somatic features and recognizable, objective indications and because they are usually very cautious to avoid being discovered."

Consequently the story of the detainees of Catania is made up of poverty, "petty theft and prostitution; of ignorance, illiteracy, and interrogation statements signed with a mere cross; of hours and hours of work in the fields. It is also made up of love affairs, of the occasional late and drunken night. It is the story of a hidden world made up of particular streets, parks, dance halls, and special movie theaters."[132] It is the story of individuals forced to deny their own nature, to report their friends to the police, accept the fact that they are condemned and despised and beg for an act of mercy. What the police called the "primo-genitor of official pederasty" was a group of individuals who practiced passive pederasty "openly and without pretence," who knew each other, even if they preferred not to be seen together for fear of scandals, as they were well-known to the townspeople, almost all of them having feminine nicknames and behavior.

This circle of Catanian homosexuals who socialized with each other superficially was seen by the Fascists as a real danger, in part because they passed syphilitic diseases, but above all, because they broke up families and corrupted "young, sexually normal persons, thus harming the integrity of the race and morality."[133] There was a prevailing belief that a homosexual's experiences in adolescence, perhaps even a violent ones, led irremediably to being infected by this "vice." This belief was supported by personal stories of many passive pederasts of Catania, who had been subjected to sexual violence as children and who, since then, had "gradually and perhaps without realizing it, resigned themselves to their destiny." The police chiefs of Sondrio and Palermo as well were convinced that homosexuality was "a serious danger for the younger genera-tion."[134] Both were determined to root out "the shameful vice of pederasty" which undermined the Fascist educational plan to form new, strong and virile Italians, "degraded the nobility of the human race and represented a real social danger."[135]

The story of the Catanian detainees ended on May 28, 1940, when, on a proposal of the police chief and with the Duce's approval, it was decided to free the 56 pederasts on the island of San Domino and change the remaining sentence to two years of cautioning. The Fascist authorities were not driven by indulgent pity but by problems of overcrowding: when France was defeated it was decided to send more dangerous individuals than the homosexuals to San Domino, namely, the anti-Fascist Italians who had fought in Spain on the side of the republican army, and had been interned in French concentration camps at the end of the Spanish civil war.

The Catania affair is useful for understanding some of the attitudes and lifestyles of homosexuals that were common in the rest of Fascist Italy as well. Above all, we can understand their difficulty in finding places to get together freely without being criticized by neighbors and running into police surveillance. Their meeting places were either secret and private or completely impersonal, like streets and movie theaters, coffee shops and beaches, parks and public urinals. The public's widespread hostility and the fear of police repression drove them to defend their reputation by living in semi-secrecy. Specific areas emerged in many towns where homosexuals could approach and meet heterosexuals or solicit passers-by. These activities were more evident in big cities where less attention was given to individual behavior by the community, and where it was easier to be anonymous.

Paolo Valera wrote that by the end of the 1800s some public areas in Milan had already become meeting places for pederasts, for example "between the entrance to the *Galleria Vittorio Emmanuele* and the area around the *Duomo*": here "there was a host of boys and older youths who dressed with feminine care, eyeing passers-by and guessing which ones desired them. Their voices were effeminate, they called themselves Ernestina, Adalgisa, Edvige and Cleofe and their homes were open like those of prostitutes." Besides parks and streets there were private premises, hotels, restaurants and coffee shops for men only. In 1879 Valera wrote that "the followers of Oscar Wilde have been present in Milan for some time, and those who lead a society life know everything that goes on in these male alcoves."[136] More often than not these rooms were mixed rather than exclusive, as they received not only homosexual clients but bisexual and heterosexual ones as well. Differently from what happened in other European cities, there were not meeting places for homosexuals, owned by homosexuals and run by homosexuals, with homosexual employees and patronized exclusively by homosexuals,"[137] but meeting places where pederasts could find male partners, for the most part occasional.

Often these meeting places lacked refinement. In Catania, for example, after repressive police measures, the number of for-men-only dance halls dropped drastically; nevertheless, Don Pasqualino's was still open in 1929: "a bare hovel" where "women never enter" and where an out-of-tune organ plays popular dance music and the clients in rags and tatters dance among themselves, taking turns playing the parts of male or female."[138] The hall was a place where adults in search of homosexual relationships could meet needy youths who were very pleased to receive money and a bit of friendliness. "After dropping their fiancées off at home, the men" spent a brief moment of intimacy with pederasts in the Piazza Sant'Antonio dance hall, in a deconsecrated church, although it cost twenty cents for every dance. The "*arrusi*" knew they could find people looking for clients, lovers or steady boyfriends there.[139] The police were perfectly aware that the "perverts" of the city hung out there wearing cosmetics "to delight" the clients in the long hours of the night, and kept the place under close surveillance but held off closing it down until May 1939. The police knew that once this decision was taken, sidewalks, beaches, gardens and movie theaters would once again be filled with homosexuals and prostitutes, creating a much more obvious scandal. However, Catania was not an exceptional case. "At the beginning of the 1900s there was a 'club for ignoramuses' in Rome, while in other towns there were private rooms where one could enter only by showing a card or giving a secret password, or bars known only by those directly interested."[140] The dance hall in Gioiamia Street in Palermo was also well known. The youths there were willing to agree to "obscene homosexual proposals" and "females were absent from the scene."[141]

The existence of these places should also be understood in relation to the repressive sexual morality reserved for women, who were rigorously confined to the home, especially in the evening. Even the Fascists' attempt to mobilize women in southern Italy was blocked by family bonds and the persistence of a traditional idea of women that prevented their participation in public life.[142] This mentality considered sexual intercourse with another man as a sort of substitute for heterosexual intercourse, or as a fleeting and episodic experience, a simple interlude in a person's normal life. In fact, pederasts nearly always had sex with men who were married or with children and who did not consider themselves homosexuals or bisexuals; on the contrary they considered themselves, real, virile males. As in the case of female prostitutes, paying for a service banished even the suspicion of possible sentimental involvement. Convinced that an active role did not compromise one's virility and consequently one's heterosexuality, contributed to preventing deep and lasting relationships based on love and reciprocal respect from forming and fostered unequal relationships with the passive partner, whose only function was to be an object of pleasure, subordinate to and dominated by the active partner. Therefore, steady couples rarely formed, even though some more affluent active partners sometimes kept their lovers close, as cooks or servants.

This rigid division between active and passive pederasts, between virile and effeminate men, was particularly widespread and part of the police's mentality as well. Therefore, sexually passive males who inverted their nature were to be punished, not homosexuals in general. It was not forbidden for men to love each other; the problem lay in their confusing of the sexual roles. The pederasts themselves did not consider their "lovers" homosexuals but "persons who prefer men" or "men who prefer pederasts." This also explains why this universe of persecuted men, which never publicly protested against its repression, never formed a spirit that might have led to the establishment of a collective subject. Pederasty in Catania continued to be "a matter of custom rather than a sign that the personal freedom of a group affirming itself in the face of the coercive limits of an ethical model imposed by the myth of race and procreation."[143]

Venice and Florence

What happened in Venice and Florence was, in some ways, unique compared to Catania. Both cities attracted an influx of foreigners, adding notably to the number of cases of pederasty. Despite the atmosphere of moral severity established by Fascism, Italy's tradition as a destination for homosexual tourism, which dated back to the age of the *Grand Tour*, had made these places famous abroad as paradises for "eccentric love affairs."[144] Venice, in particular, attracted many tourists because it was easy to find poor young men, willing to subject themselves to homosexual relationships. Financial needs and emotions mingled in relationships somewhere between prostitution and love. In Thomas Mann's masterpiece, *Death in Venice,* this latent pederasty, disguised as a search for artistic inspiration in the beauty the lagoon is interpreted from a decadent perspective. Indeed, a great number of Gustav von Aschenbachs traveled from Germany to Venice in search of young boys whose appearance recalled "the Greek sculptures of nobler times." The reincarnation of the classical aesthetics could be found in some "mortal youths" who, like Tadzio with his "lithe and youthfully perfect body," embodied the divine work of art and "the very essence of beauty."[145]

   Many homosexual intellectuals went to Venice, staying there either on a permanent basis or for short periods, including the aesthetes Jean Lorrain and Jean Cocteau, the poets August von Platen and Alfred Edward Housman, the renaissance historian John Addington Symonds, and many others.[146] One such visitor, the English writer Frederich Rolfe, known as "Baron Corvo" or "Baron Crow," who lived on the lagoon in the early twentieth century and carried out conspicuous relationships with young gondoliers, left a vivid description of how widespread and, to a certain degree, organized this homosexual tourism was. Not only were Italian youths very willing to satisfy foreigners' desires with the prospect of earning a bit of money, but an illegal brothel where tourists could always find students or unemployed youths "ready for use" was available as well.[147] Everybody knew about this trafficking. In fact, in 1908 during an anti-Austrian demonstration, some Venetians attacked the "round table house"

patronized by many Germans.[148] Although the police had begun arresting
youths "who practiced pederasty for profit" as early as 1911, measures against
the spread of male prostitution were not fully implemented until the Fascists
came to power. In 1925 the Blackshirts raided "a secret gathering of pederasts,
who met in the building of one of them," causing the police to intervene.[149] In
1927 and 1929 there had been two other roundups, leading to numerous homosexuals being sentenced to *confino comune*. Their stories are particularly significant
because a few months after their sentences had been served, they were given
confino again for five more years, and were freed only in 1939, in some cases in
1940.

According to the police, they were pederasts who prostituted themselves
with foreigners and, despite police surveillance, persisted "in their shameful
and loathsome degeneracy." In order to solicit more effectively they even dressed
as women or wore makeup and went to tourist meeting places, such as Piazza
San Marco and the Lido of Venice. Through confidential sources, the police
learned of cases of blackmailing and theft carried out against foreigners who
had had sex with these "degenerates" in hotels and rooms rented for the purpose.
Police investigations revealed a proper organization run by an Eritrean who
procured youths or sailors willing to practice "the foul trade" and who were
paid sums ranging from one to two hundred liras, not counting the extras they
could obtain by blackmailing their rich clients. This extortion and theft went
unpunished because the victims did not report them. When the homes of the
various homosexuals arrested were searched, ambiguous letters were found, as
well as photographs with the names and addresses of the foreigners and of the
other members of the group that proved how varied their clients were, mainly
foreigners and important Italian personalities. Some of these male prostitutes
periodically received money from their well-to-do admirers: for example, the
famous Italian artist Filippo De Pisis sent sums from Paris to one of the boys
in the group. Members of the aristocracy and the armed forces were involved
in the scandal as well; many of them had kept young lovers and paid them
handsomely. The police action involved various people, yet only those who
were considered guilty of pederasty for profit and those who encouraged prostitution, like the two brothers employed at the Grande bathing establishment
who rented out the cabins for lovers' meetings, were sent to *confino*. Only in one
case was an important Venetian nobleman, under surveillance since 1924 because
of his suspected "sexual degeneracy," sentenced to *confino*. Well-known pederasts
who had meetings at his place for "homosexual practices" had reduced him to
poverty. Consequently, in September 1927 the prefect of Venice decided to send
him to a *confino* for delinquents for two years and, in view of his social position,
sent him to Breganze in the province of Vicenza.[150]

After completing their sentence and returning to Venice, the former detainees, still under close surveillance, proved not to be "redeemed" and continued to frequent "circles where the vice prevailed and took to committing illicit offenses."[151] The sex trade flourished as before on the Riva degli Schiavoni or around the public urinals, and just as before, the clients who fell into the pederasts' clutches were often robbed or blackmailed, without ever reporting it to the police to avoid publicity. Thus continued the corruption of young adolescents who had been initiated into pederasty to satisfy the requests of foreigners. In 1934 another roundup led to *confino* for old and new homosexuals, accused, as always, of practicing pederasty for profit, of creating scandal, and of hindering the measures taken by the state authorities to protect public health and morality and to safeguard the race. As aforementioned, the pederasts who had already been sentenced in 1927 were therefore destined to spend ten years in the penal colonies. One servant nicknamed "Norma," who was given *confino* in 1927 and then in 1934, spent a total of thirteen years as a detainee, including several months in a solitary confinement cell for committing acts of passive pederasty.[152]

However, "due to a resurgence in the spread of pederasty, not only among the foreigners, who were temporary or permanent residents but also among locals," the police had to extend their interventions. Indeed, investigations had revealed that besides the local youths, even "previous offenders from other provinces gathered in Venice during the bathing season to solicit the foreigners given to pederasty." In the summer of 1935, two Milanese couples who practiced prostitution and theft at the same time were caught by the police: while one accompanied the person he had solicited to a room, the other entered the room furtively and robbed him.[153] In another case, in 1936, a Venetian servant whose relationship with a rich married Austrian man had caused the latter's wife to protest strongly, as she was unable to prevent her husband's "scandalous" meetings, was eventually sentenced to *confino* after having had his passport confiscated out of fear that he would flee to Austria, following the multiple invites to Innsbruck extended to him.[154] Another young servant who worked for a German baron, accompanying him on his trips around Italy, met the same end: a conscript doing military service, he was imprisoned by the army while he awaited news of the military command's sentence. However, on Mussolini's orders, it was decided to send him to *confino* for passive pederasty.[155] Another offensive against homosexuality came in December 1937, when six pederasts and their landlord were arrested in a brothel after an impromptu inspection during the night, after which they were sent to *confino*.[156]

All in all, the repression of pederasty in Venice involved a large number of people. It was important for the Fascists to defend the prestige of the city, which was a reflection on the regime for those who visited: "this indecent activity, sometimes often practiced without restraint, seriously damaged the good name and dignity of the townspeople, because these youths usually frequented the best meeting areas and the centers of Venice and the Lido." Venice, where art, culture, and society life merged, had to rid itself of its unpleasant reputation as an attraction for pederasts from all over the world. Moreover, homosexuality, as it encouraged crimes that frequently went unpunished because they were un-reported, was considered a threat to public safety.

There were numerous victims in Florence as well, where, above all, from the middle of the 1930s on, the police intensified their investigations of homo-sexual circles seeking to discover those responsible for some cases of extortion and theft.[157] The prefect of Florence summed up the police action against pederasty in three different reports titled *Prevenzione e repressione della pederastia e adozione di provvedimenti di polizia a carico di pederasti* (The Prevention and Repression of Pederasty and the Adoption of Police Measures against Pederasts), stamped with the phrase *"Presi gli ordini da S.E. il Capo del Governo"* (orders received from His Excellency the head of government), which meant that the whole file had been brought to the personal attention of Mussolini. The results of the investiga-tions were described in detail in a series of reports that are worth quoting to understand how profoundly loathed homosexuals were. In the first report dated December 3, 1936, the prefect wrote:

> Recently, following the orders of the police chief, discreet investigations have been carried out concerning some individuals given to idleness and suffering from serious psychosexual depravation. Numerous people, well known in the evil circle of pederasts and all of whom are morally dangerous for society and public security, were identified. During these investigations sexually perverted psychopaths, who up to recently were unknown to the police, were identified. . . . Attracted by easy earnings out of greed and lacking any moral conscience, they were indulging in the most complicated sexual inversions and perversions as well as the most vulgar exhibitions of prostitution. This kind of prostitution made up of dominators and domi-nated, who are given to homosexual relationships and are variously dangerous, has turned out to be so widespread and deeply rooted that it escapes repression by punitive justice. This is both because the dominator can always count on the congenital or diseased homosexual's tacit complicity, as he is obliged to keep silent so as not to reveal his own depravation, and because those who manage to hide their degenerate activity are cunning.

The police managed to identify a group of about thirty "homosexual psycho-paths" whose leader was a former *carabiniere*, "an extremely dangerous, active and passive pederast, and an exploiter of pederasts." According to the police chief, he was a pimp who exploited the sexual abnormalities of others and later blackmailed his own clients. He lived together with "several psychopaths whom he exploited" and a young lover with whom he was "morbidly" in love, to the point of jealousy. They "regularly organized obscene gatherings" in this house; besides the group of "inverts," many wealthy people—industrialists, hotel owners, doctors, noblemen, teachers, artists and booksellers—attended. Relationships were not only between prostitutes and rich clients. There were some homosexual couples with stable and lasting relationships as well. For the police they were a group of antisocial individuals who were dangerous for public morality and security because their sexual perversion often gave rise to theft, extortion and even murder. Close surveillance of these areas would prevent crimes and create advantages "of a specifically political-social nature by removing elements that were physically and morally infectious and harmful and by purging society of those who weaken the body and morals of young people." The report ended with a list of the eugenic advantages of careful preventive action:

> To strengthen, defend and ameliorate our race, it is necessary to fight the
> various causes of individual and collective degeneracy: the Fascist govern-
> ment, then, rightly attributes great importance to discipline implemented
> through force and social reclamation in its general effort to prevent
> criminality. This is accomplished by repressing environments that foster
> the development of crime and by preparing suitable preventive measures
> in an effort to increasingly improve our race.

Consequently the former *carabiniere* was sent to *confino* and despite his repeated requests for clemency and his past with the military police force, was forced to serve all the five years of the sentence.[158] His young lover suffered a similar fate: he, too, was registered as a sexual pervert who "thanks to his good looks, made friends and entered into relationships with foreign passive pederasts and upper class men for money." Fourteen other people of the group were cautioned and five just warned.

After this first operation, the investigations continued and three other men were given *confino* in 1937. Later, on January 30, 1938, the prefects report spoke of further repressive measures. He boasted to have discovered a group of

> unsuspected homosexuals who were above suspicion up to now because
> apart from their particular behavior in sexual intercourse, there was nothing
> abnormal about them. Many of them are young men, who have already
> been corrupted by these filthy relationships and who exploit the vices of
> other degenerates for money.

In all there were 38 individuals, who "suffered from serious psychosexual depravation, all of whom were morally corrupt and given to satisfying their shameful lust, whatever form it took." Even though "certain" proof that pederasty was practiced "not only as a vice but as a real trade" had been gathered about only a few of these individuals and although "there was nothing exceptional about the behavior of some of them, apart from the sexual aspect of their lives," it was, in any case, necessary and urgent to apply severe police measures in the name of "social therapy." The measures ranged from *confino* to warning and cautioning, depending on how dangerous these men "given to homosexual practices due to natural tendency or vice," were considered."[159] One of the detainees was an electrician, Giovanni B., called "Diana." He was married with two children and was well known in Florence for his "brazen display of degeneracy." According to the police chief, "Diana" was actually a sexually perverted psychopath suffering from passive pederasty who had "scandalous" relationships with men his age, whom he even approached in public places. "To be more attractive and fascinating," the police chief added, "he usually wore women's underwear, like his wife's silk stockings and panties in order to create, through his hybrid passivity, a double erotic sensation in the persons he has unnatural intercourse with, especially when they are active pederasts."[160]

Once again the police chief portrays homosexuals as passive, "hybrids" somewhere between men and women who, because of their hybrid nature, were able attract males. The pederasts profoundly introjected this idea; it was not by chance that sexual inversion was quite widespread. There were many homosexuals who tried to imitate women, almost as if they were looking for their place in a society where being virile or feminine was defined in distinctly heterosexual terms. The social stereotype of a homosexual was someone who refused his own virility and inverted his nature, taking on the features of the opposite gender. As Barbagli and Colombo have pointed out, it is a middle road between classical pederasty and modern homosexuals; in the 1930s pederasts did not have their own sexual identity, they borrowed it from women, also because they thought feminine clothes, features and behavior, and moving like a woman might more easily attract partners. However, it was a forced choice; by denying homosexuality, the prevailing culture forced homosexuals to conform to the only genders permitted: masculine and feminine. In the first case, one's homosexuality was repressed, in the latter it was made to conform to a female role. Sexual inversion resulted from this impossibility of understanding one's personal identity, from the need to "to interpret one's feelings and homoerotic desires within the framework of available categories.[161]

The Florentine electrician Giovanni B., who attempted to defend himself with the same criteria of judgment used to accuse him, is an emblematic case. With concrete evidence, he tried to demonstrate his virility. He rejected every feminine trait and mentioned his courage in war and his capacity to procreate, all of which were male characteristics. Although he admitted to having had homosexual leanings in his youth, he claimed to have made a great effort to mend his ways by taking part in the conflict in eastern Africa and by getting married and having children. Conjugal life and affection with his wife must have been enough to make the accusation inconceivable. What was more, there was no genetic precedent since no relative of his had ever "suffered from these physiological disorders."; nor did he have "the somatic features usually found in well-known pederasts: the way he walks and moves, his voice and the expression in his eyes all belong to a healthy man, like everybody else."[162] Cultural conditioning was strong enough to produce a conflict between a person's own sexual tendency and the gender role attributed to him by society. The effects of social disapproval of those who did not conform to this role triggered such a strong guilt complex that homosexuals were driven to be as "normal" as possible, to attempt to reconcile the irreconcilable, observing all the standards of virility even at the cost of denying their own identity. The only possible choice for homosexuals was to conform to the role of the dominating gender or to freely express their own sexuality and run up against public censure and repression.

In the summer of 1939, in Florence, keeping a watch on and repressing people suspected of suffering from "the degeneracy of pederasty" produced good results, as the prefect wrote in his self-satisfied report on August 16, 1939. Even though immoral behavior persisted on occasion, investigations had led to the arrest and sentencing to *confino* of a group of very young boys who hung around the areas near the Parco delle Cascine and the outskirts of the city where they practiced active pederasty on individuals "suffering from psychosexual degeneracy of a passive type," managing to extort small sums of money from them by threatening to reveal their degeneracy.[163] Despite this case, the harshest police measures were nevertheless meted out to passive pederasts in Florence as well, no matter if they were married with children. The law was more indulgent toward active pederasts who occasionally practiced pederasty for money, persuaded to do so by those "traffickers in pederasts who usually exploited the insane desires of well-to-do perverts by putting them in contact with active pederasts." There were many wealthy people among those involved, personalities prominent in the community who, thanks to their social position, could have a good word put in for them, thus avoiding police measures or managing to receive better treatment.

Such was the case of a rich man of property and hotel owner, named Vittorio B., who had already been sentenced to three months of imprisonment for indecent behavior and given five years of *confino* in 1938. He was accused of being "passive pederast who had led an immoral and scandalous life for many years, taking advantage of his wealthy financial situation to have loathsome relationships with youths who, attracted by easy money, were coerced by him to satisfy his vile lust." This rich gentleman had immediately appointed an attorney who was an expert in issues regarding homosexuality, a certain Agostino Mormino,[164] and who immediately drew up a letter against the sentence of *confino* to send to the appeals commission. The letter pointed out that Vittorio B.'s behavior

> had never offended public morality as his relationships, which are now heavily criticized, have always been of a completely private nature and limited to one or two persons. Consequently it is not a matter of continuous acts of corruption, carried out in public and with persons who do not suffer from the same illness. Everything the petitioner is reproached for has been absolutely private. For this reason and for his illness (diabetes), may the commission, whose members are nobly and benevolently magnanimous, deliver an absolutely merciful decision that completely overrules that of the Florentine commission. For his part, the petitioner formally promises that from now on, his conduct will be beyond reproach, free of perversion or abnormality.

However, the appeal was rejected, as its justifications were interpreted as further proof of guilt: even if Vittorio B.'s perverted behavior was due to a physical abnormality, he was not to be considered any less dangerous for public morality. Mormino then did his best to have his client transferred to a colony on the mainland, closer to Rome and less severe than the Tremiti islands. Thanks to the editor of the *Popolo di Roma* who put in a good word for him, he was able to achieve this in the summer of 1938.[165]

Ottone Rosai, the well-known Florentine artist, was much more famous than the hotel owner Vittorio B., yet he ended up in the clutches of the police as well; despite his adherence to Fascism, his *squadrista* and *teppista* past, and his tall and strong grenadier build, all of which should have been a fairly secure cover for "his profound but irregular relationships."[166]

Reported to the police as a passive pederast by his young lovers themselves, who declared he had "continuous abnormal intercourse" with them, nevertheless Rosai managed to escape arrest. Because they had not found serious enough probative elements to confirm his "psychosexual depravity" and because this "highly esteemed artist, of high literature culture" led a very withdrawn life, the *carabiniere* thought they should simply warn him. So on February 24, 1938, his party card was confiscated but he did not receive a legal warning. The prefect sent a note to the Ministry of the Interior at the beginning of March, explaining why he had been so indulgent: no measure had been taken "also keeping in mind Rosai's record as a former serviceman decorated for military valor and his having been a Fascist of the "first hour," as well as the distinction he had acquired as an artist." Three years later, the prefect returned to Rosai's case in a note sent to Buffarini Guidi, referring once again to his "past that was not entirely limpid either morally or politically," and pointed out that, also thanks to his "intimate relationships with some local personalities, he had been able to obtain recognition of higher worth with a special appointment as Professor."[167]

Another fortunate homosexual with connections was Ugo S., a "Fascist of the first hour" who had already been suspended from the NFP in 1929 on the grounds that he was a moral disgrace to the party but had then been readmitted in 1932 with the justification that "groundless accusations" had been level against him. Sentenced in March 1937 to five years of *confino* because he was believed to be an active and passive pederast, he was acquitted after just two months thanks to his influential acquaintances and the intervention of his friend, the prefect Giovanni Battista Marziali, the one who was really behind Ugo S.'s successful career.[168] Alberto M., important party official and former political secretary of the Fascist Party of Grenoble, was, on the contrary, less fortunate. Police investigations had turned up "evidence that left no doubts" about his passive pederasty. Warned in February 1938, Alberto M. had turned to the senator Dino Perrone Compagni who, however, was unable to prevent the issuing of a warning for Alberto M., nor the confiscation of his party card. Senator Alfredo Di Frassineto, also intervened, without success, on the part of Alberto M., begging the police chief Arturo Bocchini "to take the petitions of the former Fascist Party secretary of Grenoble into benevolent consideration." Despite his influential acquaintances, his *squadrista* past and his longtime devotion to Fascism,[169] he had not yet managed to be accepted back in the NFP in July 1940. However, the former party official did not give in: in a statement to Bocchini, he enumerated his merits as a Fascist, animated by faith and veneration for the Duce, and appended a list of important personalities ready to give ample information on his incorruptible morality, but also on his "constant and marked love of the fair sex that has given me a reputation as a womanizer as well as chivalrous disputes and quite serious diseases." Not even this time did he manage to convince the authorities, also because there was new proof of his "psychopathic abnormality," in fact he had escaped a severer sentence only because the father of one of his young victims did not report him to the police.

Special Cases

Catania, Venice, and Florence are examples that give us a good overall picture of the atmosphere during Fascism. However, it is worth dwelling upon some single cases as well, as they give a greater understanding of the Fascist policy regarding homosexuals. One of these concerns a Vercelli milkman,[170] who was under police observation because of his "extremely cordial friendship" with an

alleged pederast, the owner of a movie theater where he had been employed
for some years. Although the police investigations did not manage to gather
concrete proof of the milkman's perverse activities, the fact that "many people
believed he had homosexual relationships" was deemed sufficient reason to
take police measures against him. It was taken for granted that, in the room at
the back of the milk-shop, he committed "lustful acts with local youths afflicted
with the same vice, some of whom he himself had corrupted and set on the
road to homosexual prostitution." Without proof or charges made by those
concerned, and since the acts had occurred in places that were not open to the
public, it was impossible to start criminal proceedings. Nevertheless, in the
name of public morality, the poor milkman was cautioned and his shop closed
down. This was still not enough: on Mussolini's direct orders he was given a three-
year sentence of *confino* at San Domino and, as he had no criminal precedents,
his file was recorded among those of the political detainees.[171]

As we have seen, homosexuals were often easy prey for extortionists because,
in order to hide their own "crime," they ended up paying the people who blackmailed them. For example, Pietro P. was sacked by the director of the National
Agency for School Assistance (L'Ente nazionale per la mutualità scolastica)
where he was employed as a cashier, because he had stolen large sums of money.
The investigations revealed that he had been led to stealing by some ex-convicts
with whom he had had sexual intercourse and who had repeatedly threatened
him and asked him for money. According to the commander of the *carabinieri* of
Rome, although Pietro P. was married and had three children he suffered from
pederasty, something he had acquired while in prison during the First World
War. In order to avoid having "his unnatural sexual intercourse" and "his
abnormal state as a passive pederast," revealed, he had been forced to steal
money to pay his blackmailers, and had even attempted suicide out of desperation. He was saved from prison by a rich uncle who paid back the stolen money in
part together with the president of the National Agency for School Assistance,
Agostino Lanzillo himself, who covered the story up so as not to discredit the
agency with the scandal of a public trial. However, since he was considered
capable of committing crimes in order to satisfy his homosexual desires, Pietro P.
was sentenced with *confino* in June 1934, while criminal proceedings were started
against his extortionists. The report of the Political Police's (Polizia Politica)
informers on the affair reveals significant opinions on pederasts:

> The band of pederasts to whom Pietro P., employee of School Assistance,
> generously paid such large sums, has been sent up for trial by the courts of
> Rome for the crime of extortion. P. is taking civil action against the pederasts.
> The distressing display of pederasty is spreading: Alfredo F. who is known

to be a expert on this activity, explains that it is widely practiced in Venice, Turin and Milan, places and centers he often visits as a variety artist. When asked which social class was afflicted with this disease, he answered that all classes have active and passive subjects; that the affluent pay handsomely for these services. Considering the sums paid by Pietro P. for his sexual affairs, the question arises spontaneously: where did he get the money? The answer will promptly be given. The police have put their finger on an extremely important problem. Our nation must not be infected by this foul vice. We're merely at the beginning of an exceptionally disgusting phenomenon.[172]

Confino did not, however, help to cure the treasurer of his "foul vice"; he was transferred to five different places because he continued to raise suspicion by keeping company with young boys.[173] Those who were guilty of extortion were given *confino* as well, because they were acquitted at their trial for insufficient proof. One of these was the aforementioned variety artist, Alfredo F., who performed in women's clothes. He had been cautioned before for passive pederasty and was thought to be responsible for the suicide of the sacristan of the church of Santo Spirito, from whom he had continued to extort money after having had an intimate relationship with him. Alfredo F. acknowledged he was "afflicted with passive pederasty" and openly declared he sometimes felt "the need to have sexual intercourse with active males." However, he noted that if homosexuality were reason enough for a serious security measure like *confino*, then "the islands used for this purpose would be chock-full of sick persons, because famous psychiatrists have proved that homosexuals are ill, and very often suffer terribly because of their illness." Despite his self-defense, in October 1934 he was sentenced to *confino* for five years, first on the island of Lampedusa and then Ustica where, once again accused of obscene acts and breaking the rules, he was destined to stay until January 3, 1941.[174]

In the case of a farmer from Voghera sent to *confino* in 1940 by the provincial commission of Pavia, the accusation of homosexuality was prompted by political motives as well. The unfortunate man was not only accused of being afflicted with passive pederasty, but of criticizing the regime and the militia, particularly the Fascist demographic policy. When talking with some young soldiers, he had foolishly said that there were too many people in Italy, that there was not enough room for everybody, and that big families were in financial difficulty. This conversation was repeated in the barracks and reported to the officers, who held it to be a clear sign of defeatism and antinationalism. Once the police were informed of what had happened, they intervened immediately, and after verifying that the incautious "chatterbox" had also tried to solicit the soldiers because he was afflicted with passive pederasty, they recommended police measures. The provincial commission decided that this amoral individual who had spoken against the regime just to "fulfill his depraved desire," should be given *confino* at once and sent to Pisticci to do manual labor as part of the Fascist *bonifica* campaign.[175]

The crime of pederasty was combined with political motivations in the case of Otello A. as well: "defamation of the race." Having arrived in eastern Africa in 1935 where he opened an eating-house, Otello A. had "lost all sense of morality and had indulged passively in acts of pederasty." And what was more, he had carried them out with a native with whom he had a turbulent relationship, at least judging from the trial. In fact, he himself sued young Abraha G. for insulting and threatening him. After being arrested, the native declared he had hurled a bottle at Otello as a reaction because he was no longer willing to satisfy Otello's desires for passive pederasty.[176] Thus thorough investigations were begun to decide whether it was necessary to bring the Italian home because of his depraved instincts. The relationship between the two lovers was well known to the white and Eritrean community. The police organized an ambush to catch the two lovers in the act. One evening in December 1937, two police officers lay in wait in front of Otello's house. Abraha soon arrived and entered. At that point the officers informed the commander of the Adi Ugri company to send men to the house in the middle of the night and knock repeatedly on the door. "Otello was frightened and asked what was up, and when he was answered "police," he said to wait a moment while he lit a candle." On the contrary, in the few seconds he had, he tried to let the young Eritrean escaped through the back door, but an officer was waiting there for him armed with a pistol and arrested the two lovers. Consequently Otello A. was sent back to Italy and sentenced to only two years of *confino*, as his past as a good Fascist was taken into consideration.[177]

In other cases, the police managed to discover a group of homosexuals by pure chance. In the spring of 1938, following investigations of a theft at the municipal gas company of Genoa, the police discovered that an employee of the company had a photograph of one of his colleagues, Francesco C., in women's clothes. The police superintendent, who boasted that he had "studied forensic medicine and psychology, immediately summoned the suspect to the police station and after interrogating him, was convinced of his homosexuality: "it was enough to look him in the face to be convinced that this suspect was undoubtedly a passive pederast." The police superintendent immediately invited the suspect "to give him the name of the first priest who had raped him," because experience had led him to be absolutely sure of this particular as well. Seeing the accused's reticence, the officer threaten to enter him in the police records, "officially registering him as a pederast" and warned, at the same time promising to save him and eliminate his file only after he confessed his crime. The unfortunate Francesco C. therefore declared his homosexuality; however, to his great surprise, within a few days he was served a police warning and dismissed from the Fascist business union. His heated protests were totally ignored as was the appeal he sent to Mussolini together with the medical certificates of three specialists who vouched for "the absence of any feminine features or signs of passive pederasty in the subject." On the contrary, in July, the prefect wrote to the Ministry of the Interior that "following the instructions given by this Honorable Ministry to repress the degenerating phenomenon of pederasty, more serious police measures are being taken against Francesco C."[178]

However, in some cases *confino* was a light punishment in relation to the crimes committed. This was particularly common in the case of influential, wealthy, and well-known citizens who managed to avoid being reported to the police, evaded trials and possible sentences by receiving support from the upper echelons of the regime. Such was the case with a rich attorney from Molfetta, considered "a really dangerous and habitual pederast" who, "by corrupting people and giving them generous amounts of money," always managed to conceal his "crimes against public morality and his evil deeds." After managing, once again, to stop the parents of a little boy he had raped from taking legal action, by paying them five thousand liras, the prefect of Bari decided to present the matter to the provincial commission that sentenced him to five years of *confino* in October 1937. At this point the plea in his favor by the president of the Court of Assizes of Brescia was useless because Bocchini decided that on this occasion "it was impossible to show clemency to such a filthy wretch."[179] In other cases *confino* was used to set an example "to curb those who abandon themselves to indecent and unseemly practices" to the detriment of their social position and the moral aims pursued by the regime. It was exactly for this reason that the administrative director of the *Gazzetta del Mezzogiorno*, who had never had any problems with the police, was given *confino* for practicing "acts of pederasty with a soldier, where the airman had been played the male role."[180]

The story of Domenico R., a young salesman at a lottery stall in Salerno, who was sentenced to five years of *confino* for passive pederasty, is different. The police declared him "fully aware of his filthy tendency. Instead of correcting it, he is content in letting it dominate him, and encourages it in every way. He has no restraint over his obscene and wanton ways that he displays in public, thus emphasizing his degeneration even more." When his request to join the PNF was rejected with the reason that his sexual tendencies were "a real danger for the moral health of the race," Domenico R. openly challenged the accusations, also criticizing the claim that homosexuality was harmful to national interests.

His opinion did not change in *confino*, where he continued to denounce the contradiction between the regime's determination to redeem those affected by pederasty and the decision to keep them all together on islands purposely reserved for them.[181] A post office clerk from Pola had similarly rebellious reaction. He disputed the sentence of *confino* that he had received as a result of his relationship with a sailor, claiming it was illegitimate. In his opinion, pederasty did not justify applying police measures since only in a broad interpretation did the code expressly define pederasty as a threat to national interests or an act of hostility against the State. Therefore only cases involving slander and notorious pederasts were punishable, but even in this case *confino* was excessive, since these individuals were surely not a danger to public security. His reasoning was in some ways accepted by the Appeal's commission that decided to reduce his *confino* sentence to just six months. He was, however, immediately fired from his job at the post office.[182]

The case of Luigi M., known as "the sissy" ("a femminella"), is quite sad. At the age of fifty-two, having asked in vain for medical treatment, he died in *confino*. He had committed a long series of offenses and had already been warned a number of times,[183] and in February 1938 had been given *confino* for five years by the provincial Board of Naples because he was believed to be a passive pederast who, considering his age and the fact that he was "no longer able to offer himself," had organized a "trade of underage men." This "sordid activity," aimed at offering young boys to rich clients, was aided by some accomplices who had the job of proposing homosexual meetings to pederasts, preferably foreigners passing through the town. "*Femminella*" acted as a go-between in the Umberto I Arcade, offering his own home for money. He was subjected to close surveillance by the police, who managed to arrest him at his home. He and one of his accomplices were given *confino*, while the father of the underage boy was warned to check his son's behavior more regularly. When Luigi M., who was seriously ill, was in *confino* on the island of Lampedusa, he requested special medicine free of charge, but only received a generic one, similar to what had been prescribed. In October 1939 he suffered a cerebral thrombosis that left him paralyzed on the right side of his body. The many letters his sister sent to the Ministry of the Interior asking for a pardon or transfer for this elderly man, who was now ill and paralyzed, were of no effect. Only on December 7, 1939, in the jail in Agrigento where he had been taken for a medical examination, it was established that he was too seriously ill to endure *confino*. However, by then it was too late. He died there, barely two days after his medical examination.[184]

Priests, on the other hand, were given special treatment: after informing the *Direzione generale culti* (General Administration of Religions), the police recorded the facts regarding *immoral priests* separately, and once they were sent to *confino*, they were almost always considered political detainees.[185] The case of Father Rodolfo S. is quite interesting. He was accused of an indecent assault on a minor, while being himself the victim of extortion by someone who had found out about it, a certain Alessandro P., who had threatened to tell the pope and the editor of the daily *Il Piccolo* what had happened and had managed to receive large sums of money from the priest. To avoid the scandal of a public trial, the affair was settled by sending Alessandro P. to *confino comune* on the island of Lampedusa and the priest to one for political detainees on one of the Tremiti islands. Father Rodolfo very soon became the new parish priest of the islands and thus also a member of the disciplinary board of the colony, a position that permitted him to decide the punishments for his own fellow-sufferers. However, he was definitively freed, following the recommendation of the bishop of Fiume.[186]

From the many files regarding the use of *confino* for repressing pederasty, the cases of three Milanese men are particularly important for understanding the attitude of Fascism toward homosexuality. Arturo Z., his brother-in-law Pietro C and Abele S. were arrested in Germany in 1935 because they were suspected of illegally smuggling currency. However, when they were tried, it emerged during the hearing that Abele S. and Arturo Z. had gone to Germany together, bound by a homosexual relationship. Unaware that the German penal code expressly provided for the offense of pederasty, the couple openly declared the nature of their relationship and were immediately accused of this new crime. They then naively defended themselves by stating their ignorance of the law and proceeded to "disgustingly, in a way that was unworthy of every Italian," proclaim that not only homosexuality was not forbidden by law in Italy, but it was officially condoned and practiced in all social classes. Having escaped a sentence at the trial thanks to the intervention of a consul who had taken steps to prevent "serious damage to the prestige of the nation," the two artless Milanese men were sent back home and, on Mussolini's orders, were sentenced to three years of *confino* "for making fallacious and slanderous statements about the Italian nation to foreign judges."[187] The same fate befell the third member of the group, Pietro C., who after being judged to be mentally unbalanced, was sent to a mental home when he returned to Italy after serving his sentence in Germany.[188] This tragicomic affair clearly shows that the absence of a specific article concerning homosexuality in the Rocco Code did not exclude the offense; on the contrary it was a crime so harmful to the prestige of the nation and so serious that not even the laws were to mention it.

Fascist action squads from La Spezia on the occasion of the March on Rome, October 1922. (Central State Archive, Rome, Mostra della Rivoluzione Fascista, b. 148, Authorization 1223.43.10)

Right: Souvenir postcard from the regional assembly of the Italian Fasci di Combattimento, Emilia-Romagna, 1921. (Central State Archive, Rome, Mostra della Rivoluzione Fascista, b. 190, Authorization 1223.43.10)

FASCI ITALIANI DI COMBATTIMENTO

ADVNATA REGIONALE EMILIA - ROMAGNA

"German male pederast." (in Cesare Lombroso, "Album criminale germanico," Lombroso Museum, Turin)

Left: Stadio dei Marmi. (photos by Anthony Majanlahti)

La rivista del generale : L'armata è una gran famiglia. Voi siete tutti miei nipoti !

(*Le Rire* - Parigi)

"The Homosexual Army." The caption reads: "The General's Review: The Army is one big family. You are all my children." Satirical cartoon about the Eulenburg scandal, 1906–9. (in Giuseppe Senizza, *Corruzione sessuale e crudeltà germanica*)

(Neue Gluklichter) - Vienna.

"Liebenberg Castle." Satirical cartoon about the Eulenburg scandal, 1906-9. (in Giuseppe Senizza, *Corruzione sessuale e crudeltà germanica*)

Pederasta passivo e rapinante

"Passive pederast thief." (in Abele De Blasio, *Usi e costumi dei camorristi*)

"Soldato Giglione, professional passive pederast" shown with his finger to his lip and with a sidelong glance intended to seduce. (Lombroso Museum, Turin)

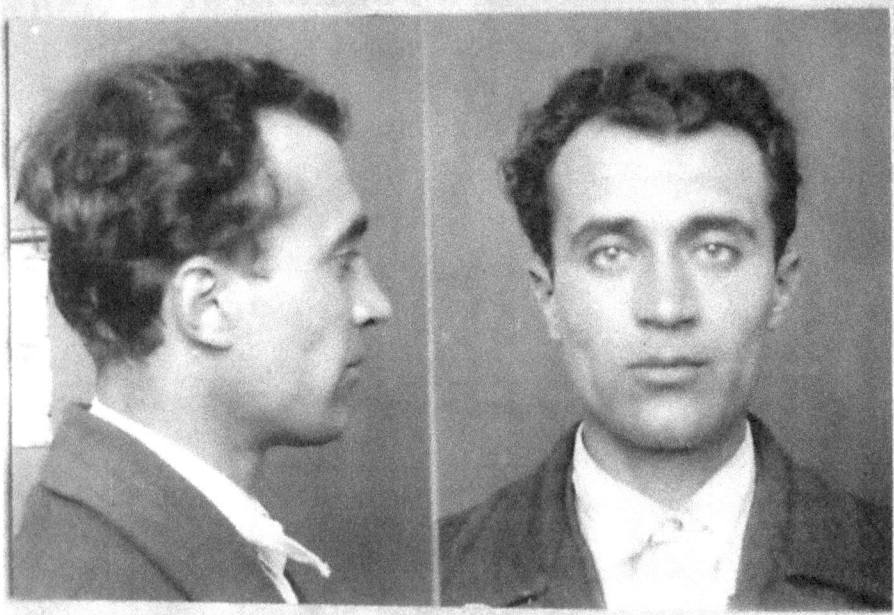

Biographical card of the *confinato politico* Emanuele Bonanno, interned for pederasty. (Central State Archive, Rome, Confino Politico, b. 128, Authorization 1223.43.10)

Biographical card of the *confinato politico* Domenico Romiti, interned for pederasty. (Central State Archive, Rome, Confino Politico, b. 878, Authorization 1223.43.10)

Cover of *In Africa Orientale* by Giovanni Longetti. (Fry Collection, Department of Special Collections, University of Wisconsin–Madison)

This postcard documents and compares the activities of the 42nd Infantry Regiment in North Africa during the First World War and the Fascist period. (Fry Collection, Department of Special Collections, University of Wisconsin–Madison)

E. M. Vardaro, "135th Legion MVSN 'Gran Sasso' Teramo." (Fry Collection, Department of Special Collections, University of Wisconsin–Madison)

The tank speech, August 16, 1934. Benito Mussolini in the Field Marshall uniform of the MVSN addressing the troops from atop a tank named after Damiano Chiesa. (Central State Archive, Rome, Segreteria Particolare del Duce, Attività del Duce, b. 12, f. 27, Authorization 1223.43.10)

Benito Mussolini reviews Rome's garrison troops on the occasion of the king's birthday, November 11, 1932. Angelo Manaresi and Achille Starace can be seen behind him. (Central State Archive, Rome, Segreteria Particolare del Duce, Attività del Duce, b. 9, f. 33, Authorization 1223.43.10)

The Mussolini family at Villa Tor-
lonia, Rome, 1930. *From left to right*,
Mussolini's wife Rachele holding
Anna Maria, Benito with Romano,
Edda, Bruno, and Vittorio. (Central State Archive, Rome, Authorization 1223.43.10)

A bare-chested Duce on
the slopes of Monte Ter-
minillo, February 17, 1937.
(Central State Archive,
Rome, Segreteria Partico-
lare del Duce, Attività del
Duce, b. 15, f. 1, Autho-
rization 1223.43.10)

M. D'Ercoli, "Distretto militare di Nola" (The Recruiting Office in Nola). Young bourgeois men enter the barracks in civilian clothes and leave as soldiers in uniform. (Fry Collection, Department of Special Collections, University of Wisconsin–Madison)

USANZE MONDANE

— Perchè quella signora si è messa sul dorso della mano, alici, cetriolini sotto aceto e mostarda?
— È tanto brutta, che nessuno altrimenti, le baciava la mano.

TIPI: NUMERO UNO

"The Latest Fashion." The caption reads: "Why is that woman wearing anchovies, pickles, and sweet relish on the back of her hand? She is so ugly that no one would kiss her hand otherwise." (Fry Collection, Department of Special Collections, University of Wisconsin–Madison)

"Tipi: numero uno" (Types: Number One), a satirical cartoon. (in Carlo Scorza, *Tipi . . . Tipi . . . Tipi . . .*)

Filipo De Pisis, "Reclining Nude, February 8, 1931." (in Rodolfo Pallucchini, ed., Filippo De Pisis: *Testo di Marco Valsecchi*)

Portrait of Aldo Mieli by Joao Saaverda Machado, published in *Archeion*, 1940. (courtesy of the National Library of Medicine)

5

Madmen or Criminals

Homosexuals and homosexuality are seen as kinds of "evil": but an evil that has been removed and transferred to a place where it is "something else." That is, where it becomes monstrous, devilish and degrading.

PIER PAOLO PASOLINI,

Il carcere e la fraternità dell'amore omosessuale

Prostitution and Delinquency: Homosexuals on Trial

Institutions such as jails and insane asylums were also used to repress homosexuality. As we have seen, despite the lack of any specific article against homosexual relationships, one could be condemned for indecent behavior or solicitation, two crimes that had acquired a very broad meaning during the dictatorship, including, of course, any violation of the Fascist standard of virility. Consequently, an analysis of the legal proceedings gives us an official idea of what was sexually unacceptable and helps us delineate the model of masculinity that Fascism sought to defend, as well as society's perception of "normal" sexuality. Through their sentences, courtrooms condemned homosexuality and delineated proper sexual conduct, creating a standard of virility. Trials established *The Boundaries of Eros*,[1] defining the borders of sexual practices: what was licit or illicit, normal or abnormal, usual or transgressive. With the criminalization of homosexuality, sexual behavior in general was subjected to legal control; masculinity was disciplined and heterosexuality defended. The sentences delivered in the courts were closely connected to social norms and evoked an unwritten code of virility that reinforced a standard of manliness. Angus McLaren wrote, "The trials of those men who were considered transgressive or homosexual are precious sources of information because they explicate the nuances, though often variable, which were inherent in the injunction of these men."[2]

These sources can be applied to the case of Fascist Italy as well. During the twenty years of Fascism there were still many homosexuals condemned for indecent behavior and solicitation, although it appears from legal statistics, especially after the implementation of the Rocco Code, that there was a notable decrease in offenses against public morality.[3] An analysis of the sentences delivered in the courts of Rome shows how legal action did not limit itself to protecting the community from those who offended public morality, but rather worked to repress various kinds of "scandalous" behavior, regardless of whether they represented an offense to public morality or not. Homosexuality was blameworthy and to be condemned, and even if a homosexual was not discovered in wanton behavior, he was a disturbing factor for morality. He was considered a degenerate, a threat to society. By analyzing his behavior and lifestyle, medical reports served as proof of his crime. Judgments hinged, then, more on an investigation of the accused's nature rather than the actual crime committed. As Foucault rightly pointed out, "expert psychiatric opinions allowed one to pass from action to conduct, from an offense to a way of being, and to make this way of being appear as nothing other than the offense itself," to punishing the criminal instead of the crime.[4] The homosexuals were judged more for their irregular behavior than for any infringement of the law. Sexual practices that represented transgressions of "normality" and did not have procreation as their aim were to be repressed and punished because they defiled respectability and the dominating standard of virility. Sentences, medical reports, and trials were all important instruments for the implementation of an "apparatus of normalization," which would individuate and repress every anomaly. The completely abstract concept of decency and the lack of specific definitions for obscenity and public morality made it possible for each court to determine which sexual behaviors were transgressive. Canosa wrote, "The courts transferred the inevitable prejudices of their members to there legal activity, prejudices that were mostly identical to those of the average citizen, full of prudery in everything concerning sex and little inclined to justify 'public' displays related to it."[5]

The magistrates' courts and the different sections of Rome's criminal courts sentenced homosexuals accused of indecent behavior or solicitation for licentious purposes to light punishments, usually limited to a few months of imprisonment. The Fascist regime criticized judges for being too lenient toward those guilty of sexual offenses and urged them to support "the Regime's efforts to foster an increase in the Nation's birthrate, its moral soundness, and fruitful development."[6]

Of greater curiosity than the severity of the actual sentences inflicted on homosexuals is the fact that many sentences were delivered without sufficient evidence and sometimes without the requisites necessary to consider the act an offense. For example, one Roman "passive pederast" was sentenced to six months of imprisonment for indecent behavior because he had been accused, in an anonymous letter, of making obscene proposals to some passers-by. After only two hearings he was acquitted for insufficient proof.[7] At other times, courts freely expressed their hostility toward homosexuals, passing exclusively moral sentences that went beyond the legal sphere. What was actually being judged were forms of behavior that, although they clearly did not break the law, were censurable as infringements of ethical rules.

The legal affairs of some individuals give clear proof of how the distinction between crime and sin became somewhat hazy in courtrooms. In his sentencing of two men accused of indecent behavior, "for carrying out unspeakably obscene acts in a public bus" one judge declared that the trial was "terribly serious from a moral point of view,"[8] even if the men were later acquitted on the grounds of insufficient proof. What happened to two other unfortunate men condemned for indecent behavior is even more important for understanding how legality and morality became closely intertwined under the Fascist judiciary. The two young men, who were caught kissing by a guard, in full daylight, in the public gardens, were rash enough to deny what had happened. They then insulted the police officer and resisted arrest, adding insult to a public official to their charges. Despite all this, the appeals judge, who believed there was no proof of licentious intentions, was lenient and repealed their previous sentence of five years, removing the offense from their records and giving them a simple fine for having offended public decency.[9] Also, in this case the sentence was not so much intended to punish or repress behavior that was considered socially dangerous, but rather to make a clear distinction between right and wrong behavior—obviously, two men kissing in public was wrong.

In addition to upholding the law, judiciary action was a means of prescribing standards of male behavior. In their sentences, judges took the morality of the accused into account. Morality and social standing were closely related; many sentences differed, in fact, depending on the social position and level of respectability of the accused. The case of the army captain Corrado M. is a typical example. He was caught in a Roman movie theater committing obscene acts with a boy, who was very different from him "in age and social class." Although the captain fled to avoid capture while the boy gave a full confession to the *carabinieri*, the army officer was fully acquitted because according to the judge, Corrado M. had all the principal features of a virile man and conformed to the predominant model of masculinity. He had "the best references, regarding not only his noble duty as an army officer but also his *moral qualities*, which show he is "*an honest, correct and well-balanced gentleman*. And as what has been said about him speaks well of the boy, whose *normality* was confirmed by the medical report recorded in the proceedings, also in reference to his sexual life, the Court acquits them of the accusation. Thus it has been decided in Rome in the court hearing of 10-12-1934."[10] Once again the contrast between "gentlemen and scoundrels" was used as a criterion to establish the male identity and normal virile behavior.

The diffusion and pervasiveness of the regime's repression and its influence and conditioning of the police force become evident when looking at these hearings. Fascism's ideology encouraged the persecution of homosexuals at the hands of local authorities, and it provided justification for their homophobic prejudices. Although, in general, the court sentence regarding homosexuals were not extremely severe, when it came to homosexual prostitution the regime waged war: police officers in plainclothes were purposely given orders to loiter around public urinals, where they were to let unknowing prostitutes make advances, and then handcuff and report them or simply put their names down in the police records and let them go.[11] Homosexual prostitutes were targeted by police determined to free the town of this disgusting and overly conspicuous scourge. Clients were considered marginal unless they had sex with very young prostitutes, a crime that fell under the category of corrupting minors and entailed much harsher sentences than did indecent behavior. Those accused of pederasty defended themselves by trying, in every possible way, to show that their young victims were already quite experienced at selling their bodies and readily submitting to "obscene actions" with rich adults. If examinations of the body confirmed that the minor was accustomed to unnatural sexual intercourse, he was considered to be already morally corrupt, thus saving the accused person from a long imprisonment.[12] Therefore, minors who were not even fifteen years old could be accused of indecent behavior as well, even if they had been persuaded to practice pederasty by much older persons. The determined level of corruption of these boys almost always depended on their social condition: if they had been abandoned, if they were uneducated, poor, or practicing prosti-tution, they were considered depraved, independent of their age. On the other hand, the sons of wealthy parents, that is, of "gentlemen" who were able to afford a good attorney, were considered uncorrupted and too young to understand their wrongdoings.

This is proven by the trial against Alfredo P., who had had sexual intercourse, "against nature and passively," with some boys in a publicly visible cave. He was sentenced to a year and eight months for corrupting minors, for infecting them with blennorrhea, and for obscene acts. However, the boys involved in the case were acquitted and deemed to have been morally uncorrupted before the events. They were well-mannered schoolboys who attended lessons regularly and had agreed to Alfredo P.'s requests only to get a bit of cash and because they had been solicited and sexually excited with obscene talk. The judge maintained, "The tendency toward anal intercourse by individuals who have reached a certain level of degradation after experiencing a whole range of sexual desires is explainable; but not here in the case of young boys who have just passed puberty and were lured into having sexual intercourse against nature when aroused by the lust of an experienced pederast." Therefore, in this case, "as it was a sordid deed," it was necessary to give "special punishment to the depraved subject," who had "sullied the minds of creatures who had just entered puberty." The medical examination was further proof of Alfredo P.'s guilt, as it showed he had "all the local features of perversion," while the anal region showed "signs of chronic, habitual pederasty."[13] The absurd conviction that someone who was already corrupt could not be corrupted shows how preconceived morals were used as the basis for distinguishing normal behavior from abnormal. The judge was more concerned with defending values than protecting individuals: it was not the adolescent who needed to be protected but virility itself.

Legal documents attest to the extent of underage prostitution. Sometimes these minors were only ten years old, yet they agreed to homosexual intercourse for money, cigarettes or food. Up until to the middle of the twentieth century pederastic relationships were still very widespread in Italy. Since it was difficult for young men to have sexual encounters with girls, who were afraid of being irreparably compromised before marriage, it was almost inevitable that boys had their first experiences with either prostitutes, servants, boys their own age, or adult men. However, sex with a prostitute required money for boys who were poor, while accepting a man's proposals could be useful to earn a few liras and give relief to their own sexual instincts. However, they had to abandon the vice eventually in order to maintain their gender identity, when their adolescence ended and they took on an active role as procreating males and began a new life with a wife and children. Umberto Saba's *Ernesto* is a clear example of this. In Trieste at the end of the nineteenth century, a sixteen-year-old, still free of certain taboos, was initiated to sex quite naturally, spontaneously, and innocently by an older man. The experience did not prevent him from loving women and having a happy marriage. This did not mean that such "unseemly" intercourse was accepted or legitimized. On the contrary, the climate of homophobia led to the belief that homosexuality was "dangerous stuff." It was necessary, then, to behave as though "it was all a secret; that nobody, not even the air, knew about it or suspected anything." Most importantly, *Ernesto* illustrates how the model that had regulated sexual intercourse between males and females for centuries had to be respected. Even if the rigid distinction between who was

active and who was passive had begun to break down between the partners
who wanted a more reciprocal and symmetrical relationship, Ernesto's lover
received the youth's proposal to reverse the roles as "wrong and offensive":

> It isn't nice, he said, to do it with a man. It's something you do only with
> boys before they start growing beards, and before (he was about to say but
> stopped in time) going with women. How could you enjoy it with me, who
> has a moustache, as you can see (and he stroked it). If I were a boy of your
> age I would willingly change over. — Couldn't you shave it off? Ernesto
> asked. But even before saying it, he realized he was about to say something
> silly. — It wouldn't be any use, the man answered, I would still be a man.[14]

Besides poverty and squalor, it was the morality of the age as well, with
its taboo on sex before marriage and the fact that "respectable" women were
excluded from public life that led many adolescents to make a practice of
prostitution and prepare them for homosexual affairs.[15]

> It's true that most of these boys give themselves for money, but far from
> being disgusted by these acts the boys get satisfaction from them. They are
> a substitute for sexual intercourse with women, something they would
> naturally prefer in most cases.[16]

The "*Ragazzi di vita*" whom Pasolini described in the 1950s were already
quite numerous during Fascism,[17] as Benigno Di Tullio documented in his 1927
study. The researcher pointed out the "troubling increase" in homosexuality,
pedophilia, and above all of male prostitution involving minors, which he
attributed to a number of "economic, social and degenerative causes." He gave
the example of a Roman working-class district where the police had arrested
twelve boys accused of carrying out libidinous acts with and raping other children
from eight to twelve years old, who had offered themselves to the accused and
engaged in "passive pederasty for small sums of money, from half a lira to one
or two liras at the most, for a piece of bread or small presents."[18] The secretary
of the Rome Center for Studies on Juvenile Delinquency (Centro romano di
studi sulla deliquenza minorile), Falcone Lucifero, a researcher on sexual crimes
committed by the young, who was convinced that the crimes were principally
due "to the tumultuous period of puberty,"[19] expressed a similar opinion. When
analyzing the whole population of the detention homes in 1932, however, Lucifero
ascertained that of the 305 boys in the institutions and penitentiaries for juveniles,
almost all of those who had committed sex crimes, second in number to those
condemned for theft, came from southern Italy. About half of these sex crimes
had been carried out against children of the same sex and of more or less the
same age. He concluded, then, that homosexuality was common among minors,

who together with pederasts and above all prostitutes, were believed to have an innate disposition for sexual crimes.

The association of "homosexuality with criminality" as an innately determined tendency was deeply rooted. The stories reported by the crime news helped to strengthen this belief. The number of occurrences of theft, blackmail, and extortion crimes with which these "perverts" were associated left no doubt as to the validity of this theory. Years before, Lombroso had maintained that homosexuality and crime were associated by way of a common atavistic quality and "moral insanity," which derived from inherited genetic defects. This parallel was evident for Lombroso, who believed "the congenital, the habitual, and the occasional homosexual corresponded exactly to the born criminal, the criminaloid, the habitual, and the occasional criminal."[20] Pederasts could be subdivided into different groups: temporary, occasional, mad, or naturally born inverts. The last were incorrigible and had to be kept in insane asylums indefinitely, or at least until their sexual activity ended. It was easy to pick them out because their "special features, typical of the other sex" were impressed on their faces or bodies. Even in the absence of particular exterior signs, their mentality was "completely abnormal, very often criminal and above all strange."[21] Homosexuality also influenced behavior, attitudes, and manners, because "other than being expressed through a perverted, brutal, and carnal tendency, inverted sexual feelings condition the entire psyche of an individual. Pederasts often give themselves false names, wear women's clothes and hair styles, and have falsetto voices."[22]

In some ways, the sources available to historians have tended to strengthen this image of "homosexuals as criminals" and led to an exaggeration of their actual involvement in criminal activities. Naturally, this depends on the nature of the documents the research consults. For example, police records and the judicial acts of the Ministries of the Interior and Justice, both of which gave precedence to defending public order, a categorical imperative in the years of the dictatorship. Consequently, these sources should be approached with care. As Mario Sbriccoli warns, "an efficient legal system creates many more files than a transgressive society."[23] This explains why the homosexual underworld has been associated with criminality; however, those who left behind more tracks, that is, those accused of criminal actions, should not overshadow all those who had no run-ins with the police and who seem to have led quite normal lives. Despite this caveat, it is undoubtedly true that the repressed lifestyle that homosexuals were forced to live helped to increase the number of crimes they committed. Being social outcasts and living secret lives often created the kind of existential conditions in which crime was necessary for survival. Homosexuality was confined to a subterranean world made up of people excluded from the rest of society, driven to brutishness and crime. The impossibility of expressing one's sexual tendencies led homosexuals to look for support and help from individuals who often exploited them for illicit ends. For example, male prostitution nurtured an entire social niche at the margins social respectability. The criminalization and moral condemnation of sexuality and the homophobia of society facilitated extortion practices against those who wanted to keep their sexual "anomaly" hidden; in particular, those who managed to live parallel lives by giving the impression of being absolutely upright, virile, and masculine men. The difficulty of finding a stable partner due to the lack of for-men-only meeting places, and the fact that homosexuals could not live their love affairs serenely and naturally, increased the willingness to resort to meetings with "professional pederasts" who, besides receiving a little cash as payment, often subjected their clients to theft and robbery.

The police kept homosexual circles under close surveillance and control. Their actions continued to be influenced by Lombrosian prejudices despite the strong criticism they had received from the academic world. This is most likely because Salvatore Ottolenghi, Lombroso's faithful assistant, had instilled a strict methodology based on a rigid criminological positivism at the Forensic Science School, where he served as director from 1902 to 1928.[24] The preventive approach was based on the conviction that certain individuals were anthropologically disposed to crime. This category included homosexuals, whose deviated nature caused "laziness, theft, drunkenness and crime."[25] Ottolenghi thought the police needed to be equipped with all the instruments necessary to identify these criminals anthropobiologically, and he had given clear indications on how they were supposed to react when confronted with them.[26] He provided the trainees at the Forensic Science School with examples of pederasty, pointing out the way they spoke in falsetto and their feminine gestures and attitudes. It comes as no surprise, then, that (as we can see in table 4) many of those among the prisoners in the Regina Coeli jail accused of extortion, indecent behavior, and corruption of minors, were entered as "homosexual delinquents" after being studied and measured in the laboratory.

Each type of sexual behavior was considered an indication of criminality and was scrupulously recorded in the biographical files of the ex-convicts; the specific word "sensuality" appeared in the part reserved for mental characteristics, and was qualified by one of several adjectives: marked, common, anomalous (pederasty: active, passive; passional, professional), violence, lust.[27] Naturally, confinati also had biographical files with identifying photographs, fingerprints, the measurements of anatomic and functional features, and so on, as well as a category, "mental attitudes," under which any sexual deviance was recorded. In cases of passive pederasty, there were always indications about the subject's

Table 4. Forensic Science School:
Recorded cases of homosexuals

YEAR	CASES
1927	18
1928	17
1929	57
1930	87
1931	92
1932	42
1933	69
1934	116
1935	92
1936	76
1937	86
1938	124
1939	153
Total	**1,029**

From *Bollettino della Scuola Superiore della Polizia Scientifica e dei servizi tecnici annessi.*

Source: Table cited in M. Ebner, "The Persecution of Homosexual Men under Fascism, 1926–1943," in *Family and Sexuality: The Private Sphere in Italy, 1860–1945,* ed. P. Wilson (London: Palgrave-Macmillan, 2004), 144.

behavior and physiognomy that served to draw up a final moral judgment that was largely based on stereotypes. Pederasts were always described as perverse, debauched, inconstant, lazy, and unreliable individuals. They were also portrayed as liars who evaded work and had no sense of morality, modesty, or decency, who tended to commit offenses against public morality and the integrity of the race, and had feminine behavior, voices, and movements, as well as "womanish instincts and attitudes."

Giuseppe Falco, who succeeded Ottolenghi at the head of the Forensic Science School, was also convinced that "homosexuality, or sexual inversion" "motivated offenses or events that, even if they are not technically crimes, upset public order and clash with modesty and public morality."[28] His long experience had led him to believe that "there are many homosexuals, forming a class that can be directly or indirectly dangerous, either because they upset public order or because they offend modesty or commit crimes, which they rarely commit themselves but of which they are often the victims (murder or other crimes against persons). Homosexuality is revealed in these subjects through acts of pederasty, in particular, passive pederasty; sometimes they act as real prostitutes, sometimes they are victims exploited by parasites who are often violent ex-convicts, capable of extortion, blackmail, and crimes."[29] It was the task of police officers and medical examiners to individuate the sexual psychopathy underlying these crimes.

The association of sexual deviance with criminal behavior spurred various scholars to conduct research on the world of male prostitution, an environment in which the link became more apparent. For example, Giuseppe Vidoni, director of the criminal anthropology laboratory of Genoa, maintained that male prostitution created serious social problems and was clearly dangerous because of the negative influence it had on young people: it was "a substitute for crimes and quite often the most favorable breeding-ground for organized crime in big cities." Specific research needed to be carried out in the field, accompanied by sexual education, as well as an efficacious battle against juvenile delinquency.[30] Mieli had also treated the problem in *Rassegna di studi sessuali*,[31] in an effort to debunk theories linking male prostitution and homosexuality. According to him, a male was driven to prostitution for financial reasons, not sexual ones; the only real homosexual was the client. Male prostitution was a form of "social degeneration" to be fought with every means possible. It was "usually a locus of organized crime," where crimes against property and persons were organized and carried out. Not considering blameworthy those who usually went with female prostitutes even though they were married, and on the other hand strongly condemning those who preferred the company of males, turned many delinquents, who sought to make a profit from blackmailing their clients, to prostitution. In their blackmail, they exploited the fact that "public opinion was often hypocritical and objected" to homosexual relationships. Clients became the victims of extortion, suffered violence and threats, and paid handsomely in order to keep their vices a secret. To put an end to these crimes, it was necessary to cast off "the impunity that delinquent prostitutes enjoy under the aegis of laws and regulations."[32] For Mieli, the victims themselves should be convinced to report their persecutors to the police without fear of being subjected to false moralism. They should be guaranteed that the trials would not be made public and that their identities would be kept secret.

The growing concern about male prostitution was principally due to the hypocritical mentality of the Fascist period and its attempt to conceal everything regarding homosexuality. Because of its public nature, male prostitution became the main target of Fascism's repression. On the other hand, as we have seen, semi-secret places for males only were often tolerated. So, whereas female prostitution, regulated and controlled by the state, remained a means of escape from the rigid standards of bourgeois respectability the "disgusting scourge of male prostitution,"[33] a locus for criminality, had to be severely forbidden and carefully supervised.

Jail

Jails, as male segregated institutions, are a point of enquiry in the history of the repression of homosexuality. Incidentally, jails, often used as instruments against pederasts, were also known as places that could encourage the urge to satisfy sexual desire with other detainees, and create a particular situation where heterosexual individuals gave way to homosexual practices. Numerous studies on institutions for males only, like boarding schools, ships, prison camps, barracks, colonies, and monasteries strengthened the belief that jails were capable of spreading pederasty, so much so that in the nineteenth century many scholars categorized homosexuality, along with other "acquired psychopathic sexual disorders,"[34] as a kind of degeneration caused by environmental factors. If "boarding-school friendships" were already considered dangerous, places where adult men were shut up and forced to live without contact with women posed even an even greater threat. "Pederasty as compensation" was more dangerous,[35] because it struck individuals who were usually heterosexual, leading to a vice that could not always be corrected. For De Napoli, it was necessary to limit communities of men as much as possible because "*semem retentum*" sometimes led to sexual inversion, above all, in those who were in some way predisposed. Forel suggested following the example of the Norwegian merchant navy that allowed its officers to live on board with their wives; it was also advisable for barracks to be near towns so that the servicemen "would remember that there were women in the world as well" when on leave.[36] Also, the army's medical draft check-up was seen as an useful way of individuating and rejecting possible pederasts. Military regulations called for disciplinary companies where homosexuals could be sent for the entire duration of their military service. In this way, "contagion" could be prevented without, however, managing to cure "these unfortunate persons," who left these special companies irrevocably "corrupted."[37]

The experience of captivity during the First World War gave further proof of how segregation might lead to homosexual relationships among the prisoners. A description of the lives of so many soldiers who fell into the enemy's hands clearly proved this:

> One saw contorted faces, dull eyes, tottering bodies; heard infantile talk and was amazed that these beings had once been men. Sordid friendships arose: more often than not inspired by similarities with women loved or

known in the past, by physical attraction or an attractive personality, by
the custom of dancing that the prisoners enjoyed immensely; pederasty
was revealed in all its forms, from the most subtle to carnal possession.
Bonds that in normal life would have become friendship took on the
features of degeneracy: a glance, a handshake, even an unwitting caress;
all involved sex. Jealousy, envy, gossip and rivalry arose. . . . In many cases
there was an almost complete inversion of tastes, desires, and expressions:
men who gesticulated and spoke like women, who danced obscenely like
female cabaret dancers, who let themselves be courted and dominated by
their admirers: little street women would not have been more trivial than
they.[38]

Persio Falchi's lively portrayal of how an individual's tendency toward
pederasty found "its most ideal breeding ground in prison camps, as confirmed
by experiments," led Dr. Amedeo Dalla Volta to study cases where obligatory
confinement drove "predisposed individuals into the arms of homosexuality,"
impressing a "lighter or darker erotic shade on the friendships of hundreds of
afflicted men who shared the same suffering."[39] However, these relationships
were just an interlude for the prisoners who were free of "morbid passions"
before the war and who returned to their normal sex life once they went back
home. In fact imprisonment aggravated "already recognized sexual perversion
or brought it out of latency," leaving all the others "sexually undamaged." For
example, after a long imprisonment, one young infantry officer, "who had
extraordinarily beautiful and feminine features," "looked back with shame . . .
for having desired to embrace some of his more masculine companions"; these
images of the past "struck him only as the memory of a horrible but unlikely
dream."[40] For Dr. Vito Massarotti as well, "the occasional homosexual" carried
out these unnatural acts because he had no other outlet for his heterosexual
needs, which did not mean he had the "mental deviation of the congenital
homosexual" or that he really loved his partner.[41] On the contrary, it was much
more difficult for the men who saw combat to return to a normal sex life again,
since the memory "of their tough life as soldiers" was unlikely to fade, and "the
state of depravation into which they had entered got worse and worse through
the most degrading eroticism."[42]

However, the environment where pederasty flourished most alarmingly was
jail. This at least was Raffaele Conforti's opinion after visiting penal institutions
in 1860 where the prisoners, who "worked together and were kept away from
the fair sex, fell in love with one other, abandoning themselves to a foul and
incorrigible vice that caused the death of many of them."[43] The prisoners, who

were forced to stay for long periods without any contact with women, were prey to strong homosexual temptations in jail, where sexual continence was required for many years. Altiero Spinelli gave proof of this in his memoirs when speaking of the Santa Maria in Gradi jail in Viterbo. He discreetly describes the attraction he felt for a youth in the cell next to his, whom he nicknamed Charis ("beauty" in Greek) and who was "just over eighteen years old."[44] His attractiveness and adolescent grace had aroused a deep affection in Spinelli, and "the absence of women in his life evidently contributed to riveting his attention more intensely on the physically and psychologically ephebic features" of the boy. Little by little, their relationship turned into that particular bond between master and slave typical of the pederasty of antiquity and "analyzed by Plato in *Symposium*," to the point that the two of them had decided to report in sick so as to be able to spend a few days in the same room and realize "the union of their bodies." This step was too daring. Spinelli was frightened, but above all he was bothered by the fact that such behavior was considered "shameful." As a result, he decided not to carry out their plans and suffered "all night for the sacrifice." Spinelli noted that the Communist Party's rigid ideals of respectability had stopped him. Although its idea of sexual morality was not so different from that of the Fascists,[45] the reasons underpinning the Communists' uncompromising condemnation of all "abnormal" behaviors differed from those of the Fascists. Both sides believed that political credibility had to be gained by living irreproachably, without transgressions or immoral behavior, but for the Communists, conforming to the prevailing morality helped one not to arouse suspicion, to fit into society. Spinelli, who did not want to compromise his relationship with the party, was well aware he risked condemnation if he gave way to his homosexual desires:

> The Communists in particular, who were nonconformists in so many other ways, were completely puritanical with regard to homosexual relationships. . . . If news of our intimacy had leaked out of the infirmary and reached the community, we would both have been outlawed and branded with an implacable mark of shame. I was already in some difficulty with the party, and I did not want to allow other reasons beyond the plain and simple ones of politics and doctrine to influence that relationship.

However, more often than not, homosexuality in jail was not so "pure." Bullying and tormenting often led to acts of sodomy, where the younger detainees were often forced to satisfy the whole dormitory. One old man serving a life sentence justified his behavior, saying: "If you others don't help us, who can give us relief? You are here as our women because you look more like them!" Arturo Dellepiane, a political detainee, also bore witness to this in his memoirs:

After the nine o'clock "roll call," some detainees get busy and prepare a special pallet in the secluded corner near the toilet; they are also careful to shut the place off from sight with a blanket, and the day's newest detainee who has arrived is pushed behind this kind of curtain. However, the curtain is so makeshift that what happens behind it can easily be seen. The men, degraded to brutes, fling themselves on the half-naked youth and give free rein to their pent-up, maybe long repressed lust, taking turns with frenzied impatience. The fact that most of the Sicilians and I protest and rebuke them is quite useless against people like these, who seem possessed by a kind of paroxysm. I do not know if what I see is an aberration of sexual feelings caused or prompted by the environment; I only know that the scene left me profoundly and indelibly disgusted.[46]

Tullio Murri's novel *Galera* (Jail) brought great public attention to the problem. After spending eighteen years in jail for murdering his brother-in-law, Tullio, a lawyer, described the reality he had seen inside. The tale of young Cesarino, who was forced to become homosexual because he was mocked and continually tormented and who died in jail due to the violence he had suffered from the various prisoners, is terribly sad. The book was to have a far-reaching effect, also because public opinion had followed the "Murri case" with almost morbid passion since the early 1900s.[47] The novel deplores the inhuman living conditions of the prisoners. Murri himself asked Mussolini to end cell segregation, sending him a letter that was published by the Milanese review *Il Fascio*.[48] The success of *Galera*, which was reprinted seven times in the space of a few years, helped to open a debate on the issue. The story of Cesarino, a young man considered a pederast for his shy and genteel appearance and for this reason obliged to pass from one jail to another and to suffer every kind of outrage, was also criticized and accused of being a literary exaggeration. On the contrary, Murri was convinced of the effect of "homosexual passions" and sustained that among prisoners "there had not been a brawl that did not have this abject jealously as its final and secret motive."[49] Dr. La Cara, a convinced supporter of the organicist theory of homosexuality, believed that Murri's novel was credible, even though in his opinion it was "immediately clear that the seed of pederastic perversion was germinating in the subconscious of this unfortunate young man (unfortunate, not a martyr); jail happened to be the motive to make it explode, but it would have come out even had he been free."[50]

Furthermore, Murri's book inspired the doctor of the Regina Coeli jail, Benigno Di Tullio, to make a careful study of pederasty, "a sexual issue of greater interest and intensity in jails."[51] The real problem within penitentiaries arose from professional passive pederasts, known to everyone and capable of prostituting themselves behind bars as well. When they entered jail, there was "a kind of competition among the convicts to have these pederasts in their cells or at least in one nearby."[52] In comparison to the number of congenital homosexuals and habitual homosexuals, there were many more occasional homosexuals, most of whom were heterosexuals who had become active pederasts but who, once out of jail, "almost always returned to normal sexuality." Far more damaging, however, were the effects that jail had on congenital and latent homosexuals. A life of confinement and segregation would certainly lead them, first, to practice pederasty occasionally, and then, little by little, to habitual and inveterate homosexuality, "a state in which they will remain even after returning to society."[53]

After six years of studies, Giulio Andrea Belloni reached a slightly different conclusion in his investigation of sexual problems in jail, and of acquired pederasty in particular,[54] Belloni maintained that in jails "eros fell, reaching the darkest and saddest depths of its degradation," until it slips from normality into homosexuality. Consequently, it was wrong to uphold that pederasty in jail struck only those who were already homosexuals or potentially so, because there were many more men attracted to these practices than was usually believed.[55] Confinement was not supposed to trigger latent inclinations but to correct them, and furthermore, the assumption that occasional homosexuals quietly returned to their normal heterosexual lives again upon release was not true either. The ex-convict returned to civil society with a "new criminal potential," since he would no longer hesitate to follow the forbidden habits he had already practiced in jail.[56] Instead of serving to redeem delinquents, jail made them more dangerous, corrupting their instincts and "spreading their depravation." To avoid spreading homosexuality, it was necessary to put three prisoners in each cell and allow conjugal visits. However, the only real solution was to create work colonies like those in *confino* where the prisoners' wives could visit as well.[57]

A place where the germ of pederasty might thrive was unacceptable to the Fascists; jail had to be an institution for the repression of homosexuality, not its proliferation. To show their total faith in Fascism, quite a few penitentiary directors accused Murri of exaggerating. His description of jails as places where homosexuality spread was false and injurious; he just told "vulgar tall tales" that were "mere exaggeration." Fortunately, however, "these publications of speculation had stopped with the climate and discipline of Fascism." Everyone had his own suggestion on how to "efficaciously attack pederasty." Nevertheless, worried about the importance the regime gave to virility, Giovanni Novelli, chief executive of the Institutions of Prevention and Punishment (Istituti di prevenzione e pena), ordered an investigation in 1936 "into the extremely serious issue of pederasty in jails," asking all jail directors to send a detailed report on

the number of prisoners suspected of pederasty, and of every case there had
been in the last five years. He wanted to know "if [the prisoners] had an outlet
for their unfortunate tendencies," and what ideas and suggestions they could
offer on the means necessary to weaken "this serious problem that often attracts
the attention of scholars."[58] The answers tell a lot about the conception of
homosexuality at the time and give a national overview of its diffusion in jails,
asylums for the criminally insane, penitentiaries, reformatories, reform centers,
farming colonies, and homes for the physically and mentally disabled. A re-
occurring theme in these reports is the difficulty experienced in managing the
homosexuals who destabilized life in jail and created an infinite number of
problems; they caused fights and jealousy, exasperating and "nauseating" the
other prisoners who had not yet "completely lost their sense of morality."
Furthermore, there was clearly widespread indifference to the problem, or rather,
an attempt to avoid an alarming tone, because the jail authorities considered
homosexuality completely natural, something that commonly occurred in
any exclusively male community, like barracks, ships, boarding schools, and
monasteries. Pederasty in penitentiaries was mainly due to the total lack of a
normal sex life that, with the passing of time, drove the prisoners to search out
a substitute for heterosexual intercourse in unnatural practices. The third point
insisted on the usual distinction between passive and active pederasts, the former
being really "dangerous and evil," because they were incurable and capable of
soliciting and corrupting their fellow prisoners. They were the ones responsible
for spreading homosexuality among the convicts who were driven to acts that
they would normally never do.

The "sexual degeneration" of passive pederasts could be confirmed through
an accurate medical examination, after which their "sordid disease" could be
recorded in police files, so that they could be sent to penal colonies where, at
least at night, they would be isolated. The jail personnel as well, who had been
in direct contact with the prisoners for years, were easily able to distinguish
them. Passive pederasts were easy to individuate: "Their bearing and way of
walking, their taste for elegant clothes and dressing up, the femininity of their
every action, the flirtatiousness of their every gesture. However, besides these
things that even a nonexpert can recognize, there are other signs that distinguish
passive pederasts: their red-rimmed eyes surrounded by dark circles, their rather
pale faces and awkward gait, their stealthy glances toward their objects of desire,
and the unmistakably weak character of those who are ready to let themselves
be dominated by any masculine or overbearing man." Furthermore, passive
pederasts were often reported "by their fellow prisoners and even by active
pederasts themselves," because they were considered "contemptible individuals."
Often the derision, contempt, and torment of the other prisoners drove them

to openly confess "their weakness and to ask for protection." The remedy was to completely isolate them in separate cells, where "objects like bottles etc." would be banned, "since their pole-like shape would make it easier for a passive pederast to indulge in his vice."

Many penitentiaries also attempted to analyze the causes of homosexuality, often using medical studies to support their opinions. Most of them considered passive pederasty an incurable congenital disease, while active pederasty was considered an acquired vice. Therefore, a distinction was made between "constitutional pederasty (also known as pederasty by inclination) and occasional pederasty (also known as prison pederasty)."[59] The former, suffering from a natural sexual inversion, were real clinical cases, antisocial and psychopathic individuals like persons suffering from tuberculosis or trachoma, who had to be isolated, continuously watched, or sent to special institutes or sections for disabled persons where they would be given treatment. Specialized buildings had to be prepared for all the pederasts, with gymnasiums, swimming pools, and workplaces, and with numerous prison personnel purposely selected and trained to prevent any act of sodomy;[60] or homosexuals were to be gathered in special cell-divided sections in the asylums for physically and mentally disabled persons, well separated from the others and kept under greater check. There would have been two advantages: on one hand, the fear of being confined to these penitentiary buildings or to the special sections for pederasts would serve as a deterrent against the vice, and, on the other hand, since no other country possessed these special prisons, by taking such measures "Fascist Italy would undoubtedly acquire further merit for the morality and soundness of its customs." Few of these prison directors, offended by the "adverse nature" of these individuals, took their unfortunate lives into consideration. Imprisonment in special institutes for degenerates would have destroyed their reputations forever, impressed "an indelible brand" on them, and degraded "their personalities even more, making the desired process of regeneration more difficult than ever."

Besides the "constitutionally passive homosexuals," there were occasional active pederasts whose homosexuality was not congenital but was brought about by the environment in prison, where forced sexual abstinence or the presence of "sexual psychopaths" made everyone a potential active pederast. In this case, it was a temporary and curable anomaly that could be limited with severe punishment and would stop as soon as the prisoner regained his liberty. After studying the psychic state of criminals, the director of the Fossombrone was convinced that, in general, "active sexual impulses when serving a sentence were a specific characteristic of violent criminals (murderers, robbers, etc.), while the loathsome passive pederast was a petty thief (a bag-snatcher, someone sentenced for indecent acts)." Furthermore, because submitting someone to acts of sodomy was considered one of the worst insults in the world of organized crime, there were many inmates who fell victim to the bullying of some criminal or another who was unable to control his "erotic exuberance."[61] Thus, there was a third category of pederasts, made up of those who were called "greenhorns": prisoners who "because of their young, ephebic appearance, were sought after by their companions and became victims of the older ones, who were ready to get their revenge on and torment anyone who attempted to resist them. In order to escape these acts of oppression, some were obliged to ask for protection or favors from more overbearing and domineering individuals who in turn expected to satisfy their own lust on these young prisoners as compensation. What to do then with these individuals?

There were also some more banal, yet feasible suggestions, such as increasing surveillance and lighting, providing every room with a spy-hole so that the prisoners could be constantly watched, and keeping a careful check on bathrooms and places where the prisoners gathered. However, in the end, isolating the pederasts was deemed to be the best solution. Every prison was required to have a special section sufficiently separated from the others and equipped with single cells; in the event that it was not possible to create such a structure, some type of space for isolation was required.[62] Nevertheless, some directors realized it was necessary not to segregate these prisoners indefinitely and proposed keeping them separated only at night and giving them a special badge as prisoners to be subjected to special supervision in crowded and well-supervised quarters during the day. Others claimed that the best solution was to put them in cells with morally sound elderly prisoners who no longer felt sexual urges; or to assign them to cells holding from four to eight prisoners, all chosen from persons of excellent conduct, with wives and children, who regularly attended religious services and who had not been sentenced for, or accused of, sexual offenses. The director of the Avigliano criminal reformatory proposed keeping them in ice-cold places because "corrupted cells are less active and the body is calmer" in such temperatures. Following the adage that "idle hands are the devil's tools," one approach to the problem was to subject the pederasts to hard labor and tiring sports, and to drastically reduce their rest hours. Mandatory gymnastics and exhausting jobs would expend their energy and limit their sexual urges. An assiduous educational effort was also necessary with the aim of redeeming at least occasional pederasts: lectures and lessons on sexual hygiene, scientific teachings on the consequences of unnatural sexual practices, sermons and special religious instruction that would help "degenerate individuals feel the disgrace and shame of remaining a slave to such a filthy vice and a laughing-stock to the community." It was considered important to make them aware of "the threat that unnatural sexual practices pose to individuals and the species, to show them the degradation they have fallen into by offending divine law so abominably"; and lastly, to instill "a moral, religious and patriotic sense" as well as the exaltation of masculine, military qualities, into the younger ones especially." It was the task of the doctor, the prison director, and the chaplain to make homosexuals feel "loathing for these filthy acts that are against the Divine laws of nature and society," by explaining how practicing pederasty causes serious illnesses: disorders of the eyes, dizziness, and tabes dorsalis, which can sometimes lead to progressive paralysis." Teaching, religious instruction, the distribution of "sound and moral" books among the prisoners, as well as forbidding any obscene talk or the circulation of porno-graphic publications would limit these immoral acts.

Others suggested psychological curative measures aimed at strengthening the will power of homosexuals, to be carried out by the doctors of the peniten-tiaries or through frequent therapeutic out-patient visits. The doctor was supposed to arouse a "profound feeling of nausea" in the homosexual, "by accompanying the moral impressions with heavy medications." This would touch the prisoner's soul, instilling a guilt complex in him, implanting him with a profound sense of morality. Hospitalization in special sections of an asylum for the criminally insane would help passive pederasts, whose homosexuality was due to morbid alterations "of the spirit, a congenital and degenerative vice, epilepsy, an acquired insanity, imbecility, arrested development, or a genital aberration." The director of the Cagliari prison was sure that this might solve the problem of homo-sexuality: "For this reason I believe that before long the shameful scourge of pederasty will be eliminated, marking another victory for the Fascist Regime." However, not everyone was so confident. Indeed there were many who called for harsher measures and the strict application of prison regulations, in particular Art. 165 No. 12, which punished obscene acts against public morality,[63] thus, a return to the traditional approach of repression.

Likewise, Riccardo Conti, Novelli's successor as the new director of the Institutions of Prevention and Punishment, faced the moral and disciplinary problem of homosexuality in prisons and also proposed sending pederasts to establishments for the physically and mentally disabled. In the larger peniten-tiaries, they were, however, already "kept separated in a special section, where, under the names of various artists, the entreaties of their companions in vice and depravity could be heard from one cell to another." Couples of "abnormal individuals" often formed in prison, where the active pederast offered "his darling" gifts, food, and cigarettes, taking care to satisfy his every desire. Fre-quently, there were cases of jealousy and fights, which broke out because somebody dared to approach a passive pederast already under the protection of another prisoner. Conti's description of the "prison world" was made even more evocative by the portrayal of a "young elegant homosexual or

male-female," "with languid eyes," "floating and effeminate movements, who
had been put into isolation."[64] In fact, by making him believe that his behavior—
"customary and esteemed in the times of ancient Greek, and therefore not
shameful"—was not blameworthy, they had been able to extort a confession
from him.[65] The unfortunate youth, nicknamed Messicana, had confirmed the
clear distinction between active and passive pederasts to the director, noting,
however, that, "these two faculties are often coupled in the same individual."
While active pederasts keep their names, passive ones, "in other words the
feminine types, conventionally called T.A. (Ti-a)," had feminine nicknames
and dressed "like women with necklines that plunged down their backs,"
"almost all of them had a male lover" and were principally young, although
there were also "married men whose wives sometimes did not know about their
husbands' vice and depravity." They recognized one another by some special
gestures: "asking for a match, offering a cigarette, going up to a urinal, or asking
for information." Many prostituted themselves and preferred to do so with "a
degenerate foreigner looking for sodomitic satisfaction." Conti considered this
long confession further proof that "all inverted and perverted subjects, exhibition-
ists, sadists, masochists, and homosexuals," were a "special class of degenerates"
who, "due to their constitutional abnormality," could not "escape the imperative
of their organic defect, "and so tended inevitably to continue committing the
same obscene acts and to return to prison with surprising regularity.[66]

Insane Asylums

As we have seen in their reports, prison directors frequently suggested locking
pederasts up in insane asylums with the double function of segregation and
therapy, of treatment and social defense. As it were, some homosexuals responsible for crimes, but not considered to be in full possession of their faculties due
to their sexual anomaly, were not sent to prison at all. Instead, they were put
directly into asylums for the criminally insane. Indeed, when the judges had to
deal with cases of homosexuality, they were faced with "a specific kind of crime
that is in itself a revelation and sign of mental disorder, according to the most
recent scientific discoveries in relation to psychopathy"; consequently, "anyone
who is unfortunately compelled to act in a certain way spurred by his peculiar
structure," does not "possess the ability to act on will."[67] The fact that most of
the medical and psychiatric studies on homosexuality were based on analyses of
pederasts in normal or criminal insane asylums, suggests that there was a rather
conspicuous number of them confined to these institutions, and shows, above
all, that committing them was a well-established procedure.[68]

The birth of the abnormal, as Foucault maintains,[69] was a result of the medicalization of deviation, of the attempt to explain exceptions rationally, in so much as they are were no longer seen as examples of unconventionality but as forms of mental alteration. Lombroso-like studies on the figure of the genius, as well as those directed at defining and classifying sexual perversions, all had a similar approach and were aimed at understanding every behavior that represented a deviation from the norm. In this way, psychiatry acquired scientific, as well as social and moral, values; social, because it contributed to keeping a check on homosexuals and marginalizing deviation; moral, because it established the rules for correct behavior. Therefore, homosexuality entered the sphere of pathology, and from time to time was branded as "a moral disease," "psychodegeneration," "sexual neurosis," and "aberration of the genetic sense." Committing homosexuals to insane asylums functioned to isolate, analyze, and cure them. They were viewed as sexual psychopaths, dissolute individuals equivalent to lunatics and criminals, whose anomalous nature drove them inexorably to break the rules of sexual behavior. As Mario Galzigna pointed out, "homosexuals, often referred to with veiled and cautious terms, were committed during the first half of the [nineteenth] century as well. Occasionally, the investigating magistrate would ask the director of an insane asylum to attentively observe cases where a special kind of physical disease (for example 'a syphilitic disease of the anus') might reveal 'an illness of a suspicious nature.'"[70] Homosexuality was considered an irrational form of love—"unreason transformed into delirium of the heart, madness of desire"[71]—and little by little took its place among the stratifications of madness.

A careful analysis of the nosological files kept in the various psychiatric hospitals would be necessary to reconstruct the Fascist regime's use of insane asylums as a repressive instrument against homosexuals. The complexity of the research would require a special, separate study that would help to quantify the extent of the phenomenon, and to understand what life was like for homosexuals in insane asylums through the personal stories of single individuals and what the likelihood of them being reintegrated into society was. Although such an endeavor is outside of the scope of this particular study, analyzing some particular cases may be useful for understanding the conceptual categories and the scientific background that influenced the work of psychiatrists, as well as the criteria used to determine the presence of the "terrible vice" and the therapies considered the most efficacious for treating the "disease." The medicalization of homosexuality was a means for justifying, on pseudo-scientific grounds, a political agenda aimed at improving the population, by opposing all those whose behavior jeopardized the demographic growth of the nation.

The progressive broadening of psychiatric control to new morbid disorders and deviating behavior not only caused a substantial increase in the number of those committed to insane asylums,[72] but gave psychiatric institutes a further task: to establish and defend the rules of sexual conduct. Certain forms of sexuality, "abuses of the senses" were considered to be the origin or result of many mental disorders, in particular onanism and homosexuality. The immorality of a person had to be ascertained through careful observation. If it were not treated or repressed, it could give rise to mental illnesses and become a serious threat to society. With this double function of treating an individual's mental illness and eliminating the danger he represented, the insane asylum, a place for committing undesirable individuals and those who upset the established order from society, served a supportive function for the police force as well. A substantial school of historiography has highlighted this very aspect of social control, the disciplining and repressing of deviation, carried out thanks to medical knowledge and the use of insane asylums. The works of Foucault and Klaus Dörner, which trace the connection between the attempt to control deviation and the formulation of social norms, both underline how insane asylums were instrumental for rejecting and excluding those who were "different." They also note how, little by little, the objective of treatment was overshadowed by the imperatives of social control and segregation.[73] Insane asylums were transformed into hospital-prisons, used to repress various forms of behavior that, although they did not openly break the law, were considered dangerous and abnormal, the result of the uncontrolled instincts of weak and easily influenced individuals. Psychiatry's interest in homosexuality and prostitution led to a great increase in the number of individuals considered morally degenerate being interned in insane asylums.

Their moral depravity, along with a desire to satisfy their "insane" passions through any means possible, placed homosexuals in a particular category of deviants, who were considered dangerous yet not easily definable as lunatics. Diagnosing them was often uncertain. As part of a vast range of people whom the medical and legal worlds called antisocial, they were sent to prison or committed to insane asylums, depending on the case.[74] Conflicts of jurisdiction between the medical and judicial systems were frequent, but in some circumstances, the two interacted. Police officers, judges, and psychiatrists all cooperated to decide how socially dangerous subjects should be treated; not by chance, homosexuals who had been sentenced more than once for theft or indecent behavior were committed to insane asylums and removed once and for all from society.[75] The ease with which one might be committed was considered an efficacious means of pressuring homosexuals to keep their behavior out of the public eye. During the Fascist regime, the Giolitti law of February 14, 1904 (No.

36), which provided for obligatory commitment in an insane asylum for danger-ous, mentally ill persons or for those who "create public scandal[,] was still in force." Yet, a simple request, presented to the judge together with a medical certificate and an attested affidavit, on the part of a relative, tutor, or "anyone else in the interest of sick persons or society" was enough to commit an individual. In other urgent cases, an individual could be committed at the direct behest of local police authorities. After a period of observation, the director of the mental hospital wrote a report on "the nature and degree of the illness," on the basis of which the court could authorize commitment or issue an order for the "imme-diate discharge" of the individual.[76]

The direct link between the threat that one posed to society and their being committed was evident in the laws relating to insane asylums. For many psychiatrists this relation was worrisome. For example, Leonardo Bianchi main-tained that "hospitals for mental illness should be real hospitals for treatment and not institutes for isolating and confining sick people, which is the function of the police; whether one represents a danger or not is of secondary impor-tance."[77] Furthermore, the laws reveal that there was also a close link between the family and insane asylums. In fact, relatives could rid themselves of an un-wanted family member, proposing commitment for those who, as often happened with homosexuals, broke the moral rules and upset domestic peace with their indecent and scandalous behavior. In some cases, insane asylums ended up taking those refused by their families, freeing the community of the disturbance caused by these undesirable figures. The mental hospital had the task of changing the individual, treating his mental illness and correcting his abnormal behavior; however, besides aiming at rehabilitation, it was given the important function of classifying and forming clinical knowledge by dividing patients according to their mental disorders and the danger they posed, as well as carrying out close surveillance. Patients were continually analyzed, both anthropologically and mentally. Through physiognomic descriptions and anthropometric measure-ments, their behavior was checked and their attitudes and moods were recorded so as to verify possible improvements and to have a clear picture of how their stay in the hospital was progressing.

Psychiatrists paid close attention to their patients' sexuality as well; any irregular or deviant sexual expression was seen a symptom of a worsening, pathology and was grounds for confinement. Patients were subjected to scrupu-lous observations aimed at finding out the duration of their immoral behavior and justifying the use of harsher correctional measures. In his reconstruction of the vicissitudes of a fictional friar who lived at the beginning of the 1900s, Paolo Sorcinelli shows that homosexuality was an important aspect for diagnosing a patient.[78] The presence of a "perverted sexual tendency of the pederastic sort" could be further proof of insanity and could confirm any suspicion of moral madness. Practicing sodomy, a clear expression of the abnormal tendencies of a person under psychiatric observation, was often decisive evidence for choosing whether to confine an individual in a mental hospital or leave him with the police. The problem of "moral madness" had been a matter of debate among psychiatrists for some time. They did, however, agree that homosexuality was a form of hereditary degeneration: "The lack of sexual activity or homosexual experience becomes the consequence, not the cause, of being low born. They are children of prostitutes, drunkards, delinquents, or lunatics, determined by heredity a priori as capable only of inadequate, offensive, and disorderly behavior. This is why the insane asylum is the only place suitable for a pederast to go on living in disgrace, marginalized from society."[79] Doctors, who cooperated in defending society from immorality and deviation, were expected to contribute to the fight against crime as well. With the arrival of forensic psychiatry, psychiatrists tried to influence trials: in their capacity as medical-legal experts, they studied the accused person in order to determine his responsibility in the crime and to establish a link between the crime and the offender's insanity.[80] Their reports are, thus, a useful historical source for understanding both psychiatric practice and how deviation was treated.[81]

In the case of homosexuals, the reports were used to clarify the extent to which the accused had been conditioned by his sexual tendency in the moment in which he committed the crime, as well as if it had altered his mental faculties to the point of making him incapable of understanding the crime committed. Thus, the inquest could proceed and be completed within the mental hospital, where it was decided, through interrogations, analyses, and observation if the criminal should be held responsible for his actions. In this case, the criminal was not condemned for the crime, but was committed so that he might be cured. However, criminal insane asylums increasingly tended to become repressive instruments to shut up those considered "irrecoverable." The case of a Genovese patient illustrates how psychiatry was instrumentally exploited in order to marginalize incorrigible criminals from society. Because of his criminal record, Giovanni Battista P. was committed in 1933. He had already been condemned by the Turin court to five years of imprisonment for multiple accounts of grand larceny and for having criminal associations with a gang who, according to the accusation, solicited and robbed sexual perverts. During these "unnatural sexual unions," one of the delinquents would come out from under the bed, and unbeknownst to the unfortunate person, steal his money. Giovanni Battista P. was first sent to jail in Genoa, and then, after a few months, to the Aversa mental hospital, which was considered a more suitable place to cure his perverse nature.

The lack of an evident reason for this transfer, shows how widespread the use of criminal insane asylums was during the Fascist regime.[82] With the new penal code and penitentiary regulations issued in 1931, the regime had reformed the law on criminal insane asylums, in which "the absolute presumption of danger" posed by all those who had been acquitted of legal proceedings due to insanity was established; they were to be automatically committed and carry out their sentences in a criminal insane asylum, by now, a kind of alternative institution to prison. Thanks to the Fascist regime's emphasis on defending society from mental illnesses and contagion by the degenerate acts of insane and abnormal individuals, the function of insane asylums was broadened to include antisocial and immoral people, in addition to the insane. Valeria Pezzi's study of the Reggio Emilia mental hospital during the Fascist period reveals that, despite continuity with the preceding period, greater attention was given to imprisonment during Fascism; "behavioral orthopedics" and "social control" were extended, giving deviation a much wider interpretation than ever before. The author states that "the preventive measures applied to defend the race, which psychiatrists had begun to yield to, in their tone and proposals ended with a call for places to be built that could socially isolate morally corrupt or dangerous subjects. Fascism's defense of the race and psychiatry's labeling abnormality as a social danger converged in a new cultural tendency of internment and social defense."[83]

Repression was used in insane asylums against sexual deviants as well, along with persistent moral persuasion. Psychiatrists found treating homosexuals complicated because it was their very nature that determined their sexual tendency. There was no treatment capable of guaranteeing sure results for these subjects, whose instinct dominated their will. However, some kinds of treatment seemed to have positive effects on persons whose homosexuality seemed to be a symptom of a mental disorder or a weakened nervous system. Hypnosis was held to be the most efficacious treatment to cure cases of occasional homosexuality. As Schrenck von Notzing's research on sexual perverts showed, the foul habits of the patients could be interrupted through repeated hypnotic sessions and by persuading them to have sexual intercourse with female prostitutes under the effect of alcohol.[84] The remedies proposed by many psychiatrists were the source of controversy. Some maintained that only through marriage and constant contact with women could the perverse nature of homosexuals be changed.[85] Their "abnormal" instincts had to be repressed with "psychological therapy, through the association of ideas": they had to be persuaded to link sexual activity to normal psychological mental images, to associate sensations of pleasure with heterosexual intercourse. Even more criticized were the proposals to castrate or sterilize sexual perverts put forward by those who thought it was a form of hereditary degeneration that could only be cured through drastic measures. Ferdinando De Napoli, for example, considered the radiological sterilization of testicles and ovaries a useful method for preventing "individuals who were ill and not fit for begetting offspring from procreating."[86]

Eugenic concern, the fear that this serious "abnormality" could be transmitted from father to son,[87] circulated in scientific circles as well, where a debate arose on this subject after the sterilization of homosexuals had been introduced in some American states, Scandinavian countries, and Nazi Germany. Thanks above all to Catholic influence, these practices were never implemented in Italy.[88] The so-called "moral therapy" was better received; it tried to rouse "normal" sexual stimuli through attentive education, based on explaining the negative effects of "unnatural practices." The aim was to cause such a profound feeling of disgust at the very idea of relapsing into homosexual behavior that the "perverse" desire would be inhibited, or at least "limit this morbid act, which invincibly arouses compassion, not without repugnance, in a normal man." Even better effects would be achieved if "artificial changes of hormonal stimuli" were associated with "educative, preventive treatment."[89]

The aim of committing someone to an insane asylum was to progressively moralize his sexuality through tenacious, influential treatment. Rehabilitation was to be achieved through a process in which norms were interiorized and the afflicted accepted the sexual role given to him by society. Insane asylums carried out scrupulous "moral treatments," which were intended to "normalize" the mentally disturbed through control, conforming behavior, and the imposition of a healthy, balanced, and productive lifestyle. Principles of hygiene and morality were combined in a therapeutic plan aimed at rehabilitating all those whose insanity derived from their immoderate passions.

Apart from the results these institutes might reach in treating sexual anomalies, they were useful places for segregating "deviant" individuals. The doctors themselves were aware of the inefficaciousness of certain treatments on homosexuals, as the director of the Montelupo Fiorentino criminal mental hospital confessed. Despite the great effort he had put into treating fifteen passive and active pederasts, he had not succeeded in correcting their "deviation." In the end, he limited himself to intensifying the ergotherapy and busying them in isolated work in order to distract their "attention from insane purposes." The director of the criminal mental hospital of Barcellona Pozzo di Giotto was also rather skeptical about treating homosexuals. He ordered the hospital's personnel and guards to report every episode of sodomy immediately and to keep a constant eye on the new arrivals, paying particular attention to any possible pederastic tendency and following "the callow youths step by step, those effeminate ones with rather undeveloped sexual organs, with small testicles, thick lips, developed breasts, curvy, broad hips." This scrupulous monitoring led to discovering 25 pederasts out of a total of 471 patients (5.3 percent), most of whom were youths from twenty to thirty years old, coming mainly from southern Italy. A close watch was kept over all of them, and they were put in dormitories with companions who were absolutely averse to pederastic practices, while some were kept isolated and employed in services where it was possible to keep a constant eye on them. The hospital director did not really believe it was possible to cure their "morbid degeneration." He was convinced that it was not easy to eliminate "deviations of the erotic sense," because all his attempts to cure homosexuality had failed, except in cases where it was the result of other mental disorders or was simply a momentary sexual aberration. Indeed, the mental hospital of Barcellona Pozzo di Giotto had subjected the pederasts to hypnosis, psychoanalytic therapy, and medical treatment by prescribing bromide, special diets, and gymnastics. However, as the results were discouraging, the treatment was abandoned and unremitting supervision and isolation were chosen to fight this serious phenomenon.[90] Sometimes these "deviations of the erotic sense" were not even expressed, as in the case of a sixteen-year-old boy, "a mentally degenerated (passive) homosexual" whose father had him hospitalized in the Santa Maria della Pietà hospital for the mentally ill in Rome. In 1939, after five years under observation, the director decided to discharge him, as he had not shown relevant signs from a sexual point of view, had not given proof of his perversion, and on the whole had behaved extremely well. The director of the mental hospital thought it was inhuman not to grant him another opportunity, "especially considering that he has never been dangerous . . . in the legal sense."[91]

In some cases, because of the great presence of homosexuals in asylums, doctors, nurses, and guards were accused of encouraging or of being directly involved in pederastic practices.[92] During the Fascist period, resorting to the accusation of homosexuality was not limited only to insane asylums but was widespread and often used for political motives.

6

The Political Use
of Homosexuality

Nothing arouses the indiscreet interest of petty law-abiding societies more than
the sincere demands to keep one's public and private lives separate.

GIORGIO BASSANI,
Gli occhiali d'oro

The New Fascist Policy

During the Fascist period, homosexuality—the accusation of practicing it—
became a common weapon for attacking one's political adversaries. Accusing
an adversary of homosexuality served to remove politically troublesome individuals or to have others, often public figures, dismissed, threatened, or blackmailed. Whether the person was actually a homosexual or not mattered very
little. Interestingly, however, some influential personalities (whether in politics,
culture, or economics) who were notoriously homosexual were tolerated, or at
least not persecuted, and in some cases continued to receive the greatest respect.
The ambiguous treatment of pederasts, always hovering somewhere between
sin and crime, vice and illness, allowed for a certain freedom of action that
enabled the authorities to judge the most suitable measures to take; in some
cases, absolute intransigence or, in others, the broadest tolerance. The regime
tended to prefer to resolve the most embarrassing cases quickly and painlessly
by postponing decisions, sparking clashes between various authorities over
whose competence it was and often shelving proceedings that in any case were
always gradual and preceded with warnings, reprimands, and threats.

Discretion, the maintaining of the social order and the supreme arbiter during Fascism, made homosexuality into a weapon for political battles. Such accusations were not infrequent. In fact, with the repression of free political confrontation within the PNF, slander spread like wildfire, striking any and all dissent, any deviation from the regime's official line, any voice out of harmony with the chorus.[1] Once Fascism's opponents were eliminated and civil society — the locus for the formation of individuals and the free expression of ideas — was gagged and blindfolded, only Fascism remained to absorb the moods and aspirations of the people, who had no other outlet. As Gramsci foresaw in 1926, "with the totalitarian system the Fascists aim to set up, conflicts that have no other outlet will manifest themselves within Fascism itself."[2] In fact, as noted by Emilio Gentile as well, clashes and rivalries continued to characterize the PNF: "behind the mythical sacredness of the totalitarian state, there was a silent battle among the 'potentates' of the Fascist oligarchy, each one defending his own territory against the ambitions of others and aiming to extend the range of his own hegemony."[3] Backstairs conflicts among party officials (*gerarchi*) were constant and in some cases bitter, with each man eager to climb to power by throwing discredit on his political adversaries. The internal struggles and discrepancies among the differing faces of Fascism were often expressed in the form widespread blackmail and slander, meant to cast political rivals in a bad light.

In the wake of Emilio Gentile's studies, Salvatore Lupo analyzed the new instruments adopted in the political struggle created by the totalitarian regime. When the Fascists came to power, politics changed. These changes were not, however, merely bureaucratic and administrative. Fascism's hostility toward the old liberal system, which had been defined by a paralyzing counterpositioning of parties, prompted it to project a government in which change and conservation cyclically alternated in order to continuously renew the ruling class and guarantee an internal dynamism capable of preventing sclerosis and realizing the myth of permanent revolution, necessary for totalitarianism. Nevertheless, centralized decision making and the vertical control of the hierarchical ladder did not eliminate competition and localism, nor did they put an end to clashes among groups and lobbies. The thing to change was the way in which these conflicts over power, whose existence was denied by the regime, were resolved and expressed. Hence the conspicuous use of anonymous letters, secret documents and plots, secretly authored by various factions. As Salvatore Lupo wrote, "The changing of the guards in the PNF's provincial federations was more often than not brought about by swindles, sex scandals, and improbable accusations, and was meant to express the Fascists' disgust for old politics, for a virus that could be reawakened at any moment in the government buildings of the capital and throughout the provinces, even within the regime, the PNF or among the most faithful Blackshirts."[4] In short, the political battle went from being a public debate over programs, tendencies, and values into veiled accusations about people's private lives; confrontation between political ideas gave way to conflicts over moral conduct.

In a dictatorial regime, in which power was ever more consolidated in the hands of Mussolini, every attempt to gain the favor of the Duce seemed justified and served to maintain one's position. Mussolini himself, determined to put an end to the wrangling and fights, which were dangerous for party unity, forcefully pronounced the following condition: "Clashes between men are not allowed because there are no conflicts regarding our aims."[5] His policy in regard to his regime was *divide et impera*: a system of rivalry and distrust, conflicting ambitions, suspicion, and slander aimed at weakening the power of the most influential *gerarchi* and rising above them as the arbitrator of their fights. Creating a number of minor characters in constant rivalry with one another and indebted to the Duce for their success fortified Mussolini's charisma as a leader and prevented the emergence of any other strong personality capable of winning approval and becoming in some way an alternative to the Duce himself. The competition among the various "Ducettes" and the clashes among the PNF factions strengthened the myth of Mussolini.[6] However, the Fascist leader vividly remembered the damage caused by the excessive power of local *ras*, once so powerful that they influenced and halted his political plans. It was fundamental that he shrewdly exploit these personal and group conflicts. Although in apparent contradiction with the goal of party unity, these conflicts represented an important instrument of power and totalitarian domination insofar as they prevented the formation of any rival positions of power and fostered vitality within the regime. Thus, two objectives were achieved by this rapid rotation of positions that gave everyone the impression they could be substituted from one day to another; however, at the same time it drove them all to do their utmost to become indispensable, with the false hope they could avoid the changeover.

In order to facilitate substitutions, the Fascists made marked use of the practice of gathering information on influential figures, at times using it in their favor, at others against them. Continuous fear of falling victim to the slander of one's political adversaries fostered a climate of suspicion in which everyone spied and was spied on at the same time.[7] When useful, Mussolini himself used dossiers and anonymous reports, scrupulously compiled through information received from the Polizia Politica, to remove a *gerarca* from office or make him more malleable.[8] Those who were closest to him knew very well how unscrupulous he was in using confidential information to get rid of someone: "Only in the last few years did he decide to be more considerate when dealing with these cases: forewarning of the dismissals, farewell letters and expressions of gratitude."[9]

Always knowing the actions of those who had responsibilities within the regime was a means of controlling his entourage and keeping a tight hold on them. One's private life became a particularly important aspect from a political point of view since accusations of illegally making money, corruption, leading an immoral life, or breaking the rules of Fascist virility could all quickly end a brilliant career. Within this framework, homosexuality as well became an important weapon against those who strayed from the ideal of masculinity prescribed by the regime. Merits and demerits depended directly on one's virility or lack thereof: those who had not taken part in the First World War, those who led dissolute lives or were unmarried, those who did not have children or had unfaithful wives risked disciplinary measures and, above all, became potential targets for their adversaries or for anyone looking to defame them. From the highest levels of the party hierarchy, as in the case of Augusto Turati, down to the lowest levels, as in the case of the *podestà* of the small village of Sgurgola,[10] accusing someone of homosexuality was quite common in political disputes.

Personality battles based on mud-slinging and struggles among *gerarchi* determined to show off their own group to the detriment of others brought to light a number of cases of deplorable behavior and worked to discredit the party and its officials. The fact that the Fascist political party had little credibility with the public made the cult of the Duce stronger, but also had the adverse effect of damaging public consensus toward the regime.[11] However, Mussolini realized how damaging these scandals were, and was only officially "in favor of absolute moral intransigence" toward those with political and administrative offices, according to De Felice; in practice, this rule was applied only in the case of less important figures, when the police report did not cause a stir and when it served to give the impression of a regime ready to intervene harshly against anyone who did not fulfill his duty. On the contrary, Mussolini was much more indulgent in cases where more prominent figures were involved: it was better to suppress the scandal and prevent any doubts about the official image of a Fascist regime composed of absolutely upright men, who were entirely devoted to their work and their families, who led exemplary lives fully respecting the standards of bourgeois respectability. Behind closed doors, the weaknesses of the *gerarchi* were used by the Duce to remove those guilty of immoral or illegal behavior, although he rarely took official measures against them.[12]

In addition to having the task of watching subversives, the Polizia Politica was employed to keep an eye on the Fascist officials themselves. Their phones were tapped and their public and private behavior was scrupulously noted. Farinacci complained about this "harmful" system to Mussolini: "The so-called OVRA [the Fascist secret political police] has created dismay and suspicion among the best men of our regime. . . . [T]here isn't a minister, *gerarca*, or

unblemished Fascist who is not subjected to surveillance and control in everything he does or says."[13] The number of documents making up the dossiers on
the various *gerarchi* is enormous, as those of the Duce's personal secretariat attest.
Even leading figures in the regime provided themselves with a more or less
considerable number of their own informers who gathered information about
their rivals. These documents, which were almost always handed over to the
police in order to ruin an opponent, added even more information to the police
records.[14] Every morning, the police chief gave Mussolini the most interesting
confidential reports relating slander or truths about the misdeeds and political,
financial, and sentimental activities of different *gerarchi* of the regime.[15] Bocchini
acquainted Mussolini with the weak points of almost all his men and armed
him with information to use against any of them who was gaining too much
political prestige.[16] From the marginalia including Mussolini's comments and
the possible measures to take, it appears that love affairs, transgressions, and
unfaithfulness particularly aroused the Duce's interest. A person's morality was
a more decisive factor than his educational record in his rise or fall within the
Fascist hierarchy. In the rather morbid attention given to apparently insignificant
and banal facts, heroism and morality are blended together and conflated.
Extremely detailed descriptions of the sexual habits, company, and private
behavior of his officials were given ample coverage in the reports. Being the
manifestation of a common ideal, lifestyle took on a fundamental importance
for the regime, as in monastic and military institutions. As Nicolò Zapponi pointed
out, "among the most imperceptible, yet visceral reasons for the success of
Fascism, there was a relatively widespread readiness to believe that could be
found in matters concerning *lifestyle.*"[17]

In this framework, private affairs, like age, sexual tendency, and civil status
were given a new public and political importance.[18] The accusation of homosexuality, then, acquired special importance because it could mean one's immediate expulsion from the party and all the consequences this involved. The
difficulty of proving one's innocence facilitated slander and the organization of
plots aimed at destroying various *gerarchi* politically. Breaking the Fascist rules
of virility called for serious punishment, though perhaps not always as severe as
Nazi repercussions; one need only think of the execution of Röhm's storm
troopers ordered by Hitler. Although the level of Nazi violence toward its
enemies—political adversaries, Jews, gypsies, Jehovah's witnesses, the mentally
ill, and homosexuals—cannot be compared to that of the Fascists, accusing a
person of pederasty both in Germany and Italy was used for the benefit of
public opinion to justify measures whose goal was different from that declared.
Mussolini once said: "I'm interested in men from the waist up only."[19] And it
is indeed true that, despite his apparent moral severity, he did not give much

importance to erotic-sentimental aspects, regarding which he was quite permissive, beginning with his own behavior. Nevertheless, he knew he could use that which regarded men "from the waist down" for political purposes. Sexual weaknesses that fell outside the "sound" heterosexual appetite of Fascist males did not go unnoticed by Mussolini, who used them as a tool for domination. In short, the erotic habits of those who worked with him were irrelevant only if they did not deviate from the period's ideal of virility.

Thus, the employment of spies and informers, which had grown well out of proportion, was widely used by the regime, which had constructed an unprecedentedly well-knit and widespread network of espionage.[20] It was a suffocating and invasive system that controlled every minute aspect of the citizens' private lives and searched out their most intimate secrets. Mimmo Franzinelli wrote, "The road of informers is paved with sordid desires and back-room rivalries, with the dreams of greatness of those who establish intimate relationships with the authorities in order to play out personal vendettas. Personal interests and less than praiseworthy feelings spurred many ordinary people to spread rumors and suspicions, arouse doubts, machinate tricks, insinuate slander, exaggerate village gossip, and throw discredit on personal enemies by cynically exploiting the act of reporting to the police."[21] Informing was used at all levels to oust *gerarchi* or comrades, but also to keep a check on and blackmail figures belonging to spheres that were not always aligned with Fascism, such as the church or the monarchy. The unsuspected informers gained the trust of their interlocutors and were able to collect precious information. It was natural, then, for Fascists to use homosexual informers as well, to keep a check on pederasts and extort secrets from them.

Homosexuals and the Polizia Politica

Homophobic prejudice was so deeply rooted that even the Polizia Politica ended up considering pederasts deviators and, as such, potential subversives whose circles were possible anti-Fascist dens requiring close observation. Not surprisingly, homosexuality was listed as a specific category, often referred to in the personal files of people watched by the police precisely for their "particular" sexual tendency. These Polizia Politica files disappeared, most likely during the great looting of documents that occurred after the fall of the Fascist regime. However, it is known for certain that some agents were specifically charged with the task of investigating those who deviated from the standards of Fascist virility. The Polizia Politica were not motivated by moral concerns; they were not interested in discovering the largest possible number of homosexuals, but in finding out how many of them were anti-Fascists. Informers who were declared homosexuals were paid by the police to carry out these particular assignments and, in some cases, a person's homosexuality was itself used as leverage in order to convince him to collaborate with the police. The threat of measures could be used to persuade the victim to begin spying as an informer paid by Bocchini. For example, in the case of Gerhard Dobbert, the respected German teacher of political economy, the discovery of "a dark side of his personality," "his homosexual tendencies with a special fondness for young boys," and his involvement in a trial for corrupting minors, left him at the mercy of the police chief who offered him help in exchange for his services as an informer. In order to save his reputation and not compromise his career, Dobbert agreed to be a spy. However, shocked by the days passed in prison and upset by the tragic turn the affair had taken, he took his life a few days later.[22]

There is not sufficient proof to maintain that these homosexual informers were driven to collaborate with the Polizia Politica because they themselves were threatened or blackmailed. Nevertheless, working as spies allowed them a higher standard of living than what they could normally afford and guaranteed them a freedom that was impossible for other citizens, in their sexual lives as well. These privileges were surely important to these informers, who, for the most part, had lived in the milieu of D'Annunzio and Futurism, and were accustomed to adventurous and extravagant lifestyles. Reluctant to conform to rigid moral norms, perennially restless, and, in many ways, frustrated and disappointed by the fact that their youthful expectations had not been realized, they let themselves be enticed by the police and agreed to become spies. Alessandro Pozzi, Vittorio Terracini, Italo Tavolato, and Friz Kusen were some of the known homosexual informers used to obtain information in social circles, which were otherwise inaccessible to police.

Pozzi, informer No. 316, had been a follower of Filippo Corridoni and was in favor of Italy's intervention in the First World War, in which he fought as a volunteer at only sixteen years of age. Later, he was a legionnaire with D'Annunzio in Fiume and was present at the 1919 gathering of Fascists in Piazza San Sepolcro. He took part in the activities of the Milanese Fascist Party and gained the friendship of Mario Giampaoli, but ended up by paying the consequences of his patron's political decline.[23] Expelled from the Fascist Party after the purge of 1929, Pozzi could not find work as a freelance journalist and had suffered a serious nervous breakdown. After various attempts at suicide, he was hospitalized in an insane asylum. It was in this period that he was recruited as an informer. Indeed, at the beginning of 1930 he was already spying on his former friends, the dissident followers of Giampaoli, whom Mussolini had decided to get rid of once and for all.[24]

The lifestyle he enjoyed thanks to his new activity as an informer is described in detail by Giovanni Comisso, his comrade in adventure at the time of Fiume. He enjoyed luxury, travel, sports cars, parties, and wild entertainment, and he ran in affluent social circles: a golden life with unlimited money to spend with his young "friends," whom he did not hesitate to report to the police when they were suspected of anti-Fascism.[25] He did not hide his bisexuality—he loved "women and young men without distinction"—knowing full well his role as a spy would ensure his impunity. This arrogant attitude became irksome. Yet everyone, police authorities included, were obliged to put up with his excesses.[26] Moreover, Pozzi used his knowledge of the unconventional sexual preferences of important people in the Milanese federation to throw suspicion on the new federal direction, or to gain power through blackmail and the threat of scandal. Comisso describes him as "an impossible man, dominated by a sexual and dietary insatiability and political passion. Slightly crippled by a car accident, he boasted that this handicap was the result of a heroic action. He carried out his work with a dreadful and grotesque imagination. He could never be trusted. That is why I could not bear him."[27] Comisso also describes Pozzi's gruesome death in November 1944: well known to anti-Fascists, he was arrested when Mussolini fell and freed after a few months, but he was later abducted from his house in Serrada di Folgaria by a group of partisans who, "after beating him, took him to a sawmill and sawed him to pieces while he was still alive."[28]

Vittorio Terracini, a Jewish tradesman from Turin, was another Polizia Politica informer actively engaged in supplying information about homosexuals. There is some confusion surrounding his political past. According to one rather implausible account, Terracini had supported nationalism and taken part in the actions of the anti-Bolshevik movement as a young man. But it is much more likely that he had been a subversive with communist ideas and a union organizer of barbers in Turin. It is known for certain that he was involved in Masonic and Fascist circles. Terracini's troubles began in 1927 when, together with his brother Augusto and his friend Claudio Colisi Rossi, a former provincial secretary of the Turin Fascist Party, he was implicated in forging Treasury bonds. Police investigations showed him to be a "morally repugnant individual," because he was a "well-known and incorrigible pederast." Because of his moral conduct, the prefect suggested that his apparent Fascist sentiments be doubted.[29] However, he managed to get out of trouble by collaborating with the Polizia Politica, who set him up in the network of informers working for Police Commissioner Renzo Mambrini, the person responsible for the OVRA subsection in Turin as well as espionage activities in France.[30] That the Polizia Politica considered Terracini a homosexual, despite his denials, was cause enough to consider him part of the Anti-Fascist Concentration:[31] in fact, he had struck up a friendship with another "individual devoted to pederasty," Luigi Torzo Campaner,[32] an important left-wing member of the PSI (Italian Socialist Party), formerly in *confino* but at the time in France, where he had adventurously escaped.[33] It was in Paris that Terracini approached Campaner, taking him to Nice in 1932 and providing him with financial support, while using him to obtain information on the anti-Fascists and creating discord within the Concentration.[34] In one of his reports, Terracini spoke of his relationship with Torzo and explained the reason for some of his "Parisian friendships and attitudes":

> This is how I "caught" Gino [Torzo] and bound him to me irremediably. Unfortunately I had not foreseen the impossible: that he . . . would fall madly in love with me. I was unaware that I had such good qualities! Naturally, and I hope you do not need me to swear to this, I led him up to the "right point" and then told him NO, and, as it always happens, this strengthened his love and my power over him. He continues to hope that one day or another I shall give in. How disgusting! But he is as jealous as a cat in spring, and every now and then makes scenes with me that are revolting. When I really do not know what to do, I send him to a professional or someone to let himself go . . . and then he calms down for a short while. So now I have finally explained everything. . . . He is completely mad and degenerate; but he is extremely valuable and will be useful for a long time.

While in Nice, Terracini tried to connect with another anti-Fascist, Alfredo Quaglino, an engineer, who had interrupted his activities with the Polizia Politica and joined the political exiles working against their national government. However, it was not easy to exploit Quaglino's homosexuality in order to gather information from him, since "homosexuals are like a caste, even more closed than masonry and, although it is very easy to approach them, it is not so easy to become their friends without being introduced." After investigating "in the shady and eclectic places of entertainment in Monte Carlo and Cannes," Terracini realized he had been wrong in judging Quaglino a pederast; nevertheless, he managed to make friends with him and elicit his secrets.[35] In his work as an informer, discrediting Quaglino and continuously contacting representatives of the left-wing movements that were alternatives to the Socialist Party— maximalists, republicans, and anarchists—he eventually aroused the suspicions of anti-Fascists. His cover was burned and he was forced to return to Italy in haste.[36]

Recognition of his increasingly valuable service due to his "incomparable zeal," his "excellent capacities," and "absolute loyalty"[37] allowed him to become an autonomous informer of the Polizia Politica, alias Terra, No. 657, acting against the Giustizia e Libertà (Justice and Liberty) movement, communists, and above all Jews and pederasts.[38] In 1936 he handed in a scrupulous report outlining his plan of attack against Zionism and an initiative to ban Jews from public life; he was extremely conscientious in this activity and tried to make use of it to be absolved from the anti-Jewish laws when they were made, counting on his good service for the country and the regime.[39]

Terracini underscored the anti-Fascist danger that "the serious problem that homosexuality presented in every sector of the community," and summed up and explained his activity as an informer in one of these reports, written in 1937, on a well-known and respected playwright, a Roman count employed by the Ministry of Popular Culture:

> Since 1934, when reporting the troubling spread of sexual inversion, I have pointed out that another, purely political problem went hand in hand with it, namely, that most homosexuals are anti-Fascists and, as such, influence young men with harmful and defamatory propaganda against the Regime. Not to mention from the fact that the actions of these homosexuals are completely counter to the efforts of the Regime. Nowadays, as most people are paying more attention to criticism and biased rumors—in short, to everything that denigrates Fascism—it would be extremely useful to go over old papers again and have a good look at this special category of individuals. As I go along and as the opportunity presents itself, I shall indicate some well-chosen names among those who, due to their social status, prestige, or culture, are more harmful than others and do not deserve any leniency.[40]

The great quantity of information provided to Mambrini by Terracini "on disgusting pseudo-intellectual and undeniably pederastic circles" was the basis of a series of reports in which the commissioner of the OVRA described the habits and activities of homosexuals, following the stereotype then in fashion:[41] "perverts who were naturally passive," regularly associated with intellectuals and artists, most of whom were anti-Fascists. Even though the perverts did not belong to these circles socially, they managed "to worm their way in, because where this vice is involved there are neither barriers nor shame." However, homosexuals' opposition was only ideal in nature: "their aversion was purely formal," they were not actively involved, but dangerous all the same, especially because of the strong influence homosexuals managed to exert over boys:

> When a homosexual speaks, he is paid a great deal of attention due to the impression of superiority that the ordinary person still acknowledges in a "gentleman" who is well-dressed and therefore well-educated; he generously

spouts insinuations, accusations and idiotic jokes that nevertheless make
the boy laugh. The latter will be surprised, doubtful, maybe uncertain, but
some of that poison will have settled in his mind. Unconsciously he will
become a spokesman, and that paranoiac's groundless accusations will
take on another form coming from the boy, they will seem new, serious and
maybe threatening.

The greatest danger was the infiltration of homosexuals in the army, the
disastrous consequences of which were felt throughout the ranks. Furthermore,
Mambrini believed there were some who exposed pederast propaganda with a
"dual aim: anti-Fascist and homosexual":

> These are the connoisseurs of ideas! They are complicated and love danger,
> the unforeseen and what is new. They scorn experiences common to the
> masses and seek adventure in undiscovered lands. They are the pioneers,
> the explorers and the Marco Polos of homosexuality! They take up the
> campaign enthusiastically. . . . Every Sunday they drive off like missionaries
> and take their message and all the rest to the outskirts of the capital.

Mambrini made lewd comments about another homosexual, a former
lieutenant of the *carabinieri* named Raffaele Forte, whom Terracini had met in
Paris and whom he had immediately reported to the police because of Forte's
contacts with anti-Fascists and because he was "a pederast who solicited young
boys." In May 1935 Mambrini described him like this:

> He is amoral in the full sense of the word, and those who knew him very
> well were always surprised that he had been an officer in an exclusive and
> severe service like the *carabinieri*. He is a well-known pederast: active and
> passive, dangerous in the early expressions of this . . . tendency of his, as
> he loves to "initiate" 14- or 15-year-old boys, whom he submits to this
> extreme offensive by using persuasion or force! When they are a few years
> older he himself submits. He was very well known in the homosexual circles
> of Place Blanche in Paris for what he was and did, and went regularly to
> the ill-famed Cinema Cigale, where it seems he had an accident. He was
> seen in Rome doing the same thing in the gardens near the station and in
> the movie theaters already mentioned, particularly in the Tritone. In
> short, I would be very happy to apply the new German law on sterilization
> to this individual.

Under continuous surveillance from the police and forced into financial
difficulties, Forte offered to collaborate as a spy, exploiting his acquaintances
and the possibility of slipping into the ranks of anti-Fascist exiles in Paris.

However, Mambrini's comments led the chief of the Polizia Politica division, Michelangelo Di Stefano, to refuse the offer. On the contrary, they urged Mambrini to continue keeping a watchful eye on this "person who was unreliable from all points of view and who was to be avoided both for the company he kept and for his habits."[42] In their concern about the problem of homosexuality, which they considered more "topical today than ever," both Mambrini and Terracini explicitly express a link between homosexuality and anti-Fascism. Their suggestions for remediating the problem were equally explicit: "It would be beneficial to leave an incisive mark" on that environment, with warnings or more severe measures. Only with an "authoritative and timely intervention" and the registration of all pederasts in the police records could the political problem created by homosexuality be ended, thus preventing it from spreading.

Terracini had to answer for his activity as a Polizia Politica informer at the end of the war. In fact, he was arrested in May 1945 and imprisoned, first in the Regina Coeli prison in Rome, then in Naples, where he was tried by the high commissioner's office for sanctions against Fascism. The final comments of the defending attorney were so paradoxical that it is easy to understand the insuperable difficulties of this political purge, whose failure is evidenced by the inefficiency of the actions taken against Polizia Politica informers.[43] Terracini was described as an anti-Fascist and was believed to be "a victim of persecution and a tenacious enemy of Fascism" because he was a Jew. His activity as an informer, which was impossible to deny, was depicted as a noble service for his country against immoral practices, namely, homosexuality. The attorney maintained that "in an environment of immoral practices, informers can only be beneficial, and should be praised and not condemned, even if it was carried out under the imperative of OVRA."[44] Accusing persons of homosexuality is reprehensible only when unjustly used against "decent men," which in no way applies in the this case. On July 19, 1946, Terracini was granted amnesty, and his "valuable services to the Fascist Cause" were forgotten once and for all.

The journalist Italo Tavolato was another notoriously homosexual informer. He had actively taken part in the futurist movement and was famous for his articles against traditional morality in *Lacerba*. After an experience as correspondent for *Tevere* that ended with his dismissal for reasons of morality, in 1933 he was urged to enter the network of informers by the spy Valerio Benuzzi. Thanks to Tavolato's connections with foreign press circles and his excellent knowledge of German, he was given the task of supplying information about Germany's journalists, internal politics, and citizens residing in Italy. Because of his knowledge of Nazism, he was even authorized to accept secret assignments from the Gestapo and to immediately refer what he discovered about its organization and agents.[45] In addition, he diligently reported the details on the private lives of important politicians and used his contacts in the Vatican to give the names of many anti-Fascists hidden there. However, his main contacts were with foreign correspondents in Rome. These relations benefited from his "special" friendship with Goffredo Kusen, known as Friz, another Polizia Politica informer, who had been struck off the journalists' register for his immoral conduct by the federation of the German press following the discovery of his love affair with Tavolato.[46] The two lived together in the same apartment,[47] and they contributed to the dailies *Dresdner Nest* and *Dresdner Neuste Nachrichten* under the false names of Tiberio and Nettuno, respectively. They gave detailed reports on the political beliefs and the affairs and lifestyles of journalists and homosexuals residing in Rome.[48] For example, one of Kusen and Tavolato's victims was the German journalist Joachim Boettcher. Already in 1935 Mussolini himself had ordered that he be expelled from Italy, since his "immorality, his homosexuality" had become known when his activity as an informer was examined by the SIM (Servizio Informazioni Militari—Military Information Service) on behalf of the armed forces of the Reich.[49] Boettcher was later given permission to return to Italy but was put under close surveillance. However, he was expelled again in February 1942, because Kusen and Tavolato, to whom he had ingenuously proposed to become spies for Germany, reported him to the police.[50]

Many of Tavolato's numerous reports were about the homosexuality of more or less famous figures.[51] He provided a great deal of information that was to be used at the right moment to wield disciplinary actions against his victims, such as Karl Rudolf Kircher, the correspondent of the *Frankfurten Zeitung* in Rome. Tavolato himself had suggested exploiting homosexuality for political purposes. He wrote: "Kircher is a passive pederast. . . . In view of this tendency of his, it would be easy to influence him politically: if so, one could dictate what he writes as a political writer." Kircher's "Achilles' heel" made him easy to blackmail. He knew very well that he would be "done for" if the German authorities were informed of his "deviation." Kircher tried in every way to cover up this deviation in Germany, while in Italy he abandoned himself more easily to "giving free rein to his pederastic tendencies," leading a "dissolute life." Because of Tavolato's report, the German journalist was put under close surveillance, which included tailing him and checking his mail in order to accumulate proof of his "dangerous unconventionality." Kircher kept company with young students of the Accademia del Littorio (Littorio Academy) and took them with him on his trips around Italy, staying in a boardinghouse known as the "*maison de passé* for pederasts" or in small rooms subleased exclusively for that purpose. The boys received presents or small sums of money and showed affection and kindness for their benefactor. They invited him to contact them again and pretended to be related so they would not attract attention.[52] Although

Kircher was considered "politically sound and an able writer who has always shown discipline and deference," in 1939 the Ministry of the Interior ordered that he be permanently expelled from Italy because of his "moral perversion."[53]

Since each case was examined singly in order to determine a correspondent's effectiveness for enhancing the image of Fascism abroad, they were not usually expelled immediately. Before deciding on expulsion, the Ministry of Popular Culture was usually consulted. If opportune, the case was sometimes dropped so that public scandal might be avoided. Such was the case for the Estonian journalist George Popoff-Bebontoff, who had already been expelled from England for "pederastic reasons" and noted by Tavolato himself as a homosexual. The father of a twenty-five-year-old young man with whom the journalist was having a love affair intervened as well. In order to break off his son's relationship, the father threatened to involve Bocchini and have Popoff expelled from Italy. Although "the nature of the relationship between the two was evident," the Secretary of Popular Culture praised Popoff "for his serene and impartial journalism and for his anticommunist politics, which are favorable to Our Country." Because of his merit as a journalist, Popoff was exempt from expulsion. His young lover, on the other hand, received a police warning for his actions.[54]

This affair shows, once again, that political interests always prevailed in these instances. Although homosexuality had to be fought and eliminated, it was much more important to control the citizens' political ideas and safeguard the regime from possible scandals. Tavolato himself was often asked to provide information about possible subversives from the "masonry of pederasts." However, homosexuality was above all an important tool for blackmailing and controlling important people. Establishing that a person had this vice by investigating him could turn out to be a useful means of influencing the careers of *gerarchi*, comrades, or rich entrepreneurs and making any possible adversaries of the regime more pliable.

Umberto's Homosexuality

The most famous case in which the accusation of homosexuality was used for political ends is surely that of Prince Umberto, son of King Vittorio Emanuele III. His biographers were the first to face the delicate subject. In veiled allusions, they hinted that the heir to the throne's troubled love life might be due to his particular sexual tendency. For example, Silvio Bertoldi describes him as a shy young man who was intimidated by women's advances. Umberto was known as a sort of Don Giovanni, yet none of the noblewomen he kept company with claimed to have been his lover. In his biography, the prince is described as having an inconsistent character: serious but also inclined to jokes; very austere and religious but hedonistic as well; respectful of protocol, with a tendency toward intemperance; always hovering between mysticism and the senses, between temptation and repentance for his sins.

Especially during the years in Turin before his marriage, his existence was defined by society life and pleasure. He was always in the company of a small circle of friends, each of whom the crown prince gave a U-shaped diamond brooch as a sign of distinction.[55] Gianni Oliva also believed that Umberto was a man with unresolved contradictions. He portrays him as being dissatisfied and melancholy, constantly torn between his rigid upbringing and the sponta-neous tendency of his personality. These particular features aroused suspicion that he suffered from "an incomplete personality, repressed behavior, and blocked sexuality."[56] Michele Luigi Straniero's opinion was that Umberto's sexual diversity was impeded by respect for royal dignity and was a source of frustration and guilt : "The real drama of this man was his endless, inevitable sexual dissatisfac-tion, a syndrome shared by many of those whose 'different' nature forces them to hide, to feign, to precociously make a pretence of feelings that they cannot experience, to continually disguise themselves until they acquire the habit of wearing the mask like a second nature, obliged to live their lives as if it were a parody, an arduous performance."[57] Further confirmation of Umberto's "special friendships," especially with young officers, emerged from the biographies of Luchino Visconti, Umberto's close friend with whom the crown prince had apparently had a love affair when he was young. Their "restless lives" and homosexual behavior[58]—which did not, however, prevent them from intimate relationships with the other sex—had already caused a few scandals and some unpleasant difficulties in the bigoted and clerical atmosphere of Fascist Italy.[59] In addition to his liaison with Visconti, Umberto was said to have a strong liking for the French actor Jean Marais and the Italian boxer Primo Carnera.[60]

The subject of the crown prince's homosexuality drew the attention of historians and journalists; more for the sensationalism surrounding it than for any real interest in understanding the relationship between monarchy and Fascism and their reciprocal influence. Only recently has the subject left the realm of gossip so common in cases in which the affairs of royal families are concerned. This new interest has shed light on the complicated period of the civil war and the birth of the republic. The questions that De Felice had already brought up regarding the contents of the papers that Mussolini had with him when he was captured, led the French historian Pierre Milza to suppose that the Duce's "famous defense briefcase,"[61] also contained "some documents that proved the crown prince was a homosexual."[62] It is thought that, in the last few days before the war ended, the Duce selected a number of files he considered extremely important and that had been brought from Villa Feltrinelli to Milan, among which was apparently the file on the crown prince. Blackmailing Umberto was so crucial that in the tragic days that followed April 25, 1945, Mussolini thought it was advisable to take the dossier on the crown prince with him when fleeing to Switzerland. He probably intended to use it to discredit the monarchy or to take revenge for the betrayal he had suffered, knowing he could prove that Victor Emmanuel III was jointly responsible for all the decisions made by the Fascist regime, including entering the war, and demonstrate Umberto's level of "degeneracy."[63]

Despite the air of mystery that still surrounds Mussolini's capture and death and the numerous, conflicting versions of the contents of the Duce's documents, many sources claim there was a file on Umberto. According to the partisan "Bill" (that is, Urbano Lazzaro), vice-commissioner of the 52nd Garibaldi brigade, the first bulky bag that he made the Duce hand over to him when he was arrested contained a large number of documents, which Mussolini considered "of great historical importance."[64] There were four files in it: the cover of the first was entitled "Miscellaneous" and was made up of about a hundred pages; the second on Umberto of Savoy contained the proceedings of the interrogation of police officer Vincenzo Beneduce (the crown prince's orderly), typewritten poems (many of which were stupid and puerile) and letters of minor importance; the third was on the trial of Verona; and the fourth held Hitler and Mussolini's correspondence.[65] In his diary, "Comrade Bill" noted his impressions following the discovery of the file on the crown prince:

> I took the fourth and last file titled "Umberto of Savoy" from the bag.
> There were reports, some of them secret, on the crown prince's behavior
> and friendships, and I was disgusted by the police officer Beneduce's state-
> ment about Umberto of Savoy's acts of pederasty. I looked at Mussolini
> again but he turned his head away. How much filth in those sheets of
> paper![66]

The file on Umberto is missing from both the Anglo-American microfilm inventory and from the State Archives where those papers taken from Mussolini's bag are kept.[67] We can therefore suppose—and there is evidence that this may be the case—that this valuable material was removed and handed over to the Savoy family. A "brief [anonymous] report" found among the papers of the PCI (Partito comunista italiano—Italian Communist Party), preserved in the Gramsci Institute, has a detailed description of the passage of the bags seized from Mussolini and his secretary Vito Casalinovo, the list of files in the bag when Mussolini was arrested and the reconstruction of how most of the documents in the bags were stolen. Mussolini's bag alone contained the following files:

miscellaneous—50 fifty or sixty sheets; Umberto of Savoy—poems he wrote and other letters, and the report of the police officer Beneduce on Umberto's attempt to have sexual intercourse with him; the Verona trial; the Hitler and Mussolini correspondence. The anonymous author of the report believed that many of the documents had been taken by Bill, Pedro (Pier Bellini Delle Stalle), and Antonio Scappin, and that it was the latter who immediately went to Rome to speak directly to Umberto.[68] The strongest doubts about the affair concern this last detail. It is still not sufficiently clear when the file on the crown prince was given to the Savoy family, and who did so.[69]

Further confirmation that there was a dossier on Umberto's homosexuality was provided by the recently published diaries of Falcone Lucifero,[70] the minister of the Royal House from 1944 to 1946. Indeed, Mussolini had given the Polizia Politica the task of putting the prince under surveillance and of paying particular attention to his sexual habits, so that this information could be used at the right moment to throw discredit on the monarchy or force its members to submit to Fascist requests. There are still concrete traces of this in the state archives, where there are two files under the name of the Prince of Piedmont.[71] In order to win the king's favor, Italo Balbo referred explicitly to these other documents when he informed the king of the Duce's plots against the crown prince—"Mussolini had been preparing a dossier for years to show that the prince was a pederast"—and gave the king details of the documents and evidence gathered by the police at the dictator's orders. Balbo's thoughtfulness turned out to be unnecessary. He later found out that the king had already known for some time about these compromising documents on his son.[72]

We can be certain, then, that there was a file on Umberto among the those secretly held by the Duce's personal secretariat. One can easily imagine the royal family's concern. In fact, from the moment the Fascist regime fell, an anxious search for these confidential papers had begun. The evidence provided by Emilio Re, the superintendent for the archives of Lazio, Umbria, and the Marches at that time, reveals that immediately after July 25, 1943, Pietro Acquarone, the minister of the Royal House, had the "personal files and the correspondence regarding the royal family and the princes of the Savoy House withdrawn from Mussolini's confidential archives."[73] However, during the Salò Republic, information about Umberto's most intimate habits had become useful once again to intensify the conflict between the monarchy and the Kingdom of the South. It was just this dossier on the prince's homosexuality that gave rise to "the filthy scoops of a small Fascist daily paper in Alessandria, the source of the well-known insinuations that have been circulating about Umberto for so many years."[74] The Salò radio and press openly accused the viceroy of being a homosexual, giving him the nickname "Stellassa" and repeatedly making allusions about his secret habits and his lack of virility.[75] The king did not at all appreciate this defamatory campaign against the prince at such a delicate time for the Italian monarchy, which had just agreed on a difficult compromise with the anti-Fascists and was preparing to face the institutional referendum. It seems legitimate to assume that Victor Emmanuel III's reluctance to abdicate was due in part to concern about his successor, the target of such slanderous gossip. Even the solution of making Umberto his viceroy had greatly concerned the king, "considering that the Fascist government had threatened to publish a dossier on His Royal Highness, the Prince of Piedmont,"[76] all the more so because the Salò press continued to dig up dirt. Furthermore, word of the scandal had also traveled to the South, where numerous anti-Fascists were determined to liquidate the royal family. Benedetto Croce was the exception. He was one of the few who did not believe these rumors, considering them to be the result of "the Fascists' habit of slander."[77] Most people believed the many rumors about the secret documents that Mussolini had gathered, which contained "some episodes from the prince's youth that were not in conformity with his rank."[78]

The venomous comments against the heir to the throne, which continued to circulate for the whole time Umberto was viceroy, starting from June 1944, worried the monarchy's supporters as well, particularly Lucifero, the minister of the Royal House, who carried out a thorough search for the famous OVRA documents, a search that continued for a long time after the end of the war. As the institutional referendum approached, the burning issue of the dossier was again used as blackmail and as means to assist the birth of the Republic. In March 1946, right in the middle of the referendum campaign, Lucifero was informed that the long-sought-after documents had been found during the examination of the OVRA documents. Determined to get them, he had decided to bribe one of the four judges assigned to examining the documents, to the tune of millions of dollars. It was the Minister of the Interior, the socialist Giuseppe Romita, who showed Lucifero "the two bulky files" on the viceroy, one of which held the most important and compromising information on Umberto's habits, details that Bocchini had communicated directly to Mussolini in some cases. The matter was closed on April 4 when the police chief sent all the documents concerning the prince, the princess, the prince of Assia, the duke of Bergamo, and the duke of Pistoia with information on their private and sexual lives to the minister of the Royal House, who hurriedly made them disappear once and for all by burning them in his fireplace.[79] However, When Victor Emmanuel Umberto ascended to the throne upon Victor Emmanuel's abdication, just a month before the referendum, a final defamatory campaign was set in motion, once again aimed at discrediting the "May king" with the well-established accusation of pederasty.[80]

The intricate affair of the dossier on Umberto's homosexuality helps us to understand some aspects of the relationship between the Fascist regime and the monarchy. Indeed, Mussolini believed himself to be in possession of information capable of influencing the sovereign and enabling him to finally do away with the monarchy, if necessary. The "diarchy" that continued to develop over the whole duration of the regime had caused intense friction and strong ill feelings at times. Mussolini's intolerance of this parallel power, capable of impeding his unquestioned leadership, grew greater with the years and the consolidation of the dictatorship into a real totalitarian regime. The difficult compromise with the monarchy that began with the march on Rome and was confirmed during the Matteotti crisis, had reciprocally conditioned both parties: the Duce knew that resolving the institutional question and reviving the republican spirit of early Fascism would take time. Legitimizing the Grand Council through the constitution had been the first step toward providing the means necessary to put an end to the monarchy, but also toward binding it more and more to the regime and by making its members feel the precariousness of their positions. In fact, the December 1928 law changed the Grand Council's powers, stating that it needed to be consulted on any bill concerning succession to the throne and the king's powers and prerogatives. The crown was now extremely limited and its very existence ransomed. "The law determined the first serious clash between monarchy and the Fascist regime" and caused an enormous scandal in dynastic circles, as it appeared to be an obvious attempt to prevent the crown prince from ascending to the throne.[81]

With this new legislation, the dossier on Umberto's homosexuality became even more important. If Victor Emmanuel III had died, it would have led to a dynastic succession that was more favorable to the Fascist regime or even to a complete and definitive dismantling. In any case, it would give the Duce a weak king, easily coercible and forced to submit when threatened. Thanks to his "Achilles' heel," his son, the sovereign himself was easily persuaded to accept the most controversial measures. Luigi Federzoni gives further details about the purpose of the law in his memoirs:

> It was widely believed all over Italy that the Prince of Piedmont was deeply hostile to Fascism, which naturally fomented the party's disparaging campaign against him. The regime mainly tried to put the idea in people's minds that one day the prince could be prohibited from ascending the throne. In any case, it was a way of blackmailing him to make him take a more favorable attitude toward the regime. This was the aim of using that unfortunate abortion of a law, passed December 9, 1928, that was implemented superficially. The law set up the Grand Council, and at the last

moment Mussolini ordered Alfredo Rocco to add, among other illogical ideas, the provision that made the opinion of the Grand Council obligatory on the subject of succession to the Throne.[82]

Apart from Mussolini's desire to do away with the monarchy, he was indeed concerned about Umberto's presumed anti-Fascism mentioned by Federzoni, since the Duce thought the future king seemed less reliable than the present one. Information from the Polizia Politica continually referred to the prince's lack of enthusiasm for, even dislike of, the regime. Actually, the heir to the throne was hostile, above all, to the superficial aspects of the Fascist regime rather than its politics; his anti-Fascism arose from a spirit of caste, from a natural aversion to the style and histrionics of the rites imposed by the regime and from an aristocratic intolerance toward the inconsistent and coarse *gerarchi*. He was irritated by the rude behavior of the new Blackshirt political class, by their lack of manners or traditions; he found Mussolini's attitude toward the monarchy irreverent, and the attacks, the slander, and the intrusive surveillance of his private life, something he was surely aware of, unbearable. In short, the Fascists did not like Umberto because he showed he did not like them very much. It was not a simple problem to resolve. The crown prince had always been kept apart from politics and, following the axiom that "one king rules at a time in the Savoy House," had done nothing to change this situation, always managing to stay on the fringes and to not compromise himself with the regime. However, it was his very detachment that made him a threat. Once king, he could take on a different attitude toward Fascism than his father's, a more critical and autonomous attitude, aimed at asserting the monarchy's prerogatives as established by the Albertino Statute.

The growing anti-Fascist commitment of Umberto's wife, Maria José, on one hand, and Victor Emmanuel III's twenty-year-long ties with the Fascist regime on the other, forced the crown prince to waver between a critical and detached attitude in private often followed by a conciliatory one in public, with the result that he dissatisfied everyone, as emerges clearly from evidence provided by Maria José:

> Bigheaded monarchists reproached my husband for his society life; the
> regime's fanatics criticized him because he kept well away from Fascist
> activities. He was in a very delicate situation. Being the crown prince, he
> was obliged to live under the yoke of a dictatorship, and his wife's situation,
> mine, was the same! Here is a small detail of our daily life: every time we
> went somewhere, however close by, a swarm of police officers began to follow
> us, but it was only thanks to Umberto's extremely good manners that he
> put up with it politely.[83]

Objectively, Umberto ended up seeming weak and thus promising for Mussolini's hopes of eliminating the monarchy. When controversy broke out surrounding the Duce's nomination as First Marshal of the Empire, Galeazzo Ciano thought the question would be resolved once "the respectable signature was replaced by the less than respectable signature of the prince." This prospect was certainly not disagreeable to Mussolini, who was tempted to put an end to the monarchy every time friction arose, even though he did not end up respecting his deadline—"when the war in Spain ends we shall talk about it."[84] This institutional shift represented a delicate step and had to be prepared down to the last detail and carried out very carefully. The royal family had to be made unpopular, leaving it isolated. The crown prince had to be discredited, and the monarchy as an institution needed to seem like a useless anachronism. The death of Victor Emmanuel III would have been the right moment to successfully carry out such a complicated operation.[85] As Ciano describes in his diary, Mussolini's hostility toward the monarchy grew as Italy became a more totalitarian state and ties with Hitler took root with the approaching war,[86] making the crown prince's position even more precarious and escalating the Fascist campaign to collect information on his sexual deviance.[87] The dossier on Umberto's homosexuality was important to Mussolini for potentially quelling Umberto's resistance to the regime and for eventually eliminating the monarchy altogether.[88]

The proof gathered on Umberto's homosexuality was capable of damaging the careers of some of his "intimate" friends as well. In his memoirs published in the postwar period, the ex-partisan Enrico Montanari tells of how he was intensely courted by Umberto in 1927 while serving as a lieutenant in Turin. Montanari tells of how Umberto made him his intimate confidant and even gave him a valuable silver cigar-lighter with the words "Say yes!" engraved on one side. Montanari himself explains that the meaning of those words became clear the evening after the present had been given:

> The prince asked me to meet him at the Gran Madre di Dio. . . . He walked with one arm around my shoulders then suddenly drew me close to him and in a broken voice murmured: "Say yes." I was astonished, but immediately remembered his past effusions and some of the ways he behaved, which I had justified up to then with the naïve conviction that he was fond of me because of my character and disinterested loyalty. I shook his arm off violently and stared at him, astounded and indignant. My first impulse was to push him down the bank of the Po river, but commonsense prevailed. . . . He casually took me by the arm and, smiling, told me that if I betrayed him he would make me pay for it. Unfortunately, I had no other way to show I disapproved than by keeping quiet. Thus I had proof that the

rumors going around in some circles about his anomaly were well founded. Despite everything, he resorted to his "Say yes" several other times.[89]

Montanari's correspondence with Umberto and his reputation as an anti-Fascist must have caused him quite a few problems. A plan organized against him persuaded him to go out of his home in Verona on the pretext of giving him the details of an important mission, but in fact the aim was to search his apartment and confiscate the compromising letters sent to him by the crown prince.[90] Montanari was investigated without motive and sentenced to thirty days arrest in a fortress, the citations were expunged from his service and conduct book, and on May 1, 1933, his professional career was abruptly ended when the War Secretary informed him he had been discharged from permanent service until he reached his pension.[91] There is evidence of the affair in the Polizia Politica papers, which show that the letters sent to Montanari by the prince were immediately confiscated and burnt in the office of the Chief of the General Staff of the army corps, most likely to avoid blackmail.

However, it was not always easy to come across compromising documents. For example, Enrico De Simone, a cavalry officer, had managed to hide some "intimate letters" sent to him from Umberto in a strongbox, in hopes of selling them in France.[92] The most serious episode was the report a *carabiniere* made to the police about "unacceptable proposals made by the king's son," which set off an inquiry that reached the highest ranks of the *carabinieri*. Gossip and slander against Umberto were widespread. Numerous anonymous messages about his homosexuality were sent directly to the Head of Government's Cabinet, after which the police tried to determine the identity of the sender. Such was the case for a series of letters starting in 1927 and signed with the false name of Philip Anderson, which urged the Grand Council "not to allow the prince to succeed to the throne." After continuous hints at "the vice of pederasty in the Savoy House," Bocchini charged the police chief of Turin to identify the anonymous writer at all costs and to put an end to such dangerously credible rumors.[93]

The affair regarding Umberto is the most sensational case in which homosexuality was used as a political weapon against a person; however, similar accusations with the same intention of discrediting the monarchy were made against other members of the royal family as well, such as the Duke of Pistoia and the Duke of Bergamo, who were spied on and criticized for being too feminine. According to Franco Fucci, in 1935 the particular sexual tendencies of another important duke of the Savoy House were discovered by chance, during a police investigation of the murder of a *carabiniere* warrant officer in Quarto, in the province of Genoa:

The investigations led to Turin because it appeared that the officer associated with homosexuals and that the last person he was seen with was a young man from Turin, a hairdresser. The police had no difficulty in tracing the man to an important salon in Turin, which was known as a meeting place for homosexuals. A detective went there one evening, got somebody to open the door and asked for the young hairdresser. The sound of music could be heard coming from an adjoining room. The owner, who was terrified, hurried up to him and murmured: "For heaven's sake, my guests are in there!" Obviously the detective wanted to see what was going on, and on opening the door, discovered about forty men in the large salon, all nude. They were forced to dress and asked for their documents. One of them, a middle-aged man, took the detective aside to tell him that he was the duke of . . . , a member of the House of Savoy. Naturally the affair was dropped and covered up; but OVRA did not lose sight of the duke from that moment on.[94]

However, the most insistent rumors were concentrated on the presumed homosexuality of Prince Philip of Assia. A high Nazi official and husband of Mafalda, one of Victor Emmanuel III's daughters, he carried out the important function of intermediary between the Reich and the House of Savoy and was the go-between for Mussolini and Hitler as well. His rapid career and the delicate assignments he was given were due to the Führer's absolute trust in him. Hitler knew he could confidently use the King of Italy's son-in-law, because his homosexual tendencies made him susceptible to blackmail and constricted him to faithfully support Nazism and follow Hitler's orders. Proof that Prince Philip was not very virile was provided directly by the Italian chief of police who "sent Himmler abundant information on the double life that the royal son-in-law led on the isle of Capri and in Naples, in the company of disreputable men. In short, Hitler played cat and mouse with him and was always ready to do away with him when necessary."[95] Eugen Dolmann believes the Führer used the information about the prince of Assia, passed on by the Gestapo, to put pressure on Mussolini and convince him to break away from the king.[96] The Italian police knew how important surveillance of the prince was politically and kept a very close watch on him.

The first to report Philip of Assia's homosexuality was Italo Tavolato, who explained the real reasons for the massacre of the storm troopers, which the Nazis had explained as a kind of cleansing against Röhm's extremist movement. Röhm was accused of taking in "degenerates" and "homosexuals," a cancer for the purity of the Aryan race. Hitler had not ordered the massacre to get rid of homosexuals, but to establish his unquestioned leadership of the entire Nazi movement. In fact, Rudolf Hess, Baldur von Schirach, Philip of Assia, and other important *gerarchi* who were all notorious homosexuals, were not removed from their positions. Bocchini considered Tavolato's report to be reliable since "the informer is particularly competent in the matter."[97] Besides, Prince Philip's lifestyle was such that it was extremely easy to gather information on his sexual habits. In April 1935 an embarrassing mistake took place in this regard. A policeman arrested a distinguished gentleman who had tried to molest him and commit indecent acts with him in the dark of the Cola di Rienzo movie theater in Rome. When taken to the police station, the man, who was embarrassed by what had happened, surprised everyone by pulling out a blue card where the name "H.R.H. the Prince of Assia" was printed. The policemen present immediately apologized and let the prince go, being very careful not to attract too much attention as he did so.[98] The harsh persecution that was to strike Philip of Assia, culminating in his deportation to the concentration camp in Dachau, was not due to his homosexuality: Hitler believed that the prince was guilty of much more serious offenses, above all his intimate and suspicious relationship with the House of Savoy, and with his father-in-law Victor Emmanuel III, against whom the Nazi leader had decided to take revenge after his betrayal on July 25, 1943. The real victim of this sequence of hatred-inspired actions ended up being Mafalda, who was innocent, and who was destined to die of hardship and illness in Buchenwald.[99]

Vatican Scandals

The Vatican was another environment that was carefully controlled by the Fascist regime. The ties with the Holy See, sanctioned when the Concordat was signed in 1929, had not completely resolved the problems that arose when the Fascist regime started to pose a threat to the authority of the Church. The events of 1931, along with the fierce conflict over the monopoly of educating young people, were a clear sign that relations between the two were in trouble. The regime's hegemonic design clashed with the attempt of the Roman Catholic Church to safeguard faith and morality from the interference of politics. The reciprocal attempts of both to extend their influence caused friction, which was ignored at the time because the pope and the Duce were well aware of the advantages that would come from reconciliation. However, the Fascist regime needed to be informed about what was going on within the Vatican curia in order to influence the political choices of its high ecclesiastical hierarchies and foster the careers of those from within the church who were most supportive of Fascism. In November 1929 Grandi himself made it clear to Mons. Borgoncini that the Holy See's demand "that the state give up one of its most elementary faculties—the "normal activity of obtaining information about, and investigating, every citizen"—was unacceptable.[100] The Polizia Politica informers assigned to the Vatican frequently noted the moods and affairs of the Church in order to discover its weak points. It was not a new kind of espionage: in the liberal period as well the governments used informers at the Holy See; however, as Pietro Scoppola rightly noted, "the fact that this spying was carried out for so many years, being on familiar terms with influential personages, the taste for gossip, the satisfaction of reporting something that could contribute to putting the Holy See in a bad light, gave greater importance to the case of Mussolini's informers and stressed what was morally negative and blameworthy in the figure and position of informers."[101] The careful control carried out by the police informers was needed to report anyone who tried to thwart Mussolini's politics and thus foil possible anti-Fascist plots, furthermore to discover the secrets of the Vatican Secretary of State. However, spying flourished among the churchmen themselves, who were ready to launch attacks against rivals or anyone who did not respect Catholic orthodoxy. Jealousy and rivalry within the confined circle of the Vatican curia encouraged resorting to the weapon of slander, which did not even spare bishops and cardinals. Some clergymen did not limit themselves only to writing anonymous messages but even became police informers.[102]

The defamatory campaign against priests and prelates was also based on revealing private behavior that discredited the slandered person irreparably. Therefore, accusing someone of pederasty was a useful weapon for blackmail and to put an end to a career. Real scandals were about the sexual behavior of clergymen, and the Fascist regime was ready to exploit them so as to worm its way into the internal struggles in the curia and spread its influence. The first to experience how compromising even the suspicion of homosexuality was, was Mons. Riccardo De Samper, the pope's majordomo, who was removed from the papal court because he had been slandered by a relative bent on revenge related to a question of inheritance.[103] The most sensational case broke out in 1928 and involved the pope's important chamberlain, Mons. Camillo Caccia Dominioni.[104] Two young men who had been received by him several times gave risqué details of the priest's conduct, and consequently an inquiry was immediately started to ascertain the truth. The outcome of the first one, carried out by the Vatican, was in favor of Caccia Dominioni, while the second one, made by the Rome Vicariate, confirmed the serious accusations. To hush up the scandal the pope decided to send the high prelate to Sydney as one of the participants of the Eucharistic congress; however, although he had been sent away, there was still talk of the scandal after several years. Every time Caccia Dominioni was proposed for an appointment as cardinal, the more or less veiled accusations of his homosexuality were brought up again. For example, in 1929 a Polizia Politica informer reported that Caccia Dominioni's way to a cardinalate was blocked by the many enemies he had due to his position, and above all for moral reasons, because "to be blunt, he was accused of pederasty."[105] The following year the whole affair turned into an out-and-out scandal. The second inquiry on Caccia Dominioni's homosexuality had been assigned to Emanuele Brunatto,[106] a member of the Vatican secret police assigned to gather information about the prelates. Brunatto, who had been given the task by Cardinal Gasparri, had confirmed the accusations, despite pressure to modify the final results of his investigations. However, he had been accused, in turn, by Count Eduardo Aluffi the pope's Guard of Nobles, of using these inquiries of the priests to extort money from them. Brunatto had responded to these insinuations by suing Aluffi for libel, convinced he could resolve the question in court. The fact that Caccia Dominioni was also among the influential members of the pontifical court called upon to testify as witnesses led to the idea that all the "most licentious behind-the-scenes intrigues" of the affair could come to light in the trial. To avoid the trial at all costs, every effort was made to convince Brunatto not to go ahead with the proceedings, suggesting that he accept Aluffi's retraction and begging him not to show compromising documents that could create an enormous sensation. After the decision to hold a closed trial, after newspapers were forbidden to publish news about the case and after continual adjournments, the issue ended on June 6, 1930, with the withdrawal of the action, obtained with the payment of large sums of money according to a Polizia Politica informer.

The trial had been blocked, thanks to the good offices of the chief of police as well, because "there was concern that many obscene details would come to light during the public hearings." Indeed, Bocchini received information about the ecclesiastical world from Brunatto, and to avoid being involved in the affair had him warned not to boast of police and government backing and ties.[107] Although everything had been hushed up, Brunatto decided to write a book entitled *Gli anticristi nella chiesa di Cristo* (The Antichrists in Christ's Church). The numerous documents in the book served to tell "the most intimate details and off-color episodes" in the lives of many important prelates and aimed at showing the lack of justice in the Holy See, where only political interests determined the choice of men and the assignment of dioceses. The threat of a scandal once again weighed heavily on the Vatican, and the Fascist regime itself feared it would seem to be behind the move, especially after the difficult situation of 1931. Bocchini, who had been given a copy of the book, consequently thought it was necessary to forbid its publication to avoid a new conflict with the Church.[108]

This intricate affair of spying and blackmail shows how widely used the accusation of homosexuality was, both for personal advantage and for political interests. The weapon of slanderous dossiers added fresh fuel to a continuous game of moves and countermoves to strike a rival or foil possible traps. In any case, it is quite clear that the question of homosexuality was so troublesome and serious in the Vatican as well, that it encouraged resorting to any means in order to hush up a scandal. In actual fact, estimating and repressing these "blameworthy" activities were based on political rather than ethical reasons. It was a choice similar to the Fascist one, that is, to deny there was a problem as long as possible, trying to find a solution for the real or invented cases of pederasty from within their structures without making the issue public. However, it was just this strategy that made the Fascist regime and the Church more vulnerable to blackmail as it forced them to try to hush up the aspects that could damage their image, using every possible method. During the twenty years of Fascism, Catholic and Fascist morality influenced each other, often leading to intransigent and bigoted attitudes that hid behavior that did not always respect rigidly declared rules. From this viewpoint, the Fascist regime was in full harmony with the concept of respectability proposed by the Church. It was respectability at face value, aimed at safeguarding appearances, and did not reach the point of imagining ruthless and open action against homosexuals but rather avoided the problem, covering up the repression itself. Turning a blind eye to the most influential personages and avoiding possible scandals were, after all, still the quickest way to hide the pressing problem of pederasty behind a veil of hypocrisy and moralism.

On the other hand, even when the accusation of pederasty was reported openly against priests and ecclesiastics, the Fascist regime preferred to give these cases special treatment. In fact, after informing the General Administration for Religious Observances, the police noted the facts regarding immoral priests separately. In order to give them the advantage of better conditions, they were almost always considered political detainees in the rare cases they were sent to *confino*.[109] A good example of this is the case of Don Rodolfo S., accused of indecent assault on a minor and in turn, a victim of extortion by someone who had found out about it. A person called Alessandro P. had threatened to tell what had happened to the Holy Father and the editor of the local daily *Il Piccolo*, thus receiving enormous sums of money from the priest. The Secretary of Homeland Security then decided to avoid the sensation that would be caused by a public hearing and resolved the question by sending Alessandro P. to *confino comune* and the priest as a political detainee to the Tremiti islands. Very soon, Don Rodolfo became the new parish priest of the islands, thus becoming a member of the disciplinary board of the colony as well, with the task of establishing punishments for his unfortunate companions themselves. However, his new pastoral experience did not last long, because in October 1938, he was freed once and for all thanks to the good offices of the bishop of Fiume.[110]

The Party Secretaries

The accusation of homosexuality was also used as a political weapon within the PNF itself. No fewer than three party secretaries were the objects of such rumors. Even Starace, an emblem of virility, known for his sexual escapades, had to defend himself from such "defamatory" lies. An easy target for criticism and backbiting, Starace was accused of every kind of crime and depravation. The fact that he was the Fascist Party leader for so long and with such undisputed power increased the constant campaign of denigration aimed at dragging him down. The massive personal file that Mussolini kept on him in his secret records was overflowing with police reports and anonymous communications about Starace's illegal and immoral activities. The party secretary was accused of leading an unruly and dissolute private life, full of vice and lechery; mention was made of orgies with disreputable women, which, accompanied by alcohol and drug use, often ended in violence against the girls. Although Starace constantly showed off his virility and was proud of his many adulterous love affairs, many questioned his masculinity, and he was openly accused of being homosexual. His passion for sodomy was described in detail. He had practiced it since he was a boy in the Lecce national boarding school, which expelled him, so it was rumored, following an inquiry that brought to light his "addiction to passive pederasty."[111] A police informer summed up the affair: "There is the widespread belief in Lecce, where S. E. Starace spent his youth, that the party secretary is a passive pederast. He was apparently expelled from the Collegio Nazionale for this weakness. Furthermore, there is a certain Ramando in Lecce, a modest court intermediary, who openly brags about having been the first to physically exploit Starace's boyhood." These allusions to Starace's homosexuality also referred to the period he spent in the army in the First World War: "During the national meeting of the *Bersaglieri* [light infantry-men] in 1928 in Naples, which included veterans as well, there was a lot of talk accompanied by laughter about Captain Starace's war scandals. Emphasis was placed on the protection he enjoyed thanks to his INTIMATE RELATIONSHIP with General Ceccherini."

His circle of friends was criticized and discussed because, according to the police, the Gallipoli *gerarca* surrounded himself with "morally corrupt" people coming from the "lowest levels of social delinquency," like his protégé Giuseppe P., "well-known in Lecce and the province as a sexually depraved slanderer, a

corruptor of minors, a Freemason, and a pimp interested in running brothels."
An anonymous letter sent to Rachele pointed out that Starace had turned the
province of Lecce into his own fiefdom by using the provincial administrative
secretary, another "incorrigible pederast," as his informer. In addition, he was
accused of having "sexual intercourse" with a member of his private police
force, set up to gather information on Fascist *gerarchi*. And last, he was called
"henpecked" because, by then, he had become a slave to his lover, Pierisa Giri,
an attractive singer at the Carro di Tespi, to the point of becoming a laughing
stock.[112] In actual fact it was all only slander, unproved gossip used to defame a
person who was controversial and envied precisely because of his enormous
power. Bocchini's resentment of Starace was such that even unlikely and obviously invented gossip was passed on to the Duce in hopes that this very loyal
party *gerarca* would be dismissed. Mussolini, who knew the party secretary's
reputation as an "unrestrained womanizer" and called him "a great consumer
of ballerinas," did not believe these rumors; besides, he had defended Starace
against much more serious accusations, and with much more evident proof.
Starace was loyal and zealously carried out the duties assigned to him by the
Duce; he devoted maniacal attention to the work of transforming the customs
of Italians and managed the party to Mussolini's satisfaction: all these factors
led the Duce to forgive his obedient servant's vices and shortcomings.

   Although Mussolini disregarded the widespread rumors of pederasty
regarding Starace, it was not the case with another Fascist Party secretary,
Augusto Turati. The secretary was deeply resented by Farinacci's followers, who
blamed him for bringing about the latter's political defeat, and was thus destined
to fall victim to some conspiracy against him. During his years as secretary, Turati
engaged in a hard struggle against Fascists of "the first hour" who were unruly
when it came to accepting party discipline. He also attempted to curb the abuse
of power and fraud of some local *ras*, thus making himself a large number of
enemies who were plotting to have him removed.[113] The vast purge regarded
Farinacci's followers, whose power Turati hoped to weaken, ending their political
presence once and for all.[114] Farinacci, the *ras* of Cremona, had been trying to
regain leadership of the Fascist Party since 1926 and had been attacking the
new party secretary in every way possible. Besides, he and Turati, who were
poles apart in terms of their politics and their personalities, openly displayed
their reciprocal hostility, which only intensified the rivalry. This visceral hatred
manifested itself in continuous clashes and repeated attempts to isolate and
weaken each other. Farinacci considered the fight Turati had begun against the
Integralists a mortal blow to his own methods and political aims. In order to
block Farinacci's thirst for revenge, Turati openly accused him of being disloyal
and obstructive, and advised him "in a personal letter, not to upset the plans for

revolution lest he end up the lone and indigestible expression of the resulting mess."[115] Mussolini himself was irritated by Farinacci's attitude and had threatened him, saying: "Obey Turati and stop behaving like an antipope waiting for his time to come, or getting others to believe he is doing so. . . . Remember that whoever leaves the party falls into decline and dies."[116]

The fact that Farinacci was involved in the collapse of the People's Agricultural Bank of Parma through his political and financial ties with its manager, should have undermined his power even more, but Farinacci responded promptly. Still lacking the strength for a direct attack on the party secretary or a direct opposition to his politics, he directed his offensive against Turati's entourage and tried to involve him indirectly in some big scandal, all the while waiting to take more forceful action once Turati was weaker and more vulnerable. The first attack was launched against Ernesto Belloni, *podestà* of Milan, who had ties with the PNF secretary and the Duce's brother, Arnaldo. He was accused of dishonest dealings and illicit affairs, including bribes. Belloni sued Farinacci for libel, but despite several attempts to bury the case, the latter accepted the trial willingly, during which he "tore his rival to pieces" with proof in hand, which even discredited Arnaldo Mussolini.[117] Turati himself came out of the affair much weakened, and resigned from the position of national secretary of the PNF after a few months.

De Felice's interpretation of the events seems implausible. According to the historian, one of the reasons why "the best secretary the Fascist Party had had since its beginning" was toppled lies in the fact that Mussolini reproached him for not being hard enough on Farinacci.[118] Turati had indeed been wrong in not expelling Farinacci from the party when the lawsuit with Belloni came up. However, Turati had no other option than to adopt this attitude of acquiescence toward Farinacci. De Felice claims this "caused Mussolini to deeply resent Turati" and "undoubtedly contributed to his reaching the decision to remove him as leader of the PNF, especially when it became clear that Farinacci would win the lawsuit and be politically strengthened."[119] Turati knew he could not take strong action against his powerful adversary, both to avoid splitting the party, thus increasing the rupture between moderates and extremists, and not to avoid damage to Arnaldo's position. Mussolini himself was probably unwilling or unable to attack Farinacci; in fact, when the clash between the two party secretaries came to an end, the Duce sacrificed Turati without managing to mitigate Farinacci's controversial position as moralizer of Fascism and critic of the regime's vices.

In 1929, after the regime's reconciliation with the Church and the success obtained in the Plebiscite, a historical phase of Fascism closed and Turati himself realized that his cycle was coming to an end. The Duce and the PNF secretary differed on too many points for their relations to endure. Once peace reigned within the party, dissidents were gagged, and the resistance of the *ras* was repressed, there was no longer need for Turati. Furthermore, with Fascist mysticism and the cult of the Duce there was little place for an authoritative party secretary capable of overshadowing Mussolini.[120] Turati, aware of this fact, had in fact decided to leave politics with style, like Cincinnatus, and on March 19, 1929, he handed in his resignation, which was, however, rejected. His top-level position in the PNF, almost like vice-Duce, inevitably aroused resentment and envy. Many increasingly feared that his double appointment as secretary of the party and the Grand Council meant he would become the Duce's successor. In September 1930 Turati once again handed in his resignation, and this time Mussolini accepted it, convinced by then that he and the secretary disagreed on too many points: regarding for example the economy and trade unions, but also the role of the Fascist Party and how to resolve certain "moral issues." According to De Felice, Turati did not share the Duce's permissive attitude in regard to illegal or immoral crimes, against which Mussolini sometimes took no official action in order to avoid scandals. Turati, on the other hand, was convinced that this behavior would discredit Fascism in the long run and prevent the formation of a ruling class up to the tasks required of it. However, above all it would "actually encourage the spread of a double morality, formerly puritanical and bigoted but substantially lax and corrupted."[121] Turati himself was to experience the harmful effects of this approach, ending up the victim of a real moral lynching and of a conformism of the most intransigent sort.

Knowing that his rivals resented him and being well aware of how defamatory dossiers could negatively influence one's career, he himself had begun creating a personal spy network just after his appointment in order to gather information about party members that he could use at the right moment as a means of defense. His trusted friend Ernesto Gulì, head of the Polizia Politica division, provided him with proof against anyone who could harm him, and helped him set up several microphones, hidden in his office at Vidoni Palace, to record his conversations with various *gerarchi*, in order to record their most compromising affirmations.[122] Once Turati was no longer the party secretary and had become editor of *La Stampa*, he became an easy target for all those who had been waiting to take their revenge on him. Precisely to forestall any possible attack, he made a desperate and useless attempt to make peace with Farinacci.[123] In return, the new secretary, determined to definitively remove Turati from politics, organized a plot to discredit his rival once this long-awaited moment arrived. To this aim, Farinacci could count on the help of a number of persons that Turati had investigated, considering them possible profiteers or corrupt individuals; among them were Renato Ricci and Giovanni Preziosi, as well as some important figures like Costanzo Ciano, all of whom were well prepared to cooperate with Farinacci in hopes of taking their own revenge. Deprived of power, Turati was abandoned by all, just when the hardest attack on his dissolute private life was unleashed, leading to accusations of unconventional sexual behavior and pederasty.

Besides, this was not the first time that Farinacci had used such arguments to discredit a political rival. In 1917, immediately after the defeat at Caporetto, he attacked Guido Miglioli in these terms: "German, mercenary, traitor, coward, and sodomite,"[124] because he had reported Farinacci to the police for insulting a public official. After being removed as Secretary of the Fascist Party, Farinacci, staunch moral critic of the regime, also railed against the widespread immorality within the party and gathered information on the private lives of the *gerarchi*, including their homosexuality.[125]

For his "slanderous accusation" against Turati,[126] Farinacci resorted to a certain Paola Marcellino, a dressmaker of Turin, whose workshop was also used for enlivening the secretary's nights with young girls. Farinacci, also a frequenter of the "fashion house," coerced the dressmaker into confessing the intimate secrets of his political rival. Andrea Gastaldi, the federal secretary (*federale*) of Turin and a loyal follower of Farinacci, advised the dressmaker to provide proof of her lover's sexual habits. Either out of naïveté or because she was paid, she gave Gastaldi a series of ambiguous letters that alluded to Turati's homosexuality.[127] Apparently in one of these letters the former PNF secretary invited the madam once again to give him "the little boy," who was, actually, a young girl, nicknamed this way for her short haircut. However, Turati's enemies gave this expression a different meaning and considered it clear proof that he was a pederast. Once Farinacci had these compromising letters in hand, he sent Starace and Arpinati a note of three pages where he described "the complete and turbid exasperations of his sexual psychopathy." "The news spread immediately, appearing first in the foreign press and then in the Italian, albeit in a much softer version. However, the news made an enormous impression on the intermediate and upper levels of the regime, where everybody knew about the scandal that was only hinted at in public opinion clearly enough to strengthen the idea of widespread moral corruption among the *gerarchi*.

Senator Giovanni Agnelli and the editor of the *Corriere della Sera*, Aldo Borelli, were the only ones who defended Turati, who was described as degenerate, ridiculed by his colleagues in parliament, and subjected to cutting remarks by the honorable Luigi Lanfranconi. Turati urgently requested an inquiry and sent the Duce a long retraction from the woman who had accused him. The only answer he got was to be removed as editor of *La Stampa*. The Turin daily commented on the affair almost scornfully: "We say farewell to Augusto Turati with virile feeling: our thoughts go to Him who knows and sees everything, to

Him who reads human hearts with unwavering eyes." Soon after, Turati was shut away in the Sant'Agnese mental home in Rome to avoid arrest, and was later transferred to a nursing home in Ramiolo, near Parma. Finally, Starace gave him the final blow by accusing him of taking part in a suspected plot organized by Guido Cristini, president of the special court, against Mussolini and Starace himself.[128] At that point, Turati was completely discredited, removed from the party, and expelled from the Grand Council because of his "dissolute and licentious life." He was then sent to *confino* in Rhodes in 1933, where he was received with all the honors and respect appropriate to the position he had held.[129] In fact, Agnelli had suggested to Turati that he write a letter to the Duce, asking him to be sent abroad so as to tone down the sensation aroused by the affair. Agnelli believed that the former secretary could make a new life for himself without causing trouble, patiently waiting to be called back for some other political appointment and hoping "that also his enemies would be disarmed before the man who was no longer a threat."[130] The press summed up the news of his disastrous fall in a few lines. *Il Giornale d'Italia*, for example, dismissed the affair saying tersely: "The Party Secretary has been removed indefinitely for the following reason: 'In certain private letters that were made public, he used some deplorable expressions considered unacceptable, especially for someone who is invested with appointments of the Regime.'"[131]

The way the whole affair was handled was heavily criticized. As a Polizia Politica informer commented, if Turati was really an active or passive pederast who committed shameful acts on minors, he should have been brought before a court of justice, like any other citizen; otherwise, he should have been rehabilitated immediately, and those who had slandered him should have been punished.[132] The situation became even more complicated when Paola Marcellino, angry for having given Farinacci the "more or less licentious letters" that Turati had sent her, tried to reestablish the truth and "expose that puritan, Farinacci," who had exploited her for his own political interests.[133] After the letters had been published in French newspapers and as the scandal spread, Marcellino turned to Leandro Arpinati, who was then the undersecretary of the Interior, to make it clear that "a false interpretation had been given to the famous letters," contrary to the logic of common sense and to the facts." However, getting no results, the artless woman told Turati himself the whole story and signed a statement accusing Farinacci of using statements and documents that she had given him as her attorney, in violation of professional secrecy. Worried about this unexpected complication, Farinacci warned Arpinati about Turati's move to "pick himself up again"; and contemptuously threatened his rival with obvious allusions to the accusation that Turati might be a homosexual: "He had better not cross the line or mess with me . . . unlike him, I have an exclusively . . . active nature."[134] Paola Marcellino was forced to make her manservant write a declaration stating that Turati was a passive pederast and to sign a backdated letter freeing Farinacci from any obligation regarding the use of the documents she had given him.

At that point, Marcellino, completely caught in the intrigue, tried in vain to be received by the Duce himself in a desperate attempt to expose the plot organized against her. So she wrote a long memoir in Turati's defense, where she explained the truth behind the scandal to Mussolini: he was neither "a pervert" nor a "pimp," but a loyal and humble *gerarca*. To be sure that the memoir reached the Duce, she even threatened Bocchini to have it published in France. The only answer was a warning against "accusing important political personalities for the Honorable Turati's fall."[135] A few days later, after a violent quarrel with Farinacci, Paola Marcellino was sentenced to *confino* on Mussolini's direct orders, for her "scandal mongering against members of the PNF."[136] The police subjected her to continual interrogations in Lauria as well, where she had been sent to serve her two-year sentence; they confiscated all her letters and kept her under strict surveillance to find out if she had any further proof in her possession of the political plot carried out against Turati.[137] Marcellino continued to create problems. She tried to send an envelope with the memoir she had sent to Mussolini to Turati. However once the intermediary of the operation, a certain Mario Polini, had been paid the two thousand liras agreed upon, he sent the envelope directly to Farinacci instead of passing it on to Turati.[138] After trying to contact all the most important *gerarchi* to plead her cause, Paola Marcellino put herself under the protection of the police chief and bartered her silence for the promise of financial aid.[139] Once again, in June 1935, she begged Bocchini, the only one who had ever assisted during the entire affair, to find a job for her and offered to carry out work as an informer. It is likely that her request was in some way accepted, seeing that she began to earn large sums of money soon after, thanks to the information she supplied to the police.[140]

Farinacci was not the only one responsible for Turati's shameful end. Mussolini was so overwhelmed by the breadth of this squalid affair, with all its deception and blackmail, that he apparently remarked: "Now they are even ruining Turati."[141] In actual fact, Mussolini had concealed the secret moves of his *gerarchi* from the public, and when his highly respected collaborator's letters reached his desk, he did nothing to save Turati, preferring to allow him to die on the altar of virility. The basic virtue of the Fascist male could not be publicly questioned by the libertine behavior of such an important person as the former secretary of the party, even though homosexuality was only a pretext in the whole affair. Knowing well that Italians despised pederasty, the regime, which had made the glorification of virility one of its cornerstones, did not hesitate to sacrifice Turati, and banished him indefinitely to oblivion. This is further proof of how homosexuality had become an important negative factor under the regime, which in presenting it as evil itself, as the worst sin against Fascism, had turned it into a weapon of destruction. Mussolini explicitly confided to Yvon De Begnac: "I am convinced of Turati's innocence as well"; despite this, he justified the downfall of the PNF secretary saying:

> Roberto Farinacci stirred up public opinion and launched it against Turati, who, with regard to the other sex, has never been a saint. As long as he led the party I supported him. . . . For years Farinacci had been waiting for the moment to take care of him for once and all. Yvon, you say that Turati was destroyed by slander and that his homosexuality was a dark fairy tale invented by the man from Cremona against him. That might be, but in Italy, when public opinion strikes, no matter how it is organized, nothing can be done to stop it.[142]

The hypocrisy of these statements is evident: Mussolini had all the means necessary to suppress the scandal, which was organized in the upper echelons but had reached the public somewhat deflated. He could easily have rehabilitated Turati, as he would do later on with Giuriati and Starace by brushing aside the same accusations. The truth is that Turati was inconvenient; so once he had completed his political course, the best solution seemed to be to move him as far away as possible, even if the Duce claimed that he had given Turati *confino* on Rhodes and in eastern Africa "in order to save him from the brutes who wanted to tear him to pieces." He could not do anything to "calm down and wipe out the torrent of slander" that had struck Turati down.[143] On the contrary, rivalry among the *gerarchi* and their conflicts strengthened the totalitarian mechanism and helped Mussolini to increase his power. De Begnac himself considered the Turati affair as emblematic of the party's progressive loss of political content and its growing role as a center of gossip and unscrupulous ambition. Of the ugly work of defamation carried out against one of the few honest PNF secretaries, he commented:

> There is no other beast more capable of organizing the lynching of a rival than the Italian politician. . . . It should be sincerely acknowledged that this tendency toward wretchedness has become much stronger under the Fascist regime. Perhaps Italian history has never known such an organized class of people, who destroy all the rules of honest living, like the one that obeyed the orders of the many major, intermediate and minor subordinates determined to keep their power, whatever the cost of this game to state finances or to the national political class's meager tradition of courtesy.[144]

Despite Turati's initially dignified attitude when accepting his political downfall,[145] when he returned to Italy in 1937 he was kept under close surveillance up to the fall of the regime. After Rome was liberated in 1944, he was charged with carrying out activities in favor of Fascism, and prepared a defensive memoir for the purging trial in which he complained of the moral lynching to which he had been subjected. He himself had been a victim of the regime, removed from power and besmirched following accusations invented by people paid to lie. He now found himself on trial and suffering injustice twice. Since during the dictatorship he had not been able to defend himself in court, as had happened in other similar cases, and now he was being judged for his past as a Fascist,[146] without managing to get rid of that indelible label of "pederast."[147] The then-forgotten PNF secretary blamed his premature political decline on Mussolini in his book of memoirs, saying that the latter was envious of his popularity, eloquence, and charisma, which threatened to overshadow the Duce. This was confirmed by his friend Arnaldo, who explained that Turati was substituted as PNF secretary precisely because the Duce envied him, something the foreign press maintained as well.[148] According to Turati, "Mussolini was once again overcome by his unrestrained jealousy and ended up allowing the moral lynching that was being organized" against Turati himself, and, also considering the austere and bigoted atmosphere created by the Fascist regime, the Duce had not lifted a finger to save Turati from the scandal cunningly machinated by Farinacci. Turati heatedly railed at "all these worthless puritans," at "these champions of morality at all costs," who were horrified when they found out about his "nefarious" life:

> Among all those aspiring to the prize of virtue that Mussolini would certainly have set up one day, among all those Spartan women and moral eunuchs, I who have loved women since my youth and have so often laughed at rigid morality, could not but be a scandal. And these champions of purity who one day were to join up against me to denounce me to Europe as depraved and perverted, did not remember they had exchanged wives and lovers, but above all they forgot that sometimes they offered me their own women to bend me to the game of their politics or to obtain protection and complicity.[149]

From many points of view, the Turati affair is emblematic of the Fascist regime's attitude toward homosexuality, a "problem" faced by giving priority to those political considerations that served as the yardstick for establishing what measures to take against those who broke the rules of Fascist ethics.

Giovanni Giuriati, who succeeded Turati, was constantly mentioned in relation to homosexuality as well. When he was appointed, a police informer reported the comments that circulated about him within the party. Although nobody questioned his honesty, there was talk in parliamentary circles that he was a jinx, and, in particular, there were doubts about his virility. The accusation of pederasty followed Giurati, and after the vast purge he carried out in an attempt to bring order back to the Fascist Party, a real offensive was unleashed against him. His expulsion of 120,000 members from the party aroused protests and dissatisfied many Fascists, who were prepared to take revenge at any moment. Despite the Duce's growing prestige and his attempt to reorganize the party, all those who were dissatisfied with how the regime had changed expressed their criticism in the form of slander and libel. One influential official of the Polizia Politica explained why there was so much rancor against the PNF secretary in a confidential report in April 1931:

> A symptom emerges when talking to old and young Fascists: nobody dares to comment on or criticize His Excellency the Head of Government. Only the collaborators of the Duce of Fascism and the highest offices of the Regime are the object of criticism, malicious gossip, and slanderous insinuations. When the gossipers, the irresponsible plotters of the Regime do not know what to say, they spread the story of "barbed wire" around the Duce or claim that the Head of Government is unaware of, and in the dark about . . . everything! And naturally, as regards the Party, the most poisonous attacks are aimed at Giuriati, who carries out the orders he receives, and therefore the despicable, low and vulgar insinuations against the Party Secretary are noted down to shake his prestige and authority. When talking with Commendatore Mario Carli, our man Brucassi learned that the Settimelli group boasted that they had recent letters giving further proof that the Party Secretary and President of the Chamber of Deputies was a pederast. But is that possible? "—Yes! Yes! Reliable persons have these documents in hand. Some figures should not be at the top of the Regime. It would mean singing the praises of immorality!"[150]

Increasingly isolated, criticized, and impotent before this underground work of denigration, Giuriati did not succeed in remaining party leader for long. However, the reasons for his fall were political and not moral. Although Giuriati had always been considered a moderate, as Emilio Gentile pointed out, he "revealed an unexpected sense of the party and a totalitarian fervor that were to clash inevitably with the Duce's ideas on these issues and with his concept of the Fascist Party."[151] It was just his attempt to give the party an active role, along with his intransigence about moralizing it, that led to his premature political end. As had already happened to Turati, the difficult problem of dualism between state and party, between the undersecretary of the Interior and the

PNF secretary, between the prefects and the provincial party secretaries, the eternal contradictions within the regime, overwhelmed Giuriati and forced him to resign after only a year. Comments on his removal referred again to homosexuality and insinuated that he fell because he had turned Montecitorio (the seat of parliament) into a "den of pederasts." This squalid rumor seemed confirmed by the attitude of his successor and rival Achille Starace, who ordered the burning of the chair of his two predecessors' in a staged a ritual aimed at wiping out the "germ" of pederasty that had "contaminated" the office. The solemn ceremony was a spectacular way of marking a new beginning, showing his loathing for pederasty, and clearly defined the difference between his own virility and the suspected homosexuality of the preceding secretaries. The ridiculous and vulgar spectacle was commented on favorably, because "something dirty had been left in the chair as well, and Starace was smart to burn it."[152]

Clashes in the Provinces

However much the Fascist regime proudly claimed to have transformed politics from an expression of local interests to a single national program that spread from the center to the provinces, factions and hangers-on continued to clash over the margin of power that remained after the process of centralizing and normalizing. By consolidating their influence at the local level, the Fascists were able to obtain assignments and acquire political roles at a national level as well. In short, although the *podestà* was appointed from above in order to prevent provinces and municipalities from turning into arenas for the fortunes of individuals and groups who might have been favored in elections, provincial federations were still marked by bitter feuds over leadership. De Begnac has given us useful proof of how centers and provinces reciprocally influenced one another:

> All things considered, all the provincial clashes were played out in Rome. . . .
> The provinces communicated with the Capital more by train than by wire
> or post. According to their tribe, the hangers-on traveled within the walls
> of the city, where other groups of hangers-on formed. Every deputy had a
> secretary, every secretary a friend, and every friend a near relation or close
> friend tied to his own fortunes, and so on.[153]

The central authorities, sometimes feverishly, ordered inquiries and temporary administration to resolve worrisome local disputes: local regional representatives, district inspectors, and temporary administrators intervened continually to guarantee order and respect for the hierarchy in place, even in the smallest centers, which were more difficult to control and where old notables often continued to wield power through clientelism. Reshuffling was frequent in the federations of the big cities, especially in those where a predominant figure, capable of aggregating the various forces and guaranteeing a balance among the different rivals, failed to emerge.[154]

Local conflicts often markedly reflected the power games played out in Rome. The weapons used were always the same: slander, blackmail, dossiers, and plots. The political conflict was not over. Although the regime declared that peace had been made within the party, the struggle for power and also the clash between the alternative ideas of Fascism were hidden behind police reports of corruption and immoral behavior. Even in 1932, Farinacci himself observed that "the terrible evil that has often oppressed us has not ceased;" "the second a party official is in sight, a silent attack is waged against him, until reshuffling gives way to a destructive cannibalism."[155] Among the papers of the archive, which are full of these secret controversies among *gerarchi* at all levels, it is not always easy to pick out the political motive behind the clashes recorded. It often seems impossible to find one's way in this enormous sea of gossip and slander, to pinpoint the true reasons for these conflicts among factions. However, the reoccurrence of certain accusations used in these political power struggles is striking: the most common were homosexuality, mafia associations, Freemasonry, and profiteering.

De Begnac gives an "anthropological" explanation for this phenomenon based on the distinctive character of Italians, on widespread immorality, cultural backwardness, and the absence of public morals, without, however, grasping how much the dictatorial context, in its degradation of human society, had heightened the phenomenon:

> As regards respect for other people's characters, Italian customs have not made much progress. Public representatives defeated one another through defamation. Anonymous accusations rule public opinion. It is enough to create a rumor about a man who goes against the stream to eliminate the possibility of being overcome by his strength. Swindler, thief, pederast, jinx, or gigolo: the list to choose from is varied; whether the Italians belong to the ruling class or are ordinary citizens, they are extremely clever in choosing.[156]

On the whole, the police papers provide a dark cross-section of party life, revealing a large number of "sins carried out by *gerarchi*: theft, corruption, bad administration and a lot of internal and external rivalry."[157] It is not that these accusations were not used in the past as well. There were also scandals in Liberal Italy, but during Fascism, in which they were an integral part of the system, they seemed to have become the main political weapon. During the Ventennio, all explicit dialogue on programs, values, and ideologies was eliminated; all means of free expression were silenced and conformity dominated; a political rival was attacked for his private behavior because, formally speaking, there was no possibility for clashes in terms of ideas or doctrine. The political struggle thus tended to become barbarized and to encourage the creation of feverish hunts for gossip, a search for the most intimate secrets of one's rivals.

The Duce noted every accusation scrupulously, waiting for the moment to use it to bring down troublesome figures who, once removed, were ready in turn to invent rumors and use political plots in order to take revenge, exploiting the rapid rotation of appointments to counterattack. Mussolini was disappointed in the quality of those who worked with him and did not give too much weight to the disputes he settled but rose above them as a judge; in fact, he "enjoyed seeing his henchmen fighting and was amused by the display of small factions and even smaller ones entering the field to fight over the right to expel a man from the ranks."[158] The *gerarchi* were not allowed to be autonomous and were held in a constant state of uncertainty, making them increasingly aware that they could be removed from one day to another. The Duce aimed at cutting the ties of the *gerarchi* with the provinces and weakening their local power so they would have to depend directly on him, making him the only source of their success. A pattern, however, that did not help the formation of a strong, authoritative, and prepared ruling class.

Public and private immorality were on the same level in this climate, as we can gather from the affair of the former *federale* of Turin, Claudio Colisi Rossi, member of the national party leadership and of the Grand Council, whose career was destroyed by a host of slanderous accusations, maybe too many to be really credible: he had organized a group of *squadristi* who had already been expelled from the party so as to have a kind of personal militia at his disposal; he was a Mason; he had plotted to kill the new officials imposed by Rome; all this to lead the federation again, and he had taken to passive pederasty as well. Probably the only true accusation was the first, taking into consideration that the scandal broke out between 1925 and 1926, when the battle within the Turin federation to put an end to the organization and conduct of *squadristi* and *ras* was still in progress. After all, Colisi Rossi was an extremist, a radical follower of Farinacci and loyal to Cesare Maria De Vecchi, with ties to the group of middle industrialists and accommodating toward the Mutua squadristi (assistance scheme for members of the Fascist action squads), even though he claimed he had been attacked several times, "with revolvers and sticks," because of his efforts to remove them from the party.[159] The struggle to reduce this *squadrismo* was led by Mussolini, who, after dissolving them all over Italy once and for all on October 5, 1925, required that his orders be respected and that every kind of illegality be suppressed in Turin as well. This normalization wiped out the old Fascist guard of Turin, whose idea of the party "as a propelling force of initiatives to be carried out locally and autonomously" was seen as "heretical."[160] Colisi Rossi was expelled from the Fascist Party in January 1926 for indiscipline and because he was accused of disruptive activities. After a few months, when the Mutua squadristi had been dissolved and *Il Maglio*, the newspaper of the Turin Fascists, suppressed, the new provincial party secretary, Dante Maria Tuninetti, who was a former member of a Fascist action squad and a follower of Farinacci, was also involved in a financial scandal. This provided a pretext to substitute him with the more moderate Count Carlo Nicolis di Robilant. This vast purge left many discontented, in particular, Colisi Rossi's staunch followers, who continued to organize activities of political opposition.

The way to resolve the problem was to get rid of the former provincial party secretary once and for all by discrediting him morally and politically. This explains the great number of accusations, among them homosexuality, which had acquired an important political significance. Colisi Rossi was accused by his enemies of having had a "perverted" relationship with Carlo Bonservizi,[161] the brother of Nicola, the famous "Fascist martyr" who was killed in France in February 1924. To give weight to this slander, an elaborate mise-en-scène was devised and put into play by a number of accomplices. As the story went, a hotel worker in Turin informed the police he had heard low moans and suspicious noises coming from the room where Colisi Rossi was lodged; looking through the keyhole he had seen the former provisional party secretary "having sexual intercourse passively with young Bonservizi." A police officer confirmed the hotel worker's story, as he had watched this "disgusting" scene as well to verify the facts.[162] The obscene act had not taken place in public, and to avoid scandal, Colisi Rossi was not reported to the police. Nevertheless, he underwent a military inquiry. To defend himself he was obliged to exploit his merits as a fighter and show that his life up until then could not have been "more active, more masculine, more productive."[163] Besides, from the point of view of those times, virility was a distinctive feature that could be proved: masculinity was expressed in various kinds of behavior, among which one of the most important was courage in war. Although the military discipline council accepted his defense, Colisi Rossi was arrested and condemned to a year of *confino* on Mussolini's orders in October 1927. This punishment was meant to determine the end of his political career and squash any desire he may have had to recover an important role within the federation.

To the Duce, Colisi Rossi expressed his intention to be "absolutely disciplined while out of the ranks in silence,"[164] but in reality he was not planning on surrendering quite yet. To save himself he turned for help to his brother Luigi, a well-known collaborator of the Polizia Politica, who first contacted Father

Tacchi Venturi to put in a good word. Then, thanks to his ties with the police force, Luigi managed to get hold of his brother's file and gathered documents and confessions useful for exposing the whole plot, which he believed had been organized to cover up the misdeeds of the *podestà* of Turin and Count Robilant. All this triggered a hunt for the documents held by the Polizia Politica informer, as many feared they contained some dossiers against members of the federation as well.[165] The proof that cleared Claudio Colisi Rossi was sent directly to Mussolini, who, in April 1928 at Easter time, carried out an act of clemency and had him released from *confino*. Free again, the former *federale* requested, to no avail, to be admitted back in the party. Although not readmitted to the party, Colisi Rossi was given a job in the Vatican in 1930 thanks to the backing of Cesare Maria De Vecchi, for whom he had been private secretary. The Fascist police continued to keep a close watch on his private life, as this report reveals: "I have ascertained that Colisi Rossi has quite ephebic habits, meaning that he often and willingly takes home boys and adolescents instead of women. After keeping an eye on him for months I can state that he is always in the company of lads."[166] Finally free from police surveillance, Claudio Colisi Rossi died of typhoid fever on January 9, 1936, in the Sant'Agnese nursing home in Rome. There, he had been hospitalized after passing a period of time in a mental home because he was recognized as suffering from a dangerous paranoiac delirium."[167]

The accusation of pederasty was used as a political weapon to remove the *federale* of Florence as well. Rumors of the marquis Luigi Ridolfi's homosexuality—a "sodomite who lived an immoral life"—were so widespread that Starace, who had begun a campaign against bachelors, urged him to get married to put an end to the widespread rumors, which could have ruined his career after his promotion to national councilor.[168] Duke Andrea Carafa d'Andria, secretary of the *fascio* in Naples from 1925 to 1926 and consul of the MVSN was unable to avoid dismissal. The inquiry into his presumed pederasty, ordered directly by the militia's central command, turned up positive evidence, forcing the duke to resign. Although he was later rehabilitated and promoted in 1935 to the position of vice-president of the national Fascist federation of cattle and meat dealers, malicious gossip persisted, intensifying after the break up of his marriage in 1942, which was considered further proof of his homosexuality.[169]

The reputation of being a pederast was damaging and extremely difficult to shake off. For example, Renato Pergolani who was the *federale* Perugia in 1924 and later of Teramo and Marsala, had to live with continual rumors about his homosexuality. In this case as well, the fact that his marriage was annulled due to impotence made his life impossible. Once he had left Perugia to run the Terni hospital, he became the object of lewd comments and malicious gossip. By then, the scandal had become widespread. The military authorities were forced to take action against him and send his case to the disciplinary council, which removed him from the rank of officer. Pergolani, who was "humiliated and derided," was obliged to leave the city permanently as well as the hospital once and for all "to escape the comments and criticism he suffered as a result of his marriage problems and certain homosexual tendencies."[170] His bad reputation was an indelible blot on his name, even though in this case it was not an obstacle to his political career, which culminated in his appointment to the general direction of the party. Nevertheless, Starace later asked Bocchini to give him the information gathered by the police chiefs of the various cities where Pergolani had had political appointments. Certainly the Fascist Party secretary intended to use the documents he had obtained since the Sicilian deputy Alfredo Armato was reproached for having allowed Pergolani, whom he had met in Marsala, to live with him.[171] In short, anyone who had contacts with this "non-man" risked being identified as a pederast as well.

As internal conflict increased within the federations, so did the number of accusations of pederasty. This was the case in Pisa where, from 1921 to 1922, the local Fascist Party was particularly turbulent under the administration of Bruno Santini, who had ties with ex-combatants and trade unionists, and who criticized the illegality and violence of the *squadristi*. Obviously, Santini had to go; but after his resignation two other secretaries followed him, Duilio Cambellotti and Filippo Morghen, both incapable settling the disputes within the federation. A careful analysis of the affair regarding the *fascio* in Pisa reveals the political reasons for this incessant changing of the guard: Santini was a well-established member of the group of Fascist dissidents, while Morghen had ties with land-owners and big industrialists; the former had followers in town among the urban petty bourgeoisie, the latter had followers primarily in the countryside. The conflict among the Fascist leaders in Pisa, anomalous in comparison to the national one that was fought between integralists and normalizers, was more a clash between urban Fascism and the power of *ras* in rural areas. However, it is worth noting that even here, in this very complex power struggle, which came to the point of homicide—the accusation of homosexuality was used as a weapon.[172] Morghen was accused of pederasty and, although the inquiry launched by the provisional administrator Luigi Freddi turned up no concrete evidence,[173] one of Morghen's men, previously accused of having had homo-sexual relations in 1931 with the former *federale*, fell into the hands of the police. The unlucky man was sentenced to *confino* on the island of Favignana for his "immoral behavior."[174] The sentence was a warning for everyone involved: the factions had to be dismantled and the groups dispersed. The Duce demanded order in the provinces: this applied to all levels of the federation, as well as to the town administrations where the clashes between state authorities and the *gerarchi* of the Fascist Party were a continual source of tension.[175]

However, once greater control of the center over the provinces was achieved, the early conflicts for leadership, between alternative policies, extremists, and revisionists, battles between the *ras* turned into competition among the *gerarchi* over personal questions or fights for the admiration of the Duce. As the regime became stabilized, and the normalization and reorganization of the provincial Fascists diminished the instabilities within the federations, there were fewer conflicts and the rivalries were not as bitter. Nevertheless, the accusation of homosexuality was still widely used as a weapon in internal conflicts.[176] This happened in the Milan federation, where, after Mario Giampaoli fell from grace, the provincial party secretary Rino Parenti, in office from 1933 to 1939, managed "to normalize Milanese Fascism and adapt it to the requirements of national Fascism, even though some internal conflicts and especially a vestige of *sansepolcrism*, continued to survive."[177] Nevertheless, Parenti's capacity to intermediate between integralist Fascists and Milanese entrepreneurs, his ability to organize and rally the masses, and his absolute loyalty to Mussolini thwarted every attempt to attack him directly. Attempts were made to discredit him with attacks on his entourage by insinuating and spreading rumors that two of those who worked closest to him, Renzo Rezzonico and Riccardo Riva, were involved in immoral and sordid activities. The former was Parenti's private secretary, while the latter was a member of the governing body of the federation and president of the inter-union committee (Comitato intersindicale) of Milan.[178] Both were described as incorrigible pederasts in a series of anonymous letters that consequently threw suspicion on the "unspeakable" nature of their relationship with Parenti.[179] Attempts were made to stir up a scandal, as well: first Sandro Pozzi, a close friend of Rezzonico and then Roberto Rossi, press office chief of the Milan federation when Giampaoli was in office and later a Polizia Politica informer, gathered information and written proof of the intimate rendezvous and un-inhibited orgies that Rezzonico and Riva took part in, both of them totally shameless and depraved.[180] A young Fascist even protested because he had not been paid for his "male services" and asked Riva to pay the sum agreed upon while a hotel waiter stated that he had refused to serve Rezzonico's table because of the "disgustingly obscene gestures" he was making with his fellow dinners. This "evidence that Riva and his companions were pederasts initiated a mechanism to stop the scandal from breaking out, a string of coercive actions, money and job offers, and threats of arrest, anything in order to buy the silence of the witnesses or persuade them to retract.

The papers about this squalid affair reveal three significant documents on the question of homosexuality in the Fascist period. The first one contains a telling statement by a collaborator: "After all, Riva was not afraid of blackmail because he had played the male part."[181] The statement confirms what has been said regarding the passivity as the defining characteristic of the sin of homosexuality. In this rigid model, the active male is virile, even if he has intercourse with men. The second observation regards an adjective, again used in a confidential note, which describes the "Nazi habits" of those who worked closely with Parenti. The date of the report, December 1934, should not be overlooked. At this point, Italian Fascists had an idea of Nazism that seemed strongly influenced by the propaganda spread by Hitler at the time of the clash with Röhm's storm troopers. The third interesting element is the threat to inform Farinacci about the whole affair. Evidently he already had the role of moral critic of Fascism at this point.[182] In any case, the Riva–Rezzonico issue was destined to drag on for all the years that Parenti was the leader of the Milanese federation. It was fed by the resentment of the Fascists whose ambitions had been frustrated and by the desire for revenge of those who, disappointed in their aspirations to important assignments, were ready to cooperate in denigrating Parenti's two collaborators. Riva himself was hated by many, because "he had alienated the industrialists with his decidedly favorable attitude toward the people."[183] Riva was able to save himself with Parenti's help and some ties he had with important parliamentarians. Rezzonico also managed to defend himself from every accusation with the support of a member of the disciplinary court.

The protection that the *federale* offered his men prevented their incrimination. Pressed directly by Rome, where the Parenti dossier was building up, the Milan chief of police could only confirm that Riva was not highly respected, because he was a homosexual whose "sexual perversion was talked about openly, even in public places and in Fascist circles."[184] However, in the end, although Riva was indeed considered an individual "whose moral conduct was anything but clean and who was afflicted with active and passive pederasty,"[185] Bocchini limited himself to advising the greatest discretion, considering Riva's position, and in order to avoid "giving rise to regrettable difficulties that could damage the prestige of the Federation."[186] Once again, the good name of Fascism had to be safeguarded; the easiest way to resolve the problem remained the same: suppress every possible public mention.

Precisely to avoid a scandal, a Milanese shopkeeper who was guilty of publicly repeating a prostitute's comments about "Parenti's perverted tastes" was sentenced to *confino*. As the police report reads, the young man's slander seemed "quite harmful to the regime" because of its connection to the slanderous campaign against the provincial party secretary and the other members of the provincial federation. Parenti himself confirmed that it was necessary not to show leniency toward this imprudent "slanderer," which "set the precedent that a man of honor holding responsible positions in the party, can be the target of vulgar insults that seriously damage his moral and political figure without anyone being punished for it."[187] Not even this move was enough to stop gossip and reports on Rezzonico and Riva. The latter was still described "as a vulgar passive pederast," who continually associates with "handsome young men" and who discredits Fascism with his amoral behavior.[188] His long permanence in the federation meant that Parenti was also rather suspect, because many were surprised that the provincial party secretary could continue to employ a reputed homosexual. It was rumored that Rezzoncino and Riva were the real heart and soul of the federation, that they procured business for him and were the only ones capable of making decisions. Parenti, in turn, wrapped up in a morally compromising relationship where morality was compromised, was accused of blindly following their wishes. For example, Mario Di Marco, an old comrade of Giampaoli, blackmailed the federation and by threatening to go public with the information about the behind-the-scenes intrigues of some members of the governing body.[189]

This flood of gossip, anonymous letters, and accusations exasperated even the chief of the Polizia Politica in the end. Most of this "trash" had been gathered by his official representative, Roberto Rossi, who was loyal to Giampaoli and who, right from the start, had played a decisive part in building up the mountain of accusations against Parenti and his entourage. He was eventually peremptorily advised to drop the issue:

> Dearest Roberto . . . I would like to point out to you that I am completely indifferent to everything that regards these personal quarrels among local individuals. They do not interest me, nor should they. Therefore I entreat you to forget about Riva and Pozzi and all those who are for or against Riva, attending only to what can and must concern our work that, as you know, has a much higher purpose than what might regard wretched personal tantrums.[190]

The affair, which seemed closed at that point, began again in 1940, after the leadership of the federation changed hands.[191] Parenti's enemies started attacking again, accusing him of homosexuality and producing new proof aimed at striking the former provincial party secretary.[192] Parenti's followers counter-attacked with the same ammunition, accusing the new leader of the Milanese Fascist Party, Emanuele Gianturco, of pederasty.[193] As usual, it was the well-tested weapon of sexual perversion that was used: a probative case was built up to support "a series of vile accusations against the *federale*," making use of his mistress, who had been offered money. However, this time the trap was foiled and the perpetrators of the plot arrested and sent to *confino*.[194]

The Milanese case offers a cross-section of daily life in the regime's centers of provincial power and gives us a good idea of the importance Fascism gave to virility, and consequently how obsessive the rejection of homosexuality was. Just being suspected of pederasty left an indelible stamp on a person and made life extremely difficult. Belonging to the "society of pederasts," taking part in the "round table," could jeopardize a political career more than a dubious political past or unscrupulous business practices. The criterion of masculinity was the standard for ideal Fascist male behavior. Sexual conceit and macho attitudes were tolerated because they were part of the widespread image of virility.[195] A man always had to be the active one, the conqueror, and if he was married, it was normal to satisfy his instincts outside of his marriage. On the other hand, an effeminate, passive man, often a cuckold, seemed unworthy of being a Fascist; as a living symbol of the values despised by the regime, he was a person to cast out of society. In short, anyone who did not follow this model of masculinity was an easy target for his rivals.

The importance given to virility, one of the principal ideological components of Fascism, enables us to better understand why so many structural political conflicts during the life of the regime were nourished and fought with accusations of "deviated" or "perverted" sexuality. As noted, it was the quickest and most radical way to discredit one's rival "politically." This custom was extremely widespread in the provinces where only the echoes of national politics arrived and can be explained precisely by the fact that provincial public life was simplified in many ways. The more "serious" political discussion were carried out in Rome, where the political dialectic was still alive within the regime despite the constraints of the dictatorship, so much so that the two principal approaches to Fascism, integralist and moderate, authoritarian and totalitarian, were to continue confronting each other throughout the Ventennio. Clearly, these divisions affected the provincial federations as well; however, the small local *gerarchi* turned each political option, both personal and of their groups, into the immediate and concrete defense of their positions of power, acquired thanks to their siding with one or another more important *gerarca*. Thus, to defend their positions or obtain a more prestigious appointment, any weapon was permissible, but since "local quarrels" were not allowed, slander was mainly used in the clash between groups and factions. In the provinces, compared to the upper echelons of the party, there was less tolerance for the expression of one's particular interpretation of Fascism. Bottai could oppose Farinacci and criticize some aspects of the regime, just like Balbo could show his disagreement with Mussolini, but it was much more difficult for a *federale* or a mere member of the federation to start an open battle against an opponent. The sole task of the *federali* and *podestà* was to manage, administer, and control the regime's organizational nature in the provinces. Yet disputes were inevitable, even if they ended up seeming like mere struggles for power, which were fought with the ugliest means of slander and calumny.

In addition, we should not forget that Fascism constituted an entirely new political class, taken from the bourgeois and petty bourgeois, from those who had fought in the First World War and young people, all of whom abruptly substituted the entire ruling class of the old Liberal state. This new group of political personnel coming from lower social classes than those preceding them, brought into the limelight personalities who were not used to public debate and confrontation, who did not have a lot of experience in political militancy, and who brought their aggressive, controversial, and simple ways of resolving rivalries and conflicts to the political arena.[196] Immediately after the Rome congress in November 1921, Cesare Rossi himself reflected on the difficulty of turning these upstarts newly arrived at power into expert politicians, and pointed out "the gaps typical of an improvised movement of inexperienced people"—like the newborn Fascist Party—"nine-tenths of whose members had nothing to do with politics until yesterday."[197] Turati attempted to solve the problem of forming and selecting a new ruling class that was morally and culturally superior to the old liberal class by rendering the party more professional, co-opting young *avanguardisti* (members of a Fascist youth organization), and substituting the undisciplined Fascists of the "first hour" with better prepared and more presentable political personnel. Yet the attempt was not altogether successful. The legacy left by *ras* and the very real difficulty of turning delinquents and violent men used to solving problems with their fists into a ruling class was another reason for the proliferation of underground moves made up of insinuations, plots, and blackmail, and a political approach that lacked ideals.

Finally, it should be taken into consideration that Fascism was becoming more and more similar to a modern mass dictatorship, a mammoth organizational machine with two to three times the personnel than the Liberal state. During the Fascist Ventennio the number of cadres and positions increased considerably, with PNF representatives in countless organizations, bodies, and institutions of the regime. An entire party bureaucracy was instituted alongside those of the state already in existence. Between these two bureaucracies there were often overlapping areas of competence. With its constant turnover of personnel and a number of clashes and dualism, the tension between state and party became a structural characteristic of Fascism. The Fascist regime continually reproduced new bureaucracies that clashed with each other, with hierarchies that fought for power and autonomy. Competition among parties, which was the basis of the Liberal state immediately after the First World War, was substituted by clashes between institutions and administrations. In addition, the continuous enlarging of the ruling class created conflicts over who was to occupy the new places of command. The Fascist Party increasingly became a means of social climbing, which attracted people with little experience in politics, who were recruited from the higher echelons without having established any connection with party members. There were also a good number of opportunists, "eleventh-hour Fascists" who saw valuable opportunities to further their careers. The absence of free competition and a political formation marked by progressive stages encouraged many to continually resort to moral lynching in order to defeat rivals, and prevented the ruling class from establishing any strong ties with civil society, which after all, had been deprived of any ability to choose.[198] With the elimination of political parties and organizations representing the masses and their wills, the leaders imposed from high up theoretically should have had special qualities that made them loved and respected by those deprived of the right to choose their own representatives. Therefore, it is understandable that the people experienced a certain amount of satisfaction in seeing so many *gerarchi* periodically discredited, victims of slander campaigns. This also explains the gap between institutions and civil society that has led historians to interpret the approval for the regime in terms of a cult of Mussolini, "Mussolinism," and a refused Fascist bureaucracy.

Compared to Nazism and Stalinism, which substituted leaders through brute force, the Fascists did not have a "night of the long knives" or the summary trials set up by the KGB. Changings of the guard came about without any bloodshed: overly influential and inconvenient *gerarchi* were removed, often through a defamatory campaign; in some cases, a man was eliminated through promotion—*promoveatur ut amoveatur*. The Fascists who had hoped to initiate a new form of rotation and selection of the ruling class little by little curbed the substitutions in the positions of responsibility and reached a compromise between the moderate elite born under Fascism and the old pre-Fascist ruling class, and ended up by reproducing the same system of clientelism accompanied, however, by a widespread use of blackmail and slander. In a dictatorial regime where reporting something to the police often led to an attempt to suppress every scandal, all people, protected by anonymity or certain they would not have to uphold their accusations before a court, were encouraged to use slander as a political weapon. The lack of freedom created a situation where it was increasingly difficult to distinguish truth from falsehood. The internal investigations of the PNF and the disciplinary courts became forums for assessing the moral conduct of party members, for trying to safeguard the regime's prestige, and for judging how truthful these innumerable defamatory accusations were through a kind of internal trial.

Inquiries within the Fascist Party

Unfortunately the PNF files containing the documents on the inquiries within the party were destroyed or went missing after July 25, 1943. The same is true of the documents in the archives of the provincial federations. Therefore, it is difficult to analyze the overall number of inquiries, and even more so the percentage of cases where these inquiries ended with the expulsion of a *gerarca*. However, we do know that the sanctions for those who did not respect "the political and moral discipline of the Party" became progressively harsher with the years; it was not by chance that the PNF statute of 1926 established that a Fascist who was expelled had "to be outlawed from politics," while the 1929 statute outlawed him "from public life" as well. Exemplary measures were adopted for those who were considered "traitors against the Cause of the Fascist Revolution," but for those who had done something or been convicted of something that damaged "their moral figure," in this case the person involved was to be immediately expelled from the Fascist Party and removed from the appointments he held.[199] Expulsion from the party could strike anyone who "neglects his family or leads an irregular life" or "allows or facilitates extremely dangerous, poisonous germs to infiltrate the family": two statements that were vague enough to be open to free interpretation.[200] Those expulsed suffered serious career problems, in particular because the PNF membership card was necessary to have a job. Many complained that they had no means of subsistence. Having one's political career interrupted also marked a financial disaster for those who had become wealthy thanks to the party, though there was always the hope of being readmitted sooner or later. Being expelled was never considered definitive. Both the person expelled and the Fascist authorities were well aware that one day it might be useful to the party to reinstate a reprobate. For example, the fall of a fellow political personage could bring somebody previously expulsed back into favor. One only needed to wait patiently for the right moment to gain credit again and maybe be called back to carry out new political assignments. Quinto Navarra recounted: "Once a *gerarca* fell out of favor, he knew that the best way to return was to 'fascistically' obey and wait. The longer the wait the greater the reward."[201]

A parallel system of justice conducted by members of the party's disciplinary court served to give an appearance of legality to measures that were often completely arbitrary. "Numerous judges made strenuous efforts to be transferred to Palazzo Littorio, assigning themselves a task that was particularly capable of debasing their dignity": conducting justice in a political seat.[202] This judicial body, entrusted with establishing the truth about the behavior of party members and with indicating the disciplinary measures to be taken, almost always turned out to be the means for carrying out political strategies decided elsewhere. The inquiries were supposed to verify the accusations; but crimes and illegal actions often went unpunished because the measures taken served to avoid a regular trial and ended up creating privileged treatment for members of the Fascist Party.[203] Few traces of these proceedings are left in the archives, some of which concerned the "crime" of homosexuality. Nevertheless, an analysis of a couple of sensational cases provides us with an idea of the way in which *gerarchi* who were presumed pederasts were dealt with, the means used to ascertain whether they suffered from the "vice" or not, and above all the discretion used by the Fascists in these instances. As aforementioned, the repression of homosexuals was aimed mainly at individuals of lower social classes and prostitutes, while greater tact was used when dealing with members of the wealthy bourgeoisie and influential personages. Moreover, if it was a matter of deputies, senators, or national councilors, a blind eye was often turned, and when this was not at all possible, they were subjected to disciplinary measures in an attempt to keep their excessively dissolute behavior in check.

In 1929, at the request of Mussolini's cabinet, a particularly delicate inquiry was undertaken to establish whether the Honorable Liberato Pezzoli was a pederast. Pezzoli was coeditor of *Lavoro Fascista*, president of the national confederation of trade workers, a member of the Grand Council and had been elected to the chamber in the 1929. Thanks to police investigations, it was established that Pezzoli had repeatedly tried to have passive homosexual intercourse with some youths." Various witnesses testified to the deputy's immoral behavior. The receipts for sums of money paid to two employees of the Fascist trade unions were only some of the examples of evidence gathered to prove the important politician's "illness." The inquiry ended with Pezzoli's suspension from all political and trade union activities, on the grounds that his homosexuality made him morally unworthy. However, Pezzoli was formally invited to resign with a payout of a hundred thousand liras in order to hush up the whole scandal.[204] Once again, political interest prevailed over ideological consistency. Only in theory was pederasty a "sad vice" to be repressed with harsh police measures; in practice, the authorities were ready to tolerate this kind of "degeneration" in order to safeguard the reputations of the regime's representatives. Obviously, the Chamber of Deputies accepted Pezzoli's resignation, but the excessive indulgence adopted was criticized: "The Party should have had the courage to expel unworthy members publicly, not behind closed doors." In fact, Pezzoli's removal from the political scene did not last very long: after just a few months he had taken up his old activities again, parading proudly among the militia squad leaders, and as the end of the legislature approached, his name circulated freely among the possible candidates in the 1934 plebiscite. However, this would have been excessively indulgent even for a tolerant PNF, which was pleased with the reservation Pezzoli had adopted, "evidently with the aim of quelling any suspicion and rehabilitating himself in the eyes of the Party Hierarchies." In the end, Pezzoli did not make the cut among the list of new parliamentarians.[205]

Another particularly controversial inquiry involved Elio Turola, director of the Chamber of Deputies' police offices. Turola was said to have exploited his

position in order to maintain his "lascivious" behavior and his "dissolute" lifestyle by keeping company with young servicemen and personnel in service at
Montecitorio (the House of Parliament) until late at night. There had always
been gossip in parliament, but the younger members thought that the degeneration and sexual perversion had gotten out of control—"never as now had vice
and corruption reached such heights."[206] According to more malicious opinions,
Turati had always managed to save himself, despite the persistent rumors of his
passive pederasty, because Giuriati was afflicted with the same vice and could
not act against him.[207] In January 1934, when some of Turola's employees
explicitly accused him of being a homosexual, the police chief of the chamber,
Alessandro Dudan, was charged by the Head of Government's Cabinet to carry
out a thorough investigation on him.[208] Interrogations of the receptionist, the
chamber switchboard operators, and some deputies reveal an interesting
panorama that sheds light on the attitude toward homosexuality and tells us
which kinds of behavior were considered to be indisputable proof of pederasty.
For example, the questions were about the "freedom and intimacy" Turola
showed toward his employees and how offensive his behavior was to public
morality. "His morbidly abnormal partiality" for some employees at Montecitorio
and his excessive effusiveness with the doorkeeper of the Chamber of Deputies
were not only considered reproachable but were evidence enough to confirm
the suspicion of pederasty. Dudan thought there could not be "proof" of the
accusation of homosexuality, unless "there were confessions of accomplices with
photographs and documents"; however, the evidence gathered on Turola's
exaggerated fondness for his "uncouth, semi-illiterate, and corrupt subordinates,"
was an indisputable sign of "abnormality in a culturally and hierarchically
superior person." These reflections show how the model of bourgeois respectability was used to judge the private lives of citizens. A real Fascist had to behave
in an absolutely honest way in public by keeping straightforward, absolutely
martial, and virile relations with his companions. Once again, it was the superficial elements that opened the way to investigating people's souls. It was not so
important to be certain that Turola was or was not homosexual. It was important
that his behavior did not arouse suspicion. Dudan's final suggestions are also a
compendium of how these delicate issues were resolved: the police chief's opinion
was that Turola should be invited to resign and be given an appointment in the
colonies; immediately after this, "a purge of his subordinate personnel" should
be carried out, "so that the future Chamber would not be burdened with the
legacy of this hereditary defect."[209] Homosexuality was considered one of the
basest vices: its degrading aspects discredited those who were afflicted, driving
them to unrestrained excesses.

    Although the secret inquiry was carried out scrupulously and had confirmed
the accusations, Dudan was invited to interrupt the investigations and hand the

whole dossier over to Aldo Rossi-Merighi, the secretary-general of the Chamber
of Deputies. Once the proceedings had been taken away from the parliamentary
police headquarters and given directly to the party, the disciplinary committee
of the Rome federation now handling Turola's case radically changed the verdict:
after consulting Mussolini, Starace himself acquitted Turola of every accusation,
and to put an end to all unpleasant comments, not even the subordinates who
had confirmed the slanderous accusations against Turola were subjected to any
disciplinary measures. Neither the witnesses' statements nor the compromising
documents and letters were taken into consideration. The case was deflated
and buried.

Despite the pretext that the case was of a confidential nature, the public
rebelled against the regime's habit of repressing its scandals, claiming that "if
they were nipped in the bud and made public instead of hiding them, exposing
the unworthy subjects to scorn, the situation would not become so gangrenous.
The example would be useful to the institutions and would set a moral standard
for citizens. The silence surrounding these scandals is an instigation to do
wrong."[210] Everybody certainly knew very well that the use of accusations of
homosexuality was widely exploited, so much so that it was difficult to distinguish between true facts and contrived falsehoods. Notwithstanding this, as a
police collaborator observed, in Turola's case:

> Rumors say that the accusation may not have been fully proved, but the
> opinion remains, in particular because, were he innocent, he would have
> gotten rid of the subordinates who accused him. However, we should note
> that this accusation has been spreading for some time since the German
> scandals, and that in Italy as well, when it is not clear why some serious
> measure had been taken, rumors get round and the accusation of pederasty
> is believed to be true.[211]

Reassured by his complete acquittal only a few days later, Turola even
aspired to the nomination of officer of the Order of the Crown of Italy, but
Dudan's protests led Starace not to confer the decoration upon him. Nevertheless, when Turola and his wife separated, because their marriage had not been
consummated and for "obscene proposals against nature,"[212] the rumors that
Turola was homosexual became so insistent that they convinced the Speaker of
the Chamber, Costanzo Ciano, to use the information Arturo Bocchini had in
hand to open a new inquiry. After having Turola closely followed day and
night, the Polizia Politica collaborator Mario Finizio (Marius) drew up a report
describing Turola's numerous "base and degenerate actions" in detail: the
"despicable, revolting scenes," and his meetings, embraces, and effusions of
every kind with men of a "much lower social condition than his as well as with

well-known pederasts of Rome." In 1936 Turola was dismissed from his appointment as president of the police station of the Chamber of Deputies, with the excuse that the post had been abolished.

In some cases, expelling someone from the party was considered too light a measure, even though *confino* was called for only if it concerned a politically minor person, as in the case of Confucio G., struck off the membership list of the Fascist Party by the *federale* of Modena because of his "serious moral turpitude and behavior against public and private morality, and for introducing young men to the vice, after they had shed blood in a time of sacrifice and struggle. He should be kept away from any dishonest and despicable attraction." Surprisingly, the press took up the affair but did not seem satisfied and asked for an even harsher punishment:

> With all the respect due to Confucius and his Oriental followers, we express
> our vote that the various Confuciuses and Confucians of the Modena sort
> not only be expelled but immediately sent into *confino*.[213]

The author of this brief note was the deputy Egilberto Martire, a clerical–Fascist, assigned to reportage on the Vatican for the *Corriere d'Italia*, founder of the Youth Union for the Public Morality of Rome as well as the magazines *Vita* and *Il Rogo*. The journalist had been interested in the subjects of love and sexuality for years.[214] His proposal gave rise to various comments at *Montecitorio* and some predictable insinuations: "The Hon. Martire speaking of pederasts is like a loan-shark speaking of nooses."[215] The allusions to Martire's lack of morality had more to do with his ties to the Vatican and the Catholic world than his "sexual traditionalism," which the Fascists used to strengthen the image of a party dedicated to reforming the customs of Italians, defending respectability, and fostering sound principles.[216] In practice, the authorities intended to move very cautiously when repressing the "sins" of party members. *Confino*, when used, was meant to serve as a warning, to persuade them to behave "decently," and to respect the rules of Fascist ideology.

At times, such extreme measures were taken following a conflict of jurisdiction between party and state, between the police force and the disciplinary commissions of the provincial federation. Such was the case with the first president of the Udine Fascio, Antonio Bazzi, a courageous fighter decorated with the Military Cross, who had been the commander of a local action squad and had taken part in the March on Rome. His glorious past had opened the door to a career within the party and guaranteed him numerous administrative positions.[217] However, this did not stop his expulsion from the PNF after quarrels and internal issues in 1923, and then his suspension ten years later for shameful behavior. In 1941 the police found out about Bazzi's presumed homosexuality when he was accepted back into the party as a member of the federal directorate of Udine. Based on one of Starace's directives still in force, it was up to the PNF to authorize all legal actions. The investigation was taken away from the police and carried out directly by the *federale* and included crosschecked interrogations and testimonies. All of them confirmed the accusations: Bazzi was described as a passive pederast who led a "life of vices, debauchery, and depravation." Nevertheless, to save the honor of Fascism and to avoid damaging his family, a proposal was made to move him to another city, instead of taking disciplinary measures. The *federale* explained to the party secretary the reasons for, and advantages of, following this line of action:

> As a result of his past, Bazzi was acknowledged by the members of the Fascist action squad as their local commander for a long time and, as such, he worked enthusiastically for the organization and conduct of Fascist action squads and for Fascist initiatives in general. Taking this into consideration and with the intention of avoiding, especially at this time, the malicious comments that would inevitably arise and that could even indirectly damage the Party in the provinces if we resorted to the severe disciplinary measures that the present laws on pederasty call for, I would consider it fitting to limit the measure to the removal of Bazzi from all his present appointments, and, as far as his profession is concerned, have him immediately and officially transferred from the insurance company "Alleanza" to another provincial office. I reached this decision after rigorously examining the situation and the repercussions that otherwise could arise unfavorably, given the appointments Bazzi held for so many years, and not neglecting my anxiety about breaking up Bazzi's family, made up of his wife and twenty-year-old daughter. In fact, taking away his Party card would compromise the delicate position of his daughter, who teaches in a public school, besides meaning that Bazzi would inevitably lose his job, which provides his only income. However, I would like to confer on this and the whole delicate affair that Bazzi has come up against, and take the liberty of asking for an appointment.

Although the provincial party secretary suggested leniency, the PNF secretary's orders were that Bazzi was to be expelled from the party for the following reasons: "His behavior has damaged his moral figure."[218] However, not even this internal measure ended the affair. The Interior Minister later sent the case to the committee for *confino*, because police and *carabinieri* reports revealed that Bazzi's homosexual tendencies were well known in Udine, that "he was more feared than respected by the public for his moral deficiency." New interrogations confirmed the accusation of passive pederasty: witnesses said that the *gerarca* "was more attracted to men than to women," and that during sexual intercourse "he played the role of the woman and stayed underneath." Bazzi vainly tried to defend himself, denying he was a "passive" and denouncing the investigations as inaccurate, claiming it was all part of a plot against him orchestrated by the *federale*, his long-standing rival. On March 8, 1941, Bazzi was sentenced to two years of *confino* but no measures were taken against the youth with whom he had had sexual intercourse. Once again, the distinction between male/female, active/passive, dominator/dominated was used to establish a person's homosexuality.[219]

It was necessary to handle cases of foreign homosexuals with care as well, especially if they were politically useful to the Fascist regime, as is illustrated by the case of the "extremely perverted" president of the foreign press, Roberto Hodel. This Swiss journalist, who was a resident in Italy, had already been suspected of spying in 1915. No proof to confirm the suspicion had emerged from the investigations, but his private conduct had seemed quite questionable. In fact, Hodel turned out to be "addicted to homosexuality" and kept intimate relationships with Roman boys.[220] Again, in the immediate postwar period, there continued to be complaints about his "immoral" conduct. For example, the nationalist deputy Luigi Federzoni asked that this "permanent scandal for the Capital" be brought to an end:

> Is it not enough to have Italian pederasts? Must we have foreign ones as well? His home is like a brothel, a meeting place for degenerate louts, most of whom are under age. I have been told by some tenants who are nauseated by this permanent scandal that Hodel keeps some fifteen-year-old boys as lovers, and that there are noisy parties at his place day and night. Your Excellency Hon., please have this indecent man expelled from the Kingdom and have Rome purged of such obscenity.[221]

Although Hodel's "homosexual tendencies" were extremely well known, the police intervention and expulsion were not unjustifiable. In 1926, when nominated president of the foreign press association, Hodel had promised to faithfully support the regime with the condition that he would enjoy a certain impunity in relation to his sexual habits. Hodel carried out the delicate task of steering the foreign press toward pro-Fascist positions and had the secret charge of supplying confidential information to the Ministry of Popular Culture. Spying guaranteed him generous earnings and the certainty that he could continue to freely satisfy his homosexual desires.[222] Hodel had friendly relations with many of the foreigners who shared his sexual tendencies, particularly with Goffredo Kusen and Italo Tavolato, but he also had various enemies who were anxiously waiting for a specific article against homosexual relationships to be introduced into the Rocco law.[223] However, the attempts to attack him were to no avail. For the police, he had caused so much scandal and gossip about his morals that it was no longer worth bothering about him. Even when the parents of some underage boys reported him to the police, nothing was done about it. In short, as he was politically untouchable, the police could only continue to keep him under surveillance.[224]

The type of relationships he had with these young lovers emerges from the observations of the police and some of his letters. In these letters, Hodel heartbreakingly expressed his love for some boys to whom he gave small sums of money and whom he hosted in his home, or took around Italy with him. While Mussolini's protection allowed him "to take all the liberties he wanted, even the most illicit and damaging ones," the same did not apply to his partners. Thus, in 1936 two grenadiers, guilty of exchanging letters with and having "dubious" relations with Hodel, were arrested and interrogated. The presents received from Hodel and other "passive foreigners," the loving words exchanged, and the time spent in lighthearted gaiety all became counts of an indictment, as did their "alluding to sexual intercourse between men," or "stating that such sexual intercourse was preferable to that with women."[225] Consequently, the army disciplinary committee assigned the young servicemen to a specific correctional squad for pederasty. Thanks to his connections, Hodel, who came into possession of some compromising documents concerning his person, managed to avoid being directly involved. Dino Alfieri, who was the secretary of Popular Culture at the time, and Galeazzo Ciano thought, however, that the case was enough to persuade Hodel not to nominate himself for the post of foreign press president again.[226] Thus, in 1937 Hodel left his important position and paid the consequences for the "shameful way in which he made his abnormal tendencies public."[227]

According to Vittorio Terracini, a collaborator with the Polizia Politica, Hodel was also a duplicitous spy who cleverly provided confidential information while hiding behind a façade of loyalty to the regime.[228] Hodel's position became precarious in the climate of international tension preceding the outbreak of the Second World War. Nevertheless, in 1939, despite the suspicions of the Italian counterespionage and thanks to the good offices of the Swiss embassy, he managed to have the measure of expulsion revoked, and in 1941, after a brief stay abroad, was authorized to return to Italy.[229] In December 1942 Tavolato continued to provide information about him, suggesting that the door of his building be watched, "to find out what company he keeps, so as to be able to 'nab' him for political reasons, or even more easily, for homosexuality, seeing that various questionable lads often go to visit him. Some of Hodel's friends maintain that he became anti-Fascist when Italy joined forces with Germany and the Axis; and that his hatred of Germany derived from the fact that Hitler and Himmler persecuted pederasts."[230]

Hodel's friends who were attracted to the Roman boys and were "pleased that at least on this . . . article Italy had not applied counter-sanctions!" were also controlled by the police and noted in their records as pederasts.[231] At a certain point the suspicion arose that there was possibly some sort of espionage network made up of foreign homosexuals residing in Italy. The antimodernist priest Umberto Benigni, paid by the Fascist Polizia Politica, explained how this network of spies worked:

> We would not have either the time, the desire, or the duty to deal with pederasts if it were not well known that pederasty, the business of common criminal law, is the traditional bond that links so many spies and sects. Many get away with it, just because their pederasty serves, among other things, as a cover for their spying. In some countries, pederasty is a crime for public law only in certain cases; when a pederast is known to be within the law we murmur "dirty pig" and go on our way, without suspecting the rest. That is why we are watching Sandoz's place, to reach some results. It is well known that pederasts form a brotherhood and that each one knows the . . . position of the others. They talk about these things habitually; and it is enough to find a way to make one of the . . . reporters talk to discover a lot.[232]

This concern reveals a clear racist attitude that led to considering homosexuals as traitors and liars. During the Second World War this stereotype took further root. For example, Malaparte was convinced that there was "a homosexual Five Year Plan for the corruption of Europe's young men" and for carrying out military spying.[233]

The link between espionage and homosexuality led to a tragic outcome in the case of Kurt Sauer. This German art critic and cultural attaché at the Reich's embassy in Rome was arrested in June 1942 for working as an informer. Galeazzo Ciano summed up what happened in his diary, saying:

> June 9—Our SIM has discovered an espionage center at the German embassy. Dr. Sauer, the cultural attaché, has already been arrested and has confessed. He only made it clear that he did not do it for money but out of hatred for Nazism and Fascism. He passed military information to the Swiss military attaché. It seems that a German colonel, Enno von Rintelen's adjutant, is mixed up in the question as well. The Duce commented bitterly on the affair and fears it could also damage the position of the ambassador, Hans Georg von Mackensen. Bismarck spoke about the affair with d'Aieta

but did not give much importance to the incident: he says that Sauer is a pederast whose vice led him to commit this serious crime.[234]

It was precisely due to this police inspection, made to confirm Sauer's homosexuality, that a close-knit network of spies that transmitted coded information to the Soviet Union and England, passing through Switzerland, had been discovered.[235] After further investigations by the SIM, the members of the group were immediately arrested, and the Roman cell composed of the Swiss citizens Robert Steiger and Gaetano Fazio along with Sauer, all three "bound by the filthy vice of homosexuality," were sent to Regina Coeli, the Roman prison.[236] In June 1943 the special court for the defense of the state passed the sentence of death for Sauer, life imprisonment for Steiger, and thirty years of imprisonment for Fazio. At dawn on June 2, Sauer was shot by a firing squad at Forte Bravetta, while the other two were taken to Germany and interned in a concentration camp after the Germans occupied Italy.[237]

7

Bourgeois Respectability and Fascist Morality

Their naked bodies met at dawn
It was something completely natural

SANDRO PENNA

Stranezze

Homosexuality and Totalitarianism

The fact that the regime wavered between repression and laxity in relation to pederasty was largely due to its rigid view of homosexuality and its largely superficial idea of virility. As a consequence, only those whose public behavior went against the stereotype of the virile, muscular, traditionally attired, and sexually active male—such as effeminate men, transvestites, and prostitutes— were persecuted. If a homosexual did not violate this public model he was not a target of the Fascist regime, which was not actually interested in a person's sexual orientation. Paradoxically, homosexuals, in this case meaning men who are attracted to other men, were totally ignored by the regime. The only thing that worried the regime was a lack of virility. No specific Fascist books, measures, or speeches dealt with the problem of homosexuality. The sedentary bourgeois man, the English dandy, or the refined and elegant Parisian represented the negative stereotype of the nonvirile male much more than a tough *squadrista* who was attracted to young boys. An effeminate man, who was not necessarily homosexual, was despised and derided because he symbolized the negative counter-type to the new Fascist man, who was self-confident, strong, and tough.

This attitude is particularly evident in the comments made by Mussolini about the alleged passive pederasty of the deputy Domenico Bagnasco. In Turin there were insistent rumors that Bagnasco, wounded in battle, recipient of military honors, nationalist, and president of the Turin Cooperative Alliance, was "sexually deviant." For this reason, reportedly, he had been dismissed as the union leader. The Duce had quickly quashed the rumor, saying that "given Bagnasco's physique, his masculine features and bushy beard there cannot be an iota of truth in the rumor."[1] Basically, Fascism did not punish homosexuals but those who were effeminate, embracing, thus, the idea that women were inferior to men. Consequently, active pederasts and masculine-looking homosexuals were usually tolerated, or at least not persecuted, whereas passive pederasts were targeted because they were the ones that actually had the female role. However, apart from their sexual identity, those who created the greatest concern were men whose behavior was effeminate, because they propagated a negative model and jeopardized Fascism's canon of respectability as well as its proposed model of masculinity. The gender division was to be rigidly maintained so as to clearly underline the difference between men and women.

This view of homosexuality as the absence of virility and the almost non-existent interest in female sexuality, except as being there for the pleasure of men or for reproduction, is also useful for understanding Fascism's attitude toward lesbians. Pederasty was considered a transgression, a vice, a disease to be fought and hidden, but the actions against lesbianism were so radical that no one dared acknowledge its existence. Lesbianism was not sexual deviation, it was only a mental illness, a syndrome of hysteria, or at the most a sign of the devil; not surprisingly, then, many lesbians were exorcised. Therefore, repression against them was even more occult and scheming than against pederasts, but it was equally effective and pervasive.[2]

Hostility toward the "masculinized" woman was far more explicit.[3] During the Fascist period, the regime leveled a fierce attack on the emancipated woman, the "boyish" woman or *garçonne* whose movements and short haircut made her look masculine, harshly censoring French fashion advertisements and American movie stars. To a certain extent, this hostility mirrored the attack on effeminate men. Carlo Scorza wrote:

> Today I don't know why there is so much talk about the masculinization of women when it would be the case to talk about the feminization of men, or at least acknowledge that the two movements are parallel. It is true that women have invaded the field of business, taking over professions and jobs, but it is equally true that men have invaded the world of fashion, perfumes, and the trivial world of leisure and comfort.[4]

The regime instigated the fight against effeminate men, against the lifestyle of the bourgeoisie, against bachelors and married men without children, to prevent the excessive feminization of men. The regime's indifference to the homoerotic elements of *squadrismo* is probably linked to its reductive image of masculinity—essentially just a show of strength and virility. Adherence to the lifestyle and ideology of Fascism were the necessary requirements for belonging to the Fascist community. The extent to which these male groups might foster the birth or manifestation of homosexual leanings was never considered. Virility was the yardstick for measuring and judging behavior; a lack of virility was strongly condemned, but excessive sexual yearnings were also scorned, and the latter was often used to depict the negative stereotype of blacks or enemies at war, who were described as sex-hungry beasts.

One could say that military rules, manners, and behavior represented the ideal lifestyle for the whole community and the most suitable framework within which to spread a new morality based on the total subordination of individual interests to those of the nation. Oddly enough, however, this extreme exaltation of virility and bellicosity, the realization of an organized collective, the soldier-citizens, and "respectability in uniform," all of which reduced differences, when applied to homosexuals actually reduced the hostility they suffered. In fact, once again the negative model only concerned effeminate men who were seen as weaklings and pacifists. The extent to which the "bellicose spirit" was in itself a mark of virility and morality was clearly described by Eugenio Galvano in the pages of the newspaper *Popolo d'Italia*:

> Fascism is a hierarchical collective. . . . The new morality is wild; it embodies the new ethical type whether individual, class, population or race. . . . As a race the Italians are violent, bloodthirsty, instinctive, and endowed with the most important moral requisites. Vitality and virility are the corner-stones of our morality, derived from ancient Rome: for us, vitality and virility are innate characteristics. . . . For us, it is sufficient to act in order to be morally correct. Not acting leads to immorality.[5]

The totalitarian goal of permanently mobilizing the nation in an effort to create a new community, an armed nation with a disciplined and regimented population, made virility synonymous with militarization. As a result, the sexual sphere took a backseat; virility was no longer linked to a person's sexual leaning but to his ability to fight for his country. As a matter of fact, with the war, virility became a female requisite as well. In their gray-green uniforms, women were called on to defend Fascism from internal and external enemies. And while this did not eliminate gender differences, it did, however, amalgamate to a greater extent the ties between virility and heterosexual masculinity. The strong, courageous, dedicated soldier, who was always ready to sacrifice himself for his country out of faith in the values of Fascist ideology, was the prototype of the ideal Fascist regardless of his sexual identity.

The repressive instruments used by the regime against homosexuals were inevitably linked to this cultural background. For this reason they may seem inadequate and even grotesque. Although the persecution of homosexuals was much crueler in Nazi Germany, the political use of homosexuality was similar to that of Fascist Italy, and their common view of pederasty led both countries to direct their repression against the same subjects. As Francesco Saba Sardi notes, "In Hitler's Germany the weak, decadent type of homosexual was persecuted, not the vigorous barracks queen. The simpering fairies that walked the Ring boulevards and city outskirts were eliminated; they were not martial enough. The rough SA or blond SS, adored by the sergeant or the *Strumbannführer*, were considered more virile, soldier-like and trustworthy than those who devoted their time to frivolous love affairs with women. In the same way, women soldiers in the SS were given the choice between lesbianism and *Hausfrau*, that is, entering a brothel for soldiers."[6] Nazism had a stronger racist matrix, however, which in the context of a totalitarian logic led to extreme consequences and repressive measures carried out in extremely ferocious ways unknown in Fascist Italy. Thousands of homosexuals were deported, sterilized, or exterminated as the result of the Reich's public battle against degeneration. Eugenics was used to justify the most atrocious forms of annihilation of all those "unfit," because in order to improve the nation's hereditary endowment it was considered perfectly normal to sterilize or even physically eliminate those who were "different." The concept of *lebensunwertes Leben* was justified on the basis of the need to safeguard the country from the eventual transmission of diseases or dysfunctions, among them homosexuality. Nazism's biological racism flung open the doors to extermination camps for those who risked contaminating Arian blood, corrupting customs, and spreading the germ of degeneration. In a Catholic society like Italy's, "negative eugenics" was strongly criticized and, probably for this reason, Fascism's repression of homosexuality never arrived at the same inhuman cruelty as under Nazism. Nevertheless, it would be misleading to use the example of Nazi Germany as a point of comparison for totalitarian regimes. The importance that Nazism attributed to the purity of the race was so accentuated that it became an incommensurable factor capable of triggering forms of intolerance such as euthanasia and genocide that cannot be compared with countries that lacked such a deeply rooted form of biological racism.

With regard to pederasty, "the evolution of Italian totalitarianism" also had specific prerequisites, due to its particular historic background. In a country where it would have been counterproductive to trigger an open battle against homosexuals in light of its weak racial matrix, the most suitable instrument for solving the problem was to hide any deviance, to silence pederasty. As we have seen, Fascism's strategy aimed at hiding the very existence of homosexuals and the measures used to punish them. Despite the apparent inadequacy of this approach with regard to the principles of Fascism's ideology, it proved to be very effective. Pretending not to see and, at the same time, tightening control over society were effective means of stopping the spread of this dangerous form of "sexual deviance." Fascism provided no specific punishment for pederasty, but it had many cunning ways of dealing with it. The point of "repressive tolerance" was to hide persecution, which was supposed to be evident only in clamorous cases as a sort of warning to the population, thus safeguarding citizens' morality without alarming them and without giving the impression that homosexuality was common. The fact that homosexuality was treated more like a social problem than a racial one is evidenced by the fact that Fascism did not revoke the citizenship of pederasts, even when they were sentenced to *confino*, where they were kept all together, forming a sort of separate community. In this way they could express their sexual identities by continuing to dress and wear cosmetics like women, and maintaining their homosexual love affairs. Of course, that did not make the Fascist morality, based on a cunning strategy to hide the problem, less despicable. With regard to the matter of sexuality, the regime's main concern was public behavior and practices that could lead to a scandal; pederasty was to be punished only when it was publicly visible and when it ended in antisocial, effeminate conduct.

One debate that took place among the members of the provincial commission for *confino* in Rome is particularly emblematic of this last tendency. They met to discuss the case of a municipal driver, married and father of a child, whose homosexuality had been discovered in 1942 through wartime postal censorship. The commission was divided on whether or not to punish him. According to the king's magistrate and the prefect, as well as the representative of the *carabinieri*, there was not enough circumstantial evidence to justify punishment, because the "immoral homosexual act had not been made public." Furthermore, "the person charged had not been listed as being socially dangerous, because his homosexual practices took place between him and only one other person. The public authority had discovered this relationship through censorship." On the other hand, the chief of police and the militia representative were in favor of punishment and maintained that "letting a pederast who had confessed his wrongdoing, one who had written disgustingly obscene letters, go unpunished would create a dangerous precedent, which might lead to other homosexual developments, infringements of the new race laws."[7] In other words, men who hid their attraction to persons of the same sex, perhaps even marrying, managed more easily to escape the rigors of the law and police action, particularly if they had enough money to lead an apparently normal life and safeguard their respectability.

Respect for Appearances and Censorship

The only way homosexuals could hope to avoid persecution was to suppress or hide their sexual identities and take on a public appearance in conformity with the male stereotype of the period. Exterior appearance and behavior reflected the Fascist new man who, with his radically different lifestyle from the past, was walking evidence of the successful fascistization of the entire Italian society. In order to change the mentality, to reach the consciences and emotions of individuals, Fascism's totalitarian approach sought to expand the public sphere, to make the private domain public, even to the point of encroaching on sexual privacy. Nevertheless, as we have seen, Fascism advanced prudently on this treacherous ground that presented many obstacles, the chief one being the canon of bourgeois respectability. Based on a deeply rooted sense of privacy and discretion, this tradition clashed with the idea of exercising total control over people's lives. Furthermore, a good social standing, wealth, and one's declared loyalty to Fascism as well as scrupulously honest conduct in public were good guarantees that one would escape the regime's inquisitional eye and avoid problems, even if one were of a "different" sexual orientation.

A perfect example was the case of two high-level exponents in the Fascist hierarchy, Carmine Senise, the head of the police department and Leopoldo Zurlo, director of theater censorship. Their friendship, which began in childhood, lasted a lifetime. They were both from Naples, and at the beginning of the twentieth century both entered the administration of the Interior Ministry, occupying many different roles under various governments. With the advent of Fascism, after briefly working for the head office of the Health Department, they managed to secure important positions with Arturo Bocchini, a long-time friend. Zurlo was made head of the censorship of theater productions, while Senise was first appointed head of the General and Private Affairs Division and soon after deputy chief of police.[8] The two men lived together in Zurlo's apartment on Via Provana in the San Giovanni district of Rome. Their relationship was so close that once Senise, talking about his modest, anonymous cohabitation with his "fraternal and inseparable friend," described Zurlo as being "more than a brother."[9] While this is not proof of a sexual relationship, other more explicit accounts, alluding to a particular kind of relationship between the two, came from Eugen Dolmann, who was Hitler's representative in Rome and was quite knowledgeable about its homosexual circles. This is how he described Bocchini's successor as chief of police:

> Little by little, Senise lost his predecessor's enormous political influence. . . .
> By now, there were no traces of Bocchini's gentlemanly manner and social
> qualities. Unlike in the past, conversations with the new boss were only about
> the happenings in Don Carmine's large Neapolitan family; he, an incor-
> rigible bachelor, was surrounded by a host of male and female relatives. . . .
> At that time, the ministry's luxurious automobiles were left to gather dust
> in their garages; the car doors no longer opened to allow the senator to
> descend, arm in arm with his lady covered in sparkling jewels, to enjoy the
> evening breeze on the Pincio under Rome's starlit sky. Instead, in their
> place there were two men dressed in black. They, too, were elderly and
> they, too, admired the view of the eternal city. It was easy to recognize
> Carmine Senise and his inseparable friend, Zurlo, who had shared an
> unpretentious apartment for years.[10]

Dolmann, who sincerely admired Bocchini for the way he managed the
police and also because, in his opinion, he impersonated an "authentic Italian
gourmand" (epicure),[11] did not feel the same way about Senise. He described him
sourly as an opera lover who sat "every evening at the Costanzi, not in the
company of a beautiful woman, but with the head of Italian censorship. The
two men could also be seen at the Pincio, but the atmosphere was very different
from that created by Bocchini with his 'beautiful' lady friend. The two walked
back and forth under Rome's brilliant starlit sky, giving the impression they
were concentrated on their constitutional, but all the while they were conspiring
to topple the Duce and liquidate the hated Germans."[12]

Senise, a serious, precise creature of habit, gave this same impression to
Guido Leto, who spoke ironically of the chief of police's conduct. Certainly,
the important appointment he received in 1940 must have "upset some of his
deeply rooted habits, such as mealtimes and the long walks he took in all kinds
of weather with his inseparable friend and colleague, the Prefect Leopoldo
Zurlo, imitating in this the Cardinal Pacelli, whom he often met walking the
pathways of the Pincio and Villa Borghese.[13] If Leto spoke in these terms, it is
easy to imagine what sort of gossip circulated inside and outside the ministry
about the relationship between Senise and Zurlo. In particular, in 1943 when
doubts about the police chief's loyalty to the regime increased and the cata-
strophic outcome of the war and Fascism became ever more evident, the insinuations were transformed into open accusations. The secret service within the
Duce's personal secretariat, set up by Mussolini and Guido Buffarini-Guidi in
February 1943 to gather information about and keep watch over politicians,[14]
reported that Zurlo was the "target of many sarcastic comments," because he
was considered a homosexual and therefore his cohabitation with the Police
Chief was extremely suspect.[15] However, most of the reports concerned Senise,

the real target, because he was thought to be a traitor connected with the anti-
Fascists. Many of the anonymous letters written about him denounced his
"immoral" conduct in private and his suspected pederasty linking him with
Zurlo.[16] One particularly venomous letter ended, for example, with the following
harsh words: "The present Chief of Police is morally corrupt. He is a pederast
and for many years has lived together with his Excellency Zurlo, who is his girlfriend. He also has sexual intercourse with Zurlo's sister. Some young police officers have homosexual relations with him, and that is why they have become
rich and powerful, feared by all. If he becomes aware that someone is suspicious
he will destroy him. Do you think this is sufficient to kick him out as he deserves,
or are you going to wait for him to bury the Duce?"[17]

With the downfall of Fascism and proclamation of the armistice, the lives
of these two friends took a tragic turn. The chief of police was arrested, because
the Germans considered him a dangerous traitor who had conspired against
Mussolini. Senise himself recalled that terrible September 23, 1943, when, after
days of worry for fear of being murdered, he was captured by the SS and
separated from his lifetime companion: "I was allowed to have someone call
Zurlo, but the sight of him broke my heart. Tears ran down his face but he didn't
say a word. I asked Alianello and Querci to take him home; at the time, the
separation was the only comforting thing possible for the noble friendship that
had linked us for so long."[18] Zurlo did everything possible to save his friend,
from whom he hadn't had any news for a long time. He implored the Duce to
get the Germans to set him free.[19] Soon after Senise's arrest, the Fascists published
a leaflet openly accusing the former police chief of treason and depicting him
as a "worshiper of Priapus, slave to a clearly manifested form of sexual inversion."[20] When the war ended, Senise was freed and tried for his actions within
the police force.[21] Zurlo, who had not taken part in the Social Republic, was
able to avoid the purge thanks to the scrupulous way in which he had performed
his role as theatrical censor. He went back to a quiet, anonymous life far from
the limelight.[22]

The particular behavior of these two important *gerarchi*, two bachelors who
lived together and were very different from the male stereotype widespread at
the time, clearly shows how Fascism was more concerned with the political usefulness of its servants than with their private lives. Senise and Zurlo's private
behavior was tolerated, because they were both useful bureaucrats for the regime,
skilled in dealing with the most intricate matters and capable of getting their
jobs done without causing scandal. For instance, Mussolini did not approve of
Zurlo's bachelorhood, and given the "unbreakable demographic rules," he did
not make him a senator,[23] but at the same time, he appreciated Zurlo's professional capabilities, the intelligent and subtle censorship he performed without

sensationalism or excess. The police chief, too, was criticized for his behavior in private, which, as he himself admitted was the complete opposite of his predecessor's lifestyle. Bocchini was considered "a Fascist for his exterior behavior; I was always considered anti-Fascist for my different conduct, but in the end we had the same idea of the police force's objectives."[24] Nevertheless, the Duce considered him a model official, even if in carrying out his job, he was inspired more by a profound sense of state than any real bond with Fascism. Cesare Rossi described Senise as a devout Catholic and fervent monarchist, part of the "cult of state," with a "well-developed juridical sense" and so respectful of formal legality that he was unable to see the negative aspects of Fascism.[25] Senise's selflessness, the zeal with which he faced even the most delicate matters, the experience accumulated in the pre-Fascist period and then during Fascism, made him a key figure for the regime and gave him an enormous amount of power. Therefore, it was neither easy nor advisable to attack this "odd" couple, despite the many rumors that circulated about their homosexual relationship.

On the whole, the Senise–Zurlo case highlights once again an inevitable contradiction between the totalitarian desire to transform Italians into a virile population and the ever-constant priority given to the political outcome of matters. In fact, the "supremacy of politics," typical of totalitarian regimes, resulted not only in assigning political importance to private matters and trying to orient people's conduct according to ideology, but also in placing matters of strategic political importance before ideology. Theoretical statements might be disregarded or adapted for political purposes. The political use of homosexuality is a perfect example of this phenomenon. The Senise–Zurlo affair showed exactly how morality changed depending on social origin and the political role of the people involved. Fascists were fairly tolerant with party leaders, intellectuals, and important men; in other words, with those with whom they had to be more indulgent so as to avoid dangerous scandals or those who were necessary for the regime.

Special consideration was reserved for artists whose sexual "peculiarities" were commonly thought to be typical of their eccentric personalities.[26] Their immoral behavior, however, was to be hidden behind a façade of respectable public conduct. In reality, their freedom of action was restricted by careful censorship. Artists could only refer to homosexuality by making direct or indirect hints or veiled references, or using ironic metaphors that did not tarnish Fascism's macho, homophobic rhetoric. As Dell'Orto has rightly noted, tolerance was granted to artists in exchange for "never mentioning the motives for their intellectual exploration of certain arguments, for drawing a veil of lies over the 'different' experiences, which were at the roots of their creativity."[27] Thus, homosexuals continued to remain in the shadows, and even if they were not labeled as being immoral, corrupt perverts, they were "inept heroes" who were at the most to be pitied.[28]

Because homosexuality was a prohibited subject, the homosexual artist felt denied and rejected, as if a part of him, of his feelings and his sexuality, which were fundamental components of his art, were completely eliminated. On the other hand, Fascism's intention of keeping homosexuality in the dark was implemented through intense censorship meant to respect people's inhibitions and safeguard the heterosexual code. Some interesting comments regarding the censorship of the "kind of love that dares not say its name" is to be found in Zurlo's memoirs.[29] In June 1931 he was given the difficult task of heading the theater review board.[30] Zurlo was convinced that the degree of obscenity varied depending on the period, the culture, and the moral sensibility of the reader. Consequently, he thought it was justifiable to be quite permissive in censoring books but much stricter with theatrical works, because they were educational and directed at a vast public that was not always well educated. He maintained that "at the theater a sort of collective mind is formed of the average intelligence that is lower than that of the more enlightened public, and whose morality— whether hypocritical or not—is more traditional and exigent."[31]

Other restrictions on theatrical productions that involved homosexual love affairs were imposed by higher-ranking officials who often prohibited scripts already approved by the censor. Thus, even Oscar Wilde's very successful plays did not obtain the placet. The reason given was that the public, which instinctively despised sexual inversion and worshiped "physical strength, which is often the shell for moral strength," would not welcome the works of an author whose very name "evoked memories of foulness and raised, once again, the question as to whether, with the current state of science, Dante would have had the right to place Brunetto Latini and his friends in the third circle of Hell."[32] Decadentism, the reaction to Victorian bourgeois respectability, and the birth of sexology had induced some reckless directors to think they could adapt books like *De Profundis* for the stage, but to raise the curtain on such a reality was considered, to say the least, unseemly. The censors even rejected the idea of performing a readapted version of *The Portrait of Dorian Gray* from which every reference to homosexuality had been removed. The author's plea to Zurlo to obtain permission for such "an unusual work, so full of contrasting elements and apparent 'double meanings' that it could easily degenerate into ambiguity or rise to moral heights" was to no avail:

> For obvious reasons of contingency and censorship . . . I have removed all
> of the gruesome episodes that make the story so original, but unfortunately
> so odd, and I have also carefully avoided that sort of "dual sexuality" that

hovered throughout. . . . I may have erred from an "aesthetic" point of view, but I think there is no doubt that from an ethical point of view the work is improved. From a literary standpoint my efforts may be questionable, but from the censor's viewpoint the script can now "work," in my opinion.

However, despite the suitable readaptation, both Zurlo and the minister, Alessandro Pavolini, rejected the play, claiming that people would flock to the theater attracted solely because of "that harmful element," which unbeknownst to them had been removed.[33] There was a long list of works that dealt with homosexuality and did not obtain permission. In 1942, for example, *Casa delle Muse* by Nino Bolla was rejected because the plot alluded to a "sexual psychopath" and because Maria Melato, the main actress, would have refused to interpret such a part. Furthermore, somber atmosphere created by the war called for distracting the public with light, enjoyable entertainment and not anguishing, sad, existential dramas.[34] As for works that dealt with hermaphroditism and transvestites, it was up to science and religion to concern themselves with such matters, not art:

> Saint Bernadino of Siena may evoke scandalous scenes of sodomy in public because his listeners are prepared to condemn this sin. From his podium, a professor may illustrate nature's errors because he knows that the students accept the disgusting sight for the purpose of scientific investigation. But when the theater speaks — and in this case for a long time — of this unspeakable squalor for the sole purpose of triggering disgust, though it may be accompanied by pity, it is intolerable. In this case, even without censorship aesthetics saves ethics.[35]

Safeguarding morality was supposed to be the main task of the censor and the police regulation Testo Unico P.S. served to establish the most typical and frequent cases of violation. Punishment for those who did not comply ranged from simple script revisions, to more or less substantial cuts, to banning. Because of frequent attempts to circumvent the censor's prescriptions through slight changes or other expedients, it was the police's job to ascertain that they were properly followed.

Government censorship also attacked cinema, literature, photography, music, and all printed material. Censorship was harsh enough that it often led to the production of works that were already in line with the prevailing directives. This widespread initiative to moralize was aimed at enhancing the image of Fascist Italy as the domain of order and well-being where, thanks to Mussolini, all the "awful" material and immoral things had been obliterated; it was also meant to regenerate costumes, as part of a larger plan to build the new man, built on healthy and righteous values and customs. The comments of Philip Cannistraro about the "propaganda of integration" provide an insight into fully understanding the regime's effort to create an atmosphere in which Italians might easily interiorize behavioral rules, an atmosphere in which modernity and tradition, innovative moral events and values of the past alternated to better form the Italian soul.[36] As Balbino Giuliano wrote:

> Today our souls are all divided a bit between desire and regret, between the need to keep on searching for new sensations and nostalgia for past motifs, everything is a bit too citified or countrified, the anxious longing for new ideas and a return to the serenity of ancient ideas. The contradiction can only be resolved in the culture of Fascism.[37]

The directives, which were maniacally issued to the press in the form of the well-known press releases, were intended to transmit a virile image of Italians. The figure, however, that most symbolized masculinity was Mussolini. His strong, youthful looking, athletic constitution was continually highlighted by Fascism's media machine. Italians were bombarded with photos of the Duce in various guises: sportsman, horseman, tireless worker, tamer of ferocious beasts, airplane pilot, and motorcycle racer.[38] Speaking of the less virile aspects of his life was forbidden. No emphasis was to be given to the useless entertainments he allowed himself sometimes, such as dancing and small talk. It was also forbidden to mention his age, his illnesses or even the wounds he suffered in World War I, for fear that news of the syphilis that obliged him to leave the front might get out.[39] The intention to transmit a perfect image of Fascism through the media also meant the censorship of deplorable phenomena like homosexuality.

The general list of offenses that were not to be publicized by the media included crimes against public morality and decency, as well as crimes against the family and the integrity and health of the race. Newspapers were obliged to refrain from reporting exceedingly upsetting events and were not to mention pederasty, infanticide, or other vices linked to the sexual sphere. There was to be no mention of tragic acts of passion or news that was "particularly gruesome and disgusting, or that revealed unnatural events even if committed under extenuating circumstances."[40] Publicity had to adapt to these same rules and refrain from advertising medicines or cures for impotency and other sexual dysfunctions. Crimes and dirty stories disappeared from novels,[41] whereas vices and "sexual perversions" could only be treated when set in a decadent country like France or a distant, exotic land of the Orient. Images of hysterical, emancipated, and boyish women, typical of foreign fashion, were to be eliminated,[42] while the bellicose image of men was to be enhanced. Photographs of fat and depleted men, the product of a decadent, bourgeois culture and mentality, were not to be published.[43] A strict puritan attitude, whose fervent application "went beyond mere censorship as it is commonly understood, was at the basis of the campaign against vice and perversion."[44]

Particular attention was focused on erotic, scandalous narratives whose success appeared to threaten Fascist morality. In the wake of the "crusade" launched in 1910 by Prime Minister Luigi Luzzatti,[45] Fascism immediately waged a war against pornography. It blocked the sale of erotic postcards and even pseudo-scientific novels or books that dealt with sex. Of course, this campaign in defense of morality was applauded by the Church, which was forever at war against sinful manners and behavior. However, in some cases the regime's determination bordered on ridiculousness. For example, the regime ordered the confiscation of reproductions of famous paintings of great artistic worth, such as the *San Sebastian* by Sodoma and Titian's *Venus*, or such literary classics as Casanova's *Memoires*, Apollinaire's *Le tres Don Juan*, and several works by Oscar Wilde, Maupassant, and Prévost. The repression hit novels by Pitigrilli and Mariano Mariani, as well as scientific publications and obviously all works that regarded homosexuality, like *Amori diabolici* by Senizza and Fabiani's *Sodoma e Gomorra*. Faced with this excessive zeal that raised much protest, the chief police inspector, Emilio De Bono, sent out a memorandum in which he asked his police officers not to be terribly rigorous, in other words, not to transform the safe-guarding of public decency into an action of indiscriminate censorship.[46]

The regime found reliable allies in the battle against indecent publications among the leagues for public morality, which still in 1929, suggested removing all evil and frivolous books from libraries and destroying such "poisonous ones as *The Art of Love* by Ovid along with obscene books like *Gli amori degli uomini* by Paolo Mantegazza."[47] Local magazines joined the chorus in favor of recovering greater morality and decency and against the negative influence of foreign ways that undermined the traditional virility of Italians. Critics attacked the confusion of gender, greater independence for women, attacks on male superiority, and the figure of the foreign homosexual artist.[48] In fact, the "pederast Dadaist artist who read Cocteau and copied Picasso"[49] was the target of caustic satire in Maccari's *Il selvaggio* or Longanesi's *L'italiano*; whereas English or French literary men were depicted as effeminate dandies, types very similar to Wilde, Gide, Proust, and Valéry. Young people were not to read the works of such men, because even in the sexual sphere, indecency was propagated due to the influence of foreign literature, which were bearers of vice and perversion. In order to assert the virile nature of Fascism it was necessary to end "childless marriages or scarcely reproductive marriages, which waver between elective affinity and sexual inversion," by stigmatizing those French literary type novels full of listless, ineffectual men lacking determination, shunted between wife and lover or lovers, introspective men with Freudian insecurities, psychopaths, and weak men who are dominated, devastated, emasculated losers."[50] As

Alessandro Augusto Monti commented in *Costruire* after the *tabarin* (nightclubs) were closed down:

> In Rome nightclubs, nude variety shows, cocaine and the "Maisons de passé" are dreadfully out of style as is Malthusianism, divorce, and pederasty, all things that are modern and elegant things that must not take hold on this side of the Alps.[51]

During the 1930s, as Fascism's totalitarian tentacles reached further into all sectors of cultural production, action against all literature considered immoral became so invasive that transgressive novels became increasingly less scabrous and provocative and lost their irreverent, anticonformist charge.[52] The elimination from mass circulation of this literary genre was combined with extensive censoring of works by writers such as Guido da Verona, Umberto Notari, and Luciano Zuccoli. When the control of literary production moved from the Interior Ministry to the newly created Ministero per la stampa e la propaganda (Propaganda Ministry) monitoring became more widespread. A specific department for censorship was set up to guarantee the strict supervision of literary production and create a cohesive set of regulations.[53] Thus, in the space of a few years, Fascism appeared to extinguish the interest in sexual perversion that had so fascinated late nineteenth-century intellectuals, but in actual fact, the journals, books, series and encyclopedias dedicated to the study of sexuality, which had developed with the advent of sexology, were closed down and censored.[54]

The reasons for the seizure of Pier Leone Ticchioni's *Suicidio di un estete* (Suicide of an aesthete), which centered on a love affair between two men, give an idea of the regime's parameters of censorship. In spite of the fact that in the introduction the author condemned the "evil love affair" and quoted Oscar Wilde, according to whom "moral or immoral books did not exist. Books are either well written or badly written," the prefect of Milan had no doubts: the work should be censored "owing to its abnormal contents that went against the nation's moral order." In vain, Ticchioni insisted that his intention was not to defend or indulge "this wretched passion" that he had described and which ended in suicide, highlighting the "condemnation that nature has in store for every human aberration." However, the prefect stood his ground:

> The novel, whose plot develops around a homosexual love affair, is against the healthy principles of moral order that our legislation defends and therefore against the policy that the national government continues to follow in defense of morality and public decency.[55]

Giuseppe Orioli, a Florentine bookseller, also ran into trouble with government censors. Following the depression he had turned his bookshop on the Lungarno delle Grazie into a publishing house specializing in books by English writers that had been forbidden. Between 1929 and 1937, Orioli was able to print twelve unabridged works, including D. H. Lawrence's *Lady Chatterley's Lover* and the works of Norman Douglas, who was a great friend of his.[56] Besides their cultural interests, the two men shared an attraction to young boys, a passion they thought they could account for through literary expression, defying the convention of the period. However, Orioli's undertaking as a publisher ended abruptly, due to some difficulties he encountered but mainly because of the introduction of the racial laws. In 1939 he had to leave Italy and was sent to Lisbon, where he died in 1942, alone and destitute.

Literary censorship became more rigorous with the introduction of the anti-Semitic laws and the antibourgeois campaign. In 1938 the *bonifica libraria* was launched in an effort eliminate the works of Jewish writers, but also to continue monitoring the cultural sphere and censoring immoral literature.[57] Among the authors not welcome in Italy were those who had studied homosexuality — Lombroso and Mieli, Foà and Hirschfeld, as well as writers like Pitigrilli or da Verona whose success depended largely on their having dealt with audacious subjects freely and openly.[58] The idea of transmitting an entirely Fascist culture to the new generations led to a more careful supervision over literature for the young. From this point of view, controlling the publication of books that dealt with sexuality took on a political importance because, as Fernando Mezzasoma wrote, "politics were sought in areas that appeared to be far from the political scene; in everything that reflected a particular orientation on matters important to the regime's agenda, such as religious tendencies, the health of the family as an institution, attachment to one's land or the nobility of human labor; social teamwork or the spirit of discipline; the tenacity that must typify a Fascist education."[59] Therefore, censorship had to be intensified regarding neo-Malthusian publications, pornographic material, and "pseudoscientific" works that divulged information about perversions and sexual inversion. Thus, in 1939 a number of "immoral and antisocial" books were confiscated, several publishing houses were closed, and some people were exiled to *confino* or received a warning because they had encouraged this "sordid activity that ran counter to the regime's efforts to regenerate tradition and morality."[60] As a result of this prim morality and Fascist censorship, a total silence fell over homosexuality, creating a taboo that was so deeply rooted that it lasted well beyond the end of the war.

The War, the Scourge of Virility, and Moral Rigor

The regime also often adopted a double standard in its puritanism, a double morality that was tolerant toward the rich and important and very strict with regard to the common person. For Fascism, a regimented population implied the rigorous control of sexuality. Any form of free expression of one's personality might be threatening to the nation. The instincts of the masses had to be restrained and channeled to keep them from turning into forms of rebellion. The sexual ethics proposed for the community were extremely severe: lust, lechery, and perversions were dangerous vices to be fought with any means. It was the duty of every citizen to show decency, respectability, and restraint. As Pier Giorgio Zunino wrote, "In substance it was an unassailable fact and was downright manifest that the principles of order and control over society were one with traditional sexual morality."[61] However, ordinary ethics did not apply in official circles: the elite enjoyed the privilege of a free, more permissive morality. It suffices to take as an example the private life of the Duce, who was allowed all kinds of sexual freedom. His son, Romano Mussolini, was known to have tried to calm down his jealous mother, Rachele, saying, "Mamma, papà isn't just any Tom, Dick, or Harry. Papà is papà! You must understand, women love him."[62] Thus, whereas adultery did not exist officially in Fascist Italy, Mussolini's affair with Claretta Petacci was not a secret and was considered a weakness that made him seem more human. It was understandable for such a virile man and represented a legitimate breach of the rules for such a figure who was, after all, above morality and laws.[63]

For Zunino, the new Fascist ruling class's double standards were not only a privilege they had surreptitiously stolen because they were in power, but they also came to be a charismatic sign of their indisputable superiority with respect to the masses. Those who governed the country had to distinguish themselves and prove they were above ordinary morality by clearly violating the ethics of the collectivity: "Those who only had to answer to history, those who were *legibus solutus* in the management of the state, were also so in regard to the current behavioral norms. In this way and for subsequent superficialities, sexual freedom became not only an attribute but a distinguishing mark of power. It was not a simple exception in the name of an abstract *raison d'état* but was seen as a positive choice in order to establish the ruling class more securely in society and make it more powerful. These behavioral models were, in the end, an expression of the government's legitimacy and, in turn, also that which legitimized it."[64] Zunino's observations, however, do not seem entirely convincing. Perhaps it is an exaggeration to state that "parallel to the exaltation of a collective morality, there was a reverse exaltation of immorality for the elite."[65] In reality, the ruling class was allowed to behave immorally within certain parameters. Their transgressions were tolerated and even looked on with a sort of satisfaction if they reflected the Fascist model of virility, but if it involved homosexuality, not even the most powerful person escaped negative judgment. This is evidenced by the fact that these scandals were always quickly buried.

The clear-cut distinction between imposed behavioral rules for all and the sexual practices allowed the few, between public virtue and private vice, was such that the intransigence of such statements did not always correspond to what was commonly practiced. Officially, Fascism preached austerity and sexual moderation, but behind the façade these rules were violated very frequently. Actually, despite the great importance given to the family, to monogamy, and to procreation within marriage, the number of illegitimate children continued to increase. In other words, the extramarital affairs of husbands usually resulted in a smile, not a punishment. As Marta Boneschi has noted, "Males are allowed to lead very libertine private lives as long as they maintain a public façade of respectability."[66] Prostitution was legalized in the same way; brothels were authorized and controlled so as to save appearances. Prostitutes were condemned in public, but their societal function was acknowledged and accepted.[67]

The wide gap between proposed ideals and reality, between theory and accepted practice is not particular to Fascism in comparison with democratic societies, which are defined by their pluralism. However, in claiming to embody the absolute truth, dictatorships are under more stress to represent a model of perfection without vices or corruption. In spite of the fact that the exaggerated puritanism remained a statement of principles that was largely disregarded, the necessity to preach total inflexibility where morality was concerned lent the regime a sad and gloomy aura. Augusto Turati, a protagonist during the Ventennio, was witness to the dreary, severe atmosphere that reigned in the years following the march on Rome. He considered the "lack of smiling faces" and the priggish façade typical aspects of Fascism:

> Fascist rhetoricians claimed that a whole new lifestyle was to be developed, both in public and private; and the more miserable and corrupt reality became, the louder the warnings and instigation were. Catos could be found preaching on every street corner, proclaiming the need for strict moral conduct: the healthiness of the family, the fervor of actions, and the nobility of the spirit. The party leaders' wives were all Cornelias and their husbands chaste Josephs. . . . In other words, a world of virtuous people, an arcadian paradise where nobody envied their neighbor and preferred to disappear from the eyes of men rather than give in to temptation.[68]

With the onset of World War II the atmosphere grew even more austere and intransigent. Exhibitions of amusement, luxury, and lust were inadmissible in the face of the poverty and hardship affecting the general public. The frivolous and dissolute lifestyle of the *gerarchi* needed to be toned down to show solidarity with civilian populations suffering financial difficulties and the commitment of the soldiers fighting the war. Polemics between the army and draft dodgers that arose during World War I had to be avoided at all cost. The regime's greatest concern was caused by the profligate "moral pederasty" of those who continued to spend heedlessly in order to satisfy their desires but remained untouchable because of their social or political standing. The moral atmosphere had to be intensified. In a rigorous effort to stop the spread of this dissoluteness, greater control over people's conduct in private had to be exercised. During times of both war and peace, the most influential people regularly violated the rules of Fascist ethics without any consequences. By resorting to a number of clientelistic expedients they were able to disobey the prescribed behavior. A perfect example was the case of the Marchese Lottieri Lotteringhi della Stufa. In 1942 the office for civil mobilization sentenced him to the mines in Carbonia (Sardinia) "for his worldly, extremely immoral temperament (he was rumored to be effeminate and sickly, and to have unnatural vices) and because his lifestyle was too scandalous." However, thanks to some acquaintances, he was able to avoid the order because of a medical visit that proclaimed him unfit for work owing to "physical and mental disorders." Even this was taken as an insult by his family, who believed it was unacceptable for a nobleman of his stature to stoop so low and perform such humble work.[69] Most of the time, however, it was not necessary to threaten those whose conduct was immoral with work in the mines; they usually got a light scolding, which certainly did not stop them from continuing their usual lifestyle. In the case of the son of the governor of Rome, Prince Gregorio Boncompagni Ludovisi, Mussolini himself issued an order to "call him and tell him clearly that he must give up his extremely disorderly and peculiar lifestyle." Nevertheless, the prince took no heed of the warning, so when the war broke out, the Duce decided to call him to arms and in 1942 also took into consideration the possibility of issuing an official warning.[70]

With the birth of the Salò Republic and the Fascist attempt to reaffirm their identity, the already difficult wartime climate was worsened by an eruption of brutality and cruelty. The Fascist symbol of death was once again flaunted like it had been in the days of *squadrismo*, but now it was accompanied by an air of gruesomeness and ferocity hitherto unknown. It was this transformation of values, this estrangement from the life of the rest of the country and loss of consensus that inverted the image of the Fascists, transforming them into a hateful internal enemy, despised and stereotyped as inhuman monsters. As Marco Tarchi rightly comments, "in the vortex of bombings, retaliations, ambushes, and police roundups that dot the difficult months of Mussolini's republic, many of the Fascist volunteers gradually and angrily became aware that people saw them as *abnormal*; the same people who had been united in their consensus now became fearful and, at times, openly hostile."[71] The desperate awareness of the population's hostility is clearly expressed in the Black Brigade's official chant:

Women don't want us anymore
because we wear black shirts
They say we are good for the prisons
they say we are good for chains
To love a Fascist is not a good idea
better a weakling without a flag
one who'll save his skin
one without blood in his veins!

The collapse of Fascist ideals marked the tragic end of the myth of the Blackshirts as conquerors and seducers, the highest expression of masculine attractiveness and living symbols of virility; now the women who had loved them, conquered by their explosive virility were giving them the cold shoulder. Once the war was over and for many years after, the idea of the Salò Fascists as the sum of everything negative, the emblem of negative values, and the manifestation of the kind of degeneration power brings with it, led people to use homosexuality as a metaphor for cruelty, perversion, and the corruptness of dictatorships. In the field of literature and cinema, Fascists—and Nazis—were presented as grotesque executioners, addicted to all kinds of vices and depravity. Ruthless homosexuals appear as torturers in Roberto Rosselini's film *Roma, città aperta* (*Rome: Open City*, 1945), Luchino Visconti's *Caduta degli dei* (*The Damned*, 1969), Liliana Cavani's *Il portiere di notte* (*The Night Porter*, 1974), Pier Paolo Pasolini's *Salò o le centoventi giornate di Sodoma* (*Salò, or the 120 Days of Sodom*, 1975), and Bernardo Bertolucci's *Novecento* (*1900*, 1976),[72] as well as in Vasco Pratolini's book *Cronache di poveri amati* (*Chronicle of Poor Lovers*, 1947) just to mention a few of the best known works. Oddly enough, the same negative stereotype of homosexuality spread by the Fascists is adopted by these works, transferring the image from the persecuted to the persecutors. The pathological image of "pederasts" as dangerous, degenerate, and perverse individuals is applied to Fascists and Nazis, with the idea that such torturers must also have been homosexuals. The parallel ends up making homosexuals, the real victims, into perpetrators. Such a depiction risks obscuring or erasing the reality of the persecution of homosexuals that was so ferociously carried out by the regime.[73]

There are some works, however, that give a more faithful and critical perspective of the persecution suffered by homosexuals under Fascism. Giorgio Bassani's *Gli occhiali d'oro* (*The Gold-Rimmed Spectacles*, 1958) and Ettore Scola's film *Una giornata particolare* (*A Special Day*, 1977) are good examples. Scola's film tells the story of the marginalization and isolation of two "deviants." The story takes place on the day of Hitler's visit to Rome in 1938 and shows the violent infringement of the public sphere on the private lives of a man and a woman;

the woman is relegated to the role of wife, mother, and housewife, while the man, a homosexual and former Eiar announcer, dismissed because his voice is not sufficiently masculine, is exiled to *confino* at Carbonia because of his "depraved tendency."[74] Following Bassani but emphasizing other aspects, Piero Chiara in his book *Il balordo* (1967) narrates the story of an ordinary citizen who is sentenced to *confino* by the regime because he is suspected of being a homosexual. As a result, he is shunned and mocked by everyone including his own daughters.

During the period of the Salò Republic, several episodes of violence that were characterized by their perverse and homoerotic nature, as in the case of the atrocious torture practiced by the Koch gang, fueled the equation of Fascism with homosexuality. However, the events involving Gino Bardi, one of the commanders of the armed guards at Palazzo Braschi, clearly demonstrate that the regime's harsh attitude toward homosexuals was constant. The squad commander Bardi, head of the Confederation of Fascist merchants, was appointed on September 15, 1943, to the position of federal commissioner for Rome, and along with the consul general, Guglielmo Pollastrini, formed the Armed Guards of the Revolution. This organization was supported by Urbe's republican *fasci*, and its task was to "combat anti-Fascist activities, seize hidden weapons, and carry out repressive action against the Jews and traitors of the Revolution." The guards performed all sorts of violent and abusive actions against presumed anti-Fascists, who were subjected to abuse, torture, and intimidation in the basement of Palazzo Braschi. Bardi's ferocity, however, wasn't only directed against presumed antiregime activists; his victims also included anyone who had offended him by casting doubts about his virility. By torturing and threatening people, he tried to get the names of those who had "gossiped about him, accusing him of being a homosexual."[75] There was much talk about Bardi's relationship with some of the young men in the guards, which fueled rumors of his sexual abnormality. In fact, in order to silence these "slanderous insinuations" he had asked the party to defend him in public.[76] In November 1943, given the excesses committed by the Palazzo Braschi guards, Mussolini ordered the disbandment of Rome's Fascist armed guards. All of its members were arrested and tried for coercion, unlawful restraint, abuse of power and public function, unlawful entry, injury, and abuse.[77] The investigation revealed the use of illegal means to obtain confessions, including "beatings, lacerated and contused wounds, the violent fracture of the base of the anus in males, the burning of pubic hair in females, depriving victims of food for long periods, making victims drink urine, etc." and confirmed the accusation of pederasty for Bardi.[78] Fascism's attitude toward homosexuality, then, had remained substantially unchanged; Bardi's pederasty was considered a "more serious offense" than the other crimes he committed as commander of the armed guards.

Tradition and Modernity

This excursus of the regime's last years and the focus on the continuing prejudice against homosexuality aims to highlight Fascism's ambiguous attitude toward the relationship between tradition and modernity, between safeguarding respectability and the propelling force of totalitarianism, between Catholic morality and the hope of creating a new man. The "problem" of pederasty shows how repressive action—although implemented by Fascism in a wider and more invasive way than in the past, thanks to its more rigorous control over society and the greater harshness of its police force—centered on a general strategy of concealment, which was, in some ways, contrary to the totalitarian plan to anthropologically transform Italians. By focusing on the exaltation of virility and the health and strength of the race, the regime was driven to undertake harsher and more widespread actions against pederasty. However, this ideological novelty was not supported by equally innovative instruments and modalities of repression. By deciding not to introduce specific antihomosexual measures into the penal codes, Fascism's sphere of action was limited to traditional courses of action. This also weakened the new moral significance with which the regime wanted to imbue its battle. Homophobia was nourished by long-standing prejudices and a legacy of values that dated back to before the dictatorship; the old custom of avoiding the problem and covering it up prevailed. The Fascist attitude toward homosexuals corresponded to the values of the average Italian and to the "Italietta" of a narrow-minded bourgeoisie, symbolically represented in Alberto Moravia's *Indifferenti* (1929),[79] which was not terribly interested in the problem and preferred scorn and isolation so as not to see the harsher aspects of the repression.

The Fascist model of virility and its project of creating a new man, which implied the rejection and condemnation of homosexuality, found an obstacle in the bourgeois canon of respectability, which defended the private sphere from political interference. Fascism was very aware of this. In fact, during the Ventennio, the pathway to totalitarianism was punctuated—in fits and starts— by antibourgeois battles. The bourgeois mentality so threatened Fascism because in its individualism it could produce a lack of heroism and even effeminacy. In fact, only the strongest critics of bourgeois respectability, the most intransigent and truly convinced supporters of a totally Fascist society—as for example, Carlo Scorza, commander of the Fascist youth group and the last PNF leader—called for a wide open battle against pederasty.[80] As for the masses who gave substantial support to the regime, they preferred to cover up the problem without resorting to harsh repressive measures, even if they continued to despise and isolate homosexuals.

The tension between the conservative bourgeois mentality and the propelling force of totalitarianism to implement a thorough anthropological revolution was present throughout the entire period of Fascist rule with continuous friction between the safeguarding of traditional morality and the desire to create new values. The antibourgeois campaign that Mussolini launched during the second half of the 1930s to accelerate the totalitarian experiment was inherent in Fascism from the very beginning and was based on all-out hostility toward the "bourgeois mentality," which Yvon De Begnac described as "the perfect antithesis of the heroic and Fascist conception of life."[81] The criticism of the liberal ruling class advanced by the *squadrista* movement clearly contained aspects that were anti-bourgeois, as arrogantly expressed here by the Ragusa Fasci di Combattimento:

> Bourgeoisie! In this miserable historic period, you are trying to hold on to the characteristics of the old feudal tradition. . . . You are a bunch of idle, pipe smoking, senile, emasculated beings. Your features are contorted into the most ridiculous expressions, your hands glitter like the seventh of the Ten Commandments, your fat is stained with the blood of 500,000 martyrs. You are monsters, you are beasts and you always have been. You are responsible for the internal conflicts. For this, you shall pay. Poor cowards, may you continue to grow pale. The Fascists, whom yesterday you thought your saviors have always been your enemies.[82]

The harsh criticism of the "dandy," of his fashionable lifestyle and "snobbishness" and the lack of virility among the upper classes,[83] continued to be expressed throughout the Fascist period by a series of intolerant and pro-Italy magazines and was reproposed periodically by party leaders and even Mussolini himself. The Fascist hostility toward the comfortable life and its exaltation of frenetic activeness, its attack on the private sphere, and its promotion of community participation in public life clashed with many of the values inherent in bourgeois ethics. The campaign launched in the 1930s[84] was therefore only the official announcement of the "trial against of the bourgeoisie"[85] that had begun long before Fascism came into power.

Therefore, I think we can agree with Emilio Gentile's observations on the studies of sexuality and masculinity carried out by George Mosse. By stressing the role of respectability as an indispensable instrument for conforming the collective behavior to the regime's directives, Mosse ended up neglecting the contrasting aspects between Fascist morality and bourgeois respectability in an unconvincing correlation between the Fascists and the bourgeois.[86] As a result, Mosse overly reduced the image of the Fascist to an indiscriminate Western, bourgeois model of masculinity, without placing enough emphasis on the difference between the hyper-virile, aggressive Italian *squadrista* or the equally heroic and soldierly German SS and the middle-aged man, "the clean-cut Englishman or the all-American boy," whose values were self-control, honesty, and modesty.[87] However, even if the two levels—Fascist and bourgeois—should be kept separate, the one doesn't exclude the other. Within the sphere of morality and, in particular, sexual morality, Fascism always expressed a sort of ambiguity between tradition and innovation, between the elements that belong to bourgeois respectability and the propelling force of totalitarianism that aimed to create a new morality. The antibourgeois campaign itself points to the existence of a widespread and deeply rooted mentality that was distinguishable from that imposed by the regime. Indeed, there was significant opposition to the Fascist implementation of what Gentile has called "respectability in uniform." This is demonstrated by the repeated appeals to reduce resistance and eliminate "dead ground."[88] Mosse himself, in spite of the fact that he considered Fascism the ideal bourgeois revolution, stressed the fact that its definition of masculinity inevitably created friction with bourgeois respectability:

> The tension between the ideal of masculinity and family life—wrote Mosse—was common to all forms of Fascism: on the one hand there was the covenant among males that was believed to determine the destiny of the state; on the other, the virtues of a bourgeois family life that Fascism promised to protect.[89]

The "affected and soppy life of the middle-class," like the one represented in the book *Cuore*, clashed with the militaristic activeness proposed by the regime; similarly, family and loved ones were an "impediment to Fascism's goal of a warlike, virile education."[90] Certainly, as the totalitarian process accelerated the tension increased between the military model, based on virile heroism, and the bourgeois model, based on a peaceful home life. The design to transform Italians' lifestyle, their behavior in public and private, and even their way of dressing and eating, created contempt of the middle-class temperament, which came to be seen as the main obstacle to the spread of Fascist ideals, including the fundamental value of virility. In other words, to restore "the virile spirit, which one needs in order overcome the terrible trials that await it,"[91] it was necessary to eliminate effeminacy from the bourgeois lifestyle. The goose step was introduced to strengthen soldiers' military character; the use of the second-person singular *lei*, "a baroque effeminacy" of foreign origin, was to be replaced with the more virile Italian word *voi*; and the handshake, "a bourgeois greeting, effeminate and extremely unattractive," needed to be replaced with the more energetic, martial Roman salute.[92] It was necessary to prove one's masculinity by having a prolific marriage, by taking part in sports competitions and athletic games, by having a proud and imposing presence, and by leading an austere lifestyle without many amenities or useless foreign-type entertainments, by displaying a strong, athletic, vigorous masculine body, and by being ready for war and combat. Therefore, the bourgeois type was ridiculed, criticized, and mocked. He was described as being impotent or homosexual, a spineless coward; a ridiculous example of an insignificant, outmoded, frivolous man. Exhibitions were organized so that everyone could see images, photographs, and vignettes of these "degenerates."[93] The middle-class man was the antihero, who, like Sor Pampurio, a character from *Il Corrierino*, was sad, frustrated, and obsessed with all the things he was unable to do. According to an article in the publication *Gerarchia*,

> Bourgeois morality is the morality of slippers, armchairs, and skullcaps; the antibourgeois morality is the morality of soldiers fighting in the trenches, of the hero and the apostle. The antibourgeois is a soldier, the soldier is a hero, the hero is an emperor, and the emperor is a Fascist.[94]

Therefore virility was the only attribute of the real Fascist, mobilized both in civilian and military life, ready to conform himself entirely to the new political creed.

The deep hostility that the antibourgeois campaign had encountered among the middle class clearly shows how difficult it was to try to modify the character of Italians. Police informers found criticism to be rampant and unsparing, even when it came to Mussolini, of whom it was said "for some time now he has been exaggerating with the novelties, and if they are not his ideas, he should at least put a stop to them."[95] The fact that people began to doubt that the Duce's authorship of the project to militarize citizens' public and private lives according to Fascist rules is in itself significant. As usual, the responsibility of imparting unwelcome directives was unloaded on the *gerarchi*, who kept the true feelings of the Italians from the Duce. In actual fact, Mussolini was determined to accelerate the permanent revolutionary process in hopes of penetrating a society that appeared to be completely watertight against political interference within family households.[96] On March 18, 1934, during the regime's second five-year assembly, the Duce clearly explained the importance of this totalitarian plan, which De Felice later described as the "most explicit public attack against the bourgeoisie":[97]

> Anti-Fascism is over, but there is a danger that could, however, pose a threat to the Regime; this threat is represented by what is commonly called the "bourgeois spirit"; in other words, the spirit of satisfaction and accommodation, with a tendency to be skeptical, compromising, to prefer an easy

life, to be a careerist. A bourgeois Fascist is a person who thinks that nothing more can be done, that enthusiasm is annoying, that there are too many parades, that the time has come to settle down, that one child is enough and that support from the home is the most important exigency. I do not exclude the existence of bourgeois temperaments. I deny that they are Fascists. The Fascist creed is heroism, the bourgeois creed is selfishness. There is but one remedy against this danger: the principle of continuous revolution. The principle must be entrusted to the young in years and at heart. It keeps the intellectually lazy away, while it keeps the people's interest wide awake; it does not mobilize history but strengthens it. In our minds the Revolution is a creation that alternates the gray fatigue of the day-to-day construction with dazzling moments of sacrifice and glory. Having undergone the labors that follow a war, it is already possible to see, and will become more and more visible, the physical and moral changes that have come over the Italians. This is where the fourth great era of the Italian people begins; the era that future historians will call the Era of the Black-shirts. This will be the first totally Fascist era of people born and brought up in the environment we created. They will be endowed with the virtues that grant populations their superiority worldwide.[98]

The new Fascist, strong and virile, had not yet been fully realized but thanks to the party's pedagogical efforts, the "spiritual redemption of the middle class,"[99] and the substitution of the old ruling class with the new generation, born and brought up within the regime, it would finally be possible to transform the totalitarian state into a totalitarian society.[100] However, given the persistent defense of privacy from political interference, where the sexual sphere was concerned it was not easy to achieve this goal.

As Gentile has demonstrated, despite its limits and imperfections, the plan to subjugate the individual to the goals of the regime in the Fascist "totalitarian experiment" did have a logical consistency of its own and a clear ideological theorization.[101] The desire to standardize human behavior, the continuous effort to shape the bodies and minds of Italians so as to transform them into a strong, virile people ready to fight for the nation's greatness, the spasmodic attention given to the creation of the soldier–citizen, were all necessary objectives for the success of Fascism. From this point of view, as the war approached, even Mussolini could see that the outcome would be a failure, a disaster he disdainfully and bitterly attributed to the Italian people themselves, who were incapable of making the regime's totalitarian characteristics theirs. The failure of the anthropological revolution depended on the very nature of the "material to be molded":

It's the raw material that I lack. Even Michelangelo had to have marble
for his statues. Had he only had clay he would have been no more than a
potter. A population that has been an anvil for centuries cannot become
a hammer in just a few years.[102]

Fascism had had too little time, and the nature of Italians themselves was
too inconsistent for the dream of transforming their character to come true:

I dreamt a lot about the qualities of the Italian people, and I thought during
these past twenty years that I had tempered them for sacrifice and given
them back a sense of national unity that they had lost centuries ago. It was
nothing more than a great dream! Today I must convince myself that I
made a big mistake when I believed that. Twenty years cannot suffice to
bury centuries of history that saw only a succession of factions.[103]

The totalitarian ambition to create a new man collapsed when it had to
undergo the real trials of a war, suddenly highlighting the gap between myth
and reality.

Even if the inevitable distance between aspirations and the realization of
these aspirations is not a characteristic particular to totalitarian regimes, all the
same, the breadth of this distance is of historical importance. Juan J. Linz rightly
notes that the disagreement among experts as to the extent of the totalitarianism
of Italian Fascism is partly dependant on "the greater emphasis given, on the
one hand, to the ideological formulations and monism of the normative system
promulgated by the regime and, on the other, to the real actions of the government and the social reality during Fascism. The more importance we give the
first aspect, the more we shall tend to consider the Italian regime totalitarian.
The more we focus on the second, the more we shall doubt the totalitarian
nature of that regime."[104] However, in my opinion, an analysis of the points of
contact between theoretical statements and practical applications, the interaction
between ideology and political action may help us to better understand Fascism.
In the case of homosexuality, for example, by studying behavior it is possible to
trace the mentality, reasoning, and ideology and thus to grasp the new Fascist
attitude toward pederasty and, at the same time, sense the influence of a
centuries-old tradition that had delegated the protection of morality to the
Catholic Church, an entity whose norms were mainly interested in safeguarding
appearances in order to avoid scandals that might upset public opinion.
"Bourgeois respectability" had consolidated itself on these behavioral standards.
Fascism, in an effort to transform itself into "respectability in uniform," tried
unsuccessfully to mold itself according to its values of courage, strength, and
virility. The Fascists believed that virility itself, whose eternal nature did not

prevent it from manifesting itself in new ways or from redefining the male stereotype on the basis of these sudden changes and innovations, would have been capable of harmonizing tradition and modernity. Supposedly, the regime's task was to correct and cure the "wrongs of our contemporary civilization."[105] Confronting the negative aspects of modernity—included here is homosexuality—did not mean taking on an antimodern attitude but rather protecting some traditional values that would be integrated into the ethos of the Fascist state. This defense of traditional morality masked a fear of disorder and uncontrolled changes. As such, regulating citizens' sexual lives was fundamental. However, not even the Strapaese group, which considered pederasty the perverse outcome of modernity, took their contempt of homosexuals to extremes: in fact, the caricature and mocking of pederasts did not prevent collaboration with artists such as Comisso and Rosai, whose "particular" sexual leaning was no mystery.

The reference to traditional morality—emblematically expressed in the campaign to increase rural settlements and exalt peasant life as an example of correct behavior, proper ethical rigor, and perfect virility—introduces the complex subject of the relationship between the sexual moralities of Fascism and the Church that was so deeply ingrained in the souls of Italians that it created an obstacle to the regime's totalitarian design. Indeed, the need to avoid total conformity to Catholicism and the aim to carry out an anthropological regeneration of Italians created a great deal of strife between Fascism and the clergy, a situation that worsened during the later years of the regime.

On the contrary, at the beginning of the Fascist era, the pressure of the Leagues for Public Morality, and above all the need for reconciliation with the Church, had encouraged the formulation of a plan to reform morality and customs in line with traditional values. Concerned about modernity, the ecclesiastical authorities were somewhat satisfied because the libertine atmosphere of Fascism's early years was being followed by a decidedly conformist, moralist attitude with "stricter public behavioral rules," without, as Wanrooij notes, reaching the point of "officially acknowledging Catholic doctrine in the field of ethics."[106] Despite the Concordat, the differences between Fascism and the Church did not subside. The fiery dispute in 1931 over the education of the younger generation is a clear example of this.[107] As regards sexual morality, the divergence did not stem so much from a different way of considering sexuality but more from the rivalry over which side had the monopoly of preparing, spreading, and defending morality. The Holy See found it difficult to bear the Fascist attempt to interfere with citizens' private lives, since this had always been its exclusive domain. Therefore, it was ready to go to battle in order to safeguard its authority from the regime's totalitarian design to establish the limits of correct sexual conduct and subordinate families to the needs of the state. For this very reason, the Church took a stand against Rinaldo Pellegrini, founder of the Archivio politico di medicina fascista (Fascist medical archives) and supporter of a strictly Fascist morality in the sexual sphere as well. The regime was obliged to repudiate him even if the reasoning of this scholar followed a certain logic: "If Fascism believes that everything is within the state and nothing lies outside the state, it is evident that the state must watch over the morality and sexual lives of its young people, orient their lives toward its own ends, and, where necessary, correct and modify them irrespective of their traditional and denominational educational backgrounds with which its ends do not always coincide."[108]

Catholicism and Fascism shared many values: the fight against urbanization, the demographic policy to raise the birthrate, the strict division of gender, and the subordinate role of women. At the same time, the Church attributed a divergent significance to following mandatory rules: procreation, for example, was the exclusive aim of marriage and not a means for providing the state with more soldiers; as a matter of fact, the clergy openly criticized the education of young people, which was focused mainly on their physical and military preparation. Above all, the Vatican did not conceal its great concern about the preeminent role Fascism granted the state; "the state," said Pius XI in May 1929, on the eve of the Concordat, "that claims it will absorb and swallow up the individual and the family to annihilate them; the state that claims it is bringing up conquerors for the sake of conquering."[109] Just a few months later, in his encyclical *Divinis Illius Magistri*, the pontiff launched a new attack against those who "dared to maintain that children belong to the state even before they belong to their families, and that the state has exclusive rights over their education."[110] Although these attacks were harsh, neither the Church nor Fascism really wanted to aggravate the situation. Pius XI was well aware of the advantages obtained in the Concordat with the regime. Meanwhile, Mussolini stressed the need to enhance the study of religion at school so as to give students "a sense of virility, power, and conquest,"[111] but at the same time he tried to avoid an open clash with the Vatican, since he knew how deeply rooted Catholicism was among the population. He tried to reconcile the totalitarian project with Catholic morality, the cult of political religion with Christian rites, for as long as possible.[112] During the Ventennio, Catholic morality conditioned Fascist morality and vice versa. The result was an ambiguous attitude toward morality and private life, a mixture of tradition and innovation with elements of reinstatement linked to Catholic doctrine and innovative elements typical of a totalitarian state. Although it was difficult to harmonize these two contrasting forces, on the whole, cooperation between Church and state prevailed where the control and orientation of citizens' moral lives were concerned, and in most cases the Fascist regime did not object to the clergy's dominance over sexual morality, as demonstrated by its line of conduct toward homosexuals. In the end, the regime delegated educational actions against pederasty to priests, confessors, and the members of Azione cattolica and reserved all forms of punishment, official warnings, admonitions, imprisonment, and exiling of people to *confino* for itself, whenever public order was at stake. According to John Lauritsen and David Thorstad, who studied the movement for homosexuals' rights, "the real position of the Fascists regarding sexual matters was clearly expressed in their slogan 'moral purity' and their ideal was the sexual repression of families as decreed by Christian virtue. With regard to morality, Fascism was equivalent to Christian totalitarianism."[113] This definition could be misleading, however, in understanding Fascism, which, with its totalitarian ideology, had religious aspects and presented itself as a true religion, but was in actual fact secular and not traditional. The "moral purity" that led to the rejection of homosexuality did not express a "Christian virtue" but the "virtues" of the new Fascist man. The design was to create the new Italian by limiting the individual's freedom to choose his sexual leaning; the purpose of strict male–female ideals was to safeguard the sexes and the virility of a "totalitarian community." Consequently, the condemnation of pederasty stemmed more from political than from moral or religious reasoning: for the Fascist totalitarian experiment, homosexuality was not really a sin or a vice, but it represented a permanent danger for its "respectability in uniform" concept based on the ethics of collective virility. The homosexual was the new man's enemy and was equal to the individualist and hedonist bourgeois. It is more correct, then, to trace the regime's efforts to circumscribe sexuality, within the family and for the purpose of procreation, to its anthropological revolution. This plan was destined to disappear with the end of the regime, but it involved millions of Italians for two decades. Thus, despite the failure of the totalitarian experiment, Fascism's homophobic prejudices took root in people's minds and created lasting effects on postwar Italian society.

Notes

Abbreviations

ACS	Archivio centrale dello Stato
ASR	Archivio di Stato di Roma
CAP	Corte d'appello penale
CPC	Casellario politico centrale
MI	Ministero dell'Interno
Min.Cul.Pop.	Ministerio della Cultura Popolare
MVSN	Milizia volontaria per la sicurezza nazionale (Volunteer Militia for National Security, usually called Blackshirts)
PCM	Presidenza del Consiglio dei ministri
PNF	Partito nazionale fascista (National Fascist Party)
Pol.Pol.	Polizia politica fascicoli personali
Pol.Mat.	Polizia politica fascicoli per materia
PS	Pubblica sicurezza
RSI	Repubblica sociale italiana
SA	Sturmabteilungen (Squadre d'assalto, Storm Troopers)
SIM	Servizio informazioni militari (Military Information Service)
SIS	Servizi informativi e sicurezza
SPD, CO	Segreteria particolare del duce, Carteggio ordinario
SPD, CR	Segreteria particolare del duce, Carteggio riservato
UCP	Ufficio confino politico
b.	busta
f.	fascicolo
s.f.	sotto fascicolo

Introduction

1. See F. Tamagne, *A History of Homosexuality in Europe: Berlin, London, Paris, 1919–1939* (New York: Algora, 2004).

2. G. Chauncey, *Gay New York: Gender, Urban Culture, and the Making of the Gay Male World, 1890–1940* (New York: Basic Books, 1994).

3. J. Butler, *Gender Trouble: Feminism and the Subversion of Identity* (New York: Routledge, 1990).

4. R. W. Connell, *Masculinities* (Cambridge: Polity Press, 1995).

5. D. Herzog, "Hubris and Hypocrisy, Incitement and Disavowal: Sexuality and German Fascism," *Journal of the History of Sexuality* 11, no. 1–2 (2002): 3–21. See also E. D. Heineman, "Sexuality and Nazism: The Dubly Unspeakable?" *Journal of the History of Sexuality* 11, no. 1–2 (2002): 22–66.

6. A. Timm, "Sex with a Purpose: Prostitution, Venereal Disease, and Militarized Masculinity in the Third Reich," *Journal of the History of Sexuality* 11, no. 1–2 (2002): 223–55. See also J. Roos, "Backlash against Prostitutes' Rights: Origins and Dynamics of Nazi Prostitution Policies," *Journal of the History of Sexuality* 11, no. 1–2 (2002): 67–94.

7. See C. Ross, *Naked Germany: Health, Race and the Nation* (Oxford: Berg, 2005).

8. G. Robb, *Strangers: Homosexual Love in the Nineteenth Century* (New York: Norton, 2004).

9. N. Z. Davis, "Women's History in Transition: The European Case," *Feminist Studies* 3, no. 3–4 (1976): 83–103.

10. J. W. Scott, "Gender: A Useful Category of Historical Analysis," *American Historical Review* 91, no. 5 (1986): 1053–75. The issue is also taken up in Italy, see P. Di Cori, "Dalla storia delle donne alla storia di genere," *Rivista di storia contemporanea* 4 (1987).

11. *Memoria: Rivista di storia delle donne*, no. 27 (1989); ten years later scholars researching the history of the family and gender identity began to take such an interest in the subject that in 1998 a special seminar on male identity was organized (see A. Arru, ed., *La costruzione dell'identità maschile nell'età moderna e contemporanea* [Rome: Biblink, 2001]). More recently the subject was dealt with in an issue of *Genesis*, the periodical of the Italian Society of Historical Works ("Mascolinità," *Genesis* 2 [2003]). Also the *Journal of Modern Italian Studies* dedicated a special issue to the theme of Italian masculinities (edited by B. Wanrooij, vol. 10, no. 3 [September 2005]).

12. "Tendenze e caratteri della storiografia sul maschile," *Rivista di storia contemporanea* 1 (January 1991): 3–18.

13. On approaches to men's studies and the history of masculinity, see H. Brod, *The Making of Masculinities: The New Men's Studies* (Boston: Allen and Unwin, 1987); F. Mort, "Crisis Point: Masculinities in History and Social Theory," *Gender and History* 6, no. 1 (1994): 124–30; and J. Tosh, "What Should Historians Do with Masculinity?" *History Workshop Journal* 38, no. 1 (1994): 179–202.

The only specific book that tries to trace the history of masculinity in Italy comes from a conference in Bologna in 1998 on gender and masculinity (see *Genere e mascolinità: Uno sguardo storico*, ed. S. Bellassai and M. Malatesta [Rome: Bulzoni, 2000]). The work has the merit of providing a broad and detailed picture of the problem, but it does not show the development of masculinity in the various historical periods consistently. Recently, Sandro Bellassai tried to reconstruct the history of masculinity in Italy in the twentieth century, providing interesting ideas but overemphasizing the interconnectedness of modernity, the crisis of masculinity, and the glorification of virility (see his *La mascolinità contemporanea* [Rome: Carocci, 2004]). For some interesting critical considerations on foreign works "on the [Fascist] political body and the policy of bodies," see S. Luzzatto, "La cultura politica dell'Italia fascista," *Storica* 12 (1998): 57–80.

14. J. D'Emilio, *Making Trouble: Essays on Gay History, Politics, and the University* (New York: Routledge, 1992), 109–10.

15. See P. Dogliani, entry "omosessualità," in V. De Grazia and S. Luzzatto, eds., *Dizionario del fascismo* (Torino: Einaudi, 2003), 2:264–65.

16. The term "homosexuality" does not appear in Italian language dictionaries at the end of the 1800s and the beginning of the 1900s, which almost always include the word "sodomy" and sometimes "pederasty." I shall use the expression "pedophilia" and not "pederasty" to indicate the attraction to adolescents, because although the word "pederast" derives from the Greek roots *pais* (adolescent) and *eratos* (lover), it is still used today to refer to homosexuals and especially to effeminate ones. During the twenty years of Fascism the term "pederast" was widely used with this particular meaning.

17. According to Dennis Altman, the term "homosexual" should be used as an adjective to describe a kind of behavior, not as a noun to describe a person (see his *Homosexual: Oppression and Liberation* [New York: Avon, 1973]).

18. "You understand that in homosexuality, just like in heterosexuality, there are all shades and degrees, from Platonic love to lust, from self-denial to sadism, from radiant health to sullen sickliness, from simple expansiveness to all the refinements of vice. Inversion is only one expression. Besides, between exclusive homosexuality and exclusive heterosexuality there is every intermediate shading" (A. Gide, *Corydon*, trans. R. Howard [Urbana: University of Illinois Press, 2001], 18).

19. Obviously, this does not mean that these kinds of behavior are inevitably linked to homosexuality; for example, a transsexual or transvestite may not be attracted to persons of his own sex.

20. See M. S. Kimmel, "Masculinity as Homophobia: Fear, Shame and Silence in the Construction of Gender Identity," in *Theorizing Masculinities*, ed. H. Brod and M. Kaufman (Thousand Oaks, Calif.: Sage, 1994), 119–41. On the history of homophobia, see also D. Wickberg, "Homophobia: On the Cultural History of an Idea," *Critical Inquiry* 27 (2000): 42–57.

Chapter 1. The Making of the Virile Italian

1. Thanks to military medical visits it was possible to diagnose rickets, since the large number of men who were deformed suffered mainly from deficiencies caused by malnutrition. For more information about the physical condition of Italian youths, see B. Farolfi, "Antropometria militare e antropologia della devianza" (1876–1906), in *Storia d'Italia: Annali 7. Malattia e medicina*, ed. F. Della Peruta (Turin: Einaudi 1984), 1181–222.

2. See G. Bonetta, *Corpo e nazione: L'educazione ginnastica, igienica e sessuale nell'Italia liberale* (Milan: Franco Angeli, 1990). Gaetano Bonetta analyzes the ideological relevance the human body acquired in unified Italy through physical, moral, and health education. The body, strengthened by gymnastics and made pure by strict sexual ethics, was the preferred instrument for political intervention and was used by the young state to give itself a national identity and discipline.

3. See G. L. Mosse, *The Image of Man: The Creation of Modern Masculinity*, Studies in the History of Sexuality (New York: Oxford University Press, 1996).

4. Filippo Tommaso Marinetti uses the expression in the supplement to Antonio Beltramelli's book *L'uomo nuovo Mussolini* (1926) to describe Mussolini's typical Italian look. See G. Pini and D. Susmel, *Mussolini, l'uomo e l'opera* (Florence: La Fenice, 1954), 2:8.

5. Mosse stresses that the plan to create the new man originated during the French Revolution. The Jacobeans tried to mobilize the population by spreading the idea that the revolution could create "a new man and a new nation" (G. L. Mosse, "Fascism and the French Revolution," *Journal of Contemporary History* 1 [1989]: 5–8).

6. Giovanni Giolitti, 1842–1928; five-time prime minister between 1892 and 1921; Liberal Party.

7. To quote Gentile on this point: "Modernist nationalism considered a 'Revolution of the spirit' necessary for creating a 'new man,' and new intellectual, political and moral aristocracies capable of ruling and dominating modern life and maintaining the superiority of the spiritual powers against the development of the material powers" (E. Gentile, "La nazione del fascismo alle origini del declino dello stato nazionale," in *Nazione e nazionalità in Italia: Dall'alba del secolo ai nostri giorni*, ed. G. Spadolini [Rome: Laterza 1994], 69–70).

8. E. Gentile, *The Origins of Fascist Ideology, 1918–1925* (New York: Enigma, 2005), 375.

9. A. Asor Rosa, "La cultura," in *Storia d'Italia dall'unità ad oggi* (Turin: Einaudi, 1975), 4:2:1237.

10. G. Papini, "La necessità della rivoluzione," *Lacerba* 8 (April 15, 1913).

11. Asor Rosa, "La cultura," 1146.

12. See E. Gentile, *Il mito dello Stato nuovo: Dal radicalismo nazionale al fascismo* (Bari: Laterza, 1999).

13. B. Mussolini, "Discorso al IV Congresso del PNF," (22-6-1925), qtd. in Gentile, *The Origins of Fascist Ideology*, 350.

14. S. Gatto, "Della cultura fascista," *Bibliografia fascista* (May 1926), quoted in E. Gentile, *The Sacralization of Politics in Fascist Italy* (Cambridge, Mass: Harvard University Press, 1996), 97.

15. See G. L. Mosse, *Nationalism and Sexuality: Middle-Class Morality and Sexual Norms in Modern Europe* (Madison: University of Wisconsin Press, 1988). On the palingenetic aspirations of Fascism, see R. Griffin, "Il nucleo palingenetico dell'ideologia del 'fascismo generico,'" in *Che cosa è il fascismo? Interpretazioni e prospettive di ricerca*, ed. A. Campi (Rome: Ideazione, 2003), 97–122.

16. See G. Sasso, *Tramonto di un mito: L'idea di progresso tra Ottocento e Novecento* (Bologna: Il Mulino, 1988).

17. See E. Fromm, *Escape from Freedom* (New York: Farrar and Rinehart, 1941).

18. See Mosse, *The Image of Man*, 3–16. According to Mosse, "in modern times stereotypes found their utility within the spheres of the overall search for symbols that would enable people to embody the abstract in the face of the upsetting changes of modernity" (5). On stereotypes, see also S. L. Gilman, *Difference and Pathology: Stereotypes of Sexuality, Race and Madness* (Ithaca: Cornell University Press, 1985).

19. See E. Corradini, "Mens sana in corpore sano," in *L'ombra della vita* (Naples: Parrella, 1908), 13–18.

20. Corradini, "Le Olimpiadi," in ibid., 2.

21. See Corradini, "L'unità della vita," in ibid., 7. On the new educational plan built around the well-balanced development of the mind and the body, see A. Mosso, *Mens sana in corpore sano* (Milan: Treves, 1903). On the widespread resonance of Angelo Mosso's book in Italy, see G. Volpe, *Italia moderna* (Florence: Sansoni, 1973), 347; and S. Lanaro, *Nazione e lavoro: Saggio sulla cultura borghese in Italia 1870–1925* (Venice: Marsilio, 1988), 59–63.

22. Corradini, "L'unità della vita," 6.

23. See Bonetta, *Corpo e nazione*, 71–207. According to Bonetta "as a result of this nationalistic, restrictive and highly demanding undertaking, the physical education program that was to be introduced had a decidedly military–nationalistic aim, the most suitable for training middle-class 'civilians' and military soldiers, combatants for national progress who would be ready to sacrifice themselves at the workplace and on the battlefield in the supreme interest of the country. Thus, physical education in schools was deprived of gymnastics as a sporting event as well as its more civilized sociological characteristics" (139).

24. See G. Conti, "Il mito della 'nazione armata,'" *Storia Contemporanea*, December 6, 1990, 1149–95.

25. In A. Salucci, ed., *Il nazionalismo giudicato dai Letterati, Artisti, Scienziati, Uomini politici e Giornalisti italiani* (Genoa: Libreria Editrice Moderna, 1913), 28.

26. E. Corradini, "La marcia dei produttori," in *L'Italiana*, ed. Società Anonima (Rome, 1916), vii, 117.

27. On the concept of sport as proposed in the magazine *Il Regno*, see G. Papini, "Le feste dell'energia (Il Concorso ginnico di Firenze)," 29 (June 12, 1904); "I giuochi romani," 30 (June 19, 1904); "Olimpiadi internazionali e giuochi romani," 31 (June 26, 1904); "Le Olimpiadi a Roma," 32 (July 3, 1904); "L'antisocialismo dello sport," 34 (July 17, 1904).

28. "La Patria e lo Sport 'vigor di vita,'" in *Il Tricolore*, qtd. in A. Todisco, *Le origini del nazionalismo imperialista* (Rome: Berlutti, n.d.), 12–14. According to *Il Tricolore*, physical reinvigoration and more vital energy would make Italy and its army strong and victorious.

29. F. T. Marinetti, "Prefazione futurista a 'Revolverate' by Gian Pietro Lucini," in *Teoria e invenzione futurista*, ed. L. De Maria (Milan: Mondadori, 1983 [1968]), 23–30.

30. Corradini, "Mens sana in corpore sano," 14.

31. G. E. Rusconi, introduction to J. M. Hoberman, *Politica e sport: Il corpo nelle ideologie politiche dell '800 e del 900* (Bologna: Il Mulino, 1988), 13. John Hoberman states that in

their doctrines, only some political ideologies express and maintain "the specific traits of the sportsman's temperament (idealized): competitive aggressiveness, awareness of physicality, ascetic indifference to pain and ethical contents" (129). On the link between sport and aggressiveness see N. Elias and E. Dunning, *Quest for Excitement: Sport and Leisure in the Civilizing Process* (Oxford: Blackwell, 1986).

32. "Ordine del giorno sul problema della scuola," from the nationalist Congress of Florence (December 3–5, 1910) and the Rome Congress (December 20–22, 1912), qtd. in P. M. Arcari, *Le elaborazioni della dottrina politica nazionale fra l'unità e l'intervento (1870–1914)* (Florence: Marzocco, 1934), 9, 22.

33. S. Pivato, *I terzini della borghesia: Il gioco del pallone nell'Italia dell'Ottocento* (Milan: Leonardo, 1991), 124. See also Pivato's "Ginnastica e Risorgimento: Alle origini del rapporto sport/nazionalismo," *Ricerche storiche*, May–August 1989, 249–79; S. Giuntini, *Sport, scuola e caserma dal Risorgimento al primo conflitto mondiale* (Padua: Centro Grafico Editoriale, 1988); and C. Papa, "Borghesi in divisa: Sport e nazione nell'Italia liberale," *Zapruder* 4 (May–August 2004), 26–38.

34. On the images of athletic leaders and the political athlete as the "risk-taking nationalist," and "as a phenomenon, the Fascist political athlete is founded upon the unchallenged authority of the body, which is in turn invested with the virtually sacred authority of instinct," see Hoberman, *Politica e sport*, 96, 63; and L. Di Nucci, "L'eroe atletico nell'epoca delle masse: Note sulla cultura del tempo libero nella città moderna," *Società e Storia*, December 1986, 867–902.

35. On the ideal male figure chosen by Western culture to create the model of masculinity, see Mosse, *The Image of Man*, 17–39. According to Mosse, modern masculinity was established at the end of the eighteenth century when, with the birth of the new bourgeois society, a "stereotype of manliness emerged that we recognize even today." During the eighteenth century, the concept of masculinity underwent a revision process that reproposed a de-eroticized model of Greek beauty. Therefore, once Greek sculpture was deprived of its sensual charge, it became socially acceptable and could be used to convey new political instances.

36. S. Sighele, "Virtù antiche e virtù moderne," in *Idee e problemi di un positivista* (Milan: Sandron, 1907), 386–88.

37. Corradini, "Le Olimpiadi," 2–3.

38. See L. Canfora, *Le vie del classicismo* (Bari: Laterza, 1989).

39. See "Ragazzi a Olimpia," *FMR*, September 26, 1984, 93–122; C. Bianchi, "Il nudo eroico del fascismo," in *Gli occhi di Alessandro: Potere sovrano e sacralità del corpo da Alessandro Magno a Ceausescu*, ed. S. Bertelli and C. Grottanelli (Florence: Ponte alle Grazie, 1990), 154–69. On the aggressive, martial image of the Fascist see M. Isnenghi, "Il volto truce dell'Italiano Nuovo," in *Immagini e retorica di Regime* (Milan: Motta, 2001), 17–20.

40. G. Mazza, *Il paradosso dei sessi* (Milan: Alfieri, 1939), 134.

41. The contempt of Christianity's defeatist and servile morality expressed by the nationalists was actually based on criticism of the negative influence exercised by Judaism on Christianity. See Corradini, "Sion e Roma," in *L'ombra della vita*, 169–74; and F. Coppola, "Il mito democratico e l'imperialismo," *Politica* 2 (January 1919), reprinted in F. Perfetti,

Il nazionalismo italiano (Milan: Edizioni del Borghese, 1969), 265–68. Furthermore, the nationalists were convinced admirers of paganism, which they considered the foundation of classicism and in opposition to "the deliquescence and cowardice of the centuries-old Nazarene submission." This reference to paganism was to have a lasting influence on twentieth-century political thought. The image of a superior male—whose strength, heroic morality, and ability to dominate, face, and win challenges freed him from the moral shoestrings of weaklings—was to strongly influence not only nationalism but also some aspects of Fascism. See F. Filippi, *Una vita pagana: Enrico Corradini dal superomismo dannunziano a una politica di massa* (Florence: Vallecchi, 1989); and J. Evola, *Imperialismo pagano* (Todi: Atanor, 1928).

42. F. Coppola, "Virtù latina e furore barbarico," in *La crisi italiana* (Rome: L'Italiana, 1916), 126.

43. Corradini, "Mens sana in corpore sano," 13–18.

44. M. Morasso, "A proposito di un rapimento in automobile," *Il Marzocco* (December 21, 1902).

45. M. Morasso, *La nuova arma: La macchina* (Turin: Fratelli Bocca, 1905), 253.

46. M. Morasso, *L'imperialismo nel secolo XX: La conquista del mondo* (Milan: Treves, 1905), 369; see also Morasso's *Il nuovo aspetto meccanico del mondo* (Milan: Hoepli, 1907).

47. Nationalists repeatedly reiterated the parallel between competitive sport and warfare. According to them, in fact, if games teach warfare, then war itself becomes a game. This aggressive force released in sport conceals a strong imperialist craving and an intense desire to dominate; see J. A. Hobson, *Imperialism: A Study* (Ann Arbor: University of Michigan Press, 1965), and *The Psychology of Jingoism* (London: G. Richards, 1901).

48. See L. Borghi, *Educazione e autorità nell'Italia moderna* (Florence: La Nuova Italia, 1974).

49. P. Turiello, *Politica contemporanea* (Naples: Luigi Pierro editore, 1894), 98–101; see also A. Gibelli, *Il popolo bambino: Infanzia e nazione dalla Grande Guerra a Salò* (Turin: Einaudi, 2005).

50. E. Corradini, "Domenico Trentacoste," in *L'ombra della vita*, 238.

51. E. Corradini, *La Patria lontana* (Milan: Società Anonima Editoriale, 1920 [1910]), 50.

52. Mosse, *The Image of Man*, 58.

53. Mosse, *Nationalism and Sexuality*, 128. On the link between sport and masculinity, see J. A. Mangan, ed., *Making European Masculinities: Sport, Europe, Gender* (London: Frank Cass, 2000).

54. E. Corradini, "Come parlano i sociologi positivisti" and "Le opinioni degli uomini e i fatti dell'uomo," in *La vita nazionale* (Siena: Lumachi, 1923 [1907]), 54, 92–93. Fascism took up this counter-position between "*red-blooded men* (interventionists, volunteers, the *arditi*, and the Fascists)," and *white-blooded men* (neutralists, shirkers, and anti-Fascists); see M. Carli, *Fascismo intransigente* (Florence: Bemporad and Figlio, 1926), 88–89.

55. G. Papini, "I consigli di Amleto," *Hermes* 5 (1904), reprinted in *La cultura italiana del '900 attraverso le riviste Leonardo, Hermes, Il Regno*, ed. D. Frigessi (Turin: Einaudi, 1979), 428.

56. On the non-Socialist antibourgeois polemics, which began in 1879 with the publication of Pietro Ellero's book *La tirannide borghese*, see D. Settembrini, *Storia dell'idea antiborghese in Italia 1860–1989* (Rome: Laterza, 1991).

57. Gentile, *Il mito dello Stato nuovo*, 251.

58. S. F. Romano, *Le classi sociali in Italia* (Turin: Einaudi, 1963), 204–5.

59. G. Papini, "Chi sono i socialisti? I. Socialismo e Borghesia," *Il Leonardo* 5 (February 22, 1903), reprinted in *La cultura italiana del '900 attraverso le riviste*, 121.

60. On the importance of modernity and industrialization for the birth of a generational conscience, see S. N. Eisenstadt, *From Generation to Generation; Age Groups and Social Structure* (Glencoe, Ill.: Free Press, 1956); and J. Savage, *Teenage: The Creation of Youth, 1875–1945* (New York: Viking, 2007).

61. See R. Wohl, *The Generation of 1914* (Cambridge, Mass.: Harvard University Press. 1979), 210. According to Wohl, "around the end of the nineteenth century the idea of generational rebellion began to crystallize into a cluster of attitudes that can be called the ideology of youth" (205). Therefore, "we can say that the rise in generational consciousness was one of the side effects of the coming of mass society. It was, like the concept of class, a form of collectivism and determinism, but one that emphasized temporal rather than socioeconomic location" (207).

62. See G. L. Mosse, *La cultura dell'Europa occidentale* (Milano: Mondadori, 1986), 38–39. "These were middle-class youths, most of them under thirty years of age, in rebellion against their elders"; see G. L. Mosse, *Masses and Man: Nationalist and Fascist Perceptions of Reality* (New York: Howard, 1980).

63. Prezzolini described his youth this way: "I did not want to admit that reality was enough to negate my contempt of the past and the middle class world since being supported by that world enabled me to despise and offend it" (G. Prezzolini, *L'italiano inutile* [Milan: Rusconi, 1994], 102). Giuseppe Bottai also admitted that the Futurist revolution against the bourgeoisie was carried out by "so-called bourgeois elements because they were born bourgeois but had already surpassed it" (G. Bottai, "Stratificazione borghese," *I nemici d'Italia*, October 30, 1919).

64. See A. De Bernardi, "Il mito della gioventù e i miti dei giovani," in *Il secolo dei giovani: Le nuove generazioni e la storia del Novecento*, ed. P. Sorcinelli and A. Varni (Rome: Donzelli, 2004), 55–79. See also G. Borgna, *Il mito della giovinezza* (Rome: Laterza, 1997); M. Degl'Innocenti, *L'epoca giovane: Generazioni, fascismo e antifascismo* (Manduria: Licata, 2002); and E. Papadia, "I vecchi e i giovani: Liberal-conservatori e nazionalisti a confronto nell'Italia giolittiana," *Contemporanea* 4 (2002), 651–76.

65. M. Morasso, "La tirannia della vecchiaia: La democrazia contro i giovani," in *Contro quelli che non hanno e che non sanno* (Milan-Palermo: Sandron, 1899), 287–88.

66. G. Papini, *Un uomo finito* (Florence, 1913), tried to create the autobiography of a whole generation. From the beginning of the twentieth century he expressed the desire to be a guide for "several hundred youths born in Italy around 1880, in other words, a part of the generation that had begun to think and act with the coming of the new century." In fact he wrote: "I would really like to become the spiritual guide of the young, the very young, the future of Italy" (G. Papini, "Campagna per il forzato risveglio," *Il Leonardo*, August 4, 1906, reprinted in *La cultura italiana del '900 attraverso le riviste*, 312–15).

67. R. Wohl, *The Generation of 1914*, 210.

68. See V. Saint-Point, "Manifesto futurista della lussuria," 1913, reprinted in *I manifesti del futurismo 1909–1913* (Rome: Empiria, 2001), 130–34.

69. See F. T. Marinetti: *Come si seducono le donne* (Florence: Edizioni da Centomila copie, 1917); *L'isola dei baci* (with B. Corra) (Milan: Facchi, 1918); *Gli amori futuristi* (Cremona: Ghelfi, 1922); *Un ventre di donna* (with E. Robert) (Milan: Vitagliano, 1922); *Novelle con le labbra tinte* (Milan: Mondadori, 1930). See also B. Corra, *Perché ho ucciso mia moglie* (Milan: Facchi, 1918), and *La famiglia innamorata* (Milan: Facchi, 1920); E. Settimelli, *Si amarono così* (Milan: Modernissima, 1920), and *Donna allo spiedo* (Milan: Modernissima, 1921).

70. R. De Felice, introduction to F. T. Marinetti, *Taccuini* (Bologna: il Mulino, 1987), xviii. On the Futurist concept of the woman and feminism see C. Salaris, *Le futuriste* (Milan: Edizioni delle donne, 1982), and *Storia del futurismo: Libri giornali manifesti* (Rome: Editori Riuniti, 1985), 52–56, 98–99.

71. F. T. Marinetti, "Democrazia Futurista: Dinamismo politico" (1919), reprinted in *Teoria e invenzione futurista*, 351.

72. See, in this regard, E. Gentile, "La politica di Marinetti," in *Il mito dello Stato nuovo*, 139–70; G. L. Mosse, "Futurismo e culture politiche in Europa: Una prospettiva globale," in *Futurismo, cultura e politica*, ed. R. De Felice (Turin: Fondazione Giovanni Agnelli, 1988), 15–29; and Marja Harmanmaa, *Un patriota che sfida la decadenza: F. T. Marinetti e l'idea dell' uomo nuovo fascista, 1929–1944* (Helsinki: Academia scientiarum fennica, 2000).

73. I. Tavolato, *Contro la morale sessuale* (Florence: Gonnelli, 1913), and "Elogio della prostituzione," *Lacerba*, May 1, 1913.

74. M. Morasso, *Uomini e idee del domani: L'egoarchia* (Milan: Bocca, 1898), 193.

75. F. T. Marinetti, "Contro l'amore e il parlamentarismo," reprinted in *Teoria e invenzione futurista*, 292.

76. F. T. Marinetti, *Mafarka il futurista* (Milan: Edizioni Futuriste di "Poesia," 1910). In this work Marinetti took the contrast between love and war, between sentimentalism and heroism to such extremes as to imagine the "absolute and definitive capability of will power," the possibility of "procreating without a woman's womb," the ability of men to "procreate from their own flesh without the help and smelly complicity of the female matrix" (237).

77. See M. Carli, *Sii brutale amor mio!* (Milan: Facchi, 1919); and F. T. Marinetti, *L'alcova d'acciaio* (Milan: Vitagliano, 1921). On Marinetti's "aggressive priapism" based on the affinity between the warrior instinct and sexual instinct, see E. Franzina, *Casini di guerra: Il tempo libero dalla trincea e i postriboli militari nel primo conflitto mondiale* (Udine: Gaspari, 1999); and M. Isenghi, *Il mito della grande guerra* (Bologna: Il Mulino, 1997), 179–83.

78. See E. Settimelli, *Nuovo modo di amare* (Rocca San Casciano; Cappelli 1918).

79. F. T. Marinetti, "Il cittadino eroico, l'abolizione delle polizie e le scuole di coraggio," reprinted in *Teoria e invenzione futurista*, 456.

80. "Matrimony," wrote Marinetti, "discourages and suffocates the development of the child, shortens the youth and virile strength of the father, makes the adolescent effeminate. . . . Matrimony is the enemy of bravery and heroism" ("Orgoglio italiano rivoluzionario e libero amore," in *Teoria e invenzione futurista*, 372). According to the creator of Futurism, at an early age, all "mixing of boys and girls should be abolished" so that

boys' games "could be clearly male games, deprived of any affectionate softness or girlish delicacy; lively, combative, muscular and violently dynamic" (F. T. Marinetti, "Contro il matrimonio," in *Teoria e invenzione futurista*, 370).

81. According to Marinetti, female luxury caused "males to become jewelers, perfume makers, dressmakers, milliners, ironers, embroiderers, and pederasts. The *toilettite* encourages the singular development of pederasty, and soon it will be necessary to resort to the hygienic provision adopted by a Doge in Venice who obliged the beautiful Venetian women to sit in their windows and display their naked bosoms between two candles to get the men back on the right track" (F. T. Marinetti, "Contro il lusso femminile," in *Teoria e invenzione futurista*, 547).

82. On the Futurist goal of building a masculine society based on the exaltation of virility and the contempt of homosexuality, and on this *"male homosexual panic"* generated by the way in which the futurists conceived of their relationships with women, who could transform heterosexual males into "pederasts" but at the same time were necessary for transforming boys into men and men into patriots, see B. Spackman, *Fascist Virilities: Rhetoric, Ideology, and Social Fantasy in Italy* (Minneapolis: University of Minnesota Press, 1996), 7–16.

83. See E. Settimelli, *Processi al futurismo per oltraggio al pudore* (Rocca San Casciano; Cappelli 1918).

84. Marinetti, *Taccuini*, 366.

85. Ibid., 465.

86. F. T. Marinetti and B. Corra, *L'isola dei baci: Romanzo erotico-sociale* (Capri: La Conchiglia, 2003), 129.

87. F. T. Marinetti, "Guerra sola igiene del mondo," reprinted in *Teoria e invenzione futurista*, 282–83.

88. "Grande serata futurista," *Lacerba*, December 15, 1913.

89. See F. T. Marinetti and A. Palazzeschi, *Carteggio* (Milan: Mondadori, 1978), 45, letter 53, April 1911. Paolo Prestogiacomo notes that Palazzeschi "apparently wanted to omit this postscriptum even sixty years after he had written it. By saving it from destruction as Marinetti did at the time despite his friend's explicit wishes, we have been able to unveil the deep shadows that shroud Palazzeschi's biography. What can be deduced is not much, but there was the faint sign of a particular type of friendship." Marinetti himself in his autobiographical memories described Palazzeschi as "overly effeminate, a mamma's boy," but still continued to praise him and value his work. See F. T. Marinetti, *La grande Milano tradizionale e futurista* (Milan: Mondadori, 1969), 95.

90. S. Sighele, *Eva moderna* (Milan: Treves, 1910), 9.

91. S. Sighele, *La donna e l'amore* (Milan: Treves, 1913), 106.

92. Mosse, *Nationalism and Sexuality*, 190. See also A. M. Banti, *L'onore della nazione: Identità sessuali e violenza nel nazionalismo europeo dal XVIII secolo alla grande guerra* (Torino: Einaudi 2005).

93. Sighele, *La donna e l'amore*, 18. Antifeminism was so deeply rooted in nationalism that even Sighele, a strenuous defender of improving conditions for women, criticized feminism and remained culturally prejudiced against women. In his opinion, from the

national point of view "love was a woman's destiny and maternity her duty. The vitality of a population was measured by the capability and desire of its women to give birth to healthy children and the capability and desire of its men to defend the country. Motherhood was woman's patriotism; it was her way of fighting and sacrificing themselves for their country." Even his proposals encouraging female emancipation stemmed from a kind of male paternalism. He wrote: "Considering women weak, inferior beings—as they really are—we should protect them; this should be the psychology of strong, superior men" (see Sighele, *Idee e problemi di un positivista*, 173).

94. E. Corradini, "Delle baccanti e del femminismo," *Il Regno* 30 (June 19, 1904). On Corradini's opposition to female suffrage, see his "Le culture artificiali," *Il Regno* 4 (March 8, 1906).

95. M. Morasso, *Uomini e idee del domani*, 305.

96. S. Sighele, *La coppia criminale* (Turin: Bocca, 1909 [1892]), 217–18.

97. See G. Papini, *Maschilità* (Florence: Libreria della Voce, 1915), esp. 41 and 93–97.

98. Mosse, *The Image of Man*, 67–68. For an analysis of gender relationships between the nineteenth and twentieth centuries and the need to assert a male identity by imposing heterosexual masculine canons, see A. McLaren, *The Trials of Masculinity: Policing Sexual Boundaries, 1870–1930* (Chicago: University of Chicago Press, 1997).

99. E. Corradini, "Per coloro che risorgono," *Il Regno* 1 (1903), reprinted in *La cultura italiana del '900 attraverso le riviste*, 442.

100. A. Campodonico, "I risorgenti dell'oggi e i risorti di ieri," *Il Regno* 1 (1903), reprinted in *La cultura italiana del '900*, 445.

101. E. Corradini, "Liberali e nazionalisti," December 1913, in *Discorsi politici (1902–1923)* (Florence: Vallecchi, 1925), 182.

102. Corradini, "La marcia dei produttori," 92.

103. According to Corradini, for example, words like "freedom," "democracy," "reformism," "indicated much more than their political content, they were the inclination of men" (E. Corradini, "Le elezioni della vittoria," in *Diario postbellico* [Rome: Stock, 1924], 115).

104. "Il nemico della Patria," *L'Idea Nazionale* (May 14, 1915), qtd. in *La stampa nazionalista*, ed. F. Gaeta (Bologna: Cappelli, 1965), 530.

105. E. Corradini, "Giolitti," May 16, 1915, qtd. in *I nazionalisti*, ed. A. D'Orsi (Milan: Feltrinelli, 1981), 126.

106. "Nitti non sa governare," *L'Idea Nazionale* (June 9, 1920), qtd. in *La stampa nazionalista*, 235.

107. E. H. Gombrich, *Meditations on a Hobbyhorse and Other Essays on the Theory of Art* (London: Phaidon, 1963), 139.

108. E. Gentile, *Storia del partito fascista, 1919–1922: Movimento e milizia* (Rome: Laterza, 1989), 524–25.

109. On the alleged sexual violence on Giacomo Matteotti, see M. Canali, *Il delitto Matteotti: Affarismo e politica nel primo governo Mussolini* (Bologna: il Mulino, 1997), 42–44.

110. B. Mussolini, *Opera Omnia*, ed. E. Susmel and D. Susmel (Florence: La Fenice, 1951–53), 21:236.

111. Gentile, *Storia del partito fascista*, 483. See also M. Piazzesi, *Diario di uno squadrista toscano 1919-1922* (Rome: Bonacci, 1980).

112. Art. 3 of the "Regolamento di disciplina della milizia fascista," qtd. in D. Bartoli, *Il volontario delle camicie nere* (Rome: Luzzatti, 1933), 26.

113. Mosse, *Masses and Man*, 240.

114. For further considerations on this matter, see C. Saraceno, "Costruzione della maternità e della paternità," in *Il regime fascista: Storia e storiografia*, ed. A. Del Boca, M. Legnani, and M. G. Rossi (Rome: Laterza, 1995), 475-97.

115. L. Ellena, "Mascolinità e immaginario nazionale nel cinema italiano degli anni Trenta," in *Genere e mascolinità: Uno sguardo storico*, ed. S. Bellassai and M. Malatesta (Rome: Bulzoni, 2001), 249.

116. On the representation of youth used to create the image of the ideal Fascist, see L. Malvano, "Il mito della giovinezza attraverso l'immagine: Il fascismo italiano," in *Storia dei giovani: L'età contemporanea*, ed. G. Levi and J. C. Schmitt (Rome: Laterza, 1994), 311-48. For a useful, but not always convincing, analysis of iconographic culture in Fascist Italy and the use of advertising as an instrument used to consolidate gender identities, see K. Pinkus, *Bodily Regimes: Italian Advertising under Fascism* (Minneapolis: University of Minnesota Press, 1995). On the body of the Duce as the model of the ideal male and best example of Fascist virility, see M. Isenghi, "Il corpo del duce," in *L'Italia del fascio* (Florence: Giunti, 1996), 405-19; S. Luzzatto, *Il corpo del duce: Un cadavere tra immaginazione, storia e memoria* (Turin: Einaudi, 1998); G. Di Genova, ed., *L'uomo della provvidenza: iconografia del Duce 1923-1945* (Bologna: Bora, 1997); G. Gori, "Model of Masculinity: Mussolini, the 'New Italian' of the Fascist Era," *International Journal of History of Sport*, December 1999, 27-61; and J. A. Mangan, ed., *Superman Supreme: Fascist Body as Political Icon—Global Fascism* (London: Frank Cass, 2000).

117. See G. M. De Marinis, *Resurrezione Eroica: L'Italiano Nuovo* (Naples: Pironti, 1929); L. Ferretti, *Il volto dell'Italia virile* (Florence: Barbera, n.d. [1934]), and *Esempi e idee per l'italiano nuovo* (Rome: Libreria del Littorio, 1930).

118. G. Maggiore, "Maschilità del fascismo," in *Un regime e un'epoca* (Milan: Treves, 1929), 139 and 141. On the need to counter "the loss of the virility that the Fascist regime is attempting to restore," see M. Palazzi, "La Famiglia nello Stato fascista: Autorità dell'uomo," *Critica fascista* 10 (May 15, 1933).

119. M. Carli, "Sfemminilizzare la mondanità," in *Antisnobismo* (Milan: Morreale, 1929), 101.

120. E. Galvano, "Natura e morale," *Il Popolo d'Italia*, September 26, 1934.

121. W. Reich, *The Mass Psychology of Fascism* (New York: Farrar, Straus and Giroux, 1970); C. E. Gadda, *Eros e Priapo (Da furore a cenere)* (Milan: Garzanti, 1995); B. Wanrooij, "Mobilitazione, modernizzazione, tradizione," in *Storia d'Italia: Guerre e fascismo*, ed. G. Sabatucci and V. Vidotto (Rome: Laterza, 1997), 4:379-439; A. Capone, "Corporeità maschile e modernità," in *Genere e mascolinità*, 195-221. According to Capone, "the male search for a new collective body" originated in the physical decadence, isolation, and sexual indifference brought about by a mass industrial society that questioned "the identity structures that had been constructed during modernity" (200). In my opinion, Capone

underestimates the importance of the religious aspects of Fascist ideology and therefore exaggerates in interpreting this subconscious male need to belong to a collective body as the key to consensus of the regime.

122. B. Mussolini, "Il compito dei medici," *Il Popolo d'Italia*, January 29, 1932. On the Fascist plan to regenerate the Italians, see E. Gentile, "'L'uomo nuovo' del fascismo: Riflessioni su un esperimento totalitario di rivoluzione antropologica," in *Storia e interpretazione del fascismo* (Rome: Laterza, 2002), 235–64; L. La Rovere, "Rifare gli italiani: L'esperimento di creazione dell' 'uomo nuovo' nel regime fascista," in *Annali di storia dell'educazione e delle istituzioni scolastiche* 9 (Brescia: La Scuola, 2002), 51–77; see also S. Setta, *Renato Ricci: Dallo squadrismo alla Repubblica Sociale Italiana* (Bologna: il Mulino, 1986); and L. Pazzaglia, "La formazione dell'uomo nuovo nella strategia pedagogica del fascismo," in *Chiesa, cultura e educazione in Italia tra le due guerre*, ed. L. Pazzaglia (Brescia: La Scuola, 2003), 105–46.

123. G. L. Mosse, *La nazione, le masse e la nuova politica* (Rome: Di Renzo, 1999), 43.

Chapter 2. The Discovery of Homosexuality

1. The origin of the strategy to hide situations probably can be traced to St. Paul in his Letters to the Ephesians: "But among you there must not be even a hint of sexual immorality, or of any kind of impurity, or of greed, because these are improper for God's holy people" (Ephesians 5:3, New International Version).

2. See M. Daniel and A. Baudry, *Gli omosessuali* (Florence: Vallecchi, 1974), 9–10.

3. On the contradictory tendencies of the nineteenth century, an era when Victorian puritanism and middle-class decency went hand in hand with anticonformist, transgressive, libertine situations, see P. Gay, *Education of the Senses*, vol. 1 of *The Bourgeois Experience, Victoria to Freud* (New York: Oxford University Press, 1984), and *Schnitzler's Century: The Making of Middle-Class Culture, 1815–1914* (New York: Norton, 2002).

4. M. Foucault, *Society Must Be Defended: Lectures at the Collège De France, 1975–76* (New York: Picador, 2003).

5. See G. Canguilhelm, *The Normal and the Pathological* (New York: Zone Books, 1989).

6. M. Foucault, *The History of Sexuality* (New York: Vintage Books, 1988), 37.

7. Ibid., 43. These considerations of Foucault were endorsed and developed by other scholars as well, above all by the English historian Jeffrey Weeks, according to whom the end of the nineteenth century marked the critical point in time when a clear homosexual identity was determined; see J. Weeks, *Coming Out: Homosexual Politics in Britain from the Nineteenth Century to the Present* (London: Quartet Books, 1990). By the same author, see also *Sex, Politics, and Society: The Regulation of Sexuality since 1800* (London: Longman, 1984); *Sexuality and Its Discontents: Meanings, Myths and Modern Sexualities* (London: Routledge, 1985); and *Against Nature: Essays on History, Sexuality, and Identity* (London: Rivers Oram, 1991).

8. On the criticism of Foucault's postulations, see M. Barbagli and A. Colombo, *Omosessuali moderni: Gay e lesbiche in Italia* (Bologna: il Mulino, 2001), 223–25. Some historians, such as Randolph Trumbach and Alan Bray, date the appearance of homosexuals at

the beginning of the eighteenth century with the advent in London of the so-called
Molly Houses; others, like Michel Foucault, Jeffrey Weeks, Lillian Faderman, and John
D'Emilio, place the date at the end of the nineteenth century with the advent of medical
investigation, the growth of the cities, the reorganization of families, and the development
of capitalism; lastly, some scholars even hypothesize the existence of a "proto-homosexual
personality" in the Middle Ages. On the different positions about the birth of modern
homosexuals see Barbagli and Colombo, *Omosessuali moderni*, 232–35; M. Duberman,
M. Vicinus, and G. Chauncey, eds., *Hidden from History: Reclaiming the Gay and Lesbian Past*
(New York: Meridian, 1989), 9; K. Plummer, ed., *The Making of the Modern Homosexual*
(London: Hutchinson, 1981); G. Chauncey, "From Sexual Inversion to Homosexuality,"
Salmagundi 58 (1982), 114–46; D. F. Greenberg, *The Construction of Homosexuality* (Chicago:
University of Chicago Press, 1990); J. D'Emelio, "La storia gay: Un nuovo settore di
ricerca," *Rivista di storia contemporanea*, January 1, 1991, 88–105; D. Altman et al., *Homo-sexuality, Which Homosexuality? International Conference on Gay and Lesbian Studies* (London:
Gmp Publishers, 1989); and R. Norton, *The Myth of the Modern Homosexual: Queer History
and the Search for Cultural Unity* (London: Cassell, 1997).

9. See M. Foucault, *Abnormal: Lectures at the Collège De France, 1974–1975* (New York:
Picador, 2003).

10. Foucault, *The History of Sexuality*, 26.

11. In his museum for criminal anthropology, Cesare Lombroso collected photo-graphs of homosexuals; see C. Lombroso, *L'uomo delinquente: In rapporto all'antropologia, alla
giurisprudenza ed alla psichiatria*, 5th ed. (Turin: Bocca, 1897), table 47, 2–5, and G. Co-lombo, *La scienza infelice: Il museo di antropologia criminale di Cesare Lombroso* (Turin: Bollati
Boringhieri, 2000), 243–44. On photos of transvestites preserved in the criminological
museum of Rome see L. Schettini, "Immagini truccate," *Zapruder* 5 (September–December
2004): 65–69. On the use of hermaphrodites as an attraction see A. Zuccarelli, "Zefthe
Akaira: La donna–uomo esposta in Napoli nel maggio 1892, e l'ermafroditismo," *L'anomalo*
1 (1893): 78–92. On the relationship between science and entertainment see C. Gallini, *La
sonnambula meravigliosa: Magnetismo e ipnotismo nell'Ottocento italiano* (Milan: Feltrinelli, 1983).

12. See G. Hekma, "'A female soul in a male body': Sexual Inversion as Gender
Inversion in Nineteenth-Century Sexology," in *Third Sex Third Gender*, ed. G. Herdt (New
York: Zone Books, 1993), 213–40; H. Kennedy, "The 'Third Sex' Theory of Karl Heinrich
Ulrichs," *Journal of Homosexuality* 6 (1980–81): 103–11, and *Ulrichs: The Life and Works of
Karl Heinrich Ulrichs, Pioneer of the Modern Gay Movement* (Boston: Alyson, 1988); M. Consoli,
"Karl Heinrich Ulrichs," *Cronache Lucane*, September 25, 1988; and G. Dall'Orto, "Karl
Heinrich Ulrichs (1825–1895): Il nonno del movimento gay," in *C'era una volta un secolo fa*,
supplement to *Babilonia* 135 (July–August 1995): 41–46. On the influence of Ulrichs on
Italian and foreign scholars see V. Massarotti, *Nel regno di Ulrichs: Appunti e considerazioni
sull'omosessualità maschile* (Rome: Bernardo Lux Editore, 1913).

13. A. La Cara, *La base organica dei pervertimenti sessuali e la loro profilassi sociale* (Turin
1924 [1902]), 3.

14. A. Forel, "Etica e tormento di un omosessuale distinto," in *Etica sessuale—con
un'appendice: Esempi di conflitti etici e sessuali presi dalla vita* (Turin: Bocca, 1909), qtd. in P. Pedote

and G. Lo Presti, *Omofobia: Il pregiudizio anti-omosessuale dalla Bibbia ai giorni nostri* (Viterbo: Stampa Alternativa, 2003), 76.

15. G. A. Belloni, *L'eros incatenato: Studio sul problema sessuale penitenziario* (Milan: Bocca, 1939), 42.

16. See L. Benadusi, "Lecito e illecito: Nascita della sessuologia e invenzione delle perversioni nell'Italia tra Ottocento e Novecento," *Zapruder* 6 (January–April 2005): 28–43.

17. A. Tardieu, "Étude médico-legale sur les attentats aux moeurs" [1857], qtd. in J. P. Aron and R. Kempf, *Il pene e la demoralizzazione dell'Occidente* (Florence: Sansoni, 1979), 36–37. The authors highlight the fact that doctors and jurists treated homosexuality with disgust, and they maintain that the removal of such indecent matters led directly to open condemnation. Thus "panting was followed by anger," silence by vociferous condemnation of all forms of sexual deviation. In my opinion, this position—which led them to openly criticize Foucault, guilty of stating that knowledge conveyed the truth about sexual freedom—is overly rigid and places too much importance on fear and repression compared to the desire to know and understand.

18. N. De Aldisio, introduction to G. Poderecca, *Sessualità e politica della Germania imperiale* (Rome: Bottega dell'antiquario, n.d. [1934]), 5–6.

19. On the crisis of masculinity between the nineteenth and twentieth centuries see A. Maugue, *L'identité masculine en crise au tournant du siècle 1871–1914* (Paris: Rivages, 1987), and "The New Eve and the Old Adam," in *A History of Women in the West*, vol. 4, *Emerging Feminism from Revolution to World War*, ed. G. Fraisse and M. Perrot (Cambridge, Mass: Belknap Press of Harvard University Press, 1993), 515–32; E. Showalter, *Sexual Anarchy: Gender and Culture at the Fin de Siècle* (London: Virago Press, 1992); J. Le Rider, *Modernité viennoise et crise de l'identité* (Paris: Presses Universitaires de France, 1990); M. S. Kimmel, "The Contemporary 'Crisis' of Masculinity in Historical Perspective," in *The Making of Masculinities: The New Men's Studies*, ed. H. Brod (Boston: Allen and Unwin, 1987), 121–53; and M. Pustianaz and L. Villa, eds., *Maschilità decadenti: La lunga fin de siècle* (Bergamo: Sestante, 2004).

20. See S. L. Gilman and E. J. Chamberlin, eds., *Degeneration: The Dark Side of Progress* (New York: Columbia Universty Press, 1985).

21. In this regard, see P. Penta, "Dei varii studii pubblicati sui pervertimenti sessuali dai primi sino ai più recenti dei giorni nostri," *Archivio delle psicopatie sessuali* 1 (1896): 9–15, 111–17; and G. Dall'Orto, *Leggere omosessuale* (Turin: Edizioni Gruppo Abele, 1984).

22. See A. Tamassia, "Sull'inversione dell'istinto sessuale," *Rivista sperimentale di freniatria e di medicina legale* 4 (1878): 97–117.

23. For studies of hermaphroditism, see L. Benadusi, "Dalla paura al mito dell'indeterminatezza: Storia di ermafroditi, travestiti, invertiti e transessuali," in *Transessualità e scienze sociali*, ed. E. Ruspini and M. Inghilleri (Naples: Liguori, 2008), 19–48; B. Wanrooij, *Storia del pudore: La questione sessuale in Italia 1860–1940* (Venice: Marsilio, 1990), 191–94; D. Di Meglio, *L'invisibile confine tra ermafroditismo e omosessualità* (Rome: Melusina, 1990); and M. T. Caffaratto, *L'ermafroditismo umano: Storia clinica, medica e legale* (Saluzzo: Minerva medica, 1963).

24. A. Zuccarelli, "La misteriosa 'donna barbuta' arrestata dalla questura di Napoli: Un altro caso di 'inversione dell'istinto sessuale' un uomo," *L'anomalo* 14 (1917): 122–30.

25. On the longevity of the monosexual model, whereby women were simply a less perfect version of men and on the tardy assertion of a bipolar sexuality based on the priority of sexual differentiation versus gender, see T. Laqueur, *Making Sex: Body and Gender from the Greeks to Freud* (Cambridge, Mass.: Harvard University Press, 1990).

26. P. Penta, "Caratteri generali, origine e significato dei Pervertimenti Sessuali dimostrati con le autobiografie di Alfieri e di Rousseau e col dialogo 'Gli amori' di Luciano," *Archivio delle psicopatie sessuali*, f. 1 (1896): 1. The works of Pasquale Penta were based on the degeneration models that, following Lombroso, were used to explain the causes of sexual perversions; see P. Penta, *I pervertimenti sessuali nell'uomo* (Naples: Luigi Pierro editore, 1893), and "In tema di pervertimenti sessuali: Documenti umani. Lettere di amore tra individui dello stesso sesso," *Rivista di psichiatria forense* 3 (1900): 69–89.

27. C. Lombroso, "L'amore nei pazzi," *Archivio di psichiatria, scienze penali ed antropologia criminale* 2 (1881): 32.

28. Mosse, *Nationalism and Sexuality*, 39.

29. See S. Venturi, *Le degenerazioni psico-sessuali nella vita degli individui e nella storia della società* (Turin: Bocca, 1892); and P. Fabiani, *Il problema dell'omosessualità e di tutte le degenerazioni sessuali innanzi alla scienza* (Naples: Società Ed. Partenopea, 1900).

30. G. Obici and G. Marchesini, *Le "amicizie" di collegio: Ricerche sulle prime manifestazioni dell'amore sessuale* (Rome: Dante Alighieri, 1898), 251; see also E. Mandolini, "Amicizie e omoerotismo," *Rassegna di studi sessuali* 6 (1923): 393–99.

31. E. Morselli, *Sessualità umana: Secondo la psicologia, la biologia e la sociologia* (Turin: Bocca, 1931), 154–57.

32. P. Valera, *Milano sconosciuta* (Milan: Bietti, 1931 [1879]). The chapter "Sodoma e Gomorra" was eliminated from subsequent editions, whereas in 1931 new passages were added, including "Gli invertiti a Milano," taken from other publications by Valera; see E. Ghidetti, introduction to P. Valera, *Milano sconosciuta rinnovata* (Milan: Longanesi, 1976), xiv–xxi.

33. On the attitude Paolo Valera and the Italian left had toward homosexuality between the nineteenth and twentieth centuries, see G. Dall'Orto, "La rivoluzione contro gli omosessuali e la contro-rivoluzione sessuale del socialismo," *Lotta continua*, January 14, 1982. On the person and works of Valera see C. Botta, "Paolo Valera e gli 'abissi plebei' di Milano fin de siècle: Immagine e realta sociale," *Rivista di storia contemporanea* 1 (1988): 3–36.

34. P. Valera, *Amori bestiali* (Milan: La Folla, 1923 [1884]), 74. Valera expressed great indignation about the hypocrisy of those who had professed friendship and admiration of Oscar Wilde but paid him back after the trial with hate and contempt. At the same time, he stated his true condemnation of this "degenerate repulsive being": "May the memory of the man disgust everyone until the day when disgust for such abominable acts shall have disappeared. The pederast of all London pederasts is revolting after many years. The society of the Oscar Wildes is too obscene, too nauseating, too filthy to let live. May the memory of him be persecuted everywhere" (88). See also Valera's *I*

gentiluomini invertiti: Echi dello scandalo di Milano. Il caposcuola Oscar Wilde al processo con i suoi giovanotti (Milan: Floritta, 1909).

35. On the image of the typical androgine during Decadentism see C. Gatto Trocchi, ed., *Androgino: Il mito, l'arte, la merce* (Perugia: Galeno, 1997), 10; and R. Bussone, *Arte e costume nell'Occidente romantico e decadentista: Il volto non ufficiale del XIX secolo nella letteratura e nelle arti figurative. Le visioni, le perversioni, i sentimenti, gli incubi degli artisti e le immagini nascoste della società* (Turin: Celib, 1993); but above all A. J. L. Busst, "The Image of the Androgine in the Nineteenth century," in *Romantic Mythologies* (London: Routledge and Kegan Paul, 1967); and F. Monneyron, "Estetismo e androgino: I fondamenti estetici dell'androgino decadente," in *Androgino*, ed. A. Faivre and F. Tristan (Genoa: Ecig, 1986), 283–311. On the fragility of men due to their simultaneous adoration and contempt of women, present in some of D'Annunzio's and Pirandello's works, see R. Alonge, *Donne terrifiche e fragili maschi: La linea teatrale D'Annunzio-Pirandello* (Rome: Laterza, 2004).

36. M. Praz, *La carne, la morte e il diavolo nella letteratura romantica* (Milan: La Cultura, 1934), 320–31.

37. Valera, *Milano sconosciuta*, 159.

38. Ibid., 210. During the Fascist era, the popular national magazine *L'Italiano* went back to considering homosexuality a modern vice and a fashionable aesthetic pose. Published in an article significantly titled "Morte del '900," "called '900 because the plan was to be completely modern, dynamic, and devoid of tradition. In order to be modern, the poor thing . . . was favorable toward hermaphrodites and pederasts and adored mulattos . . . and could never say no to a Jew" (L. Longanesi, "Morte del '900," *L'Italiano* 12–13 [1927]: 3).

39. See P. Bourdieu, *Masculine Domination* (Stanford: Stanford University Press, 2001).

40. See L. A. Hall, *Hidden Anxieties: Male Sexuality, 1900–1950* (Cambridge: Polity Press, 1991). The author highlights the tension between the proposed model of masculinity and the real-life experience of men, based on a study of letters written by some men to Dr. Marie Stopes. In her opinion, anxiety and phobias are typical of the male universe, because men find it impossible to emulate the prototype of the normal male.

41. Maximilian Harden, editor of *Die Zukunft*, accused Eulenburg of being homosexual with the intention of putting an end to a sort of international brotherhood of pederasts, but his action actually led to the biggest scandal of the reign of Wilhelm II. On this affair and the outcome of the Moltke-Harden-Eulenburg trials, 1907–9, see I. V. Hull, *The Entourage of Kaiser Wilhelm II 1888–1918* (New York: Cambridge University Press, 1982); and P. Jungblut, *Famose Kerle: Eulenburg—Eine wilhelminische Affäre* (Hamburg: MännerschwarmSkript Verlag, 2003).

42. For a careful analysis of the satirical cartoons published in the international press on the Eulenburg case see J. D. Steakley, "Iconography of a Scandal: Political Cartoons and the Eulenburg Affair in Wilhelmin Germany," in Duberman, Vicinus, and Chauncey, *Hidden from History*. On the use of homosexuality as an instrument to defame an enemy and the cartoons published in Italian newspapers on the effeminacy of the German army, see M. Hirschfeld, *Sittenge-schichte des Weltkrieges* (Berlin: Verlag für Sexualwissenschaft Scheider and Co., 1930).

43. In the publication *La Tradotta*, for example, there were evident references in rhyme to the enemy's sexuality: "Manfredi, che in Sicilia occupò il trono, / Per un Tedesco era abbastanza buono: / Biondo era, e bello e di gentile aspetto, / Però con la sorella andava a letto. / Oggi i tedeschi sono meno belli, / ora amoreggiano persin con i fratelli. / Ché la storia, sia antica o nuova sia, / quand'è tedesca è una sudiceria" (R. Simoni, "Paginette scelte di storia tedesca," *La Tradotta* 6 [May 2, 1918], qtd. in M. Isenghi, *Giornali di trincea 1915–1918* [Turin: Einaudi, 1977], 164).

44. S. Fasulo, "I pervertiti dell'Imperatore. Da Krupp allo Stato maggiore tedesco," *Il Popolo d'Italia*, April 11, 1918.

45. G. Podrecca, *Sessualità e politica della Germania imperiale* (Rome: Bottega dell'antiquario, n.d. [1934]), 37, previously printed with the title *La tavola rotonda in Germania* (Rome, 1919).

46. Ibid., 145.

47. G. Senizza, *Corruzione sessuale e crudeltà germanica* (Florence: Istituto Editoriale "Il Pensiero," n.d. [1917]). Senizza maintained that "the German holds women in contempt because he loves strength, violence, and brutal virility. His sexual leanings tend to be homosexual or sadistic, and his politics tends to be imperialist or militarist absolutism" (123). Therefore, in Germany, the "erotic color-blindness" present in other parts of the world, went from "individual to group, from sporadic to endemic," to the point that even the case of "Harden's Round Table" did not arouse true indignation at home. Instead, "homosexuality" even came to be seen as a sign of ethnic superiority.

48. L. M. Bossi, *La cultura dei tedeschi e quella degli Alleati* (Venice: Libreria Editrice Nazionalista, 1917), 16.

49. F. Paoloni, "I sudekumizzati del socialismo," *Il Popolo d'Italia* (1917), qtd. in A. Ventrone, *La seduzione totalitaria: Guerra, modernità, violenza politica (1914–1918)* (Rome: Donzelli, 2003), 181.

50. See A. Bravo, ed., *Donne e uomini nelle guerre mondiali* (Rome: Laterza, 1991). Regarding World War I as the perfect example of a masculine-military war compared to the "feminine" World War II, considered so because of the greater involvement of civilians, see the article by Ernesto Galli della Loggia, "Una guerra 'femminile'? Ipotesi sul mutamento dell'ideologia e dell'immaginario occidentale tra il 1939 e il 1945," in *Donne e uomini nelle guerre mondiali*, ed. A. Bravo (Rome: Laterza, 1994).

51. On soldiers' martial fantasies and their excitement about going to war see J. Bourke, *An Intimate History of Killing: Face-to-Face Killing in Twentieth-Century Warfare* (New York: Basic Books, 1999).

52. See E. Showalter, "Rivers and Sasson: The Inscription of Male Gender Anxieties," in *Behind the Lines: Gender and the Two World Wars*, ed. M. R. Higonnet, J. Jenson, S. Michel, and M. C. Weitz (New Haven: Yale University Press, 1987), 61–69; and E. J. Leed, *No Man's Land: Combat and Identity in World War I* (Cambridge: Cambridge University Press, 1979).

53. See L. Lattes, *Gli omosessuali nell'esercito* (Rome: Tipografia Enrico Voghera, 1917).

54. The concept of homoeroticism is used here with the meaning given it by Paul Fussell, who uses this word "to mean a sublimated, 'chaste' form of temporary homosexuality" (Fussell, *The Great War and Modern Memory* [New York: Oxford University

Press, 1975], 272). On the exaltation of violent, aggressive virility among the German troops see K. Theweleit, *Male Fantasies* (Minneapolis: University of Minnesota Press, 1987–89). On violence and militarism as specific characteristics of virility see L. B. Iglitzin, "War, Sex, Sports, and Masculinity," in *War: A Historical, Political and Social Study*, ed. L. L. Farrar Jr. (Santa Barbara, Calif.: Abc-Clio, 1978); E. J. Leed, "Violenza, morte e mascolinità," *Ventesimo secolo* 9 (September–December 1993): 243–72; and B. Ehrenreich, *Blood Rites: Origins and the History of the Passions of War* (New York: Metropolitan Books, 1997), 117–32.

55. G. L. Mosse, *Fallen Soldiers: Reshaping the Memory of the World Wars* (New York: Oxford University Press, 1990). According to Mosse, "The First World War tied nationalism and masculinity together more closely than ever before and, as it did so, brought to a climax all those facets of masculinity that had merely been latent and that now got their due. Trench warfare freed aggression from restraint as men went over the top in order to take the enemy's trench" (110).

56. See F. Thébaud, "The Great War and the Triumph of Sexual Division," in *A History of Women in the West*, vol. 5, *Toward a Cultural Identity in the Twentieth Century*, ed. F. Thébaud (Cambridge, Mass.: Harvard University Press, 2000), 21–75; and M. De Giorgio, "Dalla 'Donna Nuova' alla donna della 'nuova Italia,'" in *La Grande Guerra: Esperienza, memoria, immagini*, ed. D. Leoni and C. Zadra (Bologna: Il Mulino, 1986), 307–32.

57. The literature of the nationalists often compares cars to women as something to be harnessed and dominated. In Marinetti's works this *transfert* between cars and women also takes on sexual importance. In *L'alcova d'acciaio* the auto-machineguns symbolize the "agile steel women who run around singing, happy to be possessed and to possess the lengthy tortuous body of the road with lesbian virility." While the armored car is the "fast alcove of steel created to receive the naked body of my naked Italy that I now gracefully drag by its pretty little feet into you!" (F. T. Marinetti, *L'alcova d'acciaio* [Milan: Vitagliano, 1921], 80, 284).

58. P. Mantegazza, *Fisiologia dell'amore* (Florence: Marzocco, 1939 [1873]), 248.

59. A. Mosso, "Le cagioni dell'effeminatezza latina," *Nuova Antologia: Rivista di scienze, lettere ed arti*, f. 22 (November 16, 1897): 249–65. According to Mosso, physical activity, open-air games, and sport could help "distract boys from effeminacy." See also M. Nani, "Fisiologia sociale e politica della razza latina: Note su alcuni dispositivi di naturalizzazione negli scritti di Angelo Mosso," in *Studi sul razzismo italiano*, ed. A. Burgio and L. Casali (Bologna: Clueb, 1996), 29–60.

60. On the homosexuality of English men see C. Pettinato, *Questi inglesi* (Milan: Bertieri, 1943).

61. A. Ventrone, *La seduzione totalitaria: Guerra, modernità, violenza politica (1914–1918)* (Rome: Donzelli, 2003), 155.

62. See N. Pende, *Bonifica umana razionale e biologia politica* (Bologna: Cappelli, 1933); and C. Ipsen, *Dictating Demography: The Problem of Population in Fascist Italy* (Cambridge: Cambridge University Press, 1996).

63. According to Renzo Villa, criminal anthropology is in fact a sort of "reverse, negative anthropology in which the protagonist is not a generally and tautologically defined

subject: it is an anthropology of the opposite, of the borders and limits within which the so-called 'normal' subject closes and defends himself like a kind of besieged species" (Villa, *Il deviante e i suoi segni: Lombroso e la nascita dell'antropologia criminale* [Milan: Franco Angeli, 1985], 8).

64. The anthropologist Lorenzo Giuliano prowled the public toilets of Turin, for example, hoping to "discover some homosexuals worthy of study" (Giuliano, "Facile modo per riconoscersi fra omosessuali," report given in 1906 at the sixth Congress of Criminal Anthropology, qtd. in *Babilonia* 36 [1986]).

65. A. De Blasio, "Sul tatuaggio di prostitute e pederasti," *Archivio di psichiatria, scienze penali ed antropologia criminale* 27 (1906): 41–45.

66. A. Nicefero, *Il gergo nei normali, nei degenerati e nei criminali* (Turin: Bocca, 1897), 37, 46, and all of chap. 3.

67. See R. Corso, *La vita sessuale nelle credenze, pratiche e tradizioni popolari italiane* (Florence: Olschki, 2001 [1914]), and *Per lo studio dei pregiudizi sessuali del popolo italiano* (S. Maria Capua Vetere: La Fiaccola, 1925); A. De Blasio, *Usi e costumi dei camorristi* (Naples: Luigi Pierro editore, 1897); and E. Mirabella, *Mala vita: Gergo, camorra e costumi degli affiliati* (Naples: Perrella, 1910).

68. On the tendency of physiognomy to emerge as a process of signifying that, through a study of the face, gave certain meanings to behavior, see D. Pick, *Faces of Degeneration: A European Disorder, 1848–1918* (Cambridge: Cambridge University Press, 1989); and P. Magli, *Il volto e l'anima: Fisiognomica e passioni* (Milan: Cde, 1995).

69. See G. Colombo, *La scienza infelice*, qtd. in U. Levra, ed., *La scienza e la colpa: Crimini, criminali, criminologi. Un volto dell'Ottocento* (Milan: Electa, 1985).

70. For a detailed reconstruction of how sexual inversion was treated in the *Archivio di antropologia criminale* see N. Milletti, "Analoghe sconcezze: Tribadi, saffiste, invertite e omosessuali: Categorie e sistemi sesso/genere nella rivista di antropologia criminale fondata da Cesare Lombroso (1880–1949)," *DWF* 4 (October–December 1994): 50–122.

71. According to Tardieu, "a revolting physiognomy, rightly suspicious that betrays pederasts" easily recognizable because of their smell and their "sordid filth"; visible because of their outward appearance; easy to pick out because of their shrill, effeminate voices; recognizable to the touch because of their funnel-shaped anuses and "tiny, fragile members withered at the top." On Tardieu's portrait of the sodomite, see A. Corbin, "Cries and Whispers," in *A History of Private Life*, vol. 4, *From the Fires of Revolution to the Great War*, ed. M. Perrot (Cambridge, Mass.: Harvard University Press, 1990), 640.

72. Massarotti, *Nel regno di Ulrichs*, 7.

73. L. Pasolli, "Sessualità maschile e sessualità femminile," *Rassegna di studi sessuali* 1–2 (1930).

74. See F. De Napoli, *Sesso e amore nella vita dell'uomo e degli altri animali* (Turin: Bocca, 1927), 359; A. Signorelli, *Sesso, intersesso, supersesso: Specchi per tutti e per ognuno* (Rome: Tipografia Coop. Sociale, 1928), 17; and P. Babina, *Corruzione della donna: Responsabilità dell'uomo* (Milan: Istituto di propaganda libraria, 1942), 32. The comparison between women and passivity is virtually infinite; on an attempt to prove this image scientifically, see D. F. Noble, *A World without Women: The Christian Clerical Culture of Western Science* (New

York: Knopf, 1992); V. P. Babini, F. Minuz, and A. Tagliavini, *La donna nelle scienze dell'uomo: Immagini del femminile nella cultura scientifica italiana di fine secolo* (Milan: Franco Angeli, 1986); V. P. Babini, "Un altro genere: La costruzione scientifica della natura femminile," in *Nel nome della razza: Il razzismo nella storia d'Italia 1870–1945*, ed. A. Burgio (Bologna: il Mulino, 2000), 475–89; and B. Wanrooij, "'La carne vedova': Immagini delle sessualità femminile," *Belfagor* 42, no. 4 (1987): 454–56.

75. According to Mario Mieli, within a heterosexual male chauvinist ideology, the active partner in a homosexual relationship can define himself "doubly male" because he is a person who "feels heterosexual twice over: he reassures himself of this and would knock the teeth out of anyone who called him a 'fairy'"; see Mieli, *Elementi di critica omosessuale* (Milan: Feltrinelli, 2002 [1977]), 129–30.

76. George Chauncey, in his study of male homosexual subculture in New York, found that up until the end of the Second World War, of the men studied, those who had sexual relationships with other men did not feel that their virility was threatened if they had the active role; see Chauncey, *Gay New York: Gender, Urban Culture, and the Making of the Gay Male World, 1890–1940* (New York: Basic Books, 1994). The antithesis between active and passive, between virile and effeminate, was not therefore only a characteristic of Mediterranean countries, although it probably lasted longer there; see G. Dall'Orto, "Mediterranean Homosexuality," in W. R. Dynes, ed., *Encyclopedia of Homosexuality* (New York: Garland, 1990), 2:796–98; and R. Trumbach, "Gender and the Homosexual Role in Modern Western Culture: The 18th and 19th Centuries Compared," in Altman, *Homosexuality, Which Homosexuality?* 149–70.

77. Proteus, "Recensione ad Amore verso persone del proprio sesso," *Rassegna di studi sessuali* 4 (1922): 242.

78. A. E. Housman, "Praefanda," *Hermes* (October 1931), 208.

79. M. A. Raffalovich, *L'uranismo: Inversione sessuale congenita. Il processo Oscar Wilde* (Turin: Bocca, 1896), 7.

80. A. Gide, *Corydon* (Milan: Tea, 1995 [1920]). In the book Gide stressed his disgust of sexual inversion, effeminacy, and sodomy and tried to demonstrate the compatibility between pederasty, masculinity, and martial values.

81. M. Proust, *In Search of Lost Time* (New York: Modern Library, 2003), in particular volume 4, *Sodom and Gomorrah* (1922). On Proust's attempt to establish an equivalence between homosexuality and Jewishness see H. Arendt, *Le origini del totalitarismo* (Milan: Edizioni di Comunità, 1997[1951]), 113–19; J. Recanati, *Profils Juifs de Marcel Proust* (Paris: Buchet-Chastel, 1979); and Mosse, *Nationalism and Sexuality*, 137–38.

82. In 1897 Proust challenged the writer Jean Lorrain to a duel because the latter accused him of being homosexual. Just around ten years later Proust was ready to challenge another friend who hadn't denied similar insinuations emphatically enough.

83. See A. De Blasio, "La secrezione lattea nei pederasti passivi," *Archivio di psichiatria, scienze penali ed antropologia criminale* 25 (1904): 152–54.

84. Massarotti, *Nel regno di Ulrichs*, 11. The same attitude was used with respect to lesbians, subdivided, in turn, into active and passive partners; in other words, the masculine partner and feminine partner. Their body structure was analyzed to see whether a

highly developed clitoris was the cause of their hypervirlity; see N. Milletti, "Analoghe sconcezze," 61. On how much this model was interiorized by the lesbians see S. Aleramo, *Lettere d'amore a Lina* (Rome: Savelli, 1982).

85. On the diagnosis of pederasty on the basis of the physical and morphological characteristics of the anus, see L. Martinau, *Le deformazioni vulvari ed anali prodotte dal Saffismo, dalla Deflorazione e dalla Sodomia* (Rome: Capaccini, 1896); and G. Ziino, entry "Stupro e attentati contro il pudore e il buon costume," heading 4, "Della venere contro natura," in *Il digesto italiano: Enciclopedia metodica e alfabetica di legislazione, dottrina e giurisprudenza diretta da Luigi Lucchini* (Turin: Utet, 1899–1903), 22:951–63. For a criticism of this approach and on the lack of probative value of these signs, see F. Pacini, *Di alcuni pregiudizi in medicina legale* (Florence: Tipografia cooperativa, 1876), 2; and M. Carrara, "I caratteri locali della violenza carnale e delle perversioni sessuali," *Riforma medica* 19 (1922): 440–41.

86. F. Corinaldesi, "In tema di deflorazione (perizia extra-giudiziale)," *Archivio di antropologia criminale psichiatria e medicina legale*, annual supplement (1936): 207.

87. See G. Falco, "Su alcune anomalie sessuali," *Rivista di Medicina Legale e di Giurisprudenza Medica* 7-8 (July–August 1919): 100–106, and 9–10 (September–October 1919): 133–37. Falco continued to support the need to "prune the forest of so-called sure signs of passive pederasty that have been handed down to us especially from Tardieu and his pupils" (Falco, *La sessuologia nel codice penale italiano* [Milan: Società palermitana editoria medica, 1935], 158).

88. G. L. Mosse, *Toward the Final Solution: A History of European Racism* (New York: H. Fertig, 1978).

89. Mosse, *Nationalism and Sexuality*, 187.

90. M. Pollak, "Male Homosexuality—or Happiness in the Ghetto," in *Western Sexuality: Practice and Precept in Past and Present Times*, ed. P. Ariès and A. Béjin (New York: Basil Blackwell, 1985), 40–61.

91. In his confession to Paolo Mantegazza, a homosexual confirmed that "any pederast who is endowed with self-respect refrains as much as possible from satisfying his desires not so much because he fears the provisions of the criminal code but because he is concerned about his public reputation" (Mantegazza, *Gli amori degli uomini*, 14th ed. [Milan: Ed. Mantegazza, 1910 (1885)], 285).

92. See Mussolini, "Il compito dei medici"; Mussolini delivered the speech at the inauguration of the National Congress of the Fascist Doctors' Syndicate.

93. R. Maiocchi, *Scienza italiana e razzismo fascista* (Florence: La Nuova Italia, 1999), 57–64, and *Scienza e fascismo* (Rome: Carocci, 2004), 139–204. On the mobilization of doctors implemented by the regime and on their readiness to actively work in order to achieve the regime's aims, see also A. Morelli, "La 'missione' del medico negli anni '30," in *Libere professioni e fascismo*, ed. G. Turi (Milan: Franco Angeli, 1994), 139–75.

94. See R. A. Nye, *Masculinity and Male Codes of Honor in Modern France* (New York: Oxford University Press, 1993). According to Nye, when French sexology is compared with the sexology of the rest of Europe, considerable differences emerge that help explain why in this sphere France contributed only marginally to the modern views of sexuality based on understanding and tolerance. The bourgeois ideals of male honor markedly

influenced the determination of a rigid image of masculinity and created social reactions to perversions based on the projection of deeply felt male anxieties about the bodies and souls of those who had unconventional sexual habits (100). In my opinion, the same can be said for Italy. The two countries shared a profound aversion to pederasty, which was looked upon with far greater indulgence in other countries.

95. I. Bloch, *La vita sessuale dei nostri tempi nei suoi rapporti con la civiltà moderna* (Turin: Sten, 1913), 1.

96. See J. Boswell, *Christianity, Social Tolerance, and Homosexuality: Gay People in Western Europe from the Beginning of the Christian Era to the Fourteenth Century* (Chicago: University of Chicago Press, 1980). Boswell demonstrates how in ancient times people did not feel the need to to explain the etiology of homosexuality, because this type of behavior was not considered strange or abnormal. On this interpretation cf. M. Kuefler, ed., *The Boswell Thesis: Essays on Christianity, Social Tolerance, and Homosexuality* (Chicago: University of Chicago Press, 2006).

97. See A. Niceforo, *Le psicopatie sessuali acquisite e i reati sessuali* (Turin: Bocca, 1898).

98. Mantegazza, *Gli amori degli uomini*, 148–53.

99. La Cara, *La base organica dei pervertimenti sessuali*, 10–13. The link between old age and perversion had already been postulated by Silvio Venturi in his book *Le degenerazioni psico-sessuali* (Turin: Bocca, 1892) and was largely based on considerations made by Arthur Schopenhauer in *The World as Will and Representation* [1884]. According to the German philosopher, this "hateful and utterly revolting monstrosity" was nature's remedy for preserving the species from the damage caused by procreating at an elderly age and thus encouraged pederasty, "something totally foreign to and inconceivable at a virile age"; see Schopenhauer, *Metaphysics of Love of the Sexes*, in *The Works of Schopenhauer*, ed. W. Durant (New York: Simon and Schuster, 1928).

100. La Cara, *La base organica dei pervertimenti sessuali*, 18, 105.

101. See G. Viola, *La costituzione individuale* (Bologna: Cappelli, 1932).

102. See N. Pende, "I fattori biopatologici della criminalità," *La scuola positiva*, pt. 1 (1935): 315, "Le applicazioni della endocrinologia allo studio dei criminali," *La scuola positiva*, pt. 1 (1923): 145ff., "La biotipologia umana," *Scienza e vita* 2 (1924), and ed., *Trattato di biotipologia individuale e sociale* (Milan: Vallardi, 1939).

103. See N. Pende, "Endocrinologia e psicologia," *La medicina italiana* 2 (1920): 7–15, and "La scheda biotipologica individuale nella medicina preventiva e nella politica sociale," *Atti della Società Italiana per il Progresso delle Scienze*, Venice, September 12–18, 1937 (1938), 283–86.

104. N. Pende, "La scienza dell'ortogenesi," *Difesa sociale* (March 1940): 257.

105. Pende, member of the High Council for Public Health Education and enrolled in the PNF from April 1924, was appointed medical consul of the MVSN and subsequently made senator; see Archivio centrale dello Stato, Casellario politico centrale (hereafter ACS, CPC), b. 1005, f. 509.058 "Pende Gr. Uff. Prof. Nicola." On Pende's relationship with the Fascist regime and the link between his ideas and the racist theories proposed by the regime, see G. Cosmacini, "Clinici, biologi, igienisti ebrei e la "nuova medicina dell'Italia Imperiale," in *Cultura ebraica e cultura scientifica in Italia*, ed. A. Di Meo (Rome:

Editori Riuniti, 1994), 69–82; G. Cosmacini, "Scienza e ideologia nella medicina del Novecento," in *Storia d'Italia: Annali 7. Malattia e medicina*, ed. F. Della Peruta (Turin: Einaudi, 1984), 1262–68; G. Israel and P. Nastasi, *Scienza e razza nell'Italia fascista* (Bologna: il Mulino, 1998), 210–25, 274–86; Maiocchi, *Scienza italiana e razzismo fascista*, 31–57, 225–41; A. Gillette, *Racial Theories in Fascist Italy* (London: Routledge, 2002); and C. Pogliano, *L'ossessione della razza: Antropologia e genetica nel XX secolo* (Pisa: Edizioni della Normale, 2005).

106. Qtd. in E. Garin, *Cronache di filosofia italiana 1900–1943* (Bari: Laterza, 1955), 493–94.

107. N. Pende, *Scienza dell'ortogenesi* (Bergamo: Ist. italiano arti grafiche, 1938), 10.

108. According to Pende one of the main factors of homosexuality was a pathological hyperfunctioning of the thymus gland, particularly if associated with constitutional hyperthyroidism; see his "Deviazione dell'istinto sessuale nei soggetti ipertimici," in various authors, *Tre lezioni di sessuologia* (Rome: Castaldi, 1931), 26–31.

109. See N. Pende, *Endocrinologia: Patologia e clinica degli organi a secrezione interna* (Milan: Società editrice libraria, 1949 [1916]), 271.

110. N. Pende, preface to G. Marañon, *L'evoluzione della sessualità e gli stati intersessuali* (Bologna: Zanichelli, 1934 [1929]), vi.

111. In 1938 the government approved the foundation of the institute for human regeneration and orthogenesis of the race, of which Pende was appointed director, see ACS, Segreteria particolare del duce, Carteggio ordinario (hereafter SPD, CO), f. 509.168/2, "Milano Reale Società di Igiene," s.f. "Istituto centrale di bonifica umana, di ortogenesi e di terapia naturista." Regarding the influence of Pende on the initiatives organized by the regime on race and orthogenesis, see A. Mignemi, "Profilassi sanitaria e politiche sociali nel regime per la 'tutela della stirpe.' La 'mise en scéne' dell'orgoglio di razza," in *La menzogna della razza: documenti e immagini del razzismo e dell'antisemitismo fascista*, ed. D. Bidussa (Bologna: il Mulino, 1994).

112. See E. Steinach, *Vita e sesso: Un capitolo di endocrinologia sessuale* (Milan: Mondadori, 1941).

113. G. Lombroso-Ferrero, *La genesi e la cura dei reati sessuali nella endocrinologia* (Rome, 1924). The same opinion was expressed by Mario Carrara who suggested operating on homosexuals and then having them follow a pharmacological cure based on organotherapy.

114. De Napoli, *Sesso e amore*, 192–93.

115. See E. Tinto, *Innesti Voronoff e fenomeni sessuali* (Rome: Edoardo Tinto ed., 1930); and G. Bizzarrini, *Gli innesti animali e la loro distinzione secondo Giard: Alcune osservazioni su quanto scrive Voronoff* (Siena: S. Bernardino, 1938). In 1944 the Danish endocrinologist Karl Vernaet, affirming that such practices were already widely used in concentration camps, requested authorization to emasculate and then use homosexuals interned in Nazi concentration camps for his experiments involving the implantation of artificial glands and the transplantation of hormones.

116. On the way Mussolini used this word as a synonym for "seeming younger and more virile," see A. Simonini, *Il linguaggio di Mussolini* (Milan: Bompiani, 1978), 25. For

some opinions expressed regarding Voronoff's experiments, see P. Buonuomo La Rossa, "Il problema del 'ringiovanimento,'" *Rassegna di studi sessuali* 6 (1922): 349–54; U. Cerletti, "In tema di ringiovanimento," *Gerarchia*, June 6, 1923, 1050–52, and July 7, 1923, 1114–18; G. Cesena, "Le recenti ricerche di S. Voronoff," *Difesa sociale*, March 3, 1924, 71–72; and N. Pende, "La verità scientifica su Voronoff e le sue esperienze," *Gazzetta degli Ospedali e delle Cliniche* 9 (1924).

117. Morselli, *Sessualità umana*, 49; see also his "Gli innesti di Voronoff e la neuropsichiatria," *Quaderni di psichiatria* 5–6 (1924). For Giuseppe Vidoni's hormone-based theory as an explanation of homosexuality, see G. Vidoni, "Contributo allo studio delle dismorfie endocrine: Continuazione e fine," *Archivio di antropologia criminale* 41 (1921): 545–671.

118. In order to disprove the validity of these experiments, some decided to transplant a testicle from a homosexual to a heterosexual man to see if he would lose his attraction to women. Others, to avoid the emotional effects, performed these transplants of testicles on homosexuals who were led to think they were undergoing a hernia operation. On the different applications of these endocrinological experiments, see P. Rondoni, *Sessualità e ringiovanimento secondo le ricerche sperimentali moderne* (Bologna: Zanichelli, 1922).

119. See Marañon, *L'evoluzione della sessualità e gli stati intersessuali*. Marañon's theories were taken up and developed by another important scholar of homosexuality, Leonidio Ribeiro, who received the Lombroso award and was appointed director of the Institute for Identification in Rio de Janeiro; see L. Ribeiro, *Omosessualità e endocrinologia* (Milan: Bocca, 1940).

120. See Proteus, *Anomalie sessuali e ghiandole endocrine* (Rome: Edoardo Tinto ed., 1928).

121. O. Weininger, *Sesso e carattere* (Turin: Bocca, 1912 [1903]). For Weininger's theory of bisexuality, see also M. Lodi, *La teoria della bisessualità di Otto Weininger: Saggio critico* (Bologna: Clueb, 1990); and C. Sengoopta, *Otto Weininger: Sex, Science, and Self in Imperial Vienna* (Chicago: University of Chicago Press, 2000).

122. The inventory of the books from the Duce's library is kept in the state archives. On the influence of Weininger in Italy and how Fascism adopted his ideas, see A. Cavaglion, *Otto Weininger in Italia* (Rome: Carucci, 1982). Most of all, Mussolini appreciated Weininger's considerations on the nature and influence of women and, speaking with Emil Ludwig, he said, "Weininger was right on the main point, although he exaggerated in the end. He clarified many things for me" (Ludwig, *Colloqui con Mussolini* [Milan: Mondadori, 2001 (1932)], 147).

123. Marañon, *L'evoluzione della sessualità e gli stati intersessuali*, 143.

124. See De Napoli, *Sesso e amore*, and "La bisessualità latente come carattere individuale costante e consecutiva opoterapia antiomosessuale," *Rassegna di studi sessuali* 4 (1923): 229–45.

125. De Napoli, *Sesso e amore*, 493. According to De Napoli, from a somatic point of view, the original hermaphroditism of the embryo usually disappeared at the third month of life in the womb, while it disappeared from the mind with puberty. In hermaphrodites this process did not occur, whereas in homosexuals the original bisexuality resurfaced and the gender characteristics reappeared, atrophied and latent.

126. See De Napoli, "La bisessualità latente," 242–43. According to De Napoli, the cure for sexual inversion—"the most miserable of the various deformations of sexual instinct and erotic sentiment"—should be endocrinological, not psychological, and should consist of administering, by means of testicular organotherapy in males and ovaric organotherapy in females, "the elements missing with respect to the sex the individual was supposed to be."

127. According to Alberto Cavaglion, "only by keeping in mind the Weininger-Freud combination, and only if we consider the former a sort of 'poor man's Freud,' will it be possible to grasp the reason behind the incredible popularity of *Sesso e carattere* and *Intorno alle cose supreme*; it is an epidemic that has not taken place in other European cultures, which right from the start, have been more willing to accept the psychoanalytical doctrine" (Cavaglion, *Otto Weininger in Italia*, 19).

128. According to Michel David, the influence of Marañon "as a substitute for Freud" in our country was considerable because "in him there was something of Freud and something of Jung with biological overtones that were more familiar to Italian scientists" (M. David, *La psicoanalisi nella cultura italiana* [Turin: Boringhieri, 1974], 22). On Marañon's relationship with Freud see G. Marañon, *Il problema dei sessi* (Rome: Astrolabio, 1945), 18–19.

129. Michele Levi was one of the strongest supporters of the bisexuality theory. He advocated the substitution of the *uniqueness* of the sexes with the tenet of *intersexuality*; see M. Levi, *Elementi per uno studio clinico dell'intersessualità* (Bologna: Cappelli, 1936). On Marañon's debt to Weininger, see M. F. Canella, introduction to Marañon, *L'evoluzione dell'intersessualità e degli stati intersessuali*, xix–xxi.

130. On Weininger's success in Italy thanks to his reference to the works of Lombroso, see N. Harrowitz, "Lombroso come fonte per Weininger: una questione di influenza," in G. Sampaolo, *Otto Weininger e la differenza: Fantasmi della ragione nella Vienna del primo Novecento* (Milan: Guerini e Associati, 1995), 99–110.

131. See G. Tallarico, "Virilizzare l'uomo femminilizzare la donna," *Razza e civiltà* 5–7 (July–September 1942), 203–13.

132. Signorelli, *Sesso, intersesso, supersesso*, 33–34.

133. Ibid., 52.

134. Ibid., 78. On the image of Mussolini as combining the best characteristics of masculinity and femininity, see L. Passerini, "Costruzione del femminile e del maschile. Dicotomia sociale e androginia simbolica," in *Il regime fascista: Storia e storiografia*, ed. A. Del Boca, M. Legnani, and M. G. Rossi (Rome: Laterza, 1995), 498–506.

135. Preface to Raffalovich, *L'uranismo*, 8. According to the author, inverts from birth, being less inclined to vice than perverts, deserved greater respect. Therefore, doctors treating inversion had to be very careful not to transform inversion into perversion, creating "womanizers" or unhappy husbands and fathers; consequently, chastity and not the imposition of a "normal" sexuality was the only remedy for homosexuality.

136. G. Moglie, *Manuale di psichiatria ad uso dei medici e degli studenti* (Rome: Pozzi editore, 1940 [1930]), 233.

137. Ibid., 234; see also Moglie's *La psicopatologia forense ad uso dei medici, dei giuristi e degli studenti in conformità ai nuovi codici* (Rome: Pozzi, 1938).

138. See L. Ellero, "Smarrita gente. Perizie medico-legali," in *Opere* (Bologna: Zanichelli, 1927), 2:83–91, an examination of Erminio Fiori, hospitalized in 1908 for the psychopathic syndrome typical of an exhilarated maniac. See also A. Murri, *Saggio di perizie medico-legali* (Bologna: Zanichelli, 1928).

139. See G. G. Perrando, "Impotenza psichica o psicopatica motivo di annullamento matrimoniale: Note ad una perizia," *Archivio di antropologia criminale* 47 (1927): 905–47. Perrando suggested considering serious degenerative constitutional cases, such as homosexuality, sufficient reason to annul a marriage; the proposal, however, was not accepted in all courts.

140. Eugenio Tanzi, one of Italy's most famous neurologists, included homosexuality among mental illnesses because those whose homosexuality was not temporary but total and definitive were "paranoic imbecilles" whose illness depended on a "sexual color-blindness" and their inability to bring the "aim of love" into focus because their sexual instinct had suffered an arrest during childhood; see E. Tanzi and E. Lugaro, *Trattato delle malattie mentali* (Milan: Società editrice libraria, 1923 [1914]).

141. S. De Sanctis and S. Ottolenghi, *Trattato pratico di psicopatologia forense per uso dei medici, giuristi e studenti* (Milan: Società editrice libraria, 1920), 1:371.

142. Morselli, *Sessualità umana*, 164. For the works of Morselli, see P. Guarnieri, *Individualità difformi: La psichiatria antropologica di Enrico Morselli* (Milan: Franco Angeli, 1986).

143. For a detailed study of these matters, see L. Benadusi, "Per una storia dell'omosessualità nell'Italia del Novecento: Gli studi psicanalitici," *Storia e problemi contemporanei* 37 (September–December 2004): 183–203.

144. David, *La psicoanalisi nella cultura italiana*, 14.

145. See S. Freud, *Tre saggi sulla teoria della sessualità* (Milan: Mondadori, 1970 [1905]); published in English as *A Case of Hysteria: Three Essays on the Theory of Sexuality and Other Works*, ed. James Strachey (London: Vintage, 2001). According to Freud, homosexuality was a form of narcissism and was due to an arrest of sexual development during childhood caused by the individual's escape from the Oedipus complex, through which the fear of incest determined the renunciation of one's own sex.

146. See G. Modena, "Psicopatologia ed etiologia dei fenomeni psiconeurotici: Contributo alla dottrina di S. Freud," *Rivista sperimentale di freniatria e medicina legale delle alienazioni mentali* 45, no. 34 (1908): 657–70, and 46, no. 35 (1909): 204–18.

147. Ibid., 215.

148. R. G. Assaglioli, "Trasformazione e sublimazione delle energie sessuali," *Rivista di Psicologia Applicata* 7 (1910): 228–36. *La Voce* had already published an article by Assaglioli that reported Freud's ideas about sexuality and homosexuality and expressed appreciation of "the extraordinary practical importance" of the new theory on psychoanalysis; see R. G. Assaglioli, "Le idee di Sigmund Freud sulla sessualità," *La Voce* 9, "La questione sessuale," February 10, 1910, 262–63.

149. See G. Prezzolini, "Un po' di bibliografia," *La Voce* 9 (February 10, 1910).

150. See David, *La psicoanalisi nella cultura italiana*, 29–51; and P. C. Masini, "Una inchiesta della polizia fascista sulla scuola psicoanalitica," in *Mussolini: La maschera del dittatore* (Pisa: Biblioteca Franco Serantini, 1999), 127–37.

151. E. Weiss, *Elementi di psicoanalisi* (Pordenone: Studio Tesi, 1985 [1931]).

152. From an article by Bragaglia that appeared in *Critica fascista*, November 15, 1932, qtd. in David, *La psicoanalisi nella cultura italiana*, 51.

153. See M. Durst, "Gli studi di psicologia nell'Enciclopedia Italiana," in *La psicologia in Italia: I protagonisti e i problemi scientifici, filosofici e istituzionali (1870–1945)*, ed. G. Cimino and N. Dazzi (Milan: Led, 1998), 609–50.

154. Servadio, who had tackled the subject of sexuality as soon as he began working with the esoteric group Ur, believed psychoanalysis could be of great importance for sexology. He deserves credit, among other things, for having focused attention on child sexuality, for having discovered the origin of many perversions, for not having limited the sexuality to the functions of the genitals, and for considering sexuality a fundamental aspect in the origin of several types of psychoneuroses and some psychotic forms; E. Servadio, "Psicoanalisi e sessuologia," *Rivista di psicologia: Normale e patologica* 4 (October–December 1936): 219–25.

155. See David, *La psicoanalisi nella cultura italiana*, 257–59. According to David, "Freud's influence in Italy on sexual matters for the first fifty years of the twentieth century should not be overestimated," because only a few individual cases were actually affected, while there was virtually no influence at the community level.

156. C. Musatti, entry "omosessualità," in *Dizionario di criminologia*, ed. E. Florian, A. Niceforo, and N. Pende (Milan: Vallardi, 1943), 2:602–3.

157. Ibid.

158. See G. Dall'Orto, "Un pioniere gay: Aldo Mieli," *Babilonia* 57 (June 1988): 52–54.

159. "Statuto della Società italiana per lo studio delle questioni sessuali," in the appendix to H. Ellis, *Lo scopo dell'eugenica* (Rome: Leonardo da Vinci, 1922).

160. "We shall avoid taking final decisions in any particular sense; we believe, in fact, that in science all opinions should be accepted and assessed. To stop in the face of certain crystalized forms would be in contradiction with the very principles of scientific inquiry, whether expressing ultraconservative conventionalism or subversive liberalism," "Società italiana per lo studio delle questioni sessuali," *Rassegna di studi sessuali* 6 (1922), 273.

161. See Wanrooij, *Storia del pudore*, 96.

162. See ACS, CPC, b. 3271, f. 24106, "Aldo Mieli." According to the police, Mieli had a "subtle personality, was quite well educated and of mediocre intelligence"; from April 2, 1911, he was no longer watched, because for several years he had not been active in politics.

163. See C. Pogliano, "Aldo Mieli, storico della scienza (1879–1950)," *Belfagor* 5 (September 30, 1983): 546.

164. A. Mieli, preface to *Il libro dell'amore* (Firenze 1916), qtd. in Dall'Orto, "Un pioniere gay," 54.

165. According to Claudio Pogliano, Mieli feared that the absolute supremacy of

idealism would "end by censuring a group of subjects in the areas considered to be 'low' human experiences" (Pogliano, "Aldo Mieli," 548).

166. According to Mieli "not only where homoeroticism is concerned but in many other matters connected with the sexual problem, superstition and prejudice are present and errors are made"; the job of educators is not, then, "to repeat things they have heard people say without any foundation but continue studying the matter, always keeping in mind justice and human kindness" (A. Mieli, "Per una educazione degli educatori," *Rassegna di studi sessuali* 1 [1922]: 41).

167. A. Mieli, "Ai lettori," *Rassegna di studi sessuali* 1 (1921): 3.

168. Among the most notable were Assaglioli, Baglioni, Carrara, Corso, De Pisis, Ellis, Ferrando, Ferri, Foà, Hirschfeld, Levi-Bianchini, Levi, Limentani, Michels, Morselli, Ottolenghi, Pende, Prezzolini, Sergi, Tavolato, and Varisco.

169. See C. Susani, "Una critica alla norma nell'Italia del fascismo," in E. Venturelli, ed., "Le parole e la storia: Ricerche su omosessualità e cultura," in *Quaderni di critica omosessuale* 9 (Bologna: Il Cassero, 1991), 112. I don't agree entirely with the idea that *Rassegna* was, in the intention of its editor, an extremist publication. Mainly because the creation of strong ties with the "movement for the liberation of homosexuals" could have limited the publication's circulation and damaged its highly scientific profile.

170. Susani and Dall'Orto hypothesize that Proteus was Mieli, whereas Wanrooij thinks that Pende was behind the pseudonym; see Wanrooij, *Storia del pudore*, 212.

171. Proteus, in reviewing Pende's book *Le debolezze di costituzione. Introduzione alla patologia costituzionale* (Rome 1922), reported on and praised the way homosexuality was conceived, but he stressed the need to place greater relevance on the distinction between a homoerotic tendency and homosexual acts; see Proteus, review of N. Pende, "Le debolezze di costituzione," *Rassegna di studi sessuali* 6 (1922), 366–67.

172. The Latin term *proteus* refers intentionally to a soothsaying marine god who undergoes multiple transformations. It is also a synonym for a fickle or wily man.

173. A. Mieli, review of S. Placzek, *Das Geschlechtsleben des Menschen*, *Rassegna di studi sessuali* 2 (1926): 202.

174. See A. Mieli, "Sociabilità, famiglia e sessualità in un libro recente," review of H. Blüher, *Die Rolle der Erotik in der männlichen Geschellschaft*, *Rassegna di studi sessuali* 1 (1921): 29–40.

175. A. Mieli, review of H. Licht, *Beiträge zur antiken Erotik*, *Rassegna di studi sessuali* 4 (1925): 163.

176. See G. Franceschini, *La vita sessuale* (Milan: Hoepli, 1923), and *Igiene sessuale ad uso dei giovani e delle scuole* (Milan: Hoepli, 1929).

177. A. Mieli, "Un fatto di cronaca e le amenità di un cronista," *Rassegna di studi sessuali* 1 (1922): 39–41.

178. Proteus, "La legge degli errori e l'indirizzo costituzionalistico in sessuologia," *Rassegna di studi sessuali* 6 (1921): 300–312, and "Moralità e sessualità," *Rassegna di studi sessuali* 6 (1922): 333–349; later combined in Proteus, *Moralità e sessualità* (Rome: Edoardo Tinto, 1928).

179. Proteus, "Le nuove vedute sulla genesi e sul significato dell'istinto sessuale," *Rassegna di studi sessuali* 3 (1921): 129.

180. See Proteus, "Secrezione interna e sessualità," *Rassegna di studi sessuali* 5 (1921): 239-53.

181. Ibid., 253.

182. Proteus, "A proposito di un nuovo libro sulle anomalie sessuali," *Rassegna di studi sessuali* 4 (1921): 177.

183. Proteus wrote: "Deviations from normal processes, the so-called abnormalities make up the biological variants according to the Gauss-Quatelet law on organically based anomalies and pathological events: in other words, categories of phenomena that I find it hard to qualify as moral or immoral. Is a healthy man a moral man and a sick man immoral? Is a man of average height moral and a dwarf or a giant immoral?" (Proteus, "Moralità e sessualità," 6).

184. Ibid., 11.

185. Ibid., 12-13.

186. Ibid., 22. According to Proteus, "except for cases of offense to another person's physical and moral character, the classification into moral or immoral did not apply to manifestations of sexuality" (23).

187. Ibid., 25. These concepts were to be developed a few years later in the *Rassegna di studi sessuali* by the Polish anthropologist Bronislaw Malinowski, who deserves credit for developing the foundations of cultural relativism; see B. Malinowski, "Antropologia e scienza sessuale," *Rassegna di studi sessuali, demografia ed eugenica* 1 (1929): 105-8, and *Etica e vita dei selvaggi: Amore matrimonio e vita familiare presso gli indigeni delle isole Trobriand, Nuova Guinea inglese. Descrizione etnografica* (Milan: Palladis, 1932), published in English as *The Sexual Life of Savages in North-Western Melanesia: An Ethnographic Account of Courtship, Marriage, and Family Life among the Natives of the Trobriand Islands, British New Guinea* (London: Routledge and Kegan Paul, 1929).

188. Proteus, "Moralità e sessualità," 27.

189. Ibid., 28.

190. Ibid., 29.

191. Ibid., 29-30. Proteus had already denounced the climate of *"social persecution"* that homosexuals were subjected to.

192. Ibid., 30.

193. Pende's relationship with the regime was fairly sound; in 1925 Pende took part in the Meeting for Fascist Culture or the Meeting of the Fascist Institutes of Culture; see the list of participants qtd. in E. R. Papa, *Fascismo e cultura* (Venice: Marsilio, 1974), 161-62.

194. For a criticism of Proteus's position see L. Limentani, "Appunti sopra l'onore sessuale," *Rassegna di studi sessuali* 1 (1923): 26-32. On the concept of sexual inversion as "an evil symptom of social degeneration and an abnormality of the biopsychic functions," toward which it was necessary not to be indulgent, see F. Travagli, "L'istinto sessuale della donna moderna," *Rassegna di studi sessuali* 2 (1927): 72-78; and E. Morselli, "Continenza, astinenzae moralità," *Rassegna di studi sessuali* 1 (1927): 31.

195. Review of A. Gide, *Corydon*, in *Rassegna di studi sessuali* 2 (1925): 78. Subsequently, Santino Caramella also treated the matter in "Problema dell'omosessualità nell'opera di André Gide," published in *Rassegna*.

196. Proteus, "A proposito di un nuovo libro sulle anomalie sessuali," 179.

197. Proteus, "Secrezione interna e sessualità," 250.

198. A. Mieli, review of E. Morselli, *La psicoanalisi*, and H. Stoltenhoff, *Kurzes Lehrbuch der Psychoanalyse*, *Rassegna di studi sessuali* 2 (1926): 207.

199. See E. Carpenter, *The Intermediate Sex* (London: Swan Sonnenschein, 1908).

200. G. Ferrando, "Edward Carpenter e il problema sessuale," *Rassegna di studi sessuali* 3 (1921): 143. Carpenter, one of the founders of English socialism, was actually the first scholar who saw homosexuality as being based on love and a loving relationship, shifting the attention to sentiment. In his opinion, homosexuals did not need to be cured, and certainly not punished, but helped to understand their nature.

201. Carpenter, *The Intermediate Sex*, qtd. in J. Lauritsen and D. Thorstad, "Il primo movimento per i diritti degli omosessuali (1864–1935)," in various authors, *Gay gay: Storia e coscienza omosessuale* (Milan: La Salamandra, 1976), 81. On Carpenter, see S. Rowbotham and J. Weeks, *Socialism and the New Life: The Personal and Sexual Politics of Edward Carpenter and Havelock Ellis* (London: Pluto Press, 1977).

202. A number of studies have been devoted to Hirschfeld and the activities of the CSU; the most rigorous from a historical point of view include E. Mancini, *Magnus Hirschfeld and the Quest for Sexual Freedom: A History of the First International Sexual Freedom Movement* (New York: Palgrave, 2010); C. Wolff, *Magnus Hirschfeld: A Portrait of a Pioneer in Sexuology* (London: Quartet, 1986); J. Lauritsen and D. Thorstad, *Per una storia del movimento dei diritti omosessuali (1864–1935)* (Perugia: Savelli, 1979), originally published as *The Early Homosexual Rights Movement (1864–1935)* (New York: Times Change Press, 1974); and J. D. Steakley, *The Homosexual Emancipation Movement in Germany* (New York: Arno Press, 1975).

203. Hirschfeld, who even before Hitler's rise to power had been attacked and threatened because of his activity and because he was a homosexual Jew, was obliged to leave Germany in 1933 after the Nazis closed down the institute and burned the entire library. He sought refuge in France.

204. See M. Hirschfeld, "La riforma sessuale su base scientifica: Discorso d'apertura del I Congresso internazionale per la riforma sessuale," *Rassegna di studi sessuali* 5 (1921): 229–38. Hirschfeld showed the congress participants Richard Oswald's film *Andres als die Andere* (Different from others), in oppostion to article 175 of the criminal code. The film also described the lives of homosexuals.

205. A. Mieli, "Tentativi di riforma sessuale in Italia," *Rassegna di studi sessuali* 5 (1921): 266. See also his "Congresso Internazionale per la riforma sessuale basata su fondamenti scientifici tenuto a Berlino dal 15 al 19 settembre 1921," *Rassegna di studi sessuali* 5 (1921): 222–23.

206. For Mieli's impressions after his stay in Berlin, including his visits to popular homosexual haunts, see his "Un viaggio in Germania. Impressioni e appunti di uno storico della scienza," *Archivio di storia della scienza* 4 (1926): 342–81.

207. Ibid., 344–45.

208. Qtd. in Pogliano, "Aldo Mieli," 550.

209. Because of Germany's financial problems due to the devaluation of the mark, it was decided to hold the second International Congress on Sexual Reform in Germany and not in Rome, as previously established.

210. Mieli commented favourably on the March 15 conference in 1922 in the Reichstag, held by the "well-known homosexual Hirschfeld" and Kopp, the head of the Berlin police, on the need to remove the paragraph against homosexuals from the new draft of the criminal code. He expressed his full support of the just cause and stated that "the solution to the problem does not lie only within the law, albeit important, but rather in the acknowledgement that there are people who, from a sexual point of view, are different from others. It is in the general interest of all that the efforts of Dr. Hirschfeld and the activity of the CSU, of which we are members, be fully successful" (A. Mieli, "La discussione dell'omosessualità al Reichstag," *Rassegna di studi sessuali* 2 [1922]: 125–26).

211. See A. Mieli, "Patologia sessuale," *Rassegna di studi sessuali* 2 (1921): 81–94. According to Mieli, it was necessary to replace Krafft-Ebing's (1880) book on homosexuality *Psycopathia sexualis*, which by 1918 had reached its fifteenth edition, with Hirschfeld's *Sexual pathologie* (1918–21).

212. Ibid., 86.

213. See Numa Praetorius (according to Dall'Orto, the pseudonym of Eugen Wilhelm, but probably, as Nerina Milletti maintains, the pseudonym chosen by Hirschfeld), "La questione dell'omosessualità in Germania nell'ultimo cinquantennio," *Rassegna di studi sessuali* 3 (1922): 148–57.

214. Ibid., 155.

215. A. Mieli, "Società italiana per lo studio delle questioni sessuali," *Rassegna di studi sessuali* 4 (1926): 322. The Italian society had relations with other similar organizations in The Hague, London, and Prague besides the CSU.

216. This group coordinated by Mieli proposed the study of homosexuality in Italy, guaranteeing professional secrecy and anonymity for anyone helping with the investigation and research of intermediate sexual forms. Doctors, jurists, educators, and law enforcement officials could work together to acquire information on the measurements of homosexuals' bodies, on their overall number, on trials and inquiries that involved sexual inversion, and, in particular, on the violence and blackmailing of homosexuals.

217. Given the political situation in Italy in 1930 it was decided to hold the second International Congress on Sexology in London.

218. See S. Baglioni, "Lo stato attuale degli studi sessuali in Italia," *Rassegna di studi sessuali* 1 (1926): 1–5.

219. In Mieli's opinion, as a result of the resolute legislative activity carried out by the Fascist regime regarding sexuality, the publication *Rassegna* would be able to let people abroad know about the "immense work the government had started doing in the sexual sphere. Apart from how Italy was judged abroad, it had certainly renewed life from head to foot and given Italy a boost that would ensure it a hitherto unknown level of respect"; see A. Mieli, "Legislazione sessuale," *Rassegna di studi sessuali* 4 (1926): 346.

220. In criticizing a "pointlessly sentimental *idealism*," Mieli was also attacking "a political party that believed it was bringing back idealism (without knowing what this word meant philosophically, confusing *idealism* and *ideal*) as the foundation for a sociological and political system devised by lunatics"; see A. Mieli, review of C. Lombroso, "L'uomo delinquente," *Rassegna di studi sessuali* 4 (1924): 288.

221. See A. Mieli, "Il problema della natalità e la tassa sui celibi e Il matrimonio dei sifilitici, dei tubercolosi, degli omosessuali etc.," *Rassegna di studi sessuali* 1 (1922): 37–39. According to Mieli, homosexuals should be discouraged from marrying and having children. The tax on unmarried men should not be introduced, and in the same way it was wrong to encourage population growth through "immoral marriages" without being able to guarantee "a strong and healthy lineage."

222. Mieli, "Legislazione sessuale," 349.

223. See Archivio storico dell'Enciclopedia italiana Giovanni Treccani, correspondence of Nicola Parravano (in charge of the section on chemistry).

224. Pogliano, "Aldo Mieli," 553.

225. The Leonardo da Vinci publishing house produced a series called "Società e sesso" that included books on homosexuality as well as a collection of articles previously published in the journal *Rassegna di studi sessuali*. On the vicissitudes concerning Mieli, his library, and his transfer to France after having setttled charges of bankruptcy thanks to proceeds from the sale of a building that belonged to him, see G. Dall'Orto, "Un pioniere gay."

226. ACS, CPC, b. 3271, f. 24106 "Aldo Mieli." In February 1930 Mieli was listed in the border control index and in the bulletin of subversives hiding abroad as a dangerous socialist who needed to be arrested. Since he did not create any problems from a political point of view, he was able to renew his passport but was still kept under careful surveillance. According to the fiduciary of the Polizia Politica Valerio Benuzzi, Mieli was an "adversary of the Regime, above all of its demographic policy," but even though he was not a Fascist, his political conduct was not cause for great suspicion. ACS, Polizia Politica fascicoli personali (hereafter Pol.Pol.), b. 843, f. "Mieli Aldo."

227. On Mieli's relationship with Chiappini and Pisani and their continuous attempts to exploit his financial assets, see ACS, Pol.Pol., b. 291, f. "Chiappini Gino."

228. A. Mieli, "Digressions autobiographiques," in *Archives internationales d'Histoire des sciences*, qtd. in Dall'Orto, "Un pioniere gay," 54. Mieli died in solitude in Argentina on February 16, 1950, from a brain hemorrhage. The many letters from those who thanked him for his activity are preserved at the University of Buenos Aires. They were proof that his work would never be forgotten by the many homosexuals who found comfort and support in the *Rassegna di studi sessuali*. In scientific circles as well, colleagues greatly appreciated his effort to study sexual inversion. For example, Giuseppe Vidoni acknowledged that "since Aldo Mieli began publishing his *Rassegna di studi sessuali*, the problem of homosexuality has been so widely treated in Italy that to refer to the result of studies and research—past and present—and to repeat the criticism and synthesis of said works would be entirely out of place and out of time" (G. Vidoni, *Per lo studio della prostituzione maschile* [Nocera Inferiore: Tipografia del Manicomio, 1923], 1).

229. Some of the works published on homosexuality by the *Biblioteca dei curiosi* had the following titles: 8) *L'amore omosessuale*; 15) *Filosofia delle psicopatie sessuali*; 21) *Saffo poetessa di Lesbo*; 27) *Anomalie sessuali e ghiandole endocrine*; 32) *La bisessualità latente*; 36) *Moralità e sessualità*; 41) *La riforma sessuale su base scientifica*; 48) *Innesti Voronoff e fenomeni sessuali*; 58) *Tre lezioni di sessuologia*.

230. E. Tinto, *Dizionario di sessuologia* (Rome: Edoardo Tinto, 1932), 1:iii.

231. E. Tinto, *Quinta dispensa del Dizionario di sessuologia*, entry "Anomalie" (Rome: Edoardo Tinto, 1933), 124.

232. Even today in the Biblioteca nazionale in Rome, many books on sexual matters published in the early twentieth century are kept in a separate room called the Biblioteca Riservata.

233. See G. Falco, *La sessuologia nel codice penale italiano*, 8.

234. ACS, *P.S. G1 1912–1945*, b. 24, f. 260, "Lega universale per la riforma sessuale."

Chapter 3. Sodomy: Sin or Crime

1. Pius XI, *Casti Connubi*, December 31, 1930, in *Acta Apostolicae Sedis*, 22:560. On how to divulge the encyclical to the laity, see A. Vermeersch, *Catechismo del matrimonio cristiano secondo l'enciclica "Casti Connubi"* (Turin: Marietti, 1931).

2. On politics as religion, see E. Gentile, *Politics as Religion* (Princeton: Princeton University Press, 2006). On the evolution of the relationship between Church and Fascism, in particular concerning the concept of family, see C. Dau Novelli, *Famiglia e modernizzazione in Italia tra le due guerre* (Rome: Studium, 1994).

3. See also G. Coppelli, *Forti e puri* (Como: Cavalleri, 1941). For the Catholic educational model of a virile, courageous, and heroic Christianity that by means of warlike, military language tried to form a *militia Christi* whose weapons were to be prayer, invocations, and supplications, see F. De Giorgi, "Linguaggi totalitari e retorica dell'intransigenza: Chiesa, metafora militare e strategie educative," in *Chiesa, cultura e educazione in Italia tra le due guerre*, ed. L. Pazzaglia (Brescia: La Scuola, 2003), 55–103; and A. Ponzio, "Corpo e anima: Sport e modello virile nella formazione dei giovani fascisti e dei giovani cattolici dell'Italia degli anni Trenta," *MondoContemporaneo* 3 (2005): 51–104.

4. F. A. Vuillermet, *Siate uomini, alla conquista della virilità* (Turin: Lice, 1930).

5. Ibid., 183.

6. R. De Felice, *Mussolini il duce: Lo Stato totalitario 1936–1940* (Turin: Einaudi, 1996), 144.

7. See M. Foucault, *Power/Knowledge: Selected Interviews and Other Writings 1972–1977* (New York: Harvester Wheatsheaf, 1980).

8. According to Foucault "by making sex into that which, above all else, had to be confessed, the Christian pastoral always presented it as a disquieting enigma: not a thing which stubbornly shows itself, but one which always hides" (Foucault, *History of Sexuality*, 35).

9. P. Lucà Trombetta, *La confessione della lussuria* (Genoa: Costa and Nolan, 1991), 141. On this subject, see also J. Delumeau, *Sin and Fear: The Emergence of a Western Guilt Culture, 13th–18th Centuries* (New York: St. Martin's Press, 1990).

10. See, for example, Giuseppe Antonelli's manual of pastoral medicine, in which sodomy was expressly dealt with; G. Antonelli, *Medicina pastoralis in usum confessariorum et curiarum ecclesiasticarum* (Rome: Pustet, 1920 [1905]), 2:203–5. Also Father Gemelli, in his medical manual for confessors, devoted a chapter to "perversions of the sexual instinct";

see A. Gemelli, *Non moechaberis: Disquisitiones medicae in usum confessariorum* (Milan: Vita e pensiero, 1923 [1910]), chap. 4, "De sexualibus aberrationibus earumque cura."

11. Monsignor Bouvet, *Venere ed imene al Tribunale della penitenza: Manuale dei confessori* (Livorno: L'Informazione, 1994 [1885]).

12. See ibid., 1–2.

13. See ibid., 56–57.

14. See ibid., 65, 68.

15. Don R. Louvel, *Il libro secreto dei preti. Trattato di castità* (Viterbo: Scipioni, 1995) [Milan, 1880], 64.

16. Ibid., 65.

17. See R. Ruiz Amado, *Ai confessori, educatori e padri di famiglia sopra la educazione alla castità* (Turin: Marietti, 1909). Harsh criticism of this exaggerated appraisal of chastity came from Alberto Orsi, who stated that chastity was nothing other than a sexual aberration or the preamble to the most disgusting perversions; see A. Orsi, *Lussuria e castità: Saggio di psicologia del pudore* (Sesto San Giovanni; Madella, 1915).

18. See A. Gemelli, *La tua vita sessuale: Lettera ad uno studente universitario*, 7th ed. (Milan: Vita e Pensiero, 1946 [1941]).

19. Gemelli was against an open debate on some delicate issues such as homosexuality. For this reason he judged the *Rassegna di studi sessuali* a "dangerous journal . . . that, although it contains some good articles, is not recommendable"; see A. Gemelli, "Ciò che può fare la famiglia per l'educazione dei giovani alla purezza," *Vita e pensiero* 13 (1927): 88.

20. Gemelli, *La tua vita sessuale*, 98.

21. A. Gemelli, "Quaestio de hermaphroditis quoad ordines sacros suscipiendos" (1943), qtd. in David, *La psicoanalisi nella cultura italiana*, 104–5.

22. A. Arrighini, *La nuova medicina delle passioni: Ad uso dei Confessori, Educatori e Moralisti* (Turin: Marietti, 1934), 186.

23. See ibid., 158–59.

24. Ibid., 192.

25. The code of canon law promulgated by Benedict XV came into force on May 19, 1918. It was made up of five books, the last of which dealt with criminal law and therefore crimes against public decency and public morality. Article 2058 defined sodomy as follows: "sodomia est coitus carnalis non servata debita diversitate sexsus, seu maris cum mare, aut feminae cum femina"; see *Institutiones iuris canonici ad usum utriusque cleri et scholarum*, vol. 5, *De Delictis et Poenis*.

26. See A. d'Avack, entry "Omosessualità" (diritto canonico), in *Enciclopedia del diritto*, supervised by C. Mortati and F. Santoro-Passarelli (Varese: Giuffrè, 1980), 92–95; and G. Caputo, "Omosessualità e diritto canonico," in *Quaderni di critica omosessuale* 3 (Bologna: Il Cassero, 1988), 60–68.

27. See S. Raiteri, *Venti sentenze della Sacra Rota* (Milan: Barletti Editore, 1973), 167–71; and A. C. Jemolo, *Il matrimonio nel diritto canonico* (Milan: Vallardi, 1941), 325–26. In theory homosexuality could justify dispensation for a marriage ratified but not consummated or an annulment due to impotence only in cases in which there were

mental or bodily defects that, by themselves, were already associated with the presence of sexual inversion.

28. See on this matter L. Crompton, *Byron and Greek Love: Homophobia in Nineteenth-Century England* (London: Faber and Faber, 1985); F. Tamagne, *Histoire de l'homosexualité en Europe* (Paris: Seuil, 2000); and G. Robb, *Strangers: Homosexual Love in the Nineteenth Century* (New York: Norton, 2004).

29. Cesare Beccaria was one of the promoters of this hypothesis: he did not intend to "minimize the horror that these crimes rightly deserve," but to render the punishment against "Attic love" less severe, doing everything possible to prevent it; see C. Beccaria, *Dei delitti e delle pene* (Harlem, 1766), 150ff.

30. In 1791 the French constituent assembly had already decided not to consider sodomy a crime. This innovation was then assimilated into the Napoleonic Code and exported to Italy, Belgium, and Spain. On the legal treatment of homosexuality in Europe, see F. Leroy-Forgeot, *Histoire juridique de l'homosexualité en Europe* (Paris: Puf, 1997). On the codes in Italy before unification, see various authors, *Diritto penale dell'Ottocento: I codici preunitari e il codice Zanardelli* (Padua: Cedam, 1999).

31. G. Raffaelli, "Nomotesia penale, Napoli 1820–1826," 2:113ff., qtd. in R. Canosa, *Sesso e Stato: Devianza sessuale e interventi istituzionali nell'Ottocento italiano* (Milan: Mazzotta, 1981), 113.

32. The Austrian universal criminal code of 1803 (adopted also in Lombardy and the Veneto) punished unnatural libidinous acts with imprisonment ranging from six months to a year. Subsequently, after the brief Napoleonic period, the new code of 1815 brought back homosexuality as a crime. Article 129 of the 1852 code also considered homosexuality a crime. Meanwhile, the Church's state article 178 of the *Regolamento su i delitti e sulle pene*, promulgated on September 20, 1832, by Gregory XVI, punished those "guilty of consummating unnatural sexual intercourse with indefinite imprisonment"; see also C. Caramelli, *Commento al regolamento penale gregoriano* (Macerata: Mancini, 1844).

33. See G. Dall'Orto, "La 'tolleranza repressiva' dell'omosessualità: Quando un atteggiamento legale diviene tradizione," in *Omosessuali e Stato*, ed. Arci gay nazionale (Bologna: Cassero, 1988), 37–57.

34. Article 425 of the criminal code for the Kingdom of Sardinia, dated November 20, 1859, was identical to article 439 of the previous code, dated October 26, 1839.

35. Ziino, "Stupro e attentati contro il pudore e il buon costume." Article 425 established that unnatural libidinous acts committed with violence were punishable by imprisonment for at least seven years, while acts committed without violence were punishable by up to ten years of forced labor.

36. On the modifications introduced by the deputyship's decree of February 17, 1861, to the Sardinian-Piedmontese code and the different proposals to extend it to the rest of the nation without, however, abrogating the article on unnatural libidinous acts, see M. Da Passano, "Il problema dell'unificazione legislativa e l'abrogazione del codice napoletano," in *Codice per il Regno delle Due Sicilie (1819)—Ristampa anastatica* (Padua: Cedam, 1996), lxix–clxiii.

37. "Relazione presentata a S. A. R. il Principe Luogotenente dalla Commissione per gli studii legislativi, istituita con decreto del 6 febbraio 1861," in V. Cosentino, *Il codice penale del 20 novembre 1859 con le successive modifiche per le provincie napoletane–siciliane e quelle generali per tutto il Regno* (Naples: Sarracino, 1879–1880), xiii. On the whole matter, see D. Petrosino, "Omosessualità e diritto: un percorso tra storia, modelli culturali e codice in Italia," *Rivista di sessuologia* 2 (1992), 150.

38. On Mediterranean homosexuality, see G. Dall'Orto, "Mediterranean Homosexuality," in *Encyclopedia of Homosexuality*, ed. W. Dynes (New York: Garland, 1990), 2: 796–98.

39. C. Malaparte, *The Skin* (Marlboro: Marlboro Press, 1988), 127.

40. A. De Blasio, *Usi e costumi dei camorristi* (Naples: Luigi Pierro editore, 1897), 154. Mantegazza also reported that, particularly in Naples, "the pederasts simulate nuptial rites with the same pomp as ordinary weddings and the participants even go so far as to pretend they are pregnant, experience fake births and motherhood" (Mantegazza, *Gli amori degli uomini*, 278). On the *figliata*, see also E. Ballone, *Uguali e diversi: I travestiti come e perché* (Milan: Mazzotta, 1978), 92.

41. See F. Del Greco, *Elemento etnico e psicopatie negli italiani del Mezzogiorno* (Rome: Tip. dell'Unione Coop., 1895). For a critique of this point of view, see F. De Luca, *L'elemento etnico nei reati di libidine: Considerazioni per l'Italia, con speciale riguardo ad alcune città siciliane* (Catania, 1909). The author was trying to confute the idea of those who maintained that the large number of crimes committed against public decency and the many unnatural libidinous acts committed in Catania and Siracusa were due to the Hellenic origin of the Etnean provinces.

42. A. Niceforo, *Italiani del Nord e Italiani del Sud* (Turin: Bocca, 1901), 8.

43. See R. Romanelli, *Il comando impossibile: Stato e società nell'Italia unita* (Bologna: Il Mulino, 1988); on these matters see also G. Galasso, *L'altra Europa, per un'antropologia storica del Mezzogiorno d'Italia* (Milan: Mondadori, 1982); J. Schneider, ed., *Italy's "Southern Question": Orientalism in One Country* (Oxfrord: Berg, 1998); and N. Moe, "'This Is Africa': Ruling and Representing Southern Italy, 1860–1861," in *Making and Remaking Italy: The Cultivation of National Identity around the Risorgimento*, ed. A. R. Ascoli and K. von Henneberg (Oxford: Berg, 2001), 119–53.

44. "Relazione presentata a S.A.R.," viii.

45. For a detailed reconstruction of the debate that led to the decision to decriminalize unnatural libidinous acts committed without violence, see Canosa, *Sesso e Stato*, 114–15.

46. Homosexuality was still considered a crime in the military criminal codes. Both the army (art. 273, army criminal code) and the navy (art. 297, navy military code), in force until 1941, established harsh punishment for unnatural libidinous acts; see S. Messina, "L'omosessualità nel diritto penale," *Ulisse, l'omosessualità e la società moderna* 18 (Spring 1953): 671–76.

47. Zanardelli did not accept the proposal to make a clear distinction between natural rape and unnatural rape, because in this matter it was necessary to maintain as much modesty as possible, and it was better "not to enter into detail and distinctions"; qtd. in

Rivista penale 5–6 (1875): 528–29. Article 331 of the criminal code on sexual assault also involved unnatural rape; in fact, it clearly noted "the violent physical copulation with one person on top of another of the same or a different sex"; whereas article 338, which punished offense to public decency and morality because of acts committed in a public place or exposed to the public, was also applied in the case of homosexual behavior; see Cassazione di Roma, *Sentenza Serino,* January 15, 1890, in *Giurisprudenza penale* 18 (1891): 201.

48. Qtd. in P. Tuozzi, "I delitti contro il buon costume e l'ordine delle famiglie," in *Enciclopedia di diritto penale italiano,* ed. E. Pessina (Milan: Società Editrice Libraria, 1909), 9:175–76. On the debate that led to the abolition of unnatural libidinous acts as a crime see also Chamber of Deputies, *Relazione della commissione* (. . .) *sul disegno di legge* (. . .), *22 November 1887* (Rome: Stamperia Reale, 1888), 259–60.

49. On the relationship between sin and crime, morality and law during the liberal period see P. Prodi, *Una storia della giustizia: Dal pluralismo dei fori al moderno dualismo tra coscienza e diritto* (Bologna: Il Mulino, 2000), 450ff. On the multifaceted nature of this process of construction, regarding the sexual sphere, of a private area that was not affected by the state's interference, see D. Rizzo, "L'impossibile privato: Fama e pubblico scandalo in età liberale," *Quaderni storici* 112, no. 1 (April 2003): 215–42, and *Gli spazi della morale: Buon costume e ordine delle famiglie in Italia in età liberale* (Rome: Biblink, 2004); and P. Wilson, ed., *Family and Sexuality: The Private Sphere in Italy, 1860–1945* (London: Palgrave Macmillan, 2004).

50. Camera dei deputati, *Progetto del Codice penale per il Regno d'Italia e disegno di legge che ne autorizza la pubblicazione,* Relazione ministeriale (Rome: Stamperia Reale, 1887), 1:213–14 (session November 22, 1887), my italics.

51. G. Tolomei, "Delitti contro il buon costume e contro l'ordine delle famiglie secondo il nuovo codice penale," *Rivista penale* 4 (October 1889): 319.

52. On the debate that began in the early years of the twentieth century as to the different ways Catholicism and Protestantism influenced the spread of homosexuality, see "L'omosessualismo in Francia e in Germania," *Rivista penale di dottrina, legislazione e giurisprudenza* 4 (April 1909): 518–19.

53. Dall'Orto, "La 'tolleranza repressiva' dell'omosessualità." The author's interpretation seems to agree with the reasons behind the differences between Catholic and Protestant countries. Dell'Orto maintains, albeit sometimes with excessive simplicity, that the theory of predestination typical of Calvinism, which tends to substantiate the presence of the grace of God even in private situations, is conducive to considering the repression of "immoral" sexual acts vitally important in order to save the whole community. The state has the duty of publicly punishing and condemning homosexuality without concealing its existence. In comparison, Catholicism places the Church in charge of granting salvation to repentant sinners; and as a result, homosexuality is hidden inside confessionals and never receives proper criminal punishment.

54. Chamber of Deputies, *Progetto per il codice penale per il Regno d'Italia,* 213–14, my italics.

55. See G. Carmignani, *Teoria delle leggi della sicurezza sociale,* vol. 1 (Pisa: Nistri, 1831).

56. A. Pozzolini, *Dei delitti contro il buon costume e l'ordine delle famiglie* (Milan: Vallardi, n.d.), 6.

57. G. Bruni, "È necessaria la repressione penale dei delitti contro natura?" appendix to Raffalovich, *L'uranismo*, 105–11.

58. See ibid., 108–10.

59. Ibid., 111.

60. Tuozzi, "I delitti contro il buon costume e l'ordine delle famiglie," 172, 175.

61. F. Puglia, *I reati di libidine e contro i buoni costumi* (Naples: Anfossi, 1886), 91. However, according to the author, "when the unnatural sexual act is consummated in private with the partners' consent, all of the elements typical of a crime are lacking."

62. A. Nicefero, "Le disposizioni penali per i reati sessuali," excerpted from *Foro Penale* (Rome: Bertero, 1896), 4–5. According to Niceforo, homosexuality should not be decriminalized, because it was contagious and could therefore corrupt perfectly normal people; see Nicefero, *Le psicopatie sessuali*.

63. Ziino, "Stupro e attentati contro il pudore e il buon costume," 952. The author thought it was immoral to include both rape and pederasty in the same article on sexual assault. In his opinion, men were driven to have sexual intercourse with women because of a natural need, and while this did not exculpate those guilty of sexual assault, "it extenuated the crime removing all that was base and despicable. The same cannot be said for pederasty, which is always a shameful act and in any case a degeneration of human nature, both for the active and the passive partner" (907).

64. See E. Morselli, preface to P. Viazzi, *Sui reati sessuali: Note ed appunti di psicologia e giurisprudenza* (Turin: Bocca, 1896), xix.

65. Ibid., 202.

66. Actions in support of the introduction of legal measures against homosexuality were evermore sporadic while there were still heated discussions about the criminal responsibilities of pederasts who committed crimes; see L. Ferrante-Capetti, *Reati e psicopatie sessuali* (Turin: Bocca, 1910); and G. Cusani, *Il pentalogo, o delle cinque leggi penali nei reati di carne: Studio legale psicologico sociale* (S. Maria di Capua Vetere: Di Stefano, 1910).

67. See Dall'Orto, "La 'tolleranza repressiva' dell'omosessualità." According to Dall'Orto, this "social pact" obliged homosexuals to conduct a "double life" such that "up until 1971 Italian society managed to prevent the formation of groups of individuals who made their diversity the reason for a crusade that would lead to the birth of a liberation movement for homosexuals."

68. On the approach of the Rocco code see P. Ungari, *Alfredo Rocco e l'ideologia giuridica del fascismo* (Brescia: Morcelliana, 1974).

69. See G. Neppi Modona and M. Pelissero, "La politica criminale durante il fascismo," in *Storia d'Italia. Annali 12. La criminalità*, ed. L. Violante (Turin: Einaudi, 1997), 784–86.

70. See ACS, Ministero di Grazia e giustizia *Gabinetto*, b. 1, Verbale no. 1, November 30, 1927, "Discorso di Rocco di presentazione alla Commissione del Progetto Preliminare del Codice Penale."

71. Ministero della Giustizia e degli affari di culto, *Lavori preparatori del codice penale e del codice di procedura penale* (Rome: Tipografia delle Mantellate, 1928), 2:206. This article concerned the crime of indecent behavior and was placed in Book II—"Dei delitti in

ispecie. Titolo VIII" — "Dei delitti contro la moralità pubblica e il buon costume. Capo secondo" — "Delle offese al pudore e all'onore sessuale."

72. *Lavori preparatori del codice penale e del codice di procedura penale*, Acts of the ministerial commission in charge of giving an opinion on the preliminary draft of the new criminal code, introductory remarks by S. E. Giovanni Appiani, chairman of the commission, Rome 1929, vol. 4, pt. 1, 394–96.

73. See ibid., 407–8.

74. *Lavori preparatori del codice penale e del codice di procedura penale*, Observations and proposals to the draft of the new criminal code, Rome 1928, vol. 3, pt. 4, 10; for other opinions, see 7–11. The only person who expressed some doubts as to the criteria adopted in treating sexual crimes was Professor Ugo Conti, of the University of Pisa, who ended his comments recommending not to confuse morality with law and not to be excessively strict in the punishment.

75. Ibid., 43. Professor Giuseppe Maggiore, spokesman for the special royal commission of the lawyers' association of Palermo, regarding the preliminary draft of the new criminal code, was in favor of punishing homosexual relationships (article 528) but suggested eliminating the grounds of public scandal as had been done for incest: "these are crimes that most seriously offend moral sensibilities and should be punished whether or not they are followed by a public scandal."

76. On all of these opinions, see ibid., 39–44.

77. ACS, Ministero di Grazia e giustizia *Gabinetto*, b. 10, f. 10, "Relazioni sul progetto preliminare," Royal Lawyers' Commission, January 1927–May 1928, Report on the preliminary draft of the new criminal code by the Royal Lawyers' Commission of Alessandria.

78. ACS, Ministero di Grazia e giustizia *Gabinetto*, b. 9, f. 9, "Pareri sul progetto preliminare" University, November 1927–March 1928, Report on the preliminary draft of the new criminal code by Emanuele Carnevale, Law Faculty of the University of Palermo.

79. See "Civiltà cattolica," September 1927, quaderno 1854, 487.

80. Azione cattolica italiana, "Note, rilievi e proposte sul progetto preliminare di un nuovo codice penale," Rome 1928, in ACS, Ministero di Grazia e giustizia *Gabinetto*, b. 7, f. 6, "Personalità varie—osservazioni in arrivo (sul progetto preliminare) October 1927–June 1928."

81. Ibid., 3.

82. Announcements by the government at the IV International Congress on Moral Education (1926), qtd. in ibid., 4.

83. Ibid., 12.

84. See G. Agnese, *Con quale mezzo vedo possibile il risanamento dei costumi e il progresso morale di una moderna Nazione: Proposta di un codice dei costumi* (Turin: Ditta Eredi Botta, 1929), 19–21.

85. Associazione italiana di medicina legale, "Brevi appunti raccolti fra i professori di Medicina Legale per ritocchi di indole tecnica al progetto del Nuovo Codice Penale" (Genoa, n.d.), 10.

86. Proteus, "Intorno ad un articolo del progetto del nuovo codice penale," *Rassegna di studi sessuali demografia ed eugenica (Genesis)* 3 (1927): 212. According to the author, it was absurd to require harsher punishment for habitual homosexuals who deserved a more understanding attitude because, unlike incidental homosexuals, their behavior was caused by a congenital problem.

87. Ibid., 215.

88. See *Lavori preparatori del codice penale e del codice di procedura penale*, Acts of the ministerial commission in charge of giving an opinion on the preliminary draft of the new criminal code, Minutes of the commission's sessions, book II of the draft, Rome 1929, vol. 4, pt. 3, 169–72.

89. *Lavori preparatori del codice* . . . , Acts of the ministerial commission . . . , Minutes of the commission's session and summary of the commission's work, Rome 1929, vol. 4, pt. 4, 377.

90. *Lavori preparatori del codice* . . . , Acts of the parliamentary commission called upon to give an opinion on the draft of the new criminal code, III subcommittee, minutes no. 2, session of December 10, 1929, Rome 1930, vol. 6, 608.

91. See *Lavori preparatori del codice* . . . , Final draft of a new criminal code with the report of the Minister of Justice, the Honorable, Alfredo Rocco, Report on books II and III of the draft, Rome 1929, vol. 5, pt. 2, 314–15.

92. V. Manzini, *Trattato di diritto penale italiano secondo il codice del 1930* (Turin: Utet, 1936), 7:252. According to Manzini, the legislator had decriminalized homosexuality because it was considered "the task of morality, and not law, to condemn unnatural acts that were not violent, abusive or scandalous" (255). Manzini had made the same considerations in the first edition of his work, *Trattato di diritto penale italiano* (1908).

93. Ibid., 254. According to Manzini, the legislator, having decided not to include article 528 against homosexual relationships in the code, had however considered unnatural libidinous acts obscene and had therefore included them as being offensive to public decency; the only change with respect to article 528 was the necessary requisite of a public place instead of public scandal (376). It should be noted that after the Second World War and after several editions of his work, Manzini still had numerous supporters. Even the avant-garde journal *Scienza and Sessualità*, which was harshly criticized for its publications in the early 1950s regarding the subject of homosexuality, published Manzini's opinion on unnatural libidinous acts because his words had "served to warn society about certain immoral phenomena that were to be seriously condemned"; see A. Gabrielli, "Delitti sessuali," *Quaderni di "Scienza and Sessualità"* 12 (1953): 88–89. On the problems of this journal see G. Rossi Barilli, *Il movimento gay in Italia* (Milan: Feltrinelli, 1999), 26–27.

94. M. Manfredini, *Delitti contro la moralità pubblica e il buon costume: Delitti contro la famiglia* (Milan: Vallardi, 1934), 73.

95. In an exaggerated version of this same reasoning, Manfredini believed that female homosexuality was not punishable in so much as it did not endanger the conservation of the species since lesbians could generate children by having, like it or not, sexual intercourse with men. "Therefore, there was no radical violation of the laws of nature to justify criminal action" (76).

96. Ibid., 74.

97. Ibid., 76. According to Manfredini the decidedly degenerative nature of homo-sexuality made it a corrupt libidinous act even when committed with the full consensus of the partners (218–19).

98. See ibid., 43, 129. Filippo Manci was of the same opinion. According to him, "unnatural" sexual intercourse performed by a husband against the will of the wife should be punished "because that is contrary to nature and the natural and legal aims of marriage and it furthermore offends the dignity and self-esteem of the woman, whereas normal sexual intercourse, even if against the will of the wife, should not and cannot be punished" (F. Manci, *Reati sessuali* [Turin: Bocca, 1927], 112).

99. G. A. Fanelli, *Preliminari per un codice domestico* (Rome: Siae, 1935), 32–33.

100. Ibid., 23.

101. "L'omosessualismo in Francia e in Germania," 518.

102. G. Perrando, *Manuale di medicina legale* (Naples: Idelson, 1921), 134–35.

103. A. Dalla Volta, *Trattato di medicina legale* (Milan: Società editrice libraria, 1933), 1:308.

104. Niceforo, "Le disposizioni penali per i reati sessuali," 5.

105. Manzini, *Trattato di diritto penale*, 252.

106. G. Guareschi, "Note comparative fra i codici penali italiano e tedesco nei rispetti dei reati di indole sessuale," in *Archivio di Antropologia Criminale Psichiatria e Medicina Legale*, f. supplementare (Turin, 1936), 275–91.

107. Moreover, the German code of 1935 worsened the punishment of homosexuals with sentences that ranged from ten years of forced labor to life imprisonment.

108. Ibid., 288. In addition, the author criticized the German code because it pun-ished pederasty but completely ignored lesbianism, which was widespread in Germany even if it was less of an antisocial problem than male homosexuality.

109. On crimes against morality, the Rocco code introduced a considerable novelty in the defense of lineage. Heading X of the code was concerned with crimes against the integrity and health of lineage so as to "protect the continuity and health of the race, an essential condition for the development and health of the Italian nation"; see *La legislazione fascista 1929–1934* (Senato del Regno e Camera dei deputati, legislatura XXVIII), 235.

110. See E. Altavilla, *Delitti contro la persona: Delitti contro l'integrità e la sanità della stirpe* (Milan: Vallardi, 1934), 310; *Lavori preparatori del codice penale*, Acts of the ministerial commission in charge of giving an opinion on the preliminary draft of a new criminal code; introductory report by S. E. Giovanni Appiani, chairman of the commission, vol. 4, pt. 1, 413–14; and G. Falco, *I delitti contro l'integrità e la sanità della stirpe* (G.U.F. Mussolini, Naples 1937).

111. Only in hindsight, when the racial laws came into force, was the racial matrix of these new articles of the code devoted to crimes against the "integrity and health of the lineage," recognized by Carlo Costamagna, one of the regime's most illustrious jurists, author of the text on the "doctrine of Fascism" and editor of *Lo Stato*. In 1939, at a meeting on race and the law, he linked racism with the Rocco code of 1930; see

C. Costamagna, "*Razza* e diritto al convegno italo-tedesco di Vienna," *Lo Stato* 10, no. 3 (March 1939): 141–46.

112. G. Benvenuto, *I delitti contro l'integrità e la sanità della stirpe* (Naples: La Toga, 1934), 7.

113. See in this regard L. Cabitto, "Un caso di automascolinizzazione totale," *Archivio di Antropologia Criminale Psichiatria e Medicina legale* 6 (November–December 1932): 733–38; and G. Cucco, "Su di un caso di autoevirazione," *Archivio di Antropologia Criminale Psichiatria e Medicina Legale* 2 (March–April 1936), 194–98. Until a few years ago in Italy sex change operations were forbidden precisely on the basis of this article in the Rocco code that punished anyone who performed acts that brought about the sterility of another person, whether the intervention had been agreed on or not. For this very reason, many transsexuals had to go to Casablanca or Copenhagen for the operation. Transvestites were punished according to article 85 of the Police Force's Single Text that forbade appearing in public in disguise.

114. "Perversioni," *Il popolo d'Italia*, November 7, 1926 (my italics).

Chapter 4. The Repression of Homosexuality

1. B. Mussolini, *Spirito della rivoluzione fascista*, ed. G. S. Spinetti (Milan: Hoepli, 1937), 70.

2. See P. V. Cannistraro, *La fabbrica del consenso: Fascismo e mass media* (Rome: Laterza, 1975.

3. B. Mussolini, "Il discorso dell'Ascensione," in *Scritti e discorsi di Benito Mussolini dal 1927 al 1928* (Milan: Hoepli, 1934), 51.

4. ACS, SPD, carte della cassetta di zinco autografi del Duce the b. 4, f. "Discorso del Duce alla Camera (discorso dell'Ascensione), materiali e appunti autografi del Duce."

5. See the section "Doctrine of Fascism," written in part by Giovanni Gentile and in part by Mussolini, in *Enciclopedia Italiana Treccani* (Milan: Istituto enciclopedia italiana, 1932), 847–48. The Fascist totalitarian concept of state was thus summarized by Mussolini: "Fascists believe that the state is everything, and nothing human or spiritual exists, even less is of value, outside the state. Fascism is totalitarian in this sense" (848).

6. A. Rocco, *La formazione dello Stato fascista (1925–1934)* (Milan: Giuffrè, 1938), 797–98.

7. A circular letter headed "For Morality and Public Safety," no. 12985.2/18138, sent by Mussolini to the prefects of the Kingdom on October 30, 1928, and a copy to the general headquarters of the *carabinieri*, in Archivio di Stato di Milano, *Gabinetto prefettura* I versamento, b. 225 "Moralità Pubblica." In the circular, Mussolini invited the police force to continue their energetic action to protect morals by curbing the feverish "search for new kinds of pleasure"; forbidding pornographic publications; repressing the neo-Malthusian tendency; limiting alcoholism, the use of drugs, and prostitution; and fighting vagrancy, usury, and gambling.

8. See Gentile, *The Origins of Fascist Ideology*, 356.

9. On the ever-decreasing distinction between public and private spheres, see M. Salvati, *L'inutile salotto: L'abitazione piccolo borghese nell'Italia fascista* (Turin: Bollati Boringhieri, 1993).

10. Canosa, *Sesso e Stato*, 198.

11. E. Goffman, *Asylums; Essays on the Social Situation of Mental Patients and Other Inmates* (Garden City, N.Y.: Anchor Books, 1961), xiii, 4.

12. See *Conversazioni con Lévi-Strauss, Foucault, Lacan*, ed. P. Caruso (Milan: Mursia, 1969); and M. Foucault, *Sorvegliare e punire: Nascita della prigione* (Turin: Einaudi, 1976).

13. R. De Felice, *Intervista sul fascismo* (Bari: Laterza, 1999), 90.

14. Mussolini, "Il discorso dell'Ascensione," 45.

15. Mussolini, *Opera omnia*, 19:230.

16. Mussolini, "Il discorso dell'Ascensione," 53–54. For a careful reconstruction of Mussolini's use of medical metaphors see F. Rigotti, "Il medico-chirurgo dello Stato nel linguaggio metaforico di Mussolini," in *Cultura e società negli anni del fascismo*, various authors (Milan: Cordani, 1987), 501–17.

17. Mussolini, "Il discorso dell'Ascensione," 60.

18. D. Grandi, *Bonifica umana* (Rome: Ministero di Grazia e Giustizia, 1941).

19. Qtd. in E. Lussu, *La catena* (Florence: Vallecchi, 1945), 84.

20. See L. Musci, "Il confino fascista di polizia: L'apparato statale di fronte al dissenso politico e sociale," in *L'Italia al confino 1926–1943: Le ordinanze di assegnazione al confino emesse dalle Commissioni Provinciali dal novembre 1926 al luglio 1943*, ed. A. Dal Pont and S. Carolini (Milan: La Pietra, 1983), xxi–ci. Thanks to a careful analysis of documents, Musci's work gives a detailed reconstruction of the use of *confino* during the Fascist period. The author rightly emphasizes the importance of the preventive measure, even though, in my opinion, it may be exaggerated to consider *confino* "the keystone of the whole [repressive, Fascist] system" (xciii).

21. ACS, Ministero dell'Interno, Direzione Generale P.S., Divisione Polizia, Atti amministrativi, fascicoli personali di confinati mafiosi e comuni, fascicoli personali di ammoniti e diffidati politici e comuni 1895–1945 (hereafter *Confino Comune*), b. 10, categoria 11504, "Assegnazione al confino—Massime (fino al 1933)": report on administrative security measures by Franco De Chiara (deputy police superintendent), sent by the prefect of Frosinone to the police division on January 21, 1933.

22. *Domicilio coatto* was established for the first time on August 15, 1863, together with other exceptional measures to repress banditry ("legge Pica," "the Pica law," No. 1409). On *domicilio coatto*, see I. Mereu, "Cenni storici sulle misure di prevenzione nell'Italia 'liberale' (1852–1894)," in *Le misure di prevenzione*, various authors (Milan: Giuffrè, 1975), 200–201; and L. Violante, "La repressione del dissenso politico nell'Italia liberale: Stati d'assedio e giustizia militare," *Rivista di storia contemporanea*, 4 (1976): 48ff.

23. G. Amato, *Individuo e autorità nella disciplina della libertà personale* (Milan: Giuffrè, 1967), 240.

24. G. Rosadi, *Del Domicilio Coatto e dei delinquenti recidivi* (Florence: Bocca, 1900), iv.

25. On November 5, 1926, before leaving the Ministry of National Security, Luigi Federzoni handed over a series of repressive measures to the cabinet. One of these called for the substitution of *domicilio coatto* with *confino*, which would provide for both common-law and political offenses. These measures became part of the Testo Unico, whose main goals had already been summed up by Federzoni on September 5, 1925:

"The affirmation of police authority as distinct and autonomous from penal authority, . . . and this criterion shall be applied to the institutions that deliver the cautioning and those that give *confino*, and also regards the setting up of the organization called on to carry them out; the police are to enforce administrative injunctions; . . . the interests of public morality are to be preeminent over all private interests" (ACS, MI, Direzione Generale P.S., *Divisione Polizia Amministrativa e sociale 1919–1926*, Miscellanea, b. 2, f. 5 "Riforma legge P.S. — 1925").

26. P. Carucci, "Arturo Bocchini," in *Uomini e volti del fascismo*, ed. F. Cordova (Rome: Bulzoni, 1980), 72–73. For the changes to police law with the Testo Unico, see also P. Carucci, "L'organizzazione dei servizi di polizia dopo l'approvazione del Testo Unico delle leggi di Pubblica Sicurezza nel 1926," *Rassegna degli archivi di Stato* 1 (1976): 98.

27. ACS, MI, Direzione Generale P.S. *Massime*, b. 93, categoria Li, "Leggi e regolamenti" f. 41, "Regolamento per la legge di P.S.," circular for the prefects and chiefs of police of the kingdom, No. 10.12982, of July 3, 1940, whose subject is the "Nuovo regolamento per l'esecuzione della legge di P.S. in sostituzione di quello approvato con R.D. 21 gennaio 1929-VII no. 62."

28. Musci, "Il confino fascista di polizia," xxii.

29. On the continuity between the juridical authoritarianism of the post-Risorgimento state and "its overall exasperation by the Fascist regime," see A. Aquarone, *L'organizzazione dello Stato totalitario* (Turin: Einaudi, 1995).

30. Compared to the preventive measures of the liberal state, one of the main novelties introduced by the Testo Unico, which was changed without being substantially modified in 1931, was the composition of the provisional board: in particular, the figure of a court president was not provided for.

31. Art. 181 of the Testo Unico, 1931.

32. The board of appeal was made up of the undersecretary of state of the Ministry of National Security who presided, the chief of police, the court attorney at the Appeals Court of Rome, a general of the *carabinieri*, and a general from the MVSN.

33. Qtd. in S. Carolini, "Gli antifascisti italiani dal confino all'internamento 1940–1943," in *I campi di concentramento in Italia. Dall'internamento alla deportazione (1940–1945)*, ed. C. Di Sante (Milan: Franco Angeli, 2001), 133.

34. Lussu, *La catena*, 77–78.

35. See D. Petrini, "Il sistema di prevenzione personale," in *Storia d'Italia, Annali 12. La criminalità*, ed. L. Violante (Turin: Einaudi, 1997), 902–3.

36. On cases in which people acquitted by ordinary judges were then sent to *confino*, see "Al confino! In margine a certe assoluzioni," *Il popolo di Roma*, December 15, 1928.

37. L. Grimaldi, introduction to *Il popolo al confino: La persecuzione fascista in Sicilia*, S. Carbone and L. Grimaldi (Rome: Istituto poligrafico e zecca dello Stato, 1989), 48–49.

38. ACS, MI, Telegrammi ufficio cifra in partenza, circular to the prefects no. 29,746 of November 26, 1926. See also the other telegraphic circulars sent to the prefects of the kingdom by the chief of police Bocchini and the undersecretary of National Security, Giacomo Suardo, between November 8 and 26, 1926.

39. In 1937 Mussolini authorized a reportage to be carried out on the *confino* colonies, precisely to change the negative judgment that the American public had formed of the repression practiced by the Fascist regime against political adversaries. Stefano Bricarelli's photo reportage on the designer and journalist Paolo Garetto was supposed to appear in *Life* magazine, but it was never published because the description of daily life there was overly sugar coated. See S. Bricarelli, "Fai vedere come vivevano: Dall'archivio di un grande fotografo degli anni Trenta un inedito reportage sui confinati del regime a Ponza," *Storia illustrata*, 359 (October 1987): 24–33; also about this affair, see D. Caraföli and G. M. Padiglione, *Il viceduce: Storia di Arturo Bocchini capo della polizia fascista* (Milan: Rusconi, 1987), 138–40. Also the report on *confino* by Mino Maccari, 1930, and published by *La Stampa* of Turin was supposed to give a soothing image of "Mussolini's vacation." However, the purpose was not fully achieved because, despite the censors' cuts and the changes, the people were made aware of facts and situations that had been ignored up to then by the regime's press. See M. Maccari, *Visita al confino* (Marina di Belvedere: Cultura Calabrese, 1985).

40. Mussolini, "Il discorso dell'Ascensione," 58.

41. Legally speaking there was no difference between the two measures, the special office that dealt with *confino politico*, set up in 1927 was dependent on Section 1 of the general and confidential affairs division, while Section 2 of the police division was in charge of *confino comune*. The judiciary police division that had always dealt with *domicilio coatto* had merged into a single police division together with the administrative and social police division in January 1927 like it had been before October 1919.

42. In many cases, it was believed best to remove persons already condemned for theft or murder from society. When the prefect, Mori, was given full powers for the fight against organized crime in Sicily, it was applied to a large number of Mafia men as well. See G. Antoniani Persichilli, "Le misure di pubblica sicurezza. Dal domicilio coatto al confino di polizia," *Temi ciociara* 5 (1978): 107–21.

43. ACS, Telegrammi ufficio cifra in partenza, circular No. 28,942, November 18, 1926, to the prefects of the kingdom and a copy to headquarters of the *carabinieri*. Guido Corso also stressed that the Fascists believed "social and political threats were similar, both worthy of being fought on the same level and with the same means in order to protect political and social order"; see G. Corso, *L'ordine pubblico* (Bologna: Il Mulino, 1979), 284. According to Giuseppe Maggiore, every kind of crime in a totalitarian state had to be considered a political crime because even common delinquents violate and damage the honor of the state with their behavior; see G. Maggiore, "Diritto penale totalitario nello Stato totalitario," *Rivista italiana di diritto penale*, 2–3 (1939): 157.

44. See ACS, *Confino Comune*, b. 8, ff. "Affari di massima relativi ai confinati comuni: Situazione numerica colonie; capienza colonie; richieste locali." In 1925 Francesco Crispo Moncada, who was then the chief of police, urged the Ministry of National Security to reopen some of the *confino* colonies again, seeing that "there had been an increase in the number of people assigned to them, especially after the arrival of the national government." In July 1926 Crispo Moncada once again denounced the serious inconvenience caused by the excessive number of detainees in what he called an

"increasingly alarming situation, due to the numerous new cases of *confino*, the consequence of a firmer application of the law" (ACS, *Confino Comune*, b. 1, f. "Colonie confinati di polizia affari generali anno 1930," s.f. 3 "Lavori di ampliamento e di adattamento dei locali nelle colonie di confino").

45. ACS, MI, Direzione Generale P.S., Divisione A.G.R., Ufficio confino politico (hereafter UCP), Affari Generali, b. 11, f. "Divisione dei confinati comuni dai confinati politici." On December 17, 1926, Mussolini decided to separate political detainees from criminal detainees, thus changing his first decision. Consequently, some islands were mainly colonies for political detainees, above all because they were more secure and living conditions were less difficult, while there were more criminals in other colonies.

46. The "Manchurians" were also called *pascolo abusivo* ("illegal grazing") because, as they were not truly political detainees, they were held in a place reserved for others. See A. Spinelli, *Come ho tentato di diventare saggio* (Bologna: Il Mulino, 1988), 234–43, for further information about the origins and meaning of the term "Manchurian," given to "drunkards, criminals and poor wretches" sent to *confino politico* because "by chance they let themselves go in outbursts of anger against the Duce or the regime." The term was also foisted on those who had given up anti-Fascism and had cooperated with the police in order to be free again. See also Maccari, *Visita al confino*, 79–80, for more about this "dark area made up of social rejects, who have been given an undeserved political label by absolutely occasional circumstances, or by the wrong criteria applied by some provincial board when deciding on *confino*."

47. The pride in being persecuted for one's ideals increased the contempt for those who were treated "like pariahs in India" and considered to be an added disturbance to the already difficult life in the colony. See G. Amendola, *Un'isola* (Milan: Rizzoli, 1980), 112, for more about this rigid separation and about the two big but different dormitories on the island of Ponza, one for political detainees and the other for Manchurians, who were "persons given *confino* for various reasons, often for individual expressions of anti-Fascism, being rowdy, unruliness and shouting against the Duce when drunk."

48. M. Magri, *Una vita per la libertà: Diciassette anni al confino politico di un martire delle fosse Ardeatine* (Rome: Puglielli, 1956), 34–36. Also Angelo Sorgoni believed that "the regime was used to considering its political adversaries as common delinquents, using attestations and rejecting any difference between political and common offenses, which was confirmed by penal law as well" (A. Sorgoni, *Ricordi di un ex confinato: Un socialista recanatese dal 1898 alla liberazione* [Urbino: Argalia, 1975], 130).

49. For example, Point No. 9 of the permanence card for Ustica established that *confinati politici* were forbidden from associating with *confinati comuni*. Gramsci, who had been in *confino* on Sicily since December 1926, noted that it was "a shame that it was forbidden to have any contact with beings reduced to such an exceptional life"; the *confinati comuni* who were kept in unimaginably bad physical and moral conditions, "would have provided for a unique psychological and folkloristic study" (A. Gramsci, *Lettere dal carcere* [Turin: Einaudi, 1971], 13).

50. U. Terracini, *Al bando dal Partito: Carteggio clandestino dall'isola e dall'esilio* (Milan: La Pietra, 1976), 8.

51. See P. Rossi, "L'antagonismo psicologico di classe tra i detenuti," *Rivista di psicologia normale, patologica e applicata* 1–2 (January–June 1943): 111–24.

52. R. Spadafora, *Il popolo al confino: La persecuzione fascista in Campania* (Naples: Athena, 1989), 15.

53. G. De Luna and M. Revelli, *Fascismo/Antifascismo: Le idee, le identità* (Florence: La Nuova Italia, 1995), 72.

54. Emilio Franzina wrote: "Although approval was quite widespread and 'Mussolini's Italians' embodied the meaning simply by acting and operating (like conformists) in conformity with the 'hierarchical' decisions coming from above, the presumed extent of this consensus should be seen in proportion to the opposite aspect of approval (dissent), and not only for dialectical reasons. Choosing the viewpoint of the 'controllers' (the police, the various repressive political branches from the militia to OVRA, etc.), in other words, putting ourselves in the shoes of those who had to deal with the quality and quantity of 'approval,' including coercion and persecuting dissent, we can reach a more balanced reconstruction of the social categories that made up both sides from a documentary and historiographic point of view" (E. Franzina, "Proteste sociali nel Veneto fra le due guerre," in *Geografia e forme del dissenso sociale in Italia durante il fascismo 1928–1934*, ed. M. Chiodo [Cosenza: Luigi Pellegrini Editore, 1990], 302).

55. For an example of this position that tends to theorize mass dissent and protest against the Fascist regime, often as a controversial answer to De Felice's idea of approval of the regime, see N. Tranfaglia, ed., *Fascismo e capitalismo* (Milan: Feltrinelli, 1976); G. Quazza, *Resistenza e storia d'Italia: Problemi e ipotesi di ricerca* (Milan: Feltrinelli, 1976), and "Il fascismo: Esame di coscienza degli italiani," in *Storiografia e fascismo*, various authors (Milan: Franco Angeli, 1985), 7–24; and the essay by L. Casali, "E se fosse dissenso di massa? Elementi per un'analisi della conflittualità politica durante il fascismo," *Italia contemporanea* 144 (1981): 101–20. In my opinion, the most recent historiographic tendency tries to reach a more balanced position between stressing approval and overestimating dissent, maintaining that in many cases consent was not active and substantial but passive and formal, precisely for fear of incurring the vast repressive action of the regime.

56. G. Santomassimo, "Antifascismo popolare," *Italia contemporanea* 140 (1980): 55, and see his "Classi subalterne e organizzazione del consenso," in *Storiografia e fascismo*, 99–117. Gianpasquale Santomassimo rightly notes that the behavior of these individuals considered "misfits" by the police "is outside the usual pattern and may be ambiguous and subject to discordant interpretations" due to their nature. However, in my opinion he is wrong in overemphasizing the political nature of this behavior, and thus in considering it a kind of anti-Fascism.

57. See S. Corvisieri, *La villeggiatura di Mussolini: Il confino da Bocchini a Berlusconi* (Milan: Baldini Castoldi, 2004).

58. The permanence card was called a "statement of submission" in some colonies and gave an even stronger impression of total subordination to, and dependence on, the authorities' control. The detainees were obliged to keep the card with them at all times and show it when requested.

59. As Ettore Franceschini notes, usually the detainees were allowed to go into public places, but if someone had it out for them, a policeman was ready to charge them with infringement. He would arrest them and report them to the judiciary for violating the rules of *confino*. After one of these episodes, if one happened to ask the police, "But can we go or not to the shops?" they answered with a shrug, "At your own risk." See H. France, *Il domicilio coatto: Il cosiddetto Confino di Polizia. Come l'ho visto io* (Rome: Morara, 1956), 51.

60. Gramsci, *Lettere dal carcere*, 50.

61. The detainees themselves preferred the islands without the army present. On the continual abuse of power committed by the soldiers on supervision in the colonies, as well as memoirs on *confino*, see ACS, *Confino Comune*, b. 19. Violence against the delinquents in *confino* was particularly ferocious as well; for example, at Ustica, after some violation or other, "they ended up in the "ditch" as the disciplinary prison was called, where unfortunately they were slapped, punched, kicked, and whipped. The moaning of those poor wretches was heard even in the houses nearby" (G. Scalarini, *Le mie isole* [Milan: Franco Angeli, 1992], 101).

62. See Musci, "Il confino fascista di polizia," lxxx–lxxxi.

63. The executive regulations for *confino* set down a whole series of punishments ranging from simple reprimands to more serious measures: forbidding the detainees to go out, obliging them to stay in the dormitories for extended periods, putting them in solitary confinement cell with a plank-bed to sleep on, withholding half of their daily allowance, and limiting their food to bread and soup. Furthermore, those who disobeyed the regulations of *confino* could be arrested and reported to the judiciary authorities; in this case, the *confinato* was almost certainly condemned and ended up serving a further period of imprisonment. See "Regulations for implementing the Testo Unico," January 21, 1929, royal decree No. 62, title 37: "On the treatment of detainees in *confino* and the discipline of the *confinati*," Art. 343.

64. G. Damiani, *Il domicilio coatto* (Palermo: Giannitrapani, 1905), 30–31.

65. E. Mirabella, "Nevrosi e domicilio coatto," *Archivio di Psichiatria, Neuropatologia, Antropologia criminale e Medicina legale* 26, no. 1–2 (1904): 147.

66. In fact, ninety-six people accused of pederasty appeared before the provincial board for *confino politico*, but eight of these were not given *confino* for three possible reasons: the board fell back on a simple cautioning, the accusation was not sufficiently proved, or the men were finishing their draft service.

67. The documents in the ACS reveal that the first cases of people given *confino* for pederasty date back to 1927, while the last cases were recorded as late as the Second World War. The police were concerned that homosexuals could "take advantage of the state of war" to vent their "sexual perversion"; see ACS, *P.S. A1 1940*, b. 45, f. "Dino G."

68. Actually there are forty-four files in the central state archives on delinquents given *confino* for pederasty, but six of them were sentenced twice. These files had never been consulted and were discovered by sifting through the 178 file cabinets (containing over twenty-five hundred files) that made up the unfortunately incomplete material on *confino* for delinquents.

69. See ACS, *Confino Comune*, b. 23, f. "Elenco pederasti presenti nelle colonie di Ustica e di Favignana."

70. ACS, UCP, Fascicoli Personali, b. 391, f. "Salvatore F." The police were constantly concerned about avoiding a scandal caused by the free expression of "perverse" attitudes. For example, the police justified the measure in the case of a detainee from Catania: "he copulates with persons of the same sex and publicly parades his degeneration and causes scandal through the way he walks, gesticulates and wears cosmetics. He is a serious threat to morality. We recommend *confino* for the maximum length of time possible"; ACS, UCP, Fascicoli Personali, b. 128, f. "Emanuele B."

71. Homosexuals themselves were convinced that their behavior was morally blameworthy and out of compliance with the dictates of Fascism. Not surprisingly, then, a *confinato politico* interned for passive pederasty wrote to the Duce saying: "I promise I will learn to be a worthy Italian Fascist." Another detainee, fully aware that he was not "one of Mussolini's perfect Italians" firmly repeated his commitment to henceforth "live the fruitful and happy life appropriate to the New Italian"; ACS, UCP, Fascicoli personali, b. 624, f. "Giuseppe M."

72. Police action to repress homosexuality was only constant and widespread in some cities, like Catania for example, where as many as forty-six men (more than half of the overall number of homosexuals given *confino politico*) were sent to *confino* for pederasty in 1939.

73. Cautioning was a kind of house arrest limited to a few hours in the daytime and that implied the obligation to have a permanent job. However, paradoxically it was just this measure that created serious difficulty at work for those who received it, both because obligations imposed that seriously limited the mobility of the person cautioned, and because few employers were prepared to take on a cautioned person. On the contrary, a police warning was a kind of sermon given by the chief of police to persuade a person to refrain from acting in a certain way, in order to avoid more serious measures.

74. The more limited use of *confino* in comparison to other police measures is evident in the case of Florence, where only eleven of the sixty-one "pederasts" judged by the provincial board between 1936 and 1939 were given *confino politico*, while thirty-four were cautioned and sixteen simply given a talking to by the police chief.

75. ACS, UCP, Affari generali, b. 1, f. 1 (1926–30) "Varie," R. prefecture of Potenza, prefect Dinale, December 28, 1929, subject: *confinati comuni*.

76. A homosexual, who was employed at the *Popolo d'Italia* during the Ventennio, gave an interview in the 1980s where he confirmed that by saving appearances it was possible to avoid the repression carried out by the regime against pederasty and evade police intervention: "It was enough to do it in private and nobody said anything. It was enough to observe the standard sobriety and morality and they were not interested in it. The reason why they used severe measures against certain homosexuals was that besides setting a bad example to others, besides showing they were like that, they were almost always against the Fascist regime"; qtd. in Rossi Barilli, *Il movimento gay in Italia*, 21–22.

77. ACS, UCP, Fascicoli personali, b. 1084, f. "Giuseppe Z."

78. See Dall'Orto, "La 'tolleranza repressiva' dell'omosessualità," 37–57. In my opinion, it can be misleading to apply the term "tolerance" to the Fascist context, because although it is associated with repression, it risks equating silence with some kind of acceptance of diversity.

79. M. Barbagli, *Sotto lo stesso tetto: Mutamenti della famiglia in Italia dal XV al XX secolo* (Bologna: Il Mulino, 1984), 412. Lucetta Scaraffia points out that nonaggressive ritual forms were used to confirm sexual hierarchies. For example, "some rituals of inversion— men dressed up as women and vice versa—were periodically useful to confirm and stigmatize any transgressions of the established borders: the function of these customs was to keep the division of genders very clear" (L. Scaraffia, "Essere uomo, essere donna," in *La famiglia italiana dall'Ottocento ad oggi*, ed. P. Melograni [Rome: Laterza, 1988], 210–11).

80. P. Dogliani, *L'Italia fascista 1922–1940* (Milan: Sansoni, 1999), 282–83.

81. For example, Dall'Orto maintains that "the Fascist regime's explicitly racist policy against homosexuals lasted three years: from 1936 to 1939" and "came about openly to ape Nazi Germany" (G. Dall'Orto, "Omosessualità e razzismo fascista," in *La menzogna della razza. Documenti e immagini del razzismo e dell'antisemitismo fascista*, ed. D. Bidussa [Bologna, 1994], 139). The author also firmly repeats this idea in "Il paradosso del razzismo fascista verso l'omosessualità," in *Nel nome della razza. Il razzismo nella storia d'Italia 1870–1945*, ed. A. Burgio (Bologna: Il Mulino, 2000), 515–28.

82. On the changes brought about in the private lives of citizens by the attempt to transform the Italians into a population of warriors ready to fight for the greatness and territorial expansion of the new Fascist empire, see M. G. Knox, "Conquest, Foreign and Domestic, in Fascist Italy and Nazi Germany," *Journal of Modern History* 56, no. 1 (March 1984): 1–57. For more on the link between the escalation of the war and the increasingly severe repressive action directed against homosexuals, see M. Ebner, "The Persecution of Homosexual Men under Fascism 1926–1943," in *Family and Sexuality: The Private Sphere in Italy, 1860–1945*, ed. P. Wilson (London: Palgrave-Macmillan, 2004), 139–56.

83. According to Dall'Orto, "extending the policy of defending the race to homosexuals" led to "classifying over eighty homosexuals as *confinati politici* instead of *confinati comuni*" (Dall'Orto, "Omosessualità e razzismo fascista," 139). Gianfranco Goretti reached the same conclusion. Goretti considered the 1938 racial laws, with the use of *confino politico* for pederasts, as the turning-point for the repression of homosexuals in Fascist Italy. See G. Goretti, "Il periodo fascista e gli omosessuali: Il confino di polizia," in *Le ragioni di un silenzio: La persecuzione degli omosessuali durante il nazismo e il fascismo*, Circolo Pink (Verona: Ombre Corte, 2002), 64.

84. Consequently the number of political detainees on the Tremiti islands increased greatly, passing from seventeen at the beginning of 1936 to 438 in December 1937. In July, 1937, the detainees in the Tremiti colonies staged a noteworthy insurrection by refusing to give the Roman salute (also called the Fascist salute). As a result, it was decided to remove all the *confinati comuni* (about two hundred) in order to better control the *confinati politici*. Later on, when the Ponza colony was closed in July 1939, the number of political detainees

in the Tremiti colonies increased even more because the Ponza detainees were transferred partly to Ventotene and partly to the Tremiti islands. See ACS, UCP, Affari Generali, b. 28, "Tremiti—saluto romano."

85. See ACS, UCP, Affari generali, b. 12, f. "Capienza," s.f. "Tremiti."

86. See ACS, *Confino Comune*, b. 43, "Biagio C." In his novel *Galera*, Tullio Murri writes of an episode that gives the impression that pederasty had been practiced on the Tremiti islands since their establishment as a *domicilio coatto*. An old habitual delinquent who had been in *domicilio coatto* for many years on the Tremiti islands reported that there he had practiced "the profession that everyone considers the most shameful—even for women, for a cent"; in fact, on those islands there was "a cave hollowed out by the waves, a deep cave on the seashore, used by the detainees for the filthiest of vices" (T. Murri, *Galera* [Milan: Modernissima, 1928 (1920)], 14–15).

87. The police inspector-general Giuseppe Consone (III zona OVRA), charged with carrying out the inquiry, had denied these accusations. However, he suggested that the pederast in question be sent to another colony "for obvious reasons." See ACS, *Confino Comune*, b. 25, f. "Relazione di inchiesta a Tremiti del 15-9-36 circa accuse mosse sull'andamento della colonia di confino."

88. Magri, *Una vita per la libertà*, 174.

89. See Barbagli and Colombo, *Omosessuali moderni*. On the debate in response to Barbagli and Colombo's book, see "Modelli di omosessualità," *Genesis* 3, no. 1 (2004): 183–200.

90. ACS, UCP, Fascicoli personali, b. 772, f. "Antonio P."

91. ACS, UCP, Fascicoli personali, b. 576, f. "Giuseppe L.P."

92. In Salerno as well, three individuals in *confino* for passive pederasty had been previously subjected to a medical examination to prove their "degeneration." We should note that a rectal analysis to check for homosexuality was used for a draft check-up as well. In fact, on the basis of Art. 30 of the E. A. code, the individuals who were recognized as being afflicted with sexual mental disorders were considered permanently unfit for military service. Consequently, some detainees had been rejected precisely because they were considered passive pederasts.

93. The file on Barbaro M. is very interesting because it contains criticism of police activity, but also an extremely severe judgment of homosexuality. Barbaro's brother defended him. He considered it inadmissible for a person to be violently separated from his family and forced to spend so many years on an isolated island because of gossip, or only because he was well mannered and had smooth skin, without a beard, scars, or wrinkles, which emphasized how delicate his face was. However, at the same time, he was convinced that it was necessary to harshly repress "the debauched persons who had fallen into the Abyss of vice" through *confino*. Furthermore he stressed he was ready to wash his hands of his brother once it was proved he was a pederast, accepting his removal in order to ease "the perpetual shame of his presence." Thus, "if I had known my brother suffered from this vice I would have called for the most serious measures for him. As a doctor and a Fascist, I approve of the Fascist government's healing work in the social field and its defense of the race. I would feel freed of any duty to care for an individual

who turned out to be a proven sexual degenerate, despite our blood ties." See ACS, UCP, Fascicoli personali, b. 675, f. "Barbaro M."

94. ACS, UCP, Fascicoli personali, b. 1068, f. "Salvatore V." Not by chance, the detainee had already been admitted to a mental home and kept there for about three weeks under observation. When he appealed against the measure of *confino*, he wrote in his defense: "I have never suffered such an illness, I feel myself to be a man both physically and morally."

95. ACS, UCP, Fascicoli personali, b. 466, f. "Placido G."

96. See ACS, *Confino Comune*, b. 78, f. "Giovanni I." Giovanni I.'s case is one of the few in which a detainee was ready to acknowledge his homosexuality openly. This teacher of Italian admitted "being no angel," but also pointed out that "they have exaggerated and still exaggerate" about him. However, in his opinion repressing pederasty was illegitimate because a homosexual was not so out of his own volition and was not socially dangerous even though he had "a mental state that was not completely normal and that derived from a kind of partial insanity."

97. See ACS, UCP, Fascicoli personali, b. 878, f. "Domenico R."

98. Homosexuals were given *confino* on the basis of Art. 181, No. 3 of the police law since they engaged in or showed the intention of engaging in an activity "that would damage national interests."

99. ACS, UCP, Fascicoli personali, b. 574, f. "Giuseppe L. M."

100. The position of this tailor from Piacenza was also aggravated by friction with a known Fascist. Driven by jealousy, he had sent offensive letters to an official of the GIL (Italian Fascist Youth Movement), inviting him not to associate with his young friend anymore "because he said the boy belonged to him." Although there had been "rumors for some time" about the official's homosexuality, no measures had been taken against him, while the poor tailor, who was not a member of the PNF, was distanced from the boy once and for all and sentenced to *confino*. In this case as well, the attorney's defense had no effect; he had maintained that it was more suitable not to use repressive but rehabilitative measures, and proposed that his client be admitted to an asylum for his mental deficiency. ACS, UCP, Fascicoli personali, b. 11, f. "Dante A."

101. ACS, UCP, Fascicoli personali, b. 90, f. "Giuseppe B." On his testimony and life in *confino*, see G. Dall'Orto, "Ci furono dei 'femminella' che piangevano quando venimmo via dalle Tremiti! Intervista a un omosessuale confinato nel periodo fascista," *Babilonia*, 50 (1987): 26–28.

102. See ACS, *Confino Comune*, b. 48, f. "Rosario C." For a brilliant literary reconstruction of the consequences of being accused of homosexuality, see P. Chiara, *Il balordo* (Milan: Mondadori, 1967).

103. There is only one case in which a mother in serious financial difficulty with a sick husband and several children to care for thought it more convenient for her own son to stay in *confino*, despite her sorrow over the separation. After her son's complaints that there was no work at San Domino, she answered him: "My dear son, I have finally received your caring letter. I shall answer your question by saying that we do not want you at home, and you want to be helped as Mimi's mother did because you don't believe

what I write to you? Mimi's mother doesn't have a husband and so naturally she must go on leave. Don Attilio says that you must help yourself, you are no longer a boy that needs help. He says that you shouldn't bother us, we cannot accept your lifestyle. Don't disturb us anymore, we have enough to bear here at home, with family problems. . . . Why do you want to change islands, aren't there others like you, as well? If you are on this island it means that it is the right one for you" (ACS, UCP, Fascicoli personali, b. 941, f. "Vincenzo S.").

104. ACS, UCP, Fascicoli personali, b. 128, f. "Emanuele B." The appeal was rejected, even though it was reduced to a cautioning after his father and sister died so that he could assist his mother who was seriously ill.

105. ACS, UCP, Fascicoli personali, b. 127, f. "Maurizio B."

106. As stressed in the preceding chapter, it is not completely anachronistic to imagine that groups committed to defending the rights of homosexuals may have arisen in the early 1900s, seeing that at the end of the 1800s and during the Weimar Republic these kinds of organizations had arisen in Germany. With the arrival of Fascism in Italy, it was definitely not possible to imitate the German trend, an exception to the rule in Europe that was destined to end with rise of the Nazis to power.

107. See Dall'Orto, "Ci furono dei 'femminella' che piangevano quando venimmo via dalle Tremiti," 26–28.

108. Amendola, Un'isola, 152–53.

109. G. Ansaldo, L'antifascista riluttante: Memorie del carcere e del confino 1926–1927 (Bologna: Il Mulino, 1992), 352.

110. A. Misuri, "Ad bestias!" Memorie di un perseguitato (Rome: Edizioni delle catacombe, 1944), 226. On sodomites in confino, "with peroxide-blond hair, wearing tight pants that cling to their hips and flashy, golden sandals," see also I. Marusso, Domicilio coatto 1940 (Florence: Edizioni Cynthia, 1963), "Il Sodomita," 20–23, and "Il Negro," 64–66.

111. Spinelli, Come ho tentato di diventare saggio, 238–39.

112. C. Fiori, Una donna nelle carceri fasciste (Rome: Editori Riuniti, 1965), 296.

113. G. Goretti, "Un 'pederasta' catanese al confino," in Le ragioni di un silenzio, Circolo Pink 127.

114. We can see that there is the stamp "Seen by the Duce" or "Orders taken from the Head of Government" on many of these documents regarding detainees in confino for pederasty. In fact, in many cases the measure was taken on Mussolini's orders while the confino location was decided by Bocchini, the chief of police.

115. See V. Brancati, Don Giovanni in Sicilia (Milan: Mondadori, 2002 [1941]), Il bell'Antonio (Milan: Bompiani, 1979 [1949]), and Paolo il caldo (Milan: Mondadori, 2001 [1955]).

116. On this affair, see A. Dalla Volta, "Una associazione a delinquere nel reato di violenza carnale contro natura," Zacchia, 1–6 (1929): 1–12.

117. Catania Court of Assizes, sentence of February 2, 1929. There were twenty-two accused, but considering the reticence and fear of reporting the violence suffered, the number of persons involved was probably much higher.

118. Ibid., 11. According to Dalla Volta, "the perversion and precocious corruption" of these young victims was due to their wretched living conditions, as well as the criminal

gang's violence and their death threats, and "also maybe to the difficulty the boys had in finding an adequate heterosexual outlet for their instincts, which were already awakened and precociously stimulated." The only remedy to put an end to this criminal activity and corruption was to enhance institutions for the protection and defense of children and increase the supervision of ill-famed places in the city by cleaning up some dangerous districts and closing some suspect places of entertainment.

119. See ACS, *Confino Comune*, b. 43, f. "Biagio C."

120. See ACS, *Confino Comune*, b. 114, f. "Pietro P." The repressive action of the Catania police indirectly fostered the birth of an organization dedicated to extorting money from homosexuals. In 1934 another individual was given *confino* because he tried to pass as a police office. Together with his friend, who purposely solicited pederasts, the two of them would then surprise them in the act and make them pay the fine on the spot.

121. The Catania pederasts were given *confino* with various sentences; those sentenced with the order of February 2, 1939, were sent to Favignana, Lampedusa, and Ustica and were formally considered *confinati comuni*. It was only after they were transferred to the Tremiti islands that they were recorded as *confinati politici* although they were treated in the same way as delinquents. In March 1939 the chief of police decided to group all the pederasts of Catania at San Domino, giving instructions that "all the papers relative to the repression of *Pederasty in Catania* be passed to *Confino Politico*. The same must also be done for the personal files of the Catania pederasts." Those given *confino* with the order of April 11, 1939, and May 8, 1939, were therefore sent directly to the Tremiti islands and considered political detainees. See ACS, *Confino Comune*, b. 24, "Affari per provincia relativi ai confinati comuni — 1937-1939," f. "Catania."

122. A Sicilian term indicating a passive homosexual, often used when referring specifically to young homosexuals who prostitute themselves. See G. Dall'Orto, "Le parole per dirlo: Storia di undici termini relativi all'omosessualità," *Sodoma* 3 (Spring–Summer 1986): 81–95.

123. On sexual morality, the value of virginity and prostitution in Sicily, in addition to Giuseppe Pitrè's numerous studies on Sicilian customs, see A. Cutrera, *Storia della prostituzione in Sicilia* (Milan: Sandron, 1903); G. Fiume, "Le patenti di infamia: Morale sessuale e igiene sociale nella Sicilia dell'Ottocento," *Memoria*, 17 (1986): 71–89; and J. Schneider, *La vigilanza delle vergini* (Palermo: La Luna, 1987). On brothels for sodomites in Catania, see F. De Luca, *L'elemento etnico nei reati di libidine* (Catania, 1909), 17. For female chastity, see M. Giovannini, "Female Chastity Codes in the Circum-Mediterranean: Comparative Perspective," in *Honor and Shame and the Unity of the Mediterranean*, ed. D. D. Gilmore (Washington, D.C.: American Anthropological Association, 1987), 61–74. For the life and social conditioning in Sicily in the 1930s, see C. Gower Chapman, *Milocca, a Sicilian Village* (Cambridge: Schenkman, 1971).

124. According to De Martino "ethnic homosexuality went hand in hand with the seclusion of women in southern culture. Freer and sunny, homosexuality in the South seemed due more to chance meetings than to psychological determinism, but in reality it was culturally codified and rigidly split into active and passive roles of behavior: the 'male' ['il maschio'] and the 'faggot' ['recchione'] who may be a bit effeminate; the

older man and the little boy, who had to be given a gift. The question of recompense in this last relationship (a traditional relationship extending from the Greek-Latin model) was linked to the tradition of ethnic retribution rather than with real prostitution"; see G. De Martino, "Le tarantate del Salento e l'omosessualità," *Babilonia* 15 (June 1984): 16; see also G. De Martino, "Topa," *Babilonia* 8 (1983): 24.

125. See ACS, UCP, Fascicoli personali, b. 996, f. "Umberto T." The teacher, Umberto T., had already been the center of a scandal in April 1938, when two youths robbed him. During the trial that ended with the two boys being condemned, it emerged that their meeting was due to an unnatural "sexual union."

126. On the personal affair and professional career of the Chief of Police Alfonso Molina, see ACS, Direzione Generale P.S., *Divisione Personale PS (1890–1966)*, versamento 1959, b. 31 and b. 31 bis, f. "Molina Alfonso (comm.)." Molina was removed from his position as chief of police of Catania on August 5, 1943, and immediately afterward he risked being sent to a concentration camp by the Allied powers. Even Molina—who had stubbornly fought to prove his virility—was overcome by a fit of crying, showing "his complete lack of any sign of masculine dignity." He was saved thanks to the good offices of the bishop of Catania and a few days later he was recalled to service as the regional inspector of police for eastern Sicily. Later on, in 1944, he was subjected to the judgment of the "High commissioner for sanctions against Fascism" (*L'Alto commissario per sanzioni contro il fascismo*) and proposed for purging because of his history as a Fascist: he had been an efficacious instrument of the police oppression set up by the Fascist regime, he had been an overzealous member of the board for *confino*, he had ties with *gerarchi* and well-known spies of the OVRA, and he had persecuted anti-Fascists for many years. He had carried out harsh repression against subversives in Salerno and had struck up a friendship in Avellino with the prefect Tullio Tamburini "with whom he had orchestrated enthusiastic Fascist activities." Molina justified himself for these accusations maintaining that his activity had not been typical of a dedicated Fascist, but of a severe official, devoted to the laws and his superiors, inflexible and relentless, harsh and energetic when fighting crime and immoral behavior that pimps and delinquents of every kind exploited to prevent social activities from being carried out freely. Thus, in January 1946, after two trials, Molina was acquitted once and for all, but only after being removed from Catania, where he was hated by the people for his harshness and for his close ties with Fascism. Because of his age and the length of service he went into retirement. However, the professional career of this chief of police, who passed unscathed through every change of government from 1910 to 1946, saw its apex on May 10, 1949, when the Ministry of National Security decided to award him the silver medal for civil bravery, after he had attained two testimonials for special merit, two commendations and six bonuses.

127. ACS, *Confino Comune*, b. 94, f. "Salvatore M."

128. Molina denounced the worsening situation saying: "The local police, alarmed by the spreading degeneracy in this city, have intervened to put a stop to, or at least curb this serious sexual aberration that offends morality and is disastrous for the health and improvement of the race but unfortunately the means adopted have proved to be insufficient. Medical examinations, detainment, and heightened surveillance of

entertainment halls and the streets are no longer enough. The pederasts have become more cautious and resort to a host of makeshift alternatives in order to avoid police supervision."

129. ACS, UCP, Fascicoli personali, b. 923, f. "Salvatore S." In some cases the accused defended themselves from the accusation of pederasty by maintaining they had provided proof they were virile men; that they were active and not passive; that they were married and had children. On the contrary, Molina believed this was just another examples of how passive pederasts "adapt to playing the male part when they do not find a male to satisfy their filthy perverse desires." See ACS, UCP, Fascicoli personali, b. 285, f. "Giovanni C."

130. A detainee openly declared that he had been approached by some wealthy individuals who, with their money and cunning, had used him. He was an innocent "victim of one of the many who go around the city of Catania unpunished and un-hindered because they are rich! The consequences fall on the many wretches who are dragged into the abyss of suffering by these unconscionable people." In relation to the resentment of the Catanian *femminelli* for the fact that active pederasts did not suffer the same treatment, see the evidence gathered by Dall'Orto in "Ci furono dei 'femminella' che piangevano quando venimmo via dalle Tremiti."

131. ACS, *Confino Comune*, b. 125, f. "Francesco S."

132. G. Goretti, *Catania 1939*, in E. Venturelli, ed., "Le parole e la storia: Ricerche su omosessualità e cultura," in *Quaderni di critica omosessuale* 9 (Bologna: Il Cassero, 1991), 121.

133. ACS, UCP, Fascicoli personali, b. 865, f. "Domenico R."

134. ACS, UCP, Fascicoli personali, b. 547, f. "Roberto L."

135. ACS, UCP, Fascicoli personali, b. 9, f. "Matteo A." The prefect of Palermo thought that pederasty "undermined the moral framework of young people and damaged physical integrity by encouraging people to be dissolute and depraved, in contrast with the regime's dictates on the education of young people."

136. P. Valera, *Milano sconosciuta* (Milan: Bietti, 1931 [1879]), 159–60, and by the same author see *I gentiluomini invertiti. Echi dello scandalo di Milano* (Milan: Floritta, 1909).

137. Barbagli and Colombo, *Omosessuali moderni*, 180. According to Barbagli and Colombo, the Italian case is atypical precisely because an older model of homosexuality, based on the active/passive contraposition and mixed and unplanned meeting places, resisted here longer than in other European countries. In relation on the situation in cities like Berlin and Paris, where vast homosexual communities flourished, with places of entertainment and secret spots only for men, see M. Bollé, ed., *Eldorado: Homosexuelle Frauen und Männer in Berlin, 1850–1950* (Berlin: Frölich and Kaufmann, 1984); and G. Barbedette and M. Carassou, *Paris Gay 1925* (Paris: Presses de la Renaissance, 1981).

138. A. Dalla Volta, "Una associazione a delinquere," 5.

139. For a description of the dance hall in Piazza Sant'Antonio, see G. Goretti and T. Giartosio, *La città e l'isola: Omosessuali al confino nell'Italia fascista* (Rome: Donzelli, 2006); Goretti, *Catania 1939*, 122; and "Un 'pederasta' catanese al confino," 125, where the person interviewed says: "We often went there. It was a hall in Piazza Sant'Antonio for men

only. You could find boys who were looking for *arrusi*, which is what we call homosexuals, there. Sometimes the police arrived, the vice-squad, and for reasons of public scandal they could give you trouble."

140. Barbagli and Colombo, *Omosessuali moderni*, 257. The authors also give the testimony of some homosexuals who explain that during the Fascist period "there were 'L'Eduardin,' 'La Primavera,' 'La Cà Bianca' or 'Da Mamma Rosa,' in Milan, entertainment halls that some elderly people still remember, where you could dance, watch variety shows and meet up with other men" (179). Besides these places, there were also dwellings everywhere that were used as meeting places for pederasts, and rooms rented for amorous meetings.

141. See ACS, UCP, Fascicoli personali, b. 524, f. "Nunzio H." In May 1939 the police made a raid here and arrested five people, who were subsequently sent to *confino*.

142. Involving women in the regime's mass organizations inevitably fostered a change in customs. Considering the difference between North and South, city and country, and younger and older generations, it is not surprising that there was strong resistance and difficulty in encouraging female activism. On the Fascist attempt to safeguard the traditional role of women and the virtues of domestic life, but at the same time proposing new models of female conduct, necessary to rally women for activities outside the realm of the household, see V. De Grazia, *Le donne nel regime fascista* (Venice: Marsilio, 1993); M. Fraddosio, "Recensione al volume di Victoria De Grazia—Le donne nel regime fascista," *Storia contemporanea*, 2 (1995): 335–44; and H. Dittrich-Johansen, *Le "militi dell'idea": Storia delle organizzazioni femminili del Partito Nazionale Fascista* (Città di Castello: Olschki, 2002).

143. Grimaldi, introduction to *Il popolo al confino*, 38.

144. R. Peyrefitte, *Eccentrici amori* (Milan: Longanesi, 1967 [1949]). For an in-depth analysis of the development of heterosexual and homosexual tourism in Italy, see L. Benadusi, "Turismo, omosessualità e fascismo," *Storia e problemi contemporanei* 43 (2006): 55–80; I. Littlewood, *Sultry Climates: Travel and Sex since the Grand Tour* (London: John Murray, 2001). On Italy seen by foreigners as a place where one can relive the Hellenic ideal of pederasty, see C. Bertelli, "La penisola ermafrodita," in *Storia d'Italia, Annali 2. L'immagine fotografica 1845–1945* (Turin: Einaudi, 1979), 84–86; and R. Aldrich, *The Seduction of the Mediterranean: Writing, Art and Homosexual Fantasy* (London: Routledge, 1993).

145. T. Mann, *Death in Venice* (New York: Ecco, 2004), 52, 82. For autobiographical interpretations of this story by Thomas Mann, see M. Krull, *Nella rete dei maghi: Una storia della famiglia Mann* (Turin: Bollati Boringhieri, 1993), 172; *Letters of Thomas Mann, 1889–1955*, ed. R. Winston (Berkeley: University of California Press, 1990); and A. Heilbut, *Thomas Mann: Eros and Literature* (London: Macmillan, 1996).

146. On the homosexual adventures of these intellectuals in Venice, whose "short trips abroad meant above all freedom—a momentary escape from the accepted morality that . . . made them feel prisoners," see P. Grosskurth, *John Addington Symonds: A Biography* (London: Longmans, 1964), and *The Memoirs of John Addington Symonds* (London: Hutchinson, 1984); A. von Platen, *Tegebücher*, ed. R. Görner (Zurich: Manesse, 1990);

P. Quennell, *Byron in Italy* (London: Collins, 1951); and R. P. Graves, *A. E. Housman: The Scholar-Poet* (Oxford: Oxford University Press, 1981).

147. See A. J. A. Symons, *Alla ricerca del Baron Corvo* (Milan: Longanesi, 1966); *The Quest for Corvo: An Experiment in Biography* (New York: New York Review of Books, 2001); G. Dall'Orto, "Erotismo in gondola," *Pride and Guide* 4 (October 1999): 18–19; and D. Boni, *Geografia del desiderio: Italia immaginata e immagini italiane nelle opere di Frederick Rolfe, Vernon Lee, Norman Douglas* (Capri: La Conchiglia, 2003).

148. See D. Weeks, *Corvo* (London: Joseph, 1971), 306–8. Consequently, the owners decided to move the brothel to Padua.

149. See V. Manzini, *Trattato di diritto penale italiano, secondo il codice del 1930* (Turin: Utet, 1936), 7:253.

150. ACS, CPC, b. 3428, f. 110490. When this Venetian count had served his *confino* sentence he went to Milan, but was immediately forced to return to Venice because he had lured some soldiers into vice with his "perversion." Thanks to Rocco's good offices, he obtained a passport in November 1930 and moved to Paris. However, he attracted the attention of the Polizia Politica in the French capital because he was considered "a very strong adversary of the Regime" with ties to anti-Fascist exiles. Therefore, in February 1933 Michelangelo Di Stefano again asked one of his informers in Paris for "news of this dirty pig"; see ACS, Pol.Pol., b. 23, f. "Conte M.A."

151. Later on, the police dealt with some cases by preventing detainees guilty of pederasty and solicitation from returning to Venice after they had served their sentences, stating that it was a "city with a lot of foreign tourists." See ACS, *Confino Comune*, b. 3, the opinion of the prefect of Venice, June 24, 1936.

152. See ACS, *Confino Comune*, b. 76, f. "Angelo G." Arrested as many as ten times for continually infringing the regulations of *confino* from June 1927 to May 1940, "Norma" was free for only a few days.

153. Informed by a communication, the police carried out a roundup, managing to arrest three of the four Milanese in question. They were immediately sent to *confino*. See ACS, *Confino Comune*, b. 45, f. "Paolo C." and b. 54, f. "Mario C."

154. See ACS, *Confino Comune*, b. 171, f. "Remo V." The file on this Venetian waiter is particularly interesting. There is a note from the Ministry of National Security that reads, "the pederasts in *confino* are all at the Police," thus confirming the instructions to give *confino comune* instead *confino politico*.

155. See ACS, *P.S. A1 1936*, b. 10, f. "Ugo B."

156. See ACS, *Confino Comune*, b. 66, f. "Bruno F."

157. On June 17, 1933, the Court of Assizes of Florence sentenced them to twelve years and four months of imprisonment, a fine of 1,700 lire, and three years of probation.

158. See ACS, UCP, Fascicoli personali, b. 657, f. "Eugenio M."

159. Five were sent to *confino*, sixteen proposed for cautioning and ten for police warning. However, in the end, only thirteen were cautioned because the provincial board decided to give a police warning to two students instead of cautioning them. For one of the individuals, an important citizen, every measure was suspended. Bocchini then communicated the names of the seven pederasts who were members of the Fascist

Party to the vice-secretary of the PNF and their membership cards were immediately
withdrawn.

160. ACS, UCP, Fascicoli personali, b. 117, f. "Giovanni B."

161. Barbagli and Colombo, *Omosessuali moderni*, 261. According to the authors,
many changes that were important for the formation of the modern homosexual came
about with the passage from a traditional model of pederasty to one based on the inversion
of genders. "However much sexual inverts make up a premodern form of interpreting
desires and homoerotic behavior, in some ways they have prepared the ground for the
birth of gays and lesbians" (267).

162. See ACS, UCP, Fascicoli personali, b. 117, f. "Giovanni B."

163. On Mussolini's orders, three of those arrested were sent to *confino* on San Domino,
while five were merely cautioned. The overall number of men given *confino* by the
provincial board of Florence from 1936 to 1939 was thirteen, while about fifty were
cautioned or warned.

164. According to the Polizia Politica, the attorney Agostino Mormino, a former
assistant editor of *Il Popolo*, a member of don Sturzo's team and *pars magna* of the legal
department of the Banco di Santo Spirito, was a pederast who had always carried out
his profession in the Catholic clerical sphere. He had continued his contacts with some
representatives of the Italian Popular Party and informed Sturzo and exiles of "intimate
news against the Regime"; see ACS, Pol.Pol., b. 870, f. "Mormino avv. Agostino."

165. See ACS, UCP, Fascicoli personali, b. 144, f. "Vittorio B." The complaints of
the other detainees who were not so fortunate as to enjoy preferential treatment went
unheeded once the recommendation was verified, Vittorio B. was immediately transferred
to Agnone in the province of Campobasso. On August 16, 1939, after a year of *confino*,
he was acquitted and forbidden to go to Florence. After he was released, an anonymous
letter sent to the police accused him once again of having homosexual relationships
with underage students. However, despite this accusation, his prohibition from Florence
was revoked in June 1940.

166. L. Paciscopi, *Gli anni discontinui: Seduto al caffè con Rosai e Conti* (Florence: Giubbe
Rosse, 1992), 26. On the existential disquiet of Rosai, who found it difficult to reconcile
virile Fascist rhetoric with his strong homosexual inclination, see L. Benadusi, "Comisso,
Rosai e de Pisis: L'arte di vivere nell'Italia fascista," in *Omosapiens: Studi e ricerche sugli
orientamenti sessuali*, ed. D. Rizzo (Rome: Carocci, 2006), 135–52; P. Santi, *Ritratto di Rosai:
Lineamenti di un'esistenza* (Bari: De Donato, 1966); and E. Weiss, "Una dolente bellezza,"
in *Ottone Rosai*, ed. L. Cavallo (Milan: Mazzotta, 1995), 22–27.

167. ACS, *P.S. A1 1942*, b. 99, f. "Rosai Ottone." Nevertheless, the police thought
that Rosai should be put under careful surveillance. On August 19, 1941, the Minister for
National Security wrote to the prefect of Florence: "With regard to the artist Rosai
Ottone, please order that he be put under surveillance, and inform the Minister of any
noteworthy emergency."

168. Although he had continuously been accused of pederasty, in 1943 Ugo S. was
nominated sole administrator of a joint-stock mining company. The prefect of Florence
considered this further proof that the commercial representative had always managed

to get by because he had been a long-standing member of the PNF and had established friendships with many old Fascists. The prefect wrote: "Those who know are starting to suspect that it will be impossible to strike him because he is so well protected, especially among the members of the hierarchy." See ACS, UCP, Fascicoli personali, b. 949, f. "Ugo S."; Pol.Pol., b. 1266, f. "Ugo S." and *P.S. A1 1937*, b. 43, f. "Ugo S."

169. Since 1920 Alberto M. had taken part in numerous punitive missions and was consequently appointed vice commander of the *squadristi* in 1921 and, later, head of the *fascio* of Santa Brigida.

170. The repression of pederasty was particularly intense in Vercelli; the information gathered at the central state archives reveals that there were as many as twenty-three detainees from this province. Many people were cautioned and warned but unfortunately their personal files are missing. The only one still there is that of this political detainee sentenced in 1939.

171. See ACS, UCP, Fascicoli personali, b. 511, f. "Felice G."

172. ACS, Pol.Pol., b. 959, f. "Pietro P. Cav."

173. ACS, UCP, Fascicoli personali, b. 753 and *P.S. A1 1934*, b. 29, f. "Pietro P." Pietro P.'s wife as well fought in every possible way to prevent her husband from being brought to trial. It was not by chance that she wrote a letter begging the Duce to accept her dowry title of forty thousand liras as compensation for the damage and allow her family to be saved. She herself, "all of whose sentiments as a woman, mother, and wife had been offended," had forgiven her husband, "victim of an illness that must have taken control of his actions and dragged him into dishonor."

174. ACS, *Confino Comune*, b. 68, f. "Alfredo F." Alfredo F., who had continually carried out extortions, also fell victim of a swindle. He had lavished money on self-styled brigadiers and others who had guaranteed his immediately acquittal from the cautioning and had given him a false permit to enable him to go home late in the evening. The inquiry revealed that some police officers were responsible as well; however, the measures taken were limited to a cautioning for a former vice brigadier and a reprimand for a police sergeant. See ACS, Pol.Pol., b. 521, f. "Alfredo F."

175. ACS, UCP, Fascicoli personali, b. 901, f. "Antonio Ettore S."

176. It is curious to note that there was deep-rooted hostility toward homosexuals in Eritrea as well. The locals sang "scornful songs at the immoral couple. One went like this: 'Abrahà, Abrahà, Otello suacalò,' which meant in Italian: 'Abrahà, Abrahà, Otello is calling you.' Another was: 'Uoddì fitaurari mi gurtì fanà, cancello chifotò cham signorina,' which means: 'son of fitaurari with a clean face, you open the gate like a young lady.' Abraha's father also found out about his son's relationship with his fellow countryman Otello, and when he came to Adi Quala he said he wanted to kill his son. Then he took him away to Tembien." See ACS, UCP, Fascicoli personali, b. 9, f. "Otello A."

177. See ibid. A Roman driver suffered the same fate. Seen several times in the company of young colored soldiers, and accused of having homosexual relationships with racially "inferior" individuals, he was sentenced to *confino*. See ACS, UCP, Fascicoli personali, b. 154, f. "Luigi B." and *P.S. A4*, b. 68, f. "Luigi B."

178. ACS, *Confino Comune*, b. 149, f. "Francesco C." The unfortunate man managed to get off with nothing more than a police warning because the reports of some medical experts established that he was "clinically ill, for neurological reasons, and not out of sexual perversion for vice or predilection."

179. ACS, *Confino Comune*, b. 160, f. "Pasquale M."

180. ACS, *P.S. A1 1940*, b. 13, f. "Umberto A."

181. ACS, UCP, Fascicoli personali, b. 878, f. "Domenico R."

182. ACS, *Confino Comune*, b. 43, f. "Loris C."

183. Luigi M.'s problems with the law began in 1903 when he was sentenced for injury. Alternating periods of imprisonment for common-law offenses with the provisions imposed by police measures for pederasty followed. This was the reason why cautioning had been proposed for him in 1907, but the delegated judge had decided not to apply the measure. However, he was cautioned in 1910, 1927, and 1934, and was accused each time of being a "passive, violent, overbearing pederast and a usurer." ACS, *Confino Comune*, b. 99, f. Luigi M."

184. There is another case of the death of a detainee confined for passive pederasty. Enrico T., sentenced in 1938 by the provincial board of Ancona to five years of *confino*, had a foot amputated due to gangrene in the prison infirmary and died in 1940 of a brain haemorrhage. See ACS, *Confino Comune*, b. 135, f. "Enrico T."

185. See ACS, *P.S. A1 1939*, b. 8, f. "Sacerdoti immorali" and *Reverendo giù le mani: Clero e reati sessuali negli anni Trenta e negli anni Novanta* (Ragusa: La Fiaccola, 2000). On the Vatican's intervention to save priests sentenced to *confino* for "shameful acts," see also C. M. De Vecchi di Val Cismon, *Tra Papa, Duce e Re* (Rome: Jouvence, 1998), 86. Some homosexuality-related scandals in religious circles had already broken out in the early 1900s, and had given rise to harsh invectives against the immorality of priests and ecclesiastical celibacy. See U. Notari, *Il maiale nero: Rivelazioni e documenti* (Milan: Arte e Lavoro, 1907); A. Costa, *Turpitudini umane* (Milan: L'autore Ed., 1907); and E. Bossi [Milesbo], *La degenerazione professionale del clero cattolico* (Naples: Società editrice partenopea, 1919).

186. ACS, UCP, Fascicoli personali, b. 919, f. "Don Rodolfo S." On the contrary, Alessandro P. was less fortunate, as he was given *confino* for three years but was admitted to the insane asylum of Agrigento, only to be discharged because it was believed that he was feigning the neurological symptoms. Although he was paralyzed after an epileptic attack, he was still considered a faker who deserved three months of solitary confinement in the Bari prison. Alessandro P. was arrested again for insulting the prison guards and died mysteriously in the Palermo prison on October 25, 1939. See ACS, *Confino Comune*, b. 111, f. "Alessandro P."

187. See ACS, UCP, Fascicoli personali, b. 934, f. "Abele S." and b. 1084, f. "Arturo Z." Nothing was achieved by declaring they were victims of a misunderstanding, caused by their poor knowledge of German and by an attempt not to contradict his fellow-sufferer, who had chosen to acknowledge a nonexistent homosexual relationship.

188. See ACS, Pol.Pol., b. 310, f. "Pietro C." The ingenuity of the two Milanese men was disconcerting for their family members as well. In a phone call tapped by the

Servizio speciale riservato, Arturo. Z.'s sister spoke to Abele S.'s sister, saying: "But can anybody be so idiotic as to go and confess such a thing? I could knock my head against the wall. To testify and sign! Do you understand what they have done? They're crazy!" She went on, saying: "They will hush the whole thing up and if you say something you'll end up in prison, too. These things have to be kept hidden, because they don't want the papers talking about it. They don't want scandals like this. If they arrested them for this, they will give them *confino*."

Chapter 5. Madmen or Criminals

1. G. Ruggiero, *The Boundaries of Eros: Sex Crime and Sexuality in Renaissance Venice* (Oxford: Oxford University Press, 1985).

2. A. McLaren, *The Trials of Masculinity: Policing Sexual Boundaries 1870–1930* (Chicago: University of Chicago Press, 1997), 36. On the use of legal sources in the history of gender, see also G. Alessi, "L'uso del diritto nei recenti percorsi della gender history," *Storica* 15 (1999): 105–21.

3. See A. Spallanzani, *Statistiche giudiziarie* (Milan: Giuffrè, 1933). On the reasons for this decrease, see R. Canosa, *Storia della criminalità in Italia 1845–1945* (Turin: Einaudi, 1991), 305–7.

4. M. Foucault, *Abnormal: Lectures at the Collège De France, 1974–1975* (New York: Picador, 2003), 16. See also his "L'évolution de la notion 'd'individu dangereux' dans la psychiatrie légale du XIXe siècle," in *Dits et écrits*, vol. 3 (Paris: Gallimard, 1994).

5. Canosa, *Sesso e Stato*, 146.

6. Ministerial circular, qtd. in G. Neppi Modona, "La magistratura e il fascismo," in *Fascismo e società italiana*, ed. G. Quazza (Turin: Einaudi, 1973), 145.

7. Archivio di Stato di Roma (hereafter ASR), Tribunale di Roma, *Sentenze Penali*, sentenza n.984, 21-02-1930, n.1865/1929 appello registro generale.

8. ASR, Tribunale di Roma, *Sentenze Penali*, sentenza n.4419 del 17 dicembre 1934, n.609/1934 app. reg. gen.

9. ASR, Tribunale di Roma, *Sentenze Penali*, sentenza n.930 del 17 marzo 1934, n.54/1934 registro generale.

10. ASR, *Sentenze Penali*, sentenza n.4279 del 10 dicembre 1934, n.672/1934 app. reg. gen. Also in the case of an employee at the American Consulate, who was reported to the police for indecent behavior because he had been caught by a police officer while molesting a little boy in a train compartment, his "excellent moral record" made him "incapable of committing illicit acts against minors." Consequently, the judge decided to acquit him, accepting the defense of the accused, who declared he had "fondled" the boy to "confirm that the boy's muscles had developed from doing sport" (ASR, *Sentenze Penali*, sentenza n.2170 del 24 aprile 1930, n.72/1929 app. reg. gen.).

11. During the trial of two homosexuals who had been seen while behaving indecently in a public urinal, the Supreme Court of Appeals confirmed that similar behavior was an offense against public morality, and that in regard to the requisite of being in public, urinals were undoubtedly public places. The sentence of five months on probation

was confirmed, but the punishment was remitted (ASR, *Sentenze Penali*, sentenza n.3533 del 25 ottobre 1934, n.191/1934 app. reg. gen.).

12. The last paragraph of Art. 530 of the penal code states that, when the corruption of minors was involved, the offense was not punishable if the minor was already morally corrupt.

13. ASR, *Sentenze Penali*, sentenza n.1275 del 19 aprile 1934, n.884/1934 app. reg. gen.

14. U. Saba, *Ernesto* (Turin: Einaudi, 1979 [1975]), 30-31.

15. According to Giovanni Dall'Orto, the spread of homosexuality among adolescents was also due to the Mediterranean mentality that allowed boys to experiment with homosexuality for a period; furthermore, he believed that the "compensation homosexuality" of those who had limited opportunities for heterosexual intercourse when young was predominantly a "rural homosexuality," because it was practiced mostly by country people. See G. Dall'Orto, "Credere, obbedire, non 'battere,'" *Babilonia* 36 (May 1986): 13-17.

16. N. Praetorius, "À propos de l'article du dr. Laupts sur l'homosexualité dans les 'Archives' du 15 avril 1908," qtd. in Barbagli and Colombo, *Omosessuali moderni*, 243.

17. See P. P. Pasolini, *Ragazzi di vita* (Milan: Garzanti, 1955), and *Una vita violenta* (Milan: Garzanti, 1959). Pasolini believed that the real change in customs and lifestyles, the real "anthropological revolution" of the Italians, did not come about with the end of the Fascist regime but later, in the 1960s, with the economic boom and rise of a consumer society. The rapid changes caused by the "violent homologation of industrialization" led to the lumpenproletariat moving progressively into the middle classes, while the alternative culture of boy prostitutes ready to practice "both heterosexual and homosexual prostitution" and go with "whores or faggots, when they were only nine or ten years old" disappeared once and for all. However, by giving great importance to the changes brought about by a consumer society, Pasolini tended to underestimate the effect of Fascism, which he believed was limited to changing only the appearances and external behavior of the Italians, without really modifying their mentality: Fascism "imposed gestures and actions, demanded submission, but was not capable of changing the old human models, other than on a superficial level." On popular rural culture in the early postwar years, the failure of the totalitarian Fascist design and the changes caused by the economic boom, see some various articles now collected in *Scritti corsari* (Milan: Garzanti, 1993), in particular Sandro Penna: "'Un po' di febbre': Ebreo-tedesco and l'articolo delle lucciole."

18. B. Di Tullio, "Nella delinquenza minorile: reati sessuali e prostituzione maschile," taken from *Bollettino dell'amministrazione carceraria* 4 (Rome 1927): 2.

19. According to him, statistics on crimes from 1922 to 1927 clearly show that most of those sentenced for sexual offenses belonged to the age group between fourteen and eighteen years old. See F. Lucifero, "Epoca puberale e reati sessuali," taken from *Scuola Positiva*, f. 5-6 (Milan: Vallardi, 1934), 4.

20. Lombroso divided delinquents up into five groups: 1) anthropological criminals (born criminals); 2) occasional criminals; 3) insane criminals; 4) criminals of passion; 5) habitual criminals. The various kinds of homosexuality in some way or other led back to these groups as well.

21. C. Lombroso, "Du parallelisme entre l'homosexualité et la criminalité innée," *Archivio di psichiatria, scienze penali ed antropologia criminale* 27 (1906): 378–81. Lombroso believed that the link between pederasts and criminals could be found in another sign common to both, epilepsy.

22. C. Lombroso, *L'uomo delinquente: In rapporto all'antropologia, alla giurisprudenza ed alle discipline carcerarie* (Turin: Bocca, 1924), 203, an abridgement of the last edition, published between 1897 and 1900. The parallel between homosexuality and criminality was taken up again by Mario Carrara, according to whom studies on homosexuality provided proof of the anthropological nature of the origins of crimes. In both cases, it was the hormone secretions that influenced nervous excitability, driving the subject to pederasty or crime. See M. Carrara, "La genesi, la profilassi e la cura dei 'reati sessuali' nella criminologia generale," *Rassegna di studi sessuali* 4 (1924): 245–51.

23. M. Sbriccoli, "Fonti giudiziarie e fonti giuridiche: Riflessioni sulla fase attuale degli studi di storia del crimine e della giustizia criminale," *Studi storici* 2 (April–June 1988): 491–501.

24. On the lack of practical application of Lombroso's ideas and criminal anthropology's paltry contribution to science, see R. Villa, *Il deviante e I suoi segni: Lombroso e la nascita dell'antropologia criminale* (Milan: Franco Angeli, 1985), 228–35. In his scrupulous work, the author rightly stresses that there was "a partial recovery" of criminal anthropology in forensics labs, above all during the Fascist regime. However, in my opinion this recovery was not only partial. In particular, preventive police measures put into effect Lombroso's axiom that criminality was biologically written and therefore completely separate from the actual realization of a crime. There was an anthropological danger inherent in the very nature of criminals, which could be found by the criminal laboratory department by using the instruments provided by medicine, physiognomy, anthropometry, dactyloscopy, and legal photography. On the forensics school and its links with Lombroso's theory, see S. Ottolenghi, "L'opera di Cesare Lombroso e la polizia scientifica," in *L'opera di Cesare Lombroso nella scienza e nelle sue applicazioni*, various authors (Turin: Bocca, 1906), 220–37. On Lombroso's influence during the Fascist regime, see M. Gibson, *Born to Crime: Cesare Lombroso and the Italian Origins of Biological Criminology* (Westport: Praeger, 2002).

25. L. Salerno, ed., *Enciclopedia di polizia* (Milan: Bocca, 1938), 701.

26. See, in addition to the various volumes of the *Bollettino della Scuola Superiore della Polizia Scientifica e dei servizi tecnici annessi*, 11 volumes from 1917 to 1939, S. Ottolenghi, "Nuove ricerche sui rei contro il buon costume," *Archivio di psichiatria, scienze penali ed antropologia criminale* 9 (1888), "La classificazione morale dei detenuti" and "Caratteri psicologici di tre pseudo-ermafroditi," *Atti della società di Medicina legale*, no. 4.

27. S. Ottolenghi, "La nuova 'Cartella Biografica dei Pregiudicati' adottata dall'amministrazione di P.S.," *Atti della società romana di antropologia*, f. I, Rome (1905). On the Fascist regime's valorization of the structure that Ottolenghi had given to the forensics department, see S. Ottolenghi, "Polizia e fascismo," *Bollettino della Scuola Superiore di Polizia e dei servizi tecnici annessi*, f. 18 (1928): 160–67.

28. G. Falco, *La sessuologia nel codice penale italiano* (Milan: Società palermitana editrice medica, 1935), 125–26.

29. Ibid., 129–30.

30. See G. Vidoni, *Per lo studio della prostituzione maschile* (Nocera Inferiore: Tipografia del Manicomio, 1923).

31. A. Mieli, "Per la lotta contro la delinquenza collegata a manifestazioni sessuali," *Rassegna di studi sessuali e di eugenica* 3 (1926), 256–61.

32. Ibid., 260.

33. E. Morselli, *Sessualità umana secondo la psicologia, la biologia e la sociologia* (Turin: Bocca, 1931), 49.

34. See Niceforo, *Le psicopatie sessuali*; F. De Sarlo, "L'origine delle tendenze immorali," in *Saggi di filosofia* (Turin: Clausen, 1896); and H. Ellis, *Psicologia del sesso* (Palermo: Sandron, 1913).

35. A. Gandin, *Omosessualità maschile e femminile: Male—cause—rimedi* (Rome: Mediterranee, 1949), 29.

36. A. Forel, *La questione sessuale esposta alle persone colte* (Turin: Bocca, 1923), 324.

37. La Cara, *La base organica dei pervertimenti sessuali*, 4.

38. P. Falchi, *Un anno di prigionia in Austria* (Florence: Libreria della Voce, 1918), 24. In the 1920 edition, Falchi confirmed that homosexual practices took place in the prison camps "quite freely, as though an expression of normal love"; consequently, "very few [of his] many companions in misfortune managed to escape it." On Falchi's description of a love affair between two prisoners, see the chapter "Amori dietro il reticolo" (83–90).

39. A. Dalla Volta, *Catamnesi dei prigionieri di guerra: Contributo allo studio della psicologia del dopoguerra* (Turin: Bocca, 1920), 314. See also his *Studi di psicologia e di psichiatria sulla prigionia di guerra* (Florence: Ricci, 1919).

40. Ibid., 317.

41. V. Massarotti, *Nel regno di Ulrichs: Appunti e considerazioni sull'omosessualità maschile* (Rome: Bernardo Lux Editore, 1913), 16.

42. Dalla Volta, *Catamnesi dei prigionieri di guerra*, 319. The author believed that the main consequence of the war was, borrowing an expression from Mosse, the "brutalization" of life, because "the war undoubtedly accustomed a vast generation to violence, and in particular sexual violence."

43. R. Conforti, *Intorno al diritto di punire e al codice criminale del Regno italico* (Turin: Franco e figli, 1860), 27.

44. See Spinelli, *Come ho tentato di diventare saggio*, 171–73.

45. On the position of the Italian left toward homosexuality, see F. Giovannini, *Comunisti and diversi: Il PCI e la questione omosessuale* (Bari: Dedalo, 1980), 45–51; and G. Dall'Orto, "La rivoluzione contro gli omosessuali e la contro-rivoluzione del socialismo," *Lotta continua*, January 14, 1982. For communist morality, see S. Bellassai, *La morale comunista: Pubblico e privato nella rappresentazione del PCI (1947–1956)* (Rome: Carocci, 2000); and A. Tonelli, *Politica e amore: Storia dell'educazione ai sentimenti nell'Italia contemporanea* (Bologna: il Mulino, 2003).

46. A. Dellepiane, *Alle case rosse: Memorie di un recluso politico* (Milan: La Prora, 1945), 99. The episode regards what happened to a young detainee of the Tremiti islands when in transit to the Foggia prison.

47. See T. Murri, *Galera* (Milan: Modernissima, 1928 [1920]). On the legal implications and influence on public opinion of the Murri case, see N. Tranfaglia, "Un delitto di gente per bene: Il processo Murri (1902–1905)," in *Storia d'Italia. Annali 12: La criminalità*, ed. L. Violante (Turin: Einaudi, 1997), 525–52; and V. P. Babini, *Il caso Murri: Una storia italiana* (Bologna: il Mulino, 2004).

48. Letter sent to Mussolini and published in *Il Fascio*, Milan, February 13, 1926.

49. Murri, *Galera*, 316–17.

50. La Cara, *La base organica dei pervertimenti sessuali*, 120. De Napoli also believed that forced chastity could be the cause of sexual inversion, as individuals who already had this tendency became homosexual in the absence of women, even though they went back to being "themselves again as soon as the need for the brief perversion ceased" (De Napoli, *Sesso e amore*, 444).

51. B. Di Tullio, "Spunti sulla vita e sulla patologia sessuale nelle carceri," *Rassegna di studi sessuali e di eugenica* 5 (1925): 180.

52. Ibid., 181.

53. Ibid., 187.

54. G. A. Belloni, *L'eros incatenato: Studio sul problema sessuale penitenziario* (Milan: Bocca, 1939). The author maintained that "occasional" homosexuality in prison could become "habitual" and eventually lead to a real form of "homosexuality that was securely, if not permanently, acquired" (48).

55. According to Belloni, homosexuality was extremely common in prison. Havelock Ellis may have exaggerated when he proposed that the number of cases of pederasty reached 80 percent, but many underestimated the situation. It is very likely that over 20 percent of the total number of prisoners were pederasts (see Belloni, *L'eros incatenato*, 57–59). Homosexual prisoners could be divided into three categories: young novices who were victims of the violence of other prisoners, "normal men" blinded by forced abstinence from regular sexual intercourse, and "proven inverts" ready to lead astray the other uncorrupted prisoners (51).

56. Ibid., 71.

57. Many scholars were in favor of allowing prisoners to have sexual intercourse with their wives or with prostitutes, also taking into consideration the high number of cases of pederasty and the spread of the worrying "scourge" of onanism. The debate on this problem arose primarily at the beginning of the 1930s; in fact, the *Rivista di diritto penitenziario* published various articles on the issue: see B. Leòn y Leòn, "Il problema della funzione sessuale negli istituti penitenziari," 5 (1930); S. Cicala, "Sesso e pena," 1 (1931); L. Thòt, "Il problema sessuale nelle carceri," 6 (1931); C. Di Maria-Gomez, "Sui rapporti coniugali in carcere," 6 (1932); R. Vozzi, "Contro la concessione sessuale nelle carceri," 6 (1932). See also G. Scaglione, "Il problema della funzione sessuale negli istituti penitenziari," *Rassegna di studi sessuali* 4 (1930): 305–8.

58. Confidential ministerial circular sent to all prison directors on March 6, 1936, titled *Pratiche pederastiche*, in ACS, Ministero di Grazia e giustizia, *Direzione Generale per gli Istituti di Prevenzione e Pena*, b. 10, f. 44 "Segreteria," s.f. 1 "Pratiche pederastiche."

59. For example, Emilio Tucchi, director of the Cagliari prison, made a distinction

between clinical homosexuals and those who were so because of environmental factors. The former were passive pederasts who "are the cause of temptation for normal convicts in prison, because when the latter are overcome by sexual frenzy due to prolonged sexual abstinence, they adapt themselves to the substitutes. The younger and better-looking these accomplices are, the less disgust they feel." On the contrary, the latter were "normal men who abandon themselves to acts of depravation due to the constrictions they are subjected to." The most dangerous in this "monstrous parody of pure love" were those "who sell themselves to those willing to pay. They have no moral sense, they sell their bodies like any prostitute, and if someone does not pay them, they have no qualms about resorting to illegal measures."

60. Before the Fascists came to power, the Alghero penitentiary was reserved specifically for pederasts.

61. Emanuele Mirabella observed that, in prison, the old Camorra members used lewd songs to initiate the younger prisoners into the mysteries of the sect, especially into pederasty and sodomy. See E. Mirabella, *Mala vita: Gergo, camorra e costumi degli affiliati* (Naples: Perrella, 1910); and A. De Blasio, *Usi e costumi dei camorristi* (Naples: Luigi Pierro editore, 1897).

62. The cubicle sections were special prison divisions made up of small, individual and separate rooms, with small cells, three by two meters, where single prisoners were shut up and kept in complete isolation. These buildings with the cubicle or Hauburnian system had been highly criticized, to the point that continuous segregation in cells was considered inhumane and was abolished. However, almost all the directors proposed using them for pederasts, who were to be included among the prisoners indicated by Art. 44 of the new regulations for reform schools and penitentiaries, for whom isolation was obligatory, as they were not suited for living together with others. On segregation in cells, see S. Longhi, "Limiti e modalità del regime cellulare nel sistema penitenziario moderno," *Rivista penale* 8 (1930): 865–70; and G. Novelli, "Note sulla segregazione cellulare," *Rivista di diritto penitenziario: Studi teorici e pratici* 1 (1931): 105–17.

63. The regulations for penitentiaries and reform schools, June 18, 1931 (787), did not expressly punish homosexual relationships, against which sanctions were applied in any case with Art. 165 on indecent behavior and acts against public morality.

64. R. Conti, *Il mondo delle prigioni* (L'Aquila: Stabilimento tipografico aquilano, 1938), chap. 11: "Pederastia: Confessioni d'un degenerato," 103–13.

65. Ibid., 106.

66. Ibid., 153. Conti ended his book by praising the arrival of Fascism and extolling the Duce's work of instilling a new spirit in the Italians: "A Man who knew how to mold the new national spirit and face the imminent danger was needed. Divine Providence, watching over the destiny of our Fatherland, has offered us the Hero of our race, He who was to lead the Nation to the highest goals: the Duce! . . . Having taken up the reins of the State, the Duce molded Italy's new psyche and strengthened the Nation from every point of view" (204).

67. See R. Pogolotti, "Configurazioni criminali con carattere psicopatico," *Archivio di antropologia criminale* 6 (November–December 1933): 726–49.

68. Lombroso himself tried to fight homosexuality right from his first experience in the insane asylum in Pavia and took great interest in the problem of tribadism, "a disgraceful practice" that was difficult to eradicate. Lombroso's use of bromide and camphor on patients, increase of supervision, and even cauterizing the clitorises of patients turned out to be fruitless. In his opinion, the cause of female homosexuality depended on epilepsy and cretinism. The only possible solution was to expel "the old cretin who had originally introduced tribadism into the asylum." See C. Lombroso, "Del tribadismo nei manicomi," *Archivio di psichiatria, scienze penali e antropologia criminale* (Turin, 1885), 6:218–21.

69. See M. Foucault, Valerio Marchetti, Antonella Salomoni, and Arnold I. Davidson, *Abnormal: Lectures at the Collège De France, 1974–1975* (New York: Picador), 2003.

70. M. Galzigna, "Soggetti e dispositivo nell'archivio della follia," in *L'archivio della follia: Il manicomio di San Servolo e la nascita di una Fondazione. Antologia di testi e documenti*, ed. M. Galzigna and H. Terzian (Venice: Marsilio, 1980), 68.

71. See M. Foucault, *Madness and Civilization: A History of Insanity in the Age of Reason* (New York: Vintage Books, 1988), 208.

72. The number of inmates of insane asylums increased fourfold in Italy from 1880 to 1910, going from 12,210 to 54,311, and continued to rise, from 60,127 in 1926 to 96,423 in 1941. See G. Modena, *Le malattie mentali in Italia* (Rome: Tip. operaia romana, 1928); and R. Canosa, *Storia del manicomio in Italia dall'unità ad oggi* (Milan: Feltrinelli, 1979), 154–57.

73. Foucault, *Madness and Civilization*; K. Dörner, *Madmen and the Bourgeoisie: A Social History of Insanity and Psychiatry* (Oxford: Blackwell, 1981). See also M. Cagossi, "Tra Dörner e Foucault: Storia sociale e critico-strutturalismo della psichiatria," *Archivio di psicologia neurologia e psichiatria* 3 (July–September 1977): 409–17. Although Dörner criticized Foucault's theories, according to which bourgeois society completed the work of creating a "reign of silence" over the mad, the idea of asylums as institutions that functioned for the dominating social classes, which used them as repressive instruments to be applied almost exclusively to individuals of subordinate classes, is repeated by both authors. Power and domination were practiced, mainly on the destitute, through the use of medical knowledge. Dörner, in particular, underscored the fact that insane asylums were an answer to the "unreason" of those who put the order of capitalist-bourgeois society at risk, which thus provided itself with a useful way of segregating and excluding them. According to Canosa as well, psychiatric power was useful for isolating the social levels that class interests or political motives had caused to be considered marginal or dangerous for public order. In his opinion, insane asylums were institutions offering refuge rather than medical care, "structures that handled the illness and continued to obey their own laws as places of exclusion, laws that were closer to those of prisons than those of hospitals" (Canosa, *Storia del manicomio*, 186).

74. Psychiatrists tended to justify internment in insane asylums, passing it off as a useful instrument to prevent homosexuals from being "dragged into criminality . . . by their abnormal licentiousness" (P. Gonzales, "Due casi di pervertimento sessuale," *Archivio di Psichiatria, Neuropatologia, Antropologia criminale e Medicina legale* 1–2 [1904]: 38).

75. See for example D. Centini, "Sull'inversione sessuale," *Rassegna di studi psichiatrici* 3 (1935): 833ff.

76. Discharging patients also had to be authorized with a court ruling requested by the director of the asylum, or by relatives, guardians, or free citizens, in the last three cases after hearing the director's opinion.

77. Qtd. in Canosa, *Storia del manicomio*, 158.

78. See P. Sorcinelli, *La repressione ambigua: Il caso giudiziario e psichiatrico di un finto frate agli inizi del '900* (Milan: Franco Angeli, 1989), and "Dagli archivi della follia alla storia della società," in *Emarginazione, criminalità e devianza in Italia fra '600 e '900*, ed. A. Pastore and P. Sorcinelli (Milan: Franco Angeli, 1990), 145–65.

79. H. Terzian, "La formazione di un archivio dell'emarginazione e della follia: Prospettive di ricerca e riflessioni," in *L'archivio della follia*, ed. M. Galzigna and H. Terzian, 32.

80. See M. Galzigna, "Crimine e coscienza: Nascita della psichiatria forense," in *La follia, la norma, L'archivio: Prospettive storiografiche e orientamenti archivistici*, ed. M. Galzigna (Venice: Marsilio, 1984), 17–47; and V. P. Babini, "La responsabilità nelle malattie mentali," in *Tra sapere e potere: La psichiatria italiana nella seconda metà dell'Ottocento*, various authors (Bologna: Il Mulino, 1982), 135–98.

81. See R. Villa, "Perizie psichiatriche e formazione degli stereotipi dei devianti: Note per una ricerca," in *Follia, psichiatria e società*, ed. A. De Bernardi, 385–402; and I. Virotta, *La perizia nel processo penale italiano* (Padua: Cedam, 1968).

82. See G. Di Marco, "Criminalità e follia. Nascita del manicomio criminale in Italia," *Fogli di informazione* 20 (1975): 102–22; and A. Manacorda, *Il manicomio giudiziario Cultura psichiatrica e scienza giuridica nella storia di un'istituzione totale* (Bari: De Donato, 1982).

83. V. Pezzi, "Il San Lazzaro negli anni del Regime (1920–1945)," *Contributi*, 19–20, *Regime e società civile a Reggio Emilia 1920–1946* (Reggio Emilia: Biblioteca Municipale "A. Panizzi," 1986), 1:505.

84. See S. Von Notzing, *La terapia suggestiva delle psicopatie sessuali con speciale riguardo all'inversione sessuale* (Turin: Bocca, 1897); and A. Luzenberger, *Sul meccanismo dei pervertimenti sessuali e loro terapia* (Rome: Capaccini, 1897).

85. These remedies were strongly criticized. For example, the psychiatrist Auguste Forel believed that those who encouraged such marriages were committing a crime. The law, then, should have "proceeded rigorously against such unions and not against sexual intercourse between adult males" (Forel, *La questione sessuale esposta alle persone colte*, 356–57).

86. De Napoli, *Sesso e amore*, 1012.

87. Homosexuals themselves were afraid they would transmit their "misfortune" to their children. In fact, their doctors often urged them to have intercourse with women; one of them asked: "But have I the right to undertake such a cure? And, once cured, what if I beget unfortunate children who sadly inherit this mental anomaly of mine!? How much I would have to curse my selfish lack of foresight!!!" (Mantegazza, *Gli amori degli uomini*, 282).

88. See for example E. Goldberg, "La sterilizzazione eugenetica dello Stato di Utah," *Archivio di antropologia criminale* 2 (May–June 1936): 336–40. On the matter of

eugenics in Italy, see C. Pogliano, "Scienza e stirpe: eugenica in Italia (1912–1939)," *Passato e presente* 5 (1984): 61–97, and "Eugenisti, ma con giudizio," in *Nel nome della razza: Il razzismo nella storia d'Italia 1870–1945*, ed. A. Burgio (Bologna: Il Mulino, 2000), 423–42; C. Mantovani, *Rigenerare la società: L'eugenetica in Italia dalle origini ottocentesche agli anni Trenta* (Catanzaro: Rubbettino, 2004); and Francesco Cassata, *Molti, sani e forti: L' eugenetica in Italia* (Torino: Bollati Boringhieri, 2006).

89. G. Mariani, *La questione sessuale: Fisiopatologia, sociologia e legislazione sociale* (Milan: Istituto editoriale scientifico, 1926), 46.

90. ACS, Ministero di Grazia e giustizia, *Direzione Generale per gli Istituti di Prevenzione e Pena*, b. 10, f. 44 "Segreteria," s.f. 1 "Pratiche pederastiche."

91. On the whole affair, see G. Riefolo and T. Losavio, "Tra Ottocento e Novecento: La psichiatria italiana attraverso i documenti clinici di S. Maria della Pietà," in *L'ospedale dei pazzi di Roma dai papi al '900: Lineamenti di assistenza e cura a poveri e dementi*, ed. A. L. Bonella (Bari: Dedalo, 1994), 2:164–65.

92. For example, in 1923 an inquiry was carried out in the Aversa insane asylum by legal authorities to check if acts of sodomy between patients were in fact frequent. After the inspection, the rumor was considered groundless because it had been started by a revengeful patient with a life sentence who was "paranoiac and famous for frenzied activity" and who had been "caught with the insane intention of committing lustful acts on a young patient"; see ACS, Ministero di Grazia e giustizia, *Direzione Generale per gli Istituti di Prevenzione e Pena*, b. 11, f. 56, s.f. 5/5, "Manicomi criminali" and f. 57, "Ispezioni ed inchieste." On the frequency of such accusations, see Sorcinelli, *La repressione ambigua*, 73; and Pezzi, "Il San Lazzaro negli anni del Regime (1920–1945)," 448–53.

Chapter 6. The Political Use of Homosexuality

1. Mussolini extolled the monolithic nature of the party saying: "Fascism does not allow heterodoxy. . . . Fascism won because it has always put a stop to tendencies, factions and even simple differentiations: it is a monolithic block" (B. Mussolini, "Viatico per il 1926," *Gerarchia* [January 1926]).

2. "Il Terzo Congresso del Partito Comunista d'Italia," qtd. in *Mussolini il fascista: L'organizzazione dello Stato fascista, 1925–1929*, ed. R. De Felice (Turin: Einaudi, 1995), 4. De Felice was one of the first to understand that the monolithic nature of Fascism was purely superficial, stressing the difficult search for balance among its various elements, with the clash of personalities and allied groups. On "dialectics among the varying Fascist currents," see R. De Felice, *The Jews in Fascist Italy: A History* (New York: Enigma, 2001), 56–57.

3. E. Gentile, *La via italiana al totalitarismo: Il partito e lo Stato nel regime fascista* (Rome: La Nuova Italia, 1995), 180.

4. S. Lupo, *Il fascismo: La politica in un regime totalitario* (Rome: Donzelli, 2000), 24. According to Lupo, the fact that there were many PNF members who were first expelled and then readmitted, progressively increased the recourse to the use of "policy of dossiers." The permanent conflict among the Fascist ranks involved political life, from the center

to the provinces, and "ideological polemics—radicalism versus moderatism, early Fascism versus recent Fascism, the real or falsified merits of the period prior to the march on Rome—slowly gave way to moral controversies regarding the public, private, and even sexual spheres" (325).

5. Qtd. in A. Turati, *Ragioni ideali di vita fascista* (Rome: Berlutti, 1926), 103.

6. See E. Gentile, "Mussolini: I volti di un mito," in *Storia e interpretazioni del fascismo* (Rome: Laterza, 2002), 134.

7. Farinacci, who was probably the most important exponent of this policy based on control and blackmail, maintained emblematically that "every Fascist must be a carabiniere to the next." See "Roberto Farinacci ai fascisti cremonesi," *Il Regime fascista* (November 1, 1927), qtd. in Lupo, *Il fascismo*, 260. Mussolini himself, who was spied on by the Polizia Politica because Bocchini had his phone calls tapped and transcribed, openly acknowledged the importance of this widespread control of top *gerarchi* and confided to Emil Ludwig: "Most of the important positions in the country are covered by able Fascists. What they don't already do out of loyalty, they do out of fear because they know they are being controlled" (E. Ludwig, *Colloqui con Mussolini* [Milan: Mondadori, 2001], 84).

8. According to Cesare Rossi, "Mussolini was always delighted with espionage intrigues and plots against others, and was extremely indulgent toward the informers who worked for him. Naturally, given his intrinsically factious nature, he demanded the hangman's noose for rival informers. . . . Considering his attitude toward low-level informers, it is perfectly clear how zealous he was. He enjoyed it and meddled in this murky police work whenever he could" (C. Rossi, *Trentatré vicende mussoliniane* [Milan: Meschina, 1958], 278–79). On the surveillance of top PNF officials ordered by Mussolini in order to keep them under control and know how to attack them when necessary, see also De Felice, *Mussolini il fascista*, 349.

9. Rossi, *Trentatré vicende mussoliniane*, 426.

10. In May 1937, the *podestà* of Sgurgola was the victim of an anonymous letter sent to the Ministry of National Security, in which he was accused of turning the workmen's club premises into a billiard room and a place where adults and boys practiced pederasty. The statement requested that this unworthy *podestà*, "who had preached free love up to 1926," be immediately replaced in order to put an end to "this despicable round table." See ACS, *P.S. C2A 1937*, b. 5, f. "Movimento sovversivo antifascista—Frosinone."

11. On the progressive rise of the cult of Mussolini to the detriment of Fascism, see S. Colarizi, *L'opinione pubblica degli italiani sotto il regime* (Rome: Laterza, 1991), 161–66.

12. See R. De Felice, *Mussolini il duce: Gli anni del consenso 1929–1936* (Turin: Einaudi, 1996), 203–4.

13. ACS, Segreteria particolare del duce, Carteggio riservato (hereafter SPD, CR), b. 40, f. "Farinacci Roberto," Farinacci's letter to Mussolini on January 20, 1932.

14. The practice of setting up one's own efficient system of spies had begun even before the Fascists came to power. During the period of *squadrismo*, the various *ras* had set up their own networks of informers, which they maintained for long periods to use against their party rivals; see A. Lyttelton, *The Seizure of Power: Fascism in Italy, 1919–1929* (London: Routledge, 2004). Balbo, Turati, Farinacci, Starace, and other *gerarchi* had

invented a number of secret police forces, and there was often friction between their own informers and those of the Polizia Politica. Farinacci admitted openly that "every *gerarca* forms the nucleus of his informers against his personal enemies," creating "a dishonest confusion of misunderstandings, insinuations, slander and suspicion" (ACS, SPD, CR, b. 40, f. "Farinacci Roberto," Farinacci's letter to Mussolini, January 20, 1932).

15. Mussolini spent the first part of the morning in talks with the chiefs of the various police services (*carabinieri*, OVRA, and the police force); information from the police force and the reports of the spies were "the most urgent subjects to be examined in the daily mechanism of a totalitarian state." See Q. Navarra, *Memorie del cameriere di Mussolini* (Milan: Longanesi, 1946), 134–35. Nino D'Aroma was also amazed at the particular attention Mussolini paid to police reports: "I told Mussolini I was amazed at his morbid curiosity for police reports, the kind of rubbish and falsehoods that certain people put down periodically on paper to regularize a monthly check. He always justified himself by saying that gossip—as he called it—teaches a lot" (N. D'Aroma, *Mussolini segreto* [Bologna: Cappelli, 1958], 126–27).

16. Bocchini knew that, especially for the men who were capable of threatening the undisputed rule of the Duce, "it was necessary to have the papers ready to be able to strike them," and he patiently gathered information to be used when Mussolini suddenly decided to remove somebody; see A. Turati, *Fuori dall'ombra della mia vita: Dieci anni nel solco del fascismo*, ed. A. Fappani (Brescia: Centro Bresciano di Iniziative Culturali, 1973), 86–87.

17. N. Zapponi, *Stili di vita fasciti: L'arte di sopravivere*, in *L'economia domestica—secc. XIX–XX*, ed. G. Aliberti (Pisa: Istituti editoriali e poligrafici internazionali, 1995), 174. Zapponi rightly stresses that by becoming increasingly intrusive, this "Fascist style" tended to turn into oppressive formalism that "stiffened and straightened out the eccentric the threatening and eccentric ethics of its origins, with the starch of discredited bourgeois virtues" (179). In some cases, it was precisely the attention that the regime paid to formalities and lifestyles that led to misleading interpretations, which tended to reduce Fascism to an attempt to achieve an ideal of aesthetic perfection. See, for example, R. J. Golsan, ed., *Fascism, Aesthetics, and Culture* (Hanover: University Press of New England, 1992); and S. Falasca Zamponi, *Fascist Spectacle: The Aesthetics of Power in Mussolini's Italy* (Berkeley: University of California Press, 1997).

18. See L. Benadusi, "Private Life and Public Morals: Fascism and the 'Problem' of Homosexuality," *Totalitarian Movements and Political Religions* 2 (Autumn 2004): 171–204.

19. See C. Rossi, *Mussolini com'era* (Rome: Ruffolo, 1947), 199. According to D'Aroma, Mussolini was continually informed about the behavior of the *gerarchi* in private and quipped: "men must be observed and judged from their belts up. The rest is nobody else's business" (D'Aroma, *Mussolini segreto*, 427).

20. On the organization of the Fascist Polizia Politica, the secret services and particularly the OVRA, see E. Rossi, *La pupilla del duce, l'Ovra* (Parma: Guanda, 1956); G. Leto, *Ovra: Fascismo-antifascismo* (Bologna: Cappelli, 1952), and *Polizia segreta in Italia* (Rome: Vito Bianco, 1961); M. Franzinelli, *I tentacoli dell'Ovra: Agenti, collaboratori e vittime*

della polizia politica fascista (Turin: Bollati Boringhieri, 2000); F. Fucci, *Le polizie di Mussolini: La repressione dell'antifascismo nel "ventennio"* (Milan: Mursia, 2001); R. Canosa, *I servizi segreti del duce: I persecutori e le vittime* (Milan: Mondadori, 2001); and M. Canali, *Le spie del regime* (Bologna: il Mulino, 2004).

21. M. Franzinelli, *Delatori: Spie e confidenti anonimi; L'arma segreta del regime fascista* (Milan: Mondadori, 2002), 10.

22. During Dobbert's long stay in Italy, he published a book titled *Economia fascista*, in which he openly praised corporatism. However, the police suspected he was providing financial information to the German Minister of Foreign Affairs and consequently kept a close watch on him. See ACS, Pol.Pol., b. 446, f. "Dobbert Gerardo" and P.S. *A4*, b. 111, f. "Dobbert Gherard."

23. On the accusations that Pozzi was a homosexual, see ACS, SPD, CR, b. 40, f. "Farinacci Roberto," Farinacci's letter sent to Giuriati on October 30, 1931. After the fall of Giampaoli, Pozzi tried to establish ties with his successor, Rino Parenti, attempting to find a place for himself in the new Milanese federation and striking up friendships with various *gerarchi* in order to be able to influence their political choices. For more biographical details, see ACS, Polizia politica fascicoli per materia (hereafter Pol.Mat.), b. 5, f. 2 e ACS, P.S. *A1 1929*, b. 22, f. "Pozzi Alessandro." See also his letters sent in the summer of 1944 to the Duce and to other important *gerarchi*, in ACS, SPD, CO, RSI, b. 55, f. 4641 "Pozzi Alessandro" and ACS, *Segreteria del Capo della Polizia*, RSI 1943–1945, b. 17, f. "Pozzi Alessandro."

24. Pozzi's recruitment was like that of many of the "Fascists of the first hour" who, after the early movement and its aspirations ended with the formation of the regime, preferred being recycled as political informers to the difficult road of dissention. Despite this, Pozzi was always nostalgic for the origins of Fascism, its boldness, nonconformity, and continual commitment to revolution. In this regard, his report on Aldo Bordoni, the founder of the Milanese "Volante" squad, the first Fascist action squad, is emblematic; see ACS, Pol.Pol., b. 167, f. "Bordoni Aldo."

25. Pozzi did not limit himself to reporting boys, who were mainly from the slums and with whom he had been relationships, but provided detailed information on former legionnaires, reconstructing their biographies and reporting on their political tendencies. See for example his report in ACS, Pol.Pol., b. 263, f. "Castelbarco Visconti conte Pier Filippo."

26. See N. Naldini, *Vita di Giovanni Comisso* (Turin: Einaudi, 1985), 150.

27. G. Comisso, *La mia casa di campagna* (Milan: Lerici, 1968), 174. Comisso's deep resentment toward Pozzi was mainly due to intense rivalry in love.

28. Ibid., 117. Nico Naldini's reconstruction of Pozzi's murder does not correspond exactly with Comisso's: "At one o'clock in the afternoon a group of partisans entered his house, dragged him nude from the bed where he was sleeping with his housekeeper, beat him first with a club then tried to slit his throat with a knife they had picked up in the kitchen, but only made a shallow cut. They then beat him again with the club and shot him with a revolver, wounding him mortally; however, he still had the strength to struggle and call for help while he fell down the stairs outside the house. He was buried on

November 28 in the cemetery of Serrada under a big rock. A few days later, the *Corriere* published his obituary notice" (Naldini, *Vita di Giovanni Comisso*, 210–11). Ferdinando Gerra also gives us a profile of Pozzi similar to Comisso's: "Sandro Pozzi lived habitually in Milan and did not practice any profession except that of spying for the Ministry of National Security and as an OVRA agent. He practiced political blackmail as well, and these activities had always earned him enough to live on, as well as to purchase a house in Folgaria. During the partisan struggle he was killed by the partisans"; see "Fondo Fiumano Gerra," a comment on the book by S. Pozzi, *Guido Keller: Nel pensiero, nelle gesta* (Milan: Ed. Mediolanum, 1933), in Rome's Biblioteca nazionale.

29. ACS, Pol.Mat., b. 181, f. 11 "Falsificazione monete, biglietti e titoli di Stato."

30. On Mambrini and the network of informers who worked under him, see Canali, *Le spie del regime*, 65–66, 73–75.

31. Although Terracini had always tried to deny his homoerotic tendencies, justifying some aspects of his behavior with the need to infiltrate homosexual anti-Fascist circles, the police considered him a pederast anyway. In December 1935, it was not by chance that, when Di Stefano gave him the task of keeping watch on one homosexual, he commented: "Please ask 'Terra' if he knows him. They are colleagues!!" (ACS, Pol.Pol., b. 1436, f. "Villano della Polla").

32. ACS, CPC, b. 981, f. "Campaner Luigino detto Torzo." Torzo was up against the police in Nice as well, this time due to his homosexuality: in fact, in 1933 the police stopped him because he had been "caught in an entertainment hall patronized by perverts."

33. In July 1930, Torzo managed to pass the border at Ventimiglia with the help of an Turinese industrialist who hid him in his car in a trunk; see ACS, Pol.Pol., b. 634, f. "Gritti Mario e Edoardo."

34. ACS, Pol.Pol., b. 224, f. "Campaner Torzo Luigi." Torzo Campaner had relations with Nitti, Rosselli, Nenni, Modigliani, and other Socialists, but he was critical toward the Concentration, a position that Terracini tried to exploit to divide the anti-Fascists.

35. See ACS, Pol.Pol., b. 74 A, f. "Quaglino Alfredo."

36. On Terracini's activities as an informer, see Canali, *Le spie del regime*, 150–51.

37. Bocchini's report on Terracini, sent to the Ministry of National Security on December 2, 1938, in ASR, *Corte d'appello*, II versamento, corte d'assise speciale, b. 85, f. "Terracini Vittorio."

38. The deposition of the archivist Domenico Farese of the general police headquarters, taken at the trial before the High Commissioner for Sanctions against Fascism, on July 19, 1945. Farese stated: "Terracini very often spoke of various subjects and especially about Jews and pederasts, sometimes even about communism and communists. His reports were almost always against Jews"; see ASR, *Corte d'appello*, II versamento, corte d'assise speciale, b. 85, f. "Terracini Vittorio." The archivist's statements were later confirmed by the Vice Chief of Police Saverio Caccavale at the trial against Guido Leto.

39. See ACS, *P.S. A1 1938*, b. 52, f. "Terracini Vittorio" and ACS, *Demorazza*, b. 30, f. "Terracini Vittorio."

40. ACS, Pol.Pol., b. 1494, f. "Guglielmo Z."

41. See ACS, Pol.Pol., b. 43, f. "Alberto A."

42. ACS, Pol.Pol., b. 520, f. "Forte Raffaele." Francesco Nudi asked Di Stefano what he thought of a possible job for Forte with the OVRA, explaining that in Paris he had been in contact "with Torzo Gino, Morosini (first name unknown), and with a certain Terracini, a confidential representative of the Ministry sent to Stresa with two other informers when the well-known Conference took place"; alongside the report, Mambrini wrote: "*all well-known pederasts including Forte*," expressing his disappointment about using the former carabiniere.

43. See H. Woller, *I conti con il fascismo: L'epurazione in Italia 1943-1948* (Bologna: Il Mulino, 1997); and Canali, *Le spie del regime*, 494–555. It is strange to note that the only official who was not readmitted to the police force after the purge was Alessandro Baggio Ducarne; however, the decision did not depend on his activity as an informer within the Polizia Politica but because he had "shown homosexual tendencies" (511–12).

44. ASR, *Corte d'appello*, II versamento, corte d'assise speciale, b. 85, f. "Terracini Vittorio."

45. ACS, Pol.Mat., b. 44, f. 7, s.f. "Germania polizia." In November 1933, Tavolato was invited to collaborate with the German Polizia Politica precisely because of his past as a journalist, his long activity in public and political affairs in favor of an agreement between Italy and Germany and his knowledge of German.

46. ACS, *Alto commissariato per le sanzioni contro il fascismo (1944-1947)*, title XII (Affari delle sezioni disciplinari contro gli appartenenti e i fiduciari dell'Ovra), f. XII-11-668, "Italo Tavolato." Kusen was described as "an individual with a superficial character," who "suffered from the illness of pederasty." Kusen maintained that he was struck off the German press register because of his hostility toward Nazism; however, in actual fact it seems that the reason was "for his homosexual tendencies more than for political reasons." See ACS, Presidenza del Consiglio dei ministri, Servizi informativi e sicurezza (hereafter PCM, SIS), *Alto Commissario per le sanzioni contro il fascismo*, petitions of OVRA informers, b. 12, f. 208 "Kusen Goffredo."

47. ACS, *P.S. A1 1937*, b. 44, f. "Tavolato Italo."

48. In the postwar period, Tavolato and Kusen were called on to answer for their actions but, like many other informers of the Polizia Politica, they appealed to be struck off the list of OVRA informers. In June 1947 Tavolato's appeal was rejected, but Kusen's was accepted because "his activity as an informer was in the field of military counter-espionage, rather than in diplomatic circles"; see ACS, PCM, SIS, Alto commissariato per i reati fascisti, Ricorsi Confidenti OVRA b. 11, f. 173 "Italo Tavolato" and b. 12, f. 208 "Kusen Goffredo."

49. ACS, *P.S. A4 (spionaggio)*, b. 65bis, f. "Boettcher Joachim." Mussolini had given orders "to send him away for pederasty." As a result, the prefect of Genoa explained the reasons for his removal, saying: "Boettcher was invited to leave Italy because of his immoral behavior. In fact, the aforementioned person's conduct had become incompatible with the good and honest principles of Chiavari's people, who had made unfavorable comments about him for some time."

50. ACS, Pol.Pol., b. 16A, f. "Boettcher giornalista tedesco."

51. By the end of 1939, Tavolato had already sent as many as 693 reports.

52. ACS, Pol.Pol., b. 685, f. "Kircher Rudolf." The letters sent by the boys to Kircher portray a pederastic relationship that was, in any case, affectionate and friendly, despite differences of age and financial conditions. The boys thanked him for his attentions, they complained because he no longer sought them, and they invited him to fix more appointments. They would be pleased to meet him again and there was often a hint of jealousy toward the fortunate boy whose turn it was to accompany him on his trips around Italy. The financial factor was ever present and at times the cause of resentment. Somebody reminded Kircher of his promise to give him a pair of shoes, someone else complained because he had not sent money. For example, one youth, who was embittered because he had not been contacted any more, wrote to him: "This is how you show all the affection and respect you had for me. Yet I am quite fond of you, outside of personal interests, and you did not understand this. Go ahead and enjoy yourself with Tino and Ettore. You wanted to deny me a small amount of money, I hoped to receive at least a letter from you. It's clear you don't think of me any more, I'm sorry about that. If you still care about my friendship write to me, and if 50£ upset you, send me less."

53. ACS, Ministerio della Cultura Popolare (hereafter Min.Cul.Pop., Reports (1922–1945), b. 10, f.105 "Kircher Rudolf Karl."

54. ACS, Pol.Pol., b. 1055, f. "Popoff-Bebontoff George."

55. See S. Bertoldi, *Umberto: Da Mussolini alla Repubblica storia dell'ultimo re d'Italia* (Milan: Bompiani, 1983), 45–47; and A. Petacco, *Regina: La vita e i segreti di Maria José* (Milan: Mondadori, 1997), 51–55.

56. G. Oliva, *Umberto II: L'ultimo re* (Milan: Mondadori, 2001), 5. On the prince's "blocked sexuality," seen as the key to interpreting Umberto's life, see G. Speroni, *Umberto II: Il dramma segreto dell'ultimo re* (Milan: Rusconi, 1992).

57. M. L. Straniero, *Maria José la regina di maggio* (Milan: Peruzzo, 1985), 158.

58. See G. Prosperi, "Vita irrequieta di Luchino Visconti, parte II, Lo mandarono sotto le armi perché non combinasse altri guai," *La Settimana Incom Illustrata* 7, no. 14 (March, 1951).

59. On Visconti's homosexuality and its influence on his artistic production, see G. Rondolino, *Luchino Visconti* (Turin: Utet, 1981), 63. According to the author, it was just the search for greater freedom that drove Visconti to France in order to associate with Cocteau and Gide's circles, where homosexuality was tolerated and even exalted. On Visconti's experience in Paris, see also R. Renzi, *Visconti segreto* (Rome: Laterza, 1994), 27–29; and B. Villien, *Visconti* (Milan: Vallardi, 1996), 22. On his relationship with Umberto, see G. Servadio, *Luchino Visconti* (Milan: Mondadori, 1980).

60. According to Michele Luigi Straniero, Umberto had invited Carnera to his villa where, after bathing in the swimming pool, "he courted Carnera insistently, the outcome of which is uncertain" (Straniero, *Maria José*, 128–30). This incident—moreover unconfirmed—was described by Arrigo Petacco as well in *Regina*, 95. On Umberto's deep admiration for Carnera, who was to call his firstborn Umberto out of devotion to the prince, see A. Santini, *Carnera* (Milan: Mondadori, 1984), 187, 219.

61. See R. De Felice, *Il rosso e il nero*, ed. P. Chessa (Milan: Baldini and Castoldi, 1995), 144. For a detailed reconstruction of the affair regarding this bag and the questions

about its contents, see G. Contini, *La valigia di Mussolini: I documenti segreti dell'ultima fuga del duce* (Milan: Rizzoli, 1996).

62. P. Milza, *Mussolini* (Rome: Carocci, 2000), 946. The historians, including Milza, concentrated mainly on the correspondence between Mussolini and Winston Churchill, which was thought to be in the Duce's bag as well.

63. Before fleeing toward the Swiss border, Mussolini ordered that some of the documents of his archives be transported in a zinc box on a small truck at the end of the line traveling toward Como. He himself was carrying the more compromising documents, important for his self-preservation in a light brown leather bag when he was arrested by the partisans; see G. F. Bianchi, "L'odissea del camioncino fantasma," *Tempo Illustrato*, June 16, 1962. According to D'Aroma, Mussolini selected and gathered over two hundred confidential and personal documents in the last months of the Italian Social Republic. For "the correspondence affair," see D'Aroma, *Mussolini segreto*, 436–45.

64. P. L. Bellini Delle Stelle and U. Lazzaro, *Dongo ultima azione* (Milan: Mondadori, 1962), 177.

65. Contini, *La valigia di Mussolini*, 53–54.

66. U. Lazzaro, *Il compagno Bill: diario dell'uomo che catturò Mussolini* (Turin: Sei, 1989), 136.

67. See ACS, SPD, "Carte della valigia."

68. I consulted the unabridged version published on January 25, 1996, by *L'Unità*. This thesis about who stole the bag was confirmed by the written testimony of the parish priest of Gera Lario, don Franco Gusmeroli, who had been entrusted with Mussolini's bag. Stefano Tunesi, given the task of depositing the bag at the agency of the Cassa di Risparmo bank in the Lombard province of Domaso, also confirmed that the files had been tampered with. Recently, the political commissioner of the 52nd Garibaldi brigade, Michele Moretti "Pietro," declared that he had seen Urbano Lazzaro take one of the big file-holders containing documents from Mussolini's bag, in don Franco Gusmeroli's vestry. Thanks to the help of the Damaso bank manager's daughter, the violated files were sealed again with wax. On the whole affair and its various witnesses, see G. Cavalleri, *Ombre sul lago: Dal carteggio Churchill-Mussolini all'oro del PCI* (Casale Monferrato: Piemme, 1995), 181–85, 200–201. Lazzaro obviously denied he had stolen the papers concerning Umberto: "I did not take the dossier on Umberto. I was not present when it was stolen and I've kept my mouth shut about the name of the person responsible for 55 years. There were only four of us who knew where the papers were in the church in Gera: myself, Pier Bellini delle Stelle 'Pedro,' the parish priest don Franco Gusmeroli, and Scappin. I believe it was Scappin who betrayed my confidence"; qtd. in R. Festorazzi, *I veleni di Dongo* (Rome: Il Minotauro, 2004), 202.

69. There is conflicting evidence about the fact that the file on Umberto of Savoy, containing information about the prince's sexual tastes, had ended up in Rome. The opinion that Urbano Lazzaro handed the dossier about the "May king" to Umberto himself seems to be strengthened by partisan Bill's proven loyalty to the monarchy and by the fact that the bank manager of Damaso, Luigi Runi, received a diploma of knighthood from the minister of the Royal House, Falcone Lucifero. However, according to

some newspapers it was the other partisan, Pier Bellini Delle Stelle, who went to Rome after April 25 and talked to the king. It could have been General Raffaele Cadorna, the commander of the corps of volunteers for freedom, who gave the dossier back to Umberto, as Mussolini's bag had been entrusted to him on May 16; the Anglo-Americans themselves could have done the same. Despite the uncertainty about who indeed handed the dossier over to the Savoy family, according to the testimony of the Honorable Filippo Meda, the file on Umberto was "effectively taken to Rome"; see Cavalleri, *Ombre sul lago*, 182–83. The affair was also reconstructed by Luciano Regolo, who is overly absolutory at times, and ends up justifying every choice the monarchy made regarding the Duce's threat to use "the presumed secrets" in the dossier on Umberto; see L. Regolo, *Il re signore: Tutto il racconto della vita di Umberto di Savoia* (Milan: Simonelli, 1998), 401–5.

70. F. Lucifero, *L'ultimo re: I diari del ministro della Real Casa 1944–1946*, ed. F. Perfetti (Milan: Mondadori, 2002).

71. The papers of the Polizia Politica on Umberto, which are kept in the Archivio centrale dello Stato and are grouped into two files, contain a detailed series of information that provides further proof of how attentively the public and private lives of the heir to the throne were spied upon. Continual references were made to how incompatible the married couple were and to the prince's adulterous love affairs, which were the cause of heated arguments with his wife. Furthermore, special attention was paid to the couple's difficulty in having a child and to the delicate question of Umberto's homosexuality; see ACS, Pol.Pol., serie B., b. 19, f. "Principi di Piemonte" and f. "Principe Umberto." For example, some of these reports regarded Umberto's chauffeur, who was "given the task of collecting young boys and then taking them the Palace for the Prince," and reported that the crown prince had been insistently requested "to dismiss his chauffeur, as both his masculinity and morality were called into question by his makeup and outfits." The fact that Umberto "was considered a notorious pederast" even in aristocratic circles themselves was hinted at in other reports.

72. See D. Bartoli, *La fine della monarchia: Vittorio Emanuele III, la regina di maggio* (Milan: Mondadori, 1946), 302–3. On the "shameful accusations" against the Prince of Piedmont that had spread among the Fascist authorities since 1927, see also C. M. De Vecchi di Val Cismon, *Il Quadrunviro scomodo* (Milan: Mursia, 1983), 116.

73. See E. Re, *Storia di un archivio: Le carte di Mussolini* (Milan: Edizioni del Milione, 1946), 8. Mussolini himself wrote: "Badoglio's police officers who took away the correspondence of the Crown and servicemen (it's understandable why) did not bother at all about the other files" (20).

74. Bertoldi, *Umberto*, 87. On the newspaper campaign organized by Pavolini against Victor Emmanuel and Umberto, see also M. Mureddu, *Il Quirinale del Re* (Milan: Feltrinelli, 1977), 132. In an interview granted to Nino Bolla on April 21, 1944, Umberto himself alluded to these accusations. When asked, "The slanderous campaign against the Monarchy did not spare Your Royal Highness and doesn't now, is that so?" he answered: "I don't care at all about what professional slanderers might write about me. They know very well that I can't argue in my situation!" After which, pointing a straight finger at a photograph of Umberto and Maria José with their four children, he added:

"This is the best answer to the attacks against me!" (N. Bolla, *Colloqui con Umberto II* [Rome: Fantera, 1949], 28).

75. On March 1, 1945, *Il popolo di Alessandria*, the republican Fascist Party weekly of that city, was entirely given over to Umberto "Stellassa," with photographs and insinuations about him.

76. ACS, PCM, Gabinetto Brindisi—Salerno 1943–44, b. 8, cat. 3.6, report of the General Officer, Commanding Officer, Royal Carabinieri, General Giuseppe Pièche, of April 8, 1944. See also A. Ungari, *In nome del re: I monarchici italiani dal 1943 al 1948* (Florence: Le Lettere, 2004), 50–52.

77. Lucifero, *L'ultimo re*, 132. Croce thought that the accusations against Umberto should be minimized, because "if the prince had this defect and were Julius Caesar—seeing as how Julius Caesar did have it—what would it matter? As a matter of fact, if only the Prince had it and were Julius Caesar!"

78. Ibid., 10.

79. See ibid., 515–17, 521.

80. For example on May 11, General Arnaldo Azzi publicly called Umberto II "King pederast" during a political rally in Piazza del Popolo in Rome, giving rise to a bitter controversy (see ibid., 536). The film director Carlo Lizzani gives a similar account in a documentary about Luchino Visconti: in 1946 he was present at a political meeting in Piazza del Popolo, where Pietro Nenni addressed the people present asking them: "Do you want a king who's a pederast?" Again in the inflamed period of the political battle before the institutional referendum, Randolfo Pacciardi, secretary of the Republican Party, warned the crowd who had gathered to attend his rally in Siena that "In a monarchic regime, the people have to suffer a king even if he is an idiot and a pederast"; see E. Montanari, *La lotta di liberazione: Illusioni e realtà* (Florence: Il Fauno, 1970), 140.

81. See B. Mussolini, *Storia di un anno: Il tempo del bastone e della carota* (Milan: Mondadori, 1945 [1944]), 176. Ciano wrote in his diary that the law on the Grand Council had profoundly alarmed the members of the royal family, so much so that Maria José first went first to him, and then to Mussolini, to ask how it would effect succession to the throne (G. Ciano, *Diario 1937–1943*, ed. R. De Felice [Milan: Rizzoli, 1996], 150, 251).

82. L. Federzoni, *L'Italia di ieri per la storia di domani* (Milan: Mondadori, 1967), 225–26. On the whole affair and the testimony of Umberto II and Victor Emmanuel III, see De Felice, *Mussolini il fascista*, 305–8. In a communication to the newspapers, Mussolini even reached the point of stating explicitly that Umberto was not to be called "Crown Prince" but only "Prince of Piedmont," and was to be indicated as "Highness" and never as "Royal Highness," probably so that his succession to the throne would not be taken for granted.

83. L. Straniero, *Maria José*, 92.

84. Ciano, *Diario*, 120. Ciano also recorded in his notes on June 18, 1938: Mussolini "speaks against the monarchy that he calls 'a block brake for the regime.' He is thinking of eliminating this item as well, after the war in Spain" (149). Barely a month later Mussolini spoke to his son-in-law again of the "need to get rid of the Savoys at the first chance," and stated: "It took all my patience with this monarchy dragging us back. They

have never done anything in favor of the regime. I'm still waiting. The king is 70 and I hope nature will help me" (159).

85. On the relationship between the king and Fascism and the various phases of the plans Mussolini made to put an end to the monarchy after conquering Ethiopia, see De Felice, *Mussolini il duce: Lo stato totalitario*, 14–45.

86. Mussolini's resentment toward the king increased after Hitler visited Italy, and it led to violent friction and clashes in 1939. Ciano continually refers to this in his diary and quotes the Duce's harsh words against the monarchy on March 27: "If Hitler had had such a fool of a king in his way he would never have been able to take Austria and Czechoslovakia" (Ciano, *Diario*, 273). On June 3, he said, "I'm beginning to think it's time to put an end to the Savoy House. It's enough to rally two provinces, Forlì and Ravenna: 250,000 men, to get rid of them; or it may just be enough to stick up a poster" (306). The antagonism between Mussolini and the king became even more violent during the period before the war. Indeed, the issue of the supreme command for the direction of war operations irritated the Duce, who did not hide the fact that "when the war was won," he wanted "to get rid of a monarchy that he did not like and could no longer bear," May 14, 1940 (431). On June 6, 1940, Mussolini stressed the same point: "When the war is over I'll tell Hitler to get rid of all these absurd anachronisms, the monarchies" (440).

87. Giovanni Artieri wrote: "Umberto attracted the hostility of the party and the state police, who were to follow all the possible ways to destroy his reputation by attempting to put together inflammatory dossiers, following the old Italian custom of attributing the person under attack with homosexuality or the evil eye" (G. Artieri, *Umberto II e la crisi della monarchia* [Milan: Mondadori, 1983], 642).

88. At the beginning of May 1942, the Polish ambassador to the Holy See sent miscellaneous news to the Foreign Office, including a "special dossier [on Umberto] prepared by the party in order to thwart his ambitions by threatening to make some compromising documents about his private life public"; qtd. in V. Vailati, *1943–1944: La storia nascosta* (Turin: G.C.C., 1986), 78.

89. Montanari, *La lotta di liberazione*, 74.

90. See ibid., 75–85. The affair was also summed up by Ludovico Martinelli, an OVRA informer who was used by the police because of his connection to Montanari to extort information from him and to obtain further news about Umberto's private life (the report was sent to the Polizia Politica on November 9, 1933). The affair ended up involving the army, a counterespionage branch of the *carabinieri*, and the Polizia Politica; see ACS, Pol.Pol., b. 19/B, f. "Principe di Piemonte."

91. See Montanari, *La lotta di liberazione*, 86–90. For confirmation of this sudden change of opinion regarding Montanari after the letters were seized, see ACS, Ministero della Difesa, *Direzione Generale per Ufficiali*, libretti personali degli ufficiali b. 2497, f. "Montanari Enrico." After the war, Montanari sent a request to the Ministry of War to have his position reviewed, without result. In December 1969, the Board for the Politically Persecuted (*la Commissione perseguitati politici*), a subsidiary office of the Prime Minister, acknowledged him as a victim of political persecution with the full right to request that

his military career be renovated, but once again, the Ministry of Defense rejected his request; see Montanari, *La lotta di liberazione*, 159. The prince also told Montanari he had suffered the effects "of the Verona incident," as he had been ordered to remove all the anti-Fascists from his court, use the Roman salute, and accept that a postal office, whose real function was censorship, be set up in his Naples residence (see 100).

92. ACS, Pol.Pol., b. 426. De Simone, being an anti-Fascist, used his secret to get money from Umberto but also to defend himself from the police.

93. ACS, Pol.Pol., b. 29, f. "Anderson Philus." Other accusations regarding Umberto's pederasty are in ACS, *P.S. 1934*, b. 13, f. "Offese a S.E. il Capo del Governo." Although Romano Mussolini did not believe there was a dossier "on Prince Umberto's particular tendencies," he confirms to us that the Fascist regime intended to protect the crown prince from a possible scandal about his private life, in order to obtain advantages in exchange. In his opinion, even in the tragic hours preceding the night of the Grand Council on July 24, 1943, Mussolini relied on the confidence of the crown prince, whom he had "always protected and whom he had even got out of a scandal fifteen years [before]"; see R. Mussolini, *Il duce mio padre* (Milan: Rizzoli, 2004), 25.

94. Fucci, *Le polizie di Mussolini*, 302.

95. E. Dolmann, *Roma nazista 1937–1943* (Milan: Rizzoli, 2002), 27. Dolmann adds that despite Prince Philip of Assia's exceptional services to Nazism, Himmler "had no doubts at all about his double nature. On one hand, a general of the SA, the son-in-law of a king on the other; husband and father on the right, a regular visitor to Capri on the left: how could he be trusted? However, it was just for this reason that Himmler had such a firm hold on the prince, who would be careful not to rebel openly or double-cross him" (122).

96. See ibid., 275.

97. ACS, Pol.Mat., b. 40, f. "Germania." The note about Tavolato written in pencil by Bocchini provides further confirmation that the chief of police knew about the private lives of the spies and gives an indication of how he thought about using this information.

98. See ACS, Pol.Pol., b. 19/B, f. "Principe d'Assia." The Polizia Politica were immediately informed about the episode; furthermore, Bocchini reconstructed the prince's movements in order to be certain that what had happened was true.

99. For testimony of Philip of Assia's life and the persecution both he and Mafalda of Savoy suffered at the hands of the Nazis, see the memoirs of their son, Enrico: E. D'Assia, *Il lampadario di cristallo* (Milan: Longanesi, 1992). On Mafalda, see also R. Barneschi, *Frau Von Weber: Vita e morte di Mafalda di Savoia a Buchenwald* (Milan: Rusconi, 1995); M. Safier, *Mafalda di Savoia d'Assia: Dal bosco dell'ombra* (Turin: Teca, 1998); C. Siccardi, *Mafalda di Savoia: Dalla reggia al lager di Buchenwald* (Milan: Paoline, 1999).

100. Copy of a memo from Grandi *Per S.E. il Capo del Governo* sent De Vecchi il 19-11-1929, qtd. in C. M. De Vecchi di Val Cismon, *Tra Papa, Duce e Re*, ed. Sandro Setta (Rome: Jouvence, 1998), 22–23.

101. P. Scoppola, *La Chiesa e il fascismo: Documenti e interpretazioni* (Bari: Laterza, 1971), 145.

102. On espionage within the Vatican, including ecclesiastics who worked as

informers, see Franzinelli, *Delatori*, 114–34; and C. M. Fiorentino, *All'ombra di Pietro: La Chiesa cattolica e lo spionaggio fascista in Vaticano 1929–1939* (Le Lettere, Firenze 1999).

103. ACS, Pol.Pol., b. 424, f. "De Samper Riccardo." It appears that the accusation of pederasty was actually used against De Samper by internal adversaries in the Vatican in order to get rid of him and stop his nomination to cardinal.

104. On his life, his ecclesiastic career, and his position in regard to Fascism, see Fiorentino, *All'ombra di Pietro*, 161–62.

105. Initially one of his principal adversaries was Mons. Giuseppe Pizzardo, who had called for the investigation. But in 1931 he had an disagreement with the commander of the Vatican police force, who denounced "the male adventures of Caccia Dominioni." In 1938 informers of the Polizia Politica reported how rumors that the important prelate was a pederast continued circulate within the Vatican, despite having been nominated cardinal in the consistory of December 16, 1935; see ACS, Pol.Pol., b. 210, f. "Caccia Dominioni Camillo."

106. Emanuele Brunatto, a journalist and professor, was a member of the PNF and manager of a bookstore, the Libreria della littorio, in Rome. Having converted after a meeting with padre Pio, he had decided to defend the priest from Pietralcina and fight against his persecutors within the Vatican. With the task of spying on the prelates, he had gathered a good deal of information on them, which he promptly related to Bocchini, who wanted to know all the backstage gossip and facts within the Vatican in order to be able to influence the conclave's selection of the pope. At the end of 1930, Brunatto had moved to Paris as the representative manager of the Zarletti society, with the overt task of spying for the SIM. Known as an unscrupulous and venal person, it was suspected that he was playing both parties. When the war started, he was expulsed from France in September 1939, but after the occupation of France he returned to work for the German military. See ACS, Pol.Pol., b. 195, f. "Brunatto Emanuele"; *P.S. A4*, b. 70, f. "Brunatto Emanuele"; SPD, CO, f. 546.417 "Brunatto Emanuele" and SPD, CR, RSI, b. 36, f. "Brunatto Emanuele."

107. On April 21, 1930, Brunatto wrote a letter to Bocchini, telling him that he had information regarding the case against Aluffi, in particular about a situation within the Vatican that involved Caccia Dominioni being blackmailed by two young men. Bocchini warned him to be careful not to implicate Fascism. According to some police informers, Mussolini himself ordered the press not to report on the trial and then buried the entire scandal following the solicitation of Father Tacchi Venturi.

108. On all these events, see ACS, Pol.Pol., b. 24, f. "Aluffi Pentini Edoardo" and Pol.Pol., b. 195, f. "Brunatto Emanuele."

109. See ACS, *P.S. A1 1939*, b. 8, f. "Sacerdoti immorali" and *Reverendo giù le mani: Clero e reati sessuali negli anni trenta e negli anni novanta*, La Fiaccola, Ragusa. On the Vatican's initiatives to save priests who had been sentenced to *confino* for "sordid deeds," see also C. M. De Vecchi di Val Cismon, *Tra Papa, Duce e Re*, ed. Sandro Setta (Rome: Jouvence, 1998), 86. Some scandals within the religious sphere and of a homosexual nature had already broken out in the first years of the twentieth century and had

prompted harsh invectives against the immorality of preists and ecclesiastical celibacy, see U. Notari, *Il maiale nero: Rivelazioni e documenti* (Milan, 1907); A. Costa, *Turpitudini umane* (Milan, 1907); and E. Bossi (Milesbo), *La degenerazione* professionale *del clero cattolico* (Naples, 1919).

110. ACS, UCP., Fascicoli Personali, b. 919. Alesandro P. was less forturnate. Sent to *confino* for three years, he was then recovered in an insane asylum in Agrigento, and then discharged after being accused of feigning neurological symptoms. Despite having remained paralyzed after an epileptic attack, he was still accused of faking symptoms and was punished to three months in solitary confinement in a prison in Bari. Arrested again for offending his warders, he died mysteriously in prison in Palermo on October 25, 1939 (see ACS, *Confino Comune*, b. 111).

111. On the accusations of homosexuality directed at Starace, see A. Spinosa, *Starace* (Milan: Rizzoli, 1981), 205; and R. Festorazzi, *Starace: Il mastino della rivoluzione fascista* (Milan: Mursia, 2002), 104–5. According to the latter, "the rumors that Starace had practiced homosexual activities in his youth must have been quite worrying for the high *gerarchi*, seeing that there is a curious report among the OVRA papers that regards a puzzle magazine whose only wrong was to place Starace's name near the word 'pederasty,' a few coordinates away from each other in a crossword puzzle. The combination, which was evidently quite casual, seemed inopportune and so the report was sent out." Arrigo Petacco, however, has a hypothesis that seems less convincing. According to Petacco, Starace himself had launched the "defamatory" campaign against his own continual and unrestrained adventures with women, to defend himself from "the worst insult that can be addressed to a Fascist," that is, being a pederast, and "to reassure the Duce about his virility." See A. Petacco, *L'archivio segreto di Mussolini* (Milan: Mondadori, 2001), 64–65.

112. All these accusations are in ACS, SPD, CR, b. 94, f. "Achille Starace" and Pol.Pol., b. 92A–93A–94A.

113. For example, as far back as 1928, Emilio Settimelli wanted to take revenge for his expulsion from the party, and consequently organized a movement of opinion and a "combative coalition," which aimed to remove Turati from the leadership of the PNF and have him replaced by Carlo Sforza, who was closer to the extremists. See A. Scaratino, *"L'Impero": Un quotidiano "reazionario-futurista" degli anni venti* (Rome: Bonacci Editore, 1981), 90.

114. On Farinacci's complaints to Turati about how his friends were treated and for a series of measures taken against some members of the Cremona Fascist Party, see ACS, *Archivio Farinacci*, b. 36, f. "Augusto Turati," letter of August 20, 1926.

115. Y. De Begnac, *Taccuini mussoliniani*, ed. Francesco Perfetti (Bologna: Il Mulino, 1990), 461–62. In another letter to Farinacci, on October 31, 1929, Turati reproached him for dividing the party and encouraging the spread of suspicion and slander, because "slapping your hand hard on your capacious bag of papers, you solemnly declared you possessed documents with serious accusations against men of the government and party." Turati continued, "You must do without this private collection . . . that you keep jealously in your drawers like loaded pistols to summarily judge those you consider your adversaries." See ACS, SPD, CR, b. 40, f. "Farinacci Roberto."

116. Ibid.

117. Mussolini had tried to avoid the trial by setting up a commission of inquiry made up of three senators, but Belloni was not satisfied with the outcome and sued Farinacci, who was given a full acquittal at the trial, while Belloni was expelled from the party and sentenced to five years of *confino*. See ACS, SPD, CR, b. 80, f. "Belloni on. Ernesto," s.f. 2, "Assegnazione al confino"; SPD, CR, b. 42, f. "Farinacci Roberto," s.f. 16, "Questione Belloni 1929–1931" and PCM *1928-30*, b. 1132, f. 1/5-1 s.f. 8162, "Vertenza On/li Belloni e Farinacci." On the dispute between Turati and Farinacci due to the Belloni case, see ACS, SPD, CR, b. 40, f. "Farinacci Roberto," a meeting held at Palazzo Littorio on March 5, 1930, with Turati, Farinacci, Arpinati, Arnaldo Mussolini, Starace, and Melchiori present. On the relationship between Farinacci and Arnaldo, the involvement of the latter in the scandal and the Duce's resentment for the outcome of the affair, see SPD, CR, b. 41, f. "Farinacci Roberto," s.f. 7, "Rapporti col dottor Arnaldo 1926–1932"; and B. Mussolini, *Vita di Arnaldo* (Milan: Tip. del Popolo d'Italia, 1932).

118. De Felice, *Mussolini il duce: Gli anni del consenso*, 200.

119. Ibid., 131–32, 202–3. It is not by chance that De Felice tends to downplay Mussolini's responsibility with regard to Turati's political liquidation, and maintains that in some way the Duce was also a victim of Farinacci's initiative. This seems quite unlikely since he had all the means to counterattack Farinacci, and since a plot of that magnitude could not have been successful without Mussolini's consent.

120. Turati had acquired such great prestige in just a few years that he became a threat for Mussolini himself and ended up being a victim of the cult of the Duce that he himself had fostered. Philip Morgan rightly points out the contradiction between Turati's promotion of the myth of the leader who demands blind submission to his will and his concept of the creative, self-aware party; see P. Morgan, "Augusto Turati," in *Uomini e volti del fascismo*, ed. F. Cordova (Rome: Bulzoni, 1980), 493.

121. De Felice, *Mussolini il duce: Gli anni del consenso*, 205.

122. According to what some OVRA informers reported, Turati had set up his own police force to get rid of his rivals. "He was clever enough to place the most perceptive members of his personal Polizia Politica force at the Viminale [Ministry of National Security] and in the party headquarters. Turati placed his most loyal friend, who dated back to their time in Brescia, the accountant Gulì," who was his shield at the Viminale, because "he provided [Turati] with the curricula vitae of all the top *gerarchi* and notables, which he relied on to defend himself with." ACS, Pol.Pol., b. 101A, f. "Turati," s.f. 1 and 2.

123. See *Carteggio Arnaldo—Benito Mussolini* (Florence: La Fenice, 1954), 217.

124. For Farinacci, the trial was a means of increasing his notoriety. The court rejected the accusations, claiming no crime had been committed. Not content with this success, Farinacci continued to slander Miglioli, writing that he hoped "the dishonorable sodomite of Soresina would disappear from society." Farinacci's insults caused legal action to be taken immediately against the editors of *La Squilla*, the daily involved in the battle against Miglioli, but the trial came up only on November 27, 1918, and in the euphoria of the recent victory, the court acquitted the accused once again.

125. For example, in the case of a rich attorney of Padua who was discovered by the vice squad while behaving indecently with other men, Farinacci's intervention, together with his assistant Paolo Toffanin, helped the attorney to avoid *confino*. The unfortunate person paid money to be considered mentally unstable and interned in a home. See ACS, Pol.Pol., b. 1352, f. "Toffanin Paolo" and Pol.Pol., b. 1252, f. "Enrico S."

126. In all accounts of the affair, everyone thought the accusation against Turati was incredibly defamatory. Both those who sided with the former party secretary and those who accused him expressed profound disgust for homosexuality, considering it "despicable" behavior. Even in August 1944, the High Commissioner for punishing the crimes and illicit acts of the Fascist regime (l'Alto Commissariato per le punizioni dei delitti e degli illeciti del fascismo) believed rumors that Turati—"the former secretary of the Fascist Party who was lacking from the moral viewpoint as well"—corrupted minors. See ASR, *CAP Speciale*, b. 135, f. "Turati Augusto."

127. On Marcellino and Farinacci's plot to strike Turati, "who is so harmful to the party with his scandalous and unworthy life," see ACS, *Archivio Farinacci*, b. 29, f. 1759 "Paola Marcellino," Marcellino's letters to Farinacci, July 21 and 28, 1932. Farinacci accused Marcellino of having received 150,000 liras for the letters. She defended herself by claiming that she had been tricked into handing them over, that she had been made to believe that Turati was ready to have her sent to a place of *confino* in order to get rid of her, and therefore only an expert attorney like Farinacci could defend her. With regard to what Turati wrote in some of his letters to Marcellino, see ACS, Pol.Pol., b. 60 A, f. "Marcellino Paola."

128. Immediately after Turati was removed from office, Cristini was forced to resign from his position as president of the special court for the defense of the state and wrote to Mussolini: "As always, I obey Your Excellency's orders, certain that I have served the Duce loyally and honorably. I know of the document that has been given to you, which is supposed to show my falsehood. However, not only did I not lie but on the contrary, for reasons of my office, I intended to discover a plot that others knew nothing about." Note that Cristini, who was harshly criticized for his extremely dissolute life, was also accused of being a "sexual pervert." See ACS, SPD, CR, b. 82, f. "Cristini Guido" and Pol.Pol., b. 347, f. "Cristini avv. Guido."

129. In fact, Mussolini had asked the governor of the island to reserve the treatment and honors proper to a state minister for this important person in *confino*, making his exile as bearable as possible.

130. ACS, SPD, CR, b. 96, f. "Turati Augusto," Agnelli's letter to Alessandro Chiavolini, December 6, 1932.

131. *Il giornale d'Italia*, December 1, 1932.

132. ACS, Pol.Pol., b. 101 A, f. "Turati Augusto" report of December 6, 1932.

133. Ibid., a confidential report sent from Milan on October 2, 1932. Paola Marcellino said she had been driven to "smear Augusto Turati's name," and that the letters the secretary of the PNF had written to her had been falsified to this end, that the originals referred to "episodes that did not at all harm the dignity, honor, or prestige of the politician and citizen."

134. ACS, SPD, CR, b. 42, f. "Farinacci Roberto," s.f. 15, "Carteggio Farinacci gabinetto Min. Interni," s.s.f. "Denunzia contro On. Farinacci da parte della signora Paola Marcellino," Farinacci's letter to Arpinati, September 2, 1932.

135. With regard to this complicated affair involving a cross fire of blackmail and reciprocal slander, and to Marcellino's attempt to gain Turati's pardon, see ACS, Pol.Pol., b. 60 A, f. "Marcellino Paola" and UCP, Fascicoli personali, b. 615, f. "Marcellino Paola."

136. Again it was Farinacci who intervened, pressuring the chief of police of Turin to intervene so that Paola Marcellino would no longer be in a position to cause him problems. See ACS, UCP, Fascicoli personali, b. 615, f. "Marcellino Paola," Farinacci's letter to the Turin chief of police, April 19, 1933, and the police chief's telegram where he informed the Ministry of National Security of the need to "remove her to avoid the scandal she aims to spread sooner or later." The prefect of Turin, Umberto Ricci, then suggested taking an administrative measure against Paola Marcellino in order to avoid a trial and hush up the affair; consequently, the Turin dressmaker was given *confino* with an injunction of May 8, 1933.

137. Once again on Mussolini's orders, Turati's doctor, Giovanni C., was also warned not to support Marcellino in her scandalmongering and to abandon any action in defense of his friend. In fact, this Turin doctor had been involved in the scandal because many thought he was Turati's lover. See ACS, Pol.Pol., b. 306, f. "Giovanni C."

138. As Bocchini was worried about the possible political implications of the affair, he suggested to Mussolini not to inform the law offices about the fraud suffered by Marcellino. Consequently, Mussolini decided to end the whole affair by sending Mario Polini to *confino* with an injunction on March 3, 1934. See ACS, UCP, Fascicoli personali, b. 814, f. "Polini Mario." The fact that Mussolini intervened in such an unimportant affair reveals both his maniacal attention to even the slightest details and the deep concern he still felt for the Turati affair.

139. ACS, UCP, Fascicoli Personali, b. 615, f. "Marcellino Paola," letters written to Bocchini.

140. See ACS, Pol.Pol., b. 775, f. "Paola Marcellino."

141. Turati, *Fuori dall'ombra della mia vita*, 14.

142. De Begnac, *Taccuini mussoliniani*, 470–71. Mussolini had commented on Turati's "so called erotic incident" to the new chief editor of *La Stampa* saying: "There are some situations where one can't help intervening. Turati let himself be ruined." And then he added: "You are young. I advise you to be cautious with skirts, especially with those of women who are no longer young because, like the old infantries, they hold their ground." See A. Signorotti, *"La Stampa" in camicia nera 1932–1943* (Rome: Volpe Editore), 1968, 16–17.

143. De Begnac, *Taccuini mussoliniani*, 472.

144. Y. De Begnac, *Palazzo Venezia: Storia di un regime* (Rome: La Rocca, 1950), 556.

145. The governor of the Aegean Islands reported to Rome that Turati behaved most correctly on Rhodes, without ever complaining about how he had been treated, and on the contrary saying: "For five years I preached discipline. The Chief has struck me. I said nothing about it." See ACS, SPD, CR, b. 96, f. "Turati Augusto," s.f. 3.

146. ASR, *CAP Speciale*, b. 135, f. "Turati Augusto," Turati's letter, November 20, 1947. The trial ended with a sentence for his activity within the Fascist regime; however, Turati was left free, living an almost secluded life in Rome while waiting to benefit from the amnesty.

147. Suffice to consider that even in August 1944, the chief of police of Rome sent a report on Turati to the High Commissioner for the Punishment of Fascist Crimes (l'Alto Commissione per le punizioni dei crimini fasciti), reconstructing the events of the summer in 1932, saying that "after acquiring proof against him of pederasty and puerophilia, the party had him interned in a nursing home, evidently to hush up a scandal that would have involved a lot of top political personalities of that period in a public debate." See ASR, *CAP Speciale*, b. 135, f. "Turati Augusto."

148. Turati, *Fuori dall'ombra della mia vita*, 142–46.

149. Ibid., 100–101.

150. On this report and others where reference is made to Giuriati's presumed homosexuality, see ACS, Pol.Mat., b. 151, categoria M.9, f. 5, "PNF direzione." For Giuriati, see also SPD, CR, b. 47, f. 242/R "Giuriati Giovanni."

151. E. Gentile, introduction to G. Giuriati, *La parabola di Mussolini nei ricordi di un gerarca* (Rome: Laterza, 1981), xxxiii.

152. ACS, Pol.Pol., b. 101 A, f. "Turati Augusto," the comment of a Polizia Politica informer, October 6, 1932.

153. De Begnac, *Palazzo Venezia*, 190. Furthermore, De Begnac points out that Mussolini always tried to prevent small provincial islands dominated by a single undisputed chief from forming again.

154. Using the data provided by Mario Missori, Lupo analyzes the logic and frequency of the turnover mechanism carried out in the various provincial federations, and discovers strong instability above all where the political devitalization of the provinces was not accepted and in the federations of the big cities where provisional administrations were frequent. See Lupo, *Il fascismo*, 317–22.

155. ACS, SPD, CR, b. 40, f. "Farinacci Roberto," Farinacci's letter to Mussolini, January 20, 1932.

156. De Begnac, *Palazzo Venezia*, 452.

157. Colarizi, *L'opinione pubblica degli italiani sotto il regime*, 19.

158. De Begnac, *Palazzo Venezia*, 165.

159. The Mutua squadristi was the toughest group of the Turin Fascist squads. In 1924 it was made up of about six hundred militants, most of whom had already committed crimes and were ready for any kind of violence. When Colisi Rossi led the federation, he tried to discipline them but suffered violence and harsh protests in return. However, once expelled from the party, he reunited with them in order to set up a political following and return to power.

160. E. Mana, "Dalla crisi del dopoguerra alla stabilizzazione del regime," in *Storia di Torino*, vol. 8, *Dalla Grande Guerra alla Liberazione (1915–1945)*, ed. N. Tranfaglia (Turin: Einaudi, 1998), 178.

161. Carlo Bonservizi was unscrupulous and rather ambiguous, making money off his brother's name, spending a lot, and getting up to his neck in debt; his relationship with Mussolini and the police was not clear, but he certainly enjoyed the Duce's financial protection. See ACS, Pol.Pol., b. 165, f. "Bonservizi Carlo."

162. See ACS, *PS A1 1927*, b. 9, f. "Colisi Rossi e Bonservizi." On those who thought up the plot and what went on behind the scenes of the affair, see also the statement of Italo Fiocchetti, special vice-secretary of the provincial party secretary of Robilant in ACS, SPD, CR, b. 38, f. 242/R, "Colisi Rossi comm. Claudio."

163. ACS, UCP, Fascicoli personali, b. 265, f. "Colisi Rossi Claudio," letter sent by Colisi Rossi to Col. Giuseppe Ceccarini on October 2, 1927.

164. See ACS, SPD, CR, b. 38, f. 242/R, "Colisi Rossi comm. Claudio."

165. Count Gaschi and Captain Pietro Rabbia, the two squad members who testified against Claudio Colisi Rossi in March 1928, threatened his brother Luigi with weapons, inviting him to hand over all the compromising documents in his possession. See ACS, Pol.Pol., b. 506, f. "Fiocchetto Italo." On these documents about numerous political and financial people in Turin, gathered by Claudio Rolisi Rossi, see ACS, Pol.Pol., b. 316, f. "Colisi Rossi Claudio," confidential report, January 15, 1932.

166. ACS, Pol.Pol., b. 316, f. "Colisi Rossi Claudio," confidential report, December 12, 1931.

167. The various cases of Fascists who ended up in insane asylums, entitles one to suppose there was a sinister use of internment for political ends, or as an alternative measure to prison and *confino*.

168. See ACS, PNF, Senatori e consiglieri nazionali, b. 25, f. "Luigi Ridolfi," Ridolfi's answer to Starace sent on January 29, 1934. On his work as *federale* aimed at normalizing the federation and putting an end to the internal disagreements without reaching too harsh a clash with Tamburini's faction, see M. Palla, *Firenze nel regime fascista (1929–1934)* (Florence: Olschki, 1978), 165–67.

169. See ACS, Pol.Pol., b. 241, f. "Carafa d'Andria Andrea." In February 1942, the prefect of Naples denied the accusation of pederasty made once again against Carafa d'Andria when he was appointed director of the local Sepral, deeming it merely vulgar slander. See ACS, *P.S. A1 1942*, b. 27, f. "Carafa d'Andria Andrea."

170. ACS, Pol.Pol., b. 991, f. "Pergolani Renato." A confidential representative of the Polizia Politica commented on the affair saying: "Effeminate, they call him Renée. He had appointments in the party. He got married. A very rich, nice girl, but she had the marriage annulled because of his proven impotence. The printed memorandum (1928–) of the attorney Andreani of Perugia for that law court draws a picture of the NON MAN that makes one shudder. He is considered a pederast in Umbria, has no friends, and is kept at a distance. On the contrary, he boasts of friends at Palazzo Vidoni where he was recently entrusted with directing the Marsala *Fascio*" (report of March 15, 1931).

171. See ACS, Pol.Pol., b. 46, f. "Armato Alfredo."

172. Not even the intervention of the provisional administrator, Luigi Freddi, was capable of bringing order back within the Pisa federation: Morghen was arrested on

April 19, 1924, for complicity in the murder of Ugo Rindi, an anarchist and printer, who was killed in a Fascist reprisal. To prevent the two factions in conflict from prevailing, Freddi proposed removing Santini from Pisa as well. The battle between these two Fascist sects in Pisa ended on October 22, 1924, when Morghen was released from prison once and for all, but despite this, comments on the clash with the dissidents continued. For the whole affair see M. Canali, *Il dissidentismo fascista: Pisa e il caso Santini 1923–1925* (Rome: Bonacci, 1983).

173. See ACS, Pol.Pol., b. 869, f. "Morghen avv. Filippo," report of the prefect of Rome, July 21, 1928. The prefect had verified the truth of the information provided by a Polizia Politica informer who had sent the following report on Morghen in June: "The militia consul, Att. Morghen, former political secretary of the Pisa federation, later resigned from this appointment because he feared that his wife had started a scandal related to his pederasty. Morghen broke off relations with his wife and settled in Rome where he continued to practice his *profession*! In fact he opened a house for a certain Modesto B., a dreadful individual and pederast who supplied boys and was known to the police."

174. See ACS, *P.S. A1 1935*, b. 10, f. "Modesto B." and Pol.Pol., b. 122, f. "Modesto B." The police continued surveillance on him, and because they were suspicious of his friendship with young students they decided to send him to a place of *confino*.

175. In these cases as well, the accusation of homosexuality was particularly common. For example, the *podestà* of Verona, Vittorio Raffaldi, was the target of a flood of anonymous letters in which he was called "thief, traitor and pederast." However, thanks to the prefect, the inquiry regarding the *podestà* was stopped, even though the anonymous letters aimed at discrediting Raffaldi's reputation were still circulating at the time he was replaced. In one of these, sent to Mussolini in November 1928, the affair was thus commented: "Your Excellency, finally Verona has been freed of Raffaldi, of the old mole, the extremely subtle rodent, thief and whoremonger and furthermore a pederast! A coward and traitor. Now that the handsome *podestà* has gone, this thief should be exposed to public ridicule. Unsigned but an honest person, a patriot, a serviceman who properly reveres you." See ACS, SPD, CR, b. 90, f. "Raffaldi Vittorio."

176. In particular, from 1921 to 1926, the federations were extremely unstable. Most of the secretaries stayed in office for less than a year. There were radical changes in the federations soon after the elections in April 1924 and before the Matteotti crime, when new secretaries (a 60 percent changeover) were appointed in forty-five federations out of seventy-five. Later on, the most consistent changes took place after elections and changes in the PNF leadership. For statistics on the federations, see E. Gentile, *Fascismo e antifascismo: I partiti italiani fra le due guerre* (Florence: Le Monnier, 2000), "Appendice," ed. R. Suzzi Valli, sec. 3, 486–93; and M. Missori, *Gerarchie e statuti del PNF: Gran Consiglio, Direttorio nazionale, Federazioni provinciali: Quadri e biografie* (Rome: Bonacci, 1986).

177. I. Granata, "Il regime fascista: Peculiarità milanesi," in *Milano durante il fascismo 1922–1945*, various authors (Milan: Cariplo, 1994), 61. Parenti was successful in his work as a "normalizer" thanks to the support of Starace, whom he had provided with the proof necessary to strike Mario Giampaoli.

178. Thanks to Parenti, Rezzonico became secretary of the Federal Directorate, the Directorate of the *Fascio* of Milan, and the Provincial *Dopolavoro* association. Later, he was appointed militia leader as well. Through these various appointments he managed to earn large sums of money. See ACS, Pol.Pol., b. 1114, f. "Rezzonico Renzo." Riva also exploited his ties with Parenti to better his position: he was a member of the provincial council for the economy, advisor for the courier "L'Espresso," secretary of the union of accountants, and later an advisor for Philips. His financial situation was particularly prosperous, but many of his financial actions, especially those linked to his appointment as the auditor of "Snia Viscosa" seem to have been illicit speculations. See ACS, Pol.Pol., b. 1132, f. "Riva Riccardo."

179. See ACS, SPD, CR, b. 48, f. "Parenti Rino."

180. Rossi obtained compromising statements and letters by guaranteeing the witnesses immunity, offering them money, or simply by threatening to use the information in his possession to report them to the police.

181. ACS, Pol.Pol., b. 1132, f. "Riva Riccardo," report from Milan, December 4, 1933.

182. See ibid., report of December 29, 1934. In order to press for an inquiry, threats to inform Farinacci of the affair were made with the certainty that the small-time Cremona *ras* would manage to obtain justice by creating a scandal and removing these "depraved and abnormal" men from the Milanese federation. A few months later, the former secretary of the union of accountants, whom Riva had succeeded, actually pressed Farinacci to begin a slander campaign within the Milanese federation. See report of May 8, 1935. On the information Farinacci received directly from his informers about "what everyone was saying about the provincial party secretary from a moral point of view," see Biblioteca nazionale braidense di Milano, Fondo archivistico Roberto Farinacci, b. Milano, f. 115 "Situazione Fascismo Milanese."

183. ACS, Pol.Pol., b. 1132, f. "Riva Riccardo," report, April 23, 1935.

184. ACS, Pol.Pol., b. 1132, f. "Riva Riccardo," the police chief of Milan's report, April 27, 1935.

185. Ibid., memorandum on Riccardo Riva, April 7, 1935, by Di Stefano and sent to the undersecretary of the Ministry of National Security, who sent it to Bocchini. The report continued: "Dr. Riva himself was apparently nicknamed 'the warty young lady' in the Randaccio Fascist action squad, and it happened that the second-in-command of the Milan Fasci Giovanili once mockingly called Riva 'Lady Riccarda' in public. Further confidential information reveals that in 1933 he held after-school lessons and courses for weak students at his own home and that he ended up being involved in disgusting episodes, to the point that he was threatened with reports to the police for corruption, for something that was apparently hushed up at that time; and finally, the information that he presently kept a boy nicknamed Fifi, who had been a member of the Randaccio *squadristi*, and that they organized lewd orgies together with other boys, in his present home."

186. Ibid., the police chief's note sent to the Minister of National Security, May 1, 1935.

187. ACS, UCP, Fascicoli personali, b. 551, f. "Lanza Pier Federico," Parenti's letter to Starace, September 11, 1935. The boy's father tried to accredit the idea that his son was not responsible, making him out to be a deranged, mentally ill alcoholic, and proposed letting him avoid *confino* and sending him to a insane asylum instead. Consequently, the boy was held under observation but was considered undeserving of internment and was sentenced to three years of *confino*. The board of appeal reduced his sentence to just one year but rejected the request to annul the measure, because "even if he is mentally defective, his behavior links up with a slander campaign that has gone on for some time against various people of the PNF."

188. ACS, Pol.Pol., b. 1132, f. "Riva Riccardo," reports, August 3, 1937, and April 18, 1939.

189. ACS, Pol.Pol., b. 438, f. "Di Marco Mario."

190. ACS, Pol.Pol., b. 1132, f. "Riva Riccardo," message sent on March 13, 1939.

191. The changing of the guard in the federation gave new impulse to all those who had tried for years to bring down Parenti; when Starace was replaced by Muti as leader of the PNF, Parenti's position was weakened even further. Consequently, in March 1940, Rossi tried for the umpteenth time to expose homosexual members of the federation, fearing that the case would be shelved again, and attempted to prevent the proof gathered on Rezzonico and Riva's "immoral" conduct from reaching Parenti.

192. See ACS, Pol.Mat., b. 223, categoria Q.27, f. 3, "Personalità del PNF." Although Parenti had been removed as leader of the Milan federation when Starace fell in 1939, his political career was not compromised; on the contrary, after a short time he was appointed president of CONI, then in August 1942 he was prefect in Como, and during the Republic of Salò he was appointed head of the province of Sondrio.

193. See ACS, PNF, Situazione politica ed economica delle province, b. 6, f. "Milano."

194. The plan against Gianturco, with his lover as acting as an accomplice, was organized by the former local federation inspector together with an ex-*squadrista*. The three of them were sentenced to *confino* for slander against the *federale* with an injunction on October 7, 1940, but in June 1941, Mussolini reduced the remaining period of punishment to a two-year period of cautioning. After a few months, following the changes that took place in the federation when Gianturco was replaced, their cautioning was annulled as well. See ACS, UCP, Fascicoli personali, b. 98, f. "Berra Cesare"; b. 840, f. "Racah Eva"; b. 1056, f. "Ventura Riccardo."

195. With regard to the sexual habits of the *gerarchi*, see G. Fusco, *Playdux: Storia erotica del fascismo* (Rome: Tattilo Editore, 1973). For Mussolini's love affairs, his continual adulterous affairs, and his relations with women, see Navarra, *Memorie del cameriere di Mussolini*, 199–213.

196. For example, the 1924 elections brought about a considerable change in the parliament: 80 percent of the Fascist deputies were new to parliamentary activities, and 55.2 percent of the parliamentarians had run their first election (in 1929, 50.3 percent of the parliamentarians had been in their first elections). The social composition of the parliamentarians changed as well, with a drop in the number of upper-middle-class and

working-class members and a rise in urban middle-class members and farmers. See Gentile, *Fascismo e antifascismo*, 105–7, "Appendice" sec. 1.

197. "Il fascismo dopo il suo Congresso. Intervista con Cesare Rossi," *Il Popolo Romano* (November 16, 1921), qtd. in Gentile, *Storia del partito fascista*, 463.

198. The 1926 statute put an end to the election of national and provincial positions; for example, a provincial party secretary was chosen and appointed by the general secretary of the party, while beginning in 1929 provincial party secretaries were appointed and removed by the head of government on a proposal made by the party secretary.

199. On the texts of the statutes, see Missori, *Gerarchie e statuti del P.N.F.*

200. "Noterelle di moralità fascista: Delle espulsioni," *Il popolo di Romagna*, December 15, 1928.

201. Navarra, *Memorie del cameriere di Mussolini*, 147.

202. De Begnac, *Palazzo Venezia*, 165.

203. The idea of creating a more severe criminal code for Fascists, expressed by Stefano Mario Cutelli and Giuseppe L. Omarini in *Nobiltà della Stirpe*, was criticized as well, on the grounds that it would have only made sense for political offenses, not private moral ones. See Quidam, "Dal dire al fare," *Critica fascista* 16 (August 15, 1933).

204. See ACS, Pol.Pol., b. 1008, f. "On. Pezzoli Liberato."

205. Ibid., report of September 13, 1940, sent by the Roman chief of police to Bocchini, who had expressly urged him to provide information about the accusation of pederasty against Pezzoli. The police chief maintained that the former deputy had remarried and forwarded a request to be sent to the front as a volunteer in order to rehabilitate his reputation.

206. See ACS, Pol.Mat., b. 150, categoria M.2, f. 18, "Senato del Regno," confidential report, June 21, 1932. Another police informer even made an estimate of the number of homosexual deputies: "It is estimated that there are twenty-teo pederasts at Montecitorio [the Chamber of Deputies], including the Speaker and excluding Turola."

207. See ACS, Pol.Mat., b. 152, categoria M.14, f. 8, "Camera dei Deputati (1929–1931)."

208. Following a road accident, new insinuations had arisen about the "abnormal" nature of the relationship between Turola and the passenger injured in the car crash. On the accident, see ACS, PCM *1934–1936*, b. 2113, f. 20.13, s.f. 788, "Incidente automobilistico occorso al Comm. Elio Turola, direttore generale dei servizi di questura dei deputati."

209. ACS, Pol.Pol., b. 103, f. "Turola Elio," s.f. "Inchiesta personale," a report sent by Dudan to Edmondo Rossoni, undersecretary to the Prime Minister, February 6, 1934. The inquiry was to be kept secret; As a result, Dudan obliged the witnesses not to reveal information about the episode, threatening to revoke their party cards.

210. ACS, Pol.Pol., b. 103, f. "Turola Elio," confidential report, February 20, 1934. Some officials of the chamber sent an anonymous letter to Starace reporting that Turola had boasted about being protected by the party secretary. They expressed their opinion on the affair: "Your Excellency, we did not think that you would protected even the most vulgar of confirmed pederasts like Turola. It is extremely distressing to see that an immoral

person of that type can even approach the Duce because of his functions. If Turola is guilty, as he is, he must be kicked out of his post, if he is not, you should kick those who accused him out of Montecitorio"; see ACS, Min.Cul.Pop., Gabinetto, b. 5, f. 21, "Anonimi contro personalità," s.f. 76, "Contro il Comm. Turola della Camera dei Deputati."

211. ACS, Pol.Pol., b. 103, f. "Turola Elio," confidential report, February 27, 1935.

212. Some Polizia Politica informers maintained that Turola had married to hide his "passive homosexuality," and since his honeymoon had taken his lover with him. After a few months, his wife left him, "disgusted by her husband's sexual inversion," and asked for separation. See ibid., especially the report of the chief of police of Genoa sent to the Head of police on March 11, 1934.

213. Feature titled "Lapis blu," *Corriere d'Italia*, September 10, 1929.

214. See, for example, E. Martire, *La crisi dell'amore: Saggi intorno alla questione morale* (Rome: Vita, 1910), "Per la repressione della pornografia," *Archivio fascista di medicina politica* 1, no. 3 (1927): 157–60, and "Urbanesimo e pubblica moralità," *Archivio fascista di medicina politica* 3, nos. 2–3 (1929): 97–99.

215. See ACS, Pol.Pol., b. 797, f. "Martire Egilberto."

216. This former deputy of the Partito Popolare moved over to the Fascist Party and was included among the candidates of the Lista Nazionale in 1924. In March 1939, after opposing the racial laws, he was sent to a place of *confino* for five years because he accused Galeazzo Ciano of bringing bad luck and expressing defeatist ideas. See ACS, UCP, Fascicoli Personali, b. 633, f. "Martire Egilberto." On Martire, see also D. Sorrentino, *La conciliazione e il "fascismo cattolico": I tempi e la figura di Egilberto Martire* (Brescia: Morcelliana, 1980).

217. Bazzi had obtained various political appointments: he was chosen to chair the examining boards for granting certificates of participation for the March on Rome, for qualification as a *squadrista* and Sciarpa Littorio; he was appointed federal inspector, vice president, and then president of the militant Fascist group in Udine, and had twice been part of the federal directory.

218. See ACS, *P.S. A1 1941*, b. 14, f. "Bazzi Antonio." Final judgment was expressed by a board made up of the provincial party secretary, the provincial party vice secretary, and the chief of political services.

219. See ACS, UCP, Fascicoli personali, b. 78, f. "Bazzi Antonio," note, March 26, 1941. As Bazzi was not in good health, Mussolini accepted the prefect's suggestion to send this "immoral passive pederast" to a city with a hospital. He sent him to *confino* in Varese, where a brother of Bazzi who was a Polizia Politica informer could keep an eye on him and help him to start a new life. In any case, on October 28, 1942, Bazzi was released and granted probation on occasion of the twentieth anniversary of the March on Rome.

220. ACS, *P.S. A4 (spionaggio)*, b. 174, f. "Hodel Roberto," telegram October 4, 1915, from the Rome police headquarters to general police headquarters, confidential office.

221. Ibid., Luigi Federzoni's letter, November 18, 1920.

222. According to the police, a nephew of Hodel's had the task of keeping "a place for exchanges and supplies for all international inverts" in an antiquarian's shop in

Rome. See ACS, Pol.Pol., b. 660, f. "Hodel Roberto," Terracini's report, December 19, 1936.

223. Valerio Benuzzi, a collaborator with the Polizia Politica, believed that "the overall impression is that once the new code is in force, they will not just go after Holdel but that the police will want to collect information on the most notorious pederasts in order to be updated." See ACS, Pol.Pol., b. 660, f. "Hodel Roberto," informatory note, August 16, 1929.

224. ACS, *P.S. A4*, b. 174, f. "Hodel Roberto," report of Rome chief of police, February 23, 1930.

225. ACS, Min.Cul.Pop., Gabinetto, b. 11, f. 112 "Hodel Roberto."

226. ACS, Pol.Pol., b. 660, f. "Hodel Roberto," informatory note, December 10, 1936.

227. Ibid., Kusen's confidential note, August 19, 1937. According to Kusen, Hodel was actually against Fascism; however, his anti-Fascism was the most poisonous and corrosive type, crafty and immoral because it did not arise from ideological motives but from his negative opinion of Italy and Italians. He stayed in our country because here, in respect to other places, he could give free "vent to his sexual instincts."

228. Ibid., confidential notes, September 18 and 19, 1936.

229. With regard to SIM suspicions that he acted as an informer for the Swiss legation in Rome, see ACS, *P.S. A4*, b. 174, f. "Hodel Roberto."

230. ACS, Pol.Pol., b. 660, f. "Hodel Roberto," informatory note from Rome, December 17, 1942.

231. ACS, Pol.Pol., b. 575, f. "Germain René," Terracini's report, February 6, 1936.

232. ACS, Pol.Pol., b. 1201, f. "Sandoz Maurice," report, May 2, 1932.

233. See C. Malaparte, *The Skin* (Marlboro: Marlboro Press, 1988), 130, and *Mamma marcia* (Florence: Vallecchi, 1959).

234. Ciano, *Diario*, 628.

235. On this network of spies, see C. Amè, *Guerra segreta in Italia 1940–1943* (Rome: Casini, 1954), 156–57; C. De Risio, *Generali, Servizi Segreti e fascismo* (Milan: Mondadori, 1978), 184–89; and M. Franzinelli, *Guerra di spie: I servizi segreti fascisti, nazisti e alleati 1939–1943* (Milan: Mondadori, 2004), 49–57.

236. See ACS, SPD, CR, b. 341, f. "Tribunale speciale per la difesa dello Stato. Rapporti d'udienza, procedimenti penali, processi ed esecuzioni di sentenze a pena capitale," report on "Processo contro Steiger Roberto e altri 2" sent by the president of the Tribunale Speciale to the Duce on May 28, 1943.

237. ASR, *Detenuti di Regina Coeli*, deceduti anno 1943, b. 7, f. 314 "Sauer Kurt" and b. 2, f. 93 "Steiger Robert"; ACS, *PS A. 4*, b. 311, f. "Sauer Kurt" and Pol.Pol., b. 1216, f. 34 "Sauer Kurt."

Chapter 7. Bourgeois Respectability and Fascist Morality

1. ACS, Pol.Pol., b. 60, f. "Bagnasco Domenico onorevole." The fiduciaries of the Polizia Politica continued to describe him, instead, according to the widespread stereotype

of the homosexual: the Honorable Mr. Bagnasco "suffered, in fact, from a disease . . . that caused him to feel female stimuli! . . . Therefore, he gives jobs only to those who act on him . . . catering to his taste . . . passive!!" (a fiduciary from Turin on March 22, 1930). On the political career and the Duce's kindness toward this "all-time faithful follower," see also ACS, SPD, CO, b. 690, f. 209.128, "Bagnasco On. Domenico."

2. Historians paid little attention to female homosexuality during the Fascist era. For some indications on the subject, besides the documented source of Gabriella Romano, *L'altro ieri*, see R. Fiocchetto, *L'amante celeste: La distruzione scientifica della lesbica* (Florence: Estro, 1987); D. Danna, *Amiche, compagne, amanti: Storia dell'amore fra donne* (Milan: Mondadori, 1994); P. Lupo, *Lo specchio incrinato: Storia e immagini dell'omosessualità femminile* (Padua: Marsilio, 1998); B. Zimmerman, ed., *Lesbian Histories and Cultures: An Encyclopedia* (New York: Garland, 2000); N. Miletti and L. Passerini, eds., *Fuori dalla norma: Storie lesbiche nell'Italia della prima metà del Novecento* (Turin: Rosenberg and Sellier, 2007); and P. Guazzo, I. Rieder, and V. Scuderi, eds., *R/esistenze lesbiche nell'Europa nazifascista* (Verona: Ombre Corte, 2010).

3. On this third type of woman, neither a good "mother, wife, and daughter, only concerned with housekeeping and the family . . . morally and economically subjected to men," nor a sensual woman, "courtesan, the female of the male, woman without rules and outside of the law," but "a woman who can support herself with the means she makes from her own honorable work, a woman who finds herself facing men—father, brother, husband or lover—in the condition of being totally economically independent," see. U. Notari, *La donna "tipo tre"* (Milan: Società Anonima Notari, 1929). For a criticism of Notari's book that appeared in instalments on page 3 of *Il popolo di Roma* between November 18 and December 9, 1928, see I. Carpineta-Cagnoni, "La donna tipo tre: Risposta d'un'insegnante a Umberto Notari," *Il popolo di Roma*, December 15, 1928.

4. C. Scorza, "Il problema demografico e la camicia alla russa," *Costruire*, September 9, 1929, 11. According to Dario Lischi as well, this effeminate leaning was to be harshly repressed, "because besides weakening men it leads fathers to fear their responsibilities, to thoughtlessness, and in general foments all kinds of vice." By acting to reconfirm the value of virility in men, the question of women would also be resolved, because "despite their praise of feminism that puts them on equal standing with males, women are very willing to be guided by men when they know how to be . . . good leaders" (D. Lischi, "Il problema demografico: Contro tutti gli 'ottimisti imbecilli,'" in *Costruire*, September 9, 1929, 5).

5. E. Galvano, "Natura e morale," *Il Popolo d'Italia*, September 26, 1934.

6. F. Saba Sardi, "La società omosessuale," *Venus*, November 7, 1972, 40. The considerations of Francesco Saba Sardi are based not only on historical documents but also on personal experience as a detainee in the concentration camp at Buchenwald. Some studies have confirmed that the difficulty in finding an overall definition of homosexual is precisely what determined the alternating, irregular attitude of the Nazi regime in regard to the repression of homosexuality; see M. Herzer, "Nazis, Psychiatrists and Gay: Homophobia in the Sexual Science of the National Socialist Period," *Cabrino and Gay Books Bulletin* 12 (Spring/Summer 1985): 1–5.

7. ACS, Pol.Pol., b. 822, f. "M. A." The fiduciary of the Polizia Politica noted that "in cases of the kind the Ministry has always decided in favor of exile rather than *confino*," but the documentation in the archives does not provide further information on the decisions actually taken by the ministry.

8. See ACS, *Segreteria del Capo della Polizia*, Fascicoli del personale di P.S. cat. I, 1908–1947, b. 9, f. "Senise Carmine."

9. C. Senise, *Quando ero capo della polizia 1940–1943* (Rome: Ruffolo, 1946): "In the evening I used to go for a beer in Piazza del Carmine with my friend Zurlo" (48); "When I was replaced by Chierici as head of the Police, I always stayed at home where I did not receive anyone, and if I went for a walk with my inseparable friend Zurlo I always took country lanes outside the city or at the most I went to Villa Borghese where I was sure I would not meet anyone" (189); "I did not have a home of my own; I was a guest and still am in the modest home of my fraternal friend Zurlo" (193).

10. E. Dolmann, *Roma nazista 1937–1943* (Milan: Rizzoli, 2002), 59.

11. "Refined epicure, knowledgeable admirer of female beauty, Bocchini represented the authentic Italian gourmand, to be envied by the French traditional connoisseur" (E. Dolmann, *Un libero schiavo* [Bologna: Cappelli, 1968], 120).

12. Ibid., 141.

13. G. Leto, "Polizia segreta in Italia," qtd. in Fucci, *Le polizie di Mussolini*, 316–17.

14. There is not much information about the information network called "Servizio 6 X" or "yellow danger" (because of the color of the carbon copies used). We do know that it depended on the prime minister's office and was set up in February 1943 when, during a momentary crisis for the future of Fascism, there were doubts about the loyalty of the police, and it seemed necessary to set up a parallel spy network. Mussolini was extremely interested in this personal information service, which provided him with fiduciary relationships in competition with the Polizia Politica. It is interesting to note that the journalist Vittorio Foschini headed the "6 X" until he, in turn, was accused of "belonging to a group of degenerates" and of being "an immoral person who suffered from passive pederasty"; see ACS, Pol.Pol., b. 521, f. "Foschini Vittorio," informative document from Milan, March 13, 1933.

15. ACS, SPD, RSI, CR, b. 7, f. 29, "Senise Carmine," s.f. 1, fiduciary report, February 19, 1943.

16. An anonymous letter sent to Galeazzo Ciano informed him of the spiteful remarks made by Senise about him and also informed him that "Senise and Zurlo are well known because of the suspicion of pederasty that binds them"; see ACS, Min.Cul.Pop., *Gabinetto*, b. 5, f. 21, "Anonimi contro personalità," s.f. 42, "Contro il Gr. Uff. Senise e il Gr. Uff. Zurlo."

17. ACS, SPD, RSI, CR, b. 7, f. 29, "Senise Carmine," s.f. 1, letter sent to donna Rachele on 8-2-1943.

18. Senise, *Quando ero capo della polizia*, 265.

19. ACS, SPD, RSI, CR, b. 10, f. 43 R, "Zurlo Leopoldo." Senise was taken to Germany, and after being imprisoned in the camp at Dachau he was exiled to *confino* at Hirschegg in Bavaria. On Zurlo's "utmost sorrow" and his unsuccessful attempts to save

his "dearest, fraternal friend," see L. Zurlo, *Memorie inutili: La censura teatrale nel ventennio* (Rome: Edizioni dell'Ateneo, 1952), 365–67.

20. ACS, Min.Cul.Pop., *Gabinetto*, b. 117, f. 7767, "Carmine Senise, prefetto del Regno." As before, an anonymous letter to Galeazzo Ciano reported that "Senise and Zurlo were well known because of the suspicion of pederasty that binds them"; see ACS, Min.Cul.Pop., *Gabinetto*, b. 5, f. 21, "Anonimi contro personalità," s.f. 42, "Contro il Gr. Uff. Senise e il Gr. Uff. Zurlo."

21. See ASR, CAP, Sezione Istruttoria b. 73, f. "Senise Carmine."

22. The relationship between Zurlo and Senise ended with the sudden death of the former head of police. This is how Cesare Rossi described a grieving and inconsolable Zurlo as he mourned the death of Senise: "The saddest thing, the most agonizing thing for the many surviving friends of both men, is the state of abandon in which the learned and distinguished Prefect who for so many years presided over censorship of the theater with good taste, wisdom, integrity, and independence, so difficult at the time. Just think, this affectionate, continuous companionship that has lasted fifty years all of a sudden ends. . . . The other day Zurlo said with tears in his eyes: 'No, Carminuccio, this is the only wrong you should never have done to me. It was supposed to be you, younger than me, who closed my coffin. . . . Instead, you wanted to precede me. No, you should not have done it to me'" (C. Rossi, *Personaggi di ieri e di oggi* [Milan: Ceschina, 1960], 430–31).

23. On April 21, 1939, a long list of prefects nominated as senators was published, but Zurlo's name was not on the list because he was not married; on the matter see Zurlo, *Memorie inutili*, 170. Confirmation of this was also provided by Cesare Rossi, according to whom "Mussolini, who greatly admired Zurlo, could not forgive him for remaining obstinately unmarried" (Rossi, *Trentatré vicende mussoliniane*, 370). On the subsequent nomination of Zurlo as senator see ACS, PCM *1940–1943*, "Aspiranti senatori," b. 2866, f. 72, "Zurlo dott. Leopoldo."

24. Senise, *Quando ero capo della polizia*, 19.

25. Rossi, *Personaggi di ieri*, 426.

26. According to Mario Mieli, "in general, a homosexual who is an artist can be justified on the basis of the cliché that because artists are and have always been creative, anticonformist, and temperamental, they can also be 'inverts': in the end, in the eyes of those who are 'normal,' art offsets the anomaly, the sexual depravation. Homosexuality is therefore tolerated and permitted if accompanied by artistic expression, because in that way it fits in with imagination, fantasy, and sublimation and does not have a direct impact on real relationships nowadays termed 'normal'" (M. Mieli, *Elementi di critica omosessuale* [Milan: Feltrinelli, 2002], 110).

27. G. Dall'Orto, *La pagina strappata: Interviste di cultura e omosessualità* (Turin: Gruppo Abele, 1987), 6.

28. See F. Gnarre, *L'eroe negato: Omosessualità e letteratura nel Novecento italiano* (Milan: Baldini and Castoldi, 2000); C. Gargano, *Ernesto e gli altri: L'omosessualità nella narrativa italiana del Novecento* (Rome: Editori Riuniti, 2002); and H. Mayer, *Outsiders: A Study in Life and Letters* (Cambridge, Mass.: MIT Press, 1982).

29. This is the title of the chapter Zurlo devoted to the censorship of theatrical works regarding subjects against the law from a sexual point of view (Zurlo, *Memorie inutili*, 118-25).

30. Zurlo remained in charge until 1943, reviewing about eighteen thousand theatrical works. On his activity, see P. Iaccio, "La censura teatrale durante il fascismo," *Storia contemporanea* 4 (1986): 557-614, and *La scena negata: Il teatro vietato durante la guerra fascista (1940-1943)* (Rome: Bulzoni, 1994).

31. Zurlo, *Memorie inutili*, 120.

32. Ibid., 124.

33. ACS, Min.Cul.Pop., *Direzione Generale Teatro e Musica*, Office of the theatrical Censor, b. 480, f. 9056, "*Il ritratto di Dorian Gray* di Oscar Wilde di Gerardo Jovinelli (1940)."

34. See letter from Zurlo to Bolla dated October 20, 1942, in ACS, *Direzione Generale Teatro e Musica*, Office of the Theatrical Censor, b. 238, f. 4334, "Bolla Nino, *Casa delle muse*, 1942."

35. Zurlo, *Memorie inutili*, 125.

36. See Cannistraro, *La fabbrica del consenso*, 70-73.

37. B. Giuliano, *Il fascismo e l'avvenire della cultura* (Turin: Utet, 1928), 202.

38. See R. De Felice and L. Goglia, *Mussolini il mito* (Rome: Laterza, 1983); G. Di Genova, ed., *L'uomo della provvidenza: iconografia del Duce 1923-1945* (Bologna: Bora, 1997); G. Gori, "Model of Masculinity: Mussolini, the 'New Italian' of the Fascist Era," *International Journal of History of Sport*, December 1999, 27-61; and S. Luzzatto, *L'immagine del duce: Mussolini nelle fotografie dell'Istituto Luce* (Rome: Editori Riuniti, 2001).

39. See P. O'Brien, "Al capezzale di Mussolini: Ferite e malattia 1917-1945," *Italia contemporanea* 226 (March 2002): 5-29.

40. ACS, Min.Cul.Pop., *Gabinetto*, b. 3, f. 11, "Circolari ai prefetti del Regno (disposizioni alla stampa)," s.f. 59, "Cronaca nera" telegram n.6897, June 26, 1937, sent by Minister Alfieri to prefects. On other measures concerning crimes against decency see ibid., s.f.f. Massime, "Atti di libidine e uccisione di minorenni."

41. See C. E. Gadda, *That Awful Mess on Via Merulana: A Novel* (New York: G. Braziller, 1965).

42. This is what Polverelli wrote in some orders that he issued to the press 1931— *Disegni e fotografie di mode femminili*: "The Fascist woman must be physically healthy so as to have healthy children according to the 'rules of life' mentioned by the Duce in his memorable speech to doctors. Therefore all pictures of artificially thin, masculine-type women must be eliminated, because they represent the sterile type of woman common in the decadent Western civilization"; *Donne crisi*: "Publish short articles and short stories, etc. against the crisis woman." See ACS, Min.Cul.Pop., b. 155, f. 10.

43. When Italy entered the Second World War, the martial image was further emphasized, as was the warlike attitude of the Italian population, and so as not to leave anything to chance Pavolini sent precise orders to the press encouraging newspapers to publish photos of men in shorts, considered more "virile" than men wearing old-fashioned

trousers (ACS, Min.Cul.Pop., b. 75, report to journalists, September 14, 1940). Moreover, the wartime press was supposed to avoid scandalous subjects and photos of nude or seminude women so as not to weaken the temper of soldiers with dangerous erotic distractions.

44. On this excessive puritan morality adopted by Fascism in order to reinforce the tradition of family and successfully realize the fascist demographic policy, see Cannistraro, *La fabbrica del consenso*, 86–92.

45. In 1910 Luzzatti had sent around a memorandum to prefects inviting them to deploy greater energy in the repression of pornography. As a result, a true crusade was launched against immorality with such arbitrary confiscation that it generated much criticism. On this "virtuous myth" ready to limit freedom and gag art in order to curb immoral behavior, see V. Pareto, *Il mito virtuista e la letteratura immorale* (Rome 1914), now in *Scritti sociologici* (Turin: Utet, 1966). Regarding the list of publications confiscated, see ACS, *Polizia Giudiziaria 1910–1912*, b. 356, f. 12985.2 "Repressione della pornografia."

46. See A. Mieli, "Sequestro di libri e lotta contro la pornografia," *Rassegna di studi sessuali* 3 (1923): 140–44; V. Pareto, "Letteratura immorale," *Il secolo* (1923), reprinted in *Scritti sociologici*, 1175–81. Regarding the need to keep the attention focused on the censorship of erotic literature, see "Per la repressione della pornografia," *Archivio fascista di medicina politica* 3 (1927): 157–60.

47. G. Agnese, *Con quale mezzo vedo possibile il risanamento dei costumi e il progresso morale di una moderna Nazione: Proposta di un codice dei costumi* (Turin: Eredi Botta, 1929), 11.

48. According to Dario Petrosino, local magazines, despite their limited circulation, helped create or bring about the stereotype of the homosexual; see D. Petrosino, "Come si costruisce uno stereotipo: La rappresentazione degli omosessuali ne 'l'Italiano' di Leo Longanesi—1926–1929," in Circolo Pink, ed., *Le ragioni di un silenzio: La persecuzione degli omosessuali durante il nazismo e il fascismo* (Verona: Ombre Corte, 2002), 49–63.

49. Cartoon of an "Italian" on the "Santa Russia bolscevica," qtd. in ibid., 55. Malparte, too, in a short poem with the significant title "Il serpente sodomita," openly made fun of Cocteau.

50. "Discorsi agli uomini," *Critica fascista* 2 (January 15, 1933).

51. A. A. Monti, "La battaglia morale del fascismo," *Costruire* 5 (1927): 15.

52. See T. Achilli, "Le maschere dell'eros (Il romanzo trasgressivo)," in *I best seller del ventennio: Il regime e il libro di massa*, ed. G. De Donato and V. Gazzola Stacchini (Rome: Editori Riuniti, 1991), 5–15.

53. Following the creation of the Min.Cul.Pop., literary monitoring and censorship came under the authority of the Book Division, purposely set up within the general management for Italian publishers.

54. On the long list of publications confiscated, among those concerned with homosexual love affairs there were : *Antologia dell'amore turco* of Edoardo Fary, *Pervertimenti sessuali* of Clodomiro Bonfigli, *Amori bestiali* and *Milano sconosciuta* of Valera, *Dizionario di sessuologia* of Tinto, *Moralità e sessualità* of Proteus, *La parabola dell'eunuco* of Baracco, *La crudeltà tedesca e la corruzione sessuale* of Senizza, *L'uomo femmina* of De Lysle, *Le degenerazioni psicosessuali* of Perrone Capano, *Inversioni sessuali* and *Il problema dell'omosessualità* of Fabiani;

see ACS, *Divisione Polizia Amministrativa e sociale*, b. 222, f. "List of pornographic publications confiscated," s.f. 4. There was even a request to confiscate *Così parlò Zarathustra* by Nietzsche and *Diario di un seduttore* by Kierkegaard. In the case of *Psicopatie sessuali* by Krafft-Ebing, the undisputable scientific content of such a successful book induced the chief of police to provide for its release from seizure; the same thing happened with the works of Mantegazza, which, however, could not be sold over the counter.

55. Archivio di Stato di Milano, *Prefettura*, gabinetto, I versamento b. 422, f. "Censura libri e opuscoli osceni," s.f. "1930 sequestro."

56. This is how Orioli explained the aim of his publishing house: "It was my intention to offer, as I did, authors of the calibre of Lawrence, Somerset-Maugham, Richard Aldington, Norman Douglas the opportunity to say what they wanted and to see their manuscripts edited in an attractive format" (G. Orioli, *Le avventure di un libraio* [Milan: Il Profilo, 1988], 200). On the editorial activity of Orioli, see also O. De Zordo, *Una proposta anglofiorentina degli anni Trenta: The Lungarno Series* (Florence: Olschki, 1981).

57. See C. M. De Vecchi, *Bonifica fascista della cultura* (Milan: Mondadori, 1937). It is interesting to note that the Jews were said to have certain characteristics typical of homosexuals, and in some cases they were even accused openly of spreading pederasty; see T. Gatti, "Libidine, cupidigia e odio di razza degli ebrei," *La difesa della razza* 9 (1938–39): 24; G. Montandon, "Da cosa si riconoscono gli ebrei?," *La difesa della razza* 21–22 (1940): 6–7; and A. Tosti, "La razza giudaica: Amoralità e criminalità dei Giudei," *La difesa della razza* 23 (1940–41): 10.

58. ACS, Min.Cul.Pop., *Direzione Generale Stampa Italiana*, Division III, b. 130, f. "Scrittoti ebrei" and b. 56, f. 1075, "Produzione libraria italiana e straniera tradotta in italiano—revisione totale."

59. Comment by Fernando Mezzasoma, February 15, 1943, on books qtd. in Cannistraro, *La fabbrica del consenso*, 435–39.

60. See ACS, UCP, personal files, b. 987, f. "Carlo S."

61. P. G. Zunino, *L'ideologia del fascismo: Miti, credenze e valori nella stabilizzazione del regime* (Bologna: Il Mulino, 1985), 299.

62. "Una vita col cognome Mussolini senza mai pensare alla politica," interview with Romano Mussolini by Barbara Palombelli, in *Corriere della sera*, January 22, 2001, 17. For a similar testimony given by Rachele, see B. Palombelli, "Rachele Guidi and Benito Mussolini," *Corriere della sera*, August 20, 2003, 35.

63. On the exaltation, in various biographies, of Mussolini's exuberant virility that guaranteed him success with many women, see L. Passerini, *Mussolini immaginario: Storia di una biografia 1915–1939* (Rome: Laterza, 1991), 99–109.

64. Zunino, *L'ideologia del fascismo*, 299.

65. Ibid., 296.

66. M. Boneschi, *Senso: I costumi sessuali degli italiani dal 1880 ad oggi* (Milan: Mondadori, 2000), 87.

67. On prostitution during the Fascist era see O. Pagani, *L'orgasmo del regime: Le memorie della tenutaria del "circolo privato" del duce e dei gerarchi del fascismo* (Milan: SugarCo, 1976); G. Fusco, *Quando l'Italia tollerava* (Vicenza: Neri Pozza, 1995); and G. M. Padiglione,

Camerati, in camera! Storia seria ma divertente delle case chiuse sotto il fascismo (Milan: Mursia, 2003). Brothels, for example, were not to be called "houses of pleasure" but "houses of ill repute," they were never to be mentioned or reproduced in photos or on postcards, and the windows had to remain closed at all times. In other words, they existed but were not to be seen, they were busy but openly criticized and condemned.

68. Turati, *Fuori dall'ombra della mia vita*, 99–100.

69. See ACS, Pol.Pol., b. 1123, f. "Ridolfi Elena marchesa." In November 1943 Lotteringhi della Stufa was arrested and sentenced by the German tribunal in Florence to three months imprisonment. The sentence was motivated not by the fact that he was still suspected of being a "sexual pervert with congenital flaws" or "seriously suspected of being a homosexual," nor by his extremely costly lifestyle, but by a more serious offense: he had hidden some English prisoners in his villa after the armistice. In any case, on December 24, 1943, the prefect's office in Florence informed the Ministry of National Security that the German authority had granted Lotteringhi della Stufa a suspended sentence, and he had therefore been freed; see ACS, Pol.Pol., b. 734, f. "Lorreringhi della Stufa Lottieri."

70. ACS, SPD, CR, b. 128, f. "Boncompagni Ludovisi Don Gregorio" and Pol.Pol., b. 159, f. "Boncompagni Ludovisi Gregorio."

71. M. Tarchi, "'Esuli in Patria'. I fascisti nella Repubblica italiana," in *Lo straniero interno*, ed. E. Pozzi (Florence: Ponte alle Grazie, 1993), 186.

72. On the portrayal of homosexuality in moving pictures, see P. Bertelli, *Cinema e diversità, 1895–1987: Storia di svantaggio sul telo bianco; Mascheramento mercificazione, autenticità* (Reggio Emilia; Notor, 1994); D. Fernandez, *Il ratto di Ganimede: La presenza omosessuale nell'arte e nella società* (Milan: Bompiani, 2002), 318–40; and V. Russo, *Lo schermo velato: L'omosessualità nel cinema* (Genoa: Costa and Nolan, 1984), and *The Celluloid Closet: Homosexuality in the Movies*, rev. ed. (New York: Harper and Row Publishers, 1987).

73. I wish to thank Luca Prono for allowing me a prepublication reading of his article "Città aperta o cultura chiusa? The Homosexualization of Fascism in the Perverted Cultural Memory of the Italian Left," in which he analyzes, at times too polemically and anachronistically, the "homosexualization" of Fascism in some neorealist texts and in Carlo Lizzani's film *Celluloide* (1996).

74. See R. Maccari, E. Scola, and M. Costanzo, *Una giornata particolare* (Milan: Longanesi, 1977). More recently, the producer/director Ferzan Ozpteck, in his film *La finestra di fronte* (2002), depicted a Jewish homosexual in Nazi-occupied Rome.

75. See ASR, *Corte d'Assise*, CAP, b. 2635.4, "Processo Bardi Pollastrini ed altri," and b. 2635.1, "Bardi Gino."

76. In May 1940 an informer of the Polizia Politica apparently reported that Bardi had forbidden some people to enter the Caffè Aragno, because in that mileu everyone thought he was a homosexual and—continued the informer—"the news that Bardi is a pederast is apparently known to all" (ACS, Pol.Pol., b. 77, f. "Bardi Gino").

77. ASR, *Corte d'Assise*, CAP, b. 2635.4, "Trial Bardi Pollastrini ed altri": held on September 18, 1945 before the Criminal Court of the Court of Appeals in Rome.

78. Ibid., report from Giuseppe Pizzirani, High Commissioner of the Federazione dell'Urbe, sent to republican Fascist Party leader, Alessandro Pavolini, on December 3, 1943. On the trial and Bardi's attempt to get a recommendation to save himself from the accusations, see also ACS, PCM, RSI, Segreteria particolare del sottosegretario Barracu assistant to undersecretary Barracu (1943-1945), b. 4, f. 837, "Bardi Gino."

79. Translated as A. Moravia, *The Time of Indifference* (Vermont, Calif: Steerforth, 2001).

80. See C. Scorza, "Il problema demografico e la camicia alla russa." In the article, Scorza argues against the new trend of the young likened to "Brunetto Latini's last grandchildren" and ends his tirade by calling for direct action by the regime against homosexuality: "In this case the Fascist regime really has to intervene with an iron fist, zero tolerance, no exceptions" (12).

81. Y. De Begnac, *Itinerario della borghesia* (Brescia: Giulio Vannini Editore, 1940), 97.

82. A. Tamaro, *Vent'anni di storia* (Rome: Giovanni Volpe Editore, 1971 [1953]), 160.

83. See M. Carli, *Antisnobismo* (Milan: Morreale, 1929); and V. Masserato, "Profili di nuovi gagà," *Il popolo di Sicilia* (January 11, 1939).

84. The campaign against the "pacifist, pitiful, and sanctimonious" middle class was launched officially by Mussolini on October 25, 1938 in his speech to the PNF National Council in which he announced: "At the end of the year XVI I identified an enemy, an enemy of our regime. This enemy has a name, 'bourgeoisie'" (Mussolini, *Opera Omnia*, 29:189).

85. E. Sulis, ed., *Processo alla borghesia* (Rome: Edizioni Roma, 1939).

86. See Gentile, "'L''uomo nuovo' del fascismo," 235-64. In my opinion, Gentile does not clarify entirely the reasons for the failure of this experimental anthropological revolution, because he does not highlight all of the problems facing the regime—owing partly to the strongly rooted bourgeois respectability—in implementing respectability in uniform, capable of creating a "well organized, disciplined male community, ready to serve the country in its public and private life." On the link between Fascism, respectability, and bourgeois mentality, see Mosse, *Nationalism and Sexuality*. For some interesting comments on the concept of bourgeois respectability in Mosse see K. Plessini, "The Nazi as the 'Ideal Bourgeois': Respectability and Nazism in the Work of George L. Mosse," *Totalitarian Movements and Political Religions* 2 (Autumn 2004): 226-42.

87. Mosse, *The Image of Man*, 32. Even before Mosse maintained that "the new Fascist or national socialist (Nazi) man was not really so new," he stressed the "very slight difference in appearance, virile behavior, and stance between Mussolini's new man, the German Arian, the upright British, and the 'true' American" (G. L. Mosse, "Estetica fascista e società: Alcune considerazioni," in various authors, *Il regime fascista* [Rome: Laterza, 1995], 110).

88. This expression was used by Mussolini to justify the antibourgeois campaign: "We must fascistize even more what I call the dead ground of the nation's life"; "The Party's job is to clean out that ground that I can picture materially as salons, bars and taverns" (B. Mussolini, *Alla "decima legio," September 24, 1939, and *Rapporto ai gerarchi di*

Genova, September 30, 1939, in *Opera Omnia*, 312, 317). See also "Angoli morti e certe temperature," Foglio di Disposizioni no. 272 of July 31, 1934, in *Vademecum dello stile fascista* (Rome: Nuova Europa, 1939), 110.

89. Mosse, "Estetica fascista e società," 112. According to Mosse, however, it was possible to find an equal balance between Fascism's and Nazism's definition of masculinity and bourgeois respectability, reconciling their common ethics with the new totalitarian situations.

90. See G. Contri, "Bando al biberon," *Critica fascista* 4 (February 15, 1933); M. Pompei, "La Famiglia e il Fascismo: Un'inchiesta da fare," *Critica fascista* 9 (May 1, 1933); and M. Palazzi, "La Famiglia nello Stato fascista: autorità dell'uomo," *Critica fascista* 10 (May 15, 1933).

91. C. Costamagna, "La neutralità borghese e la trasformazione fascista dello Stato," *Lo Stato*, December 1938, 676.

92. See A. Gravelli, ed., "Anti Lei" (Rome, n.d.); and M. A. Matard, "L'anti-lei: utopie linguistique ou projet totalitarie?" *Mélange de l'Ecole française de Rome* 2 (1998): 971–1010.

93. See PNF, "Mostra antiborghese," *Gerarchia*, January 1, 1939, 51–54; and C. Scorza, *Tipi . . . Tipi . . . Tipi . . .* (Florence: Vallecchi, 1942).

94. F. Clarizia, "L'antiborghese," *Gerarchia*, March 3, 1939, 199.

95. ACS, Pol.Mat., b. 109, f. "PNF," fiduciary report June 22, 1938. On hostility toward the antibourgeois battle that almost risked turning into a real own-goal see Colarizi, *L'opinione pubblica degli italiani sotto il regime*, 282–87.

96. The attempt to safeguard a certain amount of freedom within the family does not necessarily mean, as Cecilia Dau Novelli maintains, that this environment was able to remain "socially autonomous" during the Fascist period and foreign to its totalitarian expectations; see C. Dau Novelli, *Famiglia e modernizzazione in Italia tra le due guerre* (Rome: Studium, 1994), 22–23.

97. De Felice, *Mussolini il duce: Lo Stato totalitario*, 96.

98. Mussolini, *Opera Omnia*, 26:192ff.

99. "Bonifica spirituale della borghesia," *Critica fascista*, January 1, 1935.

100. See L. La Rovere, *Storia dei Guf: Organizzazione, politica e miti della gioventù universitaria fascista 1919–1943* (Turin: Bollati Boringhieri, 2003).

101. See Gentile, *La via italiana al totalitarismo*. Gentile rightly notes that the "limits of Fascist totalitarianism are not sufficient to deny that it existed and had effects; in the same way the contradictions between myth and realization do not disprove the importance of the presence and function of myth in Fascist politics." Furthermore, according to the author, there are no complete or perfect totalitarian regimes, because hindrances, resistance, and limits always create "considerable conflict between myth and reality, between ambitions and results" (148–51).

102. In his diary entry of January 29, 1940, Ciano wrote down many comments made by the Duce. The tone was decidedly embittered and disillusioned against the inclinations and character of the Italians: "Have you ever seen a sheep turn into a wolf? The Italian race is a race of sheep. It will take more than 18 years to transform them. It will take 180 or perhaps 180 centuries" (Ciano, *Diario*, 391).

103. Words spoken by Mussolini to Giovanni Dolfin at Gargnano on January 1, 1944, qtd. in G. Dolfin, *Con Mussolini nella tragedia 1943-1944* (Milan: Garzanti, 1949).

104. J. J. Linz, *Fascism, Breakdown of Democracy, Authoritarian and Totalitarian Regimes: Coincidences and Distinctions* (Madrid: Instituto Juan March de Estudios e Investigaciones, 2002), 22.

105. Mussolini, "Il compito dei medici."

106. Wanrooij, *Storia del pudore*, 104. The author himself, when analyzing the relationship between Fascism and the Leagues for Public Morality, maintains that "it would be wrong to ignore how the guidelines followed by the regime in the sexual field—established more by political opportunism than by strong, unchanging moral principles—never leveled out on a purely conformist line with respect to the Church doctrines as the moralists would have liked" (101-2).

107. See M. C. Giuntella, "I fatti del 1931 e la formazione della 'seconda generazione,'" in *I cattolici tra fascismo e democrazia*, ed. P. Scoppola and F. Traniello (Bologna: il Mulino, 1975), 183-235.

108. On the whole affair and the influence exercised on sexual ethics by Catholicism and the Leagues for Public Morality see Wanrooij, *Storia del pudore*, 110-12.

109. Qtd. in *Tutte le encicliche dei Sommi Pontefici*, compiled and annotated by E. Momigliano (Milan, 1964), 855n.

110. Ibid., 851.

111. Mussolini's speech before the Chamber on the Lateran Pact qtd. in De Felice, *Mussolini il fascista*, 429.

112. Regarding the Church's attitude toward the regime's attempt to sacralize politics and politicize morality see Gentile, *Politics as Religion*, 68-109; and R. Moro, "Religione del trascendente e religioni politiche: Il cattolicesimo italiano di fronte alla sacralizzazione fascista della politica," *Mondo contemporaneo* 1 (2005): 9-67.

113. J. Lauritsen and D. Thorstad, "Il primo movimento per i diritti degli omosessuali (1864-1935)," in various authors, *Gay gay: Storia e coscienza omosessuale* (Milan: La Salamandra, 1976), 43.

Index

Benito Mussolini is referred to as "the Duce" in subentries. Page references in italics indicate illustrations.

330n.194; anus analysis to identify passive homosexuality, 44, 134–35, 352n.92; biological vs. endocrinal theories, 48–49, 53, 56, 66; censorship of literature, 77, 334n.232 (*see also* literary/theater monitoring); and civil incapacity, 57–58; clitoral analysis of lesbians, 321–22n.84; congenital disease theory, 49–50, 56–57, 60, 326n.135; constitutional theory, 49–50, 56, 77; criminal anthropology used to identify homosexuals, 41–42, 319–20nn.63–64, 320n.71; and the crisis of masculinity, 35–41, 317nn.40–41, 318n.43, 319n.55; dating of, 32, 313–14nn.7–8; degeneration model, 35–36, 38, 40–42, 45–46, 316n.26, 316n.34, 330n.194; *Dizionario di sessuologia a dispense*, 76–77, 400n.54; effeminacy/passivity as identfiers and sources of contempt, 42–45, 61, 134, 321nn.75–76, 321n.80, 321n.82; French intolerance/incomprehension, 47, 322–23n.94; Germans accused of homosexuality, 38–39, 317n.41, 318n.43, 318n.47; and gland research/transplants, 52–54, 324n.115, 325n.119; homophobia surrounding, 36, 38; homosexuality considered unnatural and abnormal, 48, 65, 67, 323n.96; hormonal theory, 50–51, 323n.108; mental illness theory, 57–58, 61, 327n.140; and modernity, 37–38, 40, 317n.38; onanism theory, 48; organic vs. psychological theories, 48–49, 54, 56, 60, 73; perversion model, 32, 47–48, 56–57, 322–23n.94, 323n.99, 326n.135; and physical activity's importance, 40, 319n.59; positivist views, 32, 40, 47, 63, 68; psychiatric vs. psychoanalytical theories, 48–49, 54, 57–58, 326n.127 (*see also* psychoanalysis);

and pure male/pure female, 55; racism and sexual diversity, 45–46, 269; scientific/medical views and interest, 31–35, 314n.8, 315n.17, 316n.26; sexual pathology theory, 73, 332n.211; and solitude/self-restraint/ostracism of homosexuals, 46, 61, 322n.91; and testicle transplants, 51–53, 86, 324n.113, 325n.118, 326n.126; and wartime homoerotic camaraderie, 39. *See also* Mieli, Aldo; *La Rassegna di studi sessuali*

dissent, 122, 348nn.54–55
Di Stefano, Michelangelo, 223, 359n.150, 375n.31, 376n.42, 391n.185
"Distretto militare di Nola" (D'Ercoli), *182*
Di Tullio, Benigno, 40, 190, 198
Dizionario di criminologia, 61
Dizionario di sessuologia a dispense (Tinto), 76–77, 400n.54
Dobbert, Gerhard, 218, 374n.22
Dogliani, Patrizia, 131
Dolmann, Eugen, 234, 276–77, 382n.95
Domenico R., 165–66
domicilio coatto (forced residence), xxi, 115–16, 124–25, 344n.22, 344–45n.25, 346n.41, 352n.86
Don Pasqualino's (Catania), 151–52
Dörner, Klaus, 206, 369n.73
Douglas, Norman, 285
Ducarne, Alessandro Baggio, 376n.43
Dudan, Alessandro, 263–64, 393n.209

education, Church vs. Fascism on, 81
Der Eigene, 71
Ellero, Lorenzo, 57
Ellis, Havelock, 35, 47, 78, 329n.168, 367n.55
Elogio alla prostituzione (Tavolato), 22
embryology, 50
Enciclopedia di diritto penale italiano, 94
Enciclopedia Italiana, x, xi, 60, 75

George L. Mosse Series
in Modern European Cultural and
Intellectual History

Series Editors

Stanley G. Payne, David J. Sorkin, and John S. Tortorice

Nazi Culture: Intellectual, Cultural, and Social Life in the Third Reich
George L. Mosse

What History Tells: George L. Mosse and the Culture of Modern Europe
Stanley G. Payne, David J. Sorkin, and John S. Tortorice

The Jews in Mussolini's Italy: From Equality to Persecution
Michele Sarfatti; translated by John and Anne C. Tedeschi

Jews and Other Germans: Civil Society, Religious Diversity, and Urban Politics in Breslau, 1860–1925
Till van Rahden; translated by Marcus Brainard

An Uncompromising Generation: The Nazi Leadership of the Reich Security Main Office
Michael Wildt; translated by Tom Lampert

www.ingramcontent.com/pod-product-compliance
Lightning Source LLC
Chambersburg PA
CBHW050232270326
41914CB00033BA/1876/J